HANDBOOK OF HYDRAULICS

OTHER McGRAW-HILL HANDBOOKS OF INTEREST

HANDBOOK OF HYDRAULICS
for the Solution of
Hydraulic Engineering Problems

ERNEST F. BRATER
Professor of Hydraulic Engineering
University of Michigan

HORACE WILLIAMS KING
Late Professor of Hydraulic Engineering
University of Michigan

Sixth Edition

McGRAW-HILL BOOK COMPANY

New York   St. Louis   San Francisco   Auckland   Düsseldorf
Kuala Lumpur   London   Mexico   Montreal   New Delhi
Panama   Paris   São Paulo   Singapore
Sydney   Tokyo   Toronto

Library of Congress Cataloging in Publication Data

Brater, Ernest Frederick, date.
  Handbook of hydraulics for the solution of hydraulic
engineering problems.

  First-4th ed. (1918–54) by H. W. King (4th ed. rev. by
E. F. Brater), published under title: Handbook of
hydraulics for the solution of hydraulic problems; 5th
ed. (1963) by H. W. King and E. F. Brater, published
under title: Handbook of hydraulics for the solution
of hydrostatic and fluid-flow problems.
  1. Hydraulics. I. King, Horace Williams, 1874–1951,
joint author. II. Title.
TC160.K5   1976   620.1'06   76-6486
ISBN 0-07-007243-4

*The editors for this book were Harold B. Crawford, Ross J. Kepler,
and Betty Gatewood, and the production supervisor was
George E. Oechsner.   It was set in Modern by Bi-Comp, Inc.*

It was printed and bound by The Book Press.

CONTENTS

LIST OF TABLES

PREFACE

It is the objective of this Handbook to present the fundamentals needed to solve hydraulics problems and to provide appropriate tables, graphs and computer techniques to facilitate solutions. Many numerical examples are included. The book has been organized to provide maximum assistance to engineers engaged in the design of hydraulic engineering projects; in addition, it is also suitable as a text, especially for courses that deal with nonuniform flow in open channels or coastal engineering. The tables that have made this book so useful to practicing engineers are also valuable teaching aids. It is only by solving many numerical problems that the student or the young engineer obtains a sound working knowledge of hydraulic engineering, and many problems would be prohibitively time-consuming without the use of the tables or a digital computer.

In addition to the inclusion of pertinent new material throughout the book, the sixth edition includes new material on the metric system and on the design of pipe networks, and a completely new section describing the applications of numerical methods and digital computers to hydraulic engineering. This section was prepared to introduce hydraulic engineers to the techniques used in programming problems for solution by digital computers. It includes ten examples of hydraulic engineering problems with flow charts, corresponding computer programs and outputs. An Appendix to the new section provides explanations of the more important numerical methods used in applying computers to hydraulic problems.

The author wishes to call attention to the vast contributions made by individual researchers, practicing engineers, and governmental organizations whose published material provides essential information for the solution of hydraulic problems. References to these many contributions are made throughout the text.

Special acknowledgement is made to my colleague, Professor E. B. Wylie, who was the principal co-author of the new section. He also prepared text material on pipe networks and made many valuable suggestions.

Ernest F. Brater

HANDBOOK OF HYDRAULICS

SECTION 1

FLUID PROPERTIES AND HYDRAULIC UNITS

This section provides information on fluid properties and quantities used to solve hydraulic engineering problems. The fluid properties and hydraulic quantities are listed in Table 1-1 together with commonly used symbols, dimensions, and basic units. The dimensions are expressed in terms of the three fundamental quantities: mass M, length L, and time T. The basic units are given in the foot-pound-second system, which is also called the U.S. Customary System (USCS), and in the metric system, which is also known as the International System (SI). The first subsection deals with fluid properties and the second with hydraulic engineering units and their conversion within and between systems. Some numerical values of fluid properties are presented in Table 1-2. Tables 1-3 to 1-13 are devoted to conversion of units, and Table 1-14 gives unit weights of materials used in hydraulic structures.

Fluid Properties. Before discussing the fluid properties, it is necessary to define the unit of mass. In the foot-pound-second system this is done as follows. A force of one pound will accelerate a mass of one slug at the rate of one foot per second per second. In the case of a 1-lb weight falling freely, a gravitational force of 1 lb produces a standard acceleration of 32.174 ft per sec per sec. Because the magnitude of the force must be equal to the product of the mass and acceleration ($F = Ma$), the 1-lb weight must possess a mass of 1/32.174 slug. Consequently, to convert weight W in pounds to mass, it is necessary to divide by the gravitational acceleration g, as shown by the equation

$$M = \frac{W}{g} \tag{1-1}$$

1-1

In the metric system the standard units of force and mass are newtons and kilograms, respectively. A force of one newton will accelerate a mass of one kilogram at the rate of one meter per second per second. The standard gravitational acceleration is 9.80665 m. per sec. Factors for converting pounds to newtons and slugs to kilograms are given in Table 1-3.

Specific weight, or *unit weight,* w is defined as the weight per unit of volume of a substance. The mass per unit of volume is called *density* ρ. It follows from the above discussion that, in the foot-pound-second system, specific weight in pounds per cubic foot may be converted to density in slugs per cubic foot by dividing by the gravitational acceleration, as shown by the equation

$$\rho = \frac{w}{g} \tag{1-2}$$

By solving either of the above equations it may be seen that g is the weight per unit of mass. In other words, one slug of mass weighs 32.174 lb. The value of g varies slightly with both latitude and altitude. The value 32.2 ft per sec per sec is sufficiently accurate for hydraulic computations. The densities and specific weights of water and some other fluids are given in Table 1-2. The specific weights of various materials are given in Table 1-14.

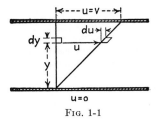

Fig. 1-1

The *specific gravity* (sp. gr.) of a substance is obtained by dividing the weight of a certain volume of the substance by the weight of an equal volume of water at 39.2°F. Values of the specific gravity of several fluids are given in Table 1-2.

The *viscosity* μ of a fluid is a measure of the relative ease or difficulty with which a particle of the fluid may be deformed. For example, heavy oil has a greater viscosity than water, and water is more viscous than air. The viscosity of a liquid decreases as the temperature increases, but the opposite is true of a gas. Assume that the space between the two horizontal plates shown in Fig. 1-1 is filled with a fluid, that the upper plate is in motion with the velocity V, and that the lower plate is stationary. Those particles of fluid which are in contact with a boundary surface will have the same velocity as the boundary. It follows that the velocity of the fluid will vary from V at the top plate to zero at the bottom one and that the velocity of any layer of fluid will be different from that of the adjacent layers. As a result, all particles of fluid will be continuously deformed by the shear stresses between adjacent layers, as illustrated in Fig. 1-1 by successive positions of a particle at a distance y from the lower plate. It has been shown by laboratory tests that for a particular fluid at a given temperature the ratio of the shear stress τ to the rate of deformation, du/dy, is constant. This constant is called the coefficient of viscosity, the dynamic viscosity, the absolute viscosity, or simply the viscosity. The preceding definition is expressed mathematically by the equation

$$\mu = \frac{\tau}{du/dy} \tag{1-3}$$

This relationship is called Newton's law of viscosity, and fluids which behave in this manner are called Newtonian fluids. Most fluids dealt with by engineers are Newtonian fluids. Some thick highly viscous fluids are non-Newtonian, meaning that the shear stress is not directly proportional to du/dy for the entire range of shear stresses.

By inserting the units for the terms in the right side of Eq. (1-3), the units of viscosity are found to be pound-seconds per square foot. Because a pound may be expressed in terms of the product of mass and acceleration (1 lb = 1 slug ft per sec²) another equivalent expression used for a unit of viscosity is a slug per foot-second. The corresponding units in the metric system are newton-seconds per meter². One pound-second per foot² is equivalent to 47.88 newton-seconds per meter² (see Table 1-3). The viscosities of a number of fluids are given in Table 1.2.

The *kinematic viscosity* ν is obtained by dividing the viscosity by the density, as shown by the equation

$$\nu = \frac{\mu}{\rho} \tag{1-4}$$

The units of kinematic viscosity, obtained by inserting the units of μ and ρ into Eq. (1-4), are feet² per second or meters² per second. One foot² per second is equivalent to 0.0929 meter² per second.

Surface tension is the property of liquids which causes capillary action in small tubes. If the liquid "wets" the surface of the tube, the liquid surface will be concave upward, and the liquid will rise, as shown by Fig. 1-2a. If the liquid does not "wet" the tube, the surface will be concave downward, causing the liquid to be depressed as shown in Fig. 1-2b. When pressures are measured by manometers, care must be exercised to avoid errors resulting from capillarity. A number of experimental values of capillary rise or fall for glass tubes of various sizes, as determined by Folsom,[1] are plotted in Fig. 1-3. The straight line shown on the graph indicates the rise that might be expected with very pure water in contact with air. Some values of surface tension of water are given in Table 1-2.

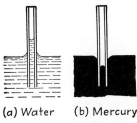

(a) Water   (b) Mercury

Fig. 1-2. Capillary tubes.

The *modulus of elasticity* E of liquids is defined as the change in pressure intensity divided by the corresponding change in volume per unit volume, as shown by Eq. (1-5). The value of

$$E = \frac{\Delta p}{\Delta V/V} \tag{1-5}$$

E for water is approximately 300,000 lb per sq in., varying slightly with temperature. This value is sufficiently high to permit the assumption that liquids are incompressible in the solution of most hydraulic problems.

The gaseous form of water is called *water vapor*, and the partial pressure due to the water vapor is called *vapor pressure*. Within a moderate range of temperatures and pressures and for conditions not too near to the point of condensation, water vapor obeys the gas laws reasonably well. For a given tem-

[1] Richard G. Folsom, Manometer Errors Due to Capillarity, *Instruments,* February, 1936, pp. 36–37.

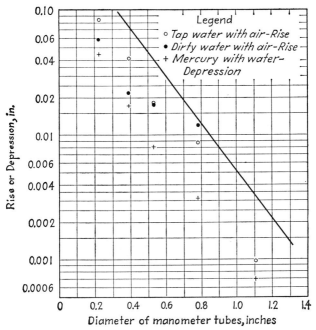

F IG. 1-3. Capillary rise and fall in glass tubes.

perature, any given space can hold only a certain amount of water vapor in the presence of a solid or liquid surface. The pressure exerted by water vapor under saturation conditions is called the *saturation pressure*, p_v. Values of the saturation pressure of water for various temperatures are given in Table 1-2.

Hydraulic Units. The purpose of this subsection is to define and provide conversion factors for all units used in hydraulic engineering. Not only are different units used for the same quantities within systems, but it is frequently necessary to convert from one system to the other. The foot-pound-second system, which is also called the U.S. Customary System (USCS), has been used in the United States and other English-speaking countries. The metric system has been used elsewhere. In the future, the entire world will undoubtedly move toward the use of the metric system in the form called the International System (SI). The SI might also be called the meter-newton-second system. The commonly used USCS units are given in Table 1-3 along with the factors for converting to the SI units and the abbreviations for both systems. The most used quantity in hydraulic engineering is discharge, for which the USCS units are cubic feet per second. These units are abbreviated as cfs, sec-ft, cu-secs, and ft³/sec. In accordance with trends toward simplification, the latter abbreviation shortened to ft³/s is the one shown in Table 1-3 and in other parts of this book. In the metric system discharge is given in cubic meters per second (m^3/s). Prefixes are commonly used in SI to modify basic units by powers of ten. For example, milli- means one thousandth, and kilo- means one thousand. The most used prefixes with their abbreviations and meanings are shown in Table 1-4. Conversion factors for many units used in hydraulics are presented in Table 1-5. Tables 1-6 to 1-13 provide numerical values of conversions between various commonly used units.

The following is a list of references on the conversion of units:

Burton Kleinberg, Introduction to Metric or SI, *Civil Engineering*, March, 1973, p. 55.

"ASTM Metric Practice Guide," ASTM Ad Hoc Committee on Metric Practice, E-380, 1966.

E. A. Mechtly, "The International System of Units, Physical Constants and Conversion Factors," NASA SP-7012, 1969.

"The International System of Units (SI)," U.S. Department of Commerce, National Bureau of Standards, Government Printing Office C13.10:330, 1971.

Table 1-1.   Fluid Properties and Hydraulic Quantities

Quantity	Symbol	Dimensions	Basic units foot-pound-second system	metric system
Length...............	l,d,D,h,H	L	Feet	Meters
Area.................	a	L^2	Feet^2	Meters^2
Volume..............	V	L^3	Feet^3	Meters^3
Time................	T,t	T	Seconds	Seconds
Velocity.............	V,v,u	L/T	Feet per second	Meters per second
Angular velocity.....	α (omega)	T^{-1}	Radians per second	Radians per second
Acceleration.........	a	L/T^2	Feet per second^2	Meters per second^2
Kinematic viscosity...	ν (nu)	L^2/T	Feet^2 per second	Meters^2 per second
Discharge............	Q	L^3/T	Feet^3 per second	Meters^3 per second
Mass................	M	M	Slugs	Kilograms
Density..............	ρ (rho)	M/L^3	Slugs per foot^3	Kilograms per meter^3
Force, weight........	F,W	ML/T^2	Pounds	Newtons
Specific weight (unit weight)...	γ (gamma)	M/L^2T^2	Pounds per foot^3	Newtons per meter^3
Viscosity............	μ (mu)	M/LT	Slugs per foot-second (pound-seconds per foot^2)	Newton-seconds per meter^2
Surface tension.......	σ (sigma)	M/T^2	Pounds per foot	Newtons per meter
Modulus of elasticity (bulk)...	E	M/LT^2	Pounds per foot^2	Newtons per meter^2
Pressure intensity.....	p	M/LT^2	Pounds per foot^2	Newtons per meter^2
Shear stress..........	τ (tau)	M/LT^2	Pounds per foot^2	Newtons per meter^2
Momentum or impulse..		ML/T	Slug-feet per second, or pound-seconds	Kilogram-meters per second
Energy or work.......		ML^2/T^2	Foot-pounds	Meter-newtons
Power...............		ML^2/T^3	Foot-pounds per second	Meter-newtons per second
Specific gravity.......	sp. gr.			

HANDBOOK OF HYDRAULICS

Table 1-2*

Fluid	Temperature, °F	Specific gravity (sp. gr.)	Specific weight w, pounds per cubic foot	Viscosity μ, slugs per foot-second	Kinematic viscosity ν, square feet per second	Pressure of saturated vapor p_v, pounds per square foot	Surface tension, $\times 10^2$ pounds per foot
Water.....	32	0.9999	62.42	0.00003746	0.00001931	12.7	0.518
	39.2	1.0000	62.427	0.00003274	0.00001687	16.9	0.514
	50	0.9997	62.41	0.00002735	0.00001410	25.6	0.509
	60	0.9990	62.37	0.00002359	0.00001217	36.8	0.504
	70	0.9980	62.30	0.00002050	0.00001059	52.3	0.498
	80	0.9966	62.22	0.00001799	0.00000930	73.0	0.492
	100	0.9931	62.00	0.00001424	0.00000739	136	0.480
	200	0.9630	60.12	0.00000637	0.00000341	1,650	0.412
Sea water..	.....	....	64				
Mercury...	32	13.60	......	0.0000355			
	68	13.55	......	0.0000328			
	80.6	13.53					
Castor oil..	50	....	......	0.0505			
	59	0.969	......	0.0315			
	68	....	......	0.0206			
Dry air at 14.7 pounds per square inch.....	32	0.00129	......	0.355×10^{-6}			
	50	0.00125	......	0.372×10^{-6}			
	59	0.00122	......	0.376×10^{-6}			
	68	0.00121	......	0.380×10^{-6}			

* Values given in this table were taken from "Handbook of Chemistry and Physics," International Critical Tables, and ASCE Manual for Hydraulic Laboratory Studies. Many of the values are averages of those obtained from various sources. Other sources of similar data are Smithsonian Physical Tables and Standard Density and Volumetric Tables of U.S. Bureau of Standards.

Table 1-3. Factors for Converting USCS Units to SI Units

LENGTH:
  Feet (ft) $\times$ 0.3048*.............. = Meters (m)
  Inches (in) $\times$ 0.0254*............ = Meters (m)
  Miles (mi) $\times$ 1609.34............. = Meters (m)
  Miles (mi) $\times$ 1.60934............. = Kilometers (km)
  Nautical miles $\times$ 1852.0*......... = Meters (m)
  Yards (yd) $\times$ 0.9144*............ = Meters (m)

AREA:
  Feet^2 (ft^2) $\times$ 0.0929030........... = Meters^2 (m^2)
  Acres $\times$ 4046.86................. = Meters^2 (m^2)
  Miles^2 (mi^2) $\times$ 2.58999........... = Kilometers^2 (km^2)

VOLUME:
  Feet^3 (ft^3) $\times$ 0.02831685........... = Meters^3 (m^3)
  Feet^3 (ft^3) $\times$ 28.31685............. = Liters†
  Yards^3 (yd^3) $\times$ 0.764555........... = Meters^3 (m^3)
  Acre feet $\times$ 1233.48.............. = Meters^3 (m^3)
  Gallons (gal) $\times$ 0.00378541........ = Meters^3 (m^3)
  Gallons (gal) $\times$ 3.78541.......... = Liters†

VELOCITY:
  Feet per second (ft/s) $\times$ 0.3048*... = Meters per second (m/s)
  Miles per hour (mi/hr) $\times$ 0.44704*. = Meters per second (m/s)
  Miles per hour (mi/hr) $\times$ 1.60934.. = Kilometers per hour (km/hr)
  Knots $\times$ 0.514444................ = Meters per second (m/s)
  Knots $\times$ 1.852*.................. = Kilometers per hour (km/hr)

DISCHARGE:
  Feet^3 per second (ft^3/s) $\times$ 0.02831685 = Meters^3 per second (m^3/s)
  Millions of gallons per day $\times$ (mgd)
    0.0438126...................... = Meters^3 per second (m^3/s)
  Acre-feet per day $\times$ 0.0142764..... = Meters^3 per second (m^3/s)
  Gallons per minute (gal/min)
    $\times$ 0.0000630902................ = Meters^3 per second (m^3/s)

FORCE:
  Pounds (lb) $\times$ 0.453592........... = Kilograms force (kgf)
  Pounds (lb) $\times$ 453.592............ = Grams (g)
  Pounds (lb) $\times$ 4.44822............ = Newtons† (N)
  Tons $\times$ 0.907185 .... = Metric tons†

PRESSURE:
  Pounds per foot^2 (lb/ft^2) $\times$ 47.8803.. = Newtons per meter^2 (N/m^2)
  Pounds per foot^2 (lb/ft^2) $\times$ 4.88243. = Kilograms force per meter^2 (kgf/m^2)
  Pounds per inch^2 (lb/in^2) $\times$ 6894.76 = Newtons per meter^2 (N/m^2)
  Pounds per inch^2 (lb/in^2) $\times$ 703.070 = Kilograms force per meter^2 (kgf/m^2)
  Millibars (mb) $\times$ 100.0*........... = Newtons per meter^2 (N/m^2)

Table 1-3. Factors for Converting USCS Units to SI Units
(*Continued*)

UNIT WEIGHT:

Pounds per foot³ (lb/ft³) × 157.0875 = Newtons per meter³ (N/m³)

Pounds per foot³ (lb/ft³) × 16.0185. = Kilograms force per meter³ (kgf/m³)

Pounds per foot³ (lb/ft³) × 0.0160185 = Grams per centimeter³ (g/cm³)

MASS AND DENSITY:

Slugs × 14.5939................ = Kilograms (kg)

Slugs per foot³ × 515.379......... = Kilograms per meter³ (kg/m³)

VISCOSITY:

Pound-seconds per foot² (lb/ft²) or

slugs per foot second × 47.8803 .. = Newton seconds per meter² (Ns/m²)†

Feet² per second (ft²/s) × 0.092903. = Meters² per second (m²/s)

---

* Exact values.

† Liters × 1000.0 = centimeters³

Liters × 0.001 = meters³

Metric tons × 1000.0 = kilograms force

Kilograms force × 9.80665 = newtons

Newtons × 100,000.0 = dynes

Newton seconds per meter² × 0.1 = poises

Table 1-4. SI Prefixes and Meanings

Prefix (abbreviation)	Meaning
Mega- (M)	1,000,000.
Kilo- (k)	1,000.
Hecto- (h)	100.
Deka- (da)	10.
Deci- (d)	0.1
Centi- (c)	0.01
Milli- (m)	0.001
Micro- (μ)	0.000001

Table 1-5. Factors for Conversion of Units

To reduce *A* to *B*, multiply *A* by *F*. To reduce *B* to *A*, multiply *B* by *G*.

Unit *A*	Factor *F*	Logarithm of *F* characteristics all positive	Logarithm of *G* characteristics all negative	Factor *G*	Unit *B*
LENGTH:					
Miles...........	5,280.*	3.72263	4.27737	.00018939	Feet
Miles...........	1,609.34	3.20665	4.79335	.00062137	Meters
Miles...........	1.60935	0.20665	1.79335	.62137	Kilometers
Kilometers...........	3,280.84	3.51598	4.48402	.00030480	Feet
Meters...........	3.2808	0.51598	1.48402	.30480	Feet
Yards...........	36.*	1.55630	2.44370	.027778	Inches
Feet...........	12.*	1.07918	2.92082	.083333	Inches
Meters...........	39.370	1.59517	2.40483	.025400	Inches
Inches...........	2.5400	0.40483	1.59517	.39370	Centimeters
Nautical miles...........	6076.115	....	....	.00016458	Feet
Nautical miles...........	1.1508	....	....	.86898	Miles
Fathoms...........	6.*	....	....	.16667	Feet
Gunter's chains...........	66.*	....	....	.0151515	Feet
Rods...........	16.5*	....	....	.060606	Feet
SURFACE:					
Square miles...........	27,878,400.*	7.44527	8.55473	.000000035870	Square feet

Square miles	640.*	2.80618	3.19382	.0015625*	Acres
Square miles	259.000	2.41330	3.58670	.0038610	Hectares
Acres	43,560.*	4.63909	5.36091	.000022957	Square feet
Acres	4,046.9	3.60712	4.39288	.00024710	Square meters
Hectares	2.47104	0.39288	1.60712	.40469	Acres
Hectares	10,000.*	4.00000	4.00000	.0001*	Square meters
Square feet	144.*	2.15836	3.84164	.0069444	Square inches
Square inches	6.4516	0.80967	1.19033	.15500	Square centimeters
Square meters	10.764	1.03197	2.96803	.092902	Square feet
VOLUME:					
Cubic feet	1,728.*	3.23754	4.76246	.00057870	Cubic inches
Cubic inches	16.387	1.21450	2.78550	.061024	Cubic centimeters
Cubic meters	35.3145	1.54795	2.45205	.028817	Cubic feet
Cubic meters	1.3079	0.11659	1.88341	.76456	Cubic yards
Cubic feet	7.4805	0.87393	1.12607	.13368	U.S. gallons
Cubic feet	6.2321	0.79463	1.20537	.16046	Imperial gallons
Cubic feet	28.317	1.45205	2.54795	.035314	Liters
U.S. gallons	231.*	2.36361	3.63639	.0043290	Cubic inches
Imperial gallons	277.274	2.44291	3.55709	.0036065	Cubic inches
Liters	61.0234	1.78550	2.21450	.016387	Cubic inches
U.S. gallons	3.7854	0.57812	1.42188	.26417	Liters
Imperial gallons	1.2003	0.07930	1.92070	.83311	U.S. gallons

* Exact values.

Table 1-5. Factors for Conversion of Units (*Continued*)

To reduce *A* to *B*, multiply *A* by *F*.   To reduce *B* to *A*, multiply *B* by *G*.

Unit A	Factor F	Logarithm of F characteristics all positive	Logarithm of G characteristics all negative	Factor G	Unit B
VOLUME (*continued*):					
Imperial gallons..........	4.5437	0.65741	1.34259	.22009	Liters
U.S. bushels..........	1.2445	0.09498	1.90502	.80356	Cubic feet
Fluid ounces..........	1.8047	0.25640	1.74360	.55411	Cubic inches
Acre-feet..........	43,560.*	4.63909	5.36091	.000022957	Cubic feet
Acre-feet..........	1,613.3	3.20772	4.79228	.00061983	Cubic yards
Acre-feet..........	1,233.5	3.09114	4.90886	.00081071	Cubic meters
Acre-inches..........	3,630.*	3.55991	4.44009	.00027548	Cubic feet
Millions U.S. gallons..........	133,681.	5.12607	6.87393	.0000074805	Cubic feet
Millions U.S. gallons..........	3.0689	0.48698	1.51302	.32585	Acre-feet
Feet depth on 1 square mile....	27,878,400.*	7.44527	8.55473	.000000035870	Cubic feet
Feet depth on 1 square mile....	640.*	2.80618	3.19382	.0015625*	Acre-feet
Inches depth on 1 square mile..	2,323,200.*	6.36609	7.63391	.00000043044	Cubic feet
Inches depth on 1 square mile..	53.333	1.72700	2.27300	.01875*	Acre-feet
VELOCITIES:					
Miles per hour..........	1.4667	0.16633	1.83367	.68182	Feet per second

Meters per second..........	3.2808	0.51598	1.48402	.30480	Feet per second
Meters per second..........	2.2369	0.34965	1.65035	.44704	Miles per hour
Knots.....................	1.1508	....	....	.86898	Miles per hour
Knots.....................	1.6878	....	....	.59248	Feet per second
DISCHARGE:					
Second-feet...............	60.*	1.77815	2.22185	.016667	Cubic feet per minute
Second-feet...............	86,400.*	4.93651	5.06349	.000011574	Cubic feet per 24 hours
Second-feet...............	448.83	2.65208	3.34792	.0022280	U.S. gallons per minute
Second-feet...............	646,317.	5.81045	6.18955	.0000015472	U.S. gallons per 24 hours
Second-feet...............	1.9835	0.29743	1.70257	.50417	Acre-feet per 24 hours
Second-feet...............	723.98	2.85972	3.14028	.0013813	Acre-feet per 365 days
Millions U.S. gallons per day...	1.5472	0.18955	1.81045	.64632	Second-feet
Inches depth per hour.......	645.33	2.80978	3.19022	.0015496	Second-feet per square mile
Inches depth per day........	26.889	1.42957	2.57043	.037190	Second-feet per square mile
Second-feet per square mile.....	1.0413	0.01758	1.98242	.96032	Inches depth per 28 days
Second-feet per square mile.....	1.0785	0.03283	1.96717	.92720	Inches depth per 29 days
Second-feet per square mile.....	1.1157	0.04755	1.95245	.89630	Inches depth per 30 days
Second-feet per square mile.....	1.1529	0.06179	1.93821	.86738	Inches depth per 31 days
Second-feet per square mile.....	13.574	1.13272	2.86728	.073668	Inches depth per 365 days
Second-feet per square mile.....	13.612	1.13391	2.86609	.073467	Inches depth per 366 days
Acre-inches per hour........	1.0083†	0.00360	1.99640	.99173†	Second-feet

* Exact values.

Table 1-5. Factors for Conversion of Units (*Continued*)

To reduce *A* to *B*, multiply *A* by *F*.   To reduce *B* to *A*, multiply *B* by *G*.

Unit A	Factor F	Logarithm of F characteristics all positive	Logarithm of G characteristics all negative	Factor G	Unit B
DISCHARGE (*continued*):					
Cubic-feet per minute.........	7.4805	0.87393	1.12607	.13368	U.S. gallons per minute
Cubic-feet per minute.........	10,772.	4.03229	5.96771	.000092834	U.S. gallons per 24 hours
U.S. gallons per minute......	1,440.*	3.15836	4.84164	.0069444	U.S. gallons per 24 hours
PRESSURES (0°C = 32°F):					
Atmospheres (mean)...........	14.697	1.16723	2.83277	.068041	Pounds per square inch
Atmospheres (mean)...........	29.921	1.47598	2.52402	.033421	Inches of mercury
Atmospheres (mean)...........	760.	2.88081	3.11919	.0013158	Millimeters of mercury
Atmospheres (mean)...........	33.901	1.53021	2.46979	.029498	Feet of water
Atmospheres (mean)...........	1.0333	0.01422	1.98578	.96778	Kilograms per square centimeter
Inches of mercury............	1.1330	0.05423	1.94577	.88261	Feet of water
Pounds per square inch.......	2.0359	0.30875	1.69125	.49119	Inches of mercury
Pounds per square inch.......	51.711	1.71359	2.28641	.019338	Millimeters of mercury
Feet of water................	62.416	1.79530	2.20470	.016022	Pounds per square foot
Pounds per square inch.......	2.3071	0.36307	1.63693	.43344	Feet of water
WEIGHT:					
Pounds.......................	7,000.*	3.84510	4.15490	.00014286	Grains

Grams.................	15.432	1.18843	2.81157	.064799	Grains
Kilograms force.......	2.2046	0.34333	1.65667	.45359	Pounds
Long tons (2,240 pounds).....	1.12*	0.04922	1.95078	.89286	Short tons (2,000 pounds)
Long tons.............	1.0160	0.00691	1.99309	.98421	Metric tons (1,000 kilograms)
Metric tons (2,204.62 pounds)...	1.1023	....	....	.90718	Short tons
POWER:					
Horsepower............	550.*	2.74036	3.25964	.0018182	Foot-pounds per second
Kilowatts.............	1.3405	0.12726	1.87274	.746	Horsepower
Kilowatts.............	8,760*	3.94250	4.05750	.00011416	Kilowatt-hours per year
Horsepower............	8,760*	3.94250	4.05750	.00011416	Horsepower-hours per year
Horsepower............	6,535	3.81524	4.18476	.00015303	Kilowatt-hours per year

* Exact values.
† Usually taken as unity.

Table 1-6. Conversion between Meters and Feet

Meters to Feet

Meters	0	1	2	3	4	5	6	7	8	9
		3.28	6.56	9.84	13.12	16.40	19.68	22.97	26.25	29.53
10	32.81	36.09	39.37	42.65	45.93	49.21	52.49	55.77	59.06	62.34
20	65.62	68.90	72.18	75.46	78.74	82.02	85.30	88.58	91.86	95.14
30	98.42	101.71	104.99	108.27	111.55	114.83	118.11	121.39	124.67	127.95
40	131.23	134.51	137.79	141.08	144.36	147.64	150:92	154.20	157.48	160.76
50	164.04	167.32	170.60	173.88	177.16	180.45	183.73	187.01	190.29	193.57
60	196.85	200.13	203.41	206.69	209.97	213.25	216.53	219.82	223.10	226.38
70	229.66	232.94	236.22	239.50	242.78	246.06	249.34	252.62	255.90	259.19
80	262.47	265.75	269.03	272.31	275.59	278.87	282.15	285.43	288.71	291.99
90	295.27	298.56	301.84	305.12	308.40	311.68	314.96	318.24	321.52	324.80

Feet to Meters

Feet	0	1	2	3	4	5	6	7	8	9
		0.305	0.610	0.914	1.219	1.524	1.829	2.134	2.438	2.743
10	3.048	3.353	3.658	3.962	4.267	4.572	4.877	5.182	5.486	5.791
20	6.096	6.401	6.706	7.010	7.315	7.620	7.925	8.230	8.534	8.839
30	9.144	9.449	9.754	10.058	10.363	10.668	10.973	11.278	11.582	11.887
40	12.192	12.497	12.802	13.106	13.411	13.716	14.021	14.326	14.630	14.935
50	15.240	15.545	15.850	16.154	16.459	16.764	17.069	17.374	17.678	17.983
60	18.288	18.593	18.898	19.202	19.507	19.812	20.117	20.422	20.726	21.031
70	21.336	21.641	21.946	22.250	22.555	22.860	23.165	23.470	23.774	24.079
80	24.384	24.689	24.994	25.298	25.603	25.908	26.213	26.518	26.822	27.127
90	27.432	27.737	28.042	28.346	28.651	28.956	29.261	29.566	29.870	30.175

Table 1-7. Conversion between Kilograms Force and Pounds

Kilograms Force to Pounds

Kilograms	0	1	2	3	4	5	6	7	8	9
		2.20	4.41	6.61	8.82	11.02	13.23	15.43	17.64	19.84
10	22.05	24.25	26.46	28.66	30.86	33.07	35.27	37.48	39.68	41.89
20	44.09	46.30	48.50	50.71	52.91	55.12	57.32	59.52	61.73	63.93
30	66.14	68.34	70.55	72.75	74.96	77.16	79.37	81.57	83.78	85.98
40	88.18	90.39	92.59	94.80	97.00	99.21	101.41	103.62	105.82	108.03
50	110.23	112.44	114.64	116.85	119.05	121.25	123.46	125.66	127.87	130.07
60	132.28	134.48	136.69	138.89	141.10	143.30	145.51	147.71	149.91	152.12
70	154.32	156.53	158.73	160.94	163.14	165.35	167.55	169.76	171.96	174.17
80	176.37	178.57	180.78	182.98	185.19	187.39	189.60	191.80	194.01	196.21
90	198.42	200.62	202.83	205.03	207.23	209.44	211.64	213.85	216.05	218.26

Pounds to Kilograms Force

Pounds	0	1	2	3	4	5	6	7	8	9
		0.4536	0.9072	1.361	1.814	2.268	2.722	3.175	3.629	4.082
10	4.536	4.990	5.443	5.897	6.350	6.804	7.257	7.711	8.165	8.618
20	9.072	9.525	9.979	10.433	10.886	11.340	11.793	12.247	12.701	13.154
30	13.608	14.061	14.515	14.969	15.422	15.876	16.329	16.783	17.237	17.690
40	18.144	18.597	19.051	19.504	19.958	20.412	20.865	21.319	21.772	22.226
50	22.680	23.133	23.587	24.040	24.494	24.948	25.401	25.855	26.308	26.762
60	27.216	27.669	28.123	28.576	29.030	29.484	29.937	30.391	30.844	31.298
70	31.752	32.205	32.659	33.112	33.566	34.019	34.473	34.927	35.380	35.834
80	36.287	36.741	37.195	37.648	38.102	38.555	39.009	39.463	39.916	40.370
90	40.823	41.277	41.731	42.184	42.638	43.091	43.545	43.999	44.452	44.906

Table 1-8. Conversion between Cubic Feet and Gallons
U.S. Gallons to Cubic Feet

U. S. gallons	0	1	2	3	4	5	6	7	8	9
		0.1337	0.2674	0.4010	0.5347	0.6684	0.8021	0.9358	1.0694	1.2031
10	1.3368	1.4705	1.6042	1.7378	1.8715	2.0052	2.1389	2.2726	2.4063	2.5399
20	2.6736	2.8073	2.9410	3.0747	3.2083	3.3420	3.4757	3.6094	3.7431	3.8767
30	4.0104	4.1441	4.2778	4.4115	4.5451	4.6788	4.8125	4.9462	5.0799	5.2135
40	5.3472	5.4809	5.6146	5.7483	5.8819	6.0156	6.1493	6.2830	6.4167	6.5503
50	6.6840	6.8177	6.9514	7.0851	7.2188	7.3524	7.4861	7.6198	7.7535	7.8872
60	8.0208	8.1545	8.2882	8.4219	8.5556	8.6892	8.8229	8.9566	9.0903	9.2240
70	9.3576	9.4913	9.6250	9.7587	9.8924	10.026	10.160	10.293	10.427	10.561
80	10.694	10.828	10.962	11.095	11.229	11.363	11.497	11.630	11.764	11.898
90	12.031	12.165	12.299	12.432	12.566	12.700	12.833	12.967	13.101	13.234

Cubic Feet to U.S. Gallons

Cubic feet	0	1	2	3	4	5	6	7	8	9
		7.481	14.961	22.442	29.922	37.403	44.883	52.364	59.844	67.325
10	74.805	82.286	89.766	97.247	104.73	112.21	119.69	127.17	134.65	142.13
20	149.61	157.09	164.57	172.05	179.53	187.01	194.49	201.97	209.45	216.94
30	224.42	231.90	239.38	246.86	254.34	261.82	269.30	276.78	284.26	291.74
40	299.22	306.70	314.18	321.66	329.14	336.62	344.10	351.58	359.06	366.55
50	374.03	381.51	388.99	396.47	403.95	411.43	418.91	426.39	433.87	441.35
60	448.83	456.31	463.79	471.27	478.75	486.23	493.71	501.19	508.68	516.16
70	523.64	531.12	538.60	546.08	553.56	561.04	568.52	576.00	583.48	590.96
80	598.44	605.92	613.40	620.88	628.36	635.84	643.32	650.81	658.29	665.77
90	673.25	680.73	688.21	695.69	703.17	710.65	718.13	725.61	733.09	740.57

Table 1-9. Conversion between Acre-Feet and Gallons
Millions of U.S. Gallons to Acre-Feet

Mil. gals.	0	1	2	3	4	5	6	7	8	9
		3.07	6.14	9.21	12.28	15.34	18.41	21.48	24.55	27.62
10	30.69	33.76	36.83	39.90	42.96	46.03	49.10	52.17	55.24	58.31
20	61.38	64.45	67.52	70.58	73.65	76.72	79.79	82.86	85.93	89.00
30	92.07	95.14	98.20	101.27	104.34	107.41	110.48	113.55	116.62	119.69
40	122.76	125.82	128.89	131.96	135.03	138.10	141.17	144.24	147.31	150.38
50	153.44	156.51	159.58	162.65	165.72	168.79	171.86	174.93	178.00	181.06
60	184.13	187.20	190.27	193.34	196.41	199.48	202.55	205.62	208.68	211.75
70	214.82	217.89	220.96	224.03	227.10	230.17	233.24	236.30	239.37	242.44
80	245.51	248.58	251.65	254.72	257.79	260.86	263.92	266.99	270.06	273.13
90	276.20	279.27	282.34	285.41	288.48	291.54	294.61	297.68	300.75	303.82

Acre-Feet to Millions of U.S. Gallons

Acre-feet	0	1	2	3	4	5	6	7	8	9
		0.326	0.652	0.978	1.303	1.629	1.955	2.281	2.607	2.933
10	3.259	3.584	3.910	4.236	4.562	4.888	5.214	5.539	5.865	6.191
20	6.517	6.843	7.169	7.495	7.820	8.146	8.472	8.798	9.124	9.450
30	9.776	10.101	10.427	10.753	11.079	11.405	11.731	12.057	12.382	12.708
40	13.034	13.360	13.686	14.012	14.337	14.663	14.989	15.315	15.641	15.967
50	16.293	16.618	16.944	17.270	17.596	17.922	18.248	18.574	18.899	19.225
60	19.551	19.877	20.203	20.529	20.854	21.180	21.506	21.832	22.158	22.484
70	22.810	23.135	23.461	23.787	24.113	24.439	24.765	25.091	25.416	25.742
80	26.068	26.394	26.720	27.046	27.372	27.697	28.023	28.349	28.675	29.001
90	29.327	29.652	29.978	30.304	30.630	30.956	31.282	31.608	31.933	32.259

Table 1-10. Conversion between Cubic Feet per Second and Gallons per Minute

U.S. Gallons per Minute to Cubic Feet per Second

Gal per min.	0	1	2	3	4	5	6	7	8	9
		.00223	.00446	.00668	.00891	.01114	.01337	.01560	.01782	.02005
10	.02228	.02451	.02674	.02896	.03119	.03342	.03565	.03788	.04010	.04233
20	.04456	.04679	.04902	.05124	.05347	.05570	.05793	.06016	.06238	.06461
30	.06684	.06907	.07130	.07352	.07575	.07798	.08021	.08244	.08466	.08689
40	.08912	.09135	.09358	.09580	.09803	.10026	.10249	.10472	.10694	.10917
50	.11140	.11363	.11586	.11808	.12031	.12254	.12477	.12700	.12922	.13145
60	.13368	.13591	.13814	.14036	.14259	.14482	.14705	.14928	.15150	.15373
70	.15596	.15819	.16042	.16264	.16487	.16710	.16933	.17156	.17378	.17601
80	.17824	.18047	.18270	.18492	.18715	.18938	.19161	.19384	.19606	.19829
90	.20052	.20275	.20498	.20720	.20943	.21166	.21389	.21612	.21834	.22057

Cubic Feet per Second to U.S. Gallons per Minute

Second-feet	0	1	2	3	4	5	6	7	8	9
		449	898	1,346	1,795	2,244	2,693	3,142	3,591	4,039
10	4,488	4,937	5,386	5,835	6,284	6,732	7,181	7,630	8,079	8,528
20	8,977	9,425	9,874	10,323	10,772	11,221	11,670	12,118	12,567	13,016
30	13,465	13,914	14,363	14,811	15,260	15,709	16,158	16,607	17,056	17,504
40	17,953	18,402	18,851	19,300	19,749	20,197	20,646	21,095	21,544	21,993
50	22,442	22,890	23,339	23,788	24,237	24,686	25,135	25,583	26,032	26,481
60	26,930	27,379	27,828	28,276	28,725	29,174	29,623	30,072	30,521	30,969
70	31,418	31,867	32,316	32,765	33,214	33,662	34,111	34,560	35,009	35,458
80	35,906	36,355	36,804	37,253	37,702	38,151	38,599	39,048	39,497	39,946
90	40,395	40,844	41,292	41,741	42,190	42,639	43,088	43,537	43,985	44,434

Table 1-11. Conversion between Cubic Feet per Second and Gallons per Day

Millions of U.S. Gallons per Day to Cubic Feet per Second

M. g. p. d.	0	1	2	3	4	5	6	7	8	9
		1.547	3.094	4.642	6.189	7.736	9.283	10.831	12.378	13.925
10	15.472	17.020	18.567	20.114	21.661	23.208	24.756	26.303	27.850	29.397
20	30.945	32.492	34.039	35.586	37.133	38.681	40.228	41.775	43.322	44.870
30	46.417	47.964	49.511	51.059	52.606	54.153	55.700	57.247	58.795	60.342
40	61.889	63.436	64.984	66.531	68.078	69.625	71.173	72.720	74.267	75.814
50	77.361	78.909	80.456	82.003	83.550	85.098	86.645	88.192	89.739	91.287
60	92.834	94.381	95.928	97.475	99.023	100.57	102.12	103.66	105.21	106.76
70	108.31	109.85	111.40	112.95	114.49	116.04	117.59	119.14	120.68	122.23
80	123.78	125.33	126.87	128.42	129.97	131.51	133.06	134.61	136.16	137.70
90	139.25	140.80	142.35	143.89	145.44	146.99	148.53	150.08	151.63	153.18

Cubic Feet per Second to Millions of U.S. Gallons per Day

Second-feet	0	1	2	3	4	5	6	7	8	9
		0.646	1.293	1.939	2.585	3.232	3.878	4.524	5.171	5.817
10	6.463	7.109	7.756	8.402	9.048	9.695	10.341	10.987	11.634	12.280
20	12.926	13.573	14.219	14.865	15.512	16.158	16.804	17.451	18.097	18.743
30	19.390	20.036	20.682	21.328	21.975	22.621	23.267	23.914	24.560	25.206
40	25.853	26.499	27.145	27.792	28.438	29.084	29.731	30.377	31.023	31.670
50	32.316	32.962	33.608	34.255	34.901	35.547	36.194	36.840	37.486	38.133
60	38.779	39.425	40.072	40.718	41.364	42.011	42.657	43.303	43.950	44.596
70	45.242	45.888	46.535	47.181	47.827	48.474	49.120	49.766	50.413	51.059
80	51.705	52.352	52.998	53.644	54.291	54.937	55.583	56.230	56.876	57.522
90	58.169	58.815	59.461	60.107	60.754	61.400	62.046	62.693	63.339	63.985

Table 1-12. Conversion between Kilowatts and Horsepower

Kilowatts to Horsepower

Kilowatts	0	1	2	3	4	5	6	7	8	9
		1.340	2.681	4.021	5.362	6.702	8.043	9.383	10.724	12.064
10	13.405	14.745	16.086	17.426	18.767	20.107	21.448	22.788	24.129	25.469
20	26.810	28.150	29.491	30.831	32.172	33.512	34.853	36.193	37.534	38.874
30	40.214	41.555	42.895	44.236	45.576	46.917	48.257	49.598	50.938	52.279
40	53.619	54.960	56.300	57.641	58.981	60.322	61.662	63.003	64.343	65.684
50	67.024	68.365	69.705	71.046	72.386	73.727	75.067	76.408	77.748	79.089
60	80.429	81.770	83.110	84.451	85.791	87.132	88.472	89.813	91.153	92.494
70	93.834	95.175	96.515	97.856	99.196	100.54	101.88	103.22	104.56	105.90
80	107.24	108.58	109.92	111.26	112.60	113.94	115.28	116.62	117.96	119.30
90	120.64	121.98	123.32	124.67	126.01	127.35	128.69	130.03	131.37	132.71

Horsepower to Killowatts

Horsepower	0	1	2	3	4	5	6	7	8	9
		0.746	1.492	2.238	2.984	3.730	4.476	5.222	5.968	6.714
10	7.460	8.206	8.952	9.698	10.444	11.190	11.936	12.682	13.428	14.174
20	14.920	15.666	16.412	17.158	17.904	18.650	19.396	20.142	20.888	21.634
30	22.380	23.126	23.872	24.618	25.364	26.110	26.856	27.602	28.348	29.094
40	29.840	30.586	31.332	32.078	32.824	33.570	34.316	35.062	35.808	36.554
50	37.300	38.046	38.792	39.538	40.284	41.030	41.776	42.522	43.268	44.014
60	44.760	45.506	46.252	46.998	47.744	48.490	49.236	49.982	50.728	51.474
70	52.220	52.966	53.712	54.458	55.204	55.950	56.696	57.442	58.188	58.934
80	59.680	60.426	61.172	61.918	62.664	63.410	64.156	64.902	65.648	66.394
90	67.140	67.886	68.632	69.378	70.124	70.870	71.616	72.362	73.108	73.854

Table 1-13. Conversion from Inches to Feet

Inches	Fractions of inches							
	0	⅛	¼	⅜	½	⅝	¾	⅞
0	.0000	.0104	.0208	.0313	.0417	.0521	.0625	.0729
1	.0833	.0937	.1042	.1146	.1250	.1354	.1458	.1562
2	.1667	.1771	.1875	.1979	.2083	.2188	.2292	.2396
3	.2500	.2604	.2708	.2813	.2917	.3021	.3125	.3229
4	.3333	.3437	.3542	.3646	.3750	.3854	.3958	.4062
5	.4167	.4271	.4375	.4479	.4583	.4688	.4792	.4896
6	.5000	.5104	.5208	.5313	.5417	.5521	.5625	.5729
7	.5833	.5937	.6042	.6146	.6250	.6354	.6458	.6562
8	.6667	.6771	.6875	.6979	.7083	.7188	.7292	.7396
9	.7500	.7604	.7708	.7813	.7917	.8021	.8125	.8229
10	.8333	.8437	.8542	.8646	.8750	.8854	.8958	.9062
11	.9167	.9271	.9375	.9479	.9583	.9688	.9792	.9896
12	1.0000	......	......	......	......	......	......	......

Table 1-14. Average Specific Weight, in Pounds per Cubic Foot,
of Various Materials Used in Construction

Substance	Weight	Substance	Weight
CLAY, EARTH AND MUD:		MASONRY AND ITS MA-TERIALS—(continued):	
Clay....................	122–162	Sand, pure quartz, dry,	
Earth, dry and loose......	72–80	loose.................	87–106
Earth, dry and shaken....	82–92	Sand, pure quartz, dry,	
Earth, dry and moderately		slightly shaken.........	92–110
rammed................	90–100	Sand, pure quartz, dry,	
Earth, slightly moist, loose	70–76	rammed...............	100–120
Earth, more moist, loose..	66–68	Sand, natural, dry, loose.	80–110
Earth, more moist, shaken.	75–90	Sand, natural, dry, shak-	
Earth, more moist, moder-		en....................	85–125
ately rammed..........	90–100	Sand, wet, voids full of	
Earth, as soft flowing mud.	104–112	water.................	118–128
Earth, as soft mud well		Stone....................	135–195
pressed into a box.......	110–120	Stone, quarried, loosely	
Mud, dry, close..........	80–110	piled.................	80–110
Mud, wet, moderately		Stone, broken, loose.....	77–112
pressed................	110–130	Stone, broken, rammed..	79–121
Mud, wet, fluid..........	104–120		
		METAL AND ALLOYS:	
MASONRY AND ITS MA-		Brass (copper and zinc)...	487–524
TERIALS:		Bronze (copper and tin)..	524–537
Brick, best pressed.......	150	Copper, cast.............	537–548
Brick, common hard......	125	Copper, rolled...........	548–562
Brick, soft, inferior.......	100	Iron and steel, cast.......	438–483
Brickwork, pressed brick,		Average...............	450
fine joints..............	140	Iron and steel, wrought...	475–494
Brickwork, medium quality	125	Average...............	480
Brickwork, coarse, inferior		Spelter or zinc...........	425–450
soft bricks..............	100	Tin, cast................	450–470
Cement, pulverized, loose.	72–105	Steel....................	490
Cement, pressed..........	115	Tin......................	459
Cement, set..............	168–187	Zinc.....................	438
Concrete, 1 : 3 : 6........	140	Mercury (32°F.).........	849
Gravel, loose.............	82–125		
Gravel, rammed..........	90–145	WOODS (DRY) *	
Masonry of granite or		White oak..............	46.4
stone of like weight:		White pine..............	25.6
Well-dressed............	165	Southern long-leaf pine....	38.1
Well-scabbled rubble, 20		Douglas fir.............	32.1
per cent. mortar.......	154	Short-leaf yellow pine.....	38.4
Roughly scabbled rubble,		Norway pine.............	30.2
25 to 35 per cent. mortar.	150	Spruce and eastern fir.....	25.0
Well-scabbled dry rubble.	138	Hemlock.................	26–32
Roughly scabbled dry		Cypress.................	29.8
rubble...............	125	Cedar...................	23.1
Masonry of sandstone or		Chestnut................	41.0
stone of like weight		California redwood.......	26.2
weighs about seven-		California spruce.........	25.0
eighths of the above.			
Mortar, hardened......	90–115		

* The weights of green or unseasoned timbers are 20 to 40 per cent greater.

SECTION 2

HYDROSTATICS

Hydrostatics is the branch of hydraulics which deals with the pressures and forces resulting from the weight of a fluid at rest. In this chapter, the principles of hydrostatics are presented and applications are made to hydraulic engineering problems. The use of these principles in cases where the fluid is in motion is discussed, and methods of determining the additional forces resulting from changes in velocity are presented.

Fluid Pressure. The force per unit area acting on a real or imaginary surface within a fluid is called *intensity of pressure*, or simply *pressure, p*. It may be demonstrated that the pressure at any point in a fluid acts equally in all directions. The force on a boundary surface re-

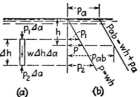

Fig. 2-1. Fluid pressure.

sulting from fluid pressure must be normal to the surface at all points because of the inability of fluids at rest to transmit shear. The pressure variation with depth within a liquid may be evaluated by considering the forces acting on the vertical prism of height Δh and cross-sectional area Δa shown in Fig. 2-1a. The summation of all the forces acting on this prism in the vertical direction, as well as in all other directions, must be equal to zero. The vertical forces consist of the weight and the force due to the pressure p_1 at the top and that due to p_2 at the bottom. It is assumed here that the fluid is a liquid and that the specific weight does not vary with pressure. The summation of the vertical forces gives

$$p_2 \, \Delta a = w \, \Delta h \, \Delta a + p_1 \, \Delta a$$

2–1

and

$$p_2 = w \, \Delta h + p_1 \qquad (2\text{-}1)$$

the downward direction of h being taken as positive. Equation (2-1) may be solved for Δh to give

$$\Delta h = \frac{p_2}{w} - \frac{p_1}{w} \qquad (2\text{-}2)$$

If p_1 is taken as the pressure at the liquid surface, Δh becomes h, the vertical distance below the liquid surface to the point where the pressure is p. Furthermore, when the pressure at the liquid surface is atmospheric pressure (p_a), p_2 is the absolute pressure at that point. The following expression for absolute pressure p_{ab} may now be obtained from Eq. (2-1):

$$p_{ab} = wh + p_a \qquad (2\text{-}3)$$

More commonly used in engineering work is the gage pressure p. The gage-pressure scale is obtained by designating atmospheric pressure as zero. The following expressions for gage pressure may be obtained from Eq. (2-3) by letting p_a become zero:

$$p = wh \qquad (2\text{-}4)$$

and

$$h = \frac{p}{w} \qquad (2\text{-}5)$$

Equations (2-3) and (2-4) are illustrated graphically in Fig. 2-1b. The expression p/w is called the *pressure head*. It expresses the depth in feet of a liquid of specific weight w required to produce a pressure p. Values of absolute pressure are always positive, whereas gage pressure may be positive or negative, depending on whether the pressure is greater or less than atmospheric. Negative gage pressures indicate that a partial vacuum exists.

Atmospheric Pressure. The variation of pressure with elevation in the atmosphere is illustrated by Fig. 2-2. The straight-line variation derived

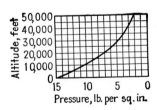

Fig. 2-2. Atmospheric pressure.

for liquids does not apply to the atmosphere (or any other gas) because the density varies with the altitude.[1] The average value of atmospheric pressure at sea level is usually taken as 14.7 lb per sq in., or 2,116 lb per sq ft.

The pressure gages used to measure atmospheric pressure are called *barometers.* A barometer of the type shown in Fig. 2-3 may be made by filling the tube with liquid, temporarily sealing the open end, inverting the tube, and releasing the seal beneath the surface of the liquid in the pan. If the tube is sufficiently long, there will be a space at the top that is empty except for the vapor of the liquid. Evaporation will take place at the liquid surface in the tube until a saturated vapor and corresponding vapor pressure p_v (see Fluid Properties, Sec. 1) exist above the liquid surface. Example 2-1 illustrates that water is an impractical liquid for barometers. The liquid generally used is mercury. Mercury not only permits the use of a shorter tube, but its vapor pressure is so low[2] that it may be neglected.

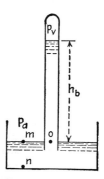

FIG. 2-3. Barometer.

Example 2-1. Determine the value of h_b in Fig. 2-3 if the liquid is water at a temperature of 70°F and p_a is 14.7 lb per sq in. If Eq. (2-1) is written first from m to n and then from n to o, it will be seen that $p_o = p_m$ and therefore that the pressure at o is atmospheric. Equation (2-2) may now be written as follows:

$$\Delta h = h_b = \frac{p_a}{w} - \frac{p_v}{w}$$

The value of p_a/w is $(14.7 \times 144)/62.3$, or 33.98 ft, the value of w being obtained from Table 1-2. The value of p_v is given in Table 1-2 as 52.3 lb per sq ft. Therefore p_v/w is $52.3/62.3$, or 0.84 ft; hence

$$h_b = 33.98 - 0.84 = 33.14 \text{ ft}$$

[1] For a detailed discussion of pressure variations in gases see L. Prandtl and O. J. Tietjens, "Fundamentals of Hydro- and Aeromechanics," pp. 29–35, McGraw-Hill Book Company, Inc., New York, 1934.

[2] "Handbook of Physics and Chemistry," 12th ed., p. 1269.

Example 2-2. Determine the value of h_b in Fig. 2-3 if the liquid is mercury at a temperature of 70°F and p_a is 14.7 lb per sq in.

The vapor pressure of mercury is negligible, so that Eq. (2-2) becomes

$$\Delta h = h_b = \frac{p_a}{w} + 0$$

$$h_b = \frac{14.7 \times 144}{13.54 \times 62.42} = 2.50 \text{ ft}$$

which is equivalent to 30 in., or 764 mm.

Manometers. Manometers are tubes attached to reservoirs, pipes, or channels for the purpose of measuring the pressure. The equations of hydrostatics are used to determine pressures from manometer readings even though manometers are most frequently used to measure pressures in moving fluids. To ensure against including forces due to acceleration in the manometer readings, it is necessary to install the tube in a wall which is parallel to the flow lines in such a manner that the flow pattern is not disturbed by the opening. When the manometers contain only the fluid in the conduit, as illustrated by Fig. 2-4a and b, they are frequently called *piezometers*. In Fig. 2-4a, the pressure at l, p_l, is equal to the pressure at the center of the pipe, p_c; consequently the value of p_c may be obtained from either of the three tubes, using Eq. (2-4) arranged as follows:

$$p_c = wh_c \qquad (2\text{-}6)$$

The left tube of Fig. 2-4a and the one shown in 2-4b may be used to measure negative gage pressures as well as positive ones. Equation (2-6) may be applied to Fig. 2-4b, knowing the pressure at l to be zero and that values of h_c measured upward from the zero datum are negative.

Example 2-3. Determine the value of h_c in Fig. 2-4a when the gage pressure at c is 50 lb per sq in. if the pipe contains water.

Solving Eq. (2-6),[1]

$$h_c = \frac{p_c}{w} = \frac{50 \times 144}{62.4} = 115 \text{ ft}$$

---

[1] Unless some particular temperature is stated, the specific weight of water will be taken as 62.4 lb per cu ft in numerical examples.

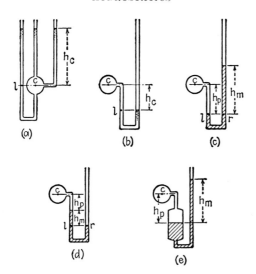

FIG. 2-4. Manometers.

Example 2-4. Determine the pressure at c in Fig. 2-4b if h_c is 6.3 ft and the pipe contains oil having a specific gravity of 0.95.

$$p_c = wh_c = -0.95 \times 62.4 \times 6.3$$
$$= -373 \text{ lb per sq ft, or } -2.59 \text{ lb/in.}^2$$

or, using the conversion factors and symbols from Table 1-3,

$$p_c = -2.59 \times 6,894.76 = -17,860 \text{ N/m}^2$$

or

$$p_c = -2.59 \times 703.07 = -1,821 \text{ kgf/m}^2$$

Piezometers are very sensitive pressure gages but are impractical for the measurement of high pressures because of the excessive length of tube required, as illustrated by Examples 2-3 and 2-4. More satisfactory manometers for the measurement of high pressures are shown in Fig. 2-4c to e. The manometer liquid most commonly used is mercury. Any liquid of greater density than the pipe fluid may be used provided that the two fluids are not miscible. Manometers of this type may be used whether the pipe fluid is a gas or a liquid and for both positive and negative pressures.

Values of h_p and h_m in Fig. 2-4c are usually read from a scale placed between the two legs of the U tube. The location of the zero of this scale fluctuates greatly with variations in the pipe pressure, thus causing some inconvenience in making the readings. This objectionable feature may be partly eliminated by the arrangement shown in Fig. 2-4e. The amount of movement of the mercury surface in the left and right tubes will be inversely proportional to the square of the diameters of the tubes. If the difference in diameters is made large, the mercury surface in the left tube will be nearly stationary and the value of h_p will then be nearly constant. For many practical purposes the scale may be marked off to give the pressure at c directly from the values of h_m.

Example 2-5. Determine the value of h_m in Fig. 2-4c if p_c is 50 lb per sq in. gage, h_p is 6 ft, the pipe fluid is water, and the manometer fluid is mercury.

Let w_p be the specific weight of the pipe fluid, and w_m the specific weight of the manometer fluid. From Eq. (2-1),

$$p_l = w_p h_p + p_c = 62.4 \times 6 + 50 \times 144$$

and from Eq. (2-4),

$$p_r = w_m h_m = 13.6 \times 62.4 \ h_m$$

Knowing p_l and p_r to be equal,

$$13.6 \times 62.4 \ h_m = 62.4 + (50 + 144)$$

from which h_m is found to be 8.9 ft.[1]

Example 2-6. Determine the value of p_c in Fig. 2-4d if h_p is 8 in. and h_m is 20 in. The pipe fluid is water, and the manometer fluid is mercury.

Equation (2-4) gives

$$p_l = w_m h_m + w_p h_p + p_c = 0$$

or

$$(13.6 \times 62.4 \times {}^{20}\!\!/_{12}) + (62.4 \times {}^{8}\!\!/_{12}) + p_c = 0$$

---

[1] Unless some particular temperature is stated, the specific gravity of mercury will be taken as 13.6 in numerical problems.

from which

$p_c = -1,460$ lb per sq ft gage, or -10.1 lb/in.² gage.

Differential manometers of the type shown in Fig. 2-5 are employed to measure the difference in pressure between two points. In both Fig. 2-5a and b it is desired to measure $p_1 - p_2$. In Fig. 2-5a the specific weight of the manometer fluid w_m is greater than that of the pipe fluid w_p, while in Fig. 2-5b the reverse is true. In the arrangement shown in Fig. 2-5a the pipe fluid may be liquid or gas, whereas in Fig. 2-5b it must be a liquid. The manometer fluid in Fig. 2-5b may, however, be

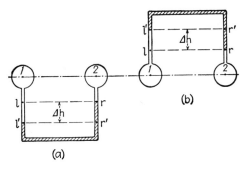

FIG. 2-5. Differential manometers.

either liquid or gas. An application of the equations of hydrostatics will show that, for either U tube of Fig. 2-5,

$$p_l' = p_r' \tag{2-7}$$

and

$$p_l - p_r = p_1 - p_2 \tag{2-8}$$

For Fig. 2-5a, Eq. (2-1) gives

$$p_l' = w_p \, \Delta h + p_l$$

and

$$p_r' = w_m \, \Delta h + p_r$$

From Eq. (2-7),

$$w_p \, \Delta h + p_l = w_m \, \Delta h + p_r$$

or

$$p_l - p_r = \Delta h(w_m - w_p)$$

and from Eq. (2-8),

$$p_1 - p_2 = \Delta_h(w_m - w_p) \tag{2-9}$$

The corresponding equation for a U tube of the type shown in Fig. 2-5b will be

$$p_1 - p_2 = \Delta h(w_p - w_m) \tag{2-10}$$

Equations (2-9) and (2-10) show that the gage becomes more sensitive as values of w_p and w_m become more nearly equal.

Pressure Forces on Plane Surfaces. In Fig. 2-6, LM represents any immersed plane surface which, if extended, would cut

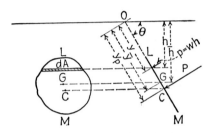

FIG. 2-6. Pressure forces on plane surfaces.

the liquid surface at O with an angle θ. Considering O the origin and OM the y axis, the pressure force dP on an elementary area dA is $wh\,dA = wy \sin\theta\,dA$. The total pressure force on the area LM is then

$$P = w \sin\theta \!\int y\,dA \tag{2-11}$$

If $\bar{y}$ is the distance of the center of gravity of the surface from O, then

$$\int y\,dA = A\bar{y}$$

and

$$P = w\bar{y} \sin\theta A$$

or letting $\bar{h} = \bar{y} \sin\theta$,

$$P = w\bar{h}A \tag{2-12}$$

The *center of pressure* is the point on the immersed surface through which the resultant pressure acts. Because the intensity of pressure increases with the depth, the center of pressure is below the center of gravity. The distance y_p from an axis through O, formed by the intersection of the plane surface LM with the water surface, to the center of pressure may be found from a summation of the moments of the elementary forces about this axis as follows:

$$y_p = \frac{\int y \, dP}{P} \tag{2-13}$$

which from the above may be written

$$y_p = \frac{w \sin \theta}{w \sin \theta} \frac{\int y^2 \, dA}{\int y \, dA} = \frac{\int y^2 \, dA}{\int y \, dA} \tag{2-14}$$

The numerator of the fraction in the above equation is the moment of inertia of the surface LM about the axis through O. This moment of inertia is equal to $Ak^2 + A\bar{y}^2$, where k is the radius of gyration of the surface. The denominator is equal to $A\bar{y}$. Substituting these values in Eq. (2-14) and reducing,

$$y_p = \bar{y} + \frac{k^2}{\bar{y}} \tag{2-15}$$

For surfaces such as are shown in Fig. 2-7, where the locus of the mid-points of horizontal lines is a straight line, the center

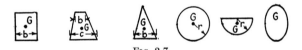

Fig. 2-7

of pressure lies on this straight line. For other surfaces, the horizontal position of the center of pressure can be obtained by taking moments as above about an axis perpendicular to the one through O. The use of the above equations is illustrated in the following examples. Problems involving fluid pressures on plane surfaces may also be solved more directly by considering the surface to be a slab with a nonuniform load equal in magnitude to the volume of the pressure-intensity diagram. Examples 2-7 and 2-8 give numerical applications of this method.

Example 2-7. Determine the magnitude and location of the resultant water-pressure force on a 1-ft section of the gate ab, shown in Fig. 2-8, (a), by the use of Eqs. (2-12) and (2-15), and (b), by loading the gate with the pressure volumes.

a. $P_l = Aw\bar{h} = 62.4 \times 12 \times 12 = 9,000$ lb $= 40.034$ N*

$$y_{pl} = \bar{y} + \frac{k^2}{\bar{y}} = 12 + \frac{(12)^2}{12 \times 12} = 13 \text{ ft} = 3.962 \text{ m*}$$

$$P_r = w\bar{h}A = 62.4 \times 6 \times 12 = 4,500 \text{ lb}$$

$$y_{pr} = \bar{y} + \frac{k^2}{\bar{y}} = 6 + \frac{(12)^2}{12 \times 6} = 8 \text{ ft}$$

Note that the latter value might have been determined by inspection because the force on the right side of ab results from

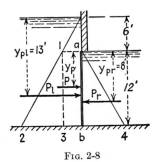

FIG. 2-8

a triangular pressure distribution, the center of gravity of which would therefore be two-thirds of its altitude from the water surface; i.e.,

$$y_{pr} = \tfrac{2}{3} \times 12 = 8 \text{ ft}$$

The resultant force P is then obtained by adding P_l and P_r as follows:

$$P = 9,000 - 4,500 = 4,500 \text{ lb (to the right)}$$

The location of P may be found by taking moments about a.

$$y_p' \times 4,500 = 7 \times 9,000 - 8 \times 4,500$$

* Conversion factors and symbols are given in Table 1-3.

and

$$y'_p = 6 \text{ ft}$$

b. Inspection Fig. 2-8 will show that the force resulting from the triangular pressure distribution 123 on the left is exactly balanced by the force on the right resulting from the pressure diagram *ab*4. Consequently, the only unbalanced pressure is a uniform intensity of $6w$ lb per sq ft on the left as shown by the pressure diagram 13*ba*. Therefore

$$P = 6 \times 62.4 \times 12 = 4,500 \text{ lb}$$

Because P is the resultant of a uniform pressure distribution, it must act on the center of gravity of the gate, i.e., 6 ft from a.

Example 2-8. Determine the magnitude and location of the pressure force on the rectangular sloping gate shown in Fig. 2-9 by three methods.

a. Using Eqs. (2-12) and (2-15),

$$P = w\bar{h}A \tag{2-12}$$
$$= 62.4 \times 8 \times 60 = 30,000 \text{ lb}$$

$$y_p = \bar{y} + \frac{k^2}{\bar{y}}$$
$$= 10 + \frac{100}{12 \times 10} = 10.83 \text{ ft} \tag{2-15}$$

b. Using Eqs. (2-11) and (2-14),

$$P = w \sin \theta \int y \, dA$$
$$= 62.4 \times 0.8 \int_5^{15} 6y \, dy$$
$$= 62.4 \times 0.8 \times 6 \left(\frac{y^2}{2}\right)_5^{15} = 30.000 \text{ lb} \tag{2-11}$$

$$y_p = \frac{\int y^2 \, dA}{\int y \, dA}$$
$$= \frac{6 \int_5^{15} y^2 \, dy}{6 \int_5^{15} y \, dy} = \frac{\left(\dfrac{y^3}{3}\right)_5^{15}}{\left(\dfrac{y^2}{2}\right)_5^{15}} = 10.83 \text{ ft} \tag{2-14}$$

c. The problem may also be solved by determining the magnitude and location of two components of the pressure force directly from the pressure loading diagrams of Fig. 2-9. Let P_1 be the force resulting from the uniform pressure of $4w$; then

$$P_1 = 4wA = 4 \times 62.4 \times 60 = 15,000 \text{ lb}$$

Note that this force is equal to the volume $1234dabc$ shown in Fig. 2-9b.

Because P_1 is produced by a pressure of uniform intensity, it must act at the center of gravity of the gate, i.e., 5 ft from ab.

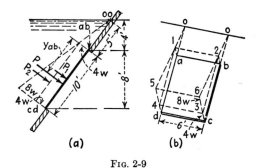

Fɪɢ. 2-9

Let P_2 be the force resulting from the triangular pressure volume 123456. The intensity of pressure varies from 0 to $8w$, the average being $4w$. Therefore

$$P_2 = 4wA = 4 \times 62.4 \times 60 = 15,000 \text{ lb}$$

Because this force is produced by triangular load, its location will be $\frac{2}{3} \times 10 = 6.67$ ft from ab.

Having P_1 and P_2, $P = P_1 + P_2 = 30,000$ lb, and the location of P may be determined by taking moments about ab as follows:

$$y_{ab}P = 5P_1 + 6.67P_2$$

from which $y_{ab} = 5.83$ ft.

Pressure Forces on Curved Surfaces. The resultant pressure force on a curved surface is made up of the sum of the small elements of force $p\, dA$, each acting perpendicular to the surface. The magnitude and location of the resultant of these elementary forces are not easily determined by the methods used for plane surfaces. The horizontal and vertical components of the resultant, however, may be readily determined and then combined vectorially.

Consider the forces acting on the prism of liquid shown in Fig. 2-10 bounded by the liquid surface *ao*, by the vertical plane surface *ob*, and by the curved surface *ab*. Acting downward on this volume is its weight W, and acting from right to left on *ob* is the horizontal force $P_H = w\bar{h}A$, where A is the area of the imaginary vertical plane surface one edge of which is *ob*. These forces must be put into equilibrium by equal and opposite forces from the curved surface *ab*. It follows then that the horizontal

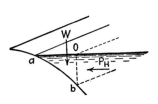

FIG. 2-10. Pressure forces on curved surfaces.

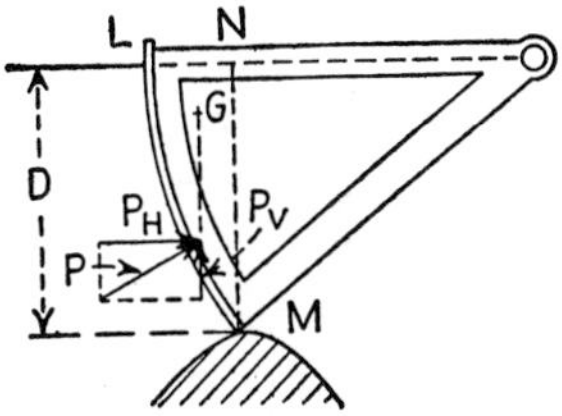

FIG. 2-11. Pressure force on taintor gate.

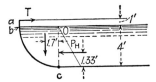

FIG. 2-12

component of the pressure force on a curved surface is equal to, and acts at the same point as, the force on a vertical plane surface formed by projecting the curved surface horizontally. Furthermore, the vertical component of the force on a curved surface is equal to the weight of the liquid above the surface and acts at its center of gravity. Similar reasoning will show that when the liquid is beneath the curved surface, the vertical component is equal to the weight of the imaginary volume of liquid above the surface and acts upward through its center of gravity. For example, the vertical component of the pressure force on the taintor gate of Fig. 2-11 is equal to the volume represented by LNM and acts upward through G as shown.

Example 2-9.   Figure 2-12 shows a section through a water tank 20 ft long.   The wall of the tank *abc* is hinged at *c* and supported by a horizontal tie rod at *a*.   The segment of the wall *bc* is a quarter circle having a 4-ft radius.

a. Determine the force *T* in the tie rod.

$$P_H = w\bar{h}A = 62.4 \times 2 \times 80 = 10,000 \text{ lb}$$

The location of *P* is $\frac{1}{3} \times 4 = 1.33$ ft above *c*.

$$P_V = W = \frac{20 \times \pi r^2 \times w}{4} = \frac{20 \times \pi \times 4^2 \times 62.4}{4} = 15,700 \text{ lb}$$

P_V acts at the center of gravity of the quarter circle which is to the left of *oc* by the amount $4r/3\pi = 1.7$ ft.   *T* may then be obtained by taking moments about the hinge as follows:

$$5T = \frac{4}{3} \times 10,000 + 1.7 \times 15,700 \qquad \text{and} \qquad T = 8,000 \text{ lb}$$

b. Determine the resultant water-pressure force on the wall.

$$P = \sqrt{(10,000)^2 + (15,700)^2} = 18,600 \text{ lb}$$

The direction and location of *P* may be found by combining P_V and P_H vectorially at their intersection.   Since all the elementary components of *P* are perpendicular to the gate and therefore pass through point *o*, it follows that *P* must also pass through *o*.

c. Determine the resultant force on the hinge, neglecting the weight of the wall.

From $\Sigma H = 0$, the horizontal component is found to be 2,000 lb and from $\Sigma V = 0$, the vertical component is found to be 15,700 lb.   The resultant force on the hinge is therefore

$$\sqrt{(15,700)^2 + (2,000)^2} = 15,800 \text{ lb}$$

Uniform Pressure on Cylindrical Surfaces.   Figure 2-13 represents a cross section of a pipe or cylinder subjected to a uniform internal hydrostatic pressure, and Fig. 2-14 represents a similar cross section subjected to a uniform external pressure.   The pressure at each point on the circumference is normal to the surface as indicated by the arrows.   The resultants of these normal pressures, on opposite sides of any diameter, are equal and in opposite directions and cause a tangential stress.   If

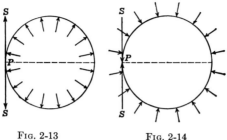

Fig. 2-13   Fig. 2-14

S is the stress in pounds per linear inch, h the static head of water in feet, and d_i the diameter of the pipe in inches,

$$S = 0.217hd_i \qquad (2\text{-}16)$$

S is tension for internal pressure and compression for external pressure.

Equation (2-16) may be used for computing the tension in pipes where h (the head to the center of the pipe) is large compared with the diameter. It may also be used for cylindrical tanks having a vertical axis and for thin circular arch dams. This formula applies to a segment of a cylinder, provided the edges are rigidly supported.

Uniform Pressure on Spherical Surfaces. If S is the stress in pounds per linear inch on the surface of a sphere subjected to uniform hydrostatic pressure, h the static head in feet, and d_i the diameter of the sphere in inches,

$$S = 0.108hd_i \qquad (2\text{-}17)$$

S will be tension when the hydrostatic pressure is applied to the inner surface and compression when applied to the outer surface.

Pressures on Spillway Sections of Dams. If still water having a depth $H + D$ were acting on the upstream face of the overflow spillway shown in Fig. 2-15, the pressure intensities could be represented by the trapezoid 1234. The effect of the velocity of the water is to increase the pressure near the bottom and decrease it at the top, so that the actual pressure distribution is similar to that shown by the dashed curved line 1-5. The increase in pressure near the bottom results from the impact of the approaching water, and the decrease near the top results from the fact that the pressure at the crest is approximately atmospheric. In computing the stability of such a section, it is on the safe side to assume that the trapezoidal pressure distribution 1234 exists. Based on these assumptions, the forces on the upstream face of the spillway are

$$P_1 = wDH \qquad (2\text{-}18)$$

and

$$P_2 = \frac{wD^2}{2} \qquad (2\text{-}19)$$

where P_1 and P_2 are in pounds per foot of length. The locations of P_1 and P_2 are shown in Fig. 2-15.

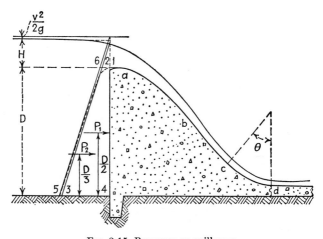

FIG. 2-15. Pressures on spillways.

In determining the stability of an overflow spillway section, it is also necessary to consider pressure forces acting on the downstream face. If the spillway slopes downward too rapidly, there is a tendency for pressures less than atmospheric to occur in the region a-b in Fig. 2-15, thus adding to the overturning moment on the section. In the region c-d, a positive pressure is produced because of the impact of the jet as it is deflected through the angle θ. The downward component of this force occurs near the location of the maximum foundation stresses, which may make it an important factor in the design. The sketch shown in Fig. 2-15 is based on the assumption that the hydraulic jump occurs downstream from the spillway. Where this is not the case, the tail-water pressure on the spillway must also be considered. Methods of determining the location of the hydraulic jump are described in Sec. 8.

Uplift Pressure on Dams. The water pressure under dams varies from a maximum at the upstream edge (b in Fig. 2-16) to a minimum at the downstream edge (f in Fig. 2-16). If there are no cutoff walls or impermeable layers in the foundation, the pressure at b is wD_u and that at f is wD_d. For homo-

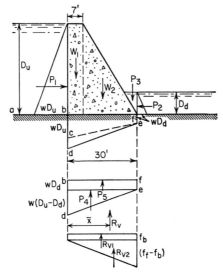

Fig. 2-16. Forces on gravity dams, Example 2-10.

geneous isotropic foundation materials the pressure will vary from b to f approximately as the straight line de. This is because the energy loss is approximately the same for each foot of distance traveled by the water. The exact form of the pressure line even for this case varies slightly from a straight line and may be determined more precisely by constructing a flow net,[1,2] by the use of hydraulic models, or by means of an

[1] A. Casagrande, Seepage through Dams, *J. New Engl. Water Works Assoc.*, June, 1937.

[2] W. P. Creager, J. D. Justin, and J. Hinds, "Engineering for Dams," John Wiley & Sons, Inc., New York, 1950.

electrical analogy.[1]   If the downstream edge of the dam were extended beyond f, as by means of an impermeable apron, the uplift pressures would be increased because the drop in pressure from wD_u to wD_d would be extended over a longer distance. On the other hand, the construction of an impervious cutoff wall vertically downward at point b would reduce the uplift pressures, as illustrated schematically by the dashed line ce. This is because the total drop in pressure from point b to point f is partly used in the energy loss as the water travels around the cutoff wall.   A reduction in uplift pressure might also be accomplished by placing a layer of impermeable material in the region ab.   This procedure would cause most of the underflow to enter the ground upstream from point a, thus creating some energy loss upstream from point b.   Measurements of uplift pressures under various conditions have been reported.[2-4] Much material of interest on this subject is also given in an article by Harza[5] and the accompanying discussions.

Stability of Dams.   Gravity dams must be designed so that they are safe against overturning and sliding.   If the material in the dam and foundation were capable of withstanding unlimited stresses, the dam would be safe against overturning provided the resultant of all forces fell within the base of the dam.   However, in order to limit the magnitude of the stresses and to ensure that the dam will maintain firm contact with the foundation over the entire base, it is required that the resultant fall within the middle third of the base.   This requirement does not necessarily assure safety against overturning because the stresses at the downstream edge may still be sufficiently large to cause failure of the material in the dam or in the foundation. If, for example, the resultant falls at the downstream end of the middle third of the base, the stresses will vary from a maximum at the downstream edge to zero at the upstream edge, assuming a straight-line variation in stresses.   The computations for a simple gravity dam are illustrated by the following example.

[1] E. W. Lane, Flow Net and Electric Analogy, *Civil Eng.* (*N.Y.*), October, 1934.

[2] Creager, Justin, and Hinds, *op. cit.*

[3] Julian Hinds, Upward Pressure under Dams, *Proc. ASCE*, March, 1938.

[4] Ivan E. Hauck, Uplift Pressure in Masonry Dams, *Civil Eng.* (*N.Y.*), September, 1932.

[5] F. A. Harza, The Significance of Pore Pressure in Hydraulic Structures, *Trans. ASCE*, vol. 114, 1949.

Example 2-10. In the gravity section shown in Fig. 2-16, $D_u = 38$ ft, $D_d = 9$ ft, and the other dimensions are as shown. The magnitudes of the forces are

$$P_1 = \frac{wD_u{}^2}{2} \qquad\qquad = 45{,}000 \text{ lb}$$

$$P_2 = \frac{wD_d{}^2}{2} \qquad\qquad = 2{,}530 \text{ lb}$$

$$P_3 = wD_d(2\tfrac{3}{8})D_d(\tfrac{1}{2}) \;=\; 1{,}530 \text{ lb}$$

$$P_4 = w\,\frac{D_u - D_d}{2}\,30 \qquad = 27{,}100 \text{ lb}$$

$$P_5 = wD_d \times 30 \qquad\qquad = 16{,}850 \text{ lb}$$

$$W_1 = 150 \times 7 \times 38 \qquad = 39{,}900 \text{ lb}$$

$$W_2 = 150 \times \frac{23 \times 38}{2} \qquad = 65{,}500 \text{ lb}$$

The resultant vertical force is determined as follows:

$$R_V = W_1 + W_2 + P_3 - P_4 - P_5 = 63{,}000 \text{ lb}$$

The summation of moments about point b is:

Clockwise

$P_1 \times \tfrac{38}{3}$	$=$	570,000
$P_3(30 - \tfrac{1}{3} \times \tfrac{9}{38} \times 23)$	$=$	43,000
$W_1 \times \tfrac{7}{2}$	$=$	140,000
$W_2(7 + 2\tfrac{3}{3})$	$=$	960,000
	$=$	1,713,000 ft-lb

Counterclockwise

$P_2 \times \tfrac{9}{3}$	$=$	7,600
$P_4 \times \tfrac{30}{3}$	$=$	271,000
$P_5 \times \tfrac{30}{2}$	$=$	253,000
	$=$	531,600

Then $\bar{x} = \Sigma M / R_V = 18.8$ ft. $= 5.72$ m*

The approximate variation in foundation stresses may then be obtained as follows, with reference to Fig. 2-16:

$$R_{V1} = 30 f_b \qquad \text{and} \qquad R_{V2} = 30\,\frac{f_f - f_b}{2}$$

* Conversion factors and symbols are given in Table 1-3.

where f_b and f_f are the foundation stresses at b and f, respectively.   Also,

$$R_{V1} + R_{V2} = R_V = 63,000 \text{ lb} = 280,000 \text{ N}*$$

Summation of moments at point b yields the following equation:

$$15R_{V1} + 20R_{V2} = 18.8 \times 63,000$$

Solution of the above equations gives

$$f_b = 510 \text{ lb/ft}^2 = 24,400 \text{ N/m}^2*$$

and

$$f_f = 3,700 \text{ lb/ft}^2 = 177,000 \text{ N/m}^2*$$

Safety against sliding requires that

$$R_H = C_f R_V \qquad\qquad (2\text{-}20)$$

where R_H is the summation of horizontal forces and C_f is the coefficient of friction between the dam and the foundation. Creager, Justin, and Hinds[1] give C_f as 0.60 to 0.75 for masonry on masonry and masonry on good rock.   For masonry on gravel, sand, and clay, they suggest 0.50, 0.40, and 0.30, respectively.

In this example the required value of C_f from Eq. (2-20) would be

$$C_f = \frac{R_H}{R_V} = \frac{P_1 - P_2}{63,000} = \frac{42,470}{63,000} = 0.675$$

which would probably be satisfactory on rock but not on unconsolidated materials.   However, this design might still be made safe against sliding by extending a concrete cutoff wall downward as in Fig. 2-15.   The principal effects of the cutoff wall are the establishment of the shear plane within the foundation material itself and the reduction of the hydrostatic uplift. For granular materials the value of C_f is greater for a plane within the material itself than for a plane between the surface of the dam and the material.   Furthermore, the reduction of the uplift pressures increases the value of R_V.   Therefore the use of a cutoff wall will increase R_H by increasing both C_f and R_V in Eq. (2-20).

* Conversion factors and symbols are given in Table 1-3.
[1] *Op. cit.*

SECTION 3

FUNDAMENTAL CONCEPTS OF FLUID FLOW

This section is included for the purpose of providing a review of the basic principles required to solve problems involving fluids in motion. The title of the section might well be *hydrokinetics*, to distinguish it from the previous section, which dealt with hydrostatics.

Virtually no problems in hydraulics can be safely solved by means of tables or formulas without a firm understanding of continuity and energy. Other problems require the application of force and momentum concepts. These basic principles will be briefly set forth in this section along with brief discussions of flow classification, the Bernoulli equation, kinetic energy and momentum correction factors, and applications of the Bernoulli equation to siphons, venturi meters, and cavitation. Two other basic topics presented in this section are dimensional analysis and similitude.

Classification of Flow. In order to determine which basic principles are applicable to particular problems it is necessary to classify flow. The various categories of flow lend themselves to presentation as a series of four pairs of alternative conditions.

The first pair of conditions to be discussed is *laminar flow* as distinguished from *turbulent flow*. In laminar flow the fluid moves in parallel layers with no crosscurrents. In the case of a circular pipe, for example, the layers are circular cylindrical tubes. The fact that, in laminar flow, fluid particles move in parallel paths was demonstrated by Osborne Reynolds[1] by introducing a thread of dye into flowing water. Turbulent flow is characterized by pulsatory crosscurrent velocities. One

[1] Osborne Reynolds, An Experimental Investigation of the Circumstances Which Determine whether the Motion of Water Shall Be Direct or Sinuous, and the Laws of Resistance in Parallel Channels, *Trans. Roy. Soc. (London)*, vol. 174, 1883.

result of the crosscurrent velocities of turbulent flow is the formation of a more uniform velocity distribution. It is shown in Sec. 6 (p. 6-7) that for laminar flow in a circular pipe the maximum velocity is twice the average velocity. For turbulent flow the maximum velocity is more of the order of 1.25 times the average velocity. The more uniform velocity found in turbulent flow is brought about by the interchange of momentum between fast-moving particles near the center and slower ones nearer the walls. One of the most important practical differences between laminar and turbulent flow is the much greater energy loss in turbulent flow. The energy which is required to produce the crosscurrent velocities must be supplied by the pump, but it is of no help in transporting the fluid through the pipe.

The criterion which distinguishes laminar flow from turbulent was also developed by Reynolds[1] and has been named the Reynolds number, R. For circular pipes flowing full, R is expressed as follows:

$$R = \frac{dv\rho}{\mu} = \frac{dv}{\nu} \tag{3-1}$$

where d is the diameter of the pipe in feet, v is the average velocity in feet per second, ρ is the density in slugs per cubic foot, μ is the viscosity in slugs per foot-second, and ν is the kinematic viscosity in square feet per second. For pipes, laminar flow occurs when $R \lessgtr 2,000$ and flow is usually turbulent when $R \gtrless 4,000$. For values of R between 2,000 and 4,000, flow is in a transition condition. The development of a Reynolds number for cases other than a circular pipe flowing full requires the use of different length terms. For example, for flow in open channels the length term may be the depth, the hydraulic radius, or one-fourth of the hydraulic radius. These variations in R are discussed in the various sections of the Handbook where the situations arise.

The physical significance of R can be understood intuitively from an examination of the terms in Eq. (3-1). For example, it is easy to visualize that a decrease in diameter will inhibit crosscurrents and, therefore, that R should also decrease. However, perhaps the best method of understanding the physical significance of this parameter is to note that R can be expressed as the ratio of an inertial force to a viscous force as

[1] *Ibid.*

demonstrated later in this section.   The inertial force represents the tendency of the fluid to develop turbulence at boundary irregularities, whereas the viscous force tends to damp out turbulence.

The numerical use of Eq. (3-1) will be demonstrated in the following example.   The example illustrates the fact that fully laminar flow rarely exists in pipes larger than 1 in. when the fluid is water.   This example also demonstrates the conversion of units into the metric system (SI) and illustrates that the value of R is independent of the system of units being used.

Example 3-1.   Determine the value of the Reynolds number for a circular pipe having an inside diameter of 1 in. when the velocity is 0.25 ft per sec and the water temperature is 70°F.

From Table 1-2,

$$w = 62.3 \text{ lb/ft}^3$$
$$\mu = 0.00002050 \text{ slugs/fts}$$
$$\nu = 0.00001059 \text{ ft}^2\text{/s}$$

Then

$$\rho = \frac{w}{g} = 1.936 \text{ slugs/ft}^3$$

and

$$R = \frac{dv\rho}{\mu} = \frac{\frac{1}{12} \times 0.25 \times 1.936}{0.00002050} = 1,970$$

or

$$R = \frac{dv}{\nu} = \frac{\frac{1}{12} \times 0.25}{0.00001059} = 1,970$$

In order to solve the problem in the metric system (SI), the quantities are first converted by use of factors from Table 1-3 as follows:

$$
\begin{array}{lll}
w = 62.3 \times 157.0875 & = 9{,}787 \text{ N/m}^3 \\
\mu = 0.00002050 \times 47.8803 & = 0.0009815 \text{ Ns/m}^2 \\
\nu = 0.00001059 \times 0.092903 & = 0.0000009838 \text{ m}^2\text{/s} \\
d = 1.0 \times 0.0254 & = 0.0254 \text{ m} \\
v = 0.25 \times 0.3048 & = 0.0762 \text{ m/s} \\
\rho = 1.936 \times 55.379 & = 997.8 \text{ kg/m}^3
\end{array}
$$

Then

$$R = \frac{dv\rho}{\mu} = \frac{0.0254 \times 0.0762 \times 997.8}{0.0009815} = 1,970$$

or

$$R = \frac{dv}{\nu} = \frac{0.0254 \times 0.0762}{0.0000009838} = 1,970$$

Another pair of categories into which flow may be classified deals with steadiness of the discharge. Flow is classified as *steady flow* when the discharge is constant with respect to time. *Unsteady flow* occurs in pipes or open channels during and following changes in valve or gate openings. Typical unsteady-flow problems involve such phenomena as water hammer in pipes, translatory waves in open channels, and the emptying of a tank. Another example of unsteady flow is the discharge of natural rivers, although during periods when there is no surface runoff[1] the change in discharge is so slow that many problems may be solved by assuming that flow is steady.

A special case of flow should be mentioned here in which the discharge varies with distance along the channel. This type of flow is called *spatially variable flow*, and it may be either steady or unsteady. Some examples of spatially variable flow are overland flow during rainstorms, flow in natural streams, and flow in side-channel spillways.

Flow may also be classified as *uniform flow* as differentiated from *nonuniform flow*. Flow is uniform if the cross-sectional area of the fluid remains constant. The term *varied flow* is frequently used as a synonym for nonuniform flow. The further distinction between *rapidly varied flow* and *gradually varied flow* is discussed in detail in Sec. 8. Some examples of nonuniform flow are flow in venturi meters, flow in natural streams, and flow above and below gates in open channels.

Continuity. One of the fundamental concepts which must be satisfied in all flow problems is continuity of flow. Continuity states the fact that no fluid is lost or gained and no cavities are formed or destroyed as the fluid passes through a conduit. When the fluid is essentially incompressible, as for liquids, and in many cases also for gases, continuity may be expressed as follows:

$$Q = a_1 V_1 = a_2 V_2 = a_n V_n \tag{3-2}$$

where Q is the discharge, a is the cross-sectional area, and V is the average velocity. Equation (3-2) may be referred to the venturi meter in Fig. 3-4.

When the fluid is compressible, the densities at the various locations must be included and the continuity equation becomes

$$\rho Q = \rho_1 a_1 V_1 = \rho_2 a_2 V_2 = \rho_n a_n V_n \tag{3-3}$$

[1] For a detailed discussion of flow in natural rivers see C. O. Wisler and E. F. Brater, "Hydrology," 2d ed., John Wiley & Sons, Inc., New York, 1959.

where ρQ represents the mass discharge in slugs per second and the values of ρ are the densities at the various sections.

For spatially variable flow continuity may be expressed as follows for incompressible fluids:

$$a_1 V_1 \pm i\,\Delta x = a_2 V_2 \qquad (3\text{-}4)$$

where i is the inflow or outflow per foot of length of conduit, and Δx is the length of the conduit between sections 1 and 2.

Energy and the Bernoulli Equation. The basic principle which is used most often in hydraulics is the law of conservation of energy as expressed by the Bernoulli equation.   All the

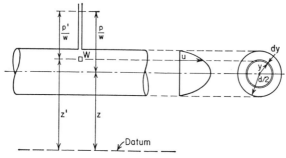

Fig 3-1. Energy of fluids in pipes.

so-called "pipe and open-channel formulas" have been developed to express the rate of energy dissipation.   Fundamental derivations of Bernoulli's equation are given in all texts.[1]   A simplified derivation will be made here which illustrates the meaning of the terms.

If a particle of fluid of weight W lb is selected anywhere in the cross section of a pipe as in Fig. 3-1, its energy may be expressed as follows:

Potential energy:

Due to position $= Wz'$

Due to pressure $= W\,\dfrac{p'}{w}$

Kinetic energy $\quad = W\,\dfrac{u^2}{2g}$

[1] See, for example, V. L. Streeter, "Fluid Mechanics," 6th ed., pp. 134–144, McGraw-Hill Book Company, Inc., New York, 1975.

Then the total energy of the particle W in foot-pounds is

$$E = Wz' + W\frac{p'}{w} + W\frac{u^2}{2g} \qquad (3\text{-}5)$$

It should be noted that the potential energy due to pressure is available only if the fluid is continuously supplied at the pressure p'. If Eq. (3-5) is divided by W, the following expression for energy in foot-pounds per pound at the location of W is obtained:

$$H' = z' + \frac{p'}{w} + \frac{u^2}{2g} \qquad (3\text{-}5a)$$

This equation is not useful unless it can be generalized so that it applies to the entire cross section. The first two terms may be generalized by noting, from Fig. 3-1, that no matter where the particle of weight W is located in the cross section

$$z' + \frac{p'}{w} = z + \frac{p}{w} \qquad (3\text{-}6)$$

in which the terms without subscripts refer to the center of the pipe.

The generalization of the kinetic-energy term is accomplished by introducing the average velocity V in place of u together with a kinetic-energy correction factor which is discussed in detail later in this section.

The expression for the energy at any point in the cross section in foot-pounds per pound is then

$$H = z + \frac{p}{w} + \alpha\frac{V^2}{2g} \qquad (3\text{-}7)$$

This expression is called the Bernoulli constant. Another useful form is obtained by multiplying Eq. (3-7) by w to obtain the energy in foot-pounds per cubic foot as follows:

$$wH = wz + p + \alpha w\frac{V^2}{2g} \qquad (3\text{-}8)$$

or, replacing w with ρg,

$$\rho gH = \rho gz + p + \alpha\frac{\rho V^2}{2} \qquad (3\text{-}9)$$

A similar derivation can be made for an open channel. Reference to Fig. 3-2 will show that Eq. (3-5a) applies to open channels as well as to pipes. The first two terms can be generalized by noting that

$$z' + \frac{p'}{w} = z + D \tag{3-10}$$

Then, introducing V and α, as for closed circuits, the following expression for the Bernoulli constant is obtained:

$$H = z + D + \alpha \frac{V^2}{2g} \tag{3-11}$$

The meaning of α, the *kinetic-energy correction factor*, can be demonstrated by writing an expression for the rate at which

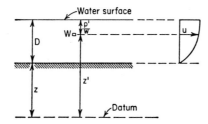

FIG. 3-2. Energy of liquids in open channels.

kinetic energy is passing any section in a pipe, in foot-pounds per second as follows:

$$Qw\alpha \frac{V^2}{2g} = w \int_0^a u \, da \frac{u^2}{2g} \tag{3-12}$$

The term on the right is an exact expression for the total kinetic energy. In this term da would be the area of an elemental ring in which the velocity is u as shown in Fig. 3-1. The term on the left includes the total discharge Q and the average velocity V. If the variation of u over the area a can be expressed mathematically, the value of α can be determined exactly from Eq. (3-12). When the shape of the cross section and the velocity variation is too complicated for expression in mathematical terms, a graphical solution may be made.

One case for which a mathematical solution for α can be made is that of laminar flow in a circular pipe. In that case the value of u from Eq. (6-14) is

$$u = \frac{p_1 - p_2}{4\mu l} \left(-y^2 + \frac{d^2}{4} \right) \tag{3-13}$$

where p_1 and p_2 are the pressures at two ends of a section of the pipe l ft long, d is the diameter, and y is defined in Fig. 3-1. For this case

$$da = 2\pi y \, dy \qquad (3\text{-}14)$$

The values of Q and V may be obtained from Eqs. (6-16) and (6-17). Inserting these values of Q, V, u, and da in Eq. (3-12) and integrating yields $\alpha = 2$. For turbulent flow in pipes, α usually is in the range from 1.01 to 1.10.[1] The value of α for laminar flow in open channels is $54/35$. It may be determined in the same manner as for pipes by making use of Eqs. (7-43), (7-45), and (7-46). For most practical problems α may be taken as unity without serious error. However, in some situations where high precision is desired, exact values of α should be used. This is especially true where α differs considerably from one point to another as in a venturi meter.

A graphical method for deriving α in cases in which a mathematical solution cannot be made has been presented by O'Brien and Johnson.[2] The procedure consists in plotting lines of uniform velocity on the cross section, after which elements of area between the lines Δa are determined and the right side of Eq. (3-12) is evaluated by adding values of $U_{av}{}^3 \, \Delta a$. The value of U_{av} is the average of the velocities bounding each increment of area.

Equation (3-7), (3-8), (3-9), or (3-11) gives the energy at any point in a flowing liquid. The law of conservation of energy is expressed by the *Bernoulli equation*, which, for closed conduits, may be stated in the form and units of Eq. (3-7) as follows:

$$z_1 + \frac{p_1}{w} + \alpha_1 \frac{V_1{}^2}{2g} = z_2 + \frac{p_2}{w} + \alpha_2 \frac{V_2{}^2}{2g} + \Sigma h_l \qquad (3\text{-}15)$$

where Σh_l is an energy loss. This equation states that the energy at one point in a fluid (point 1) is equal to the energy at any downstream location (point 2) plus the intervening losses Σh_l. The use of Bernoulli's equation will be demonstrated in the various sections of the Handbook. However,

---

[1] V. L. Streeter, The Kinetic Energy and Momentum Correction Factors for Pipes and Open Channels of Great Width, *Civil Eng.* (*N.Y.*), vol. 12, no. 4, 1942.

[2] M. P. O'Brien and J. W. Johnson, Velocity Head Correction for Hydraulic Flow, *Eng. News-Record*, Aug. 16, 1934.

several applications will be presented here to illustrate its use for basic devices such as siphons and venturi meters and for the study of cavitation.

Siphons. Shown in Fig. 3-3 is a siphon composed of three straight sections of pipe connected by elbows at points 3 and 4. If it were desired to determine the discharge through this siphon for given values of z and pipe size, the Bernoulli equation would be written from point 1 to point 5 as follows:

$$z_1 + \frac{p_1}{w} + \alpha_1 \frac{V_1{}^2}{2g} = z_5 + \frac{p_5}{w} + \alpha_5 \frac{V_5{}^2}{2g} + \Sigma h_l \qquad (3\text{-}16)$$

Then the left side reduces to z_1 because p_1/w is zero on the gage scale and V_1 is so small that it may be neglected. On the right side z_5 and p_5/w are zero, so that there remain only the kinetic-energy term and the loss term. The loss term is defined below:

$$\Sigma h_l = \begin{cases} \text{loss at entrance} \\ \text{loss at two elbows} \\ \text{loss in straight pipe sections} \end{cases}$$

As will be shown in later sections of this Handbook, all the energy losses can be expressed in terms of the velocity. Upon inserting these loss terms in Eq. (3-16), the velocity, and hence the discharge, may be computed. Knowing the discharge, the pressure can be determined by writing the Bernoulli equation from point 1 to the point where it is desired to know the pressure, including only the loss between point 1 and the point in question.

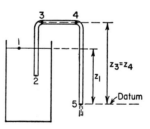

Fig. 3-3. Application of the Bernoulli equation to a siphon.

Venturi Meters. A venturi meter is a constriction in a pipe which is used for the purpose of determining the discharge. The Bernoulli equation may be written from 1 to 2 in Fig. 3-4 as follows:

$$\frac{V_1{}^2}{2g} + \frac{p_1}{w} = \frac{V_2{}^2}{2g} + \frac{p_2}{w} + h_l \qquad (3\text{-}17)$$

where V_1 is the average velocity in the pipe at 1, p_1 is the pressure at 1, V_2 and p_2 are corresponding quantities at 2, and h_l is the energy loss between 1 and 2. By rearranging terms and using the continuity relationship,

$$V_1 = \frac{d_2{}^2}{d_1{}^2} V_2$$

the following expression is obtained:

$$V_2 = \sqrt{\frac{2g(p_1/w - p_2/w - h_l)}{1 - (d_2/d_1)^4}} \qquad (3\text{-}18)$$

In the above expressions d_1 and d_2 are the diameters of the pipe and the throat of the venturi meter, respectively. The energy

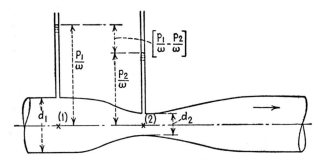

Fɪɢ. 3-4. Venturi meter.

loss is usually taken care of by using a coefficient c having a value less than 1, rather than by means of a direct subtraction, as in Eqs. (3-17) and (3-18). If this change is made and if both sides of Eq. (3-32) are multiplied by the throat area a_2, the following expression for discharge is obtained:

$$Q = ca_2 \sqrt{\frac{2g(p_1/w - p_2/w)}{1 - (d_2/d_1)^4}} \qquad (3\text{-}19)$$

The value of the term $(p_1/w) - (p_2/w)$ must be obtained by means of a differential pressure gage. Pressure gages are discussed on page 2-7. Values of c, together with other information regarding the use of the venturi meters, are given in Venturi Meters, in Sec. 12.

Cavitation. Another illustration of the energy and continuity concepts will be made by an application to cavitation.

If conditions are such that the pressure at some point in a conduit becomes very low because of a local increase in velocity or elevation, such as at the throat of a venturi meter or the highest point in a siphon, then cavitation may occur. Cavitation will begin when the pressure at any location reaches an absolute pressure equal to the saturated vapor pressure of the liquid (see Fluid Properties in Sec. 1). Usually this condition is attained by increasing the discharge to the critical condition. If discharge is increased beyond this critical condition, cavities filled with liquid vapor will alternately develop and collapse in the low-pressure region, often causing damage to the apparatus and always greatly reducing the efficiency of flow.

For the venturi meter shown in Fig. 3-4, the discharge at which cavitation will begin for a given value of p_1 may be computed by using Eq. (3-17) in conjunction with the continuity equation. Absolute pressures (see Absolute Pressure in Sec. 2) must be used rather than gage pressures, and p_2 is the vapor pressure corresponding to the temperature of the water. Values of vapor pressure for water are given in Table 1-2. The energy loss may be estimated as $0.05 V_2{}^2/2g$ (see Minor Losses in Sec. 6).

A similar situation might occur at point 4 in the siphon shown in Fig. 3-3. An increase in z_4 and/or z_1 would tend to reduce the pressure at point 4 to an absolute value near vapor pressure. The application of the Bernoulli equation would provide information about limiting conditions, although it is possible that the pipe from points 4 to 5 may cease to flow full before this limiting condition is reached.

Momentum Concepts. Another fundamental principle which is involved in many hydraulics problems involves a change in momentum and is expressed by Newton's second law of motion. For the case of steady incompressible flow, the law may be stated in the following forms:

$$F_x = \frac{M_2 V_{2x} - M_1 V_{1x}}{\Delta t} \tag{3-20}$$

$$= \frac{M_1 (V_{2x} - V_{1x})}{\Delta t} + \frac{\Delta M\ V_{2x}}{\Delta t} \tag{3-21}$$

where F_x is the force in the x direction required to change the velocity of a mass M_1 from V_{1x} to V_{2x} in a time Δt and to change the velocity of any mass added (ΔM) between points 1 and 2 in the time Δt from zero to V_{2x}. Forces and velocities

directed from left to right are considered positive.   Then the
force in Eq. (3-20) or (3-21) is the force acting on the fluid.   For
a flowing fluid Eq. (3-21) can be transformed as follows:

$$M_1 = \rho Q \, \Delta t \tag{3-22}$$
$$\Delta M = \rho i \, \Delta s \, \Delta t \tag{3-23}$$

Then

$$F_x = \rho Q(V_{2x} - V_{1x}) + \rho i \, \Delta s \, V_{2x} \tag{3-24}$$

In these equations i is the inflow per foot of length of conduit
and Δs is distance along the conduit.   The second term on the
right side of Eq. (3-24) applies to spatially variable flow and
will be given further consideration in Sec. 11.   For the case of
no addition or withdrawal of fluid, Eq. (3-24) becomes

$$F_x = \rho Q(V_{2x} - V_{1x}) \tag{3-25}$$

For precise work, correction factors are required in the momentum equation for the same reasons that the α factors are
needed to correct for the use of the average velocity in the
kinetic-energy term in the Bernoulli constant (see Energy and
the Bernoulli Equation above).   In order to illustrate the
nature of these factors, called β in this case, Eq. (3-25) may
be rewritten as follows:

$$F_x = \rho Q V_{2x} - \rho Q V_{1x} \tag{3-26}$$

Noting from the continuity relation that

$$Q = a_1 V_1 = a_2 V_2$$

Eq. (3-26) becomes

$$F_x = \rho a_2 V_{2x}^2 - \rho a_1 V_{1x}^2 \tag{3-27}$$

Then, knowing that V_x represents an average of velocities varying from zero to u_{max} (see Fig. 3-1), it may be seen that a correction factor greater than unity should be included.   The
value of β may be computed from the following equation, which
expresses the rate at which momentum is passing a cross section
of a conduit.

$$\rho a \beta V^2 = \rho \int_0^a u^2 \, da \tag{3-28}$$

For the special case of laminar flow in a circular pipe Eq. (3-28)
can be integrated after inserting values of u and V from Eqs.

(6-14) and (6-17), and the value of β is found to be $\frac{4}{3}$. For more complicated velocity variations a graphical integration is required. The method is identical with that previously described in this section for determining the kinetic-energy correction factor α. For turbulent flow in pipes values of β vary from approximately 1.01 to 1.05.[1] In most practical problems β may be taken as unity, but where precise work is desirable and possible, it may be necessary to use correct values of β.

It should be reemphasized that Eqs. (3-20) to (3-25) give the force components for a particular direction based on momentum changes in that direction. The x direction was used simply

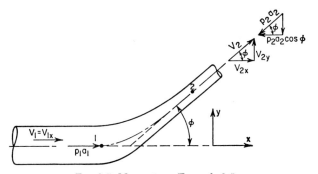

Fig. 3-5. Momentum, Example 3-5.

as a convenient illustration of the type of equation that could be written for any direction. It should be further noted that the force F_x is the summation of all forces acting on the fluid, including fluid pressure, the force due to the pressure of the conduit boundaries, friction, and gravity. The use of the momentum principle will be illustrated by the following example. Additional illustrations are given in other sections of the Handbook.

Example 3-2. In the reducing elbow shown in Fig. 3-5 the pressure at 1 is 50 lb per sq in. and V_1 is 5 ft per sec. The diameters at 1 and 2 are 12 and 6 in., respectively. Point 2 is 1.5 ft above point 1, and ϕ is 45°. Determine the horizontal

[1] Streeter, *op. cit.*

force on the reducing elbow. The discharge is[1]

$$Q = a_1 V_1 = 0.7854 \times 5 = 3.926 \text{ ft}^3/\text{s}$$

Then, from continuity, V_2 is

$$V_2 = \frac{Q}{a_2} = \frac{3.926}{0.1963} = 20.0 \text{ ft/s}$$

The pressure at 2 is obtained by writing the Bernoulli equation [Eq. (3-15)] from 1 to 2.

$$z_1 + \frac{p_1}{w} + \alpha_1 \frac{V_1{}^2}{2g} = z_2 + \frac{p_2}{w} + \alpha_2 \frac{V_2{}^2}{2g} + h_l \qquad (3\text{-}29)$$

Neglecting losses and letting the values of α be unity, Eq. (3-29) becomes

$$0 + \frac{50 \times 144}{62.4} + \frac{25}{64.4} = 1.5 + \frac{p_2}{62.4} + \frac{400}{64.4}$$

Then

$$p_2 = \frac{62.4 \times 108}{144} = 46.8 \text{ lb/in.}^2$$

Making use of Eq. (3-25),

$$\begin{aligned} F_x &= \rho Q (V_{2x} - V_{1x}) \\ &= \frac{62.4}{32.2} \times 3.926(0.707 \times 20 - 5) \\ &= 69.8 \text{ lb} \end{aligned}$$

Writing the summation of horizontal forces,

$$p_1 a_1 + E_x - p_2 a_2 \cos 45° = 69.80$$

where E_x is the force of the elbow on the water. Then, inserting numerical values,

$$50 \times 144 \times 0.785 + E_x - 46.8 \times 144 \times 0.196 \times 0.707 = 69.8$$

and

$$E_x = -4{,}645 \text{ lb}$$

This means that the elbow is acting with a force of 4,645 lb to the left against the water, or that the stresses in the pipe must resist a horizontal force to the right of this amount unless some external fastening is supplied.

[1] Areas of circles may be obtained from Table 6-3.

Dimensional Analysis[1] and Similitude. This is a procedure for arranging a number of variables into one or more dimensionless groups. For example, suppose the following variables are thought to be related to a particular flow phenomenon and it is desired to arrange them into a convenient dimensionless group π_1:

A typical length	d
Velocity	V
Density	ρ
Viscosity	μ

Assume now that π_1 is an exponential product of these variables as shown by the following equation:

$$\pi_1 = d^a V^b \rho^c \mu^{-1} \qquad (3\text{-}30)$$

The use of the negative exponent for μ is entirely arbitrary. A positive exponent or a symbolic one such as is used for the other three variables could also be employed. Then, since π_1 is dimensionless, the following relationship must exist among the dimensions of the variables:

$$L^0 M^0 T^0 = L^a \left(\frac{L}{T}\right)^b \left(\frac{M}{L^3}\right)^c \left(\frac{M}{LT}\right)^{-1} \qquad (3\text{-}31)$$

The dimensions of the variables were obtained from Table 1-1. Because each of the basic dimensions must be eliminated from the dimensionless group π_1, the following relationships must hold for the exponents:

$$
\begin{aligned}
(L) \quad 0 &= a + b - 3c + 1 \\
(M) \quad 0 &= \qquad\quad c - 1 \\
(T) \quad 0 &= \quad -b \qquad\quad + 1
\end{aligned}
$$

Simultaneous solution of the above equations yields the following results:

$$b = 1 \qquad c = 1 \qquad a = 1$$

Substitution of these values into Eq. (3-30) shows that π_1 must

---

[1] Only a single illustration of dimensional analysis will be given here. For more elaborate and detailed discussions see Hunter Rouse, "Fluid Mechanics for Engineers," pp. 1–32, McGraw-Hill Book Company, Inc., New York, 1938, or Henry L. Longhaor, "Dimensional Analysis and Theory of Models," John Wiley & Sons, Inc., New York, 1951.

have the following form:

$$\pi_1 = \frac{dV\rho}{\mu} = R \tag{3-32}$$

This dimensionless group of variables is called the Reynolds number.

If a similar dimensionless analysis is made using in succession the gravitational acceleration g, the surface tension σ, and the modulus of elasticity E, the following additional dimensionless parameters are obtained:

$$\pi_2 = \frac{V^2}{gd} = F^2 \tag{3-33}$$

$$\pi_3 = \frac{dV^2\rho}{\sigma} = W \tag{3-34}$$

$$\pi_4 = \frac{\rho V^2}{E} = M^2 \tag{3-35}$$

In the above equations F is the Froude number, W is the Weber number, and M is the Mach number. The four dimensionless numbers presented above have a particular significance which will be further explained in the following paragraphs.

The *principles of similitude* form the basis of designing models so that the results can be converted to prototypes. In order to have similarity it is first necessary that the model be geometrically similar to the prototype. Then the movement of the fluid in the model will be similar to that in the prototype if the ratios of the inertial force of the fluid to the various other forces acting on the fluid are the same in the model as in the prototype. There are four types of force acting on the fluid, those due to viscosity, gravitation, surface tension, and elasticity.

The inertial force of a fluid can be expressed in terms of the momentum equation [Eq. (3-27)] as follows:

$$F_i = \rho Q V = \rho a V^2 \tag{3-36}$$

A typical viscous force can be expressed as the product of shear stress and area as follows:

$$F_\mu = \tau a \tag{3-37}$$

and noting from page 1-3 that, for laminar flow,

$$\tau = \mu \frac{du}{dy} = \mu \frac{V}{y} \tag{3-38}$$

the friction force becomes

$$F_\mu = \mu \frac{V}{y} a \qquad (3\text{-}39)$$

The ratio of the inertial force to the viscous force can now be written

$$\frac{F_i}{F_\mu} = \frac{\rho a V^2 y}{\mu V a} = \frac{y V \rho}{\mu} = R \qquad (3\text{-}40)$$

The preceding demonstration has shown that the ratio F_i/F_μ yields a particular value of the Reynolds number R. Consequently, for similitude in so far as viscous forces are concerned, the Reynolds number must be the same in the model and prototype. A further implication is that R is a useful parameter for correlating coefficients which serve to take care of energy losses. Examples of such correlations are the friction factor f (p. 6-10) in pipe flow and the discharge coefficients of pipe orifices (p. 4-14).

The ratio of the inertial force to the gravitational force yields the Froude number, and similar ratios involving the surface tension and elastic force result in the Weber and Mach numbers, respectively.

Conversion factors for computing prototype values from model values are obtained by equating the appropriate dimensionless parameter. For example, if studies are made of a flow phenomenon involving primarily the gravitational force, the conversion factors are obtained by equating the Froude number for the model F_m to that for the prototype F_p as follows, replacing d with L to represent any typical length:

$$F_m = F_p \qquad (3\text{-}41)$$

or

$$\frac{V_m}{\sqrt{g_m L_m}} = \frac{V_p}{\sqrt{g_p L_p}} \qquad (3\text{-}42)$$

Then the velocity ratio is

$$\frac{V_p}{V_m} = V_r = \sqrt{\frac{g_p L_p}{g_m d_n}} = \sqrt{g_r L_r} \qquad (3\text{-}43)$$

Noting that the area ratio a_r is equal to L_r^2, the discharge ratio becomes

$$Q_r = \frac{a_p V_p}{a_m V_m} = g_r^{1/2} L_r^{5/2} \qquad (3\text{-}44)$$

The time ratio is obtained by replacing V with L/T; then

$$V_r = \frac{L_r}{T_r} = \sqrt{g_r L_r} \qquad (3\text{-}45)$$

and

$$T_r = \sqrt{\frac{L_r}{g_r}} \qquad (3\text{-}46)$$

Other conversion ratios can be determined in the same manner.

SECTION 4

ORIFICES, GATES, AND TUBES

An orifice is an opening with closed perimeter and of regular form through which water flows. If the perimeter is not closed or if the opening flows only partially full, the orifice becomes a weir (Sec. 5). An orifice with prolonged sides, such as a pipe 2 or 3 diameters in length or an opening in a thick wall, is called a *tube*. A *gate* is an opening in a hydraulic structure, usually including appurtenances for regulating the outflow. The same fundamental principles apply to each type of opening.

The stream of water which issues from an orifice is termed the *jet*, and the depth of water producing discharge is the *head*. An orifice with a sharp upstream edge is called a *sharp-edged* orifice. The *channel of approach* is the channel leading up to an orifice, tube, or gate, and the mean velocity in this channel is the *velocity of approach*. If

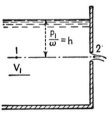

Fɪɢ. 4-1. Sharp-edged orifice.

the jet discharges into the air, the orifice is said to have *free discharge*. If the discharge is under water, it is called a *submerged orifice*. An orifice is spoken of as *vertical* or *horizontal* depending on whether it lies in a vertical or horizontal plane.

When the inner edge of the orifice consists of a sharp corner, the jet springs free, as illustrated in Fig. 4-1, and the orifice is a sharp-edged orifice. The jet issuing from a sharp-edged orifice contracts until it reaches the *vena contracta*. At the vena contracta the paths of all elements of the jet are parallel and the pressure in the jet can be assumed to be equal to that in the surrounding fluid. The vena contracta of a circular orifice is approximately $\frac{1}{2}$ diameter downstream from the inner face of the orifice plate. The area at the vena contracta, a_2 in Fig. 4-1, is related to the area of the orifice a as follows:

$$a_2 = C_c a \qquad (4\text{-}1)$$

where C_c is called the *coefficient of contraction*.

The contraction is caused by the fact that those elements of the fluid with approach from the side of the orifice have trans-

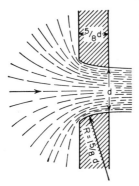

verse velocity components directed toward the center of the orifice. Therefore the nearness of boundaries, as, for example, for orifices in pipes (p. 4-14), would tend to reduce the amount of contraction and increase C_c. If one edge of an orifice is flush with a wall, the contraction on that side will be entirely eliminated. However, the contraction from the other side will be increased by approximately the same amount. Increasing the roughness of the inner face of the orifice plate would also reduce the transverse velocity components slightly. Rounding the inner edge of the orifice reduces contraction,

FIG. 4-2. Bell-mouthed orifice with rounded upstream edge.

and the contraction can be eliminated completely by shaping the orifice to conform with the form of the contracting jet as shown in Fig. 4-2.

Fundamental Equations. The Bernoulli equation (Sec. 3), written from any point in the liquid, such as 1 in Fig. 4-1, to the vena contracta (point 2), taking the datum plane through the center of the orifice, is

$$\frac{v_1{}^2}{2g} + \frac{p_1}{w} = \frac{v_2{}^2}{2g} + \frac{p_2}{w} + h_l \qquad (4\text{-}2)$$

and

$$v_2 = \sqrt{2g\left(\frac{p_1}{w} - \frac{p_2}{w} + \frac{v_1{}^2}{2g} - h_l\right)} \qquad (4\text{-}3)$$

Point 2 being located where the jet has ceased to contract, its pressure is that of the surrounding fluid. For discharge into the atmosphere, p_2 is therefore zero on the gage scale.   For large tanks, v_1 is so small that it may be neglected.   Replacing p_1/w with h and dropping the subscript of v_2, Eq. (4-3) may now be written

$$v = \sqrt{2g(h - h_l)} \tag{4-4}$$

Neglecting energy losses, the equation for the theoretical velocity becomes

$$v_t = \sqrt{2gh} \tag{4-5}$$

or

$$h = \frac{v_t^2}{2g} \tag{4-6}$$

The expression $v_t^2/2g$ is termed the *velocity head*.   Table 4-1 gives values of v_t for heads from 0 to 50 ft, and Table 4-2 gives h for velocities from 0 to 50 ft per sec.

It is convenient to take care of the energy loss by introducing a *coefficient of velocity* C_v.   Thus, instead of subtracting the energy loss as in Eq. (4-4), the expression for the velocity at the vena contracta may be written

$$v = C_v \sqrt{2gh} \tag{4-7}$$

The discharge is the product of the velocity and area at the vena contracta as follows:

$$Q = a_2 v_2 \tag{4-8}$$

Inserting the value of a_2 from Eq. (4-1) and the value of v_2 from Eq. (4-7),

$$Q = C_c a C_v \sqrt{2gh} \tag{4-9}$$

The product of the coefficient of velocity C_v and the coefficient of contraction C_c is called the *coefficient of discharge* C.   Equation (4-9) may then be written

$$Q = Ca \sqrt{2gh} \tag{4-10}$$

The energy loss may be expressed in terms of C_v by equating the expressions for v given in Eqs. (4-4) and (4-7) as follows:

$$\sqrt{2g(h - h_l)} = C_v \sqrt{2gh}$$

Then

$$h_l = (1 - C_v^2)h \tag{4-11}$$

or introducing the value of h from Eq. (4-4),

$$h_l = \left(\frac{1}{C_v^2} - 1\right) \frac{v^2}{2g} \qquad (4\text{-}12)$$

Path of Jet.   Figure 4-3 illustrates a jet discharging from a vertical orifice under a head h. x and y are, respectively, abscissa and ordinate of any point m in the path of the jet. If v is the velocity in the vena contracta, at the end of time t,

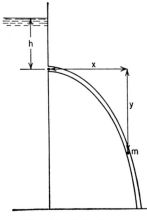

$$x = vt \qquad (4\text{-}13)$$

From the law of falling bodies,

$$y = \tfrac{1}{2}gt^2 \qquad (4\text{-}14)$$

and eliminating t from Eqs. (4-13) and (4-14),

$$x^2 = \frac{2v^2}{g} y \qquad (4\text{-}15a)$$

Fig. 4-3. Path of jet.

which is the equation of a parabola with its vertex at the orifice.   Since

$$v = C_v \sqrt{2gh} \qquad (4\text{-}7)$$

Eq. (4-15a) can also be written

$$x^2 = 4C_v^2 hy \qquad (4\text{-}15b)$$

Orifices under Low Heads.   In deriving Eq. (4-10), the head producing discharge was assumed to be the head on the center of the orifice.   Where the head on a vertical orifice is small in comparison with the height of the orifice, there is an appreciable difference between the true theoretical discharge and the discharge given by Eq. (4-10).

Figure 4-4 shows a rectangular orifice of width L and height M. h_1 and h_2 are the respective heads on the upper and lower edges of the orifice.   Neglecting velocity of approach, the theoretical discharge through any elementary strip of area $L\,dy$, discharging under a head y, is

$$dQ_t = L \sqrt{2gy} \, dy$$

which, integrated between the limits h_2 and h_1, gives

$$Q_t = \tfrac{2}{3}L \sqrt{2g} \, (h_2^{3/2} - h_1^{3/2})$$
$$(4\text{-}16)$$

When h_1 is zero

$$Q_t = \tfrac{2}{3}L \sqrt{2g} \, h_2^{3/2} \quad (4\text{-}17)$$

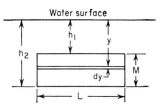

Fig. 4-4. Rectangular orifice.

which is the theoretical formula, without velocity-of-approach correction, for discharge over a weir.

Equation (4-16) gives the theoretical discharge for rectangular orifices. A similar but more complicated formula could be derived for circular orifices. For $h_1 = M$, Eq. (4-10) gives results about 1 per cent greater than Eq. (4-16), and for $h_1 = 2M$, about 0.3 per cent greater.

Equation (4-10) is generally employed for all orifices, including those discharging under low heads, deviation from the theoretical form of the formula being corrected for in the coefficient.

Discharge under Falling Head. Figure 4-5 shows a vessel filled with water to a depth h_1. The time required to lower the water surface to a depth h_2 is required. a is the area of orifice, and A is the area of water surface for a depth y. C is the coefficient of discharge. The increment of time dt required to lower the water the infinitesimal distance dy is

$$dt = \frac{A \, dy}{Ca \sqrt{2gy}} \qquad (4\text{-}18)$$

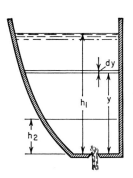

Fig. 4-5. Discharge under falling head.

From (4-18), if A can be expressed in terms of y, by integrating between limits h_1 and h_2, the time needed to lower the water surface the distance $h_1 - h_2$ can be gotten. Placing $h_2 = 0$ gives the time of emptying the vessel. Equation (4-18) applies to horizontal or inclined orifices provided the water surface does not fall below the top of the orifice. For a cylinder or prism with vertical axis, A is constant, and Eq. (4-18), after integration, becomes

$$t = \frac{2A}{Ca \sqrt{2g}} (\sqrt{h_1} - \sqrt{h_2}) \qquad (4\text{-}19)$$

Orifice Coefficients. One of the earliest experimenters on sharp-edged orifices was Hamilton Smith, Jr.[1] His values of the coefficient of discharge for round and square orifices are given in Table 4-3. There have been many subsequent investigations of circular orifices, not all of which are in agreement.

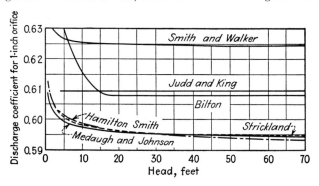

Fig. 4-6. Orifice coefficients.

Investigations by Medaugh and Johnson[2] check Smith's coefficients for orifices larger than $\frac{1}{4}$ in. in diameter within $\frac{1}{3}$ of 1 per cent. Values of the coefficient of discharge for a 1-in. orifice as determined by various investigators and plotted by Medaugh and Johnson are shown in Fig. 4-6. The differences between the values are undoubtedly not entirely due to experimental errors. Many other factors may contribute, as, for instance, the ratio of the orifice diameter to the dimensions of the tank wall, the sharpness of the edge of the orifice, the roughness of the inner surface, the orifice plate, and the temperature of the water. The effect of having the tank wall approach the orifice is to suppress contraction and therefore to make C approach the value of C_v.

[1] "Hydraulics," 1886.

[2] Medaugh and Johnson, Investigation of the Discharge and Coefficient of Small Circular Orifices, *Civil Eng.* (*N.Y.*), July, 1940, pp. 422–424.

Smith and Walker[1] found values of C_v to vary from 0.954 to 0.991 for orifices varying in diameter from 0.75 to 2.5 in., respectively. They also found a small variation with head, the above values being averages for heads varying from 1 to 60 ft.

Values of C_c for circular sharp-edged orifices were found to vary from approximately 0.67 for ¾-in. orifices to 0.614 for 2.5-in. orifices when the head is 2 ft or more. Values are slightly larger for lower heads.

If there is suppression of contraction on one side and opportunity for complete contraction on the other sides, more water will approach with velocity components parallel to the face of the orifice on these sides and cause increased contraction. This to a large extent will compensate for loss of contraction on the other side. Williams[2] found, for rectangular orifices 30 in. wide and 2 to 4 in. high with full contraction at the top and completely suppressed contraction on the two sides and bottom, that the average coefficient of discharge was 0.607. This value corresponds closely to the coefficient for orifices with complete contraction. For orifices having full contraction at the top, one side a sharp edge 6 in. from the side of the channel, and contraction suppressed at one side and the bottom, Williams secured an average coefficient of 0.611. With the above orifices, except that the top was beveled to an angle of 45°, he obtained values of C of 0.776 and 0.755, respectively. Table 4-4, from results compiled by Smith,[3] indicates the effect of suppression of contraction for small orifices. In this table, "suppressed contraction" means that the edge of the orifice coincides with the side of the channel, and "partly suppressed" means that the distance of the edge of the orifice from the side of the channel was 0.066 ft. A special case of suppressed contraction is the pipe orifice, which will be discussed later.

When the inner edge of the orifice is rounded, as in Fig. 4-2, contraction is suppressed, C_c approaches 1, and C approaches the value of C_v. Values of C_v for such orifices are approximately the same as for sharp-edged orifices.

Roughening the inner surface of the orifice plate retards the

[1] D. Smith and W. J. Walker, Orifice Flow, *Proc. Inst. Mech. Engrs.* (*London*), 1923, pp. 23–36.

[2] Unpublished experiments performed at the University of Michigan in 1928.

[3] *Op. cit.*, pp. 65–67.

velocity components along the wall which cause contraction and thus tends to increase the values of both C_c and C. Similar effects would result from having the orifice plate differ from a perfectly plane surface. If it were slightly warped outward, C_c would be increased, whereas an inward curvature of the plate would have the opposite effect (see Standard Short Tubes, p. 4-19).

The effect of the water temperature is to change the viscosity and density. Taken in conjunction with the variation of C

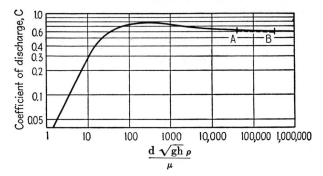

Fig. 4-7. Orifice coefficients.

with the velocity and orifice diameter shown in Table 4-3, it becomes clear that here again the Reynolds number is likely to be the coordinating factor. This was shown to be the case by Lea,[1] who plotted more than one hundred experimental values of C against R. The author's curve, derived from Lea's plotted points, is shown in Fig. 4-7. The fluids used in the tests were water, various mixtures of water and glycerin, and a number of oils. Flow is laminar for Reynolds number less than 12 and fully turbulent for R greater than 10,000, intervening values corresponding to a transition region. Except in the transition range, all points plotted by Lea show a spread of about 3 per cent. A spread of approximately 15 per cent occurs in the vicinity R equal to 1,000. The range of Reynolds numbers covered by the tests of Medaugh and Johnson is shown in Fig. 4-7 by the dashed line AB.

[1] F. C. Lea, "Hydraulics," 6th ed., Longmans, Green & Co., Inc., New York, 1942.

Investigations by Bilton[1] showed the coefficient of discharge of a circular orifice under any given head to be the same whether the jet is horizontal, vertical, or at any intermediate angle.

The extracts from tables by Fanning[2] and Bovey,[3] in Table 4-5, give coefficients of discharge for various shapes and arrangements of orifices with complete contraction. Fanning's table, compiled from experiments from several sources, contains coefficients for orifices 1 ft wide, of various heights, and under a wide range of heads. Bovey's table, prepared from his own experiments on orifices of different shapes, each with the area of a circle $\frac{1}{2}$ in. in diameter, indicates the effect of shape of opening on the coefficient.

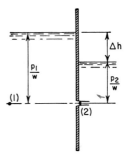

FIG. 4-8. Submerged orifice.

Submerged Orifices. Shown in Fig. 4-8 is an orifice in a tank with liquid on both sides. Application of the Bernoulli equation, taking the datum through the center of the orifice, yields Eq. (4-3) exactly in the same form as for free discharge (p. 4-2).

$$v_2 = \sqrt{2g \left(\frac{p_1}{w} - \frac{p_2}{w} + \frac{v_1^2}{2g} - h_l \right)} \qquad (4\text{-}3)$$

Noting that in this case

$$\frac{p_1}{w} - \frac{p_2}{w} = \Delta h \qquad (4\text{-}20)$$

neglecting $v_1^2/2g$, and introducing C to take care of the contraction and energy loss, the equation for discharge is

$$Q = Ca \sqrt{2g \, \Delta h} \qquad (4\text{-}21)$$

The few experiments for determining C for submerged orifices that are available indicate that the value of the coefficient is

[1] H. J. I. Bilton, Coefficients of Discharge through Circular Orifices, paper read before Victorian Institute of Engineers, April, 1908, *Eng. News*, July 9, 1908.

[2] J. T. Fanning, "Water-supply Engineering," pp. 205–206, D. Van Nostrand Company, Inc., Princeton, N.J., 1906.

[3] H. T. Bovey, "Hydraulics," p. 40, John Wiley & Sons, Inc., New York, 1909.

not greatly affected by submergence.   Table 4-6 gives values of C for sharp-edged submerged orifices, and Table 4-7 contains values of C for a submerged orifice 1 ft square with rounded corners.

Gates are openings in hydraulic structures to permit the passage of water, usually including means of regulating the

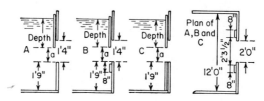

Fig. 4-9. Gates discharging freely into air.

outflow. Though gates have the hydraulic properties of orifices, there are no standards of design, and they therefore have varying degrees of contraction. The discharge may be either free or submerged. The formula for discharge, h being the head on the center of the orifice for orifices with free dis-

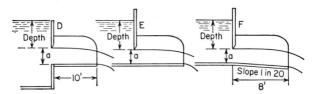

Fig. 4-10. Gates with prolonged bottoms and sides.

charge, and the difference in elevation of water surfaces for submerged orifices, is

$$Q = Ca\,\sqrt{2gh} \qquad (4\text{-}10)$$

The results of experiments on wooden models of gates shown in Figs. 4-9 and 4-10 were given by Unwin[1] and Bellasis.[1]
Table 4-8 gives C for each of these models for various depths of water above the top of the orifice.

The mean value of C for a sluice gate in the Argo dam at

[1] W. C. Unwin, Hydraulics, "Encyclopaedia Britannica," 11th ed., vol. 14, p. 41, 1912. Also, E. L. Bellasis, "Hydraulics," 2d ed., p. 68, Spon & Chamberlain, New York, 1911.

Ann Arbor, Mich., discharging without submergence under a head of about 8 ft, was found by Ward[1] to be 0.545. The

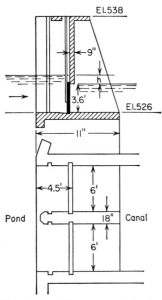

opening, 4 ft wide by 5 ft high, was between beveled piers. The base of the gate was 1 ft above the concrete floor, the bottom of the iron gate forming the top edge of the orifice.

Head gates and diversion gates usually have the general features illustrated in Fig. 4-11a. The bottom of the opening is nearly flush with the floor of the structure, the sides are flush with

Fig. 4-11a. Maxwell canal head gate.

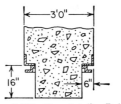

Fig. 4-11b. Pier details, Boise canal head gate.

the piers, and the noses of the piers are beveled. There is full contraction at the top.

Values of C by Newell[2] for the head gates of the Maxwell canal, Umatilla project, Oregon (Fig. 4-11a), are:

h	0.11	0.16	1.08	1.98
v	2.21	2.65	5.71	8.07
C	0.83	0.83	0.685	0.715

One gate only was open for values in the last column. For the remaining values two gates were open.

The following values of C by Steward[3] are for the main head gates of the Boise canal, Idaho. There are 8 gates, 3 ft wide by 9 ft high. Except for pier details, shown in Fig. 4-11b, the structure is similar to that shown in Fig. 4-11a.

[1] C. N. Ward, An unpublished thesis, University of Michigan, 1915.

[2] H. D. Newell, *U.S. Bur. Reclamation, Experimental Data* 9, 1916.

[3] W. G. Steward, *U.S. Bur. Reclamation, Experimental Data* 35, 1923.

G	0.67	0.72	0.76	0.80	1.10	1.40	1.45	1.57
h	7.6	8.1	7.3	7.6	5.0	7.0	9.1	12.2
v	18	16	17	17	16	18	19	21
C	0.81	0.70	0.77	0.78	0.91	0.86	0.77	0.75

G	1.85	2.13	2.22	2.85	3.41	3.75	4.46
h	7.1	7.4	9.0	9.6	7.0	5.3	6.1
v	17	18	19	19	16	15	14
C	0.81	0.81	0.78	0.78	0.74	0.81	0.68

G is the gate opening in feet. One gate only was open for values in the seventh column. For the remaining values eight gates were open.

Parker[1] discusses experiments on head gates by Bornemann,[2] Chatterton,[3] and Benton[4] and publishes formulas by each. Chatterton's formula for C for values of h below 5 ft is

$$C = 0.615 + 0.007 \times 2^{5-h} \qquad (4\text{-}22)$$

Benton gives the following formula for heads below 5 ft and widths of gate opening W up to 10 ft:

$$C = 0.7201 + 0.0074W \qquad (4\text{-}23)$$

Formulas (4-22) and (4-23) are based upon independent sets of observations. In formula (4-22) C varies only with h, and in (4-23) it varies only with W. Results by the two formulas agree quite closely for heads of 1 ft or less but differ by 10 to 25 per cent for the higher heads. Table 4-9 gives values of C computed by formulas (4-22) and (4-23).

The coefficient C for gates as given by the above formulas and tables includes the effect of velocity of approach and is to be applied directly in formula (4-21). The knowledge of the coefficient is not sufficient to justify the use of a formula which contains a separate term to correct for velocity of approach. The experiments by Newell show C to vary inversely with h at low heads and thus, in a general way, confirm Chatterton's results. Steward's results do not indicate any tendency for C to vary with h at heads above 5 ft. It appears that for gates of this type (Fig. 4-11) conditions affecting side contrac-

[1] Philip à Morley Parker, "The Control of Water," pp. 164–168, Routledge & Kegan Paul, Ltd., London, 1925.

[2] *Civilingenieur*, vol. 26, p. 297, 1880.

[3] Hydraulic experiments in the Kistna delta.

[4] *Punjab Irrigation Branch Paper* 8.

tions have very little effect on C. If the gate sill is raised above the floor of the structure, a bottom contraction is produced which will have some effect in restricting discharge.

Discrepancies in experimental results (as indicated by the formulas of Chatterton and Benton) may result from differences in:

1. Structural details which affect contraction;

2. Channel dimensions which affect velocity of approach; and particularly

3. The distance downstream from the gate at which the elevation of water surface is measured. This may affect materially the value of h.

When a *sluice gate* discharges with the jet submerged there is a characteristic dip down at the downstream side of the gate as shown in Fig. 4-12. In order to evaluate the head h on the gate, the magnitude of the depth just downstream from the gate D_s must be determined. An expression for D_s may be obtained by applying Newton's second

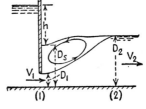

FIG. 4-12. Flow through sluice gate.

law of motion to the water in the region from 1 to 2 in Fig. 4-12. For the case of a rectangular channel having a gate extending across the entire width of the channel, the force applied to the quantity of water between 1 and 2 may be taken as the difference between the hydrostatic forces at the two ends as follows:

$$F = \frac{wD_2{}^2}{2} - \frac{wD_s{}^2}{2} \qquad (4\text{-}24)$$

The rate of change of momentum is

$$\frac{qw}{g}(V_1 - V_2)$$

where V_1 is the average velocity in the jet and V_2 is the average velocity at point 2. By equating the above expressions and making use of the continuity equations, the following value of D_s may be obtained:

$$D_s = D_2 \left[1 + \frac{2V_2{}^2}{gD_2} \left(1 - \frac{D_2}{D_1} \right) \right]^{\frac{1}{2}} \qquad (4\text{-}25)$$

Similar expressions may be obtained for channels other than rectangular or for cases where the gate width is less than the channel width. The principles involved in determining the nature of the water surface above and below the gate are presented in Sec. 8.

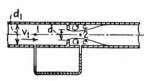

Fɪɢ. 4-13. Pipe orifice.

Pipe Orifices. A circular sharp-edged pipe orifice is shown in Fig. 4-13. The velocity at the vena contracta 2 is given by Eq. (4-3). Replacing the energy-loss term h_l with C_v as was done for orifices in tanks, Eq. (4-3) becomes

$$v_2 = C_v \sqrt{2g\left(\frac{p_1}{w} - \frac{p_2}{w} + \frac{v_1^2}{2g}\right)} \qquad (4\text{-}26)$$

In pipe orifices the velocity-of-approach factor $V_1^2/2g$ cannot be omitted. Again letting $a_2 = C_c a$ and $C = C_c C_v$, the expression for the discharge becomes

$$Q = Ca \sqrt{2g\left(\frac{p_1}{w} - \frac{p_2}{w} + \frac{v_1^2}{2g}\right)} \qquad (4\text{-}27)$$

In this form the equation requires a cut-and-try solution. However, by replacing v_1^2 with its value obtained from the equation of continuity $(Q/a_1)^2$, a_1 being the area of the pipe, the following expression for Q is derived:

$$Q = Ca \sqrt{\frac{2g(p_1/w - p_2/w)}{1 - C^2(a/a_1)^2}} \qquad (4\text{-}28)$$

The value of C varies not only with the factors which affected orifices in tanks, but also with the ratio of the orifice diameter d to the pipe diameter d_1 and with the location of the pressure taps. Tests indicate that the vena contracta is approximately half a pipe diameter downstream from the orifice.[1] When the orifice is at the end of the pipe, p_2 in Eq. (4-28) is zero and only a single pressure tap is required. Curves showing the relation between C and Reynolds number are plotted in Fig. 4-14. Portions of the curves are shown as broken lines because values of

[1] ASME, "Flow Meters: Their Theory and Application," 3d ed., 1931.

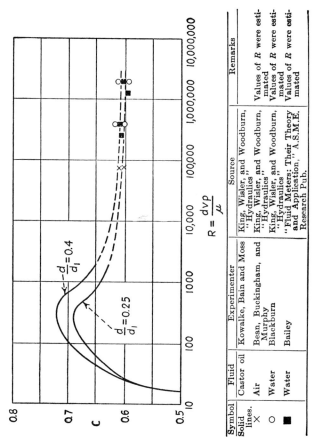

FIG. 4-14. Coefficients for pipe orifices.

Symbol	Fluid	Experimenter	Source	Remarks
Solid lines.	Castor oil	Kowalke, Bain and Moss	King, Wisler, and Woodburn, "Hydraulics"	
×	Air	Bean, Buckingham, and Murphy	King, Wisler, and Woodburn, "Hydraulics"	Values of R were estimated
○	Water	Blackburn	King, Wisler, and Woodburn, "Hydraulics"	Values of R were estimated
■	Water	Bailey	"Fluid Meters; Their Theory and Application," A.S.M.E. Research Pub.	Values of R were estimated

$$R = \frac{dv\rho}{\mu}$$

R are uncertain for the meager data available in this region. Equation (4-28) may be restated in the following form:

$$Q = Ka \sqrt{2g \left(\frac{p_1}{w} - \frac{p_2}{w} \right)} \qquad (4\text{-}29)$$

where K is defined as follows:

$$K = \frac{C}{\sqrt{1 - C^2(a/a_1)^2}} \qquad (4\text{-}30)$$

In Eqs. (4-29) and (4-30), Q is the discharge in second-feet; a and a_1 are the areas of the orifice and the pipe, respectively, in square feet; p_1 and p_2 are the pressures at the upstream and downstream sides of the orifice, respectively, in pounds per square foot; and w is the unit weight of the liquid in pounds per cubic foot. It will be noted from the derivation on page 4-14 that C takes care of the energy loss and the contraction of the jet. It follows from Eq. (4-30) that the coefficient K includes these factors as well as the velocity of approach.

Values of K for square-edged pipe orifices have been presented by the ASME[1] for three different types of pressure taps. These are flange taps, vena contracta taps, and radius taps. Flange taps are located with the center of the high-pressure tap 1 in. from the upstream face of the orifice plate and the center of the low-pressure tap 1 in. from the downstream side of the plate. For vena contracta taps, the high-pressure tap is located 1 pipe diameter, d_1, upstream from the face of the orifice plate, and the low-pressure tap is located at the vena contracta. The mean distance from the orifice plate to the vena contracta, in terms of pipe diameters, for various values of the ratio of orifice diameter to the pipe diameter, d/d_1, is given in the table on page 4-17. Radius taps are located 1 pipe diameter upstream and $\frac{1}{2}$ pipe diameter downstream from the orifice plate.

Values of K are presented in terms of the Reynolds number:

$$R = \frac{dV}{\nu} \qquad (4\text{-}31)$$

where d is the orifice diameter in feet, V is the velocity at the

---

[1] ASME, "Flow Measurement by Means of Standardized Nozzles and Orifice Plates," Power Test Codes, Supplement on Instruments and Apparatus, pt. 5, chap. 4, 1949. This supplement was prepared and published by ASME under the auspices of the Power Test Codes Committee.

orifice in feet per second, and ν is the kinematic viscosity of the fluid in square feet per second. Values of ν for water may be obtained from Table 1-2. Values of K to be used with flange taps for 6- and 10-in. pipe are shown in Fig. 4-15. These

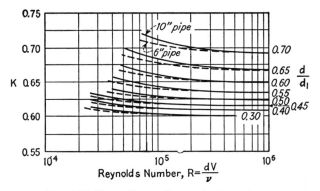

FIG. 4-15. Pipe-orifice coefficients for flange taps.

were taken from the ASME Power Test Codes, previously referred to.[1] The curves for 6-in. pipe are quite similar to

d/d_1	Distance from Orifice Plate to Vena Contracta, Pipe Diameters*
0.8	0.32
0.7	0.45
0.6	0.57
0.5	0.66
0.4	0.73
0.3	0.80
0.2	0.87

* ASME, "Fluid Meters: Their Theory and Application," pt. 1, 4th ed., 1937.

those for 3- and 4-in. pipe, while those for 10-in. pipe are similar to those for 8- and 14-in. pipe. Values of K for 2-in. pipe are somewhat lower than those for 6-in. pipe for $R < 10^5$ and slightly higher for $R > 2 \times 10^5$. If an installation of a pipe orifice is to be made without a calibration, it is recommended that reference be made to the original data for the particular pipe size, as well as to detailed installation requirements.[1]

Curves showing values of K for vena contracta taps are shown in Fig. 4-16. These curves were presented for 6-in.

[1] *Ibid.*

pipe.[1]   They are, however, nearly identical with those for other pipe diameters.

Values of K for a pipe orifice in any particular location may be expected to differ somewhat from values given in Figs. 4-15 and 4-16 unless installation recommendations are carefully followed.   Detailed instructions are available.[1]   Some of the

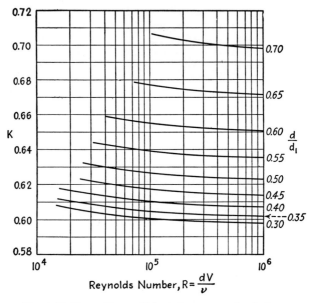

Fig. 4-16. Pipe-orifice coefficients for vena contracta taps.

more important restrictions have to do with the location of pipe fittings in the vicinity of the orifice.   For example, elbows or open valves must be located 5 pipe diameters upstream from the orifice for small values of d/d_1 and as many as 25 diameters upstream from the orifice for large values of d/d_1.   No elbow should be placed nearer than 5 diameters from the downstream side of the orifice.   Partially open valves should not be located upstream from the orifice.   Where these restrictions cannot be followed, flow straighteners must be used or the orifice must be

[1] *Ibid.*

calibrated in place. Studies regarding the effect of pipe fittings on orifice flow are being conducted, and preliminary information is available.[1]

The ISA (International Federation of National Standardizing Associations) standard orifice is also a square-edged circular-pipe orifice. The pressure taps, however, are located immediately adjacent to the orifice plate. Coefficients for this type of taps have been published by the Verein Deutscher Ingenieure, translated into English by the ASME, and recently published by the National Advisory Committee for Aeronautics.[2]

Tubes. *Borda's mouthpiece* is a short cylindrical tube projecting inward. The edge of the tube must be relatively thin and sharp to ensure perfect contraction, and its length, about $\frac{1}{2}d$, such that the jet will not touch the sides of the tube. The following are average coefficients:

$$C = 0.51 \qquad C_v = 0.98 \qquad C_c = 0.52$$

Standard Short Tube. A cylindrical tube having a length of 2 to 3 diameters with the inner end flush with a flat wall so

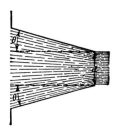

as to form a sharp-cornered entrance is called a standard short tube. In such tubes the issuing jet first contracts and then expands, filling the tube. The coefficient of contraction is considered unity. The coefficient of discharge varies from 0.78 to 0.83. The mean value generally used is

$$C = 0.82$$

Short tubes projecting inward have coefficients of discharge varying from 0.72 to 0.80. The average value is

Fig. 4-17. Convergent tube with sharp corner at entrance.

$$C = 0.75$$

Convergent short tubes are frustums of cones, as shown in Figs. 4-17 and 4-18. Figure 4-17 has the larger base flush with a flat wall forming a sharp-cornered entrance. Figure 4-18 has the entrance to the tube slightly rounded. The sides of the tube make an angle θ with the axis of the cone.

[1] "Investigation of Orifice Meter Installation Requirements," Interim Research Report, American Gas Association and ASME, March, 1951.

[2] Standards for Discharge Measurement with Standardized Nozzles and Orifices, German Industrial Standard 1952, 4th ed., *NACA Tech. Mem. 952.*

Experiments for these tubes give conflicting results. Fair average values are given by Unwin[1] as follows:

Angle θ	$0°$	$5\frac{3}{4}°$	$11\frac{1}{4}°$	$22\frac{1}{2}°$	$45°$
C, for Fig. 4-20	0.83	0.94	0.92	0.85	
C, for Fig. 4-21	0.97	0.95	0.92	0.88	0.75

Converging Bell-mouthed Orifice. If the surface of the opening is rounded to conform to the shape of the contracted

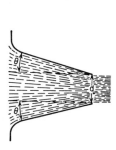

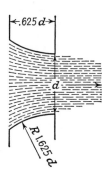

FIG. 4-18. Convergent tube with rounded corner at entrance.

FIG. 4-19. Converging bell-mouthed orifice.

jet (Fig. 4-19), C approaches unity. The following are coefficients by Weisbach[2] for $d = 0.033$ ft. Other experiments indicate that these results hold approximately for larger orifices.

h, ft	0.066	1.640	11.480	55.770	337.930
C	0.959	0.967	0.975	0.994	0.994

Diverging conical tubes are shown in Fig. 4-20a and b. The coefficient of discharge varies with the angle of divergence and length of tube. Experiments by Venturi showed discharge to be a maximum with $l = 9d$ and angle of divergence equal to 5°. If divergence is not too great, the tube will flow full. The coefficient of discharge is variable, but when so designed that the tube flows full, the following results may be obtained:

For Fig. 4-20a, $C = 1.4$
For Fig. 4-20b, $C = 2.0$

[1] W. C. Unwin, "A Treatise on Hydraulics," p. 89, A. & C. Black, Ltd., London, 1907.

[2] Julius Weisbach, "Ingenieur und Machinen-Mechanik," p. 969, 1875.

Nozzles. In 1888 John R. Freeman reported[1] the results on tests made on various types of nozzles suitable for fire hoses. Until recent years no significant change in design has been developed. In 1952 results of tests carried on at the Iowa Institute of Hydraulic Research[2] were published. These tests

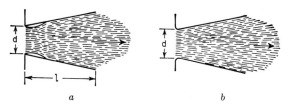

Fig. 4-20a. Diverging tube with sharp corner at entrance.
Fig. 4-20b. Diverging tube with rounded corner at entrance.

were conducted with primary attention on the efficiency of the fire stream itself. This research resulted in improved designs of both monitors and nozzles. Although the recommended nozzle design provided only a very slight decrease in energy loss in the nozzle, there was a substantial decrease in the rate of disintegration of the jet.

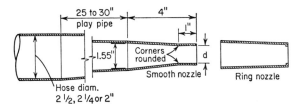

Fig. 4-21. Smooth and ring nozzles.

Two types of nozzles were reported on by Freeman, the smooth type without jet contraction and the ring type shown in Fig. 4-21. The following are mean values of coefficients of discharge for smooth nozzles as determined by Freeman:

Diameter, in.....	$\frac{3}{4}$	$\frac{7}{8}$	1	$1\frac{1}{8}$	$1\frac{1}{4}$	$1\frac{3}{8}$
	0.983	0.982	0.972	0.976	0.971	0.959

[1] Experiments Relating to Hydraulics of Fire Streams, *Trans. ASCE*, vol. 21, pp. 303–482, 1888.

[2] Hunter Rouse, J. W. Howe, and D. E. Metzler, Experimental Investigation of Fire Monitors on Nozzles, *Trans. ASCE*, vol. 117, pp. 1147–1188, 1952.

The following are mean values of coefficients of discharge for ring nozzles as determined from Freeman's experiments. The ratio of the diameter of opening to diameter just behind ring is given.

Ratio......	0.50	0.60	0.70	0.80	0.85	0.90	0.95	1.00
C..........	0.63	0.65	0.68	0.71	0.73	0.77	0.87	0.975

In Freeman's tests, as well as the Iowa tests, the velocity of approach was neglected and the coefficient of discharge was computed from the following equation:

$$Q = Ca \sqrt{2gh} \qquad (4\text{-}10)$$

where a is the area of the nozzle, and h is the pressure head just upstream from the nozzle.

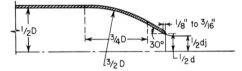

FIG. 4-22. Nozzle developed from Iowa tests.

The form of nozzle developed by the Iowa tests is shown in Fig. 4-22. Reported values of d/D, d_j/D, and C are shown below. The terms d, d_j, and D are defined in Fig. 4-22.

d/D...........	0.279	0.335	0.391	0.446	0.501	0.557
d_j/D...........	0.250	0.300	0.350	0.400	0.450	0.500
C...............	0.805	0.806	0.807	0.811	0.817	0.825
C_c*.............	0.805	0.805	0.805	0.806	0.807	0.807
C_v*.............	1.000	0.999	0.997	0.995	0.987	0.977

* Computed by the author.

Computations of C_c and C_v indicate that the energy losses are very small, as shown by the fact that values of C_v differ only slightly from unity. It may be seen from Eq. (4-12) that when $C_v = 0.977$, the energy loss is approximately 5 per cent.

Information regarding standardized nozzles which are used to measure discharge in pipes is given in Sec. 12, p. 12-18.

Submerged Tubes. Stewart[1] experimented on submerged tubes 4 ft square and 0.31 to 14 ft long under heads of 0.05 to

[1] C. B. Stewart, Investigation of Flow through Large Submerged Orifices and Tubes, *Univ. Wis. Bull.* 216, 1908.

0.30 ft. Entrance conditions included sharp edges and various degrees of suppressed contraction. Rogers and Smith[1] extended Stewart's experiments to include sharp-edged tubes 6, 8, and 10 in. square under heads of 2.2 ft and less. They found C [formula (4-21)] to vary with L/D, L being the length of tube and D the length of one side of the cross section, but to be independent of the head.

Table 4-10, obtained from the above experiments, expresses C as a function of L/p, p being the length of perimeter of the cross section of the tube. For a square tube, $p = 4D$. Though the values of C contained in Table 4-10 are derived from experiments on square tubes, they will probably apply quite accurately to other tubes which do not depart far from this form of section.

Culverts. The total loss of head in a culvert is the sum of the entrance and outlet losses, which vary with the design of the ends, plus the loss of head due to friction (p. 4-25), which varies directly with the length. It is convenient to treat culverts flowing full, with both ends submerged, as submerged tubes and to include all losses of head in the coefficient of discharge C [formula (4-21)]. To obtain the maximum discharge, the intake must be submerged to a depth equal at least to the sum of the velocity head and the loss of head at entrance. The discharge is entirely independent of the slope of the tube. It depends only on h, the difference in elevation of water surfaces at intake and outlet.

The results of 1,480 experiments on concrete-, vitrified-clay-, and corrugated-metal-pipe culverts and 1,821 experiments on concrete-box culverts were published by Yarnell, Nagler, and Woodward.[2] Experiments were conducted on pipes 12, 18, 24, and 30 in. in diameter and on box culverts 2 by 2, 3 by 3, 4 by 4, 4 by 3, 4 by $2\frac{1}{4}$, 4 by 2, 4 by 1, and 4 by $\frac{1}{2}$, all in feet. The lengths of both pipes and box culverts experimented upon were 24, 30, and 36 ft. Using the nomenclature d = diameter for pipe culverts, r = hydraulic radius for box culverts, and L = length of culvert, the following are expressions for determining C in formula (4-21):

[1] T. C. Rogers and T. L. Smith, Experiments with Submerged Orifices and Tubes, *Eng. News*, Nov. 2, 1916.

[2] D. L. Yarnell, F. A. Nagler, and S. M. Woodward, Flow of Water through Culverts, *Univ. Iowa Studies in Engineering*, 1926.

For concrete pipe, beveled-lip entrance,

$$C = \left(1.1 + \frac{0.026L}{d^{1.2}}\right)^{-\frac{1}{2}} \tag{4-32}$$

For concrete pipe, square-cornered entrance,

$$C = \left(1 + 0.31d^{0.5} + \frac{0.026L}{d^{1.2}}\right)^{-\frac{1}{2}} \tag{4-33}$$

For vitrified-clay pipe, bell end upstream,

$$C = \left(1 + 0.023d^{1.9} + \frac{0.022L}{d^{1.0}}\right)^{-\frac{1}{2}} \tag{4-34}$$

For corrugated-metal pipe,

$$C = \left(1 + 0.16d^{0.6} + \frac{0.106L}{d^{1.2}}\right)^{-\frac{1}{2}} \tag{4-35}$$

For concrete-box culverts with rounded-lip entrance,

$$C = \left(1.05 + \frac{0.0045L}{r^{1.25}}\right)^{-\frac{1}{2}} \tag{4-36}$$

For concrete-box culverts with square-cornered entrance,

$$C = \left(1 + 0.4r^{0.3} + \frac{0.0045L}{r^{1.25}}\right)^{-\frac{1}{2}} \tag{4-37}$$

Values of C, computed from the above formulas for different values of d and L, and r and L, are contained in Table 4-11.

Inasmuch as the experiments from which the above formulas were derived include only lengths of 24 to 36 ft, it would appear best, for long culverts, to apply the formulas only to a portion of the length (25 to 50 ft) and compute the head lost in the remainder of the conduit by an open-channel or pipe formula. The h to be used in formula (4-21) is then the difference in elevation of water surfaces at entrance and outlet minus this computed loss of head.

The experiments indicate that 45° wing walls used in connection with pipe culverts increase the discharge 1 to 10 per cent over that obtained with a straight end wall and that wing walls are more efficient when set flush with the edge of the pipe than when set 6 in. back from the edge. U-type wing walls used in connection with vitrified-clay pipe produced a slightly smaller discharge than that obtained with a straight end wall. The beveled lip at the entrance to concrete pipes greatly reduced entrance loss. It was found that a 24-in. clay pipe 38 ft long with a straight end wall and the bell end upstream carried about 10 per cent more water than the same culvert with a square-cornered entrance. Rounding the entrance of a 24-in. vitrified-clay-pipe culvert increased the capacity 13 per cent. It was found also that the discharge is decreased slightly by projecting the pipe through the head wall. In a square-cornered entrance there is little difference whether the pipe projects 3 in. or 2 or 4 ft. An 18-in. corrugated-metal

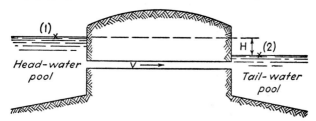

FIG. 4-23. Pipe culvert.

pipe with a 3-in. projection carries slightly more water than the same pipe with a 2- or 4-ft projection. Doubling the end area of the submerged outlet of an 18-in. vitrified-clay-pipe culvert by attaching a 10° diverging end was found to increase the discharge by 40 per cent over that obtained through the same culvert without the diverging end.

Culvert discharge may also be computed by considering the culvert as a short pipe. Bernoulli's equation written from point 1 to point 2 in Fig. 4-23, taking the datum plane at the elevation of the water surface at point 2, gives

$$H = h_e + h_f + h_o \tag{4-38}$$

In the above equation h_e is the entrance loss, h_f is the friction loss, and h_o is the loss at the outlet. The entrance and outlet losses are usually expressed in terms of the velocity head as follows:

$$h_e = K_e \frac{V^2}{2g} \tag{4-39}$$

and

$$h_o = K_o \frac{V^2}{2g} \tag{4-40}$$

where V is the average velocity in the pipe. The friction loss may be determined from the Manning formula or the Darcy-Weisbach equation as described in Secs. 6 and 7.

Straub and Morris[1] have reported values of K_e and K_o as well as values of the Manning coefficient n and the Darcy-Weisbach coefficient f, based on a series of laboratory tests on concrete- and corrugated-metal-pipe culverts. Full-scale tests were made on culverts 193 ft long for pipes flowing full and for the case of uniform flow with a free surface. Round pipes of 18-, 24-, and 36-in. diameters were used, as well as arched corrugated-metal pipes having the same perimeters as the round pipes. The dimensions of the corrugated pipe refer to the inside diameter, and the height of the corrugations was $\frac{1}{2}$ in. The entrance to the concrete culverts consisted of the groove end of a length of tongue-and-groove pipe. Tests were made with the inlet end flush with the wall of the headwater pool and also with a projecting inlet.

For the concrete pipe, design values of the entrance-loss coefficient K_e were found to be 0.10 for the flush inlet and 0.15 for the projecting inlet. These values apply to full flow and to part-full flow conditions. For corrugated-metal pipes flowing full, practical design values of K_e were found to be 0.5 for a flush entrance and 0.9 for the projecting entrance. For the case of flow with a free surface in corrugated pipes, the corresponding values of K_e were 0.4 and 0.7, respectively.

The outlet-loss coefficient K_o was found to be nearly 1.0 in all cases.

Values of the Manning n varied somewhat with the pipe size, the shape of the pipe, and the Reynolds number. Practical design values taken near the upper end of the range are 0.011 for concrete pipe and 0.025 for corrugated-metal pipe. Similar values of the Darcy-Weisbach f for concrete pipe are 0.018 for the 18-in. pipe and 0.016 for the 24- and 36-in. pipe. Corresponding values of f for corrugated-metal pipe are 0.105 for the 18-in. size, 0.090 for the 24-in. size, and 0.075 for the 36-in. size. The results obtained from Eq. (4-38), using the coefficients given above, are in close agreement with values computed from Eq. (4-21), using appropriate values of C from Table 4-11.

---

[1] L. G. Straub and H. M. Morris, Hydraulic Tests on Concrete Culvert Pipes, *Tech. Paper* 4, *Series B*, and Hydraulic Tests on Corrugated Metal Culvert Pipes, *Tech. Paper* 5, *Series B*, St. Anthony Falls Hydraulic Laboratory, Minneapolis, Minn., 1950.

Table 4-1. Theoretical Velocities in Feet per Second, for Heads of 0 to 50 Ft.   From the Formula

$$v_t = \sqrt{2gh}$$

Head in feet	.0	.1	.2	.3	.4	.5	.6	.7	.8	.9
0	0.00	2.54	3.59	4.39	5.07	5.67	6.21	6.71	7.17	7.61
1	8.02	8.41	8.79	9.14	9.49	9.82	10.14	10.46	10.76	11.05
2	11.34	11.62	11.90	12.16	12.42	12.68	12.93	13.18	13.42	13.66
3	13.89	14.12	14.35	14.57	14.79	15.00	15.22	15.43	15.63	15.84
4	16.04	16.24	16.44	16.63	16.82	17.01	17.20	17.39	17.57	17.75
5	17.93	18.11	18.29	18.46	18.63	18.81	18.98	19.15	19.31	19.48
6	19.64	19.81	19.97	20.13	20.29	20.45	20.60	20.76	20.91	21.06
7	21.22	21.37	21.52	21.67	21.81	21.96	22.11	22.26	22.40	22.54
8	22.68	22.83	22.97	23.11	23.24	23.38	23.52	23.65	23.79	23.93
9	24.06	24.19	24.32	24.46	24.59	24.72	24.85	24.98	25.11	25.24
10	25.36	25.49	25.61	25.74	25.86	25.99	26.11	26.23	26.35	26.47
11	26.60	26.72	26.84	26.96	27.08	27.20	27.31	27.43	27.55	27.66
12	27.78	27.90	28.01	28.13	28.24	28.36	28.47	28.58	28.69	28.80
13	28.92	29.03	29.14	29.25	29.36	29.47	29.58	29.68	29.79	29.90
14	30.01	30.12	30.22	30.33	30.43	30.54	30.64	30.75	30.85	30.96
15	31.06	31.16	31.27	31.37	31.47	31.57	31.67	31.78	31.88	31.98
16	32.08	32.18	32.28	32.38	32.48	32.57	32.67	32.77	32.87	32.97
17	33.07	33.16	33.26	33.35	33.45	33.55	33.65	33.74	33.84	33.93
18	34.03	34.12	34.21	34.31	34.40	34.50	34.59	34.68	34.77	34.87
19	34.96	35.05	35.14	35.23	35.32	35.42	35.51	35.60	35.69	35.78
20	35.87	35.96	36.05	36.13	36.22	36.31	36.40	36.49	36.58	36.66
21	36.75	36.84	36.93	37.01	37.10	37.19	37.28	37.36	37.45	37.53
22	37.62	37.70	37.79	37.88	37.96	38.04	38.12	38.21	38.29	38.38
23	38.46	38.54	38.63	38.71	38.80	38.88	38.96	39.04	39.13	39.21
24	39.29	39.37	39.45	39.53	39.62	39.70	39.78	39.86	39.94	40.02
25	40.10	40.18	40.26	40.34	40.42	40.50	40.58	40.66	40.74	40.81
26	40.89	40.97	41.05	41.13	41.21	41.29	41.36	41.44	41.52	41.60
27	41.67	41.75	41.83	41.90	41.98	42.06	42.13	42.21	42.29	42.36
28	42.44	42.51	42.59	42.66	42.74	42.82	42.89	42.97	43.04	43.11
29	43.19	43.26	43.34	43.41	43.49	43.56	43.63	43.71	43.79	43.86
30	43.93	44.00	44.07	44.15	44.22	44.29	44.36	44.44	44.51	44.58
31	44.65	44.72	44.79	44.87	44.94	45.01	45.08	45.15	45.23	45.30
32	45.37	45.44	45.51	45.58	45.65	45.72	45.79	45.86	45.93	46.00
33	46.07	46.14	46.21	46.28	46.35	46.42	46.49	46.56	46.63	46.69
34	46.76	46.83	46.90	46.97	47.04	47.11	47.18	47.24	47.31	47.38
35	47.45	47.52	47.58	47.65	47.72	47.78	47.85	47.92	47.99	48.05
36	48.12	48.19	48.25	48.32	48.39	48.45	48.52	48.59	48.65	48.72
37	48.78	48.85	48.92	48.98	49.05	49.11	49.18	49.24	49.31	49.37
38	49.44	49.50	49.57	49.63	49.70	49.76	49.83	49.89	49.96	50.02
39	50.08	50.15	50.21	50.28	50.34	50.40	50.47	50.53	50.60	50.66
40	50.72	50.79	50.85	50.91	50.98	51.04	51.10	51.16	51.22	51.29
41	51.35	51.41	51 47	51.54	51.60	51.67	51.73	51.79	51.85	51.91
42	51.97	52.04	52 10	52.16	52.22	52.28	52.35	52.41	52.47	52.53
43	52.59	52.65	52.71	52.77	52.83	52.90	52.96	53.02	53.08	53.14
44	53.20	53.26	53.32	53.38	53.44	53.50	53.56	53.62	53.68	53.74
45	53.80	53.86	53.92	53.98	54.04	54.10	54.16	54.22	54.28	54.34
46	54.39	54.45	54.51	54.57	54.63	54.69	54.75	54.81	54.87	54.92
47	54.98	55.04	55.10	55.16	55.22	55.27	55.33	55.39	55.45	55.51
48	55.56	55.62	55.68	55.74	55.80	55.85	55.91	55.97	56.03	56.08
49	56.14	56.20	56.25	56.31	56.37	56.43	56.49	56.55	56.60	56.65

Table 4-2. Theoretical Heads in Feet Corresponding to Velocities of 0 to 50 Ft per Sec. From the Formula

$$h_t = v^2/2g$$

Velocity in feet per second	.0	.1	.2	.3	.4	.5	.6	.7	.8	.9
0	0.000	0.000	0.001	0.001	0.002	0.004	0.006	0.008	0.010	0.013
1	.016	.019	.022	.026	.030	.035	.040	.045	.050	.056
2	.062	.069	.075	.082	.090	.097	.105	.113	.122	.131
3	.140	.149	.159	.169	.180	.190	.202	.213	.224	.236
4	.249	.261	.274	.288	.301	.315	.329	.343	.358	.373
5	.389	.404	.420	.437	.453	.470	.488	.505	.523	.541
6	.560	.579	.598	.617	.637	.657	.677	.698	.719	.740
7	.762	.784	.806	.828	.851	.874	.898	.922	.946	.970
8	.995	1.020	1.045	1.071	1.097	1.123	1.150	1.177	1.204	1.231
9	1.259	1.287	1.316	1.345	1.374	1.403	1.433	1.463	1.494	1.524
10	1.555	1.586	1.618	1.650	1.682	1.714	1.747	1.780	1.813	1.847
11	1.881	1.916	1.950	1.985	2.021	2.056	2.092	2.128	2.165	2.202
12	2.239	2.276	2.314	2.352	2.391	2.429	2.468	2.508	2.547	2.587
13	2.627	2.668	2.709	2.750	2.792	2.834	2.876	2.918	2.961	3.004
14	3.047	3.091	3.135	3.179	3.224	3.269	3.314	3.360	3.406	3.452
15	3.498	3.545	3.592	3.639	3.687	3.735	3.784	3.832	3.881	3.931
16	3.980	4.030	4.080	4.131	4.182	4.233	4.284	4.336	4.388	4.440
17	4.493	4.546	4.600	4.653	4.707	4.761	4.816	4.871	4.926	4.982
18	5.037	5.093	5.150	5.207	5.264	5.321	5.379	5.437	5.495	5.554
19	5.613	5.672	5.732	5.791	5.851	5.912	5.973	6.034	6.095	6.157
20	6.219	6.281	6.344	6.407	6.470	6.534	6.598	6.662	6.726	6.791
21	6.856	6.922	6.988	7.054	7.120	7.187	7.254	7.321	7.389	7.457
22	7.525	7.593	7.662	7.731	7.801	7.871	7.941	8.011	8.082	8.153
23	8.225	8.296	8.368	8.440	8.513	8.586	8.659	8.733	8.807	8.881
24	8.955	9.030	9.105	9.181	9.256	9.332	9.409	9.485	9.562	9.639
25	9.717	9.795	9.873	9.952	10.031	10.110	10.189	10.269	10.349	10.429
26	10.510	10.591	10.672	10.754	10.836	10.918	11.000	11.083	11.167	11.250
27	11.334	11.418	11.502	11.587	11.672	11.758	11.843	11.929	12.016	12.102
28	12.189	12.276	12.364	12.452	12.540	12.628	12.717	12.806	12.896	12.985
29	13.075	13.166	13.256	13.347	13.438	13.530	13.622	13.714	13.807	13.900
30	13.993	14.086	14.180	14.274	14.368	14.463	14.558	14.653	14.749	14.845
31	14.941	15.037	15.134	15.232	15.329	15.427	15.525	15.623	15.722	15.820
32	15.920	16.020	16.120	16.220	16.321	16.422	16.523	16.625	16.726	16.828
33	16.931	17.034	17.137	17.240	17.344	17.448	17.552	17.657	17.762	17.867
34	17.973	18.079	18.185	18.291	18.398	18.505	18.613	18.720	18.828	18.937
35	19.046	19.155	19.264	19.373	19.483	19.593	19.704	19.815	19.926	20.037
36	20.149	20.261	20.374	20.487	20.600	20.713	20.826	20.940	21.055	21.169
37	21.284	21.399	21.515	21.631	21.747	21.863	21.980	22.097	22.215	22.332
38	22.450	22.569	22.687	22.806	22.925	23.045	23.165	23.285	23.405	23.526
39	23.647	23.769	23.891	24.013	24.135	24.258	24.381	24.504	24.628	24.752
40	24.876	25.000	25.125	25.250	25.376	25.501	25.627	25.754	25.881	26.008
41	26.135	26.263	26.391	26.519	26.647	26.776	26.905	27.035	27.165	27.295
42	27.425	27.556	27.687	27.819	27.950	28.082	28.215	28.347	28.480	28.613
43	28.747	28.881	29.015	29.149	29.284	29.419	29.555	29.691	29.827	29.964
44	30.100	30.237	30.374	30.511	30.649	30.788	30.927	31.065	31.204	31.343
45	31.483	31.623	31.764	31.904	32.045	32.187	32.328	32.470	32.613	32.755
46	32.898	33.041	33.185	33.329	33.473	33.617	33.762	33.908	34.052	34.198
47	34.344	34.490	34.637	34.784	34.931	35.079	35.227	35.375	35.523	35.672
48	35.821	35.970	36.120	36.270	36.420	36.571	36.722	36.873	37.025	37.177
49	37.329	37.482	37.634	37.787	37.941	38.095	38.249	38.403	38.558	38.713

Table 4-3. Smith's Coefficients of Discharge for Circular and Square Orifices with Full Contraction

Diameter of circular orifices, feet							Head, feet	Side of square orifices, feet						
0.02	0.04	0.07	0.1	0.2	0.6	1.0		0.02	0.04	0.07	0.1	0.2	0.6	1.0
.....	0.637	0.624	0.618				0.4	.....	0.643	0.628	0.621			
0.655	0.630	0.618	0.613	0.601	0.593		0.6	0.660	0.636	0.623	0.617	0.605	0.598	
0.648	0.626	0.615	0.610	0.601	0.594	0.590	0.8	0.652	0.631	0.620	0.615	0.605	0.600	0.597
0.644	0.623	0.612	0.608	0.600	0.595	0.591	1	0.648	0.628	0.618	0.613	0.605	0.601	0.599
0.637	0.618	0.608	0.605	0.600	0.596	0.593	1.5	0.641	0.622	0.614	0.610	0.605	0.602	0.601
0.632	0.614	0.606	0.604	0.599	0.597	0.595	2	0.637	0.619	0.612	0.608	0.605	0.604	0.602
0.629	0.612	0.605	0.603	0.599	0.598	0.596	2.5	0.634	0.617	0.610	0.607	0.605	0.604	0.602
0.627	0.611	0.604	0.603	0.599	0.598	0.597	3	0.632	0.616	0.609	0.607	0.605	0.604	0.603
0.623	0.609	0.603	0.602	0.599	0.597	0.596	4	0.628	0.614	0.608	0.606	0.605	0.603	0.602
0.618	0.607	0.602	0.600	0.598	0.597	0.596	6	0.623	0.612	0.607	0.605	0.604	0.603	0.602
0.614	0.605	0.601	0.600	0.598	0.596	0.596	8	0.619	0.610	0.606	0.605	0.604	0.603	0.602
0.611	0.603	0.599	0.598	0.597	0.596	0.595	10	0.616	0.608	0.605	0.604	0.603	0.602	0.601
0.601	0.599	0.597	0.596	0.596	0.596	0.594	20	0.606	0.604	0.602	0.602	0.602	0.601	0.600
0.596	0.595	0.594	0.594	0.594	0.594	0.593	50	0.602	0.601	0.601	0.600	0.600	0.599	0.599
0.593	0.592	0.592	0.592	0.592	0.592	0.592	100	0.599	0.598	0.598	0.598	0.598	0.598	0.598

Table 4-4. Coefficients of Discharge for Rectangular Orifices 0.656 Ft Wide with Partially Suppressed Contraction

Description of contraction	Height, feet	Head, feet 1	Head, feet 3	Head, feet 5
Complete contraction	0.656	0.598	0.604	0.603
	0.328	0.616	0.615	0.611
	0.164	0.631	0.627	0.620
	0.098	0.632	0.628	0.623
	0.033	0.652	0.634	0.620
Suppressed at bottom only	0.656	0.620	0.624	0.625
	0.328	0.649	0.647	0.634
	0.164	0.671	0.668	0.666
	0.098	0.680	0.677	0.677
	0.033	0.710	0.705	0.696
Suppressed on both sides only	0.656	0.632	0.628	0.628
	0.328	0.637	0.630	0.630
	0.164	0.641	0.634	0.635
	0.098	0.653	0.643	0.639
	0.033	0.682	0.667	0.655

Description of contraction	Height, feet	Head, feet 1	Head, feet 3	Head, feet 5
Suppressed at bottom and partly on one side	0.656	0.633	0.636	0.637
	0.328	0.658	0.656	0.654
	0.164	0.676	0.673	0.672
	0.098	0.682	0.683	0.681
	0.033	0.708	0.705	0.695
Suppressed at bottom and partly on two sides	0.656	0.678	0.664	0.663
	0.328	0.680	0.675	0.672
	0.164	0.687	0.680	0.673
	0.098	0.693	0.688	0.683
	0.033	0.708	0.705	0.698
Suppressed at bottom and two sides	0.656	0.690	0.677	0.672
Complete suppression	0.656	....	0.950	

Table 4-5. Coefficients of Discharge of Various-shaped Orifices with Complete Contraction

Fanning's coefficients for vertical rectangular orifices 1 foot wide						Head, feet	Bovey's coefficients for various-shaped orifices, each 0.196 square inch in area							
Height of orifice, feet							Circle	Square		Rectangle, ratio of sides				Triangle
										4:1		10:1		
0.125	0.25	0.5	1	2	4			Sides vertical	Diagonal vertical	Long sides vertical	Long sides horizontal	Long sides vertical	Long sides horizontal	
0.622	0.616	0.611	0.605	.....	.....	1	0.620	0.627	0.628	0.642	0.643	0.663	0.664	0.636
0.619	0.614	0.609	0.604	0.609	.....	2	0.613	0.620	0.628	0.634	0.636	0.650	0.651	0.628
0.614	0.610	0.607	0.603	0.606	0.608	4	0.608	0.616	0.618	0.628	0.629	0.641	0.642	0.623
0.610	0.608	0.604	0.601	0.604	0.605	6	0.607	0.614	0.616	0.626	0.627	0.637	0.637	0.620
0.608	0.606	0.603	0.601	0.603	0.604	8	0.606	0.613	0.614	0.623	0.625	0.634	0.635	0.619
0.606	0.604	0.602	0.601	0.602	0.603	10	0.605	0.612	0.613	0.622	0.624	0.632	0.633	0.618
0.607	0.603	0.601	0.601	0.602	0.603	15	0.604	0.610	0.611	0.620	0.622	0.630	0.630	0.617
0.607	0.604	0.602	0.601	0.602	0.603	20	0.603	0.609	0.611	0.620	0.621	0.629	0.628	0.616
0.609	0.604	0.603	0.601	0.603	0.605	30								
0.614	0.607	0.605	0.602	0.606	0.609	50								

Table 4-6. Miscellaneous Coefficients of Discharge for Various Sharp-edged Submerged Orifices

The two orifices experimented on by Ellis were horizontal. All other orifices were vertical.

Dimensions of orifice in feet	Author-ity	Head in feet							
		0.3	0.5	1.0	2.0	4.0	6.0	10.0	18.0
Circle, d = .05......	H. Smith	....	.599	.597	.595	.595			
Circle, d = .10......	H. Smith	.600	.600	.600	.599	.598			
Square, .05 by .05..	H. Smith	....	.609	.607	.605	.604			
Square, .10 by .10..	H. Smith	.607	.605	.604	.603	.604			
Rectangle, l = 3.0, d = .05.	H. Smith	....	.621	....	....	.620	.620	.618	
Circle, d = 1.0......	Ellis	....	....	....	.608	.602	.603	.600	.601
Square, 1.0 by 1.0..	Ellis	....	....	....	.601	.601	.603	.605	.606
Square, 4.0 by 4.0..	Stewart	.614							

Table 4-7. Coefficients of Discharge for Submerged Vertical Square Orifice with Rounded Corners

From experiments by Ellis

Dimensions of orifice in feet	Head in feet								
	3	4	5	6	8	10	12	14	18
Square, 1.0 by 1.0.......	.952	.948	.946	.945	.944	.943	.943	.944	.944

Table 4-8. Coefficients of Discharge for Models *A*, *B*, *C*, *D*, *E*, and *F*, Figs. 4-9 and 4-10

Figure	Depth of opening in feet	Values of *C* for various depths of water above top of orifice										
		0.07	0.1	0.3	0.5	0.7	1.0	2.0	3.0	5.0	7.0	10.0
A	1.31	....	....	.597	.604	.610	.616	.618	.610	.608	.594	.592
	0.66	....	....	.632	.638	.640	.641	.640	.638	.637	.636	.634
	0.16	....	....	.691	.688	.684	.683	.678	.674	.672	.670	.668
	0.10	....	....	.711	.700	.695	.692	.688	.682	.677	.675	.672
B	1.31	....	....	.643	.650	.654	.656	.649	.636	.620	.615	.611
	0.66	....	....	.664	.670	.674	.675	.676	.674	.673	.671	.669
	0.16	....	....	.662	.681	.688	.693	.695	.694	.692	.691	.689
	0.10	....	....	.693	.700	.705	.708	.710	.705	.699	.695	.693
C	1.31	....	....	.648	.654	.658	.660	.652	.638	.622	.616	.612
	0.66	....	....	.667	.673	.676	.678	.679	.677	.674	.672	.670
	0.16	....	....	.664	.682	.690	.695	.697	.696	.693	.692	.690
	0.10	....	....	.695	.702	.707	.710	.712	.706	.699	.695	.693
D	0.656	.487	.495	.539	.562	.577	.588	.601	.601	.601	.601	.601
	0.164	.495	.550	.619	.630	.631	.630	.625	.624	.619	.612	.606
E	0.656	.487	.495	.530	.554	.573	.580	.595	.599	.602	.602	.601
	0.164	.495	.544	.600	.612	.618	.623	.627	.628	.627	.622	.617
F	0.656	.530	.535	.569	.584	.595	.600	.608	.610	.610	.609	.608
	0.164	.590	.600	.628	.640	.645	.649	.652	.651	.650	.650	.649

Table 4-9. Coefficients of Discharge C for Submerged Gates from Chatterton's and Benton's Formulas (4-22) and (4-23)

Head in feet	Authority	Width of opening in feet					
		2	4	6	8	10	12
.02	Chatterton....	.83	.83	.83	.83	.83	.83
	Benton........	.73	.75	.76	.78	.79	.81
.05	Chatterton....	.83	.83	.83	.83	.83	.83
	Benton........	.73	.75	.76	.78	.79	.81
.10	Chatterton....	.82	.82	.82	.82	.82	.82
	Benton........	.73	.75	.76	.78	.79	.81
15	Chatterton....	.82	.82	.82	.82	.82	.82
	Benton........	.73	.75	.76	.78	.79	.81
.2	Chatterton....	.81	.81	.81	.81	.81	.81
	Benton........	.73	.75	.76	.78	.79	.81
.3	Chatterton....	.80	.80	.80	.80	.80	.80
	Benton........	.73	.75	.76	.78	.79	.81
.4	Chatterton....	.78	.78	.78	.78	.78	.78
	Benton........	.73	.75	.76	.78	.79	.81
.5	Chatterton....	.77	.77	.77	.77	.77	.77
	Benton........	.73	.75	.76	.78	.79	.81
.75	Chatterton....	.75	.75	.75	.75	.75	.75
	Benton........	.73	.75	.76	.78	.79	.81
1.0	Chatterton....	.73	.73	.73	.73	.73	.73
	Benton........	.73	.75	.76	.78	.79	.81
1.5	Chatterton....	.69	.69	.69	.69	.69	.69
	Benton........	.73	.75	.76	.78	.79	.81
2.0	Chatterton....	.67	.67	.67	.67	.67	.67
	Benton........	.73	.75	.76	.78	.79	.81
2.5	Chatterton....	.65	.65	.65	.65	.65	.65
	Benton........	.73	.75	.76	.78	.79	.81
3.0	Chatterton....	.64	.64	.64	.64	.64	.64
	Benton........	.73	.75	.76	.78	.79	.81
3.5	Chatterton....	.64	.64	.64	.64	.64	.64
	Benton........	.73	.75	.76	.78	.79	.81
4.0	Chatterton....	.63	.63	.63	.63	.63	.63
	Benton........	.73	.75	.76	.78	.79	.81
4.5	Chatterton....	.63	.63	.63	.63	.63	.63
	Benton........	.73	.75	.76	.78	.79	.81
5.0	Chatterton....	.62	.62	.62	.62	.62	.62
	Benton........	.73	.75	.76	.78	.79	.81

Table 4-10. Coefficients of Discharge C for Submerged Tubes

Compiled from experiments by Stewart, and Rogers and Smith. L = length of tube; p = perimeter of cross section of tubes.

$\dfrac{L}{p}$	Condition of edges at entrance				
	All corners square	Contractions suppressed on bottom only	Contractions suppressed on bottom and one side	Contractions suppressed on bottom and two sides	Contractions suppressed on bottom, two sides and top
.02	.61	.63	.68	.77	.95
.04	.62	.64	.68	.77	.94
.06	.63	.65	.69	.76	.94
.08	.65	.66	.69	.74	.93
.10	.66	.67	.69	.73	.93
.12	.67	.68	.70	.72	.93
.14	.69	.69	.71	.72	.92
.16	.71	.70	.72	.72	.92
.18	.72	.71	.73	.72	.92
.20	.74	.73	.74	.73	.92
.22	.75	.74	.75	.75	.91
.24	.77	.75	.76	.78	.91
.26	.78	.76	.77	.81	.91
.28	.78	.76	.78	.82	.91
.30	.79	.77	.79	.83	.91
.35	.79	.78	.80	.84	.90
.40	.80	.79	.80	.84	.90
.60	.80	.80	.81	.84	.90
.80	.80	.80	.81	.85	.90
1.00	.80	.81	.82	.85	.90

Table 4-11. Coefficients of Discharge C for Culverts

d / L	0.5	1.0	1.5	2.0	2.5	3.0	3.5	4.0	5.0	6.0	7.0	8.0
Concrete pipe, beveled-lip entrance From formula (4-32)												
10	.77	.86	.89	.91	.92	.92	.93	.93	.94	.94	.94	.94
20	.66	.79	.84	.87	.89	.90	.91	.91	.92	.93	.93	.94
30	.59	.73	.80	.83	.86	.87	.89	.89	.90	.91	.92	.93
40	.54	.68	.76	.80	.83	.85	.87	.88	.89	.90	.91	.92
50	.49	.65	.73	.77	.81	.83	.85	.86	.88	.89	.90	.91
60	.46	.61	.70	.75	.79	.81	.83	.85	.87	.88	.89	.90
70	.44	.59	.67	.73	.77	.79	.81	.83	.85	.87	.88	.89
80	.41	.56	.65	.71	.75	.78	.80	.82	.84	.86	.88	.89
90	.39	.54	.63	.69	.73	.76	.78	.80	.83	.85	.87	.88
100	.38	.52	.61	.67	.71	.74	.77	.79	.82	.84	.86	.87
110	.36	.50	.59	.65	.70	.73	.76	.78	.81	.83	.85	.87
120	.35	.49	.58	.64	.68	.71	.74	.77	.80	.82	.84	.86
130	.34	.47	.56	.62	.67	.70	.73	.76	.79	.82	.84	.85
140	.33	.46	.55	.61	.66	.69	.72	.75	.78	.81	.83	.85
150	.32	.45	.53	.60	.65	.68	.71	.74	.77	.80	.82	.84
160	.31	.44	.52	.59	.63	.67	.70	.73	.77	.79	.81	.83
170	.30	.43	.51	.58	.62	.66	.69	.72	.76	.79	.81	.83
180	.29	.42	.50	.57	.61	.65	.68	.71	.75	.78	.80	.82
190	.28	.41	.49	.56	.60	.64	.67	.70	.74	.77	.80	.81
200	.28	.40	.48	.55	.59	.63	.67	.69	.73	.77	.79	.81
Concrete pipe, square-cornered entrance From formula (4-33)												
10	.74	.80	.81	.80	.80	.79	.78	.77	.76	.75	.74	.73
20	.64	.74	.77	.78	.78	.77	.77	.76	.75	.74	.73	.72
30	.58	.69	.73	.75	.76	.76	.76	.75	.74	.74	.73	.72
40	.53	.65	.70	.73	.74	.74	.74	.74	.74	.73	.72	.71
50	.49	.62	.68	.71	.72	.73	.73	.73	.73	.73	.72	.71
60	.46	.59	.65	.69	.71	.72	.72	.72	.72	.72	.71	.71
70	.43	.57	.63	.67	.69	.70	.71	.71	.71	.71	.71	.70
80	.41	.54	.61	.65	.67	.69	.70	.70	.71	.71	.70	.70
90	.39	.52	.60	.64	.66	.68	.69	.70	.70	.70	.70	.70
100	.37	.51	.58	.62	.65	.67	.68	.69	.70	.70	.69	.69
110	.36	.49	.56	.61	.64	.66	.67	.68	.69	.69	.69	.69
120	.35	.48	.55	.60	.63	.65	.66	.67	.68	.69	.69	.69
130	.33	.46	.54	.59	.62	.64	.65	.66	.68	.68	.68	.68
140	.32	.45	.53	.58	.61	.63	.65	.66	.67	.68	.68	.68
150	.31	.44	.51	.56	.60	.62	.64	.65	.67	.67	.67	.67
160	.30	.43	.50	.56	.59	.61	.63	.64	.66	.67	.67	.67
170	.30	.42	.49	.55	.58	.61	.62	.64	.65	.66	.67	.67
180	.29	.41	.48	.54	.57	.60	.62	.63	.65	.66	.66	.66
190	.28	.40	.48	.53	.56	.59	.61	.63	.64	.65	.66	.66
200	.28	.39	.47	.52	.56	.58	.60	.62	.64	.65	.66	.66

Table 4-11. Coefficients of Discharge C for Culverts (*Continued*)

L \ d	0.5	1.0	1.5	2.0	2.5	3.0	3.5	4.0	5.0	6.0	7.0	8.0
Vitrified-clay pipe, bell end upstream From formula (4-34)												
10	.83	.90	.91	.91	.90	.89	.87	.85	.80	.75	.71	.66
20	.73	.83	.86	.87	.87	.86	.85	.83	.79	.75	.70	.66
30	.66	.77	.82	.84	.84	.84	.83	.82	.78	.74	.70	.66
40	.60	.72	.78	.81	.82	.82	.81	.80	.77	.73	.69	.65
50	.56	.69	.75	.78	.80	.80	.80	.79	.76	.72	.69	.65
60	.52	.65	.72	.76	.78	.78	.78	.78	.75	.72	.68	.64
70	.49	.62	.69	.73	.76	.77	.77	.76	.74	.71	.68	.64
80	.47	.60	.67	.71	.74	.75	.75	.75	.73	.70	.67	.64
90	.45	.58	.65	.69	.72	.73	.74	.74	.72	.70	.67	.63
100	.43	.56	.63	.68	.70	.72	.73	.73	.72	.69	.66	.63
110	.41	.54	.61	.66	.69	.71	.72	.72	.71	.69	.66	.63
120	.40	.52	.60	.64	.68	.69	.70	.71	.70	.68	.65	.62
130	.39	.51	.58	.63	.66	.68	.69	.70	.69	.67	.65	.62
140	.37	.49	.57	.62	.65	.67	.68	.69	.69	.67	.64	.62
150	.36	.48	.55	.60	.64	.66	.67	.68	.68	.66	.64	.61
160	.35	.47	.54	.59	.63	.65	.66	.67	.67	.66	.64	.61
170	.34	.46	.53	.58	.62	.64	.66	.66	.67	.65	.63	.61
180	.33	.45	.52	.57	.61	.63	.65	.66	.66	.65	.63	.60
190	.33	.44	.51	.56	.60	.62	.64	.65	.65	.64	.62	.60
200	.32	.43	.50	.55	.59	.61	.63	.64	.65	.64	.62	.60
Corrugated-metal pipe From formula (4-35)												
10	.53	.67	.74	.77	.78	.79	.80	.80	.80	.79	.79	.78
20	.41	.55	.63	.68	.71	.73	.74	.75	.76	.76	.76	.76
30	.34	.48	.56	.62	.65	.68	.70	.71	.73	.74	.74	.74
40	.30	.43	.51	.57	.61	.64	.66	.68	.70	.71	.72	.72
50	.27	.39	.47	.53	.57	.61	.63	.65	.68	.69	.70	.71
60	.25	.36	.44	.50	.54	.58	.60	.62	.66	.67	.69	.69
70	.23	.34	.42	.47	.52	.55	.58	.60	.63	.65	.67	.68
80	.22	.32	.40	.45	.49	.53	.56	.58	.61	.64	.65	.67
90	.21	.31	.38	.43	.47	.51	.54	.56	.60	.62	.64	.65
100	.20	.29	.36	.41	.46	.49	.52	.54	.58	.61	.63	.64
110	.19	.28	.35	.40	.44	.48	.50	.53	.57	.59	.62	.63
120	.18	.27	.33	.38	.43	.46	.49	.51	.55	.58	.60	.62
130	.17	.26	.32	.37	.41	.45	.48	.50	.54	.57	.59	.61
140	.17	.25	.31	.36	.40	.44	.46	.49	.53	.56	.58	.60
150	.16	.24	.30	.35	.39	.42	.45	.48	.52	.55	.57	.59
160	.16	.23	.29	.34	.38	.41	.44	.47	.51	.54	.56	.58
170	.15	.23	.29	.33	.37	.40	.43	.46	.50	.53	.55	.57
180	.15	.22	.28	.32	.36	.39	.42	.45	.49	.52	.55	.57
190	.15	.22	.27	.32	.35	.39	.41	.44	.48	.51	.54	.56
200	.14	.21	.27	.31	.35	.38	.41	.43	.47	.50	.53	.55

Table 4-11. Coefficients of Discharge C for Culverts (*Concluded*)

$\frac{r}{L}$	0.2	0.3	0.4	0.5	0.6	0.8	1.0	1.2	1.4	1.6	1.8	2.0
Concrete-box culverts, rounded-lip entrance From formula (4-36)												
10	.85	.89	.92	.93	.94	.95	.96	.96	.96	.96	.97	.97
20	.76	.83	.87	.89	.91	.92	.94	.94	.95	.95	.96	.96
30	.70	.78	.82	.85	.88	.90	.92	.93	.94	.94	.95	.95
40	.65	.73	.79	.82	.85	.88	.90	.92	.93	.93	.94	.94
50	.60	.70	.75	.79	.82	.86	.89	.90	.91	.92	.93	.93
60	.57	.66	.73	.77	.80	.84	.87	.89	.90	.91	.92	.93
70	.54	.64	.70	.75	.78	.83	.86	.88	.89	.90	.91	.92
80	.52	.61	.68	.72	.76	.81	.84	.86	.88	.89	.90	.91
90	.50	.59	.66	.70	.74	.79	.83	.85	.87	.89	.90	.91
100	.48	.57	.64	.69	.73	.78	.82	.84	.86	.88	.89	.90
110	.46	.55	.62	.67	.71	.77	.80	.83	.85	.87	.88	.89
120	.44	.54	.60	.65	.69	.75	.79	.82	.84	.86	.87	.88
130	.43	.52	.59	.64	.68	.74	.78	.81	.84	.85	.87	.88
140	.42	.51	.57	.63	.67	.73	.77	.80	.83	.85	.86	.87
150	.40	.49	.56	.61	.66	.72	.76	.79	.82	.84	.85	.87
160	.39	.48	.55	.60	.64	.71	.75	.78	.81	.83	.85	.86
170	.38	.47	.54	.59	.63	.70	.74	.78	.80	.82	.84	.85
180	.38	.46	.53	.58	.62	.69	.73	.77	.80	.82	.83	.85
190	.37	.45	.52	.57	.61	.68	.72	.76	.79	.81	.83	.84
200	.36	.44	.51	.56	.60	.67	.72	.75	.78	.80	.82	.84
Concrete-box culverts, square-cornered entrance From formula (4-37)												
10	.79	.82	.83	.84	.84	.84	.83	.83	.82	.82	.82	.81
20	.72	.77	.79	.81	.81	.82	.82	.82	.81	.81	.81	.81
30	.67	.73	.76	.78	.79	.80	.81	.81	.81	.81	.81	.80
40	.62	.69	.73	.76	.77	.79	.80	.80	.80	.80	.80	.80
50	.58	.66	.71	.73	.75	.77	.78	.79	.79	.79	.79	.79
60	.55	.63	.68	.71	.73	.76	.77	.78	.79	.79	.79	.79
70	.53	.61	.66	.69	.72	.75	.76	.77	.78	.78	.78	.78
80	.50	.59	.64	.68	.70	.74	.75	.76	.77	.78	.78	.78
90	.48	.57	.62	.66	.69	.72	.74	.76	.77	.77	.77	.78
100	.47	.55	.61	.65	.67	.71	.74	.75	.76	.76	.77	.77
110	.45	.53	.59	.63	.66	.70	.73	.74	.75	.76	.76	.77
120	.43	.52	.58	.62	.65	.69	.72	.73	.75	.75	.76	.76
130	.42	.51	.56	.61	.64	.68	.71	.73	.74	.75	.75	.76
140	.41	.49	.55	.60	.63	.67	.70	.72	.73	.74	.75	.75
150	.40	.48	.54	.58	.62	.66	.69	.71	.73	.74	.75	.75
160	.39	.47	.53	.57	.61	.65	.69	.71	.72	.73	.74	.75
170	.38	.46	.52	.56	.60	.64	.68	.70	.72	.73	.74	.74
180	.37	.45	.51	.55	.59	.63	.67	.70	.71	.72	.73	.74
190	.36	.44	.50	.55	.58	.62	.67	.69	.71	.72	.73	.73
200	.35	.43	.49	.54	.57	.61	.66	.68	.70	.71	.72	.73

SECTION 5

WEIRS

A weir is a notch of regular form through which water flows. The term is also applied to the structure containing such a notch. Thus a weir may be a depression in the side of a tank, reservoir, or channel, or it may be an overflow dam or other similar structure. Classified in accordance with the shape of the notch, there are rectangular weirs; triangular, or V-notch, weirs; trapezoidal weirs; and parabolic weirs.

The edge or surface over which the water flows is called the crest of the weir. The overflowing sheet of water is termed the nappe. The depth of water producing the discharge, H in Fig. 5-1, is the head. A weir with a sharp upstream corner, or edge, so formed that the water springs clear of the crest, is called a sharp-crested weir. Sharp-crested weirs are usually made by machining a 90° angle on the inner edge of the crest. All other weirs, for want of a better term, are classed as weirs not sharp-crested, or rounded-crested weirs. A broad-crested weir may be defined as one having a horizontal or nearly horizontal crest sufficiently long in the direction of flow so that the nappe will be supported and hydrostatic pressures will be fully developed for at least a short distance. The channel of approach is the channel leading up to the weir, and the mean velocity in this channel is the velocity of approach. If the nappe discharges into the air (Fig. 5-1), the weir has free discharge. If the discharge is partially under water (Fig. 5-5), the weir is said to be submerged, or drowned.

Sharp-crested weirs are useful only as a means of measuring flowing water. Weirs not sharp-crested are commonly incorporated in hydraulic structures, and though sometimes employed to measure water, this is usually a secondary function.

Fundamental Principles

The equation for discharge over a weir cannot be derived exactly because, not only does the flow pattern of one weir differ from that of another, but the flow pattern for a given weir varies with the discharge. Furthermore, the number of variables involved is so great as to defy a rigorous analytical approach. Approximate derivations are presented in most texts.[1] These derivations show effects of gravitational forces in an approximate manner, but do not include the effects of viscosity, surface tension, the ratios of the dimensions of the weir to the dimensions of the approach channel, the nature of the weir crest, the velocity distribution in the channel of

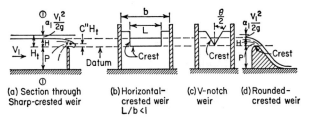

(a) Section through Sharp-crested weir

(b) Horizontal-crested weir L/b < 1

(c) V-notch weir

(d) Rounded-crested weir

FIG. 5-1. Weirs, definition sketch.

approach, and the roughness of the inside surface of the weir and approach channel. A simplified derivation will be made here to show the general nature of the relationship between the discharge and the most important variables and to demonstrate the nature of the effect of some of the variables. The derivation will be made for sharp-crested weirs, but, as will be shown later, a similar derivation would apply to weirs which are not sharp-crested.

The Bernoulli equation,[2] written from any point in section 1 of Fig. 5-1 to v, which is the center of gravity of the vena contracta of the nappe located $C'H$. above the lowest point on the crest, is

$$H + \alpha_1 \frac{V_1^2}{2g} = H_t = C'H_t + \alpha_v \frac{V_v^2}{2g} + h_l \qquad (5\text{-}1)$$

It may be seen from Fig. 5-1 and Eq. (5-1) that H_t is the total energy head above the datum on the upstream side of the weir. It includes both the potential energy H and the kinetic-energy, or velocity-of-approach, term $\alpha_1(V_1^2/2g)$. Solving Eq. (5-1)

[1] See, for example, V. L. Streeter, "Fluid Mechanics," pp. 413–417, McGraw-Hill Book Company, Inc., New York, 1962.

[2] See Energy and the Bernoulli Equation, Sec. 3.

for V_v,

$$V_v = \sqrt{2g} \sqrt{\frac{1}{\alpha_v} [H_t(1 - C') - h_l]} \qquad (5\text{-}2)$$

Introducing an arbitrary coefficient C'' to serve the combined functions of h_l, C', and α_v permits the rearrangement of Eq. (5-2) into the following simpler form:

$$V_v = C'' \sqrt{2gH_t} \qquad (5\text{-}3)$$

The discharge may be expressed as follows:

$$Q = a_v V_v \qquad (5\text{-}4)$$

The area at the vena contracta a_v may be expressed in terms of the weir opening and a coefficient of contraction as follows:

$$A_v = C_c A \qquad (5\text{-}5)$$

where A is the area of the weir opening bounded at the top by the plane of the water surface in the approach channel. Then

$$Q = C_c A C'' \sqrt{2gH_t} \qquad (5\text{-}6)$$

and letting

$$C_1 = C_c C'' \sqrt{2g} \qquad (5\text{-}7)$$

$$Q = C_1 A \sqrt{H_t} \qquad (5\text{-}8)$$

If the weir has a *horizontal crest* of length L, as shown in Fig. 5-1b,

$$A = HL$$

and Eq. (5-8) becomes

$$Q = C_1 L H H_t^{1/2} \qquad (5\text{-}9)$$

If now the coefficient is made to include the effect of velocity of approach, H_t can be replaced by H and

$$Q = CLH^{3/2} \qquad (5\text{-}10)$$

This is the general form of equation used for horizontal-crested weirs.

If the weir is a *V-notch weir*, reference to Fig. 5-1c will show that

$$A = H^2 \tan \frac{\theta}{2} \qquad (5\text{-}11)$$

and

$$Q = C_1 \tan \frac{\theta}{2} H^2 H_t^{1/2} \tag{5-12}$$

and again including velocity of approach in the coefficient,

$$Q = C_1 \tan \frac{\theta}{2} H^{5/2} \tag{5-13}$$

and letting

$$C = C_1 \tan \frac{\theta}{2} \tag{5-14}$$

the expression for discharge becomes

$$Q = CH^{5/2} \tag{5-15}$$

This is the general form of equation for V-notched weirs.

The same approximate derivation would apply to rounded-crested weirs as illustrated in Fig. 5-1d, the only difference being that the section corresponding to the vena contracta would occur at or near the crest and any contraction of the nappe would occur only at the top of the nappe.

As previously stated, the coefficient C must include the effect of all other variables except those included in Eqs. (5-10) and (5-15).

The most convenient method of including these variables can be established by dimensional analysis. In general, it can be shown that

$$C = f\left(R, W, \frac{x_1}{y_1}, \frac{x_2}{y_2}, \ldots, \frac{x_n}{y_n}\right) \tag{5-16}$$

where R is the Reynolds number, W is the Weber number (p. 3-32), and the x/y ratios indicate significant length ratio such as, for example, the head divided by the height of the weir, H/P, a roughness length divided by the head, or the side slope of a V notch. The particular parameters, indicated generally by Eq. (5-16), which are of importance for each type of weir will be discussed in detail in the appropriate subsections which follow.

Sharp-crested Weirs

All the tests on weirs of this type were made with the nappe fully aerated. When the crest length L of a horizontal weir (Fig. 5-1) is shorter than the width of the channel b and for V-notch weirs, aeration is automatic. However, for horizontal weirs extending over the full width of the channel, $L/b = 1$, air at atmospheric pressure must be provided by vents. Otherwise the air beneath the nappe will be exhausted, causing a reduction of pressure beneath the nappe, with a corresponding increase in discharge for a given head.

Horizontal Sharp-crested Weirs with $L/b = 1$. Such weirs are also described as *weirs with suppressed end contraction* because the length of the nappe at the vena contracta is the same as the length of the weir. This does not mean, however, that the discharge is the same over each unit of length of the weir, because of the reduced velocity in the boundary layer which causes a slight reduction in discharge near the walls of the channel.

A consideration of terms on the right side of Eq. (5-16) for horizontal weirs will show that a convenient method of including the variation in the velocity of approach, as well as the contraction of the jet, is to relate C to H/P. When H/P is small, the area of the approach channel is relatively large compared with the area of the nappe at the vena contracta, and the kinetic-energy term is of relatively little importance; whereas, as H/P becomes larger, the velocity in the approach channel becomes larger in relation to the velocity in the nappe.

The contraction of the nappe from the top is caused by the conversion of potential energy to kinetic energy and by gravitation. However, at the bottom of the nappe the contraction is caused primarily by the vertical component of the velocity along the inner face of the weir. When H/P is small, the contraction is relatively large, but for large values of H/P, the influence of the vertical components is smaller and there is less contraction. Thus, in regard to the velocity of approach and the contraction of the nappe, there will be a larger discharge for a given H when H/P is large, and this increase in discharge is reflected in the variation of C with H/P. Even some of the very earliest weir equations included H/P in the expression for C.

The effect of viscosity is represented in Eq. (5-16) by the Reynolds number R. This factor is related to the energy loss as well as to the velocity variation near the boundaries. The length term in the Reynolds number may be taken as either the head or the length, so that alternative forms of R are

$$R = \frac{VH}{\gamma} \qquad (5\text{-}17)$$

or

$$R = \frac{VL}{\gamma} \tag{5-18}$$

If it is noted from Eq. (5-3) that $V \propto H^{1/2}$, it may be seen that, for constant values of kinematic viscosity,

$$R \propto H^{3/2} \quad \text{or} \quad H^{1/2}L \tag{5-19}$$

Thus it is demonstrated that R itself need not appear in the equation for C to reflect the effect of viscosity, but that a term containing H or L or both can accomplish this purpose. This explains to a large extent the fact that even some of the earliest equations for C in a horizontal sharp-crested weir without end contractions contained a term involving H. For this type of weir the effect of L is apparently very small.

The surface tension affects weir discharge, particularly at low heads, because of differences both in the manner in which the nappe adheres to the weir blade and in the form of the nappe. The effect of surface tension is represented in Eq. (5-16) by the presence of the Weber number (p. 3-32), which can be written for horizontal weirs with either the head or the width as the length parameter as follows:

$$W = \frac{V\sqrt{H}}{\sqrt{a/\rho}} \tag{5-20}$$

or

$$W = \frac{V\sqrt{L}}{\sqrt{a/\rho}} \tag{5-21}$$

However, again as in the case of the Reynolds number, $V \propto H^{1/2}$, so that the effect of surface tension can be related to H [Eq. (5-20)] or to H and L [Eq. (5-21)], this being an additional reason for having H or L or both in the expressions for C.

Some values of the weir coefficients C for horizontal sharp-crested weirs with $L/b = 1$ will be presented. It would be impractical to attempt to present all the data available in the literature. Only representative data will be given to illustrate the range of values of C.

Experiments on Sharp-crested Rectangular Weirs. Early experiments in France are described by Horton.[1] In all the

[1] Robert E. Horton, Weir Experiments, Coefficients, and Formulas, *U.S. Geol. Survey Water Supply and Irrigation Paper* 200, 1907. This paper

earlier experiments on weirs only small quantities of water were available. In most cases results are given in the form of C in Eq. (5-10).

The Francis[1] experiments were performed at Lowell, Mass., in 1852. Francis had facilities for using larger quantities of water than had been available for the earlier experiments. The range of experiments was heads 0.6 to 1.6 ft; lengths of weirs 8 and 10 ft; heights of weirs 2 and 5 ft; velocities of approach 0.2 to 1.0 ft per sec.

From the Francis formula,

$$C = 3.33 \left[\left(1 + \frac{h}{H} \right)^{3/2} - \left(\frac{h}{H} \right)^{3/2} \right] \qquad (5\text{-}22)$$

h being $V^2/2g$. For velocities of approach less than 5.0 the following expression is practically equivalent to (5-22):

$$C = 3.33 \left(1 + 0.259 \frac{H^2}{d^2} \right) \qquad (5\text{-}23)$$

in which $d = P + H$.

Fteley and Stearns,[2] in 1877 and 1879, near Boston, experimented with two sharp-crested suppressed weirs, respectively 5 and 19 ft long, 3.17 and 6.55 ft high, maximum heads 0.8 and 1.6 ft. They also experimented on a weir with end contractions. The greatest velocity of approach was 1.0 ft per sec.

From the Fteley and Stearns formula,

$$C = 3.33 \left(1 + 1.5 \frac{h}{H} \right)^{3/2} + \frac{0.007}{H^{3/2}} \qquad (5\text{-}24)$$

For velocities of approach less than 2.0 the following expression gives results agreeing closely with (5-24):

$$C = 3.31 \left(1 + 0.383 \frac{H^2}{d^2} + \frac{0.007}{H^{3/2}} \right) \qquad (5\text{-}25)$$

---

gives a very complete description of most of the weir experiments performed prior to 1907, including the experiments of Francis, Fteley and Stearns, and Bazin.

[1] J. B. Francis, "Lowell Hydraulic Experiments," 4th ed., 1883. Also *Trans. ASCE*, vol. 13, p. 303, 1884.

[2] A. Fteley and F. P. Stearns, Flow of Water over Weirs, *Trans. ASCE*, vol. 12, 1883.

The Bazin[1] experiments on suppressed weirs were performed near Dijon, France, in 1886. There were in all 381 experiments. Heads varied from 0.3 to 1.7 ft, heights of weir ranged from 0.79 to 3.72 ft, and lengths of weir were 1.64, 3.28, and 6.56 ft.

From the Bazin formula,

$$C = \left(3.248 + \frac{0.079}{H}\right)\left(1 + 0.55\frac{H^2}{d^2}\right) \qquad (5\text{-}26)$$

The Frese[2] experiments were performed at Hanover, Germany, prior to 1890. Comparatively large volumes of water were used in testing weirs under a wide range of conditions.

From the Frese formula,

$$C = \left(3.288 + \frac{0.0368}{H}\right)\left(1 + 0.55\frac{H^2}{d^2}\right) \qquad (5\text{-}27)$$

Tests conducted at the University of Michigan by King[3] resulted in the following expression for C:

$$C = \frac{3.34}{H^{0.03}}\left(1 + 0.56\frac{H^2}{d^2}\right) \qquad (5\text{-}28)$$

The Rehbock[4] experiments were performed at the Karlsruhe Hydraulic Laboratory, Germany. The quantities of water used were not large, but conditions were favorable for unusual accuracy and for conducting experiments under a wide range of conditions. Rehbock also presented the results of extensive experiments by the Swiss Society of Engineers and Architects.

From the Rehbock formula,

$$C = 3.235 + \frac{1}{60H - 0.56} + 0.428\frac{H}{P} \qquad (5\text{-}29)$$

From the Swiss Society formula,

$$C = \left(3.288 + \frac{1}{92.8H + 0.49}\right)\left(1 + 0.5\frac{H^2}{d^2}\right) \qquad (5\text{-}30)$$

[1] H. Bazin, *Ann. Ponts et Chaussées*, October, 1888. Translation by Marichal and Trautwine, *Proc. Eng. Club*, Philadelphia, January, 1890. Also *Ann. Ponts et Chaussées*, 1894, first quarter.

[2] F. Frese, Versuche über den Abfluss des Wassers bei vollkommenen Ueberfällen, *Z. Ver. deut. Ing.*, 1890.

[3] H. W. King, "Handbook of Hydraulics," McGraw-Hill Book Company, Inc., New York, 1918.

[4] T. Rehbock, Discussion of Schoder and Turner, Precise Weir Measurements, *Trans. ASCE*, vol. 93, 1929. Also "Handbuch der Ingenieruwissenschaften," pt. 3, vol. 2, sec. 1, p. 58, Leipzig, 1912.

Rehbock also presented a revised formula which gives values of C that differ but little from his 1912 formula. The revised formula[1] is of interest because, to the author's knowledge, this represents the first time that the influence of H in the value of C was expressed as a corrective addition to H in the framework of the main body of the basic equation.[2] His expression for discharge is

$$Q = C_e L H_e^{3/2} \tag{5-31}$$

where

$$H_e = H + 0.004 \tag{5-32}$$

and

$$C_e = 3.22 + 0.44 \frac{H}{P} \tag{5-33}$$

The experiments of Schoder and Turner[3] were performed at Cornell University between 1904 and 1920. With the published results of these experiments were included 1,162 experiments by others. In all, 2,438 separate volumetric measurements for 152 different heads were made. Heights of weirs ranged from 0.5 to 7.5 ft, heads from 0.012 to 2.75 ft, and lengths from 0.9 to 4.2 ft. Schoder and Turner did not present their results in the form of Eq. (5-10). Therefore no equation for C, such as Eqs. (5-22) to (5-30), is available for their tests. However, an equation representing their test results is presented on page 5-10.

Tests on weirs of this type were also conducted by Kindsvater and Carter.[4] Their tests cover a range of values of H/P from approximately 0.1 to 2.5, a range of heads from 0.10 to 0.72 ft, and weir heights from 0.30 to 1.44 ft. They also varied the weir length and channel width from 0.10 to 2.68 ft. In presenting their data they adopted the method used by Rehbock [Eq. (5-31)] of including the effect of H in the main body of the equation. Kindsvater and Carter also introduced a method of including the effect of the weir length L in the main body of the equation. Their method is shown in the following three equa-

---

[1] Rehbock, *op. cit.*, p. 1149.

[2] The use of this method of presenting weir data has been adopted and refined by Kindsvater and Carter, as is shown below.

[3] E. W. Schoder and K. B. Turner, Precise Weir Measurements, *Trans. ASCE*, vol. 93, 1929.

[4] Carl E. Kindsvater and Rolland W. Carter, Discharge Characteristics of Rectangular Thin-plate Weirs, *Trans. ASCE*, vol. 124, pp. 772–822, 1959.

tions, in which the notation has been changed to correspond to
that used in this book:

$$Q = C_e L_e H_e^{3/2} \tag{5-34}$$

$$L_e = L + k_L \tag{5-35}$$

$$H_e = H + k_H \tag{5-36}$$

In the above equations k_L and k_H are factors representing the
effects of viscosity and surface tension (p. 3-32), and the
subscript e indicates "effective" values; i.e., H_e is the effective
head.   By treating the variables in this manner they were able
to obtain a single linear relationship between C_e and H/P for
all values of H.   The values of k_L and k_H were obtained by
trying successive values of k_L and k_H until the values of C_e
were obtained which were the most independent of H and L.
They did this, not only for their own data, but for several
other groups of experiments.

Their equations for C_e, with corresponding values of k_H and
k_L, are given below.

Kindsvater and Carter[1] tests:

$$C_e = 3.22 + 0.40 \frac{H}{P} \tag{5-37}$$

$$k_H = 0.003 \text{ ft} \qquad k_L = -0.003 \text{ ft}$$

Bazin tests:

$$C_e = 3.25 + 0.445 \frac{H}{P} \tag{5-38}$$

$$k_H = 0.012 \qquad k_L = 0$$

Schoder and Turner[2] tests:

$$C_e = 3.21 + 0.45 \frac{H}{P} \tag{5-39}$$

$$k_H = 0.004 \qquad k_L = 0$$

USBR tests:[3]

$$C_e = 3.22 + 0.44 \frac{H}{P} \tag{5-40}$$

$$k_H = 0.003 \qquad k_L = 0$$

[1] *Op. cit.*   See also discussion on page 5-9.   Test series 1 to 10 were used.
[2] *Op. cit.*   See also discussion on page 5-9.   Test series E and F were
used in deriving these equations.
[3] These tests were conducted by the U.S. Bureau of Reclamation with a
weir having a knife-edge rather than a square-cornered edge.   Data were
obtained by Kindsvater and Carter from a report of the Bureau.

For practical purposes as well as for comparison of results it is of interest to develop the relation between C in Eq. (5-10) and C_e in Eq. (5-34).

$$Q = CLH^{3/2} = C_e L_e H_e^{3/2}$$

Inserting values of L_e and H_e from Eqs. (5-35) and (5-36),

$$CLH^{3/2} = C_e(L + k_L)(H + k_H)^{3/2} \qquad (5\text{-}41)$$

Then

$$C = C_e \left(1 + \frac{k_L}{L}\right) \left(1 + \frac{k_H}{H}\right)^{3/2} \qquad (5\text{-}42)$$

By using this equation values of C were computed by the author from the Kindsvater and Carter tests and the USBR

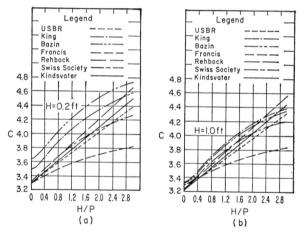

FIG. 5-2. Coefficients, horizontal sharp-crested weirs.

tests for comparison with those given by Eqs. (5-22) to (5-33). The comparisons are shown graphically in Fig. 5-2a for $H = 0.2$ ft and in Fig. 5-2b for $H = 1.0$ ft. To prevent confusion, the results of the tests of Fteley and Stearns, Frese, and Schoder and Turner are not shown. The Fteley and Stearns test results are similar to those of the Swiss Society; the Frese values of C are similar to those given by the King and Bazin equations; and as can be seen by a comparison of Eqs. (5-33) and (5-39), the Schoder and Turner tests are nearly identical with the Rehbock values. In studying the variations in test results shown by these figures, it should be realized that each of the curves represents the best fit through points which may scatter over a range of from 1.5 to 2.5 per cent on either side of the curves.

It may be seen from Fig. 5-2a and b that the Francis tests give smaller values of C than the others for all values of H. For $H = 0.2$ (Fig. 5-2a) the Bazin and King values are considerably higher than the others. Neglecting the Francis results, there is a spread of approximately 5 per cent in values of C for $H = 1$ and $H/P = 2.0$. In general, it must be concluded that even among tests for which conditions appear to be quite similar, there are rather great differences in discharges for the same head, and that although the weir is a very useful measuring device, its limitations should be recognized and understood (p. 5-29).

The computations involved in dealing with horizontal sharp-crested weirs without end contractions will be illustrated by a numerical example.

Example 5-1.　Estimate the discharge over a sharp-crested weir extending over the full width of a rectangular channel 5 ft wide if the weir blade is 3 ft high and the head is 0.84 ft.

$$\frac{H}{P} = 0.84/3 = 0.28$$

From Rehbock (1912), using Eqs. (5-29) and (5-10),

$$C = 3.235 + \frac{1}{60H - 0.56} + 0.428\,\frac{H}{P}$$
$$= 3.235 + 0.020 + 0.120 = 3.375$$

Then

$$Q = 3.375 \times 5 \times 0.84^{3\!/\!2} = 13.0 \text{ cu ft per sec}$$

The value of $0.84^{3\!/\!2}$ may be obtained from Table 5-1. From Kindsvater and Carter tests, using Eqs. (5-35) to (5-38), noting that $k_H = 0.003$ and $k_L = -0.003$:

From Eq. (5-35):

$$L_e = 5 - 0.003 = 4.997 \text{ ft}$$

From Eq. (5-36):

$$H_e = 0.84 + 0.003 = 0.843 \text{ ft}$$

From Eq. (5-37):

$$C_e = 3.22 + 0.40 \frac{H}{P}$$
$$= 3.20 + 0.11 = 3.31$$

Then, from Eq. (5-34),

$$Q = C_e L_e H_e^{3\!/\!2}$$
$$= 3.31 \times 4.997 \times (0.843)^{3\!/\!2} = 12.8 \text{ cu ft per sec}$$

Horizontal Sharp-crested Weirs with End Contractions.
When the weir length L is less than the width of the channel b, the weir opening is in the form of a notch, with the ends of the notch having sharp edges and causing contractions in the same manner as the horizontal portion of the crest. A much smaller number of tests has been made on weirs of this type than on weirs without end contractions.

Tests made by Francis[1] indicated that the effect of the end contractions could be taken care of by reducing L in Eq. (5-10) by $0.2H$. The more recent work of Kindsvater and Carter[1] indicates that this procedure is not accurate for all conditions. Efforts to compensate for the end contractions led to the development of the *Cipolletti weir*.

This type of weir has ends which are not vertical but have a slope of 1:4, horizontal to vertical. This slope was chosen to provide sufficient additional discharge to compensate for the end contractions. However, experiments by Flinn and Dyer[2] and others indicate that the side slope of the notch should be greater than 1:4.

The experimentation by Kindsvater and Carter previously reported (p. 5-9) included tests on horizontal weirs with end contractions. Their procedure provides what is probably the best available method for estimating the discharge through rectangular notched sharp-edged weirs. The results are given in the form of two figures which are reproduced here in Fig. 5-3a and b. In Fig. 5-3a is shown a curve relating k_L to L/b, and in Fig. 5-3b are shown lines of C_e versus H/P for various values of L/b, the top line being the line representing Eq. (5-37), which applies to the case of $L/b = 1$. The use of these curves will be illustrated by means of an example.

---

[1] *Op. cit.*

[2] A. D. Flinn and C. W. D. Dyer, The Cipolletti Trapezoidal Weir, *Trans. ASCE*, vol. 32, 1894.

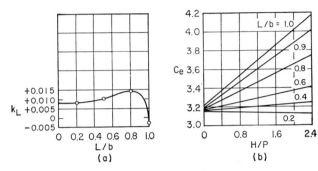

FIG. 5-3. Coefficients, horizontal sharp-crested weirs with end contractions.

Example 5-2.   A rectangular notched sharp-crested weir having a horizontal crest 3 ft long located 2 ft above the bottom is centered in a rectangular channel 5 ft wide.   Determine the discharge when the head is 0.40 ft.

$$\frac{L}{b} = \frac{3}{5} = 0.60 \qquad \frac{H}{P} = 0.40/2.0 = 0.20$$

Then, from Fig. 5-3*b*,

$$C_e = 3.19$$

From Fig. 5-3*a*, $k_L = +0.012$, and taking $k_H = 0.003$,

$$L_e = 3 + 0.012 = 3.012 \text{ ft}$$

and

$$H_e = 0.40 + 0.003 = 0.403 \text{ ft}$$

Then

$$Q = C_e L_e H_e^{3/2} = 3.19 \times 3.012 \times 0.403^{3/2}$$

and making use of Table 5-1, if desired,

$$Q = 2.47 \text{ cu ft per sec}$$

V-notch Weirs.   Triangular, or V-notch, weirs permit the accurate measurement of much lower discharges than do horizontal crested weirs.   The discharge of a notched weir increases more rapidly with the head than in the case of a horizontal crested weir.   For example, at a head of 2 ft the discharge through a 90° V-notch weir is approximately the same as that of a horizontal weir 1.5 ft long, whereas at a head of 0.1 ft the discharge of the horizontal weir is twenty times that of the 90° V-notch weir. The V-notch weir therefore presents distinct advantages where low discharges are included in the range to be measured.

The basic expression for discharge through a V-notch weir is given by Eqs. (5-13) to (5-15).

$$Q = C_1 \tan \frac{\theta}{2} H^{5/2} \qquad (5\text{-}13)$$

$$C = C_1 \tan \frac{\theta}{2} \qquad (5\text{-}14)$$

$$Q = CH^{5/2} \qquad (5\text{-}15)$$

The meanings of H and θ are given in Fig. 5-1a and c. In these equations C_1 and C must include the effect of contraction, velocity of approach, viscosity, and surface tension. Usually the velocity of approach is negligible for V-notch weirs unless H becomes very large, in which case it would be better to use Eq. (5-12).

Lenz[1] has developed a procedure for including the effect of viscosity and surface tension. His paper shows applications to his own experimental data for water and several oils, as well as to data

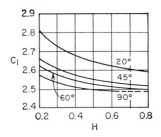

FIG. 5-4. Coefficients, V-notch sharp-crested weirs.

of other experimenters. For fluids other than water, the reader is referred to Professor Lenz's paper. For water his results are summarized by the curves shown in Fig. 5-4. Here again, the effects of viscosity and surface tension are reflected by the variation of C_1 or C with H (p. 5-6).

Another method of taking into account the effect of H for a particular weir and constant temperature is to hold C constant and let the exponent of H be such as to fit the experimental data. In that case Eq. (5-15) would be modified as follows:

$$Q = CH^n \qquad (5\text{-}15a)$$

Extensive tests conducted at the University of Michigan on

[1] Arno T. Lenz, Viscosity and Surface Tension Effects on V-notch Weir Coefficients, *Trans. ASCE*, vol. 69, pp. 759–802, 1943.

a 90° V-notch weir for water at heads varying from 0.2 to 1.8 ft resulted in the following equation[1]:

$$Q = 2.52H^{2.47} \qquad (5\text{-}43)$$

From experiments by Barr,[2]

$$Q = 2.48H^{2.48} \qquad (5\text{-}44)$$

The University of Michigan experiments were performed on a weir cut from unpolished commercial steel plate, while the Barr tests were made with a weir cut in a polished brass plate. Barr found that the discharge from his weir could be increased about 2 per cent by roughening the upstream face with an application of varnish and emery dust. Five-halves powers of numbers are given in Table 5-2.

Because the tan $(\theta/2)$ is unity for a 90° V notch, Eqs. (5-43) and (5-44) indicate that the value of C_1 in Eq. (5-13) is approximately 2.5. Using this value, the following general expression for discharge over notched weirs is derived:

$$Q = 2.5 \tan \frac{\theta}{2} H^{2.5} \qquad (5\text{-}45)$$

Experiments conducted at the University of Michigan on a $22\frac{1}{2}°$ V-notch weir yielded the equation

$$Q = 0.50H^{2.43} \qquad (5\text{-}46a)$$

Equation (5-45) gives the following equation for this weir:

$$Q = 0.50H^{2.5} \qquad (5\text{-}46b)$$

Tests made at the University of Michigan on a 60° V-notch weir gave the result

$$Q = 1.47H^{2.51} \qquad (5\text{-}47a)$$

as compared with the following expression derived from Eq. (5-45):

$$Q = 1.44H^{2.5} \qquad (5\text{-}47b)$$

Hertzler[3] gives equations derived from tests on six different 120° V-notch weirs. The average values of C and n for these

[1] The procedure for developing a weir equation from test data is illustrated by Example 13-8 in Sec. 13.

[2] James Barr, Experiments upon the Flow of Water over Triangular Notches, *Engineering*, Apr. 8, Apr. 15, 1910.

[3] R. A. Hertzler, "Determination of a Formula for the 120-deg. V-notch Weir," *Civil Eng. (N.Y.)*, p. 756, November, 1938.

weirs yield the following expression:

$$Q = 4.36H^{2.48} \qquad (5\text{-}48a)$$

whereas Eq. (5-45) gives the following result for 120° weirs:

$$Q = 4.33H^{2.5} \qquad (5\text{-}48b)$$

It may be seen from the above examples that Eq. (5-45) provides a means of deriving the discharge equation for a V-notch weir of any angle θ with a fair degree of dependability. It is especially useful in designing a weir to measure a particular range of discharges. The use of the equations for V-notch weirs is illustrated by the following example.

Example 5-3. Estimate the discharge over a sharp-crested 90° V-notch weir when H is 0.50 ft and P is 1.0 ft. The fluid is water, and the channel above the weir is 4 ft wide.

Assuming that the velocity of approach is negligible, the discharge can be estimated from Eqs. (5-14) and (5-15), together with Fig. 5-4.

From Fig. 5-4, $C = C_1 = 2.495$ and $Q = 2.495 \times 0.5^{2.5}$. Table 5-2 may be used for obtaining the five-halves powers of numbers. Then $Q = 2.495 \times 0.177 = 0.441$ cu ft per sec.

For comparison, the problem will also be solved by using Eqs. (5-43) and (5-44).

From Eq. (5-43),

$$Q = 2.52 \times 0.5^{2.47} = 0.456 \text{ cu ft per sec}$$

From Eq. (5-44),

$$Q = 2.48 \times 0.5^{2.48} = 0.446 \text{ cu ft per sec}$$

The velocity of approach is

$$V_1 = \frac{0.45}{1.5 \times 4} = 0.075 \text{ ft per sec}$$

and the velocity head is

$$\frac{V_1^2}{2g} = 0.0000875 \text{ ft}$$

This quantity is negligible compared with an H of 0.50 ft.

Submerged Sharp-crested Weirs. A profile through a submerged sharp-crested weir is illustrated in Fig. 5-5. The discharge Q over such a weir is related not only to the head on

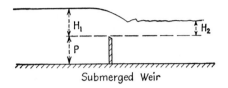

Submerged Weir

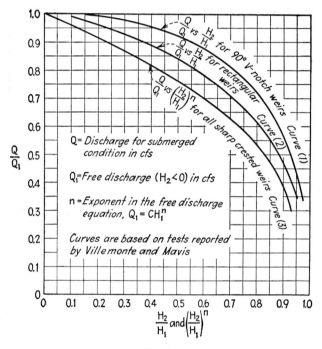

Fɪɢ. 5-5

the upstream side of the weir, H_1, but also to the head on the downstream side, H_2, and to a lesser extent, to the height of the weir crest above the floor of the channel, P. Early experiments by Francis (1848, 1883), Fteley and Stearns (1882), Bazin (1894), Cone (1916), and Cox (1928) have been summarized by Vennard and Weston.[1] They showed that the various test data could be presented in an orderly manner by selecting as variables Q/Q_1 and H_2/H_1, where Q_1 is the discharge at the head H_1, computed from the equation for free discharge (unsubmerged), which is expressed in general terms as follows:

$$Q_1 = CH_1^n \qquad (5\text{-}49)$$

By plotting Q/Q_1 against H_2/H_1, they found that the various data tended to fall on a single curve, except for small values of P/H_1.

In 1947, Villemonte[2] presented the results of a series of tests on submerged sharp-crested weirs. He conducted tests on rectangular, triangular, parabolic, cusped, and proportional weirs. He showed that the results for all types could be represented by the single equation

$$\frac{Q}{Q_1} = \left[1 - \left(\frac{H_2}{H_1} \right)^n \right]^{0.385} \qquad (5\text{-}50)$$

where n is the exponent in the free-discharge equation [Eq. (5-49)], and the other terms are as previously defined. This equation was found to satisfy all test results, with a maximum deviation of 5 per cent for some of the individual test results.

In 1949, Mavis[3] presented results of tests on rectangular, triangular, parabolic, circular, sutro, and cusped weirs. He found that a single equation could be used to express the results for all the tests. His equation with subscripts changed to conform with usage in this book is

$$\frac{Q}{Q_1} = 1 - \left(0.45S + \frac{0.40}{2^{(10-10S)}} \right) \qquad (5\text{-}51)$$

[1] John K. Vennard and Ray F. Weston, Submergence Effect on Sharp-crested Weirs, *Eng. News-Record*, June 3, 1943, p. 818.

[2] James R. Villemonte, Submerged-weir Discharge Studies, *Eng. News-Record*, Dec. 25, 1947, p. 866.

[3] F. T. Mavis, How to Calculate Flow over Submerged Thin-plate Weirs, *Eng. News-Record*, July 7, 1949, p. 65.

where S is defined as follows:

$$S = \frac{a_2 \sqrt{H_2}}{a_1 \sqrt{H_1}} \qquad (5\text{-}52)$$

In Eq. (5-52), a_2 is the weir area corresponding to H_2 and a_1 is the weir area corresponding to H_1.   Mavis also presented some interesting data which resulted from tests made in 1717 by Poleni.   It was found that Poleni's results agreed within 2 to 4 per cent with the Mavis data.

The author has plotted the curves shown in Fig. 5-5 based on the results of the work of Villemonte and Mavis.   Information regarding the experimental arrangements for the 90° V-notch weirs and rectangular weirs is given in the following table. It may be noted that the channel widths differed for the two

	Mavis	Villemonte		
Channel width........	4 ft 0 in.	3.02 ft		
P for 90° V-notch weirs	1 ft 6 in.	2.0 ft		
P for rectangular weirs	1 ft 10 in.	2.0 ft	1.0 ft	1.25 ft
Widths of notches of rectangular weirs...	1 ft 3 in.	3.02 ft	0.5 ft	1.00 ft

sets of tests, that P was different for all cases, and that rectangular weirs of four different widths were tested.   Curves 1 and 2 are composite curves based on the results of the two investigators for the 90° V-notch weirs and the rectangular weirs, respectively.   Curves 1 and 2 differ by no more than 1 per cent from the test results.

Because Eqs. (5-50) and (5-51) both indicate that Q/Q_1 is a function of $(H_2/H_1)^n$, the author has prepared curve 3, which is an average of results obtained from Eqs. (5-50) and (5-51). Results obtained from either equation differ by less than 1 per cent from curve 3.   Curve 3 may be used to compute the discharge of a submerged sharp-crested weir of any shape. This curve is also in reasonable agreement with the results of the investigations summarized by Vennard and Weston, as well as with data presented by Stevens.[1]   It should be noted, however, that for some of the weirs tested, the results could be represented more closely by an equation differing slightly from Eqs. (5-50) and (5-51) and by a curve differing slightly from curves 1 to 3.   Therefore, if great accuracy is essential, it is recommended that the particular weir, or a similar one, be tested in a laboratory under conditions comparable with field conditions. In using the curves shown in Fig. 5-5, it is recommended that H_1 be measured at least $2.5H_1$ upstream from the weir and that H_2 be measured beyond the turbulence caused by the nappe.

Example 5-4.   Determine the discharge of a 90° V-notch weir if H_1 is 0.9 ft, H_2 is 0.3 ft, and $Q_1 = 2.5H_1^{2.5}$.

a. Use curve 1 of Fig. 5-5.

$$Q_1 = 2.5 \times 0.9^{2.5} = 1.92 \text{ sec-ft}$$
$$\frac{H_2}{H_1} = \frac{0.3}{0.9} = 0.333$$
$$\frac{Q}{Q_1} = 0.972 \text{ (from curve 1)}$$
$$Q = 0.972 \times 1.92 = 1.86 \text{ sec-ft}$$

b. Use curve 3 of Fig. 5-5.

$$\left(\frac{H_2}{H_1}\right)^n = (0.333)^{2.5} = 0.064$$
$$\frac{Q}{Q_1} = 0.972 \text{ (from curve 3)}$$
$$Q = 0.972 \times 1.92 = 1.86 \text{ sec-ft}$$

Example 5-5.   Determine the discharge of a parabolic weir if H_1 is 0.8 ft, H_2 is 0.4 ft, and $Q_1 = 2.0H_1^{2.0}$.

$$Q_1 = 2.0 \times (0.8)^{2.0} = 1.28 \text{ sec-ft}$$
$$\left(\frac{H_2}{H_1}\right)^n = \left(\frac{0.4}{0.8}\right)^{2.0} = 0.25$$
$$\frac{Q}{Q_1} = 0.89 \text{ (from curve 3)}$$
$$Q = 0.89 \times 1.28 = 1.14 \text{ sec-ft}$$

Weirs Not Sharp-crested

Sharp-crested weirs, if used to obtain discharge records for comparatively long periods, are difficult to maintain.   The

[1] J. C. Stevens, Experiments on Small Weirs and Modules, *Eng. News*, Aug. 18, 1910.

crest is likely to become dulled or rusted, or it may be damaged by floating ice and debris. Under such conditions it may be advisable to use a weir with a thicker crest. It is often convenient to use an existing weir or overflow dam for measuring discharges. Weirs of various dimensions and shapes are used in hydraulic structures. When designing such structures it is important to be able to estimate approximately the discharges over these weirs (p. 2-15).

The amount of water which will pass over a weir, not sharp-crested, depends to a large extent upon its sectional form and the shape of its crest, and it is necessary to resort to experiment to determine the discharge over any particular shape. Inasmuch as the number of shapes of weirs is unlimited, it is not to be expected that experimental data are or ever will be available for them all. There are available, however, the results of several series of experiments on weirs of different cross sections which furnish much valuable information for determining discharges over weirs of the same or similar shapes.

The available experiments are not extensive enough for a comprehensive study of the effect of velocity of approach on weirs not sharp-crested. The coefficients given in this chapter probably apply more accurately where the velocity of approach is not high. From a consideration of sharp-crested weirs it appears that discharges, for high velocities of approach, will be somewhat greater than is given by formula (5-10).

Since experimental conditions will seldom be duplicated in practice, it is probable that errors may result from the general use of the coefficients given in this chapter. Extreme accuracy, however, is not always necessary in design, where uncertainty as to the exact quantity of water to be provided for may exist.

The problem of establishing a fixed relation between head and discharge, for weirs not sharp-crested, is complicated by the fact that the nappe may assume a variety of forms in passing over the weir. For each modification of nappe form, there is a corresponding change in the relation between head and discharge. The effect of this condition is more noticeable for low heads.

The nappe may undergo several of these modifications in succession as the head is varied. The successive forms that appear with an increasing stage may differ from those pertaining to similar stages with a decreasing head. The head at which the changes of nappe form occur varies with the rate of change of head, whether increasing or decreasing, and with other conditions.

Among weirs of irregular section there is a large class for which, from the nature of their section, the nappe can assume only one form unless drowned. Such weirs, it is suggested, may, if properly calibrated, equal or exceed the usefulness of the thin-edged weir for purposes of stream gaging, because of their stability of section and because the thin-edged weir is not free from modification of nappe form for low heads.

Broad-crested Weirs. A weir approximately rectangular in cross section is termed a broad-crested weir. Unless otherwise noted, it will be assumed to have vertical faces, a plane level

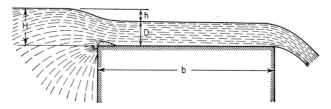

Fig. 5-6. Broad-crested weir.

crest, and sharp right-angled corners. Figure 5-6 represents a broad-crested weir of breadth b. The head H should be measured at least $2.5H$ upstream from the weir. Because of the sharp upstream edge, contraction of the nappe occurs. Surface contraction begins at a point slightly upstream from the weir.

The discharge over broad-crested weirs is usually expressed by the equation

$$Q = CLH^{3/2} \qquad (5\text{-}10)$$

Experiments on broad-crested weirs have been performed by Blackwell, Bazin, Woodburn, the U.S. Deep Waterways Board, and the U.S. Geological Survey. These experiments cover a wide range of conditions as to head, breadth, and height of weir. Considerable discrepancy exists in the results of the different experimenters, especially for heads below 0.5 ft. For heads from 0.5 to about 1.5 ft the coefficient becomes more uniform, and for heads from 1.5 ft to that at which the nappe becomes detached from the crest, the coefficient as given by the different experiments is nearly constant and equals approximately 2.63.

When the head reaches one to two times the breadth, the nappe becomes detached and the weir becomes essentially sharp-crested. The effect on discharge of roughness of the crest can be computed by applying the principles of flow in open channels.

In order to put the results of the various experiments in a form convenient for use, Table 5-3 has been prepared by graphically interpolating the results of all experiments, giving more weight to those of the U.S. Geological Survey. This table should give values of C within the limits of accuracy of the original experiments. Table 5-1 gives three-halves powers of numbers.

The effect of rounding the upstream corner of a broad-crested weir is to increase the discharge for a given head. Table 5-4 gives a résumé of experiments on this type of weir. The effect of rounding the upstream corner on a radius of 4 in. is to increase the coefficient C approximately 9 per cent. Coefficients by Woodburn[1] for flat weirs with rounded upstream corners and gently sloping crests are given in Table 5-5a.

Blackwell experimented with three weirs 3.0 ft broad having a slightly inclined crest. Inclining the crest appears slightly to increase the coefficient of discharge. The results of these experiments are rather inconsistent, especially for low heads. Table 5-5b has been obtained from Blackwell's experiments. Sloping the top of a broad-crested weir makes it similar to a triangular weir with the upstream face vertical. The coefficients given in Tables 5-6 and 5-7 will therefore be helpful in selecting coefficients for broad-crested weirs with sloping crests.

If the upstream corner of a weir is so rounded as entirely to prevent contraction, and if the slope of the crest is as great as the loss of head due to friction, flow occurs at critical depth, and discharge is given by the rational formula

$$Q = 3.087LH^{3/2} \qquad (5\text{-}53)$$

For further discussion of flow at critical depth, see Sec. 8. It should be noted that $C = 3.087$ is the maximum value of the coefficient that is obtainable for broad-crested weirs under any conditions.

Weirs of Triangular Section. Figure 5-7 represents the cross section of a weir having the upper face vertical and the lower

---

[1] J. G. Woodburn, Tests on Broad Crested Weirs, *Trans. ASCE*, vol. 96, 1932.

face inclined downward, the two faces meeting in a sharp angle which forms the crest.

Bazin has experimented with weirs of this type, 2.46 ft high, having various slopes of the downstream face. The coefficients resulting from those experiments are given in Table 5-6.

It will be observed that the coefficient for a given slope, in each case shown by the experiments, is nearly constant for heads above 0.7 ft. It seems fair to assume, therefore, that these values could be extended to higher heads with reasonable assurance. The average values of the coefficients given in

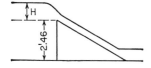

FIG. 5-7. Triangular weir.

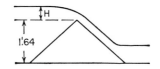

FIG. 5-8. Triangular weir.

Table 5-6, for heads above 0.7 ft, were plotted logarithmically and found to fall very accurately on a straight line. This line was then extended to include slopes of 20 horizontal to 1 vertical, from which the values given in Table 5-7 were taken. Table 5-7 may be used for computing discharges over weirs of the types shown in Fig. 5-7 for heads above 0.7 ft. These coefficients are to be used for broad-crested weirs with inclined tops only when the breadth is sufficient to prevent the nappe from springing clear. In the latter case the weir becomes in principle a thin-edged weir.

Bazin also experimented with weirs of triangular cross sections 1.64 ft high, having both faces inclined (Fig. 5-8). Coeffi-

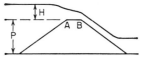

FIG. 5-9. Trapezoidal weir.

cients covering the range of these experiments are given in Table 5-8.

Weirs of Trapezoidal Section. Figure 5-9 represents a weir of trapezoidal section with both upstream and downstream faces inclined. Experiments on this type of weir were made by Bazin and the U.S. Deep Waterways Board. Bazin's experiments were all on weirs 2.64 ft high, the breadth of crest AB varying from 0.66 to 1.32 ft. Experiments on two weirs of this type, each 4.9 ft high, were performed by the U.S. Deep Waterways Board.

Coefficients covering the range of Bazin's experiments are given in Table 5-9. Table 5-10 gives coefficients resulting from the experiments by the U.S. Deep Waterways Board.

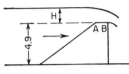

FIG. 5-10. Trapezoidal weir.

For weirs of trapezoidal cross section with sloping upstream and vertical downstream face (Fig. 5-10) there are five series of experiments by the U.S. Deep Waterways Board. All the models for these experiments were approximately 4.9 ft high, and the breadth of crest *AB* was either 0.33 or 0.66 ft. The length of all weirs was 6.58 ft. Table 5-11 gives coefficients derived from these experiments.

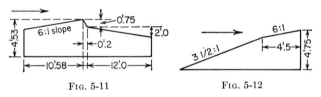

FIG. 5-11   FIG. 5-12

Weirs of Irregular Section. Figures 5-11 to 5-15 represent models of weirs experimented on by the U.S. Deep Waterways Board, under the direction of G. W. Rafter, at the hydraulic laboratory of Cornell University. From four to seven experiments were run on each model, the range of head varying approximately from 1 to 5.5 ft. Values of *C* tabulated from these experiments are given in Table 5-12.

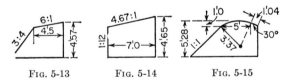

FIG. 5-13   FIG. 5-14   FIG. 5-15

Experiments for the U.S. Geological Survey, under the direction of Robert E. Horton, were performed in 1903 at the hydraulic laboratory of Cornell University to determine the coefficients of discharge of weirs modeled after various types of dams. Figures 5-16 to 5-25 show forms of crests of models experimented on. The weirs were all 11.25 ft high and either 8 or 15 ft long. The purpose of the experiments was to enable the Geological Survey to determine more accurately discharges

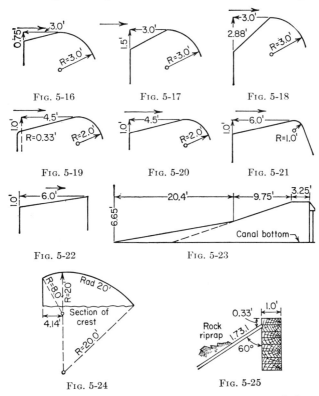

FIG. 5-16   FIG. 5-17   FIG. 5-18

FIG. 5-19   FIG. 5-20   FIG. 5-21

FIG. 5-22   FIG. 5-23

FIG. 5-24   FIG. 5-25

over weirs at gaging stations. Coefficients obtained from these experiments are given in Table 5-13.

Figure 5-24 is a cross section of the old dam at Austin, Tex. Five series of gagings of flow over this dam were made with a current meter by Taylor[1] in 1900. The range of head was from 0.42 to 1.44 ft.

[1] T. U. Taylor, The Austin Dam, *U.S. Geol. Survey Water Supply and Irrigation Paper* 40, 1900.

Figure 5-25 is a cross section of the Blackstone River dam at Albion, Mass. Five current meter measurements of the water passing over this dam were made by Dwight Porter. The head in each case was about 1 ft, and the resulting values of C vary from 3.41 to 3.94.

The last two lines in Table 5-13 give mean values of C as determined for measurement of flow over the above dams.

Spillway Sections. The typical overflow spillway section of a dam, as illustrated in Fig. 5-26, is a weir with rounded crest.

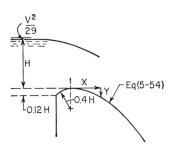

FIG. 5-26. Spillway section "standard crest."

The coefficient varies from 3.0 to more than 4.0, depending primarily on the shape of the crest, the extent of end contraction, and the head. Because of the variation in C for different weirs, it is necessary to calibrate each weir if a high degree of accuracy is desired. However, the shape of the crest is often designed as a "standard crest," which was developed[1] to fit the shape of the underside of the nappe of a sharp-crested weir. For this type of crest it is possible to coordinate the coefficients of discharge for various overflow sections to some extent. The shape of this crest may be obtained from tables[2] or from the following equation[3] for the portion of the spillway downstream from the crest:

$$Y = 0.47X^{1.80} \qquad (5\text{-}54)$$

combined with a circular curve for the upstream portion as shown in Fig. 5-26. Equation (5-54) gives the shape of the crest for $H = 1$, and all values of Y and X must be multiplied by whatever value of H is selected for the design head. It has

[1] William P. Creager, "Engineering for Masonry Dams," John Wiley & Sons, Inc., New York, 1929.

[2] William P. Creager, Joel D. Justin, and Julian Hinds, "Engineering for Dams," vol. 11, John Wiley & Sons, Inc., New York, 1945.

[3] Richard R. Randolph, "Hydraulic Tests on the Spillway of Madden Dam," *Trans. ASCE*, vol. 103, 1938; also discussion by Ettore Scimeni, p. 1113.

been shown that there is an orderly variation of the coefficient of discharge for heads above and below the design head for weirs of this type. Kirkpatrick[1] presented a curve relating C/C_0 to H/H_0 for seven TVA dams having shapes similar to the standard crest, C being the coefficient of discharge for any head H, and C_0 and H_0 corresponding values for the design head. His curve is reproduced in Fig. 5-27. A similar relationship between C/C_0 and H/H_0 developed by Randolph[2] is also shown in Fig. 5-27. Values of the coefficients of discharge for the design head, C_0, obtained for the seven TVA dams, varied from

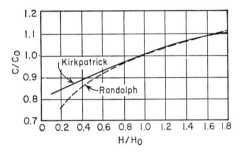

Fig. 5-27. Coefficients for spillway sections.

3.71 to 3.93, whereas the one reported by Randolph was 3.97. All the tests reported here were made on scale models and include the effect of contractions caused by piers at the ends of the crests. Kirkpatrick's tests were made through one bay of a spillway with adjacent bays closed. If, for example, a standard crest is designed for $H_0 = 15$ ft and it is assumed that the value of C_0 is 3.9, then it may be estimated from Fig. 5-27 that C for $H = 20$ is $1.05 \times 3.9 = 4.1$. Values obtained in this manner can be considered only as estimates, pending a laboratory calibration.

The Selection and Use of Weirs

Weir selection for a particular situation depends upon the range of discharges to be measured, the accuracy desired, and

[1] Hennety W. Kirkpatrick, Discharge Coefficients for Spillways of TVA Dams, *Trans. ASCE*, vol. 22, pp. 190–210, 1957.

[2] *Op. cit.*

whether or not the weir can be calibrated after installation. Most weir equations for sharp-edged weirs are not accurate for heads less than 0.2 ft; therefore, for very small discharges, a V-notch weir should be selected. On the other hand, few discharge measurements have been made on sharp-edged weirs for heads greater than 2 ft. Therefore, if a sharp-crested weir is to be used, it might be suggested that the weir be selected so that H will be between 0.2 and 2.0 ft. Weirs with rounded crests are used with much higher heads. If the weir is so located that it can be calibrated by means of volumetric or weighing tanks in the position that it will be used, exceedingly great accuracy can be expected, especially for sharp-crested weirs, and the errors will be principally those resulting from the determination of the head. When weirs are used in locations where they cannot be calibrated in place, the errors are likely to be much greater, as indicated by the difference in results obtained by various investigators for similar weirs. Table 5-14 shows the percentage of error in discharge for different discharges and dimensions of weirs resulting from various-sized errors in the measurement of head. If the head is measured too far upstream, there may be some drop in the water surface due to friction. In order to avoid errors due to drawdown at the nappe, the head should be measured at least $4H$ upstream from horizontal crested weirs and $2.5H$ upstream from V-notch weirs. A detailed discussion of various types of error which may affect weir measurements has been presented by Thomas.[1]

Heads are usually measured in a stilling well by means of a hook gage. The pipe connecting the well and channel should not project beyond the channel surface. Schoder used a cylindrical copper float in a 6-in. vertical pipe which served as a stilling well. A float stem extending above the end of the pipe had at its top a combined index and guide which traveled along a brass scale graduated to hundredths of a foot. Schoder also used a plumb bob attached to the end of a steel tape to measure the vertical distance of the water surface from a fixed mark above the channel. The gage reading corresponding to zero head should be determined with great care and checked at frequent intervals. If accuracy is essential, the head used to compute discharge should be the mean of at least 10, and

[1] Charles W. Thomas, Errors in Measurement of Irrigation Water, *Trans. ASCE*, vol. 124, pp. 319–340, 1959.

preferably 20, separate measurements made at equal intervals of about 30 sec.

Weirs for Measuring Stream Flow. Weirs of many types are used to measure the discharge of small streams. Sharp-crested weirs have the advantage that laboratory calibration conditions can be quite accurately reproduced in the field. Sharp-edged metal blades, however, require considerable maintenance, and in some cases they may be damaged by floating debris. The U.S. Geological Survey has standardized and calibrated a number of round-crested weirs specifically for stream-gaging purposes. Their Trenton and Columbus types[1] have cross sections similar to that shown in Figs. 5-1d and 5-26, thus avoiding

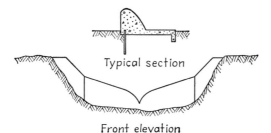

Typical section

Front elevation

Fig. 5-28. Columbus deep-notch type of weir.

the disadvantages of sharp-crested weirs. The Columbus type of deep-notch weir (Fig. 5-28) has the same cross section as the Columbus type, and in addition, the crest slopes downward toward the center to form a notch. This weir combines a large maximum capacity with good sensitivity at low discharges. It must be carefully constructed to specifications in order to assure that the rating curve derived in the laboratory will also apply in the field. In some cases standardized metal forms are used to ensure exact duplication.

When weirs are used to measure natural streams, a recording gage is used. Methods of developing such a gaging station are discussed elsewhere.[2]

[1] Equipment for River Measurements, Preliminary Report on Studies of Artificial Control, *U.S. Geol. Survey Mimeographed Circ.* 1935.

[2] C. O. Wisler and E. F. Brater, "Hydrology," 2d ed., John Wiley & Sons, Inc., New York, 1959.

Table 5-1. Three-halves Powers of Numbers

No.	.000	.001	.002	.003	.004	.005	.006	.007	.008	.009
.00	.0000	.0000	.0001	.0002	.0003	.0004	.0005	.0006	.0007	.0009
.01	.0010	.0012	.0013	.0015	.0017	.0018	.0020	.0022	.0024	.0026
.02	.0028	.0030	.0033	.0035	.0037	.0040	.0042	.0044	.0047	.0049
.03	.0052	.0055	.0057	.0060	.0063	.0065	.0068	.0071	.0074	.0077
.04	.0080	.0083	.0086	.0089	.0092	.0095	.0099	.0102	.0105	.0108
.05	.0112	.0115	.0119	.0122	.0125	.0129	.0132	.0136	.0140	.0143
.06	.0147	.0151	.0154	.0158	.0162	.0166	.0170	.0173	.0177	0181
.07	.0185	.0189	.0193	.0197	.0201	.0205	.0210	.0214	.0218	.0222
.08	.0226	.0231	.0235	.0239	.0243	.0248	.0252	.0257	.0261	.0265
.09	.0270	.0275	.0279	.0284	.0288	.0293	.0297	.0302	.0307	.0312
.10	.0316	.0321	.0326	.0331	.0335	.0340	.0345	.0350	.0355	.0360
.11	.0365	.0370	.0375	.0380	.0385	.0390	.0395	.0400	.0405	.0411
.12	.0416	.0421	.0426	.0431	.0436	.0442	.0447	.0452	.0458	.0463
.13	.0469	.0474	.0480	.0485	.0491	.0496	.0502	.0507	.0513	.0518
.14	.0524	.0529	.0535	.0541	.0546	.0552	.0558	.0564	.0569	.0575
.15	.0581	.0587	.0593	.0598	.0604	.0610	.0616	.0622	.0628	.0634
.16	.0640	.0646	.0652	.0658	.0664	.0670	.0676	.0682	.0688	.0695
.17	.0701	.0707	.0713	.0720	.0726	.0732	.0738	.0745	.0751	.0757
.18	.0764	.0770	.0776	.0783	.0789	.0796	.0802	.0809	.0815	.0822
.19	.0828	.0835	.0841	.0848	.0854	.0861	.0868	.0874	.0881	.0888
.20	.0894	.0901	.0908	.0915	.0921	.0928	.0935	.0942	.0949	.0955
.21	.0962	.0969	.0976	.0983	.0990	.0997	.1004	.1011	.1018	.1025
.22	.1032	.1039	.1046	.1053	.1060	.1067	.1074	.1081	.1089	.1096
.23	.1103	.1110	.1118	.1125	.1132	.1139	.1146	.1154	.1161	.1168
.24	.1176	.1183	.1191	.1198	.1205	.1213	.1220	.1228	.1235	.1243
.25	.1250	.1258	.1265	.1273	.1280	.1288	.1295	.1303	.1311	.1318
.26	.1326	.1333	.1341	.1349	.1356	.1364	.1372	.1380	.1387	.1395
.27	.1403	.1411	.1419	.1426	.1434	.1442	.1450	.1458	.1466	.1474
.28	.1482	.1490	.1498	.1506	.1514	.1522	.1530	.1538	.1546	.1554
.29	.1562	.1570	.1578	.1586	.1594	.1602	.1611	.1619	.1627	.1635
.30	.1643	.1652	.1660	.1668	.1676	.1684	.1693	.1701	.1709	.1718
.31	.1726	.1734	.1743	.1751	.1760	.1768	.1776	.1785	.1793	.1802
.32	.1810	.1819	.1827	.1836	.1844	.1853	.1861	.1870	.1879	.1887
.33	.1896	.1904	.1913	.1922	.1930	.1939	.1948	.1956	.1965	.1974
.34	.1983	.1991	.2000	.2009	.2018	.2026	.2035	.2044	.2053	.2062
.35	.2071	.2080	.2089	.2097	.2106	.2115	.2124	.2133	.2142	.2151
.36	.2160	.2169	.2178	.2187	.2196	.2205	.2214	.2223	.2232	.2242
.37	.2251	.2260	.2269	.2278	.2287	.2296	.2306	.2315	.2324	.2333
.38	.2342	.2352	.2361	.2370	.2380	.2389	.2398	.2408	.2417	.2426
.39	.2436	.2445	.2454	.2464	.2473	.2483	.2492	.2501	.2511	.2520
.40	.2530	.2539	.2549	.2558	.2568	.2578	.2587	.2597	.2606	.2616
.41	.2625	.2635	.2645	.2654	.2664	.2674	.2683	.2693	.2703	.2712
.42	.2722	.2732	.2741	.2751	.2761	.2771	.2781	.2790	.2800	.2810
.43	.2820	.2830	.2840	.2849	.2859	.2869	.2879	.2889	.2899	.2909
.44	.2919	.2929	.2939	.2949	.2959	.2969	.2979	.2989	.2999	.3009
.45	.3019	.3029	.3039	.3049	.3059	.3069	.3079	.3089	.3100	.3110
.46	.3120	.3130	.3140	.3150	.3161	.3171	.3181	.3191	.3202	.3212
.47	.3222	.3232	.3243	.3253	.3263	.3274	.3284	.3294	.3305	.3315
.48	.3325	.3336	.3346	.3357	.3367	.3378	.3388	.3399	.3409	.3420
.49	.3430	.3441	.3451	.3462	.3472	.3483	.3493	.3504	.3514	.3525

Table 5-1. Three-halves Powers of Numbers (*Continued*)

No.	.000	.001	.002	.003	.004	.005	.006	.007	.008	.009
.50	.3536	.3546	.3557	.3567	.3578	.3589	.3599	.3610	.3621	.3631
.51	.3642	.3653	.3664	.3674	.3685	.3696	.3707	.3717	.3728	.3739
.52	.3750	.3761	.3771	.3782	.3793	.3804	.3815	.3826	.3837	.3847
.53	.3858	.3869	.3880	.3891	.3902	.3913	.3924	.3935	.3946	.3957
.54	.3968	.3979	.3990	.4001	.4012	.4023	.4035	.4046	.4057	.4068
.55	.4079	.4090	.4101	.4112	.4123	.4135	.4146	.4157	.4168	.4179
.56	.4191	.4202	.4213	.4224	.4236	.4247	.4258	.4269	.4281	.4292
.57	.4303	.4315	.4326	.4337	.4349	.4360	.4372	.4383	.4394	.4406
.58	.4417	.4429	.4440	.4451	.4463	.4474	.4486	.4497	.4509	.4520
.59	.4532	.4544	.4555	.4566	.4578	.4590	.4601	.4613	.4624	.4636
.60	.4648	.4659	.4671	.4682	.4694	.4706	.4718	.4729	.4741	.4752
.61	.4764	.4776	.4788	.4799	.4811	.4823	.4835	.4847	.4858	.4870
.62	.4882	.4894	.4906	.4917	.4929	.4941	.4953	.4965	.4977	.4988
.63	.5000	.5012	.5024	.5036	.5048	.5060	.5072	.5084	.5096	.5108
.64	.5120	.5132	.5144	.5156	.5168	.5180	.5192	.5204	.5216	.5228
.65	.5240	.5253	.5265	.5277	.5289	.5301	.5313	.5325	.5338	.5350
.66	.5362	.5374	.5386	.5399	.5411	.5423	.5435	.5447	.5460	.5472
.67	.5484	.5496	.5509	.5521	.5533	.5546	.5558	.5570	.5583	.5595
.68	.5607	.5620	.5632	.5645	.5657	.5669	.5682	.5694	.5707	.5719
.69	.5732	.5744	.5757	.5769	.5782	.5794	.5806	.5819	.5832	.5844
.70	.5857	.5869	.5882	.5894	.5907	.5919	.5932	.5945	.5957	.5970
.71	.5983	.5995	.6008	.6020	.6033	.6046	.6059	.6071	.6084	.6097
.72	.6109	.6122	.6135	.6148	.6160	.6173	.6186	.6199	.6212	.6224
.73	.6237	.6250	.6263	.6276	.6288	.6301	.6314	.6327	.6340	.6353
.74	.6366	.6379	.6392	.6404	.6417	.6430	.6443	.6456	.6469	.6482
.75	.6495	.6508	.6521	.6534	.6547	.6560	.6573	.6586	.6599	.6612
.76	.6626	.6639	.6652	.6665	.6678	.6691	.6704	.6717	.6730	.6744
.77	.6757	.6770	.6783	.6796	.6809	.6823	.6836	.6849	.6862	.6876
.78	.6889	.6902	.6915	.6929	.6942	.6955	.6968	.6982	.6995	.7008
.79	.7022	.7035	.7048	.7062	.7075	.7088	.7102	.7115	.7129	.7142
.80	.7155	.7169	.7182	.7196	.7209	.7223	.7236	.7250	.7263	.7276
.81	.7290	.7303	.7317	.7331	.7344	.7358	.7371	.7385	.7398	.7412
.82	.7425	.7439	.7453	.7466	.7480	.7493	.7507	.7521	.7534	.7548
.83	.7562	.7575	.7589	.7603	.7616	.7630	.7644	.7658	.7671	.7685
.84	.7699	.7712	.7726	.7740	.7754	.7768	.7781	.7795	.7809	.7823
.85	.7837	.7850	.7864	.7878	.7892	.7906	.7920	.7934	.7947	.7961
.86	.7975	.7989	.8003	.8017	.8031	.8045	.8059	.8073	.8087	.8101
.87	.8115	.8129	.8143	.8157	.8171	.8185	.8199	.8213	.8227	.8241
.88	.8255	.8269	.8283	.8297	.8311	.8326	.8340	.8354	.8368	.8382
.89	.8396	.8410	.8425	.8439	.8453	.8467	.8481	.8495	.8510	.8524
.90	.8538	.8552	.8567	.8581	.8595	.8609	.8624	.8638	.8652	.8667
.91	.8681	.8695	.8709	.8724	.8738	.8752	.8767	.8781	.8796	.8810
.92	.8824	.8839	.8853	.8868	.8882	.8896	.8911	.8925	.8940	.8954
.93	.8969	.8983	.8998	.9012	.9026	.9041	.9056	.9070	.9085	.9099
.94	.9114	.9128	.9143	.9157	.9172	.9186	.9201	.9216	.9230	.9245
.95	.9259	.9274	.9289	.9303	.9318	.9333	.9347	.9362	.9377	.9391
.96	.9406	.9421	.9435	.9450	.9465	.9480	.9494	.9509	.9524	.9539
.97	.9553	.9568	.9583	.9598	.9613	.9627	.9642	.9657	.9672	.9687
.98	.9702	.9716	.9731	.9746	.9761	.9776	.9791	.9806	.9821	.9835
.99	.9850	.9865	.9880	.9895	.9910	.9925	.9940	.9955	.9970	.9985

Table 5-1. Three-halves Powers of Numbers (*Continued*)

No.	.000	.001	.002	.003	.004	.005	.006	.007	.008	.009
1.00	1.0000	1.0015	1.0030	1.0045	1.0060	1.0075	1.0090	1.0105	1.0120	1.0135
1.01	1.0150	1.0165	1.0181	1.0196	1.0211	1.0226	1.0241	1.0256	1.0271	1.0286
1.02	1.0301	1.0317	1.0332	1.0347	1.0362	1.0377	1.0393	1.0408	1.0423	1.0438
1.03	1.0453	1.0468	1.0484	1.0499	1.0514	1.0530	1.0545	1.0560	1.0575	1.0591
1.04	1.0606	1.0621	1.0637	1.0652	1.0667	1.0683	1.0698	1.0713	1.0728	1.0744
1.05	1.0759	1.0775	1.0790	1.0805	1.0821	1.0836	1.0852	1.0867	1.0882	1.0898
1.06	1.0913	1.0929	1.0944	1.0960	1.0975	1.0991	1.1006	1.1022	1.1037	1.1053
1.07	1.1068	1.1084	1.1098	1.1114	1.1129	1.1146	1.1161	1.1177	1.1193	1.1208
1.08	1.1224	1.1239	1.1255	1.1271	1.1286	1.1302	1.1317	1.1333	1.1349	1.1364
1.09	1.1380	1.1396	1.1411	1.1427	1.1443	1.1458	1.1474	1.1490	1.1505	1.1521
1.10	1.1537	1.1553	1.1568	1.1584	1.1600	1.1616	1.1631	1.1647	1.1663	1.1679
1.11	1.1695	1.1710	1.1726	1.1742	1.1758	1.1774	1.1789	1.1805	1.1821	1.1837
1.12	1.1853	1.1869	1.1885	1.1901	1.1917	1.1932	1.1948	1.1964	1.1980	1.1996
1.13	1.2012	1.2028	1.2044	1.2060	1.2076	1.2092	1.2108	1.2124	1.2140	1.2156
1.14	1.2172	1.2188	1.2204	1.2220	1.2236	1.2252	1.2268	1.2284	1.2300	1.2316
1.15	1.2332	1.2349	1.2365	1.2381	1.2397	1.2413	1.2429	1.2445	1.2461	1.2477
1.16	1.2494	1.2510	1.2526	1.2542	1.2558	1.2574	1.2591	1.2607	1.2623	1.2639
1.17	1.2655	1.2672	1.2688	1.2704	1.2720	1.2737	1.2753	1.2769	1.2786	1.2802
1.18	1.2818	1.2834	1.2851	1.2867	1.2883	1.2900	1.2916	1.2932	1.2948	1.2965
1.19	1.2981	1.2998	1.3014	1.3030	1.3047	1.3063	1.3080	1.3096	1.3112	1.3129
1.20	1.3145	1.3162	1.3178	1.3195	1.3211	1.3228	1.3244	1.3261	1.3277	1.3294
1.21	1.3310	1.3327	1.3343	1.3360	1.3376	1.3393	1.3409	1.3426	1.3442	1.3459
1.22	1.3475	1.3492	1.3509	1.3525	1.3542	1.3558	1.3575	1.3591	1.3608	1.3625
1.23	1.3641	1.3658	1.3675	1.3691	1.3708	1.3725	1.3741	1.3758	1.3775	1.3791
1.24	1.3808	1.3825	1.3841	1.3858	1.3875	1.3892	1.3908	1.3925	1.3942	1.3959
1.25	1.3975	1.3992	1.4009	1.4026	1.4043	1.4059	1.4076	1.4093	1.4110	1.4127
1.26	1.4143	1.4160	1.4177	1.4194	1.4211	1.4228	1.4245	1.4262	1.4278	1.4295
1.27	1.4312	1.4329	1.4346	1.4363	1.4380	1.4397	1.4414	1.4431	1.4448	1.4465
1.28	1.4482	1.4499	1.4516	1.4533	1.4550	1.4567	1.4584	1.4601	1.4618	1.4635
1.29	1.4652	1.4669	1.4686	1.4703	1.4720	1.4737	1.4754	1.4771	1.4788	1.4805
1.30	1.4822	1.4839	1.4856	1.4874	1.4891	1.4908	1.4925	1.4942	1.4959	1.4976
1.31	1.4994	1.5011	1.5028	1.5045	1.5062	1.5080	1.5097	1.5114	1.5131	1.5148
1.32	1.5166	1.5183	1.5200	1.5217	1.5235	1.5252	1.5269	1.5286	1.5304	1.5321
1.33	1.5338	1.5356	1.5373	1.5390	1.5408	1.5425	1.5442	1.5460	1.5477	1.5494
1.34	1.5512	1.5529	1.5546	1.5564	1.5581	1.5599	1.5616	1.5633	1.5651	1.5668
1.35	1.5686	1.5703	1.5720	1.5738	1.5755	1.5773	1.5790	1.5808	1.5825	1.5843
1.36	1.5860	1.5878	1.5895	1.5913	1.5930	1.5948	1.5965	1.5983	1.6000	1.6018
1.37	1.6035	1.6053	1.6071	1.6088	1.6106	1.6123	1.6141	1.6158	1.6176	1.6194
1.38	1.6211	1.6229	1.6247	1.6264	1.6282	1.6300	1.6317	1.6335	1.6353	1.6370
1.39	1.6388	1.6406	1.6423	1.6441	1.6459	1.6476	1.6494	1.6512	1.6530	1.6547
1.40	1.6565	1.6583	1.6600	1.6618	1.6636	1.6654	1.6672	1.6689	1.6707	1.6725
1.41	1.6743	1.6761	1.6778	1.6796	1.6814	1.6832	1.6850	1.6868	1.6885	1.6903
1.42	1.6921	1.6939	1.6957	1.6975	1.6993	1.7011	1.7029	1.7046	1.7064	1.7082
1.43	1.7100	1.7118	1.7136	1.7154	1.7172	1.7190	1.7208	1.7226	1.7244	1.7262
1.44	1.7280	1.7298	1.7316	1.7334	1.7352	1.7370	1.7388	1.7406	1.7424	1.7442
1.45	1.7460	1.7478	1.7496	1.7515	1.7533	1.7551	1.7569	1.7587	1.7605	1.7623
1.46	1.7641	1.7659	1.7677	1.7696	1.7714	1.7732	1.7750	1.7768	1.7786	1.7805
1.47	1.7823	1.7841	1.7859	1.7877	1.7896	1.7914	1.7932	1.7950	1.7968	1.7987
1.48	1.8005	1.8023	1.8041	1.8060	1.8078	1.8096	1.8115	1.8133	1.8151	1.8169
1.49	1.8188	1.8206	1.8224	1.8243	1.8261	1.8279	1.8298	1.8316	1.8334	1.8353

Table 5-1. Three-halves Powers of Numbers (*Concluded*)

No.	.00	.01	.02	.03	.04	.05	.06	.07	.08	.09
1.5	1.837	1.856	1.874	1.892	1.911	1.930	1.948	1.967	1.986	2.005
1.6	2.024	2.043	2.062	2.081	2.100	2.120	2.139	2.158	2.178	2.197
1.7	2.216	2.236	2.256	2.276	2.295	2.315	2.335	2.355	2.375	2.395
1.8	2.415	2.435	2.455	2.476	2.496	2.516	2.537	2.557	2.578	2.598
1.9	2.619	2.640	2.660	2.681	2.702	2.723	2.744	2.765	2.786	2.807
2.0	2.828	2.850	2.871	2.892	2.914	2.935	2.957	2.978	3.000	3.022
2.1	3.043	3.065	3.087	3.109	3.131	3.153	3.174	3.197	3.219	3.241
2.2	3.263	3.285	3.308	3.330	3.352	3.375	3.398	3.420	3.443	3.465
2.3	3.488	3.511	3.534	3.557	3.580	3.602	3.626	3.649	3.672	3.695
2.4	3.718	3.741	3.765	3.788	3.811	3.835	3.858	3.882	3.906	3.929
2.5	3.953	3.977	4.000	4.024	4.048	4.072	4.096	4.120	4.144	4.168
2.6	4.192	4.217	4.241	4.265	4.290	4.314	4.338	4.363	4.387	4.412
2.7	4.437	4.461	4.486	4.511	4.536	4.560	4.585	4.610	4.635	4.660
2.8	4.685	4.710	4.736	4.761	4.786	4.811	4.837	4.862	4.888	4.913
2.9	4.938	4.964	4.990	5.015	5.041	5.067	5.093	5.118	5.144	5.170
3.0	5.196	5.222	5.248	5.274	5.300	5.327	5.353	5.379	5.405	5.432
3.1	5.458	5.484	5.511	5.538	5.564	5.591	5.617	5.644	5.671	5.698
3.2	5.724	5.751	5.778	5.805	5.832	5.859	5.886	5.913	5.940	5.968
3.3	5.995	6.022	6.049	6.077	6.104	6.132	6.159	6.186	6.214	6.242
3.4	6.269	6.297	6.325	6.352	6.380	6.408	6.436	6.464	6.492	6.520
3.5	6.548	6.576	6.604	6.632	6.660	6.689	6.717	6.745	6.774	6.802
3.6	6.830	6.859	6.888	6.916	6.945	6.973	7.002	7.031	7.060	7.088
3.7	7.117	7.146	7.175	7.204	7.233	7.262	7.291	7.320	7.349	7.378
3.8	7.408	7.437	7.466	7.496	7.525	7.554	7.584	7.613	7.643	7.672
3.9	7.702	7.732	7.761	7.791	7.821	7.850	7.880	7.910	7.940	7.970
4.0	8.000	8.030	8.060	8.090	8.120	8.150	8.181	8.211	8.241	8.272
4.1	8.302	8.332	8.363	8.393	8.424	8.454	8.485	8.515	8.546	8.577
4.2	8.607	8.638	8.669	8.700	8.731	8.762	8.793	8.824	8.855	8.886
4.3	8.917	8.948	8.979	9.010	9.041	9.073	9.104	9.135	9.167	9.198
4.4	9.230	9.261	9.292	9.324	9.356	9.387	9.419	9.451	9.482	9.514
4.5	9.546	9.578	9.610	9.642	9.674	9.706	9.738	9.770	9.802	9.834
4.6	9.866	9.898	9.930	9.963	9.995	10.03	10.06	10.09	10.12	10.16
4.7	10.19	10.22	10.25	10.29	10.32	10.35	10.39	10.42	10.45	10.48
4.8	10.52	10.55	10.58	10.62	10.65	10.68	10.71	10.75	10.78	10.81
4.9	10.85	10.88	10.91	10.95	10.98	11.01	11.05	11.08	11.11	11.15
5.0	11.18	11.21	11.25	11.28	11.31	11.35	11.38	11.42	11.45	11.48
5.1	11.52	11.55	11.59	11.62	11.65	11.69	11.72	11.76	11.79	11.82
5.2	11.86	11.89	11.93	11.96	11.99	12.03	12.06	12.10	12.13	12.17
5.3	12.20	12.24	12.27	12.31	12.34	12.37	12.41	12.44	12.48	12.51
5.4	12.55	12.58	12.62	12.65	12.69	12.72	12.76	12.79	12.83	12.86
5.5	12.90	12.93	12.97	13.00	13.04	13.07	13.11	13.15	13.18	13.22
5.6	13.25	13.29	13.32	13.36	13.39	13.43	13.47	13.50	13.54	13.57
5.7	13.61	13.64	13.68	13.72	13.75	13.79	13.82	13.86	13.90	13.93
5.8	13.97	14.00	14.04	14.08	14.11	14.15	14.19	14.22	14.26	14.29
5.9	14.33	14.37	14.40	14.44	14.48	14.51	14.55	14.59	14.62	14.66
6.0	14.70	14.73	14.77	14.81	14.84	14.88	14.92	14.95	14.99	15.03
6.1	15.07	15.10	15.14	15.18	15.21	15.25	15.29	15.33	15.36	15.40
6.2	15.44	15.48	15.51	15.55	15.59	15.62	15.66	15.70	15.74	15.78
6.3	15.81	15.85	15.89	15.93	15.96	16.00	16.04	16.08	16.12	16.15
6.4	16.19	16.23	16.27	16.30	16.34	16.38	16.42	16.46	16.50	16.53

Table 5-2. Five-halves Powers of Numbers

No.	.000	.001	.002	.003	.004	.005	.006	.007	.008	.009
.00	.0000	.0000	.0000	.0000	.0000	.0000	.0000	.0000	.0000	.0000
.01	.0000	.0000	.0000	.0000	.0000	.0000	.0000	.0000	.0000	.0000
.02	.0001	.0001	.0001	.0001	.0001	.0001	.0001	.0001	.0001	.0001
.03	.0001	.0001	.0002	.0002	.0002	.0002	.0002	.0003	.0003	.0003
.04	.0003	.0003	.0004	.0004	.0004	.0004	.0005	.0005	.0005	.0005
.05	.0006	.0006	.0006	.0006	.0007	.0007	.0007	.0008	.0008	.0008
.06	.0009	.0009	.0010	.0010	.0010	.0011	.0011	.0011	.0012	.0013
.07	.0013	.0013	.0014	.0014	.0015	.0015	.0016	.0016	.0017	.0018
.08	.0018	.0019	.0019	.0020	.0020	.0021	.0022	.0022	.0023	.0024
.09	.0024	.0025	.0026	.0026	.0027	.0028	.0029	.0029	.0030	.0031
.10	.0032	.0032	.0033	.0034	.0035	.0036	.0037	.0037	.0038	.0039
.11	.0040	.0041	.0042	.0043	.0044	.0045	.0046	.0047	.0048	.0049
.12	.0050	.0051	.0052	.0053	.0054	.0055	.0056	.0057	.0059	.0060
.13	.0061	.0062	.0063	.0065	.0066	.0067	.0068	.0069	.0071	.0072
.14	.0073	.0075	.0076	.0077	.0079	.0080	.0081	.0083	.0084	.0086
.15	.0087	.0089	.0090	.0092	.0093	.0095	.0096	.0098	.0099	.0101
.16	.0102	.0104	.0106	.0107	.0109	.0111	.0112	.0114	.0116	.0117
.17	.0119	.0121	.0123	.0124	.0126	.0128	.0130	.0132	.0134	.0136
.18	.0137	.0139	.0141	.0143	.0145	.0147	.0149	.0151	.0153	.0155
.19	.0157	.0159	.0162	.0164	.0166	.0168	.0170	.0172	.0174	.0177
.20	.0179	.0181	.0183	.0186	.0188	.0190	.0193	.0195	.0197	.0200
.21	.0202	.0205	.0207	.0209	.0212	.0214	.0217	.0219	.0222	.0224
.22	.0227	.0230	.0232	.0235	.0237	.0240	.0243	.0246	.0248	.0251
.23	.0254	.0256	.0259	.0262	.0265	.0268	.0271	.0273	.0276	.0279
.24	.0282	.0285	.0288	.0291	.0294	.0297	.0300	.0300	.0303	.0309
.25	.0312	.0316	.0319	.0322	.0325	.0328	.0332	.0335	.0338	.0341
.26	.0345	.0348	.0351	.0355	.0358	.0362	.0365	.0368	.0372	.0375
.27	.0379	.0382	.0386	.0389	.0393	.0397	.0400	.0404	.0407	.0411
.28	.0415	.0419	.0422	.0426	.0430	.0434	.0437	.0441	.0445	.0449
.29	.0453	.0457	.0461	.0465	.0469	.0473	.0477	.0481	.0485	.0489
.30	.0493	.0497	.0501	.0505	.0510	.0514	.0518	.0522	.0526	.0531
.31	.0535	.0539	.0544	.0548	.0552	.0557	.0561	.0566	.0570	.0575
.32	.0579	.0584	.0588	.0593	.0598	.0602	.0607	.0611	.0616	.0621
.33	.0626	.0630	.0635	.0640	.0645	.0650	.0654	.0659	.0664	.0669
.34	.0674	.0679	.0684	.0689	.0694	.0699	.0704	.0709	.0714	.0720
.35	.0725	.0730	.0735	.0740	.0746	.0751	.0756	.0762	.0767	.0772
.36	.0778	.0783	.0788	.0794	.0799	.0805	.0810	.0816	.0822	.0827
.37	.0833	.0838	.0844	.0850	.0855	.0861	.0867	.0873	.0878	.0884
.38	.0890	.0896	.0902	.0908	.0914	.0920	.0926	.0932	.0938	.0944
.39	.0950	.0956	.0962	.0968	.0974	.0981	.0987	.0993	.0999	.1006
.40	.1012	.1018	.1025	.1031	.1037	.1044	.1050	.1057	.1063	.1070
.41	.1076	.1083	.1090	.1096	.1103	.1109	.1116	.1123	.1130	.1136
.42	.1143	.1150	.1157	.1164	.1171	.1178	.1184	.1191	.1198	.1205
.43	.1212	.1220	.1227	.1234	.1241	.1248	.1255	.1262	.1270	.1277
.44	.1284	.1292	.1299	.1306	.1314	.1321	.1328	.1336	.1343	.1351
.45	.1358	.1366	.1374	.1381	.1389	.1396	.1404	.1412	.1420	.1427
.46	.1435	.1443	.1451	.1459	.1467	.1474	.1482	.1490	.1498	.1506
.47	.1514	.1522	.1531	.1539	.1547	.1555	.1563	.1571	.1580	.1588
.48	.1596	.1605	.1613	.1621	.1630	.1638	.1647	.1655	.1664	.1672
.49	.1681	.1689	.1698	.1707	.1715	.1724	.1733	.1741	.1750	.1759

Table 5-2. Five-halves Powers of Numbers (*Continued*)

No.	.000	.001	.002	.003	.004	.005	.006	.007	.008	.009
.50	.1768	.1777	.1785	.1794	.1803	.1812	.1821	.1830	.1839	.1848
.51	.1857	.1867	.1876	.1885	.1894	.1903	.1913	.1922	.1931	.1941
.52	.1950	.1959	.1969	.1978	.1988	.1997	.2007	.2016	.2026	.2035
.53	.2045	.2055	.2064	.2074	.2084	.2094	.2103	.2113	.2123	.2133
.54	.2143	.2153	.2163	.2173	.2183	.2193	.2203	.2213	.2223	.2233
.55	.2243	.2254	.2264	.2274	.2284	.2295	.2305	.2315	.2326	.2336
.56	.2347	.2357	.2368	.2378	.2389	.2400	.2410	.2421	.2431	.2442
.57	.2453	.2464	.2475	.2485	.2496	.2507	.2518	.2529	.2540	.2551
.58	.2562	.2573	.2584	.2595	.2606	.2618	.2629	.2640	.2651	.2662
.59	.2674	.2685	.2697	.2708	.2719	.2731	.2742	.2754	.2765	.2777
.60	.2789	.2800	.2812	.2824	.2835	.2847	.2859	.2871	.2882	.2894
.61	.2906	.2918	.2930	.2942	.2954	.2966	.2978	.2990	.3002	.3015
.62	.3027	.3039	.3051	.3064	.3076	.3088	.3101	.3113	.3125	.3138
.63	.3150	.3163	.3175	.3188	.3201	.3213	.3226	.3239	.3251	.3264
.64	.3277	.3290	.3302	.3315	.3328	.3341	.3354	.3367	.3380	.3393
.65	.3406	.3419	.3433	.3446	.3459	.3472	.3485	.3499	.3512	.3525
.66	.3539	.3552	.3566	.3579	.3593	.3606	.3620	.3633	.3647	.3661
.67	.3674	.3688	.3702	.3716	.3729	.3743	.3757	.3771	.3785	.3799
.68	.3813	.3827	.3841	.3855	.3869	.3884	.3898	.3912	.3926	.3940
.69	.3955	.3969	.3984	.3998	.4012	.4027	.4041	.4056	.4070	.4085
.70	.4100	.4114	.4129	.4144	.4158	.4173	.4188	.4203	.4218	.4233
.71	.4248	.4263	.4278	.4293	.4308	.4323	.4338	.4353	.4368	.4384
.72	.4399	.4414	.4429	.4445	.4460	.4476	.4491	.4506	.4522	.4538
.73	.4553	.4569	.4584	.4600	.4616	.4631	.4647	.4663	.4679	.4695
.74	.4711	.4727	.4743	.4759	.4775	.4791	.4807	.4823	.4839	.4855
.75	.4871	.4888	.4904	.4920	.4937	.4953	.4969	.4986	.5002	.5019
.76	.5035	.5052	.5069	.5085	.5102	.5119	.5135	.5152	.5169	.5186
.77	.5203	.5220	.5237	.5254	.5271	.5288	.5305	.5322	.5339	.5356
.78	.5373	.5390	.5408	.5425	.5442	.5460	.5477	.5495	.5512	.5530
.79	.5547	.5565	.5582	.5600	.5618	.5635	.5653	.5671	.5689	.5706
.80	.5724	.5742	.5760	.5778	.5796	.5814	.5832	.5850	.5869	.5887
.81	.5905	.5923	.5941	.5960	.5978	.5996	.6015	.6033	.6052	.6070
.82	.6089	.6107	.6126	.6145	.6163	.6182	.6201	.6220	.6238	.6257
.83	.6276	.6295	.6314	.6333	.6352	.6371	.6390	.6409	.6429	.6448
.84	.6467	.6486	.6505	.6525	.6544	.6564	.6583	.6603	.6622	.6642
.85	.6661	.6681	.6700	.6720	.6740	.6760	.6779	.6799	.6819	.6839
.86	.6859	.6879	.6899	.6919	.6939	.6959	.6979	.6999	.7019	.7040
.87	.7060	.7080	.7101	.7121	.7141	.7162	.7182	.7203	.7223	.7244
.88	.7265	.7285	.7306	.7327	.7347	.7368	.7389	.7410	.7431	.7452
.89	.7473	.7494	.7515	.7536	.7557	.7578	.7599	.7620	.7642	.7663
.90	.7684	.7706	.7727	.7749	.7770	.7792	.7813	.7835	.7856	.7878
.91	.7900	.7921	.7943	.7965	.7987	.8009	.8030	.8052	.8074	.8096
.92	.8118	.8140	.8163	.8185	.8207	.8229	.8251	.8274	.8296	.8318
.93	.8341	.8363	.8386	.8408	.8431	.8453	.8476	.8499	.8521	.8544
.94	.8567	.8590	.8612	.8635	.8658	.8681	.8704	.8727	.8750	.8773
.95	.8796	.8820	.8843	.8866	.8889	.8913	.8936	.8959	.8983	.9006
.96	.9030	.9053	.9077	.9101	.9124	.9148	.9172	.9195	.9219	.9243
.97	.9267	.9291	.9315	.9339	.9363	.9387	.9411	.9435	.9459	.9483
.98	.9507	.9532	.9556	.9580	.9605	.9629	.9654	.9678	.9703	.9727
.99	.9752	.9777	.9801	.9826	.9851	.9875	.9900	.9925	.9950	.9975

Table 5-2. Five-halves Powers of Numbers (*Continued*)

No.	.000	.001	.002	.003	.004	.005	.006	.007	.008	.009
1.00	1.0000	1.0025	1.0050	1.0075	1.0100	1.0125	1.0151	1.0176	1.0201	1.0227
1.01	1.0252	1.0277	1.0303	1.0328	1.0354	1.0379	1.0405	1.0430	1.0456	1.0482
1.02	1.0508	1.0533	1.0559	1.0585	1.0611	1.0637	1.0663	1.0689	1.0715	1.0741
1.03	1.0767	1.0793	1.0819	1.0846	1.0872	1.0898	1.0924	1.0951	1.0977	1.1004
1.04	1.1030	1.1057	1.1083	1.1110	1.1137	1.1163	1.1190	1.1217	1.1244	1.1270
1.05	1.1297	1.1324	1.1351	1.1378	1.1405	1.1432	1.1459	1.1486	1.1514	1.1541
1.06	1.1568	1.1595	1.1623	1.1650	1.1678	1.1705	1.1733	1.1760	1.1788	1.1815
1.07	1.1843	1.1871	1.1898	1.1926	1.1954	1.1982	1.2010	1.2038	1.2066	1.2094
1.08	1.2122	1.2150	1.2178	1.2206	1.2234	1.2262	1.2291	1.2319	1.2347	1.2376
1.09	1.2404	1.2433	1.2461	1.2490	1.2518	1.2547	1.2576	1.2604	1.2633	1.2662
1.10	1.2691	1.2719	1.2748	1.2777	1.2806	1.2835	1.2864	1.2893	1.2923	1.2952
1.11	1.2981	1.3010	1.3040	1.3069	1.3098	1.3128	1.3157	1.3187	1.3216	1.3246
1.12	1.3275	1.3305	1.3335	1.3364	1.3394	1.3424	1.3454	1.3484	1.3514	1.3544
1.13	1.3574	1.3604	1.3634	1.3664	1.3694	1.3724	1.3755	1.3785	1.3815	1.3846
1.14	1.3876	1.3906	1.3937	1.3967	1.3998	1.4029	1.4059	1.4090	1.4121	1.4151
1.15	1.4182	1.4213	1.4244	1.4275	1.4306	1.4337	1.4368	1.4399	1.4430	1.4461
1.16	1.4493	1.4524	1.4555	1.4586	1.4618	1.4649	1.4681	1.4712	1.4744	1.4775
1.17	1.4807	1.4839	1.4870	1.4902	1.4934	1.4966	1.4997	1.5029	1.5061	1.5093
1.18	1.5125	1.5157	1.5190	1.5222	1.5254	1.5286	1.5318	1.5351	1.5383	1.5415
1.19	1.5448	1.5480	1.5513	1.5545	1.5578	1.5611	1.5643	1.5676	1.5709	1.5742
1.20	1.5774	1.5807	1.5840	1.5873	1.5906	1.5939	1.5972	1.6005	1.6039	1.6072
1.21	1.6105	1.6138	1.6172	1.6205	1.6239	1.6272	1.6305	1.6339	1.6373	1.6406
1.22	1.6440	1.6474	1.6507	1.6541	1.6575	1.6609	1.6643	1.6677	1.6711	1.6745
1.23	1.6779	1.6813	1.6847	1.6881	1.6916	1.6950	1.6984	1.7019	1.7053	1.7087
1.24	1.7122	1.7157	1.7191	1.7226	1.7260	1.7295	1.7330	1.7365	1.7399	1.7434
1.25	1.7469	1.7504	1.7539	1.7574	1.7609	1.7644	1.7680	1.7715	1.7750	1.7785
1.26	1.7821	1.7856	1.7892	1.7927	1.7963	1.7998	1.8034	1.8069	1.8105	1.8141
1.27	1.8176	1.8212	1.8248	1.8284	1.8320	1.8356	1.8392	1.8428	1.8464	1.8500
1.28	1.8536	1.8573	1.8609	1.8645	1.8682	1.8718	1.8754	1.8791	1.8827	1.8864
1.29	1.8901	1.8937	1.8974	1.9011	1.9047	1.9084	1.9121	1.9158	1.9195	1.9232
1.30	1.9269	1.9306	1.9343	1.9380	1.9418	1.9455	1.9492	1.9529	1.9567	1.9604
1.31	1.9642	1.9679	1.9717	1.9754	1.9792	1.9830	1.9867	1.9905	1.9943	1.9981
1.32	2.0019	2.0057	2.0095	2.0133	2.0171	2.0209	2.0247	2.0285	2.0323	2.0362
1.33	2.0400	2.0438	2.0477	2.0515	2.0554	2.0592	2.0631	2.0669	2.0708	2.0747
1.34	2.0786	2.0824	2.0863	2.0902	2.0941	2.0980	2.1019	2.1058	2.1097	2.1136
1.35	2.1176	2.1215	2.1254	2.1293	2.1333	2.1372	2.1412	2.1451	2.1491	2.1530
1.36	2.1570	2.1610	2.1649	2.1689	2.1729	2.1769	2.1809	2.1848	2.1888	2.1928
1.37	2.1969	2.2009	2.2049	2.2089	2.2129	2.2170	2.2210	2.2250	2.2291	2.2331
1.38	2.2372	2.2412	2.2453	2.2493	2.2534	2.2575	2.2616	2.2656	2.2697	2.2738
1.39	2.2779	2.2820	2.2861	2.2902	2.2943	2.2985	2.3026	2.3067	2.3108	2.3150
1.40	2.3191	2.3232	2.3274	2.3315	2.3357	2.3399	2.3440	2.3482	2.3524	2.3566
1.41	2.3607	2.3649	2.3691	2.3733	2.3775	2.3817	2.3859	2.3901	2.3944	2.3986
1.42	2.4028	2.4071	2.4113	2.4155	2.4198	2.4240	2.4283	2.4325	2.4368	2.4411
1.43	2.4453	2.4496	2.4539	2.4582	2.4625	2.4668	2.4711	2.4754	2.4797	2.4840
1.44	2.4883	2.4926	2.4970	2.5013	2.5056	2.5100	2.5143	2.5187	2.5230	2.5274
1.45	2.5317	2.5361	2.5405	2.5449	2.5492	2.5536	2.5580	2.5624	2.5668	2.5712
1.46	2.5756	2.5800	2.5845	2.5889	2.5933	2.5977	2.6022	2.6066	2.6111	2.6155
1.47	2.6200	2.6244	2.6289	2.6333	2.6378	2.6423	2.6468	2.6513	2.6557	2.6602
1.48	2.6647	2.6692	2.6737	2.6783	2.6828	2.6873	2.6918	2.6964	2.7009	2.7054
1.49	2.7100	2.7145	2.7191	2.7236	2.7282	2.7328	2.7373	2.7419	2.7465	2.7511

Table 5-2. Five-halves Powers of Numbers (*Concluded*)

No.	.000	.001	.002	.003	.004	.005	.006	.007	.008	.009
1.50	2.7557	2.7603	2.7649	2.7695	2.7741	2.7787	2.7833	2.7879	2.7926	2.7972
1.51	2.8018	2.8065	2.8111	2.8158	2.8204	2.8251	2.8297	2.8344	2.8391	2.8438
1.52	2.8485	2.8531	2.8578	2.8625	2.8672	2.8719	2.8766	2.8814	2.8861	2.8908
1.53	2.8955	2.9003	2.9050	2.9097	2.9145	2.9192	2.9240	2.9288	2.9335	2.9383
1.54	2.9431	2.9479	2.9526	2.9574	2.9622	2.9670	2.9718	2.9766	2.9814	2.9863
1.55	2.9911	2.9959	3.0007	3.0056	3.0104	3.0153	3.0201	3.0250	3.0298	3.0347
1.56	3.0396	3.0444	3.0493	3.0542	3.0591	3.0640	3.0689	3.0738	3.0787	3.0836
1.57	3.0885	3.0934	3.0984	3.1033	3.1082	3.1132	3.1181	3.1231	3.1280	3.1330
1.58	3.1379	3.1429	3.1479	3.1528	3.1578	3.1628	3.1678	3.1728	3.1778	3.1828
1.59	3.1878	3.1928	3.1978	3.2029	3.2079	3.2129	3.2180	3.2230	3.2281	3.2331
1.60	3.2382	3.2432	3.2483	3.2534	3.2584	3.2635	3.2686	3.2737	3.2788	3.2839
1.61	3.2890	3.2941	3.2992	3.3043	3.3095	3.3146	3.3197	3.3249	3.3300	3.3352
1.62	3.3403	3.3455	3.3506	3.3558	3.3610	3.3662	3.3713	3.3765	3.3817	3.3869
1.63	3.3921	3.3973	3.4025	3.4077	3.4130	3.4182	3.4234	3.4286	3.4339	3.4391
1.64	3.4444	3.4496	3.4549	3.4601	3.4654	3.4707	3.4760	3.4812	3.4865	3.4918
1.65	3.4971	3.5024	3.5077	3.5130	3.5183	3.5237	3.5290	3.5343	3.5397	3.5450
1.66	3.5503	3.5557	3.5610	3.5664	3.5718	3.5771	3.5825	3.5879	3.5933	3.5987
1.67	3.6041	3.6095	3.6149	3.6203	3.6257	3.6311	3.6365	3.6419	3.6474	3.6528
1.68	3.6582	3.6637	3.6691	3.6746	3.6801	3.6855	3.6910	3.6965	3.7020	3.7074
1.69	3.7129	3.7184	3.7239	3.7294	3.7349	3.7405	3.7460	3.7515	3.7570	3.7626
1.70	3.7681	3.7736	3.7792	3.7847	3.7903	3.7959	3.8014	3.8070	3.8126	3.8182
1.71	3.8238	3.8293	3.8349	3.8406	3.8462	3.8518	3.8574	3.8630	3.8686	3.8743
1.72	3.8799	3.8855	3.8912	3.8968	3.9025	3.9082	3.9138	3.9195	3.9252	3.9309
1.73	3.9365	3.9422	3.9479	3.9536	3.9593	3.9651	3.9708	3.9765	3.9822	3.9879
1.74	3.9937	3.9994	4.0052	4.0109	4.0167	4.0224	4.0282	4.0340	4.0397	4.0455
1.75	4.0513	4.0571	4.0629	4.0687	4.0745	4.0803	4.0861	4.0919	4.0978	4.1036
1.76	4.1094	4.1153	4.1211	4.1270	4.1328	4.1387	4.1445	4.1504	4.1563	4.1622
1.77	4.1681	4.1739	4.1798	4.1857	4.1916	4.1976	4.2035	4.2094	4.2153	4.2212
1.78	4.2272	4.2331	4.2391	4.2450	4.2510	4.2569	4.2629	4.2689	4.2748	4.2808
1.79	4.2868	4.2928	4.2988	4.3048	4.3108	4.3168	4.3228	4.3288	4.3349	4.3409
1.80	4.3469	4.3530	4.3590	4.3651	4.3711	4.3772	4.3832	4.3893	4.3954	4.4015
1.81	4.4075	4.4136	4.4197	4.4258	4.4319	4.4380	4.4442	4.4503	4.4564	4.4625
1.82	4.4687	4.4748	4.4810	4.4871	4.4933	4.4994	4.5056	4.5118	4.5179	4.5241
1.83	4.5303	4.5365	4.5427	4.5489	4.5551	4.5613	4.5675	4.5738	4.5800	4.5862
1.84	4.5925	4.5987	4.6049	4.6112	4.6175	4.6237	4.6300	4.6363	4.6425	4.6488
1.85	4.6551	4.6614	4.6677	4.6740	4.6803	4.6866	4.6929	4.6993	4.7056	4.7119
1.86	4.7183	4.7246	4.7310	4.7373	4.7437	4.7500	4.7564	4.7628	4.7692	4.7755
1.87	4.7819	4.7883	4.7947	4.8011	4.8076	4.8140	4.8204	4.8268	4.8332	4.8397
1.88	4.8461	4.8526	4.8590	4.8655	4.8719	4.8784	4.8849	4.8914	4.8978	4.9043
1.89	4.9108	4.9173	4.9238	4.9303	4.9369	4.9434	4.9499	4.9564	4.9630	4.9695
1.90	4.9760	4.9826	4.9891	4.9957	5.0023	5.0088	5.0154	5.0220	5.0286	5.0352
1.91	5.0418	5.0484	5.0550	5.0616	5.0682	5.0748	5.0815	5.0881	5.0947	5.1014
1.92	5.1080	5.1147	5.1213	5.1280	5.1347	5.1413	5.1480	5.1547	5.1614	5.1681
1.93	5.1748	5.1815	5.1882	5.1949	5.2017	5.2084	5.2151	5.2218	5.2286	5.2353
1.94	5.2421	5.2488	5.2556	5.2624	5.2692	5.2759	5.2827	5.2895	5.2963	5.3031
1.95	5.3099	5.3167	5.3235	5.3303	5.3372	5.3440	5.3508	5.3577	5.3645	5.3714
1.96	5.3782	5.3851	5.3920	5.3988	5.4057	5.4126	5.4195	5.4264	5.4333	5.4402
1.97	5.4471	5.4540	5.4609	5.4679	5.4748	5.4817	5.4887	5.4956	5.5026	5.5095
1.98	5.5165	5.5235	5.5304	5.5374	5.5444	5.5514	5.5584	5.5654	5.5724	5.5794
1.99	5.5864	5.5934	5.6005	5.6075	5.6145	5.6216	5.6286	5.6357	5.6427	5.6498

Table 5-3. Values of C in the Formula $Q = CLH^{3/2}$ for Broad-crested Weirs

Measured head in feet, H	Breadth of crest of weir in feet										
	0.50	0.75	1.00	1.50	2.00	2.50	3.00	4.00	5.00	10.00	15.00
0.2	2.80	2.75	2.69	2.62	2.54	2.48	2.44	2.38	2.34	2.49	2.68
0.4	2.92	2.80	2.72	2.64	2.61	2.60	2.58	2.54	2.50	2.56	2.70
0.6	3.08	2.89	2.75	2.64	2.61	2.60	2.68	2.69	2.70	2.70	2.70
0.8	3.30	3.04	2.85	2.68	2.60	2.60	2.67	2.68	2.68	2.69	2.64
1.0	3.32	3.14	2.98	2.75	2.66	2.64	2.65	2.67	2.68	2.68	2.63
1.2	3.32	3.20	3.08	2.86	2.70	2.65	2.64	2.67	2.66	2.69	2.64
1.4	3.32	3.26	3.20	2.92	2.77	2.68	2.64	2.65	2.65	2.67	2.64
1.6	3.32	3.29	3.28	3.07	2.89	2.75	2.68	2.66	2.65	2.64	2.63
1.8	3.32	3.32	3.31	3.07	2.88	2.74	2.68	2.66	2.65	2.64	2.63
2.0	3.32	3.31	3.30	3.03	2.85	2.76	2.72	2.68	2.65	2.64	2.63
2.5	3.32	3.32	3.31	3.28	3.07	2.89	2.81	2.72	2.67	2.64	2.63
3.0	3.32	3.32	3.32	3.32	3.20	3.05	2.92	2.73	2.66	2.64	2.63
3.5	3.32	3.32	3.32	3.32	3.32	3.19	2.97	2.76	2.68	2.64	2.63
4.0	3.32	3.32	3.32	3.32	3.32	3.32	3.07	2.79	2.70	2.64	2.63
4.5	3.32	3.32	3.32	3.32	3.32	3.32	3.32	2.88	2.74	2.64	2.63
5.0	3.32	3.32	3.32	3.32	3.32	3.32	3.32	3.07	2.79	2.64	2.63
5.5	3.32	3.32	3.32	3.32	3.32	3.32	3.32	3.32	2.88	2.64	2.63

Table 5-4. Values of C in the Formula $Q = CLH^{3/2}$ for Models of Broad-crested Weirs with Rounded Upstream Corner

Name of experimenter	Radius of curve in feet	Breadth of weir in feet, B	Height of weir in feet, P	Head in feet, H									
				0.4	0.6	0.8	1.0	1.5	2.0	2.5	3.0	4.0	5.0
Bazin	0.33	2.62	2.46	2.93	2.97	2.98	3.01	3.04					
Bazin	0.33	6.56	2.46	2.70	2.82	2.87	2.89	2.92					
U. S. Deep Waterways	0.33	2.62	4.57	....	2.77	2.80	2.83	2.92	3.00	3.08	3.17	3.34	3.50
U. S. Deep Waterways	0.33	6.56	4.56	....	....	2.83	2.83	2.83	2.82	2.82	2.82	2.82	2.81

Table 5-5. Values of C in the Formula $Q = CLH^{3/2}$ for Broad-crested Weirs with Crests Inclined Slightly Downward

(a)

Crest	Energy head = H_e								
	0.5	0.6	0.7	0.8	0.9	1.0	1.2	1.4	1.5
Level...................	2.78	2.79	2.80	2.81	2.82	2.83	2.85	2.85	2.85
Slope = 0.004...........	2.95	2.94	2.93	2.92	2.91	2.90	2.88	2.87	2.87
Slope = 0.026...........	3.07	3.06	3.05	3.04	3.03	3.02	3.00	2.99	

(b)

Slope of crest	Length of weir in feet	Head in feet, H						
		0.1	0.2	0.3	0.4	0.5	0.6	0.7
12 to 1............	3.0	2.58	2.87	2.57	2.60	2.84	2.81	2.70
18 to 1............	3.0	2.91	2.92	2.53	2.60	2.80	2.74	2.62
18 to 1............	10.0	2.52	2.68	2.73	2.80	2.90	2.80	2.68

Table 5-6. Values of C in the Formula $Q = CLH^{3/2}$ for Weirs of Triangular Cross Section with Vertical Upstream Face and Sloping Downstream Face

Slope of down-stream face	Height of weir in feet, P	Head in feet, H										
		0.2	0.3	0.4	0.5	0.6	0.7	0.8	0.9	1.0	1.2	1.5
Hor. Vert.												
1 to 1	2.46	3.88	3.85	3.85	3.85	3.85	3.85	3.85	3.85	3.85	3.85	3.85
2 to 1	2.46	3.48	3.48	3.49	3.49	3.50	3.50	3.50	3.50	3.50	3.51	3.51
2 to 1	1.64	3.56	3.47	3.47	3.51	3.54	3.57	3.58	3.58	3.58	3.59	3.57
3 to 1	1.64	....	2.90	3.11	3.22	3.26	3.33	3.37	3.40	3.40	3.41	3.41
5 to 1	2.46	....	3.08	3.06	3.05	3.05	3.07	3.09	3.12	3.13	3.13	3.13
10 to 1	2.46	....	2.82	2.83	2.84	2.86	2.89	2.90	2.91	2.91	2.92	2.93

Table 5-7. Values of C in the Formula $Q = CLH^{3/2}$, Being the
Mean and Extension of Experimental Results on Weirs of
Triangular Cross Section with Vertical Upstream Face
and Sloping Downstream Face

This table should be used only for heads above 0.7 ft.

Slope of downstream face	Value of C	Slope of downstream face	Value of C	Slope of downstream face	Value of C
Hor. Vert.		Hor. Vert.		Hor. Vert.	
1 to 1	3.85	6 to 1	3.07	12 to 1	2.86
2 to 1	3.54	7 to 1	3.02	14 to 1	2.80
3 to 1	3.35	8 to 1	2.98	16 to 1	2.76
4 to 1	3.21	9 to 1	2.94	18 to 1	2.72
5 to 1	3.13	10 to 1	2.92	20 to 1	2.69

Table 5-8. Values of C in the Formula $Q = CLH^{3/2}$ for Weirs of
Triangular Cross Section with Both Faces Inclined

For heads above 1.5 ft use the value of C given for a head of 1.5 ft.

Slope of up-stream face	Slope of down-stream face	Head in feet, H										
		0.2	0.3	0.4	0.5	0.6	0.7	0.8	0.9	1.0	1.2	1.5
Hor. Vert.	Hor. Vert.											
1 to 1	1 to 1	....	4.26	4.20	4.14	4.11	4.11	4.11	4.10	4.08	3.93	3.75
1 to 1	2 to 1	3.82	3.80	3.77	3.77	3.79	3.82	3.84	3.85	3.85	3.85	3.84
1 to 1	3 to 1	....	3.55	3.52	3.48	3.46	3.45	3.46	3.47	3.48	3.47	3.46
2 to 1	2 to 1	3.88	3.85	3.83	3.81	3.81	3.83	3.86	3.87	3.87	3.87	3.87
1 to 1	2 to 1	3.82	3.81	3.77	3.77	3.78	3.82	3.83	3.84	3.84	3.84	3.84
1 to 2	2 to 1	3.74	3.71	3.68	3.69	3.72	3.73	3.73	3.74	3.74	3.73	3.71
1 to 3	2 to 1	3.65	3.64	3.64	3.67	3.68	3.69	3.69	3.69	3.69	3.68	3.66
Vertical	2 to 1	3.56	3.47	3.47	3.51	3.54	3.57	3.58	3.58	3.58	3.59	3.57

Table 5-9.* Values of C in the Formula $Q = CLH^{3/2}$ for Weirs of Trapezoidal Cross Section with Both Faces Inclined

This table indicates that values of C increase slightly for heads above 1.5 ft

Slope of up-stream face	Slope of down-stream face	Width of crest in feet	Head in feet, H										
			0.2	0.3	0.4	0.5	0.6	0.7	0.8	0.9	1.0	1.2	1.5
Hor. Vert.	Hor. Vert.												
1 to 2	1 to 1	0.66	2.70	2.82	2.89	3.02	3.13	3.24	3.34	3.44	3.52	3.66	3.82
1 to 2	2 to 1	0.66	2.71	2.79	2.83	2.92	3.03	3.14	3.27	3.32	3.38	3.50	3.61
1 to 2	3 to 1	0.66	2.70	2.76	2.80	2.91	3.00	3.07	3.14	3.21	3.27	3.37	3.45
1 to 2	4 to 1	0.66	2.71	2.74	2.84	2.88	2.98	3.06	3.12	3.17	3.21	3.28	3.35
1 to 2	5 to 1	0.66	2.71	2.80	2.86	2.88	2.93	3.02	3.08	3.12	3.17	3.23	3.26
1 to 2	2 to 1	1.32	....	2.71	2.77	2.80	2.80	2.84	2.88	2.93	2.98	3.08	3.22
1 to 2	4 to 1	1.32	....	2.76	2.80	2.82	2.82	2.85	2.88	2.91	2.94	3.01	3.10
1 to 2	6 to 1	1.32	....	....	2.79	2.80	2.82	2.85	2.87	2.90	2.93	2.98	3.08
2 to 1	2 to 1	0.67	2.82	2.94	3.04	3.13	3.20	3.26	3.32	3.38	3.43	3.51	3.61
1 to 1	2 to 1	0.67	2.73	2.86	2.92	3.02	3.12	3.21	3.29	3.36	3.42	3.53	3.65
1 to 3	2 to 1	0.67	2.50	2.62	2.75	2.87	2.99	3.09	3.18	3.27	3.34	3.46	3.55
Vertical	2 to 1	0.67	2.55	2.58	2.66	2.77	2.90	2.99	3.09	3 18	3.26	3.39	3.51

* See also Table 5-10.

Table 5-10.* Values of C in the Formula $Q = CLH^{3/2}$ for Weirs of Trapezoidal Cross Section with Both Faces Inclined

Slope of upstream face	Slope of down-stream face	Width of crest in feet	Head in feet, H									
			1.6	1.8	2.0	2.5	3.0	3.5	4.0	4.5	5.0	5.5
Hor. Vert.	Hor. Vert.											
2 to 1	2 to 1	0.67	3.57	3.56	3.56	3.57	3.58	3.60	3.62	3.65	3.68	3.70
2 to 1	5 to 1	0.33	3.58	3.56	3.53	3.48	3.44	3.43	3.48	3.54	3.57	3.58

* See also Table 5-9.

Table 5-11. Values of C in the Formula $Q = CLH^{3/2}$ for Weirs of Trapezoidal Cross Section with the Upstream Face Inclined and the Downstream Face Vertical

Slope of upstream face	Width of crest in feet	Head in feet, H								
		1.0	1.5	2.0	2.5	3.0	3.5	4.0	4.5	5.0
Hor. Vert.										
2 to 1	0.33	3.85	3.82	3.79	3.77	3.75	3.73	3.70	3.67	3.64
2 to 1	0.66	3.41	3.57	3.65	3.70	3.72	3.72	3.73	3.73	3.73
3 to 1	0.66	....	....	3.57	3.57	3.57	3.57	3.57	3.57	3.57
4 to 1	0.66	....	....	3.48	3.48	3.48	3.48	3.48	3.48	3.48
5 to 1	0.66	....	....	3.39	3.39	3.39	3.39	3.39	3.39	3.39

Table 5-12. Values of C in the Formula $Q = CLH^{3/2}$ for Weirs of Irregular Cross Section

No. of figure	Head in feet, H									
	1.0	1.5	2.0	2.5	3.0	3.5	4.0	4.5	5.0	5.5
5-11	3.13	3.22	3.22	3.22	3.22	3.22	3.22	3.22	3.22	3.22
5-12	....	3.41	3.35	3.30	3.33	3.37	3.38	3.38	3.38	3.38
5-13	3.47	3.46	3.41	3.35	3.32	3.33	3.37	3.41	3.46	
5-14	....	....	....	3.44	3.39	3.38	3.38	3.39	3.41	
5-15	3.28	3.29	3.32	3.39	3.46	3.51	3.59	3.62	3.65	

Table 5-13. Values of C in the Formula $Q = CLH^{3/2}$ from Experiments at Cornell University

Experiments were made on models resembling existing dams (except that the last two experiments were made on actual dams).

No. of figure	Length of model in feet	Head in feet, H									
		0.5	1.0	1.5	2.0	2.5	3.0	3.5	4.0	4.5	5.0
5-16	7.94	....	3.30	3.32	3.36	3.40	3.43	3.48	3.53	3.62	3.72
5-16	15.97	3.32	3.44	3.46	3.42	3.41	3.46	3.50			
5-17	7.98	....	3.38	3.46	3.51	3.55	3.58	3.62	3.68	3.74	3.83
5-17	15.97	3.22	3.48	3.61	3.67	3.70	3.72				
5-18	15.97	3.15	3.45	3.64	3.75	3.82	3.87	3.88			
5-19	15.97	3.23	3.34	3.43	3.52	3.59	3.64				
5-20	15.97	3.18	3.30	3.37	3.42	3.46	3.49	3.52	3.54		
5-21	15.97	3.28	3.50	3.54	3.52	3.36	3.31	3.30			
5-22	15.97	3.53	3.54	3.55	3.50	3.35	3.27	3.25	3.25		
5-23	15.93	3.13	3.14	3.10	3.14	3.20	3.26	3.31	3.37		
5-24	....	3.09	3.11	3.33							
5-25	....	....	3.80								

Table 5-14. Errors in Weir Discharge Resulting from Errors in Measurement of Head

Discharge in second-feet Q	Error in head in feet	Weir 1 ft. long		Weir 2 ft. long		Weir 5 ft. long		Weir 10 ft. long		Right-angled V-notch wier	
		Head	Per cent. error in Q	Head	Per cent. error in Q	Head	Per cent. error in Q	Head	Per cent. error in Q	Head	Per cent. error in Q
0.05	0.001	0.06	2.6	0.04	4.0	0.02	8.0	0.01	12.0	**0.20**	**1.2**
	0.005		13.2		21.2		41.0		68.0		**6.1**
	0.010		26.6		43.6		85.0		144.0		**12.2**
0.10	0.001	0.09	1.6	0.06	2.6	0.03	5.0	0.02	8.0	**0.27**	**0.9**
	0.005		8.1		13.2		25.0		41.0		**4.6**
	0.010		16.4		26.6		51.5		85.0		**9.1**
0.50	0.001	**0.27**	**0.5**	0.17	0.9	0.09	1.6	0.06	2.6	**0.52**	**0.5**
	0.005		**2.7**		4.3		8.1		13.2		**2.4**
	0.010		**5.5**		8.7		16.4		26.6		**4.8**
	0.050		**27.3**		45.7		89.5				**23.8**
1.00	0.001	**0.44**	0.3	**0.27**	**0.5**	0.15	1.0	0.09	1.6	**0.69**	**0.4**
	0.005		1.7		**2.7**		5.0		8.1		**1.8**
	0.010		3.4		**5.5**		10.1		16.4		**3.6**
	0.050		17.0		**27.3**		53.6		89.5		**18.0**
2.50	0.001	**0.82**	0.2	**0.51**	0.3	**0.27**	0.5	0.17	0.9	**1.00**	**0.3**
	0.005		0.9		**1.5**		**2.7**		4.3		**1.2**
	0.010		1.8		**3.0**		**5.5**		8.7		**2.5**
	0.050		9.1		**14.7**		**27.3**		45.7		**12.4**
5.00	0.001	**1.32**	0.1	**0.82**	0.2	**0.44**	0.3	**0.27**	**0.5**	**1.32**	**0.2**
	0.005		0.6		0.9		**1.7**		**2.7**		**0.9**
	0.010		1.1		1.8		**3.4**		**5.5**		**1.9**
	0.050		5.6		9.1		**17.0**		**27.3**		**9.3**
10.00	0.001	**2.11**	0.1	**1.32**	0.1	**0.71**	0.2	**0.44**	**0.3**	**1.75**	**0.1**
	0.005		0.4		0.6		**1.1**		**1.7**		**0.7**
	0.010		0.7		1.1		**2.1**		**3.4**		**1.5**
	0.050		3.5		5.6		**10.6**		**17.0**		**7.3**
25.00	0.001	**3.93**	0.1	**2.45**	0.1	**1.32**	0.1	**0.82**	**0.2**	**2.53**	0.1
	0.005		0.2		0.3		**0.6**		**0.9**		0.5
	0.010		0.4		0.6		**1.1**		**1.8**		1.0
	0.050		1.8		3.0		**5.6**		**9.1**		5.0

SECTION 6

PIPES

As commonly understood in hydraulics, a pipe is any closed conduit which carries water under pressure. Usually pipes are of circular cross section. Closed conduits which normally do not flow full are generally classed as open channels. Sewers and drainage tile come under this classification.

Since the factors affecting losses of head in conduits are independent of pressure, the same laws apply to the flow of water in both pipes and open channels.

Formulas for loss of head due to friction may involve the hydraulic radius r, which is the area divided by the wetted perimeter. For circular conduits flowing full, $r = d/4$, d being the diameter. It has usually been found more convenient to write d directly into formulas for circular conduits than to use r and later substitute its value in terms of d. For this reason the common practice is to express open-channel formulas as functions of r and pipe formulas as functions of d. For convenience in tabulating formulas and arranging tables, all matter pertaining to conduits flowing full is included in this section and all matter pertaining to conduits flowing partially full is included in the following section on open channels. The word *pipe* as here used, therefore, includes all types of conduits flowing full.

The following symbols will be used in this section:

l = length of pipe, ft
d = diameter of pipe, ft
a = area of cross section of stream, sq ft
p = wetted perimeter of pipe, ft
$r = a/p$ = hydraulic radius ($d/4$ for round pipe flowing full)
V = average velocity, ft per sec

$Q = aV$ = discharge, sec-ft
h = energy loss due to friction in l ft of pipe, ft-lb per lb
$s = h/l$ = energy loss per foot of pipe
f, n, C = friction-loss coefficients
h_1, h_2, h_3, etc. = minor losses in pipes, ft-lb per lb
K_1, K_2, K_3, etc. = minor loss coefficients
μ = viscosity, slugs per ft-sec or equivalent units, lb-sec per sq ft (p. 1-2)
ρ = density, slugs per cu ft (p. 1-2)
$\nu = \mu/\rho$ = kinematic viscosity, sq ft per sec (p. 1-3)
p = pressure intensity, lb per sq ft
w = unit weight, lb per cu ft
g = gravitational acceleration, ft per sec per sec
ϵ = magnitude of wall roughness, ft

Fundamental Principles

Problems which involve steady flow in pipes require the application of the continuity and the energy principles which

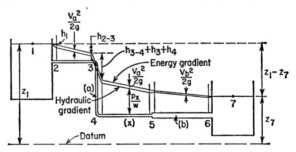

FIG. 6-1. Pipe system.

were developed in Sec. 3. The determination of forces on pipe bends or nozzles using the momentum principle was discussed in Sec. 3, page 3-13. The energy-loss term in the Bernoulli equation becomes of primary importance in pipe problems as distinct from orifices and weirs in which energy losses were shown to be relatively small. The application of the basic principles, discussed in Sec. 3, to pipes will be demonstrated for the pipe systems shown in Figs. 6-1 and 6-2. Figure 6-1 shows a pipe carrying water from one reservoir to another.

The pipe diameter is uniform in pipe a from point 2 to point 5 and in pipe b from point 5 to point 6, there being an increase in diameter at point 5. The general application of the Bernoulli equation is from point 1 to point 7, as follows:

$$\alpha_1 \frac{V_1^2}{2g} + \frac{p_1}{w} + z_1 = \alpha_7 \frac{V_7^2}{2g} + \frac{p_7}{w} + z_7 + \Sigma h_l \qquad (6\text{-}1)$$

Because points 1 and 7 are in the large tanks, the kinetic-energy terms may be neglected, and because they are located in the atmosphere, the pressure terms are zero; thus Eq. (6-1) can be written as follows:

$$z_1 - z_7 = \Sigma h_l \qquad (6\text{-}2)$$

where

$$\Sigma h_l = h_2 + h_{2-3} + h_3 + h_{3-4} + h_4 + \\ h_{4-5} + h_5 + h_{5-6} + h_6 \qquad (6\text{-}3)$$

and

$$h_2 = \text{entrance loss}$$
$$h_{2-3} + h_{3-4} + h_{4-5} = \text{total friction loss in straight sections} \\ \text{of pipe } a$$
$$h_3 = h_4 = \text{loss at bends}$$
$$h_5 = \text{loss due to sudden enlargement}$$
$$h_{5-6} = \text{friction loss in pipe } b$$
$$h_6 = \text{loss at outlet}$$

Losses at entrances, bends, enlargements, and contractions and other similar local losses are called *minor losses*, as distinguished from the friction loss in the straight sections. All the energy-loss terms can be expressed in terms of the local average velocities, as will be shown later. From continuity (p. 3-4),

$$Q = a_a V_a = a_b V_b \qquad (6\text{-}4)$$

It may be seen from Eqs. (6-2) to (6-4) that a solution can be made for $z_1 - z_7$ if the discharge is known, or since all the energy losses can be expressed in terms of the velocities, the discharge can be determined if $z_1 - z_7$ and the pipe sizes are known. A numerical example based on Fig. 6-1 is shown on page 6-25.

Two lines shown in Fig. 6-1 have not been previously mentioned. The *energy gradient* is the line showing the total energy at any point in the pipe, and the *hydraulic gradient,* or *pressure gradient,* is the line showing the pressure head, or piezometric head, at any point in the pipe. Sketching these lines is often very helpful in solving pipe problems. The energy gradient must always drop as it is traced in the direction of flow, whereas the pressure gradient may rise at locations such as point 5 in Fig. 6-1, where there is a conversion of kinetic energy to potential energy. For pipes of uniform diameter the energy loss per foot of pipe is equal to the drop in pressure gradient per foot.

Once the discharge and $z_1 - z_7$ are known in the pipe system shown in Fig. 6-1, the pressure at any point in the pipe can be determined either by placing numerical values on the graph or by writing the Bernoulli equation to the desired point. For example, to obtain the pressure at point x, the Bernoulli equation would be written from 1 to x as follows:

$$\alpha_1 \frac{V_1{}^2}{2g} + \frac{p_1}{w} + z_1 = \alpha_a \frac{V_a{}^2}{2g} + \frac{p_x}{w} + z_x + \Sigma h_l \qquad (6\text{-}5)$$

Again, neglecting V_1, noting that $p_1 = 0$, and letting $\alpha_a = 1$,

$$\frac{p_x}{w} = z_1 - \left(\frac{V_a{}^2}{2g} + z_x + \Sigma h_l \right) \qquad (6\text{-}6)$$

In the above equation $z_1, V_a,$ and z_x are known. The energy-loss term for this application consists of the following losses:

$$\Sigma h_l = h_2 + h_{2-3} + h_3 + h_{3-4} + h_4 + h_{4-x} \qquad (6\text{-}7)$$

all of which have been previously defined, except h_{4-x}, which is the friction loss in pipe a for a length extending from 4 to x. This problem is solved numerically in Example 6-3.

The pipe arrangement shown in Fig. 6-2 includes a pump in the system. The Bernoulli equation written from the water surface of the supply reservoir 1 to the center of the emerging stream 6, omitting V_1, α, and p_1 as in the previous illustration, is

$$z_1 + h_p = \frac{V_6{}^2}{2g} + \frac{p_6}{w} + z_6 + \Sigma h_l \qquad (6\text{-}8)$$

In the above equation p_6 is zero and h_p is the energy supplied by the pump in foot-pounds per pound. The energy losses are

$$\Sigma h_l = h_2 + h_{2-4} + h_3 + h_{5-6}$$

which can be identified by reference to the previous illustration. In this case the gage pressure is negative in pipe a, as shown by the location of the pressure gradient in Fig. 6-2. The meaning of h_p may be further illustrated by writing the Bernoulli equation from 4 to 5, thus:

$$\frac{V_a{}^2}{2g} + \frac{p_4}{w} + z_4 + h_p = \frac{V_b{}^2}{2g} + \frac{p_5}{w} + z_5 \qquad (6\text{-}9)$$

Then

$$h_p = (z_5 - z_4) + \frac{V_b{}^2}{2g} - \frac{V_a{}^2}{2g} + \frac{p_5}{w} - \frac{p_4}{w} \qquad (6\text{-}10)$$

where p_4/w will be a negative quantity.

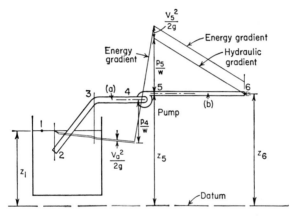

Fig. 6-2. Pipeline with pump.

Usually, in problems involving pumps, the discharge and geometric layout are known and the size of pipe and pump capacity must be determined. The solution is best made by solving for the required pump capacity for various selected pipe sizes.

Because all the terms in this form of the Bernoulli equation (see Sec. 3) have the units foot-pounds per pound, the rate at which energy E must be supplied by the pump is

$$E = Qwh_p \qquad \text{ft-lb per sec}$$

or, in terms of horsepower,

$$\text{HP} = \frac{Qwh_p}{550} \qquad (6\text{-}11)$$

Loss of Energy Due to Friction

Many investigators have sought to determine the laws governing the flow of fluids in pipes. One of the earliest expressions for energy loss in a pipe was developed by Chezy in 1775 (p. 6-14). Many other empirical formulas have been developed from test data. Most of these formulas were based on the assumption that the energy loss depends only on the velocity, the dimensions of the conduit, and the wall roughness. The work of Hagen (1839), Poiseuille (1840), and Reynolds (1883) showed that the density and viscosity of the fluid also affected the energy loss. Later, principally as the result of the work of Nikuradse (1933), it became generally recognized that the effect of roughness does not depend on the actual magnitude of the roughness, but on the ratio of the roughness size to the diameter of the pipe. Modern developments are oriented chiefly toward finding the effect of the form and spacing of roughness on energy losses.

Laminar Flow in Pipes. The laws of laminar flow in pipes were determined experimentally, independently by Hagen and

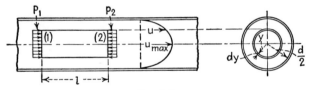

FIG. 6-3

Poiseuille. The Hagen-Poiseuille law can be developed from fundamental principles as follows. Consider the forces acting on a cylinder of fluid of length l and radius y as shown in Fig. 6-3. If steady motion exists, the force caused by the difference in pressure on the ends of the cylinder must be exactly balanced by the force resulting from the shear stress at the boundaries, as expressed by the equation

$$(p_1 - p_2)\pi y^2 = \tau 2\pi y l \qquad (6\text{-}12)$$

Simplifying and introducing the value of τ from Eq. (**1**-3), Eq. (6-12) becomes

$$(p_1 - p_2)y = -2\mu \frac{du}{dy} l$$

the minus sign being included because increments of u and y are opposite in sign, as shown in Fig. 6-3. The above equation may be solved for du and integrated as follows:

$$u = \int du = \frac{-(p_1 - p_2)y^2}{4\mu l} + C$$

The value of C may be obtained from the boundary condition that $y = d/2$ when $u = 0$. Then

$$C = \frac{(p_1 - p_2)d^2}{16\mu l}$$

and

$$u = \frac{p_1 - p_2}{4\mu l}\left(-y^2 + \frac{d^2}{4}\right) \tag{6-13}$$

This equation shows the velocity distribution for laminar flow in circular pipes to be a paraboloid of revolution. The value of u_{max} may be determined by letting $y = 0$.

$$u_{max} = \frac{(p_1 - p_2)d^2}{16\mu l} \tag{6-14}$$

The discharge is obtained by integration as follows:

$$Q = \int dQ = \int u\, dA = \int u 2\pi y\, dy$$

Substituting the value of u from Eq. (6-13),

$$Q = \frac{\pi(p_1 - p_2)}{2\mu l}\int_0^{\frac{d}{2}}\left(-y^3\, dy + \frac{d^2 y\, dy}{4}\right)$$

and

$$Q = \frac{\pi(p_1 - p_2)d^4}{128\mu l} \tag{6-15}$$

The average velocity V may be obtained from Eq. (6-15) by dividing by the area of the pipe.

$$V = \frac{(p_1 - p_2)d^2}{32\mu l} \tag{6-16}$$

It may be seen from Eqs. (6-14) and (6-16) that for laminar flow the maximum velocity is twice the average velocity. The expression for the change in piezometric head in a length l may be obtained by solving for $p_1 - p_2$ and dividing by the specific weight.

$$\frac{p_1 - p_2}{w} = h = \frac{32\mu l V}{d^2 \rho g} \tag{6-17}$$

Introducing the Reynolds number [Eq. (3-1)], the above expression becomes

$$h = \frac{64}{R} \frac{l}{d} \frac{V^2}{2g} \tag{6-18}$$

If in Eq. (6-18) the roughness coefficient f is used in place of $64/R$, the expression becomes

$$h = f \frac{l}{d} \frac{V^2}{2g} \tag{6-19}$$

which is the well-known Darcy-Weisbach[1,2] formula for flow in pipes, h being the energy loss in l ft of pipe in foot-pounds per pound. It is clear from the above that for laminar flow f is completely independent of roughness but varies only with the Reynolds number, i.e., with the relative strength of the viscous and inertial forces. The straight line shown in Fig. 6-4 is a graphical representation of the relation

$$f = \frac{64}{R} \tag{6-20}$$

The experimental work of Hagen and Poiseuille and tests by many later investigators have established the accuracy of this relationship beyond question. So well does the relation hold that the application of Eq. (6-17) to circular tubes is one of the most basic methods of determining viscosity.

The Hagen-Poiseuille law, Eq. (6-15), or the corresponding relation between f and R, Eq. (6-20), applies when R is less than 2,000. In the range of Reynolds numbers from 2,000 to 4,000, flow changes from laminar to turbulent. Values of f are uncertain in this range. If a pipeline were to be designed for flow in this range, the only safe procedure would be to assume that

[1] M. H. Darcy, "Recherches experimentales relatives au mouvement de l'eau dans les tuyaux," Mallet-Bachelier, Paris, 1857.

[2] Julius Weisbach, "Die Experimental-Hydraulik," J. G. Engelhardt, Freiberg, Germany, 1855.

flow is turbulent and to select f by extending the curves shown in Fig. 6-4.

Turbulent Flow in Pipes. When flow occurs at Reynolds numbers greater than 4,000, values of f in the Darcy-Weisbach formula [Eq. (6-19)] vary with roughness as well as with viscosity and density. Turbulent flow may be divided into three categories, namely, flow in smooth pipes, flow in the relatively rough pipes at high velocities, and flow in the transition zone between the first two categories.

For the case of flow in very smooth pipes, values of f vary with R, as shown by the lower curve of Fig. 6-4. It may be seen that this curve never becomes horizontal, which shows that the fluid properties influence the flow throughout the entire range of Reynolds numbers. Glass pipes or very smooth drawn tubing or reasonably smooth pipes having very large diameters would fall into this category.

Flow in rough pipes at large values of R is illustrated in Fig. 6-4 by the zone above and to the right of the broken line. This is called the zone of fully developed turbulence. In this zone, the f curves become horizontal, thus showing that flow is entirely independent of the fluid properties. Nikuradse[1] showed that, for pipes artificially roughened with uniform sand grains, values of f in this zone depend only on the relative roughness ϵ/d, where ϵ is the dimension of the roughness and d is the pipe diameter in the same units. He determined this by testing pipes which had been artificially roughened with sand of uniform size.

The third category of turbulent flow in pipes occurs when values of f fall in the zone between the curve for smooth pipes and the broken line in Fig. 6-4. Flow in commercial pipe usually occurs in this category. In this zone, the f curves for various values of relative roughness depart from the smooth-pipe curves at successive locations and become horizontal as they enter the zone of fully developed turbulence. It was difficult at first to apply the principle of relative roughness to commercial pipe because such a small number of experimental points extended into the zone of fully developed turbulence. This difficulty was overcome by Colebrook,[2] who developed a

[1] J. Nikuradse, "Stromungsgesetze in rauhen Rohren," *VDI-Forschungsh.* 361, 1933.

[2] C. F. Colebrook, Turbulent Flow in Pipes, with Particular Reference to the Transition Region between Smooth and Rough Pipe Laws, *J. Inst. Civil Engrs. (London)*, February, 1939.

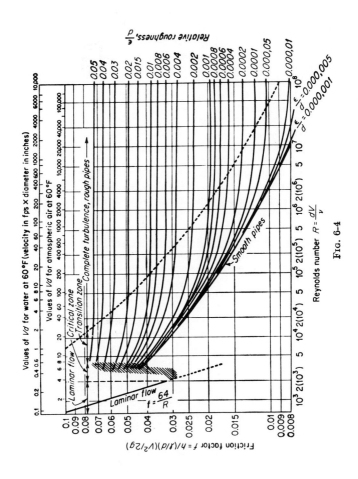

FIG. 6-4

relationship between f, ϵ/d, and R [Eq. (6-21)], which applies reasonably well to all the transition curves.

$$\frac{1}{\sqrt{f}} = -2 \log \left(\frac{\epsilon}{3.7d} + \frac{2.51}{R \sqrt{f}} \right) \tag{6-21}$$

With the aid of this equation, Colebrook[1] was able to assign roughness values to various commercial-pipe materials by comparing values of f for these pipes with Nikuradse's values for artificially roughened pipe. The broken line separating the transition zone from the zone of fully developed turbulence in Fig. 6-4 was suggested by Rouse[2]. The various curves shown in Fig. 6-4 were presented in this form by Moody.[3] Equations representing the curves in the turbulent-flow portion of Fig. 6-4, developed by Wood,[4] are presented in Sec. 13 [Eqs. (13-11) and (13-12)]. Additional values of ϵ are presented in the tabulation that follows.

It must be recognized that this method of analyzing pipe friction data has certain inherent weaknesses because it relates all types of energy dissipation caused by wall friction to that resulting from closely spaced sand grains. The turbulence mechanism near rough walls is undoubtedly affected by the longitudinal and circumferential spacing and the form of the roughness, as well as by the actual size of the roughness.[5,6] This aspect of the problem has been elucidated by Morris.[7,8] Evidence of the nonsimilarity of some types of commercial-pipe roughness and sand-grain roughness is the fact that tests sometimes show increasing values of f in the transition zone whereas

[1] *Ibid.*

[2] Hunter Rouse, Evolution of Boundary Roughness, Proceedings of the Second Hydraulics Conference, *Univ. Iowa Bull.* 27, 1943.

[3] L. F. Moody, Friction Factors for Pipe Flow, *Trans. ASME*, November, 1944.

[4] Don V. Wood, An Explicit Friction Factor Relationship, *Civil Engineering, ASCE*, December, 1966, pp. 60–61.

[5] Charles W. Harris, An Engineering Concept of Flow in Pipes, *Trans. ASCE*, vol. 115, p. 909, 1950.

[6] Victor L. Streeter and H. Chu, "Fluid Flow and Heat Transfer in Artificially Roughened Pipes," Armour Research Foundation Project 4918, Chicago, 1949.

[7] Henry M. Morris, Flow in Rough Conduits, *Trans. ASCE*, vol. 120, pp. 373–410, 1955.

[8] Henry M. Morris, Design Methods for Flow in Rough Conduits, *Trans. ASCE*, pt. 1, vol. 126, pp. 454–490, 1961.

Roughness Size for Large Pipes*

Material	Condition	Size (ϵ), ft
Concrete	Unusually rough; poor alignment at joints	0.003 −0.002
	Rough; visible form marks spalling	0.002 −0.0012
	Wood-floated or brushed surface in good condition; good joints	0.0012−0.0006
	Centrifugally cast; new; smooth; steel forms	0.0005−0.0005
	Average workmanship; smooth joints; new; very smooth; steel forms	0.0006−0.0002
	First-class workmanship; smooth joints	0.0002−0.00005
Butt-welded steel	Severe tuberculation and incrustation	0.02 −0.008
	General tuberculation	0.008 −0.0031
	Heavy brush-coated enamels and tars	0.0031−0.0012
	Light rust	0.0012−0.0005
	Hot-asphalt-dipped	0.0005−0.0002
	New smooth pipe; centrifugally applied enamels	0.0002−0.00003
Girth-riveted steel	Severe tuberculation and incrustations	0.035 −0.012
	General tuberculation	0.012 −0.0044
	Rusted	0.0044−0.0020
	New; smooth; centrifugally applied enamels	0.002 −0.0005
	Heavy brush-coated asphalts and tars	0.006 −0.003
	Hot-asphalt-dipped; brush-coated graphite	0.003 −0.001
Fully riveted steel	Severe tuberculation	0.03 −0.02
	General tuberculation	0.02 −0.007
	Fairly smooth; 3 rows longitudinal rivets	0.007 −0.0034
	Fairly smooth; 2 rows longitudinal rivets	0.005 −0.002
	Fairly smooth; 1 row longitudinal rivets	0.0034−0.001
Wood stave	Excessive growth on walls; rough projecting staves at joints	0.08 −0.001
	Used condition	0.001 −0.0009
	New; first-class construction	0.0004−0.0001
Steel†	Enamel-coated steel; 51-in. diameter	0.000016
Corrugated metal‡	Depth of corrugations ½ in. Spacing of corrugations 2⅜ in.	0.15 −0.18
Rock§	Unlined	2.0

* Values were obtained from J. N. Bradley and L. R. Thompson, Friction Factors for Large Conduits Flowing Full, by *U.S. Bur. Reclamation, Eng. Monograph* 7, 1965, except as otherwise noted.

† Maxwell F. Burke, High Velocity Tests in a Penstock, *Trans. ASCE*, vol. 120, pp. 863–896, 1955.

‡ Marvin J. Webster and Lawrence R. Metcalf, Friction Factors in Corrugated Metal Pipe, *Proc. ASCE, J. Hydraulics Div.*, September, 1959, p. 35. Value of ϵ estimated by the authors.

§ Rex Elder, Friction Factors in the Appalachia Tunnel, *Trans. ASCE*, vol. 123, pp. 1249–1274, 1958.

the Colebrook-White curves show decreasing values of f in this zone. Other tests, interpreted solely on the basis of relative roughness and the Reynolds number, are not entirely independent of the pipe diameter. The conditions mentioned above are illustrated by results obtained from corrugated-metal pipes (see Selection of Energy-loss Equation and Friction Factor, below).[1,2,3,4] The range of values of ϵ given in Fig. 6-4 and in the previous tabulation is undoubtedly due to these factors as well as to the condition of the pipe surface.

Roughness increases with age in pipes which are subject to corrosion. Ippen[5] reported one case in which observations were made on galvanized-steel pipe in which it was found that the value of ϵ was doubled within 3 years as the result of moderate conditions of use. Freeman[6] tested a number of new wrought-iron pipes and some "old, rusty" wrought-iron pipes of the same size. The roughness of his pipes was evaluated by the author, by comparison with the Nikuradse data, with the following results:

Type of Pipe	ϵ, Ft
2-in. new wrought-iron	0.00014
2-in. old rusty wrought-iron	0.003
3-in. new wrought-iron	0.00015
3-in. slightly rusty wrought-iron	0.00044
3-in. very rusty old wrought-iron	0.0031
4-in. new wrought-iron	0.00016
4-in. old rusty wrought-iron	0.0095

It may be noted that the roughness size is from twenty to sixty times larger for very old rusty pipe than for new pipe. If the relative roughness is obtained, however, and inserted in Fig. 6-4, it will be seen that the values of f for the rusty pipe are only two or three times as great as those for new pipe.

[1] L. G. Straub and H. M. Morris, Hydraulic Tests on Corrugated Metal Culvert Pipes, *St. Anthony Falls Hydraulic Lab. Tech. Paper* 5, *ser. B*, 1950.

[2] Marvin J. Webster and Laurence R. Metcalf, Friction Factors in Corrugated Metal Pipe, *Proc. ASCE, J. Hydraulics Div.*, September, 1959.

[3] Charles R. Neill, Hydraulic Roughness of Corrugated Pipe, *Proc. ASCE, J. Hydraulics Div.*, May, 1962.

[4] Jerome M. Normann and Herbert G. Bossy, Hydraulic Flow Resistance Factors for Corrugated Metal Conduits, *Federal Highway Admin.*, September, 1970.

[5] Moody, *op. cit.*, discussion by A. T. Ippen.

[6] John R. Freeman, "Flow of Water in Pipes and Pipe Fittings," ASME, New York, 1944.

Values of f for fire hose, computed from test data of the Underwriters' Laboratories, Inc., are shown in Table 6-1.

The Chezy Formula. This formula [Eq. (6-22)] was the earliest attempt to express energy loss in conduits algebraically.

$$V = c \sqrt{rs} \qquad (6\text{-}22)$$

If in this formula r is replaced by $d/4$ and s by h/l, the value of h is given by the expression

$$h = \frac{4}{c^2} \frac{l}{d} V^2 \qquad (6\text{-}23)$$

from which it can be seen that the Darcy-Weisbach formula [Eq. (6-19)] is a rearrangement of the Chezy formula, the roughness coefficients being related as follows:

$$f = \frac{8g}{c^2} \qquad (6\text{-}24)$$

From the previous discussion concerning Fig. 6-4 it may be concluded that the Chezy formula would give excellent results for flow in rough conduits at large Reynolds numbers, where the exponent of V is approximately 2. When later investigators found that this formula did not adhere to test results for smooth pipe with low velocities, other empirical formulas were devised to satisfy each particular group of tests. Only in recent years has it become generally recognized that all such tests can be unified by means of Reynolds number.

A dimensional investigation of the Chezy formula will show that the left term has the dimension L/T whereas the right side is simply $L^{1/2}$. The expression is therefore not dimensionally homogeneous and can be used in the above form only in the foot-pound-second system.

The Manning[1] Formula. Manning concluded that C in Chezy should vary with $r^{1/6}$ as follows:

$$C = \frac{1.486}{n} r^{1/6} \qquad (6\text{-}25)$$

where n is the roughness coefficient. Substitution of Eq. (6-25) in the Chezy formula [Eq. (6-22)] yields the following equation, which is in the form usually referred to as the Manning formula:

$$V = \frac{1.486}{n} r^{2/3} s^{1/2} \qquad (6\text{-}26)$$

[1] Robert Manning, Flow of Water in Open Channels and Pipes, *Trans. Inst. Civil Engrs. (Ireland)*, vol. 20, 1890.

It is obvious from the variation in values of n derived from various tests that the constant 1.486 could be written 1.49 or 1.5 with no sacrifice in accuracy. It may be noted that the exact value of the constant in the Manning equation was chosen because it is the cube root of the number of feet in one meter (3.281) and is therefore the factor required to convert to the foot-pound-second system from the metric form of the Manning formula.

For round pipes flowing full, $d/4$ may be substituted for r and the Manning formula becomes

$$V = \frac{0.590}{n} d^{2/3}s^{1/2} \qquad (6\text{-}26a)$$

A comparison of the Manning equation [Eq. (6-26)] with the Darcy-Weisbach equation [Eq. (6-19)] reveals the following relationship between n and f:

$$f = \frac{185n^2}{d^{1/3}} \qquad (6\text{-}27)$$

It is convenient to express the Manning formula, when used for pipes, in one of the following forms:

$$V = \frac{0.590}{n} d^{2/3}s^{1/2} \qquad (6\text{-}26a)$$

$$Q = \frac{0.463}{n} d^{8/3}s^{1/2} \qquad (6\text{-}26b)$$

$$h = 2.87n^2 \frac{lV^2}{d^{4/3}} \qquad (6\text{-}26c)$$

$$h = 4.66n^2 \frac{lQ^2}{d^{16/3}} \qquad (6\text{-}26d)$$

$$d = \left(\frac{2.159Qn}{s^{1/2}}\right)^{3/8} \qquad (6\text{-}26e)$$

$$d_i = \left(\frac{1{,}630Qn}{s^{1/2}}\right)^{3/8} \qquad (6\text{-}26f)$$

The solution of the Manning formula expressed in terms of the diameter in inches d_i, s, and the discharge Q [formula (6-26f)] is given in Table 6-2. It is assumed that the length of pipe is known and that the value of n has been selected. The use of this table in solving three types of problems is described:

1. *To determine d_i, s and Q being given:* Table 6-2 gives directly the diameters of pipes in inches.

2. *To determine s, d_i and Q being given:* On the page having the proper n, in the same row with the given discharge, find the diameter nearest to the given diameter. At the top of the

column will be the approximate values of s. Closer values can be obtained by interpolation.

3. *To determine Q, s and d_i being given:* On the page having the proper n, in the same column with the given s, find the diameter nearest to the given diameter. At the left end of this row will be the approximate discharge. Closer values can be obtained by interpolation.

Inasmuch as hydraulic formulas are never accurate enough to justify very close adherence to them, great exactness in interpolation is not desirable.

The values of n contained in the following table are recommended. Practically all the experimental results that have been published lie between the extremes of these values.

Values of n for Pipes, To Be Used with the Manning Formula

Kind of pipe	Variation		Use in designing	
	From	To	From	To
Clean uncoated cast-iron pipe............	0.011	0.015	0.013	0.015
Clean coated cast-iron pipe..............	0.010	0.014	0.012	0.014
Dirty or tuberculated cast-iron pipe.......	0.015	0.035		
Riveted steel pipe......................	0.013	0.017	0.015	0.017
Lock-bar and welded pipe................	0.010	0.013	0.012	0.013
Galvanized-iron pipe....................	0.012	0.017	0.015	0.017
Brass and glass pipe....................	0.009	0.013		
Wood-stave pipe.......................	0.010	0.014		
Wood-stave pipe, small diameter.........	.....	.....	0.011	0.012
Wood-stave pipe, large diameter..........	.....	.....	0.012	0.013
Concrete pipe..........................	0.010	0.017		
Concrete pipe with rough joints..........	.....	.....	0.016	0.017
Concrete pipe, "dry mix," rough forms....	.....	.....	0.015	0.016
Concrete pipe, "wet mix," steel forms.....	.....	.....	0.012	0.014
Concrete pipe, very smooth..............	.....	.....	0.011	0.012
Vitrified sewer pipe.....................	0.010	0.017	0.013	0.015
Common clay drainage tile..............	0.011	0.017	0.012	0.014
Corrugated metal ($2\frac{2}{3} \times \frac{1}{2}$).............	0.023	0.026		
Corrugated metal (3×1 and 6×1)......	0.026	0.029		
Corrugated metal (6×2 structural plate)..	0.030	0.033		
Rock, unlined..........................	0.038	0.041		
Enameled steel.........................	0.009	0.010		

The following tables will be found helpful in various solutions of the Manning formula: square roots of decimal numbers,

Table 7-17; two-thirds powers of numbers, Table 7-18; three-eighths powers of numbers, Table 7-20; areas of circles by hundredths, Table 6-4; diameters of circles in feet and inches with areas in square feet, Table 6-3. Table 6-5 gives circumferences of circles.

The Hazen-Williams Formula[1]. This formula is widely used in waterworks design. It is an empirical equation based on laboratory and field observation.

$$V = 1.318C_H r^{0.63} s^{0.54} \tag{6-28}$$

Typical values of the Hazen-Williams discharge coefficient, C_H, are given in the following table:

Type of pipe	C_H Value
Extremely smooth and straight	140
Very smooth	130
New riveted steel	110
Old riveted steel	100
Old cast iron	95
Old pipes in poor condition	60 to 80

The equation has the advantage that the coefficient C_H is not a function of Reynolds number, but has the disadvantage that it is valid only for water and is not able to account for temperature or viscosity variations.

Selection of Energy-loss Equation and Friction Factor. Only two energy-loss equations have been presented in detail, the Darcy-Weisbach equation [Eq. (6-19)] and the Manning equation [Eq. (6-26)]. Many other formulas have been used for this purpose, notably those of Hazen-Williams,[1] Tutton,[2] Unwin,[3] Scobey,[4-6] Barnes,[7] and Lea.[8] A detailed discussion of these may be found in the third edition of this Handbook.

[1] G. S. Williams and A. Hazen, Hydraulic Tables, 3d ed., rev., John Wiley & Sons, Inc., New York, 1933.

[2] C. H. Tutton, The Flow of Water in Pipes, *J. Assoc. Eng. Soc.*, vol. 23, p. 151, 1899.

[3] W. C. Unwin, "A Treatise on Hydraulics," p. 217, A. & C. Black, Ltd., London, 1907.

[4] Fred C. Scobey, The Flow of Water in Concrete Pipe, *U.S. Dept. Agr. Bull.* 852, 1920.

[5] Fred C. Scobey, The Flow of Water in Wood Stave Pipe, *U.S. Dept. Agr. Bull.* 376, 1916, rev. 1926.

[6] Fred C. Scobey, The Flow of Water in Riveted Steel and Analogous Pipe, *U.S. Dept. Agr. Bull.* 150, 1930.

[7] A. A. Barnes, "Hydraulic Flow Reviewed," Spon and Chamberlain, New York, 1916.

[8] F. C. Lea, "Hydraulics," Edward Arnold (Publishers) Ltd., London, 1909.

The Darcy-Weisbach equation, along with the concept of the variation of f with R and ϵ/d, represents a basic approach to the solution of pipe friction losses. It is dimensionally correct, its general form can be derived analytically for laminar flow (p. 6-6), and it can be used for any fluid. The Manning formula is the only one of the empirical type of energy-loss equations which is still extensively used. Numerous test results are available for the establishment of values of n. Because the Manning equation includes the hydraulic radius, it can be applied to conduits of any shape. Its principal weakness is that it can be used only for water at normal temperatures. Nevertheless, when dealing with water, results obtained with the Manning equation are undoubtedly just as accurate as those obtained from the Darcy-Weisbach equation. Indeed, because of the tendency of n to vary over a smaller range than f, there are situations in which it may be more dependable to use the Manning equation. For example, tests previously referred to [9,10] for corrugated-metal pipes resulted in values of f varying from 0.051 to 0.078, a range of 53 per cent based on the smaller value, whereas for the same tests the values of n varied from 0.0229 to 0.0248, a range of only 8 per cent based on the smaller values. Obviously, it is simpler and perhaps more accurate to use an n of 0.024 for all corrugated-metal pipes in the range of diameters and Reynolds numbers tested than to use the somewhat more cumbersome Darcy-Weisbach equation. Furthermore, extrapolation to other pipe sizes might also be more safely accomplished in this case by using the Manning equation. However, particularly for smoother pipe and large values of the Reynolds number, more dependable results can be obtained by means of the Darcy-Weisbach equation.

Although the recent developments described in Turbulent Flow in Pipes, above, have vastly improved the-understanding of the mechanics of energy dissipation in conduits, the problem is not yet fully understood, and the engineer should realize that the solution of all problems outside the laminar range must depend on the interpolation or extrapolation of experimental data determined under conditions which may have been dissimilar to that in which they will be used. For materials and pipe sizes commonly used, the curves of f and tables of n will

[9] Straub and Morris, *op. cit.*

[10] Webster and Metcalf, *op. cit.*

give good results. When unusual surfaces or very large pipe sizes are involved, and especially for very long conduits in which the energy loss becomes a vital design consideration, the literature should be searched for tests on similar conduits. The U.S. Bureau of Reclamation has presented much information on friction factors.[1] Other test results of interest have been reported by Burke[2] and Elder.[2]

The computation of energy loss will be illustrated by the following examples. Examples 13-6 and 13-7 in Sec. 13 illustrate the computations of discharge and diameter, respectively, using a digital computer.

Example 6-1. Determine the energy loss in 1,000 ft of new 24-in. concrete pipe when water at 70°F is flowing at an average velocity of 6 ft per sec (a) using the Darcy-Weisbach equation and (b) using the Manning equation.

(a) Obtaining the kinematic viscosity from Table 1-2,

$$R = \frac{dV}{\nu} = \frac{2\frac{4}{12} \times 6}{0.0000106} = 1,130,000$$

From p. 6-12, $\epsilon = 0.005$ ft. Then $\epsilon/d = 0.005/2 = 0.0025$. From Fig. 6-4, $f = 0.024$. Then, from Eq. (6-19),

$$h = f\frac{l}{d}\frac{V^2}{2g} = 0.024 \times \frac{1,000}{2} \times \frac{36}{64.4} = 6.7 \text{ ft}$$

(b) From the table on p. 6-16, $n = 0.014$. Then, from Eq. (6-26c),

$$h = \frac{2.87n^2lV^2}{d^{4/3}} = \frac{2.87(0.014)^2 \times 1,000 \times 36}{2^{4/3}} = 8.0 \text{ ft}$$

Table 6-2 may also be used to obtain this solution. First the area may be obtained from Table 6-3; then the discharge is obtained as follows:

$$Q = aV = 3.14 \times 6 = 18.85 \text{ ft}^3/\text{s}$$

Then four-way interpolation in Table 6-2 for $n = 0.014$ gives $s = 0.008$ and $sl = 8$ ft.

Example 6-2. Determine the energy loss in 50 ft of ¼-in. tubing for a liquid having a unit weight of 61.0 lb per cu ft and

[1] J. N. Bradley and L. R. Thompson, Friction Factors for Large Conduits Flowing Full, *U.S. Bureau of Reclamation, Eng. Monograph* 7, 1960.
[2] *Op. cit.*

a viscosity of 0.03 slug per ft-sec when the velocity is 0.10 ft per sec.

$$R = \frac{dv\rho}{\mu} = \frac{\frac{1}{4} \times 0.10 \times 61.0}{12 \times 0.03 \times 32.2} = 0.131$$

and from Eqs. (6-19) and (6-20),

$$h = f\frac{l}{d}\frac{V^2}{2g} = \frac{64}{R}\frac{l}{d}\frac{V^2}{2g} = \frac{64}{0.131} \times \frac{50}{\frac{1}{4} \times \frac{1}{12}} \times \frac{(0.1)^2}{64.4} = 182 \text{ ft}$$

Minor Losses

Energy losses resulting from rapid changes in the direction or magnitude of the velocity are called minor losses, or local losses. The term minor loss is appropriate for pipelines which include long reaches of uniform straight pipe. However, for short pipes it is a misnomer, because the minor losses may be greater than the friction losses.

Minor losses are usually expressed in terms of the kinetic energy and a coefficient, as illustrated by the equation

$$h_m = K_m \frac{V^2}{2g} \tag{6-29}$$

When a change in pipe size occurs, two velocities are involved and both may be included in the expression for energy loss, as will be shown for the case of enlargements and contractions. Under certain conditions, particularly for the compound-pipe problem (see Compound Pipes), it may be convenient to express the energy loss in terms of *equivalent length* of straight pipe, l_e. If the energy-loss term for minor losses given by Eq. (6-29) is equated to the loss for a straight pipe of length l_e from Eq. (6-19),

$$K_m \frac{V^2}{2g} = f\frac{l_e}{d}\frac{V^2}{2g}$$

and

$$l_e = \frac{K_m d}{f} \tag{6-30}$$

Then the actual length of pipe can be increased by the amount l_e and the total loss will be given by Eq. (6-19).

Loss at Entrance. When water enters a pipe from a reservoir, the loss is expressed as follows:

$$h_1 = K_1 \frac{V^2}{2g} \tag{6-31}$$

Values of K_1 for various conditions are given below. Additional information on entrance losses is given in the discussion of culverts on page 4-23.

Type of entrance	K_1
Square-cornered entrance flush with wall	0.5
Rounded entrance	0.04–0.2
Inward-projecting, square-cornered entrance	0.8–0.9

Loss of Head Due to Enlargement. Borda has found that the loss in pipes due to *sudden enlargement* may be represented by the theoretical formula

$$h_2 = \frac{(V_1 - V_2)^2}{2g} \tag{6-32}$$

where h_2 is the head lost and V_1 and V_2 are the velocities in the smaller and larger pipes, respectively.

This loss was also investigated experimentally by Baer,[1] Brightmore,[2] Archer,[3] and others. These experiments indicated that Borda's formula gives values of H_2 too small for the lower velocities and smaller differences in diameter and too large for the opposite conditions. Archer deduced the formula

$$h_2 = 1.098 \frac{(V_1 - V_2)^{1.919}}{2g} = 0.01705(V_1 - V_2)^{1.919} \tag{6-33}$$

This formula appears to be as satisfactory as any yet suggested. Experiments at the University of Michigan indicated that Archer's formula holds quite accurately in the limit when $V_2 = 0$.

Table 6-6 gives values of h_2 computed by formula (6-33). Table 6-7 gives a corresponding table of K_2 for use in the formula

$$h_2 = K_2 \frac{V_1^2}{2g} \tag{6-34}$$

Losses due to gradual enlargement were investigated by Parker[4] from a study of experiments by Andres, Gibson, and others.

[1] H. Baer, *Dinglers Polytech. J.*, Mar. 23, 1907.

[2] A. W. Brightmore, *Proc. Inst. Civil Engrs.*, vol. 169, p. 323, 1906–1907.

[3] W. H. Archer, Loss of Head Due to Enlargements in Pipes, *Trans. ASCE*, vol. 76, pp. 999–1026, 1913.

[4] Philip à Morley Parker, "The Control of Water," pp. 796–800, Routledge & Kegan Paul, Ltd., London, 1925.

The formula suggested by Andres for a conical enlargement may be written

$$h_2 = f \frac{V_1{}^2 - V_2{}^2}{2g} \tag{6-35}$$

where V_1 and V_2 are velocities in smaller and larger pipes, respectively, and f is an empirical coefficient depending for its value on the angle θ (θ = double the angle between the axis of the pipe and its side).

Andres gives values of f for smaller values of θ, and Gibson for values up to 90°. Their results are not entirely concordant, but the author has used them to plot a mean curve giving the results of Andres more weight for the smaller angles. The following are results obtained in this manner:

θ	2°	3°	4°	5°	6°	7°	8°	9°	10°	11°	12°
f	.033	.036	.039	.042	.046	.050	.055	.066	.078	.090	.100

θ	15°	20°	25°	30°	35°	40°	45°	50°	60°	75°	90°
f	.16	.31	.40	.49	.55	.60	.64	.67	.72	.72	.67

Using the above values of f, Table 6-8, which gives K_2 in the formula

$$h_2 = K_2 \frac{V_1{}^2}{2g} \tag{6-34}$$

has been prepared. V_1 is the velocity in the smaller pipe.

Loss of Head Due to Contraction. Merriman[1] suggests the following formula for determining the loss of head due to sudden contraction:

$$h_3 = \left(\frac{1}{c} - 1 \right)^2 \frac{V_2{}^2}{2g} \tag{6-36}$$

where V_2 is the velocity in the smaller pipe and

$$c = 0.582 + \frac{0.0418}{1.1 - r} \tag{6-37}$$

r being the ratio of the smaller to the larger diameter.

Brightmore[2] experimented on pipes 6 in. in diameter contracted to 4 and 3 in., the mean of his results being represented

[1] Mansfield Merriman, "Treatise on Hydraulics," 10th ed., p. 183, John Wiley & Sons, Inc., New York, 1916.

[2] *Loc. cit.*

approximately by the formula

$$h_3 = \frac{0.7(V_1 - V_2)^2}{2g} \tag{6-38}$$

Parker[1] suggests that formula (6-36) be used for higher velocities when the head lost is 1 ft or more, while formula (6-38) is more reliable for smaller losses of head.

Following the above suggestion, the author computed h_3 by both formulas for various velocities and diameter ratios. The results were then plotted, and curves drawn through the points by gradually changing from results obtained by formula (6-38) for lower velocities to formula (6-36) for higher velocities. Values of h_3 taken from these curves are given in Table 6-9. Corresponding values of K_3 for determining loss of head due to sudden contraction in the formula

$$h_3 = K_3 \frac{V_2^2}{2g} \tag{6-39}$$

are given in Table 6-10.

Loss of Head Due to Gate Valves. Average values of K_g for losses at gate valves, as determined by Corp and Ruble[2], are given in the table at top of page 6-24.

Loss of Head Due to Bends. The minor loss at a bend results from a distortion of the velocity distribution, thereby causing additional shear stresses within the fluid. The normal velocity distribution may not be restored for a distance as great as 25 diameters below the bend. The bend loss is considered to be the loss in excess of the loss for an equal length of straight pipe. It is expressed in terms of kinetic energy, as shown by the equation

$$h_b = K_b \frac{V^2}{2g} \tag{6-40}$$

Tests by Beij[3] indicated that the loss is a function of the relative radius (R/d = bend radius/pipe diameter) and the roughness of the pipe. Throughout the range of his tests, for Reynolds

[1] *Loc. cit.*

[2] Corp and Ruble, Experiments on Loss of Head in Valves and Pipes of One-half to Twelve Inches Diameter, *Bull. Univ. Wis., Eng. Series*, vol. 9, no. 1, p. 59, 1922.

[3] K. H. Beij, Pressure Losses for Fluid Flow in 90° Pipe Bends, *Natl. Bur. Standards (U.S.) Research Paper* RP110, *J. Res., Natl. Bur. Standards*, vol. 21, July, 1938.

Loss of Head Due to Gate Valves

Values of K_g in $h_g = K_g \dfrac{V^2}{2g}$

Nominal diameter of valve, inches	Ratio of height d of valve opening to diameter D of full valve opening					
	⅛	¼	⅜	½	¾	1
½	450	60	22	11	2.2	1.0
¾	310	40	12	5.5	1.1	0.28
1	230	32	9.0	4.2	0.90	0.23
1½	170	23	7.2	3.3	0.75	0.18
2	140	20	6.5	3.0	0.68	0.16
4	91	16	5.6	2.6	0.55	0.14
6	74	14	5.3	2.4	0.49	0.12
8	66	13	5.2	2.3	0.47	0.10
12	56	12	5.1	2.2	0.47	0.07

numbers varying from 20,000 to 300,000, he found that the bend loss was independent of the Reynolds number. Figure 6-5 is the curve plotted by Beij through his test results. These tests were run on 4-in. pipe having a roughness such that the value of f in the Darcy-Weisbach formula varied from 0.020 to 0.025. For very smooth pipe or for very large pipes, values of K_b are smaller than those given by Fig. 6-5, and the following values of K_b are suggested:[1]

R/d	K_b
1	0.23
2	0.13
4 or larger	0.08

For very rough pipe, values of K_b are likely to be larger than those given by Fig. 6-5.

[1] A. G. Anderson and L. G. Straub, Hydraulic of Conduit Bends, *St. Anthony Falls Hydraulic Lab. Bul.* 1, December, 1948.

For bends of less than 90°, Fuller[1] gave the following approximate rules:

For loss of head due to 45° bends, use three-fourths of that due to 90° bends of the same radius.

For loss of head due to 22.5° bends, use one-half of that due to 90° of the same radius.

A curve of reduction factors for bends of less than 90° given by the U.S. Bureau of Reclamation[2] shows that the 90°-bend loss should be multiplied by 0.83 for 60° bends, by 0.70 for 45° bends, and by 0.42 for 22.5° bends.

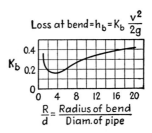

Loss at bend $= h_b = K_b \dfrac{v^2}{2g}$

$\dfrac{R}{d} = \dfrac{\text{Radius of bend}}{\text{Diam. of pipe}}$

FIG. 6-5. Energy loss in pipe bends.

The solution of a pipe problem involving minor losses is illustrated by the following example:

Example 6-3. In Fig. 6-1 pipes a and b are steel pipes having diameters of 6 and 12 in., respectively. The discharge is 3 cu ft per sec, and the fluid is water at 70°F. The radii of the bends are twice the respective pipe diameters. Pipe lengths are:

2–3	200 ft
3–4	250 ft
4–5	300 ft
5–6	300 ft

a. Determine the difference in elevations of the water surfaces in the two reservoirs $(Z_1 - Z_7)$.

Using Table 6-3,

$$V_a = 3/0.196 = 15.3 \text{ ft per sec}$$
$$V_b = 3/0.785 = 3.82 \text{ ft per sec}$$

Then

$$\frac{V_a^2}{2g} = 3.63 \text{ ft} \quad \text{and} \quad \frac{V_b^2}{2g} = 0.227 \text{ ft}$$

The various elements in the total energy loss are shown in Eq. (6-3) and identified below Eq. (6-3) on page 6-3. They will now be evaluated.

[1] W. E. Fuller, Loss of Head in Bends, *J. New Engl. Water Works Assoc.*, December, 1913.

[2] *Op. cit.*

From page 6-19: $\qquad h_2 = 0.5 \dfrac{V_a^2}{2g} = 1.8$ ft

From pages 6-9 to 6-17: $\quad h_{2-3} = f\dfrac{l}{d}\dfrac{V^2}{2g} = f\dfrac{200}{0.5} \times 3.63$

The value of viscosity is obtained from Table 1-2. Then

$$R_a = \frac{dV}{\nu} = \frac{0.5 \times 15.3}{0.0000106} = 720,000$$

From Fig. 6-4, $\epsilon = 0.00015$, and therefore

$$\frac{\epsilon}{d} = \frac{0.00015}{0.5} = 0.0003$$

Again from Fig. 6-4, $f = 0.016$. Then, from the above,

$\qquad h_{2-3} = 0.016 \times 200/0.5 \times 3.63 = 0.116 \times 200 = 23.2$ ft

and by similarity,

$$h_{3-4} = 29.0 \text{ ft} \qquad \text{and} \qquad h_{4-5} = 34.8 \text{ ft}$$

From Fig. 6-5: $\quad h_3 = h_4 = 0.2\dfrac{V_a^2}{2g} = 0.7$ ft

From Table 6-6: $\qquad h_5 = 1.9$ ft

The Reynolds number for pipe b is

$$R_b = \frac{dV}{\nu} = \frac{1 \times 3.82}{0.0000106} = 360,000$$

and from Fig. 6-4, $f = 0.0156$ and

$$h_{5-6} = 0.017 \times 300/1 \times 0.227 = 1.1 \text{ ft}$$

From Loss of Head, Due to Enlargement, above,

$$h_6 = \frac{V_b^2}{2g} = 0.2 \text{ ft}$$

Then, as shown by Eq. (6-2), the difference in the elevation of the water surfaces can be found by summation of all the losses as follows:

$Z_1 - Z_7$
$\quad = 1.8 + 23.2 + 0.7 + 29.0 + 0.7 + 34.8 + 1.9 + 1.1 + 0.2$
$\quad = 93.4$ ft

It should be noted that several of the so-called minor losses are greater than the friction loss in pipe b.

b. Find the pressure at x if the distance from 4 to x is 150 ft, $Z_1 = 200$ ft, and $Z_x = 50$ ft.

The solution of this problem is discussed on page 6-4. The summation of the energy losses shown in Eq. (6-7) can be evaluated from the values in part a of this example, except for h_{4-x}, which is

$$h_{4-x} = 0.016 \times 150/0.5 \times 3.63 = 17.4 \text{ ft}$$

Then $\Sigma h_l = 1.8 + 23.2 + 0.7 + 29.0 + 0.7 + 17.4 = 72.8$ ft. Then, from Eq. (6-6),

$$\frac{p_x}{w} = z_1 - \left(\frac{V_a{}^2}{2g} + z_x + \Sigma h_l\right)$$
$$= 200 - (3.6 + 50 + 72.8) = 73.6 \text{ ft}$$

and

$$p_x = \frac{73.6 \times 62.4}{144} = 31.9 \text{ lb per sq in.}$$

Compound Pipes

Two types of compound-pipe problems may be encountered. One type occurs in pipe networks when two or more paths are available for water flowing between two points such as 1 and 5 in Fig. 6-6. A second type, illustrated by Fig. 6-7, occurs when

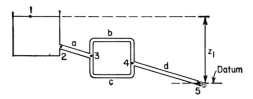

FIG. 6-6. Parallel pipes.

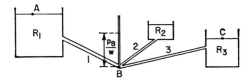

FIG. 6-7. Branching pipe system.

water can flow to or from a junction of three or more pipes from independent sources or outlets.

The first type, often called the "parallel-pipe problem," can be solved by making use of the fact that the total energy loss through the system is the same for all paths followed by the water. This will be illustrated by writing the Bernoulli equation from the water surface of the reservoir to the outlet of pipe d in Fig. 6-6, taking the datum through point 5 at the outlet of pipe d:

$$\frac{V_1^2}{2g} + \frac{p_1}{w} + z_1 = \frac{V_5^2}{2g} + \frac{p_5}{w} + z_5 + \Sigma h_l \qquad (6\text{-}41)$$

and omitting terms which are zero:

$$z_1 = \frac{V_5^2}{2g} + \Sigma h_l \qquad (6\text{-}42)$$

The expression for the energy loss may now be evaluated, first considering the path through pipe b and then that through pipe c.

$$\Sigma h_a = h_2 + h_{2-3} + h_{3(a)} + h_{3-4(a)} + h_{4(a)} + h_{4-5} \quad (6\text{-}43)$$

and

$$\Sigma h_b = h_2 + h_{2-3} + h_{3(b)} + h_{3-4(b)} + h_{4(b)} + h_{4-5} \quad (6\text{-}44)$$

where h_2, h_3, and h_4 are minor losses at the points indicated, and h_{2-3}, h_{3-4}, and h_{4-5} are friction losses. Noting from Eq. (6-42) that, because z_1 and $V_5^2/2g$ are the same no matter which path the water takes, $\Sigma h_a = \Sigma h_b$. It follows from Eqs. (6-43) and (6-44) that

$$h_{3(a)} + h_{3-4(a)} + h_{4(a)} = h_{3(b)} + h_{3-4(b)} + h_{4(b)} \quad (6\text{-}45)$$

All the terms in Eq. (6-45) can be expressed in terms of velocity, using Eq. (6-19) for the friction loss and an appropriate minor-loss equation. Then the only two unknowns will be V_b and V_c. A second equation involving continuity can then be written as follows:

$$Q_a = Q_b + Q_c = Q_d \qquad (6\text{-}46)$$

or

$$A_a V_a = A_b V_b + A_c V_c = A_d V_d \qquad (6\text{-}46a)$$

If then the total discharge is known, Eqs. (6-45) and (6-46) can be solved for the discharge in pipes b and c and the total energy drop across the system can be obtained from Eq. (6-42).

Pipe systems of the type shown in Fig. 6-7 usually require solutions by successive trials because it may not be obvious in which direction the flow occurs in one of the pipes. For example, in Fig. 6-7 it is clear that water flows out of reservoir R_1 and into R_3, but flow may be either into or out of R_2. A convenient method of starting is to assume that there is no discharge in pipe 2. This establishes the pressure head at point B as being that of the water surface in R_2. Then, by writing the Bernoulli equation from A to B and from B to C, the discharges in pipes 1 and 2 can be determined. If then $Q_1 > Q_3$, it follows that the assumed value of p_B/w must be increased, and therefore that flow must be into R_2 and

$$Q_1 = Q_2 + Q_3 \qquad (6\text{-}47)$$

If, on the other hand, $Q_1 < Q_3$, it follows that the assumed value of p_B/w must be reduced, thus causing the water to flow out of R_2 and

$$Q_1 + Q_2 = Q_3 \qquad (6\text{-}48)$$

Once the proper selection of these continuity equations has been made, the problem can be solved by assuming various pressures at B until the appropriate equation is satisfied.

Distribution Networks

Most waterline distribution networks are a complex combination of looping and branching pipelines. A direct analytical solution of pressures and flow distribution in such a network is not possible, and a trial and error procedure must be used. The most widely used procedure is that developed by Hardy Cross.[1] Other methods have also been developed to handle distribution networks, such as electronic network analyzers[2,3] and various techniques for solution on the digital

[1] Hardy Cross, Analysis of Flow in Networks of Conduits or Conductors, *Univ. of Illinois Bull.* 286, November, 1946.

[2] M. S. McIlroy, Direct Reading Electric Analyzer for Pipeline Networks, *J. Am. Water Works Assoc.*, vol. 42, April, 1950, p. 347.

[3] M. B. McPherson and J. V. Rodzidul, Water Distribution Design and the McIlroy Network Analyzer, *J. Hydraulics Div., ASCE*, vol. 84, no. HY2, April, 1958, pp. 1–15.

computer.[1-4] In this section the Hardy Cross method[5] and the nodal method[4] are briefly discussed.

Hardy Cross Solution. This method provides a procedure whereby successive corrections are systematically determined for assumed flows or pressure losses in individual pipes. The complicated network is viewed as a combination of simple circuits or loops, with each balanced in turn until compatible flow conditions exist throughout the system.

The following concepts, established in solving parallel-pipe problems (see Compound Pipes above), are applied to individual loops.

1. Continuity must be satisfied at all junctions.

2. Energy loss must be the same for all paths followed by the water, or the algebraic sum of the energy losses around any loop must be zero.

The energy losses are computed by means of one of the standard energy loss equations previously discussed, and minor losses and kinetic energy are usually neglected.

All the energy loss equations can be expressed in the following form:

$$h = kQ^n \qquad (6\text{-}49)$$

where k is a function of pipe geometry and fluid viscosity. If the Darcy-Weisbach equation Eq. (6-19) is used, $n = 2$ and $k = fl/(2g\,da^2)$. If the Manning formula Eq. (6-26) is used, $n = 2$ and $k = \ln^2/2.208r^{4/3}a^2$. If the Hazen-Williams formula Eq. (6-28) is used, $n = 1.85$ and $k = l/(1.318C_Hr^{0.63}a)^{1.85}$, where C_H is the Hazen-Williams roughness factor.

If the initial set of assumed values of discharge is designated as Q_1 and the first correction factor as ΔQ_1, then the second set of discharges is

$$Q_2 = Q_1 + \Delta Q_1 \qquad (6\text{-}50)$$

The sum of the energy losses around a loop based on the first

[1] J. H. Dillingham, Computer Analysis of Water Distribution Systems, pt. II, *Water Sewage Works*, February, 1967, pp. 43–45.

[2] M. McCormick and C. J. Bellamy, A Computer Program for the Analysis of Networks of Pipes and Pumps, *J. Institution Engineers*, Sydney, Australia, March, 1968.

[3] U. Shamir and C. D. Howard, Water Distribution Systems Analysis, *J. Hydraulics Div., ASCE*, vol. 94, no. HY1, January, 1968, pp. 219–234.

[4] V. L. Streeter, Water Hammer Analysis of Distribution Systems, *J. Hydraulics Div., ASCE*, vol. 93, no. HY5, September, 1967, pp. 185–201.

[5] Ibid.

assumptions is

$$h_1 = \Sigma k Q_1{}^n \tag{6-51}$$

and after the first correction is applied, the sum of the energy losses is

$$h_2 = \Sigma k(Q_1 + \Delta Q_1)^n \tag{6-52}$$

It is convenient to expand the right-hand term into a series and retain only the first two terms of the series as follows:

$$h_2 = \Sigma k(Q_1{}^n + n Q_1{}^{n-1} \Delta Q_1) \tag{6-53}$$

Because the algebraic sum of the losses around a loop must be zero, the right-hand terms of Eq. (6-53) can be set equal to zero and then solved for ΔQ as follows:

$$\Sigma k(Q_1{}^n + n Q_1{}^{n-1} \Delta Q_1) = 0 \tag{6-54}$$

$$\Delta Q_1 = \frac{\Sigma k Q_1{}^n}{\Sigma |k n Q_1{}^{n-1}|} \tag{6-55}$$

By use of the absolute value of the denominator in Eq. (6-55), the sign of ΔQ automatically becomes opposite to the sign of $\Sigma k Q^n$. In solving a problem, the user must adopt a sign convention for the direction of flow in the pipes around a loop. Each loop in the system is handled in the same way so that continuity is satisfied at each junction.

A step-by-step procedure is outlined below and illustrated in Example 6-4.

1. Establish the geometric configuration of the system and the coefficients for Eq. (6-49) for each pipeline in the system.

2. Assume reasonable flow rates in all pipes in such a manner as to satisfy continuity at each junction.

3. For each elementary loop in the system:

   a. Evaluate the loss in each pipe with Eq. (6-49).

   b. Find the algebraic sum of the head loss around the loop, after establishing a sign convention.

   c. Compute the sum of the quantities $n k Q_1{}^{n-1}$ from each pipe in the loop without regard to the direction.

   d. Calculate the flow adjustment for the loop from Eq. (6-55).

4. Apply step 3 to each circuit in the system, make the flow adjustments to each pipe, and repeat the process until the desired accuracy is obtained.

Example 6-4.   Determine the distribution of flow in the network of Fig. 6-8 with the inflow and outflow shown.   Also, determine the elevation of the hydraulic grade line at points 1 and 5 if the reservoir elevation is 100 ft.   There is no flow

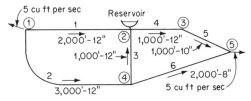

FIG. 6-8. Distribution Network.

into or out of the reservoir.   This network contains six pipes and two loops.   The Hazen-Williams formula is used, and the coefficient is assumed to be 100 in each pipe; the lengths, diameters, and values of k for each pipe are listed below.   The exponent in Eq. (6-49) is $n = 1.85$.   Flows in the counter-clockwise direction were taken as positive.

Pipe	Length, ft	Diameter, in	k	Assumed Q	ΔQ	Corrected Q
1	2,000	12	1.88	-2.5	$-.3$	-2.8
2	3,000	12	2.82	$+2.5$	$-.3$	$+2.2$
3	1,000	12	0.94	$+1.0$	$-.3$	$+0.6$
				-1.0	$+.1$	-0.6
4	1,000	12	0.94	-3.5	$+.1$	-3.4
5	1,000	10	2.29	-3.5	$+.1$	-3.4
6	2,000	8	13.51	$+1.5$	$+.1$	$+1.6$

The assumed flows with corresponding signs for the flow directions shown in Fig. 6-8 are listed in the table.   Note that the discharge in pipe 3 has a plus sign for the left-hand loop and a minus sign for the right-hand loop.   Flow corrections are computed for the left and right loops in accordance with steps 3a to 3d in the procedure outlined above.   The computed correction factors and the corrected discharges are shown in the table.   The correction factors for both loops are applied to pipe 3, and both decrease the discharge.   The process should be repeated until the pipe flows do not change significantly. In this example the flows are reasonably good after the first adjustment since it is a small system and the originally assumed flows were quite close.

Pipe no.	ΣkQ^n	ΣnkQ^{n-1}

Left loop

1	$(1.88)(2.5)^{1.85} = -10.2$	$(1.85)(1.88)(2.5)^{0.85} = 7.6$
2	$(2.82)(2.5)^{1.85} = +15.35$	$(1.85)(2.82)(2.5)^{0.85} = 11.4$
3	$(0.94)(1.0)^{1.85} = + 0.94$	$(1.85)(0.94)(1.0)^{0.85} = \underline{1.7}$
		20.7

$$\Delta Q = \frac{-(-10.2 + 15.35 + 0.94)}{20.7} = -0.3$$

Right loop

3	$(0.94)(1.0)^{1.85} = - 0.94$	$(1.85)(0.94)(1.0)^{0.85} = 1.7$
4	$(0.94)(3.5)^{1.85} = - 9.6$	$(1.85)(0.94)(3.5)^{0.85} = 5.0$
5	$(2.29)(3.5)^{1.85} = -23.3$	$(1.85)(2.29)(3.5)^{0.85} = 12.3$
6	$(13.51)(1.5)^{1.85} = +28.6$	$(1.85)(13.51)(1.5)^{0.85} = \underline{35.2}$
		54.2

$$\Delta Q = \frac{-(-0.94 - 9.6 - 23.3 + 28.6)}{54.2} = 0.1$$

The pressure level at junction 3 is $100.0 - 0.94(3.4)^{1.85} = 91.0$ ft, and at the outflow junction it is $91.0 - (2.29)(3.4)^{1.85} = 69.0$ ft. At node 1 it is $100.0 + 1.88(2.8)^{1.85} = 112.6$.

Nodal Method. In the previous example if a pump with a known head-discharge curve were located at junction 1, Fig. 6-8, and the reservoir still remains at junction 2, the method used in the example acquires another level of complexity. If the system becomes even more complex with additional connecting reservoirs, interior pumps, or valves, the previous method becomes too complicated to be useful. A junction-oriented method[1] is suggested as an alternative approach. The computations are quite lengthy for hand calculation, but the method is easily programmed for solution by digital computer.

The basic concept of the nodal method involves the evaluation of corrections to the originally assumed elevation of the hydraulic grade line at each junction in the system. Corrections are computed and applied repeatedly until the steady-state relations are satisfied throughout the system. The procedure begins with assumed values of the head at each junction in the system. Flow directions in pipes are also

[1] V. L. Streeter, Water Hammer Analysis of Distribution Systems, *J. Hydraulics Div., ASCE*, vol. 93, no. HY5, September, 1967, pp. 185–201.

indicated, but flow estimates are not needed. External boundaries must be described by a fixed flow rate, valve relationship, pump characteristic curve, fixed reservoir elevation, or other relationship. A linearized form of the pipe flow equation is then applied to each pipe at a junction, and a head correction *DH* is computed so that continuity is satisfied at the junction. Each node is treated independently, the corrections are applied, and the process is repeated. Convergence to the final result is much slower than with the Hardy Cross method. The primary motivation for using this method is to provide a capability to handle many different types of controls and boundary conditions in a system. Although the procedure is much better suited to computer solution, details are presented here along with an example.

Equation (6-49) is rewritten in the form

$$Q = Rh^{RN} \tag{6-56}$$

where $RN = 1.0/n$ and $R = 1.0/k^{RN}$. In terms of the elevations of the hydraulic grade line, this equation can be written for each pipe at a node as follows:

$$Q = R(H_j - H_i)^{RN} \tag{6-57}$$

where i indicates the node for which the equation is written, j the node at the opposite end of the pipe, and $H_j > H_i$ for flow into the node. If the initially assumed values of H were correct, the sum of the Q's would be zero at each node. Since this is not the case, a correction factor (DH) is introduced which would satisfy continuity at each node. This is done by adding DH to H_i. Then Eq. (6-57) becomes

$$Q = R[H_j - (H_i + DH)]^{RN}$$

Expanding the right-hand term and retaining only the first two terms yields

$$Q = R[(H_j - H_i)^{RN} - RN \cdot DH(H_j - H_i)^{RN-1}] \tag{6-58}$$

Equation (6-58) can be written

$$Q = A - C \cdot DH \tag{6-59}$$

where A and C have the following values:

$$A = R(H_j - H_i)^{RN} \tag{6-60}$$

$$C = R \cdot RN(H_j - H_i)^{RN-1} \tag{6-61}$$

If flow is out of the node, $H_i > H_j$ and the quantities A and C are redefined as follows:

$$A = -R(H_i - H_j)^{RN} \qquad (6\text{-}62)$$

$$C = R \cdot RN(H_i - H_j)^{RN-1} \qquad (6\text{-}63)$$

At an interior junction of two or more pipes, continuity requires that the sum of all inflows to the junction must be zero. This can be expressed

$$\Sigma A - DH\Sigma C = 0 \qquad (6\text{-}64)$$

The adjustment to the hydraulic grade line is given by

$$DH = \frac{\Sigma A}{\Sigma C} \qquad (6\text{-}65)$$

If there is a known inflow, QV_i, to the junction, Eq. (6-64) becomes

$$\Sigma A - DH\Sigma C + QV_i = 0 \qquad (6\text{-}66)$$

and

$$DH = \frac{\Sigma A + QV_i}{\Sigma C} \qquad (6\text{-}67)$$

A junction at a reservoir has a fixed elevation and therefore does not require a calculation. A pump providing flow to the system is described by its head-discharge curve. In the vicinity of the operating point a straight line

$$Q = C_1 + C_2 \, \Delta H \qquad (6\text{-}68)$$

or parabola

$$Q = C_1 + C_2 \, \Delta H + C_1 \, \Delta H^2 \qquad (6\text{-}69)$$

may be used to describe the characteristic curve, where ΔH is the head rise across the pump. If the linear Eq. (6-68) is used to describe the flow from the pump to the junction, and the suction reservoir is assumed to be at zero elevation, continuity at the junction can be expressed as follows

$$\Sigma A - DH\Sigma C + C_1 + C_2(H_i + DH) = 0 \qquad (6\text{-}70)$$

The head adjustment at the node is given by

$$DH = \frac{\Sigma A + C_1 + C_2 H}{\Sigma C - C_2} \qquad (6\text{-}71)$$

The following example illustrates one correction to each node in a simple system.

Example 6-5.   Determine the distribution of flow in the network of Fig. 6-8 with the addition of a pump to provide the inflow at junction 1.   The pump characteristics curve is shown in Fig. 6-9, and the suction reservoir is at elevation zero.   The

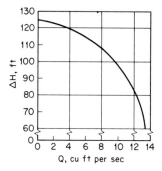

Fig. 6-9. Pump characteristic curve.

same outflow of 5 ft³/s is required at node 5, and the reservoir elevation at node 2 is 100 ft.   However, because of the specified relation between head and discharge at node 1, the input at node 1 may differ from 5 ft³/s, and inflow or outflow may be required at the reservoir.   It is assumed that this could occur without changing the elevation of the water surface.

The length and diameter of the pipes, the values of k for use in Eq. (6-49), and values of R for use in Eq. (6-56) are given in the following table.   Values of k are the same as in Example 6-4, and $RN = 1/n = 0.54$.   The node numbers with the original estimated heads are also tabulated along with the corrected heads after one iteration.   The computations for the first iteration are shown in the accompanying table.

Pipe	Length, ft	Diameter, in	k	R	Node	Estimated H, ft	Corrected H, ft
1	2,000	12	1.88	0.71	1	110	115.6
2	3,000	12	2.82	0.57	2	100	100.0
3	1,000	12	0.94	1.03	3	90	95.8
4	1,000	12	0.94	1.03	4	105	99.7
5	1,000	10	2.29	0.64	5	85	73.9
6	2,000	8	13.51	0.25			

At node 3, Eq. (6-65) is solved with values of A and C determined from Eqs. (6-60) and (6-61), respectively, for pipe 4 and from (6-62) and (6-63), respectively, for pipe 5. The same equations are used at node 4. At node 5 Eq. (6-67) is used in place of Eq. (6-63), and at node 1 Eq. (6-71) is applied. The level of the hydraulic grade line at node 2 is fixed at the elevation of the water surface (100 ft), and, therefore, no correction is needed.

Computations for First Iteration
Node 3

Pipe no.	A		C	
4	$(1.03)(10)^{0.54} =$	3.60	$\dfrac{1.03 \times 0.54(10)^{0.54}}{10}$	$= 0.194$
5	$-0.64(5)^{0.54} =$	-1.52	$\dfrac{0.64 \times 0.54(5)^{0.54}}{5}$	$= 0.164$
	ΣA	$\overline{2.08}$	$\Sigma C =$	$\overline{0.358}$

$$DH = \frac{\Sigma A}{\Sigma C} = \frac{2.08}{0.358} = 5.8$$

Node 4

2	$0.57(5)^{0.54} =$	1.36	$\dfrac{0.57 \times 0.54(5)^{0.54}}{5}$	$= 0.147$
3	$-1.03(5)^{0.54} =$	-2.46	$\dfrac{1.03 \times 0.54(5)^{0.54}}{5}$	$= 0.266$
6	$-0.25(20)^{0.54} =$	-1.28	$\dfrac{0.25 \times 0.54(20)^{0.54}}{20}$	$= 0.035$
	$A =$	$\overline{-2.38}$	$C =$	$\overline{0.448}$

$$DH = \frac{\Sigma A}{\Sigma C} = \frac{-2.38}{0.448} = -5.3$$

Node 5

5	1.52	0.164
6	1.28	0.035
	$\Sigma A = \overline{2.80}$	$\Sigma C = \overline{0.199}$

$$DH = \frac{\Sigma A + QV_5}{\Sigma C} = \frac{2.80 - 5.0}{0.199} = -11.1$$

Node 1

Pipe

	A	C
1	$-0.71(10)^{0.5} = -.246$	$\dfrac{0.71 \times 0.54(10)^{0.54}}{10} = 0.175$
2	$= -1.36$	0.147
	$\Sigma A = \overline{-3.82}$	$\Sigma C = 0.322$

$$\text{Pump Eq. (6-68):} \quad Q = 7.6,\ H = 110.0$$
$$Q = 5.8,\ H = 115.0$$
$$C_1 = 47.2,\ C_2 = -0.36$$
$$DH = \frac{-3.80 + 47.2 - 0.36(110)}{0.322 + 0.36} = \frac{3.8}{0.682} = 5.6$$

The corrected heads are shown in the table. The same procedure should be repeated until the pressure head at each node
does not change significantly. The flow in each pipe can
then be computed by use of Eq. (6-56). By use of the corrected heads in the table, the flows in pipes 1 to 6 are 3.14, 2.54,
0.54, 2.24, 3.4, and 1.45 ft^3/s. A check of continuity shows
that a balance has not been achieved. For example, the inflow
at the pump is $47.2 - 0.36 \times 115.6 = 5.6\ ft^3/s$. The outflow
at node 5 is $3.4 + 1.45 = 4.8\ ft^3/s$, and the outflow at the
reservoir is $3.14 + 0.54 - 2.24 = 1.44\ ft^3/s$, giving a total
outflow of $4.85 + 1.44 = 6.4\ ft^3/s$, which exceeds the inflow
by 0.8 ft^3/s. The second iteration reduces this inequality to
about 0.3. Several more iterations are required before continuity is satisfied at all nodes as well as in regard to the total
inflow and outflow. This same example is treated in Sec. 13,
where a computer program and solution are provided.

Table 6-1. Values of f in the Darcy-Weisbach Formula for
$2\frac{1}{2}$-in. Fire Hose

Description	Velocity in feet per second				
	4	6	10	15	20
Unlined canvas..................	.038	.038	.037	.035	.034
Rough rubber-lined cotton.........	.032	.031	.031	.030	.029
Smooth rubber-lined cotton........	.024	.023	.022	.019	.018

Table 6-2. Diameters of Pipes in Inches, from the Manning Formula, $n = 0.010$

Discharge in cubic feet per second	$s = \dfrac{h}{l} =$ drop in hydraulic gradient per foot											
	.0001	.0002	.0004	.0006	.0008	.001	.0012	.0014	.0016	.0018	.002	.003
.1	6.8	5.9	5.2	4.8	4.6	4.4	4.3	4.1	4.0	3.9	3.8	3.6
.2	8.8	7.7	6.8	6.3	5.9	5.7	5.5	5.3	5.2	5.1	5.0	4.6
.3	10.2	9.0	7.9	7.3	6.9	6.6	6.5	6.2	6.1	5.9	5.8	5.4
.4	11.4	10.0	8.8	8.1	7.7	7.4	7.1	6.9	6.8	6.6	6.5	6.0
.5	12.4	10.8	9.5	8.8	8.4	8.0	7.7	7.5	7.3	7.2	7.0	6.5
.6	13.2	11.6	10.2	9.5	9.0	8.6	8.3	8.1	7.9	7.7	7.5	7.0
.7	14.0	12.3	10.8	10.0	9.5	9.1	8.8	8.5	8.3	8.1	8.0	7.4
.8	14.7	12.9	11.4	10.5	10.0	9.6	9.2	9.0	8.8	8.6	8.4	7.8
.9	15.4	13.5	11.9	11.0	10.4	10.0	9.7	9.4	9.2	9.0	8.8	8.1
1.0	16.0	14.1	12.3	11.4	10.8	10.4	10.1	9.8	9.5	9.3	9.1	8.5
1.2	17.1	15.1	13.2	12.3	11.6	11.1	10.8	10.5	10.2	10.0	9.8	9.1
1.4	18.2	16.0	14.0	13.0	12.3	11.8	11.4	11.1	10.8	10.6	10.4	9.6
1.6	19.1	16.8	14.7	13.7	12.9	12.4	12.0	11.7	11.4	11.1	10.9	10.1
1.8	20.0	17.5	15.4	14.3	13.5	13.0	12.5	12.2	11.9	11.6	11.4	10.6
2.0	20.8	18.2	16.0	14.8	14.1	13.5	13.0	12.7	12.4	12.1	11.9	11.0
2.5	22.6	19.8	17.4	16.1	15.3	14.7	14.2	13.8	13.4	13.1	12.9	12.0
3.0	24.2	21.2	18.6	17.3	16.4	15.7	15.2	14.8	14.4	14.1	13.8	12.8
3.5	25.6	22.5	19.8	18.3	17.3	16.6	16.1	15.6	15.2	14.9	14.6	13.5
4.0	26.9	23.6	20.8	19.3	18.2	17.5	16.9	16.4	16.0	15.7	15.4	14.2
4.5	28.2	24.7	21.7	20.1	19.1	18.3	17.7	17.2	16.7	16.4	16.1	14.9
5	29.3	25.7	22.6	20.9	19.8	19.0	18.4	17.8	17.4	17.0	16.7	15.5
6	31.4	27.5	24.2	22.4	21.2	20.4	19.7	19.1	18.6	18.2	17.9	16.6
7	33.2	29.2	25.6	23.8	22.5	21.6	20.8	20.3	19.8	19.3	19.0	17.6
8	34.9	30.7	26.9	25.0	23.7	22.7	21.9	21.3	20.8	20.3	19.9	18.5
9	36.5	32.1	28.2	26.1	24.7	23.7	22.9	22.2	21.7	21.2	20.8	19.3
10	38.0	33.4	29.3	27.1	25.7	24.7	23.8	23.2	22.6	22.1	21.7	20.1
12	40.7	35.7	31.3	29.1	27.5	26.4	25.5	24.8	24.2	23.6	23.2	21.5
14	43.1	37.8	33.2	30.8	29.2	28.0	27.0	26.3	25.6	25.0	24.6	22.8
16	45.3	39.8	34.9	32.4	30.7	29.4	28.4	27.6	26.9	26.4	25.8	23.9
18	47.3	41.6	36.5	33.8	32.1	30.7	29.7	28.9	28.2	27.5	27.0	25.0
20	49.3	43.3	38.0	35.2	33.4	32.0	30.9	30.0	29.3	28.6	28.1	26.0
25	53.6	47.0	41.3	38.3	36.3	34.8	33.6	32.7	31.8	31.1	30.5	28.3
30	57.3	50.4	44.2	41.0	38.8	37.2	36.0	35.0	34.1	33.4	32.7	30.3
35	60.8	53.4	46.9	43.4	41.1	39.5	38.1	37.0	36.1	35.3	34.6	32.1
40	63.9	56.1	49.3	45.7	43.3	41.5	40.1	38.9	38.0	37.2	36.4	33.8
45	66.8	58.6	51.5	47.7	45.2	43.4	41.9	40.7	39.7	38.8	38.1	35.3
50	69.5	61.0	53.6	49.6	47.0	45.1	43.6	42.3	41.3	40.4	39.6	36.7
55	72.0	63.2	55.5	51.4	48.7	46.7	45.2	43.9	42.8	41.9	41.0	38.0
60	74.4	65.3	57.3	53.2	50.4	48.3	46.7	45.3	44.2	43.3	42.4	39.3
65	76.6	67.3	59.1	54.8	51.9	49.8	48.1	46.7	45.6	44.6	43.7	40.5
70	78.8	69.2	60.8	56.3	53.4	51.2	49.4	48.0	46.8	45.8	44.9	41.6
75	80.9	71.0	62.3	57.8	54.8	52.5	50.7	49.3	48.1	47.0	46.1	42.7
80	82.8	72.7	63.9	59.2	56.1	53.8	52.0	50.5	49.3	48.2	47.2	43.8
85	84.7	74.4	65.3	60.6	57.4	55.0	53.2	51.7	50.4	49.3	48.3	44.8
90	86.6	76.0	66.8	61.9	58.6	56.2	54.3	52.8	51.5	50.4	49.4	45.8
100	90.1	79.1	69.4	64.4	61.0	58.5	56.5	54.9	53.5	52.4	51.4	47.6
110	93.3	82.0	72.0	66.7	63.2	60.6	58.6	56.9	55.5	54.3	53.2	49.3
120	96.4	84.7	74.4	68.9	65.3	62.6	60.5	58.8	57.3	56.1	55.0	51.0
130	99.4	87.3	76.6	71.0	67.3	64.5	62.4	60.6	59.1	57.8	56.7	52.5
140	102	89.7	78.8	73.0	69.2	66.4	64.1	62.3	60.8	59.4	58.3	54.0

Table 6-2. Diameters of Pipes in Inches, from the Manning
Formula, $n = 0.010$ (*Continued*)

Discharge in cubic feet per second	$s = \dfrac{h}{l} =$ drop in hydraulic gradient per foot											
	.004	.005	.006	.007	.008	.009	.01	.015	.02	.025	.03	.04
.1	3.4	3.2	3.1	3.0	3.0	2.9	2.8	2.6	2.5	2.4	2.3	2.2
.2	4.4	4.2	4.1	4.0	3.9	3.8	3.7	3.4	3.2	3.1	3.0	2.8
.3	5.1	4.9	4.7	4.6	4.5	4.4	4.3	4.0	3.8	3.6	3.5	3.2
.4	5.7	5.5	5.2	5.1	5.0	4.9	4.8	4.4	4.2	4.0	3.9	3.7
.5	6.2	5.9	5.7	5.6	5.4	5.3	5.2	4.8	4.6	4.4	4.2	4.0
.6	6.6	6.3	6.1	6.0	5.8	5.7	5.6	5.2	4.9	4.7	4.5	4.3
.7	7.0	6.7	6.5	6.3	6.2	6.0	5.9	5.5	5.2	5.0	4.8	4.6
.8	7.4	7.1	6.8	6.6	6.5	6.3	6.2	5.8	5.5	5.2	5.0	4.8
.9	7.7	7.4	7.1	6.9	6.8	6.6	6.5	6.0	5.7	5.5	5.3	5.0
1.0	8.0	7.7	7.4	7.2	7.0	6.9	6.8	6.3	5.9	5.7	5.5	5.2
1.2	8.6	8.2	8.0	7.8	7.5	7.4	7.2	6.7	6.4	6.1	5.9	5.6
1.4	9.1	8.7	8.4	8.2	8.0	7.8	7.7	7.1	6.7	6.5	6.2	5.9
1.6	9.6	9.2	8.9	8.6	8.4	8.2	8.0	7.5	7.1	6.8	6.6	6.2
1.8	10.1	9.6	9.3	9.0	8.8	8.6	8.4	7.8	7.4	7.1	6.9	6.5
2.0	10.4	10.0	9.6	9.4	9.1	8.9	8.8	8.1	7.7	7.4	7.1	6.8
2.5	11.3	10.8	10.5	10.2	9.9	9.7	9.5	8.8	8.4	8.0	7.7	7.3
3.0	12.1	11.6	11.2	10.9	10.6	10.4	10.2	9.4	9.0	8.5	8.3	7.9
3.5	12.8	12.3	11.8	11.5	11.3	11.0	10.8	10.0	9.5	9.0	8.8	8.3
4.0	13.5	12.9	12.4	12.1	11.8	11.6	11.4	10.5	10.0	9.6	9.2	8.8
4.5	14.1	13.5	13.1	12.7	12.4	12.1	11.9	11.0	10.4	10.0	9.7	9.2
5	14.7	14.1	13.6	13.2	12.9	12.6	12.3	11.4	10.8	10.4	10.0	9.5
6	15.7	15.1	14.5	14.1	13.8	13.5	13.2	12.2	11.6	11.1	10.8	10.2
7	16.6	16.0	15.4	15.0	14.6	14.3	14.0	13.0	12.3	11.8	11.4	10.8
8	17.5	16.8	16.2	15.7	15.4	15.0	14.7	13.6	12.9	12.4	11.9	11.4
9	18.3	17.5	16.9	16.4	16.0	15.7	15.4	14.3	13.5	13.0	12.5	11.9
10	19.0	18.2	17.6	17.1	16.7	16.3	16.0	14.8	14.1	13.5	13.0	12.4
12	20.3	19.5	18.9	18.3	17.9	17.5	17.1	15.9	15.0	14.4	13.9	13.2
14	21.6	20.7	20.0	19.4	18.9	18.5	18.2	16.8	15.9	15.3	14.8	14.0
16	22.7	21.8	21.0	20.4	19.9	19.5	19.1	17.7	16.8	16.1	15.5	14.7
18	23.7	22.7	22.0	21.3	20.8	20.4	20.0	18.5	17.5	16.8	16.2	15.4
20	24.7	23.7	22.9	22.2	21.7	21.2	20.8	19.3	18.2	17.5	16.9	16.0
25	26.9	25.7	24.9	24.1	23.5	23.0	22.6	20.9	19.8	19.0	18.4	17.4
30	28.7	27.5	26.6	25.9	25.2	24.7	24.2	22.4	21.2	20.4	19.7	18.6
35	30.4	29.2	28.2	27.4	26.7	26.1	25.6	23.7	22.5	21.6	20.9	19.8
40	32.0	30.7	29.6	28.8	28.1	27.5	26.9	25.0	23.7	22.7	21.9	20.8
45	33.4	32.1	31.0	30.1	29.4	28.7	28.2	26.1	24.7	23.7	22.9	21.7
50	34.8	33.4	32.2	31.3	30.5	29.9	29.3	27.1	25.7	24.7	23.8	22.6
55	36.0	34.6	33.4	32.5	31.7	31.0	30.4	28.1	26.7	25.6	24.7	23.4
60	37.2	35.7	34.5	33.5	32.7	32.0	31.4	29.1	27.5	26.4	25.5	24.2
65	38.4	36.8	35.6	34.5	33.7	33.0	32.3	29.9	28.4	27.2	26.3	24.9
70	39.5	37.8	36.6	35.5	34.6	33.9	33.2	30.8	29.2	28.0	27.0	25.6
75	40.4	38.8	37.5	36.5	35.6	34.8	34.1	31.6	29.9	28.7	27.8	26.3
80	41.5	39.8	38.4	37.4	36.4	35.6	34.9	32.5	30.7	29.4	28.4	26.9
85	42.4	40.7	39.3	38.2	37.3	36.4	35.7	33.1	31.4	30.1	29.1	27.6
90	43.4	41.6	40.2	39.0	38.1	37.2	36.5	33.8	32.1	30.7	29.7	28.2
100	45.1	43.2	41.8	40.6	39.6	38.7	38.0	35.2	33.4	32.0	30.9	29.3
110	46.7	44.8	43.3	42.1	41.0	40.1	39.4	36.5	34.6	33.2	32.0	30.4
120	48.3	46.3	44.8	43.5	42.4	41.5	40.7	37.7	35.7	34.2	33.1	31.4
130	49.8	47.7	46.1	44.8	43.7	42.7	41.9	38.8	36.8	35.3	34.1	32.3
140	51.2	49.1	47.4	46.1	44.9	43.9	43.1	39.9	37.8	36.3	35.1	33.2

Table 6-2. Diameters of Pipes in Inches, from the Manning Formula, $n = 0.011$ (*Continued*)

Discharge in cubic feet per second	$s = \dfrac{h}{l} =$ drop in hydraulic gradient per foot											
	.0001	.0002	.0004	.0006	.0008	.001	.0012	.0014	.0016	.0018	.002	.003
1	7.0	6.1	5.4	5.0	4.7	4.5	4.4	4.3	4.2	4.1	4.0	3.7
2	9.1	8.0	7.0	6.5	6.1	5.9	5.7	5.5	5.4	5.3	5.2	4.8
.3	10.6	9.3	8.2	7.6	7.2	6.9	6.6	6.4	6.3	6.1	6.0	5.6
.4	11.8	10.3	9.1	8.4	8.0	7.7	7.4	7.2	7.0	6.8	6.7	6.2
.5	12.8	11.2	9.9	9.2	8.7	8.3	8.0	7.8	7.6	7.5	7.3	6.8
.6	13.7	12.0	10.6	9.8	9.3	8.9	8.6	8.4	8.2	8.0	7.8	7.2
.7	14.5	12.7	11.2	10.4	9.8	9.4	9.1	8.9	8.6	8.4	8.3	7.7
.8	15.3	13.4	11.8	10.9	10.3	10.0	9.6	9.3	9.1	8.9	8.7	8.1
.9	16.0	14.0	12.3	11.4	10.8	10.4	10.0	9.7	9.5	9.3	9.1	8.4
1.0	16.6	14.6	12.7	11.9	11.2	10.8	10.4	10.1	9.9	9.7	9.5	8.8
1.2	17.8	15.6	13.7	12.7	12.0	11.5	11.1	10.8	10.6	10.3	10.1	9.4
1.4	18.8	16.5	14.5	13.5	12.8	12.2	11.8	11.5	11.2	11.0	10.7	10.0
1.6	19.7	17.4	15.3	14.2	13.4	12.9	12.4	12.1	11.8	11.5	11.3	10.5
1.8	20.7	18.2	16.0	14.8	14.0	13.4	13.0	12.6	12.3	12.0	11.8	10.9
2.0	21.5	18.9	16.6	15.4	14.6	14.0	13.5	13.1	12.8	12.5	12.3	11.4
2.5	23.4	20.6	18.0	16.7	15.8	15.2	14.7	14.3	13.9	13.6	13.3	12.4
3.0	25.1	22.0	19.3	17.9	17.0	16.3	15.7	15.3	14.9	14.6	14.3	13.2
3.5	26.7	23.3	20.5	19.0	18.0	17.2	16.7	16.2	15.8	15.5	15.2	14.0
4.0	27.9	24.5	21.5	20.0	18.9	18.1	17.5	17.0	16.6	16.2	15.9	14.7
4.5	29.2	25.6	22.5	20.9	19.8	19.0	18.3	17.8	17.4	17.0	16.7	15.4
5	30.4	26.7	23.4	21.7	20.6	19.7	19.0	18.5	18.0	17.7	17.3	16.0
6	32.5	28.5	25.1	23.2	22.0	21.1	20.4	19.8	19.3	18.9	18.5	17.2
7	34.4	30.2	26.6	24.6	23.3	22.4	21.6	21.0	20.5	20.0	19.6	18.2
8	36.2	31.8	27.9	25.9	24.5	23.5	22.7	22.1	21.5	21.1	20.6	19.1
9	37.8	33.2	29.2	27.0	25.6	24.6	23.7	23.1	22.5	22.0	21.6	20.0
10	39.4	34.6	30.4	28.1	26.7	25.6	24.7	24.0	23.4	22.9	22.4	20.8
12	42.1	37.0	32.5	30.1	28.5	27.4	26.4	25.7	25.1	24.5	24.0	22.3
14	44.7	39.2	34.4	31.9	30.2	29.0	28.0	27.2	26.6	26.0	25.5	23.6
16	47.0	41.2	36.2	33.6	31.8	30.5	29.5	28.6	27.9	27.3	26.8	24.8
18	49.1	43.1	37.8	35.1	33.2	31.9	30.8	29.9	29.2	28.5	28.0	25.9
20	51.0	44.8	39.4	36.5	34.6	33.1	32.0	31.1	30.4	29.7	29.1	27.0
25	55.5	48.7	42.8	39.7	37.6	36.0	34.8	33.8	33.0	32.3	31.7	29.3
30	59.4	52.2	45.8	42.5	40.2	38.6	37.3	36.2	35.3	34.6	33.9	31.4
35	63.0	55.3	48.6	45.0	42.6	40.9	39.5	38.4	37.4	36.6	35.9	33.3
40	66.2	58.1	51.0	47.3	44.8	43.0	41.5	40.4	39.4	38.5	37.7	35.0
45	69.2	60.8	53.4	49.4	46.8	44.9	43.4	42.2	41.1	40.2	39.5	36.6
50	72.0	63.2	55.5	51.4	48.7	46.7	45.2	43.9	42.8	41.9	41.0	38.0
55	74.6	65.5	57.5	53.3	50.5	48.4	46.8	45.5	44.4	43.4	42.5	39.4
60	77.1	67.7	59.4	55.1	52.2	50.0	48.4	47.0	45.8	44.8	44.0	40.7
65	79.4	69.7	61.2	56.8	53.8	51.6	49.8	48.4	47.2	46.2	45.3	42.0
70	81.7	71.7	63.0	58.4	55.3	53.0	51.2	49.8	48.6	47.5	46.6	43.2
75	83.8	73.6	64.6	59.9	56.7	54.4	52.6	51.1	49.8	48.7	47.8	44.3
80	85.9	75.4	66.2	61.4	58.1	55.8	53.9	52.3	51.0	49.9	49.0	45.4
85	87.8	77.1	67.7	62.8	59.5	57.0	55.1	53.5	52.2	51.1	50.1	46.4
90	89.7	78.8	69.2	64.1	60.8	58.3	56.3	54.7	53.4	52.2	51.2	47.4
100	93.3	82.0	72.0	66.7	63.2	60.6	58.6	56.9	55.5	54.3	53.2	49.3
110	96.7	85.0	74.6	69.1	65.5	62.8	60.7	59.0	57.5	56.3	55.2	51.1
120	100	87.8	77.1	71.4	67.7	64.9	62.7	60.9	59.4	58.1	57.0	52.8
130	103	90.4	79.4	73.6	69.7	66.9	64.6	62.8	61.2	59.9	58.7	54.4
140	106	93.0	81.7	75.7	71.7	68.8	66.5	64.6	63.0	61.6	60.4	56.0

Table 6-2. Diameters of Pipes in Inches, from the Manning Formula, $n = 0.011$ (*Continued*)

Discharge in cubic feet per second	$s = \dfrac{h}{l}$ = drop in hydraulic gradient per foot											
	.004	.005	.006	.007	.008	.009	.01	.015	.02	.025	.03	.04
.1	3.5	3.4	3.2	3.2	3.1	3.0	3.0	2.7	2.6	2.5	2.4	2.3
.2	4.5	4.4	4.2	4.1	4.0	3.9	3.8	3.5	3.4	3.2	3.1	3.0
.3	5.3	5.1	4.9	4.8	4.7	4.6	4.5	4.1	3.9	3.8	3.7	3.4
.4	5.9	5.7	5.5	5.3	5.2	5.1	5.0	4.6	4.4	4.2	4.0	3.8
.5	6.4	6.2	5.9	5.8	5.6	5.5	5.4	5.0	4.7	4.5	4.4	4.2
.6	6.9	6.6	6.3	6.2	6.0	5.9	5.8	5.4	5.1	4.9	4.7	4.5
.7	7.3	7.0	6.7	6.5	6.4	6.2	6.1	5.7	5.4	5.2	5.0	4.7
.8	7.7	7.3	7.1	6.9	6.7	6.6	6.4	5.9	5.7	5.4	5.2	5.0
.9	8.0	7.7	7.4	7.2	7.0	6.9	6.7	6.2	5.9	5.7	5.5	5.2
1.0	8.3	8.0	7.7	7.5	7.3	7.1	7.0	6.5	6.2	5.9	5.7	5.4
1.2	8.9	8.6	8.2	8.0	7.8	7.6	7.5	6.9	6.6	6.3	6.1	5.8
1.4	9.4	9.1	8.7	8.5	8.3	8.1	7.9	7.4	7.0	6.7	6.5	6.1
1.6	9.9	9.5	9.2	8.9	8.7	8.5	8.3	7.7	7.3	7.0	6.8	6.4
1.8	10.4	10.0	9.6	9.3	9.1	8.9	8.7	8.1	7.7	7.4	7.1	6.7
2.0	10.8	10.3	10.0	9.7	9.5	9.3	9.1	8.4	8.0	7.7	7.4	7.0
2.5	11.7	11.2	10.8	10.5	10.3	10.1	9.9	9.2	8.7	8.3	8.0	7.6
3.0	12.5	12.0	11.6	11.3	11.0	10.8	10.6	9.8	9.3	8.9	8.6	8.1
3.5	13.3	12.8	12.3	12.0	11.7	11.4	11.2	10.4	9.8	9.4	9.1	8.6
4.0	14.0	13.4	13.0	12.6	12.3	12.0	11.8	10.9	10.3	9.9	9.6	9.1
4.5	14.6	14.0	13.5	13.2	12.8	12.6	12.3	11.4	10.8	10.4	10.0	9.5
5	15.2	14.6	14.1	13.7	13.3	13.1	12.8	11.9	11.2	10.8	10.4	9.9
6	16.3	15.6	15.1	14.7	14.3	14.0	13.7	12.7	12.0	11.5	11.2	10.6
7	17.2	16.5	16.0	15.5	15.1	14.8	14.5	13.5	12.8	12.2	11.8	11.2
8	18.1	17.4	16.8	16.3	15.9	15.6	15.3	14.1	13.4	12.9	12.4	11.8
9	18.9	18.2	17.6	17.1	16.6	16.3	16.0	14.8	14.0	13.4	13.0	12.3
10	19.7	18.9	18.3	17.7	17.3	16.9	16.6	15.4	14.6	14.0	13.5	12.8
12	21.1	20.2	19.6	19.0	18.5	18.1	17.8	16.5	15.6	15.0	14.5	13.7
14	22.4	21.4	20.7	20.1	19.6	19.2	18.8	17.5	16.5	15.9	15.3	14.5
16	23.5	22.5	21.8	21.2	20.6	20.2	19.8	18.4	17.4	16.7	16.1	15.3
18	24.6	23.6	22.8	22.1	21.6	21.1	20.7	19.2	18.2	17.4	16.8	16.0
20	25.6	24.5	23.7	23.0	22.4	22.0	21.5	20.0	18.9	18.1	17.5	16.6
25	27.8	26.7	25.8	25.0	24.4	23.9	23.4	21.7	20.6	19.7	19.0	18.0
30	29.8	28.5	27.6	26.8	26.1	25.6	25.1	23.2	22.0	21.1	20.4	19.3
35	31.5	30.2	29.2	28.4	27.7	27.1	26.6	24.6	23.3	22.4	21.6	20.5
40	33.1	31.8	30.7	29.8	29.1	28.5	27.9	25.9	24.5	23.5	22.7	21.5
45	34.6	33.2	32.1	31.2	30.4	29.8	29.2	27.0	25.6	24.6	23.7	22.5
50	36.0	34.6	33.4	32.5	31.6	31.0	30.4	28.1	26.7	25.6	24.7	23.4
55	37.4	35.8	34.6	33.6	32.8	32.1	31.5	29.2	27.6	26.5	25.6	24.3
60	38.6	37.0	35.8	34.7	33.9	33.1	32.5	30.1	28.5	27.4	26.5	25.1
65	39.8	38.1	36.9	35.8	34.9	34.2	33.5	31.0	29.4	28.2	27.3	25.8
70	40.9	39.2	37.9	36.8	35.9	35.1	34.4	31.9	30.2	29.0	28.0	26.6
75	42.0	40.2	38.9	37.8	36.8	36.0	35.3	32.8	31.0	29.8	28.8	27.2
80	43.0	41.2	39.8	38.7	37.7	36.9	36.2	33.6	31.8	30.5	29.5	27.9
85	44.0	42.2	40.8	39.6	38.6	37.8	37.0	34.3	32.5	31.2	30.1	28.6
90	44.9	43.1	41.6	40.5	39.5	38.6	37.8	35.1	33.2	31.9	30.8	29.2
100	46.7	44.8	43.3	42.1	41.0	40.1	39.3	36.5	34.6	33.2	32.0	30.4
110	48.4	46.5	44.9	43.6	42.5	41.6	40.8	37.8	35.8	34.4	33.2	31.5
120	50.0	48.0	46.4	45.1	44.0	43.0	42.1	39.1	37.0	35.5	34.3	32.5
130	51.6	49.5	47.8	46.4	45.3	44.3	43.4	40.3	38.1	36.6	35.3	33.5
140	53.0	50.9	49.1	47.7	46.6	45.6	44.6	41.4	39.2	37.6	36.3	34.4

Table 6-2. Diameters of Pipes in Inches, from the Manning Formula, $n = 0.012$ (*Continued*)

Discharge in cubic feet per second	$s = \dfrac{h}{l}$ = drop in hydraulic gradient per foot											
	.0001	.0002	.0004	.0006	.0008	.001	.0012	.0014	.0016	.0018	.002	.003
.1	7.2	6.3	5.6	5.2	4.9	4.7	4.5	4.4	4.3	4.2	4.1	3.8
.2	9.4	8.2	7.2	6.7	6.3	6.1	5.9	5.7	5.6	5.5	5.4	4.9
.3	10.9	9.6	8.4	7.8	7.4	7.1	6.9	6.7	6.5	6.4	6.2	5.8
.4	12.2	10.7	9.4	8.7	8.2	7.9	7.6	7.4	7.2	7.1	6.9	6.4
.5	13.2	11.6	10.2	9.5	9.0	8.6	8.3	8.1	7.9	7.7	7.5	6.9
.6	14.2	12.4	10.9	10.1	9.6	9.2	8.9	8.6	8.4	8.2	8.1	7.5
.7	15.0	13.2	11.6	10.7	10.2	9.7	9.4	9.1	8.9	8.7	8.6	7.9
.8	15.8	13.9	12.2	11.3	10.7	10.2	9.9	9.6	9.4	9.2	9.0	8.3
.9	16.5	14.5	12.7	11.8	11.2	10.7	10.3	10.1	9.8	9.6	9.4	8.7
1.0	17.1	15.1	13.2	12.3	11.6	11.1	10.8	10.5	10.2	10.0	9.8	9.1
1.2	18.4	16.1	14.2	13.1	12.4	11.9	11.5	11.2	10.9	10.7	10.5	9.7
1.4	19.5	17.1	15.0	13.9	13.2	12.6	12.2	11.9	11.6	11.3	11.1	10.3
1.6	20.5	18.0	15.8	14.6	13.9	13.3	12.8	12.5	12.2	11.9	11.7	10.8
1.8	21.4	18.8	16.5	15.3	14.5	13.9	13.4	13.0	12.7	12.4	12.2	11.3
2.0	22.2	19.5	17.1	15.9	15.1	14.5	14.0	13.6	13.2	12.9	12.7	11.8
2.5	24.2	21.2	18.6	17.3	16.4	15.7	15.2	14.8	14.4	14.1	13.8	12.8
3.0	25.9	22.7	20.0	18.5	17.5	16.8	16.2	15.8	15.4	15.1	14.8	13.7
3.5	27.4	24.1	21.2	19.6	18.6	17.8	17.2	16.7	16.3	16.0	15.6	14.5
4.0	28.8	25.3	22.2	20.6	19.5	18.7	18.1	17.6	17.1	16.8	16.4	15.2
4.5	30.1	26.5	23.2	21.5	20.4	19.6	18.9	18.4	18.0	17.6	17.2	15.9
5	31.4	27.5	24.2	22.4	21.2	20.4	19.7	19.1	18.6	18.2	17.9	16.6
6	33.6	29.5	25.9	24.0	22.7	21.8	21.1	20.5	20.0	19.5	19.1	17.7
7	35.6	31.2	27.4	25.4	24.1	23.1	22.3	21.7	21.2	20.7	20.3	18.8
8	37.4	32.8	28.8	26.7	25.3	24.3	23.5	22.8	22.2	21.8	21.3	19.8
9	39.1	34.3	30.1	27.9	26.5	25.4	24.5	23.8	23.2	22.7	22.3	20.7
10	40.7	35.7	31.4	29.1	27.5	26.4	25.5	24.8	24.2	23.7	23.2	21.5
12	43.5	38.2	33.6	31.1	29.5	28.3	27.3	26.5	25.9	25.3	24.8	23.0
14	46.1	40.5	35.6	33.0	31.2	30.0	29.0	28.1	27.4	26.8	26.3	24.4
16	48.5	42.6	37.4	34.7	32.8	31.5	30.4	29.6	28.8	28.2	27.7	25.6
18	50.7	44.5	39.1	36.2	34.3	32.9	31.8	30.9	30.1	29.5	28.9	26.8
20	52.7	46.3	40.7	37.7	35.7	34.2	33.1	32.2	31.4	30.7	30.1	27.9
25	57.3	50.4	44.2	41.0	38.8	37.2	36.0	35.0	34.1	33.4	32.7	30.3
30	61.4	53.9	47.3	43.9	41.6	39.9	38.5	37.4	36.5	35.7	35.0	32.5
35	65.1	57.1	50.2	46.5	44.1	42.2	40.8	39.7	38.7	37.8	37.1	34.4
40	68.4	60.1	52.7	48.9	46.3	44.4	42.9	41.7	40.7	39.8	39.0	36.1
45	71.5	62.8	55.1	51.1	48.4	46.4	44.9	43.6	42.5	41.6	40.8	37.8
50	74.4	65.3	57.3	53.1	50.4	48.3	46.7	45.3	44.2	43.3	42.4	39.3
55	77.1	67.7	59.4	55.1	52.2	50.0	48.4	47.0	45.8	44.8	44.0	40.7
60	79.6	69.9	61.4	56.9	53.9	51.7	50.0	48.5	47.3	46.3	45.4	42.1
65	82.1	72.1	63.3	58.6	55.6	53.3	51.5	50.0	48.8	47.7	46.8	43.4
70	84.4	74.1	65.1	60.3	57.1	54.8	52.9	51.4	50.2	49.1	48.1	44.6
75	86.6	76.0	66.8	61.9	58.6	56.2	54.3	52.8	51.5	50.4	49.4	45.8
80	88.7	77.9	68.4	63.4	60.1	57.6	55.7	54.1	52.7	51.6	50.6	46.9
85	90.7	79.7	70.0	64.8	61.4	58.9	56.9	55.3	54.0	52.8	51.7	48.0
90	92.7	81.4	71.5	66.3	62.8	60.2	58.2	56.5	55.1	53.9	52.9	49.0
100	96.4	84.7	74.4	68.9	65.3	62.6	60.5	58.8	57.3	56.1	55.0	51.0
110	99.9	87.8	77.1	71.4	67.7	64.9	62.7	60.9	59.4	58.1	57.0	52.8
120	103	90.7	79.6	73.8	69.9	67.1	64.8	63.0	61.4	60.1	58.9	54.6
130	106	93.4	82.1	76.0	72.1	69.1	66.8	64.9	63.3	61.9	60.7	56.2
140	109	96.1	84.4	78.2	74.1	71.0	68.7	66.7	65.1	63.6	62.4	57.8

Table 6-2. Diameters of Pipes in Inches, from the Manning Formula, $n = 0.012$ (*Continued*)

Discharge in cubic feet per second	$s = \dfrac{h}{l}$ = drop in hydraulic gradient per foot											
	.004	.005	.006	.007	.008	.009	.01	.015	.02	.025	.03	.04
.1	3.6	3.5	3.4	3.3	3.2	3.1	3.0	2.8	2.7	2.6	2.5	2.4
.2	4.7	4.5	4.4	4.2	4.1	4.0	3.9	3.7	3.5	3.3	3.2	3.0
.3	5.5	5.2	5.1	4.9	4.8	4.7	4.6	4.3	4.0	3.9	3.7	3.6
.4	6.1	5.8	5.6	5.5	5.4	5.2	5.1	4.8	4.5	4.3	4.2	4.0
.5	6.6	6.4	6.1	6.0	5.8	5.7	5.6	5.2	4.9	4.7	4.5	4.3
.6	7.1	6.8	6.6	6.4	6.2	6.1	6.0	5.5	5.2	5.0	4.9	4.6
.7	7.5	7.2	7.0	6.8	6.6	6.5	6.3	5.9	5.6	5.3	5.1	4.9
.8	7.9	7.6	7.3	7.1	6.9	6.8	6.7	6.2	5.8	5.6	5.4	5.1
.9	8.3	7.9	7.7	7.4	7.2	7.1	7.0	6.4	6.1	5.9	5.7	5.4
1.0	8.6	8.2	3.0	7.7	7.5	7.4	7.2	6.7	6.4	6.1	5.9	5.6
1.2	9.2	8.8	8.5	8.3	8.1	7.9	7.7	7.2	6.8	6.5	6.3	6.0
1.4	9.7	9.3	9.0	8.8	8.6	8.4	8.2	7.6	7.2	6.9	6.7	6.3
1.6	10.2	9.8	9.5	9.2	9.0	8.8	8.6	8.0	7.6	7.3	7.0	6.7
1.8	10.7	10.3	9.9	9.6	9.4	9.2	9.0	8.4	7.9	7.6	7.3	7.0
2.0	11.1	10.7	10.3	10.0	9.8	9.6	9.4	8.7	8.2	7.9	7.6	7.2
2.5	12.1	11.6	11.2	10.9	10.6	10.4	10.2	9.5	9.0	8.6	8.3	7.9
3.0	13.0	12.4	12.0	11.7	11.4	11.1	10.9	10.1	9.6	9.2	8.9	8.4
3.5	13.7	13.2	12.7	12.4	12.1	11.8	11.6	10.7	10.2	9.7	9.4	8.9
4.0	14.4	13.9	13.4	13.0	12.7	12.4	12.2	11.3	10.7	10.2	9.9	9.4
4.5	15.1	14.5	14.0	13.6	13.3	13.0	12.7	11.8	11.2	10.7	10.3	9.8
5	15.7	15.1	14.6	14.1	13.8	13.5	13.2	12.3	11.6	11.1	10.8	10.2
6	16.8	16.1	15.6	15.1	14.8	14.4	14.2	13.1	12.4	11.9	11.5	10.9
7	17.8	17.1	16.5	16.0	15.6	15.3	15.0	13.9	13.2	12.6	12.2	11.6
8	18.7	18.0	17.4	16.9	16.4	16.1	15.8	14.6	13.9	13.3	12.8	12.2
9	19.6	18.8	18.1	17.6	17.2	16.8	16.5	15.3	14.5	13.9	13.4	12.7
10	20.4	19.5	18.9	18.3	17.9	17.5	17.2	15.9	15.1	14.4	13.9	13.2
12	21.8	20.9	20.2	19.6	19.1	18.7	18.4	17.0	16.1	15.5	14.9	14.2
14	23.1	22.2	21.4	20.8	20.3	19.8	19.5	18.0	17.1	16.4	15.8	15.0
16	24.3	23.3	22.5	21.9	21.3	20.9	20.5	19.0	18.0	17.2	16.6	15.8
18	25.4	24.3	23.5	22.9	22.3	21.8	21.4	19.8	18.8	18.0	17.4	16.5
20	26.4	25.3	24.5	23.8	23.2	22.7	22.2	20.6	19.5	18.7	18.1	17.1
25	28.7	27.5	26.6	25.9	25.2	24.7	24.2	22.4	21.2	20.4	19.7	18.6
30	30.7	29.5	28.5	27.7	27.0	26.4	25.9	24.0	22.7	21.8	21.1	20.0
35	32.6	31.2	30.2	29.3	28.6	28.0	27.4	25.4	24.1	23.1	22.3	21.2
40	34.2	32.8	31.7	30.8	30.1	29.4	28.8	26.7	25.3	24.3	23.5	22.2
45	35.8	34.3	33.2	32.2	31.4	30.7	30.1	27.9	26.5	25.4	24.5	23.2
50	37.2	35.7	34.5	33.5	32.7	32.0	31.4	29.1	27.5	26.4	25.5	24.2
55	38.6	37.0	35.8	34.7	33.9	33.1	32.5	30.1	28.5	27.4	26.5	25.1
60	39.9	38.2	37.0	35.9	35.0	34.2	33.6	31.1	29.5	28.3	27.3	25.9
65	41.1	39.4	38.1	37.0	36.1	35.3	34.6	32.1	30.4	29.1	28.2	26.7
70	42.2	40.5	39.2	38.0	37.1	36.3	35.6	33.0	31.2	30.0	29.0	27.4
75	43.4	41.6	40.2	39.0	38.1	37.2	36.5	33.8	32.1	30.7	29.7	28.2
80	44.4	42.6	41.2	40.0	39.0	38.2	37.4	34.7	32.8	31.5	30.4	28.8
85	45.4	43.6	42.1	40.9	39.9	39.0	38.3	35.5	33.6	32.2	31.1	29.5
90	46.4	44.5	43.0	41.8	40.8	39.9	39.1	36.2	34.3	32.9	31.7	30.1
100	48.3	46.3	44.7	43.5	42.4	41.5	40.7	37.7	35.7	34.2	33.1	31.4
110	50.0	48.0	46.4	45.1	43.9	43.0	42.1	39.1	37.0	35.5	34.3	32.5
120	51.7	49.6	47.9	46.6	45.4	44.4	43.5	40.4	38.2	36.7	35.4	33.6
130	53.3	51.1	49.4	48.0	46.8	45.8	44.9	41.6	39.4	37.8	36.5	34.6
140	54.8	52.5	50.8	49.3	48.1	47.1	46.1	42.8	40.5	38.9	37.5	35.6

Table 6-2. Diameters of Pipes in Inches, from the Manning Formula, $n = 0.014$ (*Continued*)

Discharge in cubic feet per second	$s = \dfrac{h}{l}$ = drop in hydraulic gradient per foot											
	.0001	.0002	.0004	.0006	.0008	.001	.0012	.0014	.0016	.0018	.002	.003
.1	7.7	6.7	5.9	5.5	5.2	5.0	4.8	4.7	4.6	4.5	4.4	4.0
.2	9.9	8.7	7.7	7.1	6.7	6.5	6.2	6.1	5.9	5.8	5.7	5.3
.3	11.6	10.2	8.9	8.3	7.8	7.5	7.3	7.1	6.9	6.7	6.6	6.1
.4	12.9	11.3	9.9	9.2	8.7	8.4	8.1	7.9	7.7	7.5	7.3	6.8
.5	14.0	12.3	10.8	10.0	9.5	9.1	8.8	8.5	8.3	8.1	8.0	7.4
.6	15.0	13.2	11.6	10.7	10.2	9.7	9.4	9.1	8.9	8.7	8.6	7.9
.7	15.9	14.0	12.3	11.4	10.8	10.3	10.0	9.7	9.5	9.2	9.1	8.4
.8	16.7	14.7	12.9	11.9	11.3	10.9	10.5	10.2	9.9	9.7	9.5	8.8
.9	17.5	15.3	13.5	12.5	11.8	11.3	11.0	10.6	10.4	10.2	10.0	9.2
1.0	18.2	16.0	14.0	13.0	12.3	11.8	11.4	11.1	10.8	10.6	10.4	9.6
1.2	19.5	17.1	15.0	13.9	13.2	12.6	12.2	11.9	11.6	11.3	11.1	10.3
1.4	20.6	18.1	15.9	14.7	14.0	13.4	12.9	12.6	12.3	12.0	11.8	10.9
1.6	21.7	19.0	16.7	15.5	14.7	14.1	13.6	13.2	12.9	12.6	12.4	11.5
1.8	22.7	19.9	17.5	16.2	15.3	14.7	14.2	13.8	13.5	13.2	12.9	12.0
2.0	23.6	20.7	18.2	16.8	16.0	15.3	14.8	14.4	14.0	13.7	13.4	12.5
2.5	25.6	22.5	19.8	18.3	17.3	16.6	16.1	15.6	15.2	14.9	14.6	13.5
3.0	27.4	24.1	21.2	19.6	18.6	17.8	17.2	16.7	16.3	16.0	15.6	14.5
3.5	29.1	25.5	22.4	20.8	19.7	18.9	18.2	17.7	17.3	16.9	16.6	15.4
4.0	30.6	26.8	23.6	21.8	20.7	19.8	19.2	18.6	18.2	17.8	17.4	16.2
4.5	31.9	28.0	24.6	22.8	21.6	20.7	20.0	19.5	19.0	18.6	18.2	16.9
5	33.2	29.2	25.6	23.7	22.5	21.6	20.9	20.3	19.8	19.3	18.9	17.6
6	35.6	31.2	27.4	25.4	24.1	23.1	22.3	21.7	21.2	20.7	20.3	18.8
7	37.7	33.1	29.1	26.9	25.5	24.5	23.7	23.0	22.4	21.9	21.5	19.9
8	39.6	34.8	30.6	28.3	26.8	25.7	24.9	24.2	23.6	23.0	22.6	20.9
9	41.4	36.4	31.9	29.6	28.0	26.9	26.0	25.3	24.6	24.1	23.6	21.9
10	43.1	37.8	33.2	30.8	29.2	28.0	27.0	26.3	25.6	25.1	24.6	22.8
12	46.1	40.5	35.6	33.0	31.2	30.0	29.0	28.1	27.4	26.8	26.3	24.4
14	48.9	42.9	37.7	34.9	33.1	31.7	30.7	29.8	29.1	28.4	27.9	25.8
16	51.4	45.1	39.6	36.7	34.8	33.4	32.3	31.3	30.6	29.9	29.3	27.2
18	53.7	47.2	41.4	38.4	36.4	34.9	33.7	32.7	31.9	31.2	30.6	28.4
20	55.9	49.1	43.1	39.9	37.8	36.3	35.1	34.1	33.2	32.5	31.9	29.5
25	60.8	53.4	46.8	43.4	41.1	39.5	38.1	37.0	36.1	35.3	34.6	32.1
30	65.1	57.1	50.2	46.5	44.1	42.2	40.8	39.7	38.7	37.8	37.1	34.4
35	68.9	60.5	53.2	49.3	46.7	44.8	43.3	42.0	41.0	40.1	39.3	36.4
40	72.5	63.6	55.9	51.8	49.1	47.1	45.5	44.2	43.1	42.1	41.3	38.3
45	75.7	66.5	58.4	54.1	51.3	49.2	47.5	46.2	45.0	44.0	43.2	40.0
50	78.8	69.2	60.8	56.3	53.4	51.2	49.4	48.0	46.8	45.8	44.9	41.6
55	81.7	71.7	63.0	58.4	55.3	53.0	51.2	49.8	48.6	47.5	46.6	43.2
60	84.4	74.1	65.1	60.3	57.1	54.8	52.9	51.4	50.2	49.1	48.1	44.6
65	86.9	76.3	67.0	62.1	58.9	56.5	54.6	53.0	51.7	50.6	49.6	45.9
70	89.4	78.5	68.9	63.9	60.5	58.0	56.1	54.5	53.1	52.0	51.0	47.2
75	91.7	80.5	70.7	65.6	62.1	59.6	57.6	55.9	54.5	53.4	52.3	48.5
80	94.0	82.5	72.5	67.2	63.6	61.0	59.0	57.3	55.9	54.7	53.6	49.7
85	96.1	84.4	74.1	68.7	65.1	62.4	60.3	58.6	57.2	55.9	54.8	50.8
90	98.2	86.2	75.7	70.2	66.5	63.8	61.6	59.9	58.4	57.1	56.0	51.9
100	102	89.7	78.8	73.0	69.2	66.3	64.1	62.3	60.8	59.4	58.3	54.0
110	106	93.0	81.7	75.7	71.7	68.8	66.5	64.6	63.0	61.6	60.4	56.0
120	109	96.1	84.4	78.2	74.1	71.1	68.7	66.7	65.1	63.6	62.4	57.8
130	113	99.0	86.9	80.6	76.3	73.2	70.8	68.7	67.0	65.6	64.3	59.6
140	116	102	89.4	82.8	78.5	75.3	72.7	70.7	68.9	67.4	66.1	61.3

Table 6-2. Diameters of Pipes in Inches, from the Manning
Formula, $n = 0.014$ (*Continued*)

Discharge in cubic feet per second	$s = \dfrac{h}{l}$ = drop in hydraulic gradient per foot											
	.004	.005	.006	.007	.008	.009	.01	.015	.02	.025	.03	.04
.1	3.8	3.7	3.6	3.5	3.4	3.3	3.2	3.0	2.8	2.7	2.6	2.5
.2	5.0	4.8	4.6	4.5	4.4	4.3	4.2	3.9	3.7	3.5	3.4	3.2
3	5.8	5.6	5.4	5.2	5.1	5.0	4.9	4.5	4.3	4.1	4.0	3.8
.4	6.5	6.2	6.0	5.8	5.7	5.5	5.4	5.0	4.8	4.6	4.4	4.2
.5	7.0	6.7	6.5	6.3	6.2	6.0	5.9	5.5	5.2	5.0	4.8	4.6
.6	7.5	7.2	7.0	6.8	6.6	6.5	6.3	5.9	5.6	5.3	5.1	4.9
.7	8.0	7.6	7.4	7.2	7.0	6.8	6.7	6.2	5.9	5.6	5.5	5.2
.8	8.4	8.0	7.8	7.5	7.3	7.2	7.0	6.5	6.2	5.9	5.7	5.4
.9	8.7	8.4	8.1	7.9	7.7	7.5	7.4	6.8	6.5	6.2	6.0	5.7
1.0	9.1	8.7	8.4	8.2	8.0	7.8	7.7	7.1	6.7	6.5	6.2	5.9
1.2	9.7	9.3	9.0	8.8	8.6	8.4	8.2	7.6	7.2	6.9	6.7	6.3
1.4	10.3	9.9	9.6	9.3	9.1	8.9	8.7	8.1	7.6	7.3	7.1	6.7
1.6	10.9	10.4	10.1	9.8	9.5	9.3	9.1	8.5	8.0	7.7	7.4	7.0
1.8	11.3	10.9	10.5	10.2	10.0	9.7	9.6	8.9	8.4	8.0	7.8	7.4
2.0	11.8	11.3	10.9	10.6	10.4	10.1	9.9	9.2	8.7	8.4	8.1	7.7
2.5	12.8	12.3	11.9	11.6	11.3	11.0	10.8	10.0	9.5	9.1	8.8	8.4
3.0	13.7	13.2	12.7	12.4	12.1	11.8	11.6	10.7	10.2	9.7	9.4	8.9
3.5	14.6	14.0	13.5	13.1	12.8	12.5	12.3	11.4	10.8	10.3	10.0	9.5
4.0	15.3	14.7	14.2	13.8	13.4	13.1	12.9	11.9	11.3	10.9	10.5	9.9
4.5	16.0	15.3	14.8	14.4	14.0	13.7	13.5	12.5	11.8	11.3	11.0	10.4
5	16.6	16.0	15.4	15.0	14.6	14.3	14.0	13.0	12.3	11.8	11.4	10.8
6	17.8	17.1	16.5	16.0	15.6	15.3	15.0	13.9	13.2	12.6	12.2	11.6
7	18.9	18.1	17.5	17.0	16.6	16.2	15.9	14.7	14.0	13.4	12.9	12.3
8	19.8	19.0	18.4	17.9	17.4	17.0	16.7	15.5	14.7	14.1	13.6	12.9
9	20.7	19.9	19.2	18.7	18.2	17.8	17.5	16.2	15.3	14.7	14.2	13.5
10	21.6	20.7	20.0	19.4	18.9	18.5	18.2	16.8	16.0	15.3	14.8	14.0
12	23.1	22.2	21.4	20.8	20.3	19.8	19.5	18.0	17.1	16.4	15.8	15.0
14	24.5	23.5	22.7	22.0	21.5	21.0	20.6	19.1	18.1	17.4	16.8	15.9
16	25.7	24.7	23.9	23.2	22.6	22.1	21.7	20.1	19.0	18.3	17.6	16.7
18	26.9	25.8	24.9	24.2	23.6	23.1	22.6	21.0	19.9	19.1	18.4	17.5
20	28.0	26.8	25.9	25.2	24.6	24.0	23.6	21.8	20.7	19.8	19.2	18.2
25	30.4	29.2	28.2	27.4	26.7	26.1	25.6	23.7	22.5	21.6	20.9	19.8
30	32.6	31.2	30.2	29.3	28.6	28.0	27.4	25.4	24.1	23.1	22.3	21.2
35	34.5	33.1	32.0	31.1	30.3	29.6	29.1	26.9	25.5	24.5	23.7	22.4
40	36.3	34.8	33.6	32.7	31.9	31.2	30.6	28.3	26.8	25.7	24.9	23.6
45	37.9	36.4	35.1	34.1	33.3	32.6	31.9	29.6	28.0	26.9	26.0	24.6
50	39.5	37.8	36.6	35.5	34.6	33.9	33.2	30.8	29.2	28.0	27.0	25.6
55	40.9	39.2	37.9	36.8	35.9	35.1	34.4	31.9	30.2	29.0	28.0	26.6
60	42.2	40.5	39.2	38.0	37.1	36.3	35.6	33.0	31.2	30.0	29.0	27.4
65	43.5	41.7	40.3	39.2	38.2	37.4	36.7	34.0	32.2	30.9	29.8	28.3
70	44.8	42.9	41.5	40.3	39.3	38.4	37.7	34.9	33.1	31.7	30.7	29.1
75	45.9	44.1	42.6	41.4	40.3	39.5	38.7	35.9	34.0	32.6	31.5	29.8
80	47.1	45.1	43.6	42.4	41.3	40.4	39.6	36.7	34.8	33.4	32.3	30.6
85	48.1	46.2	44.6	43.3	42.3	41.3	40.5	37.6	35.6	34.1	33.0	31.3
90	49.2	47.2	45.6	44.3	43.2	42.2	41.4	38.4	36.4	34.9	33.7	31.9
100	51.2	49.1	47.4	46.1	44.9	43.9	43.1	39.9	37.8	36.3	35.1	33.2
110	53.0	50.9	49.1	47.7	46.5	45.5	44.7	41.4	39.2	37.6	36.3	34.4
120	54.8	52.5	50.8	49.3	48.1	47.1	46.1	42.8	40.5	38.9	37.6	35.6
130	56.5	54.1	52.3	50.8	49.6	48.5	47.5	44.1	41.7	40.0	38.7	36.7
140	58.0	55.7	53.8	52.3	51.0	49.9	48.9	45.3	42.9	41.2	39.8	37.7

Table 6-2. Diameters of Pipes in Inches, from the Manning
Formula, $n = 0.016$ (*Continued*)

Discharge in cubic feet per second	$s = \dfrac{h}{l}$ = drop in hydraulic gradient per foot											
	.0001	.0002	.0004	.0006	.0008	.001	.0012	.0014	.0016	.0018	.002	.003
.1	8.1	7.1	6.2	5.8	5.5	5.2	5.1	4.9	4.8	4.7	4.6	4.3
.2	10.4	9.2	8.1	7.5	7.1	6.8	6.6	6.4	6.2	6.1	6.0	5.5
.3	12.2	10.7	9.4	8.7	8.2	7.9	7.6	7.4	7.2	7.1	6.9	6.4
.4	13.5	11.9	10.4	9.7	9.2	8.8	8.5	8.3	8.1	7.9	7.7	7.2
.5	14.7	12.9	11.4	10.5	10.0	9.6	9.2	9.0	8.8	8.6	8.4	7.8
.6	15.8	13.9	12.2	11.3	10.7	10.2	9.9	9.6	9.4	9.2	9.0	8.3
.7	16.7	14.7	12.9	11.9	11.3	10.9	10.5	10 2	9.9	9.7	9.5	8.8
.8	17.6	15.4	13.5	12.6	11 9	11 4	11.0	10.7	10.4	10.2	10.0	9.3
.9	18.4	16.1	14.2	13.1	12.4	11.9	11.5	11.2	10.9	10.7	10.5	9.7
1.0	19.1	16.8	14.7	13.7	12.9	12.4	12.0	11.6	11.4	11.1	10.9	10.1
1.2	20.5	18.0	15.8	14.6	13.9	13.3	12.8	12.5	12.2	11.9	11.7	10.8
1.4	21.7	19.0	16.7	15.5	14.7	14.1	13.6	13.2	12.9	12.6	12.4	11.5
1.6	22.8	20.0	17.6	16.3	15.4	14 8	14.3	13.9	13.5	13 3	13.0	12.0
1.8	23.8	20.9	18.4	17.0	16.1	15.5	14.9	14.5	14 2	13.9	13.6	12.6
2.0	24.8	21.8	19.1	17.7	16.8	16.1	15.5	15.1	14.7	14.4	14.1	13.1
2.5	26.9	23.7	20.8	19.3	18.2	17.5	16.9	16.4	16.0	15.7	15.4	14.2
3.0	28.8	25.3	22.2	20.6	19.5	18.7	18.1	17.6	17.2	16.8	16.4	15.2
3.5	30.6	26.8	23.6	21.8	20.7	19.8	19.2	18.6	18.2	17.8	17.4	16.2
4.0	32.1	28.2	24.8	23.0	21.8	20.9	20.2	19.6	19.1	18.7	18.3	17.0
4.5	33.6	29.5	25.9	24.0	22.7	21.8	21.1	20.5	20.0	19.5	19.1	17.7
5	34.9	30.7	26.9	25.0	23.7	22.7	21.9	21.3	20.8	20.3	19.9	18.5
6	37.4	32.8	28.8	26.7	25.3	24.3	23.5	22.8	22.2	21.8	21.3	19.8
7	39.6	34.8	30.6	28.3	26.8	25.7	24.9	24.2	23.6	23.0	22.6	20.9
8	41.7	36.6	32.1	29.8	28.2	27.1	26.1	25.4	24.8	24.2	23.8	22.0
9	43.5	38.2	33.6	31.1	29.5	28.3	27.3	26.5	25.9	25.3	24.8	23.0
10	45.3	39.8	34.9	32.4	30.7	29.4	28.4	27.6	26.9	26.3	25.8	23.9
12	48.5	42.6	37.4	34.7	32.8	31.5	30.4	29.6	28.8	28.2	27.7	25.6
14	51.4	45.1	39.6	36.7	34.8	33.4	32.3	31.3	30.6	29.9	29.3	27.2
16	54.0	47.4	41.7	38.6	36.6	35.1	33.9	32.9	32.1	31.4	30.8	28.6
18	56.5	49.6	43.5	40.4	38.2	36.7	35.4	34.4	33.6	32.8	32.2	29.8
20	58.8	51.6	45.3	42.0	39.8	38.2	36.9	35.8	34.9	34.2	33.5	31.1
25	63.9	56.1	49.3	45.7	43.3	41.5	40.1	38.9	38.0	37.2	36.4	33.8
30	68.4	60.1	52.7	48.9	46.3	44.4	42.9	41.7	40.7	39.8	39.0	36.1
35	72.5	63.6	55.9	51.8	49.1	47.1	45.5	44.2	43.1	42.1	41.3	38.3
40	76.2	66.9	58.7	54.4	51.6	49.5	47.8	46.4	45.3	44.3	43.4	40.3
45	79.6	69.9	61.4	56.9	53.9	51.7	50.0	48.5	47.3	46.3	45.4	42.1
50	82.8	72.7	63.9	59.2	56.1	53.8	52.0	50.5	49.3	48.2	47.2	43.8
55	85.9	75.4	66.2	61.4	58.1	55.8	53.9	52.3	51.0	49.9	49.0	45.4
60	88.7	77.9	68.4	63.4	60.1	57.6	55.7	54.1	52.7	51.6	50.6	46.9
65	91.4	80.3	70.5	65.3	61.9	59.4	57.4	55.7	54.3	53.2	52.1	48.3
70	94.0	82.5	72.5	67.2	63.6	61.0	59.0	57.3	55.9	54.7	53.6	49.7
75	96.4	84.7	74.4	68.9	65.3	62.6	60.5	58.8	57.3	56.1	55.0	51.0
80	98.8	86.8	76.2	70.6	66.9	64.2	62.0	60.2	58.7	57.5	56.3	52.2
85	101	88.8	77.9	72.2	68.4	65.6	63.4	61.6	60.1	58.8	57.6	53.4
90	103	90.7	79.6	73.8	69.9	67.1	64.8	63.0	61.4	60.1	58.9	54.6
100	107	94.3	82.8	76.8	72.7	69.8	67.4	65.5	63.9	62.5	61.3	56.8
110	111	97.8	85.9	79.6	75.4	72.3	69.9	67.9	66.2	64.8	63.5	58.8
120	115	101	88.7	82.2	77.9	74.7	72.2	70.1	68.4	66.9	65.6	60.8
130	118	104	91.4	84.7	80.3	77.0	74.4	72.3	70.5	68.9	67.6	62.6
140	122	107	94.0	87.1	82.5	79.1	76.5	74.3	72.6	70.9	69.5	64.4

Table 6-2. Diameters of Pipes in Inches, from the Manning
Formula, $n = 0.016$ (Continued)

Discharge in cubic feet per second	$s = \dfrac{h}{l}$ = drop in hydraulic gradient per foot											
	.004	.005	.006	.007	.008	.009	.01	.015	.02	.025	.03	.04
.1	4.0	3.9	3.7	3.6	3.5	3.5	3.4	3.1	3.0	2.9	2.8	2.6
.2	5.2	5.0	4.8	4.7	4.6	4.5	4.4	4.1	3.9	3.7	3.6	3.4
.3	6.1	5.8	5.6	5.5	5.3	5.2	5.1	4.8	4.5	4.3	4.2	4.0
.4	6.8	6.5	6.3	6.1	6.0	5.8	5.7	5.3	5.0	4.8	4.6	4.4
.5	7.4	7.1	6.8	6.6	6.5	6.3	6.2	5.8	5.5	5.2	5.1	4.8
.6	7.9	7.6	7.3	7.1	6.9	6.8	6.7	6.2	5.8	5.6	5.4	5.1
.7	8.4	8.0	7.8	7.5	7.3	7.2	7.0	6.5	6.2	5.9	5.7	5.4
.8	8.8	8.4	8.2	7.9	7.7	7.6	7.4	6.9	6.5	6.2	6.0	5.7
.9	9.2	8.8	8.5	8.3	8.1	7.9	7.7	7.2	6.8	6.5	6.3	6.0
1.0	9.6	9.2	8.9	8.6	8.4	8.2	8.0	7.5	7.1	6.8	6.6	6.2
1.2	10.2	9.8	9.5	9.2	9.0	8.8	8.6	8.0	7.6	7.3	7.0	6.7
1.4	10.9	10.4	10.1	9.8	9.5	9.3	9.1	8.5	8.0	7.7	7.4	7.0
1.6	11.4	10.9	10.6	10.3	10.0	9.8	9.6	8.9	8.4	8.1	7.8	7.4
1.8	11.9	11.4	11.1	10.7	10.5	10.2	10.0	9.3	8.8	8.5	8.2	7.7
2.0	12.4	11.9	11.5	11.2	10.9	10.7	10.4	9.7	9.2	8.8	8.5	8.1
2.5	13.5	12.9	12.5	12.1	11.8	11.6	11.4	10.5	10.0	9.6	9.2	8.8
3.0	14.4	13.9	13.4	13.0	12.7	12.4	12.2	11.3	10.7	10.2	9.9	9.4
3.5	15.3	14.7	14.2	13.8	13.4	13.1	12.9	11.9	11.3	10.9	10.5	9.9
4.0	16.1	15.4	14.9	14.5	14.1	13.8	13.5	12.5	11.9	11.4	11.0	10.4
4.5	16.8	16.1	15.6	15.1	14.8	14.4	14.2	13.1	12.4	11.9	11.5	10.9
5	17.5	16.8	16.2	15.7	15.4	15.0	14.7	13.7	12.9	12.4	12.0	11.4
6	18.7	18.0	17.4	16.9	16.4	16.1	15.8	14.6	13.9	13.3	12.8	12.2
7	19.8	19.0	18.4	17.9	17.4	17.0	16.7	15.5	14.7	14.1	13.6	12.9
8	20.9	20.0	19.3	18.8	18.3	17.9	17.6	16.3	15.4	14.8	14.3	13.5
9	21.8	20.9	20.2	19.6	19.2	18.7	18.4	17.0	16.1	15.5	14.9	14.2
10	22.7	21.8	21.0	20.4	19.9	19.5	19.1	17.7	16.8	16.0	15.5	14.7
12	24.3	23.3	22.5	21.9	21.3	20.9	20.5	19.0	18.0	17.2	16.6	15.8
14	25.7	24.7	23.9	23.2	22.6	22.1	21.7	20.1	19.0	18.3	17.6	16.7
16	27.1	25.9	25.1	24.4	23.8	23.2	22.8	21.1	20.0	19.2	18.5	17.6
18	28.3	27.1	26.2	25.5	24.8	24.3	23.8	22.1	20.9	20.1	19.4	18.4
20	29.4	28.2	27.3	26.5	25.8	25.3	24.8	23.0	21.8	20.9	20.2	19.1
25	32.0	30.7	29.6	28.8	28.1	27.5	26.9	25.0	23.7	22.7	21.9	20.8
30	34.2	32.8	31.7	30.8	30.1	29.4	28.8	26.7	25.3	24.3	23.5	22.2
35	36.3	34.8	33.6	32.7	31.9	31.2	30.6	28.3	26.8	25.7	24.9	23.6
40	38.1	36.6	35.4	34.3	33.5	32.8	32.1	29.8	28.2	27.1	26.1	24.8
45	39.9	38.2	37.0	35.9	35.0	34.2	33.6	31.1	29.5	28.3	27.3	25.9
50	41.5	39.8	38.4	37.3	36.4	35.6	34.9	32.4	30.7	29.4	28.4	26.9
55	43.0	41.2	39.8	38.7	37.7	36.9	36.2	33.6	31.8	30.5	29.5	27.9
60	44.4	42.6	41.2	40.0	39.0	38.2	37.4	34.7	32.8	31.5	30.4	28.8
65	45.8	43.9	42.4	41.2	40.2	39.3	38.5	35.7	33.8	32.5	31.4	29.7
70	47.1	45.1	43.6	42.4	41.3	40.4	39.6	36.7	34.8	33.4	32.3	30.6
75	48.3	46.3	44.8	43.5	42.4	41.5	40.7	37.7	35.7	34.2	33.1	31.4
80	49.5	47.4	45.9	44.5	43.4	42.5	41.7	38.6	36.6	35.1	33.9	32.1
85	50.6	48.5	46.9	45.6	44.4	43.5	42.6	39.5	37.4	35.9	34.7	32.9
90	51.7	49.6	47.9	46.6	45.4	44.4	43.5	40.4	38.2	36.7	35.4	33.6
100	53.8	51.6	49.8	48.4	47.2	46.2	45.3	42.0	39.8	38.1	36.9	34.9
110	55.8	53.5	51.7	50.2	49.0	47.9	47.0	43.5	41.2	39.5	38.2	36.2
120	57.6	55.2	53.4	51.9	50.6	49.5	48.5	45.0	42.6	40.9	39.5	37.4
130	59.4	56.9	55.0	53.4	52.1	51.0	50.0	46.3	43.9	42.1	40.7	38.5
140	61.0	58.5	56.6	54.9	53.6	52.4	51.4	47.6	45.1	43.3	41.8	39.6

Table 6-2. Diameters of Pipes in Inches, from the Manning Formula, $n = 0.018$ (*Continued*)

Discharge in cubic feet per second	$s = \dfrac{h}{l}$ = drop in hydraulic gradient per foot											
	.0001	.0002	.0004	.0006	.0008	.001	.0012	.0014	.0016	.0018	.002	.003
.1	8.4	7.4	6.5	6.0	5.7	5.5	5.3	5.1	5.0	4.9	4.8	4.4
.2	10.9	9.6	8.4	7.8	7.4	7.1	6.9	6.7	6.5	6.4	6.2	5.8
.3	12.7	11.2	9.8	9.1	8.6	8.3	8.0	7.8	7.6	7.4	7.2	6.7
.4	14.2	12.4	10.9	10.1	9.6	9.2	8.9	8.6	8.4	8.2	8.1	7.5
.5	15.4	13.5	11.9	11.0	10.4	10.0	9.7	9.4	9.2	9.0	8.8	8.1
.6	16.5	14.5	12.7	11.8	11.2	10.7	10.3	10.1	9.8	9.6	9.4	8.7
.7	17.5	15.3	13.5	12.5	11.8	11.3	11.0	10.6	10.4	10.2	10.0	9.2
.8	18.4	16.1	14.2	13.1	12.4	11.9	11.5	11.2	10.9	10.7	10.5	9.7
.9	19.2	16.9	14.8	13.7	13.0	12.5	12.0	11.7	11.4	11.2	10.9	10.1
1.0	20.0	17.5	15.4	14.3	13.5	13.0	12.5	12.2	11.9	11.6	11.4	10.6
1.2	21.4	18.8	16.5	15.3	14.5	13.9	13.4	13.0	12.7	12.4	12.2	11.3
1.4	22.7	19.9	17.5	16.2	15.3	14.7	14.2	13.8	13.5	13.2	12.9	12.0
1.6	23.8	20.9	18.4	17.0	16.1	15.5	14.9	14.5	14.2	13.9	13.6	12.6
1.8	24.9	21.9	19.2	17.8	16.9	16.2	15.6	15.2	14.8	14.5	14.2	13.2
2.0	25.9	22.7	20.0	18.5	17.5	16.8	16.2	15.8	15.4	15.1	14.8	13.7
2.5	28.2	24.7	21.7	20.1	19.1	18.3	17.7	17.2	16.7	16.4	16.1	14.9
3.0	30.1	26.5	23.2	21.5	20.4	19.6	18.9	18.4	17.9	17.5	17.2	15.9
3.5	31.9	28.0	24.6	22.8	21.6	20.7	20.0	19.5	19.0	18.6	18.2	16.9
4.0	33.6	29.5	25.9	24.0	22.7	21.8	21.1	20.5	20.0	19.5	19.1	17.7
4.5	35.1	30.8	27.1	25.1	23.8	22.8	22.0	21.4	20.9	20.4	20.0	18.5
5	36.5	32.1	28.2	26.1	24.7	23.7	22.9	22.3	21.7	21.2	20.8	19.3
6	39.1	34.3	30.1	27.9	26.5	25.4	24.5	23.8	23.2	22.7	22.3	20.7
7	41.4	36.4	31.9	29.6	28.0	26.9	26.0	25.3	24.6	24.1	23.6	21.9
8	43.5	38.2	33.6	31.1	29.5	28.3	27.3	26.5	25.9	25.3	24.8	23.0
9	45.5	40.0	35.1	32.5	30.8	29.6	28.6	27.7	27.1	26.5	26.0	24.1
10	47.3	41.6	36.5	33.8	32.1	30.7	29.7	28.9	28.2	27.5	27.0	25.0
12	50.7	44.5	39.1	36.2	34.3	32.9	31.8	30.9	30.1	29.5	28.9	26.8
14	53.7	47.2	41.4	38.4	36.4	34.9	33.7	32.7	31.9	31.2	30.6	28.4
16	56.5	49.6	43.5	40.4	38.2	36.7	35.4	34.4	33.6	32.8	32.2	29.8
18	59.0	51.8	45.5	42.2	40.0	38.3	37.0	36.0	35.1	34.3	33.7	31.2
20	61.4	53.9	47.3	43.9	41.6	39.9	38.5	37.4	36.5	35.7	35.0	32.5
25	66.8	58.6	51.5	47.7	45.2	43.4	41.9	40.7	39.7	38.8	38.1	35.3
30	71.5	62.8	55.1	51.1	48.4	46.4	44.9	43.6	42.5	41.6	40.8	37.8
35	75.7	66.5	58.4	54.1	51.3	49.2	47.5	46.2	45.0	44.1	43.2	40.0
40	79.4	69.9	61.4	56.9	53.9	51.7	50.0	48.5	47.3	46.3	45.4	42.1
45	83.2	73.1	64.2	59.5	56.4	54.0	52.2	50.7	49.5	48.4	47.5	44.0
50	86.6	76.0	66.8	61.9	58.6	56.2	54.3	52.8	51.5	50.4	49.4	45.8
55	89.7	78.8	69.2	64.1	60.8	58.3	56.3	54.7	53.4	52.2	51.2	47.4
60	92.7	81.4	71.5	66.3	62.8	60.2	58.2	56.5	55.1	53.9	52.9	49.0
65	95.5	83.9	73.7	68.3	64.7	62.0	60.0	58.2	56.8	55.6	54.5	50.5
70	98.2	86.2	75.7	70.2	66.5	63.8	61.6	59.9	58.4	57.1	56.0	51.9
75	101	88.5	77.7	72.0	68.2	65.5	63.3	61.5	59.9	58.6	57.5	53.3
80	103	90.7	79.6	73.8	69.9	67.1	64.8	63.0	61.4	60.1	58.9	54.6
85	106	92.8	81.5	75.5	71.5	68.6	66.3	64.4	62.8	61.4	60.2	55.8
90	108	94.8	83.2	77.1	73.1	70.1	67.7	65.8	64.2	62.8	61.5	57.0
100	112	98.6	86.6	80.2	76.0	72.9	70.5	68.4	66.8	65.3	64.0	59.3
110	116	102	89.7	83.2	78.8	75.6	73.0	70.9	69.2	67.7	66.4	61.5
120	120	106	92.7	85.9	81.4	78.1	75.4	73.3	71.5	69.9	68.6	63.5
130	124	109	95.5	88.5	83.9	80.4	77.7	75.5	73.7	72.1	70.6	65.5
140	127	112	98.2	91.0	86.3	82.7	79.9	77.7	75.7	74.1	72.6	67.3

Table 6-2. Diameters of Pipes in Inches, from the Manning Formula, $n = 0.018$ (*Concluded*)

Discharge in cubic feet per second	$s = \dfrac{h}{l}$ = drop in hydraulic gradient per foot											
	.004	.005	.006	.007	.008	.009	.01	.015	.02	.025	.03	.04
.1	4.2	4.0	3.9	3.8	3.7	3.6	3.5	3.3	3.1	3.0	2.9	2.7
.2	5.5	5.2	5.1	4.9	4.8	4.7	4.6	4.3	4.1	3.9	3.7	3.5
.3	6.4	6.1	5.9	5.7	5.6	5.5	5.4	5.0	4.7	4.5	4.4	4.1
.4	7.1	6.8	6.6	6.4	6.2	6.1	6.0	5.5	5.2	5.0	4.9	4.6
.5	7.7	7.4	7.1	6.9	6.8	6.6	6.5	6.0	5.7	5.5	5.3	5.0
.6	8.3	7.9	7.7	7.5	7.3	7.1	7.0	6.4	6.1	5.9	5.7	5.4
.7	8.7	8.4	8.1	7.9	7.7	7.5	7.4	6.8	6.5	6.2	6.0	5.7
.8	9.2	8.8	8.5	8.3	8.1	7.9	7.7	7.2	6.8	6.5	6.3	6.0
.9	9.6	9.2	8.9	8.7	8.5	8.3	8.1	7.5	7.1	6.8	6.6	6.2
1.0	10.0	9.6	9.3	9.0	8.8	8.6	8.4	7.8	7.4	7.1	6.9	6.5
1.2	10.7	10.3	9.9	9.6	9.4	9.2	9.0	8.4	7.9	7.6	7.3	7.0
1.4	11.3	10.9	10.5	10.2	10.0	9.8	9.6	8.9	8.4	8.0	7.8	7.4
1.6	11.9	11.4	11.1	10.8	10.5	10.2	10.0	9.3	8.8	8.5	8.2	7.7
1.8	12.5	12.0	11.6	11.2	10.9	10.7	10.5	9.7	9.2	8.8	8.5	8.1
2.0	13.0	12.4	12.0	11.7	11.4	11.1	10.9	10.1	9.6	9.2	8.9	8.4
2.5	14.1	13.5	13.1	12.7	12.4	12.1	11.9	11.0	10.4	10.0	9.7	9.2
3.0	15.1	14.5	14.0	13.6	13.3	13.0	12.7	11.8	11.2	10.7	10.3	9.8
3.5	16.0	15.3	14.8	14.4	14.0	13.7	13.5	12.5	11.8	11.3	11.0	10.4
4.0	16.8	16.1	15.6	15.1	14.8	14.4	14.1	13.1	12.4	11.9	11.5	10.9
4.5	17.6	16.9	16.3	15.8	15.4	15.1	14.8	13.7	13.0	12.5	12.0	11.4
5	18.3	17.5	16.9	16.5	16.1	15.7	15.4	14.3	13.5	13.0	12.5	11.9
6	19.6	18.8	18.1	17.6	17.2	16.8	16.5	15.3	14.5	13.9	13.4	12.7
7	20.7	19.9	19.2	18.7	18.2	17.8	17.5	16.2	15.3	14.7	14.2	13.5
8	21.8	20.9	20.2	19.6	19.1	18.7	18.4	17.0	16.1	15.5	14.9	14.2
9	22.8	21.9	21.1	20.5	20.0	19.6	19.2	17.8	16.9	16.2	15.6	14.8
10	23.7	22.7	22.0	21.3	20.8	20.4	20.0	18.5	17.5	16.8	16.2	15.4
12	25.4	24.3	23.5	22.9	22.3	21.8	21.4	19.8	18.8	18.0	17.4	16.5
14	26.9	25.8	24.9	24.2	23.6	23.1	22.7	21.0	19.9	19.1	18.4	17.5
16	28.3	27.1	26.2	25.5	24.8	24.3	23.8	22.1	20.9	20.1	19.4	18.4
18	29.6	28.3	27.4	26.6	26.0	25.4	24.9	23.1	21.9	21.0	20.3	19.2
20	30.7	29.5	28.5	27.7	27.0	26.4	25.9	24.0	22.8	21.8	21.1	20.0
25	33.4	32.1	31.0	30.1	29.4	28.7	28.2	26.1	24.8	23.7	22.9	21.7
30	35.8	34.3	33.2	32.2	31.4	30.7	30.1	27.9	26.5	25.4	24.5	23.2
35	37.9	36.3	35.1	34.1	33.3	32.6	31.9	29.6	28.0	26.9	26.0	24.6
40	39.9	38.2	37.0	35.9	35.0	34.2	33.6	31.1	29.5	28.3	27.3	25.9
45	41.7	40.0	38.6	37.5	36.6	35.8	35.1	32.5	30.8	29.6	28.6	27.1
50	43.4	41.6	40.2	39.0	38.1	37.2	36.5	33.8	32.1	30.7	29.7	28.2
55	44.9	43.1	41.6	40.5	39.5	38.6	37.8	35.1	33.2	31.9	30.8	29.2
60	46.4	44.5	43.0	41.8	40.8	39.9	39.1	36.2	34.3	32.9	31.8	30.1
65	47.8	45.9	44.3	43.1	42.0	41.1	40.3	37.3	35.4	33.9	32.8	31.1
70	49.2	47.2	45.6	44.3	43.2	42.2	41.4	38.4	36.4	34.9	33.7	31.9
75	50.5	48.4	46.8	45.4	44.3	43.3	42.5	39.4	37.3	35.8	34.6	32.8
80	51.7	49.6	47.9	46.6	45.4	44.4	43.5	40.4	38.2	36.7	35.4	33.6
85	52.9	50.7	49.0	47.6	46.4	45.4	44.5	41.3	39.1	37.5	36.3	34.4
90	54.0	51.8	50.1	48.7	47.5	46.4	45.4	42.2	40.0	38.3	37.0	35.1
100	56.2	53.9	52.1	50.6	49.4	48.3	47.3	43.9	41.6	39.9	38.5	36.5
110	58.3	55.9	54.0	52.5	51.2	50.0	49.1	45.5	43.1	41.3	39.9	37.8
120	60.2	57.7	55.8	54.2	52.9	51.7	50.7	47.0	44.5	42.7	41.3	39.1
130	62.0	59.5	57.5	55.9	54.5	53.3	52.2	48.4	45.9	44.0	42.5	40.3
140	63.8	61.2	59.1	57.4	56.0	54.8	53.7	49.8	47.2	45.2	43.7	41.4

Table 6-3. Diameters of Circles in Feet and Inches; Areas in Square Feet

Diameter Inches	Feet and inches	0	⅛	¼	⅜	½	⅝	¾	⅞
0	0–0	......	.0001	.0003	.0008	.0014	.0021	.0031	.0042
1	0–1	.0055	.0069	.0085	.0103	.0123	.0144	.0167	.0192
2	0–2	.0218	.0246	.0276	.0308	.0341	.0376	.0413	.0451
3	0–3	.0491	.0533	.0576	.0621	.0668	.0717	.0767	.0819
4	0–4	.0873	.0928	.0985	.1044	.1104	.1167	.1231	.1296
5	0–5	.1364	.1433	.1503	.1576	.1650	.1726	.1803	.1883
6	0–6	.1963	.2046	.2131	.2217	.2304	.2394	.2485	.2578
7	0–7	.2673	.2769	.2867	.2967	.3068	.3171	.3276	.3382
8	0–8	.3491	.3601	.3712	.3826	.3941	.4057	.4176	.4296
9	0–9	.4418	.4541	.4667	.4794	.4922	.5053	.5185	.5319
10	0–10	.5454	.5591	.5730	.5871	.6013	.6157	.6303	.6450
11	0–11	.6600	.6750	.6903	.7057	.7213	.7371	.7530	.7691
12	1–0	.7854	.8018	.8185	.8353	.8522	.8693	.8866	.9041
13	1–1	.9218	.9396	.9575	.9757	.9940	1.013	1.031	1.050
14	1–2	1.069	1.088	1.108	1.127	1.147	1.167	1.187	1.207
15	1–3	1.227	1.248	1.268	1.289	1.310	1.332	1.353	1.375
16	1–4	1.396	1.418	1.440	1.462	1.485	1.507	1.530	1.553
17	1–5	1.576	1.600	1.623	1.647	1.670	1.694	1.718	1.743
18	1–6	1.767	1.792	1.817	1.842	1.867	1.892	1.917	1.943
19	1–7	1.969	1.995	2.021	2.047	2.074	2.101	2.127	2.154
20	1–8	2.182	2.209	2.237	2.264	2.292	2.320	2.348	2.377
21	1–9	2.405	2.434	2.463	2.492	2.521	2.551	2.580	2.610
22	1–10	2.640	2.670	2.700	2.731	2.761	2.792	2.823	2.854
23	1–11	2.885	2.917	2.948	2.980	3.012	3.044	3.076	3.109
24	2–0	3.142	3.174	3.207	3.241	3.274	3.307	3.341	3.375
25	2–1	3.409	3.443	3.477	3.512	3.547	3.581	3.616	3.652
26	2–2	3.687	3.723	3.758	3.794	3.830	3.866	3.903	3.939
27	2–3	3.976	4.013	4.050	4.087	4.125	4.162	4.200	4.238
28	2–4	4.276	4.314	4.353	4.391	4.430	4.469	4.508	4.547
29	2–5	4.587	4.627	4.666	4.706	4.746	4.787	4.827	4.868
30	2–6	4.909	4.950	4.991	5.032	5.074	5.115	5.157	5.199
31	2–7	5.241	5.284	5.326	5.369	5.412	5.455	5.498	5.541
32	2–8	5.585	5.629	5.673	5.717	5.761	5.805	5.850	5.895
33	2–9	5.940	5.985	6.030	6.075	6.121	6.167	6.213	6.259
34	2–10	6.305	6.351	6.398	6.445	6.492	6.539	6.586	6.634
35	2–11	6.681	6.729	6.777	6.825	6.874	6.922	6 971	7.020
36	3–0	7.069	7.118	7.167	7.217	7.266	7.316	7 366	7.416
37	3–1	7.467	7.517	7.568	7.619	7.670	7.721	7.773	7.824
38	3–2	7.876	7.928	7.980	8.032	8.084	8.137	8.190	8.243
39	3–3	8.296	8.349	8.402	8.456	8.510	8.564	8.618	8.672
40	3–4	8.727	8.781	8.836	8.891	8.946	9 001	9.057	9.113
41	3–5	9.168	9.224	9.281	9.337	9.393	9.450	9.507	9.564
42	3–6	9.621	9.678	9.736	9.794	9.852	9.910	9.968	10.03
43	3–7	10.08	10.14	10.20	10.26	10.32	10.38	10.44	10.50
44	3–8	10.56	10.62	10.68	10.74	10.80	10.86	10.92	10.98
45	3–9	11.04	11.11	11.17	11.23	11.29	11.35	11.42	11.48
46	3–10	11.54	11.60	11.67	11.73	11.79	11.86	11.92	11.98
47	3–11	12.05	12.11	12.18	12.24	12.31	12.37	12.44	12.50
48	4–0	12.57	12.63	12.70	12.76	12.83	12.90	12.96	13.03
49	4–1	13.10	13.16	13.23	13.30	13.36	13.43	13.50	13.57

Table 6-3. Diameters of Circles in Feet and Inches; Areas in Square Feet (*Continued*)

Inches	Feet and inches	0	⅛	¼	⅜	½	⅝	¾	⅞
50	4–2	13.64	13.70	13.77	13.84	13.91	13.98	14.05	14.12
51	4–3	14.19	14.26	14.33	14.40	14.47	14.54	14.61	14.68
52	4–4	14.75	14.82	14.89	14.96	15.03	15.10	15.18	15.25
53	4–5	15.32	15.39	15.47	15.54	15.61	15.68	15.76	15.83
54	4–6	15.90	15.98	16.05	16.12	16.20	16.27	16.35	16.42
55	4–7	16.50	16.57	16.65	16.72	16.80	16.87	16.95	17.02
56	4–8	17.10	17.18	17.26	17.33	17.41	17.49	17.57	17.64
57	4–9	17.72	17.80	17.88	17.95	18.03	18.11	18.19	18.27
58	4–10	18.35	18.43	18.51	18.59	18.67	18.75	18.83	18.91
59	4–11	18.99	19.07	19.15	19.23	19.31	19.39	19.47	19.55
60	5–0	19.63	19.72	19.80	19.88	19.96	20.05	20.13	20.21
61	5–1	20.29	20.38	20.46	20.55	20.63	20.71	20.80	20.88
62	5–2	20.97	21.05	21.14	21.22	21.31	21.39	21.48	21.56
63	5–3	21.65	21.73	21.82	21.91	21.99	22.08	22.17	22.25
64	5–4	22.34	22.43	22.52	22.60	22.69	22.78	22.87	22.96
65	5–5	23.04	23.13	23 22	23.31	23.40	23.49	23.58	23.67
66	5–6	23.76	23.85	23.94	24.03	24.12	24.21	24.30	24.39
67	5–7	24.48	24.58	24.67	24.76	24.85	24.94	25.03	25.13
68	5–8	25.22	25.31	25.41	25.50	25.59	25.69	25.78	25.87
69	5–9	25.97	26.06	26.16	26.25	26.34	26.44	26.53	26.63
70	5–10	26.73	26.82	26.92	27.01	27.11	27.20	27.29	27.39
71	5–11	27.49	27.59	27.69	27.79	27.88	27.98	28.08	28.18
72	6–0	28.27	28.37	28.47	28.57	28.67	28.77	28.87	28.97
73	6–1	29.07	29.16	29.26	29.36	29.46	29.57	29.67	29.77
74	6–2	29.87	29.97	30.07	30.17	30.27	30.37	30.48	30.58
75	6–3	30.68	30.78	30.88	30.99	31.09	31.19	31.30	31.40
76	6–4	31.50	31.61	31.71	31.81	31.92	32.02	32.13	32.23
77	6–5	32.34	32.44	32.55	32.65	32.76	32.86	32.97	33.08
78	6–6	33.18	33.29	33.40	33.50	33.61	33.72	33.82	33.93
79	6–7	34.04	34.15	34.26	34.36	34.47	34.58	34.69	34.80
80	6–8	34.91	35.02	35.13	35.24	35.34	35.45	35.56	35.67
81	6–9	35.78	35.90	36.01	36.12	36.23	36.34	36.45	36.56
82	6–10	36.67	36.79	36.90	37.01	37.12	37.23	37.35	37.46
83	6–11	37.57	37.69	37.80	37.91	38.03	38.14	38.26	38.37
84	7–0	38.48	38.60	38.71	38.83	38.94	39.06	39.17	39.29
85	7–1	39.41	39.52	39.64	39.75	39.87	39.99	40.10	40.22
86	7–2	40.34	40.46	40.57	40.69	40.81	40.93	41.05	41.16
87	7–3	41.28	41.40	41.52	41.64	41.76	41.88	42.00	42.12
88	7–4	42.24	42.36	42.48	42.60	42.72	42.84	42.96	43.08
89	7–5	43.20	43.32	43.45	43.57	43.69	43.81	43.93	44.06
90	7–6	44.18	44.30	44.42	44.55	44.67	44.79	44.92	45.04
91	7–7	45.17	45.29	45.41	45.54	45.66	45.79	45.91	46.04
92	7–8	46.16	46.29	46.42	46.54	46.67	46.79	46.92	47.05
93	7–9	47.17	47.30	47.43	47.55	47.68	47.81	47.94	48.06
94	7–10	48.19	48.32	48.45	48.58	48.71	48.84	48.97	49.09
95	7–11	49.22	49.35	49.48	49.61	49.74	49.87	50.00	50.13
96	8–0	50.27	50.40	50.53	50.66	50.79	50.92	51.05	51.19
97	8–1	51.32	51.45	51.58	51.72	51.85	51.98	52.11	52.25
98	8–2	52.38	52.52	52.65	52.78	52.92	53.05	53.19	53.32
99	8–3	53.46	53.59	53.73	53.86	54.00	54.13	54.27	54.41

Table 6-3. Diameters of Circles in Feet and Inches; Areas in
Square Feet (*Concluded*)

Diameter, feet and inches	0	⅛	¼	⅜	½	⅝	¾	⅞
8–4	54.54	54.68	54.81	54.95	55.09	55.23	55.36	55.50
8–5	55.64	55.78	55.91	56.05	56.19	56.33	56.47	56.61
8–6	56.75	56.88	57.02	57.16	57.30	57.44	57.58	57.72
8–7	57.86	58.00	58.14	58.29	58.43	58.57	58.71	58.85
8–8	58.99	59.13	59.28	59.42	59.56	59.70	59.85	59.99
8–9	60.13	60.28	60.42	60.56	60.71	60.85	60.99	61.14
8–10	61.28	61.43	61.57	61.72	61.86	62.01	62.15	62.30
8–11	62.44	62.59	62.74	62.88	63.03	63.18	63.32	63.47
9–0	63.62	63.77	63.91	64.06	64.21	64.36	64.50	64.65
9–1	64.80	64.95	65.10	65.25	65.40	65.55	65.70	65.85
9–2	66.00	66.15	66.30	66.45	66.60	66.75	66.90	67.05
9–3	67.20	67.35	67.50	67.66	67.81	67.96	68.11	68.26
9–4	68.42	68.57	68.72	68.88	69.03	69.18	69.34	69.49
9–5	69.64	69.80	69.95	70.11	70.26	70.42	70.57	70.73
9–6	70.88	71.04	71.19	71.35	71.51	71.66	71.82	71.97
9–7	72.13	**72**.29	72.45	72.60	72.76	72.92	73.08	73.23
9–8	73.39	73.55	73.71	73.87	74.02	74.18	74.34	74.50
9–9	74.66	74.82	74.98	75.14	75.30	75.46	75.62	75.78
9–10	75.94	76.10	76.27	76.43	76.59	76.75	76.91	77.07
9–11	77.24	77.40	77.56	77.72	77.89	78.05	78.21	78.38
10–0	78.54	78.70	78.87	79.03	79.20	79.36	79.52	79.69
10–1	79.85	80.02	80.18	80.35	80.52	80.68	80.85	81.01
10–2	81.18	81.35	81.51	81.68	81.85	82.01	82.18	82.35
10–3	82.52	82.68	82.85	83.02	83.19	83.36	83.53	83.69
10–4	83.86	84.03	84.20	84.37	84.54	84.71	84.88	85.05
10–5	85.22	85.39	85.56	85.73	85.90	86.08	86.25	86.42
10–6	86.59	86.76	86.93	87.11	87.28	87.45	87.62	87.80
10–7	87.97	88.14	88.32	88.49	88.66	88.84	89.01	89.19
10–8	89.36	89.54	89.71	89.89	90.06	90.24	90.41	90.59
10–9	90.76	90.94	91.11	91.29	91.47	91.64	91.82	92.00
10–10	92.18	92.35	92.53	92.71	92.89	93.06	93.24	93.42
10–11	93.60	93.78	93.96	94.14	94.31	94.49	94.67	94.85
11–0	95.03	95.21	95.39	95.57	95.75	95.94	96.12	96.30
11–1	96.48	96.66	96.84	97.02	97.21	97.39	97.57	97.75
11–2	97.93	98.12	98.30	98.48	98.67	98.85	99.03	99.22
11–3	99.40	99.59	99.77	99.95	100.14	100.32	100.51	100.69
11–4	100.88	101.07	101.25	101.44	101.62	101.81	102.00	102.18
11–5	102.37	102.56	102.74	102.93	103.12	103.31	103.49	103.68
11–6	103.87	104.06	104.25	104.43	104.62	104.81	105.00	105.19
11–7	105.38	105.57	105.76	105.95	106.14	106.33	106.52	106.71
11–8	106.90	107.09	107.28	107.47	107.67	107.86	108.05	108.24
11–9	108.43	108.63	108.82	109.01	109.20	109.40	109.59	109.78
11–10	109.98	110.17	110.37	110.56	110.75	110.95	111.14	111.34
11–11	111.53	111.73	111.92	112.12	112.31	112.51	112.71	112.90
12–0	113.10	113.29	113.49	113.69	113.88	114.08	114.28	114.48
12–1	114.67	114.87	115.07	115.27	115.47	115.66	115.86	116.06
12–2	116.26	116.46	116.66	116.86	117.06	117.26	117.46	117.66
12–3	117.86	118.06	118.26	118.46	118.66	118.86	119.06	119.27
12–4	119.47	119.67	119.87	120.07	120.28	120.48	120.68	120.88
12–5	121.09	121.29	121.49	121.70	121.90	122.11	122.31	122.51

Table 6-4. Areas of Circles by Hundredths

Diam.	.00	.01	.02	.03	.04	.05	.06	.07	.08	.09
0.0	0.000	0.000	0.000	0.001	0.001	0.002	0.003	0.004	0.005	0.006
0.1	0.008	0.010	0.011	0.013	0.015	0.018	0.020	0.023	0.025	0.028
0.2	0.031	0.035	0.038	0.042	0.045	0.049	0.053	0.057	0.062	0.066
0.3	0.071	0.075	0.080	0.086	0.091	0.096	0.102	0.108	0.113	0.119
0.4	0.126	0.132	0.139	0.145	0.152	0.159	0.166	0.173	0.181	0.189
0.5	0.196	0.204	0.212	0.221	0.229	0.238	0.246	0.255	0.264	0.273
0.6	0.283	0.292	0.302	0.312	0.322	0.332	0.342	0.353	0.363	0.374
0.7	0.385	0.396	0.407	0.419	0.430	0.442	0.454	0.466	0.478	0.490
0.8	0.503	0.515	0.528	0.541	0.554	0.567	0.581	0.594	0.608	0.622
0.9	0.636	0.650	0.665	0.679	0.694	0.709	0.724	0.739	0.754	0.770
1.0	0.785	0.801	0.817	0.833	0.849	0.866	0.882	0.899	0.916	0.933
1.1	0.950	0.968	0.985	1.003	1.021	1.039	1.057	1.075	1.094	1.112
1.2	1.131	1.150	1.169	1.188	1.208	1.227	1.247	1.267	1.287	1.307
1.3	1.327	1.348	1.368	1.389	1.410	1.431	1.453	1.474	1.496	1.517
1.4	1.539	1.561	1.584	1.606	1.629	1.651	1.674	1.697	1.720	1.744
1.5	1.767	1.791	1.815	1.839	1.863	1.887	1.911	1.936	1.961	1.986
1.6	2.011	2.036	2.061	2.087	2.112	2.138	2.164	2.190	2.217	2.243
1.7	2.270	2.297	2.324	2.351	2.378	2.405	2.433	2.461	2.488	2.516
1.8	2.545	2.573	2.602	2.630	2.659	2.688	2.717	2.746	2.776	2.806
1.9	2.835	2.865	2.895	2.926	2.956	2.986	3.017	3.048	3.079	3.110
2.0	3.142	3.173	3.205	3.237	3.269	3.301	3.333	3.365	3.398	3.431
2.1	3.464	3.497	3.530	3.563	3.597	3.631	3.664	3.698	3.733	3.767
2.2	3.801	3.836	3.871	3.906	3.941	3.976	4.011	4.047	4.083	4.119
2.3	4.155	4.191	4.227	4.264	4.301	4.337	4.374	4.412	4.449	4.486
2.4	4.524	4.562	4.600	4.638	4.676	4.714	4.753	4.792	4.831	4.870
2.5	4.909	4.948	4.988	5.027	5.067	5.107	5.147	5.187	5.228	5.269
2.6	5.309	5.350	5.391	5.433	5.474	5.515	5.557	5.599	5.641	5.683
2.7	5.726	5.768	5.811	5.853	5.896	5.940	5.983	6.026	6.070	6.114
2.8	6.158	6.202	6.246	6.290	6.335	6.379	6.424	6.469	6.514	6.560
2.9	6.605	6.651	6.697	6.743	6.789	6.835	6.881	6.928	6.975	7.022
3.0	7.069	7.116	7.163	7.211	7.258	7.306	7.354	7.402	7.451	7.499
3.1	7.548	7.596	7.645	7.694	7.744	7.793	7.843	7.892	7.942	7.992
3.2	8.042	8.093	8.143	8.194	8.245	8.296	8.347	8.398	8.450	8.501
3.3	8.553	8.605	8.657	8.709	8.762	8.814	8.867	8.920	8.973	9.026
3.4	9.079	9.133	9.186	9.240	9.294	9.348	9.402	9.457	9.511	9.566
3.5	9.62	9.68	9.73	9.79	9.84	9.90	9.95	10.01	10.07	10.12
3.6	10.18	10.24	10.29	10.35	10.41	10.46	10.52	10.58	10.64	10.69
3.7	10.75	10.81	10.87	10.93	10.99	11.04	11.10	11.16	11.22	11.28
3.8	11.34	11.40	11.46	11.52	11.58	11.64	11.70	11.76	11.82	11.88
3.9	11.95	12.01	12.07	12.13	12.19	12.25	12.32	12.38	12.44	12.50
4.0	12.57	12.63	12.69	12.76	12.82	12.88	12.95	13.01	13.07	13.14
4.1	13.20	13.27	13.33	13.40	13.46	13.53	13.59	13.66	13.72	13.79
4.2	13.85	13.92	13.99	14.05	14.12	14.19	14.25	14.32	14.39	14.45
4.3	14.52	14.59	14.66	14.73	14.79	14.86	14.93	15.00	15.07	15.14
4.4	15.21	15.27	15.34	15.41	15.48	15.55	15.62	15.69	15.76	15.83
4.5	15.90	15.98	16.05	16.12	16.19	16.26	16.33	16.40	16.47	16.55
4.6	16.62	16.69	16.76	16.84	16.91	16.98	17.06	17.13	17.20	17.28
4.7	17.35	17.42	17.50	17.57	17.65	17.72	17.80	17.87	17.95	18.02
4.8	18.10	18.17	18.25	18.32	18.40	18.47	18.55	18.63	18.70	18.78
4.9	18.86	18.93	19.01	19.09	19.17	19.24	19.32	19.40	19.48	19.56

Table 6-4. Areas of Circles by Hundredths (*Continued*)

Diam.	.00	.01	.02	.03	.04	.05	.06	.07	.08	.09
5.0	19.63	19.71	19.79	19.87	19.95	20.03	20.11	20.19	20.27	20.35
.1	20.43	20.51	20.59	20.67	20.75	20.83	20.91	20.99	21.07	21.16
.2	21.24	21.32	21.40	21.48	21.57	21.65	21.73	21.81	21.90	21.98
.3	22.06	22.15	22.23	22.31	22.40	22.48	22.56	22.65	22.73	22.82
.4	22.90	22.99	23.07	23.16	23.24	23.33	23.41	23.50	23.59	23.67
5.5	23.76	23.84	23.93	24.02	24.11	24.19	24.28	24.37	24.45	24.54
.6	24.63	24.72	24.81	24.89	24.98	25.07	25.16	25.25	25.34	25.43
.7	25.52	25.61	25.70	25.79	25.88	25.97	26.06	26.15	26.24	26.33
.8	26.42	26.51	26.60	26.69	26.79	26.88	26.97	27.06	27.15	27.25
.9	27.34	27.43	27.53	27.62	27.71	27.81	27.90	27.99	28.09	28.18
6.0	28.27	28.37	28.46	28.56	28.65	28.75	28.84	28.94	29.03	29.13
.1	29.22	29.32	29.42	29.51	29.61	29.71	29.80	29.90	30.00	30.09
.2	30.19	30.29	30.39	30.48	30.58	30.68	30.78	30.88	30.97	31.07
.3	31.17	31.27	31.37	31.47	31.57	31.67	31.77	31.87	31.97	32.07
.4	32.17	32.27	32.37	32.47	32.57	32.67	32.78	32.88	32.98	33.08
6.5	33.18	33.29	33.39	33.49	33.59	33.70	33.80	33.90	34.00	34.11
.6	34.21	34.32	34.42	34.52	34.63	34.73	34.84	34.94	35.05	35.15
.7	35.26	35.36	35.47	35.57	35.68	35.78	35.89	36.00	36.10	36.21
.8	36.32	36.42	36.53	36.64	36.75	36.85	36.96	37.07	37.18	37.28
.9	37.39	37.50	37.61	37.72	37.83	37.94	38.05	38.16	38.26	38.37
7.0	38.48	38.59	38.70	38.82	38.93	39.04	39.15	39.26	39.37	39.48
.1	39.59	39.70	39.82	39.93	40.04	40.15	40.26	40.38	40.49	40.60
.2	40.72	40.83	40.94	41.06	41.17	41.28	41.40	41.51	41.62	41.74
.3	41.85	41.97	42.08	42.20	42.31	42.43	42.54	42.66	42.78	42.89
.4	43.01	43.12	43.24	43.36	43.47	43.59	43.71	43.83	43.94	44.06
7.5	44.18	44.30	44.41	44.53	44.65	44.77	44.89	45.01	45.13	45.25
.6	45.36	45.48	45.60	45.72	45.84	45.96	46.08	46.20	46.32	46.45
.7	46.57	46.69	46.81	46.93	47.05	47.17	47.29	47.42	47.54	47.66
.8	47.78	47.91	48.03	48.15	48.27	48.40	48.52	48.65	48.77	48.89
.9	49.02	49.14	49.27	49.39	49.51	49.64	49.76	49.89	50.01	50.14
8.0	50.27	50.39	50.52	50.64	50.77	50.90	51.02	51.15	51.28	51.40
.1	51.53	51.66	51.78	51.91	52.04	52.17	52.30	52.42	52.55	52.68
.2	52.81	52.94	53.07	53.20	53.33	53.46	53.59	53.72	53.85	53.98
.3	54.11	54.24	54.37	54.50	54.63	54.76	54.89	55.02	55.15	55.29
.4	55.42	55.55	55.68	55.81	55.95	56.08	56.21	56.35	56.48	56.61
8.5	56.75	56.88	57.01	57.15	57.28	57.41	57.55	57.68	57.82	57.95
.6	58.09	58.22	58.36	58.49	58.63	58.77	58.90	59.04	59.17	59.31
.7	59.45	59.58	59.72	59.86	59.99	60.13	60.27	60.41	60.55	60.68
.8	60.82	60.96	61.10	61.24	61.38	61.51	61.65	61.79	61.93	62.07
.9	62.21	62.35	62.49	62.63	62.77	62.91	63.05	63.19	63.33	63.48
9.0	63.62	63.76	63.90	64.04	64.18	64.33	64.47	64.61	64.75	64.90
.1	65.04	65.18	65.33	65.47	65.61	65.76	65.90	66.04	66.19	66.33
.2	66.48	66.62	66.77	66.91	67.06	67.20	67.35	67.49	67.64	67.78
.3	67.93	68.08	68.22	68.37	68.51	68.66	68.81	68.96	69.10	69.25
.4	69.40	69.55	69.69	69.84	69.99	70.14	70.29	70.44	70.58	70.73
9.5	70.88	71.03	71.18	71.33	71.48	71.63	71.78	71.93	72.08	72.23
.6	72.38	72.53	72.68	72.84	72.99	73.14	73.29	73.44	73.59	73.75
.7	73.90	74.05	74.20	74.36	74.51	74.66	74.82	74.97	75.12	75.28
.8	75.43	75.58	75.74	75.89	76.05	76.20	76.36	76.51	76.67	76.82
.9	76.98	77.13	77.29	77.44	77.60	77.76	77.91	78.07	78.23	78.38

Table 6-4. Areas of Circles by Hundredths *(Continued)*

Diam.	.00	.01	.02	.03	.04	.05	.06	.07	.08	.09
10.0	78.54	78.70	78.85	79.01	79.17	79.33	79.49	79.64	79.80	79.96
10.1	80.12	80.28	80.44	80.60	80.75	80.91	81.07	81.23	81.39	81.55
10.2	81.71	81.87	82.03	82.19	82.35	82.52	82.68	82.84	83.00	83.16
10.3	83.32	83.48	83.65	83.81	83.97	84.13	84.30	84.46	84.62	84.79
10.4	84.95	85.11	85.28	85.44	85.60	85.77	85.93	86.10	86.26	86.43
10.5	86.59	86.76	86.92	87.09	87.25	87.42	87.58	87.75	87.91	88.08
10.6	88.25	88.41	88.58	88.75	88.91	89.08	89.25	89.42	89.58	89.75
10.7	89.92	90.09	90.26	90.43	90.59	90.76	90.93	91.10	91.27	91.44
10.8	91.61	91.78	91.95	92.12	92.29	92.46	92.63	92.80	92.97	93.14
10.9	93.31	93.48	93.66	93.83	94.00	94.17	94.34	94.52	94.69	94.86
11.0	95.03	95.21	95.38	95.55	95.73	95.90	96.07	96.25	96.42	96.59
11.1	96.77	96.94	97.12	97.29	97.47	97.64	97.82	97.99	98.17	98.34
11.2	98.52	98.70	98.87	99.05	99.23	99.40	99.58	99.76	99.93	100.11
11.3	100.29	100.46	100.64	100.82	101.00	101.18	101.36	101.53	101.71	101.89
11.4	102.07	102.25	102.43	102.61	102.79	102.97	103.15	103.33	103.51	103.69
11.5	103.87	104.05	104.23	104.41	104.59	104.77	104.96	105.14	105.32	105.50
11.6	105.68	105.87	106.05	106.23	106.41	106.60	106.78	106.96	107.15	107.33
11.7	107.51	107.70	107.88	108.07	108.25	108.43	108.62	108.80	108.99	109.17
11.8	109.36	109.54	109.73	109.92	110.10	110.29	110.47	110.66	110.85	111.03
11.9	111.22	111.41	111.59	111.78	111.97	112.16	112.34	112.53	112.72	112.91
12.0	113.10	113.29	113.47	113.66	113.85	114.04	114.23	114.42	114.61	114.80
12.1	114.99	115.18	115.37	115.56	115.75	115.94	116.13	116.32	116.52	116.71
12.2	116.90	117.09	117.28	117.47	117.67	117.86	118.05	118.24	118.44	118.63
12.3	118.82	119.02	119.21	119.40	119.60	119.79	119.98	120.18	120.37	120.57
12.4	120.76	120.96	121.15	121.35	121.54	121.74	121.93	122.13	122.33	122.52
12.5	122.72	122.91	123.11	123.31	123.51	123.70	123.90	124.10	124.29	124.49
12.6	124.69	124.89	125.09	125.28	125.48	125.68	125.88	126.08	126.28	126.48
12.7	126.68	126.88	127.08	127.28	127.48	127.68	127.88	128.08	128.28	128.48
12.8	128.68	128.88	129.08	129.28	129.49	129.69	129.89	130.09	130.29	130.50
12.9	130.70	130.90	131.10	131.31	131.51	131.71	131.92	132.12	132.32	132.53
13.0	132.73	132.94	133.14	133.35	133.55	133.76	133.96	134.17	134.37	134.58
13.1	134.78	134.99	135.19	135.40	135.61	135.81	136.02	136.23	136.43	136.64
13.2	136.85	137.06	137.26	137.47	137.68	137.89	138.09	138.30	138.51	138.72
13.3	138.93	139.14	139.35	139.56	139.77	139.98	140.19	140.40	140.61	140.82
13.4	141.03	141.24	141.45	141.66	141.87	142.08	142.29	142.50	142.72	142.93
13.5	143.14	143.35	143.56	143.78	143.99	144.20	144.41	144.63	144.84	145.05
13.6	145.27	145.48	145.69	145.91	146.12	146.34	146.55	146.77	146.98	147.20
13.7	147.41	147.63	147.84	148.06	148.27	148.49	148.71	148.92	149.14	149.35
13.8	149.57	149.79	150.01	150.22	150.44	150.66	150.87	151.09	151.31	151.53
13.9	151.75	151.97	152.18	152.40	152.62	152.84	153.06	153.28	153.50	153.72
14.0	153.94	154.16	154.38	154.60	154.82	155.04	155.26	155.48	155.70	155.92
14.1	156.14	156.37	156.59	156.81	157.03	157.25	157.48	157.70	157.92	158.14
14.2	158.37	158.59	158.81	159.04	159.26	159.48	159.71	159.93	160.16	160.38
14.3	160.61	160.83	161.06	161.28	161.51	161.73	161.96	162.18	162.41	162.63
14.4	162.86	163.09	163.31	163.54	163.77	163.99	164.22	164.45	164.67	164.90
14.5	165.13	165.36	165.59	165.81	166.04	166.27	166.50	166.73	166.96	167.19
14.6	167.42	167.65	167.88	168.11	168.34	168.57	168.80	169.03	169.26	169.49
14.7	169.72	169.95	170.18	170.41	170.64	170.87	171.10	171.34	171.57	171.80
14.8	172.03	172.27	172.50	172.73	172.96	173.20	173.43	173.66	173.90	174.13
14.9	174.37	174.60	174.83	175.07	175.30	175.54	175.77	176.01	176.24	176.48

Table 6-4. Areas of Circles by Hundredths (*Concluded*)

Diam.	.00	.01	.02	.03	.04	.05	.06	.07	.08	.09
15.0	176.71	176.95	177.19	177.42	177.66	177.89	178.13	178.37	178.60	178.84
15.1	179.08	179.32	179.55	179.79	180.03	180.27	180.50	180.74	180.98	181.22
15.2	181.46	181.70	181.94	182.18	182.41	182.65	182.89	183.13	183.37	183.61
15.3	183.85	184.09	184.33	184.58	184.82	185.06	185.30	185.54	185.78	186.02
15.4	186.27	186.51	186.75	186.99	187.23	187.48	187.72	187.96	188.21	188.45
15.5	188.69	188.94	189.18	189.42	189.67	189.91	190.16	190.40	190.64	190.89
15.6	191.13	191.38	191.62	191.87	192.12	192.36	192.61	192.85	193.10	193.35
15.7	193.59	193.84	194.09	194.33	194.58	194.83	195.08	195.32	195.57	195.82
15.8	196.07	196.32	196.56	196.81	197.06	197.31	197.56	197.81	198.06	198.31
15.9	198.56	198.81	199.06	199.31	199.56	199.81	200.06	200.31	200.56	200.81
16.0	201.06	201.31	201.56	201.82	202.07	202.32	202.57	202.83	203.08	203.33
16.1	203.58	203.84	204.09	204.34	204.60	204.85	205.10	205.36	205.61	205.87
16.2	206.12	206.37	206.63	206.88	207.14	207.39	207.65	207.91	208.16	208.42
16.3	208.67	208.93	209.18	209.44	209.70	209.95	210.21	210.47	210.73	210.98
16.4	211.24	211.50	211.76	212.01	212.27	212.53	212.79	213.05	213.31	213.57
16.5	213.82	214.08	214.34	214.60	214.86	215.12	215.38	215.64	215.90	216.16
16.6	216.42	216.69	216.95	217.21	217.47	217.73	217.99	218.25	218.52	218.78
16.7	219.04	219.30	219.56	219.83	220.09	220.35	220.62	220.88	221.14	221.41
16.8	221.67	221.93	222.20	222.46	222.73	222.99	223.26	223.52	223.79	224.05
16.9	224.32	224.58	224.85	225.11	225.38	225.65	225.91	226.18	226.45	226.71
17.0	226.98	227.25	227.51	227.78	228.05	228.32	228.59	228.85	229.12	229.39
17.1	229.66	229.93	230.20	230.46	230.73	231.00	231.27	231.54	231.81	232.08
17.2	232.35	232.62	232.89	233.16	233.43	233.71	233.98	234.25	234.52	234.79
17.3	235.06	235.33	235.61	235.88	236.15	236.42	236.70	236.97	237.24	237.51
17.4	237.79	238.06	238.33	238.61	238.88	239.16	239.43	239.70	239.98	240.25
17.5	240.53	240.80	241.08	241.35	241.63	241.90	242.18	242.46	242.73	243.01
17.6	243.28	243.56	243.84	244.12	244.39	244.67	244.95	245.22	245.50	245.78
17.7	246.06	246.34	246.61	246.89	247.17	247.45	247.73	248.01	248.29	248.57
17.8	248.85	249.13	249.41	249.69	249.97	250.25	250.53	250.81	251.09	251.37
17.9	251.65	251.93	252.21	252.49	252.78	253.06	253.34	253.62	253.90	254.19
18.0	254.47	254.75	255.03	255.32	255.60	255.88	256.17	256.45	256.74	257.02
18.1	257.30	257.59	257.87	258.16	258.44	258.73	259.01	259.30	259.58	259.87
18.2	260.16	260.44	260.73	261.01	261.30	261.59	261.87	262.16	262.45	262.73
18.3	263.02	263.31	263.60	263.89	264.17	264.46	264.75	265.04	265.33	265.62
18.4	265.90	266.19	266.48	266.77	267.06	267.35	267.64	267.93	268.22	268.51
18.5	268.80	269.09	269.38	269.68	269.97	270.26	270.55	270.84	271.13	271.42
18.6	271.72	272.01	272.30	272.59	272.89	273.18	273.47	273.77	274.06	274.35
18.7	274.65	274.94	275.23	275.53	275.82	276.12	276.41	276.71	277.00	277.30
18.8	277.59	277.89	278.18	278.48	278.77	279.07	279.37	279.66	279.96	280.26
18.9	280.55	280.85	281.15	281.44	281.74	282.04	282.34	282.63	282.93	283.23
19.0	283.53	283.83	284.13	284.42	284.72	285.02	285.32	285.62	285.92	286.22
19.1	286.52	286.82	287.12	287.42	287.72	288.02	288.32	288.63	288.93	289.23
19.2	289.53	289.83	290.13	290.43	290.74	291.04	291.34	291.64	291.95	292.25
19.3	292.55	292.86	293.16	293.46	293.77	294.07	294.37	294.68	294.98	295.29
19.4	295.59	295.90	296.20	296.51	296.81	297.12	297.42	297.73	298.04	298.34
19.5	298.65	298.95	299.26	299.57	299.87	300.18	300.49	300.80	301.10	301.41
19.6	301.72	302.03	302.33	302.64	302.95	303.26	303.57	303.88	304.19	304.50
19.7	304.81	305.11	305.42	305.73	306.04	306.35	306.66	306.98	307.29	307.60
19.8	307.91	308.22	308.53	308.84	309.15	309.46	309.78	310.09	310.40	310.71
19.9	311.03	311.34	311.65	311.96	312.28	312.59	312.90	313.22	313.53	313.85

Table 6-5. Circumferences of Circles by Hundredths

Diam.	.00	.01	.02	.03	.04	.05	.06	.07	.08	.09
0.0	0.000	0.031	0.063	0.094	0.126	0.157	0.188	0.220	0.251	0.283
.1	0.314	0.346	0.377	0.408	0.440	0.471	0.503	0.534	0.565	0.597
.2	0.628	0.660	0.691	0.723	0.754	0.785	0.817	0.848	0.880	0.911
.3	0.942	0.974	1.005	1.037	1.068	1.100	1.131	1.162	1.194	1.225
.4	1.257	1.288	1.319	1.351	1.382	1.414	1.445	1.477	1.508	1.539
0.5	1.571	1.602	1.634	1.665	1.696	1.728	1.759	1.791	1.822	1.854
.6	1.885	1.916	1.948	1.979	2.011	2.042	2.073	2.105	2.136	2.168
.7	2.199	2.231	2.262	2.293	2.325	2.356	2.388	2.419	2.450	2.482
.8	2.513	2.545	2.576	2.608	2.639	2.670	2.702	2.733	2.765	2.796
.9	2.827	2.859	2.890	2.922	2.953	2.985	3.016	3.047	3.079	3.110
1.0	3.142	3.173	3.204	3.236	3.267	3.299	3.330	3.362	3.393	3.424
.1	3.456	3.487	3.519	3.550	3.581	3.613	3.644	3.676	3.707	3.738
.2	3.770	3.801	3.833	3.864	3.896	3.927	3.958	3.990	4.021	4.053
.3	4.084	4.115	4.147	4.178	4.210	4.241	4.273	4.304	4.335	4.367
.4	4.398	4.430	4.461	4.492	4.524	4.555	4.587	4.618	4.650	4.681
1.5	4.712	4.744	4.775	4.807	4.838	4.869	4.901	4.932	4.964	4.995
.6	5.027	5.058	5.089	5.121	5.152	5.184	5.215	5.246	5.278	5.309
.7	5.341	5.372	5.404	5.435	5.466	5.498	5.529	5.561	5.592	5.623
.8	5.655	5.686	5.718	5.749	5.781	5.812	5.843	5.875	5.906	5.938
.9	5.969	6.000	6.032	6.063	6.095	6.126	6.158	6.189	6.220	6.252
2.0	6.283	6.315	6.346	6.377	6.409	6.440	6.472	6.503	6.535	6.566
.1	6.597	6.629	6.660	6.692	6.723	6.754	6.786	6.817	6.849	6.880
.2	6.912	6.943	6.974	7.006	7.037	7.069	7.100	7.131	7.163	7.194
.3	7.226	7.257	7.288	7.320	7.351	7.383	7.414	7.446	7.477	7.508
.4	7.540	7.571	7.603	7.634	7.665	7.697	7.728	7.760	7.791	7.823
2.5	7.854	7.885	7.917	7.948	7.980	8.011	8.042	8.074	8.105	8.137
.6	8.168	8.200	8.231	8.262	8.294	8.325	8.357	8.388	8.419	8.451
.7	8.482	8.514	8.545	8.577	8.608	8.639	8.671	8.702	8.734	8.765
.8	8.796	8.828	8.859	8.891	8.922	8.954	8.985	9.016	9.048	9.079
.9	9.111	9.142	9.173	9.205	9.236	9.268	9.299	9.331	9.362	9.393
3.0	9.425	9.456	9.488	9.519	9.550	9.582	9.613	9.645	9.676	9.708
.1	9.739	9.770	9.802	9.833	9.865	9.896	9.927	9.959	9.990	10.022
.2	10.05	10.08	10.12	10.15	10.18	10.21	10.24	10.27	10.30	10.34
.3	10.37	10.40	10.43	10.46	10.49	10.52	10.56	10.59	10.62	10.65
.4	10.68	10.71	10.74	10.78	10.81	10.84	10.87	10.90	10.93	10.96
3.5	11.00	11.03	11.06	11.09	11.12	11.15	11.18	11.22	11.25	11.28
.6	11.31	11.34	11.37	11.40	11.44	11.47	11.50	11.53	11.56	11.59
.7	11.62	11.66	11.69	11.72	11.75	11.78	11.81	11.84	11.88	11.91
.8	11.94	11.97	12.00	12.03	12.06	12.10	12.13	12.16	12.19	12.22
.9	12.25	12.28	12.32	12.35	12.38	12.41	12.44	12.47	12.50	12.53
4.0	12.57	12.60	12.63	12.66	12.69	12.72	12.75	12.79	12.82	12.85
.1	12.88	12.91	12.94	12.97	13.01	13.04	13.07	13.10	13.13	13.16
.2	13.19	13.23	13.26	13.29	13.32	13.35	13.38	13.41	13.45	13.48
.3	13.51	13.54	13.57	13.60	13.63	13.67	13.70	13.73	13.76	13.79
.4	13.82	13.85	13.89	13.92	13.95	13.98	14.01	14.04	14.07	14.11
4.5	14.14	14.17	14.20	14.23	14.26	14.29	14.33	14.36	14.39	14.42
.6	14.45	14.48	14.51	14.55	14.58	14.61	14.64	14.67	14.70	14.73
.7	14.77	14.80	14.83	14.86	14.89	14.92	14.95	14.99	15.02	15.05
.8	15.08	15.11	15.14	15.17	15.21	15.24	15.27	15.30	15.33	15.36
.9	15.39	15.43	15.46	15.49	15.52	15.55	15.58	15.61	15.65	15.68

Table 6-5. Circumferences of Circles
by Hundredths (*Concluded*)

Diam.	.00	.01	.02	.03	.04	.05	.06	.07	.08	.09
5.0	15.71	15.74	15.77	15.80	15.83	15.87	15.90	15.93	15.96	15.99
.1	16.02	16.05	16.08	16.12	16.15	16.18	16.21	16.24	16.27	16.30
.2	16.34	16.37	16.40	16.43	16.46	16.49	16.52	16.56	16.59	16.62
.3	16.65	16.68	16.71	16.74	16.78	16.81	16.84	16.87	16.90	16.93
.4	16.96	17.00	17.03	17.06	17.09	17.12	17.15	17.18	17.22	17.25
5.5	17.28	17.31	17.34	17.37	17.40	17.44	17.47	17.50	17.53	17.56
.6	17.59	17.62	17.66	17.69	17.72	17.75	17.78	17.81	17.84	17.88
.7	17.91	17.94	17.97	18.00	18.03	18.06	18.10	18.13	18.16	18.19
.8	18.22	18.25	18.28	18.32	18.35	18.38	18.41	18.44	18.47	18.50
.9	18.54	18.57	18.60	18.63	18.66	18.69	18.72	18.76	18.79	18.82
6.0	18.85	18.88	18.91	18.94	18.98	19.01	19.04	19.07	19.10	19.13
.1	19.16	19.20	19.23	19.26	19.29	19.32	19.35	19.38	19.42	19.45
.2	19.48	19.51	19.54	19.57	19.60	19.63	19.67	19.70	19.73	19.76
.3	19.79	19.82	19.85	19.89	19.92	19.95	19.98	20.01	20.04	20.07
.4	20.11	20.14	20.17	20.20	20.23	20.26	20.29	20.33	20.36	20.39
6.5	20.42	20.45	20.48	20.51	20.55	20.58	20.61	20.64	20.67	20.70
.6	20.73	20.77	20.80	20.83	20.86	20.89	20.92	20.95	20.99	21.02
.7	21.05	21.08	21.11	21.14	21.17	21.21	21.24	21.27	21.30	21.33
.8	21.36	21.39	21.43	21.46	21.49	21.52	21.55	21.58	21.61	21.65
.9	21.68	21.71	21.74	21.77	21.80	21.83	21.87	21.90	21.93	21.96
7.0	21.99	22.02	22.05	22.09	22.12	22.15	22.18	22.21	22.24	22.27
.1	22.31	22.34	22.37	22.40	22.43	22.46	22.49	22.53	22.56	22.59
.2	22.62	22.65	22.68	22.71	22.75	22.78	22.81	22.84	22.87	22.90
.3	22.93	22.97	23.00	23.03	23.06	23.09	23.12	23.15	23.18	23.22
.4	23.25	23.28	23.31	23.34	23.37	23.40	23.44	23.47	23.50	23.53
7.5	23.56	23.59	23.62	23.66	23.69	23.72	23.75	23.78	23.81	23.84
.6	23.88	23.91	23.94	23.97	24.00	24.03	24.06	24.10	24.13	24.16
.7	24.19	24.22	24.25	24.28	24.32	24.35	24.38	24.41	24.44	24.47
.8	24.50	24.54	24.57	24.60	24.63	24.66	24.69	24.72	24.76	24.79
.9	24.82	24.85	24.88	24.91	24.94	24.98	25.01	25.04	25.07	25.10
8.0	25.13	25.16	25.20	25.23	25.26	25.29	25.32	25.35	25.38	25.42
.1	25.45	25.48	25.51	25.54	25.57	25.60	25.64	25.67	25.70	25.73
.2	25.76	25.79	25.82	25.86	25.89	25.92	25.95	25.98	26.01	26.04
.3	26.08	26.11	26.14	26.17	26.20	26.23	26.26	26.30	26.33	26.36
.4	26.39	26.42	26.45	26.48	26.52	26.55	26.58	26.61	26.64	26.67
8.5	26.70	26.73	26.77	26.80	26.83	26.86	26.89	26.92	26.95	26.99
.6	27.02	27.05	27.08	27.11	27.14	27.17	27.21	27.24	27.27	27.30
.7	27.33	27.36	27.39	27.43	27.46	27.49	27.52	27.55	27.58	27.61
.8	27.65	27.68	27.71	27.74	27.77	27.80	27.83	27.87	27.90	27.93
.9	27.96	27.99	28.02	28.05	28.09	28.12	28.15	28.18	28.21	28.24
9.0	28.27	28.31	28.34	28.37	28.40	28.43	28.46	28.49	28.53	28.56
.1	28.59	28.62	28.65	28.68	28.71	28.75	28.78	28.81	28.84	28.87
.2	28.90	28.93	28.97	29.00	29.03	29.06	29.09	29.12	29.15	29.19
.3	29.22	29.25	29.28	29.31	29.34	29.37	29.41	29.44	29.47	29.50
.4	29.53	29.56	29.59	29.63	29.66	29.69	29.72	29.75	29.78	29.81
9.5	29.85	29.88	29.91	29.94	29.97	30.00	30.03	30.07	30.10	30.13
.6	30.16	30.19	30.22	30.25	30.28	30.32	30.35	30.38	30.41	30.44
.7	30.47	30.50	30.54	30.57	30.60	30.63	30.66	30.69	30.72	30.76
.8	30.79	30.82	30.85	30.88	30.91	30.94	30.98	31.01	31.04	31.07
.9	31.10	31.13	31.16	31.20	31.23	31.26	31.29	31.32	31.35	31.38

Table 6-6. Loss of Head H_2 Due to Sudden Enlargement in Pipes

d_2/d_1 = ratio of diameter of larger pipe to diameter of smaller pipe

V_1 = velocity in smaller pipe

$\dfrac{d_2}{d_1}$	Velocity, V_1, in feet per second												
	2	3	4	5	6	7	8	10	12	15	20	30	40
1.2	.01	.01	.02	.04	.06	.07	.10	.14	.21	.32	.55	1.20	2.08
1.4	.02	.04	.06	.10	.14	.18	.23	.36	.51	.78	1.36	2.96	5.14
1.6	.02	.05	.09	.14	.20	.28	.36	.55	.78	1.19	2.07	4.50	7.82
1.8	.03	.07	.12	.18	.26	.35	.45	.70	.99	1.52	2.64	5.74	9.97
2.0	.04	.08	.14	.22	.31	.41	.53	.81	1.16	1.77	3.08	6.71	11.65
2.5	.05	.10	.17	.27	.38	.51	.66	1.01	1.44	2.20	3.83	8.34	14.48
3.0	.05	.11	.19	.30	.42	.57	.74	1.13	1.60	2.46	4.27	9.29	16.14
4.0	.06	.12	.22	.33	.47	.63	.82	1.25	1.78	2.76	4.73	10.30	17.90
5.0	.06	.13	.23	.35	.49	.66	.85	1.31	1.86	2.85	4.95	10.79	18.73
10.0	.06	.14	.24	.37	.52	.70	.91	1.39	1.97	2.96	5.25	11.44	19.87
∞	.06	.14	.24	.37	.53	.71	.92	1.42	2.01	3.09	5.36	11.66	20.26

Table 6-7. Values of K_2 for Determining Loss of Head Due to Sudden Enlargement in Pipes, from the Formula

$$H_2 = K_2(V_1{}^2/2g)$$

d_2/d_1 = ratio of larger pipe to smaller pipe V_1 = velocity in smaller pipe

$\dfrac{d_2}{d_1}$	Velocity, V_1, in feet per second												
	2	3	4	5	6	7	8	10	12	15	20	30	40
1.2	.11	.10	.10	.10	.10	.10	.10	.09	.09	.09	.09	.09	.08
1.4	.26	.26	.25	.24	.24	.24	.24	.23	.23	.22	.22	.21	.20
1.6	.40	.39	.38	.37	.37	.36	.36	.35	.35	.34	.33	.32	.32
1.8	.51	.49	.48	.47	.47	.46	.46	.45	.44	.43	.42	.41	.40
2.0	.60	.58	.56	.55	.55	.54	.53	.52	.52	.51	.50	.48	.47
2.5	.74	.72	.70	.69	.68	.67	.66	.65	.64	.63	.62	.60	.58
3.0	.83	.80	.78	.77	.76	.75	.74	.73	.72	.70	.69	.67	.65
4.0	.92	.89	.87	.85	.84	.83	.82	.80	.79	.78	.76	.74	.72
5.0	.96	.93	.91	.89	.88	.87	.86	.84	.83	.82	.80	.77	.75
10.0	1.00	.99	.96	.95	.93	.92	.91	.89	.88	.86	.84	.82	.80
∞	1.00	1.00	.98	.96	.95	.94	.93	.91	.90	.88	.86	.83	.81

Table 6-8. Values of K_2 for Determining Loss of Head Due to
Gradual Enlargements in Pipes, from the Formula

$$H_2 = K_2(V_1{}^2/2g)$$

d_2/d_1 = ratio of diameter of larger pipe to diameter of smaller pipe. Angle of cone is twice the angle between the axis of the cone and its side.

$\dfrac{d_2}{d_1}$	Angle of cone													
	2°	4°	6°	8°	10°	15°	20°	25°	30°	35°	40°	45°	50°	60°
1.1	.01	.01	.01	.02	.03	.05	.10	.13	.16	.18	.19	.20	.21	.23
1.2	.02	.02	.02	.03	.04	.09	.16	.21	.25	.29	.31	.33	.35	.37
1.4	.02	.03	.03	.04	.06	.12	.23	.30	.36	.41	.44	.47	.50	.53
1.6	.03	.03	.04	.05	.07	.14	.26	.35	.42	.47	.51	.54	.57	.61
1.8	.03	.04	.04	.05	.07	.15	.28	.37	.44	.50	.54	.58	.61	.65
2.0	.03	.04	.04	.05	.07	.16	.29	.38	.46	.52	.56	.60	.63	.68
2.5	.03	.04	.04	.05	.08	.16	.30	.39	.48	.54	.58	.62	.65	.70
3.0	.03	.04	.04	.05	.08	.16	.31	.40	.48	.55	.59	.63	.66	.71
∞	.03	.04	.05	.06	.08	.16	.31	.40	.49	.56	.60	.64	.67	.72

Table 6-9. Loss of Head H_3 Due to Sudden Contraction

d_2/d_1 = ratio of larger to smaller diameter $\qquad$ V_2 = velocity in smaller pipe

$\dfrac{d_2}{d_1}$	Velocity, V_2, in feet per second												
	2	3	4	5	6	7	8	10	12	15	20	30	40
1.1	.00	.00	.01	.01	.02	.03	.04	.06	.09	.15	.29	.75	1.49
1.2	.00	.01	.02	.03	.04	.06	.07	.12	.18	.28	.54	1.38	2.74
1.4	.01	.02	.04	.07	.10	.13	.17	.27	.40	.65	1.14	2.68	4.98
1.6	.02	.04	.06	.10	.14	.20	.26	.40	.67	.89	1.56	3.44	5.97
1.8	.02	.05	.08	.13	.19	.25	.33	.51	.73	1.12	1.92	4.05	6.72
2.0	.02	.05	.09	.14	.21	.28	.36	.55	.79	1.19	2.06	4.28	7.09
2.2	.02	.06	.10	.15	.22	.30	.38	.59	.84	1.28	2.20	4.56	7.41
2.5	.03	.06	.10	.16	.23	.31	.40	.62	.88	1.34	2.30	4.76	7.71
3.0	.03	.06	.11	.17	.24	.32	.42	.65	.92	1.40	2.41	4.98	8.11
4.0	.03	.06	.12	.18	.25	.34	.44	.69	.97	1.48	2.53	5.24	8.48
5.0	.03	.07	.12	.18	.26	.35	.46	.70	1.00	1.52	2.60	5.36	8.67
10.0	.03	.07	.12	.19	.27	.36	.47	.72	1.02	1.56	2.68	5.56	9.06
∞	.03	.07	.12	.19	.27	.36	.47	.72	1.03	1.58	2.71	5.68	9.36

Table 6-10. Values of K_3 for Determining Loss of Head Due to
Sudden Contraction, from the Formula $H_3 = K_3(V_2{}^2/2g)$

d_2/d_1 = ratio of larger to smaller diameter V_2 = velocity in smaller pipe

$\dfrac{d_2}{d_1}$	Velocity, V_2, in feet per second												
	2	3	4	5	6	7	8	10	12	15	20	30	40
1.1	.03	.04	.04	.04	.04	.04	.04	.04	.04	.04	.05	.05	.06
1.2	.07	.07	.07	.07	.07	.07	.07	.08	.08	.08	.09	.10	.11
1.4	.17	.17	.17	.17	.17	.17	.17	.18	.18	.18	.18	.19	.20
1.6	.26	.26	.26	.26	.26	.26	.26	.26	.26	.25	.25	.25	.24
1.8	.34	.34	.34	.34	.34	.34	.33	.33	.32	.32	.31	.29	.27
2.0	.38	.38	.37	.37	.37	.37	.36	.36	.35	.34	.33	.31	.29
2.2	.40	.40	.40	.39	.39	.39	.39	.38	.37	.37	.35	.33	.30
2.5	.42	.42	.42	.41	.41	.41	.40	.40	.39	.38	.37	.34	.31
3.0	.44	.44	.44	.43	.43	.43	.42	.42	.41	.40	.39	.36	.33
4.0	.47	.46	.46	.46	.45	.45	.45	.44	.43	.42	.41	.37	.34
5.0	.48	.48	.47	.47	.47	.46	.46	.45	.45	.44	.42	.38	.35
10.0	.49	.48	.48	.48	.48	.47	.47	.46	.46	.45	.43	.40	.36
∞	.49	.49	.48	.48	.48	.47	.47	.47	.46	.45	.44	.41	.38

SECTION 7

STEADY UNIFORM FLOW IN OPEN CHANNELS

Reference to Sec. 3 will show that the conditions specified in the title of this section require that the discharge in the channel be constant with respect to time and that the cross-sectional area remain the same from place to place in the channel. For subcritical flow (p. 8-38), this condition can exist throughout the full length of the channel only if the outlet end of the channel is controlled so that there will be no drawdown or backwater. For supercritical flow, uniform flow can occur throughout the channel only if the water enters the channel at the uniform-flow depth from a pressure chamber and if no obstruction exists at the outlet end of the channel. Strictly speaking, this type of flow can occur only in parallel-walled channels, thus precluding all natural streams. Practically speaking, however, there are often reaches of natural streams in which flow is nearly uniform, and in many cases flow can be considered as steady in rivers for short time intervals.

The principles governing the relationship between depth slope and discharge for uniform flow depend entirely on the rate of energy dissipation due to friction. Consequently, this section deals entirely with this aspect of flow in open channels. However, because the rate of energy dissipation for gradually varied flow (p. 8-36) depends on the same variables as in the case of uniform flow, the material presented here will also be used in Sec. 8. The problems involved in steady nonuniform flow are discussed in Secs. 8 and 9, and unsteady flow in open channels is treated in Secs. 10 and 11.

Elements of a Cross Section. The more important elements of cross sections, together with the symbols that will be used to designate them, are as follows:

The *area a* always means the cross-sectional area of the stream.

The *wetted perimeter* p is the length of the line of intersection of the plane of the cross section with the wetted surface of the channel, the line abc (Fig. 7-1).

The *hydraulic radius* $r = a/p$ is the area divided by the wetted perimeter.

The *depth* D (Fig. 7-1), if not specified otherwise, refers to the maximum depth of water in the cross section.

The *top width* T (Fig. 7-1) is the term used to designate the width of cross section at the water surface.

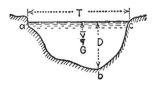

FIG. 7-1. Cross section of open channel.

The *mean depth* $D_m = a/T$ is the area of cross section divided by the top width. This term will be applied generally to all sections, but it is not literally descriptive of channels with overhanging sides, such as circular conduits flowing more than half full.

The *depth to center of gravity* $\bar{y}$ (Fig. 7-1) is the depth to the center of gravity of the cross section of the stream.

The above terms and symbols are all used in the discussions and formulas contained in this and the following section. The hydraulic radius enters into formulas involving velocity or discharge. The mean depth occurs in the criterion for indicating when flow in a channel is at critical depth (p. 8-8). The depth to center of gravity of a cross section is employed in determining hydrostatic pressures in problems involving sudden changes in depth of flow.

Sectional Forms. Most of the sectional forms used for open channels are shown in Fig. 7-2. It is convenient to have tables which facilitate the determination of numerical values of the elements of a cross section. The equations used in deriving these tables are shown for trapezoidal sections only. Similar equations were derived and used for developing the tables for circular and parabolic sections.

The *trapezoidal section* (Fig. 7-2a) is always used for earth canals. Ordinary earth sections have relatively flat side slopes, usually not steeper than 1:1 in cut and 1½:1 in fill. In rock, hardpan, or other indurated material and for lined canals, trapezoidal sections with very steep side slopes are often employed. It is not uncommon to have different side slopes on the two sides of a canal. Often the uphill side of an earth canal will have a steeper slope than the downhill side.

As indicated in Fig. 7-2a, D is the maximum depth of water and b is the bottom width of the canal. The area of the

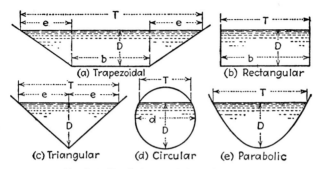

Fig. 7-2. Simple forms of channel sections.

trapezoidal section is

$$a = eD + bD \tag{7-1}$$

and letting

$$z = \frac{e}{D} \tag{7-2}$$

and

$$x = \frac{D}{b} \tag{7-3}$$

then

$$a = \left(z + \frac{1}{x}\right) D^2 \tag{7-4}$$

The wetted perimeter is

$$p = b + 2(e^2 + D^2)^{\frac{1}{2}} \tag{7-5}$$

or substituting for b and e as above,

$$p = \left[\frac{1}{x} + 2(z^2 + 1)^{\frac{1}{2}}\right] D \tag{7-6}$$

Then

$$r = \frac{a}{p} = \frac{1/x + z}{[1/x + 2(z^2 + 1)^{\frac{1}{2}}]} D = C_r D \tag{7-7}$$

Values of C_r as functions of x and z are presented in Table 7-1. The top width is

$$T = b + 2e = \left(\frac{1}{x} + 2z\right) D \tag{7-8}$$

Then the expression for mean depth becomes

$$D_m = \frac{a}{T} = \frac{1/x + z}{1/x + 2z} D = C_m D \qquad (7\text{-}9)$$

Values of C_m in terms of z and x are given in Table 7-2. The distance down from the water surface to the center of gravity is obtained by taking moments as follows:

$$a\bar{y} = bD\frac{D}{2} + eD\frac{D}{3}$$

Substituting for a, b, and e, using Eqs. (7-4), (7-3), and (7-2), respectively,

$$\bar{y} = \frac{1/2x + z/3}{z + 1/x} = C_{\bar{y}} D \qquad (7\text{-}10)$$

Values of $C_{\bar{y}}$ are given in Table 7-3.

If the slopes of the two sides of the channel are different, an average value of z used in Eqs. (7-4), (7-9), and (7-10) will give correct values of a, D_m, and $\bar{y}$, respectively, but Eq. (7-7), used with an average z, will not give exact values of r. For example, if $D = 5$, $b = 10$, and $z = 1$ and 2; from Table 7-1, using z (average) = 1.5, then $r = 3.12$, while the correct result is 3.10. For smaller differences in z, the error will be relatively less. The values corresponding to an average z obtained from Table 7-1 will usually therefore be within 1 per cent of the correct result.

The *rectangular section* and *triangular section* are special cases of the trapezoidal section. The former has $z = 0$, and the latter has $b = 0$. The rectangular section (Fig. 7-2b) is used for wooden flumes and for various types of lined conduits. Triangular cross sections (Fig. 7-2c) are seldom encountered, but channels of this form have interesting hydraulic properties.

For the rectangular section, $a = bd$, $r = bd/(b + 2d)$,

$$\bar{y} = \frac{D}{2}$$

and $D_m = D$. For the triangular section, $a = zD^2$,

$$r = \frac{zD}{2(z^2 + 1)^{\frac{1}{2}}}$$

$\bar{y} = D/3$, and $D_m = D/2$. In Table 7-1, the first column gives C_r [Eq. (7-7)] for rectangular sections, and the bottom row gives this factor for triangular sections.

Circular conduits, designed to flow partially full under normal operating conditions, are commonly used for sewers and drains and for other purposes where underground channels are required. Semicircular sections are sometimes employed for flumes and lined canals.

As indicated in Fig. 7-2*d*, D is the maximum depth of a partially filled circular conduit and d is the diameter. The area is

$$a = \left(\frac{360 - \theta}{360}\frac{\pi}{4} + \frac{\sin \theta}{8}\right) \frac{D^2}{x^2} \tag{7-11}$$

in which θ is the angle between the radii subtending the water surface and $x = D/d$. When D is replaced by xd in Eq. (7-11), the area is expressed as $C_a d^2$, where C_a is a function of x. Values of C_a for determining a are given in Table 7-4.

The wetted perimeter of a circular channel flowing part full is

$$p = \left(\frac{360 - \theta}{360}\right) \frac{\pi D}{x} \tag{7-12}$$

in which θ and x are as defined above. Then r is obtained by dividing a by p using Eqs. (7-11) and (7-12) and replacing D with xd $r = C_r d$, where C_r is a function of x. Values of C_r for computing r are given in Table 7-5. In the same manner Table 7-6 was prepared for determining the top width, T, Table 7-7 for determining the mean depth, D_m, and Table 7-8 for computing the depth to the center of gravity, $\bar{y}$.

The parabolic section (Fig. 7-2*e*) is occasionally used for lined channels, and it approximates the form assumed by many natural streams and old earth canals. The hydraulic features of parabolic channels are interesting. The equation of the section shown in Fig. 7-2*e* in terms of x and y coordinates is $x^2 = ky$, in which $k = 10$. A parabolic section can be defined in terms of the top width T and maximum depth D. Then, if $T/2$ and D are substituted, respectively, for x and y in the general equation, k can be determined, and the equation can be used to locate other points of the section.

The area of a parabolic cross section is

$$a = \frac{2D^2}{3x} \tag{7-13}$$

in which $x = D/T$, and the wetted perimeter is

$$p = \left[(16x^2 + 1)^{1/2} + \frac{1}{4x} \ln (16x^2 + 1 + 4x) \right] \frac{D}{2x} \quad (7\text{-}14)$$

Then by dividing a by p, we see that $r = C_r D$, where C_r is a function of x. Values of C_r for computing r are given in Table 7-9. The mean depth $D_m = \frac{2}{3}D$, and the depth of the center of gravity $\bar{y} = \frac{2}{5}D$.

Most Efficient Channel Section. Considered purely from the standpoint of the hydraulics of a channel, it can be seen from the Manning equation [Eq. (7-35)] that for a given area the most efficient channel will be the one with the minimum wetted perimeter. Therefore, if in the expression for the wetted perimeter given by Eq. (7-6) the depth is replaced in terms of a, z, and x from Eq. (7-4), p can be differentiated first with respect to x and then with respect to z. The first operation yields the following expression:

$$\frac{1}{x} = \frac{b}{D} = 2[(z^2 + 1)^{1/2} - z] \quad (7\text{-}15)$$

which yields the best ratio b/D for any z. The second differentiation gives $z = 1/\sqrt{3}$, which, when substituted in Eq. (7-15), gives $b/D = 2/\sqrt{3}$, thus showing that the most efficient trapezoidal section is a half hexagon. The most efficient rectangular section is that for which $b/D = 2$, as shown by letting $z = 0$ in Eq. (7-15). It may be seen from Eq. (7-15) that for flat side slopes, as would be used in earth canals, the most efficient sections have small bottom widths. All cross sections which satisfy Eq. (7-15) have forms such that semi-circles can be inscribed in them and the most efficient open-channel cross-sectional shape of all is a semicircle. Steep-sided parabolas also have a high efficiency.

Not only does Eq. (7-15) give the channel with the smallest wetted perimeter for a given area, but it therefore also gives the channel which provides a given discharge with the minimum area. Therefore the section determined from Eq. (7-15) will be the most economical section to build in so far as both excavation and canal lining are concerned. However, earth canals may involve other considerations, such as construction difficulties or maintenance problems, which make it desirable to depart from the ideal section.

Two earth-canal sections with balanced cut and fill are illustrated in Fig. 7-3. Each has the same capacity, 300 sec-ft, and all conditions except the ratio of depth to bottom width and area of section are the same for each. Figure 7-3a is the theoretically most efficient section, while Fig. 7-3b has dimen-

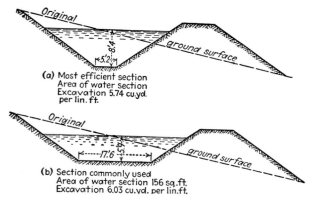

(a) Most efficient section
Area of water section
Excavation 5.74 cu.yd. per lin. ft.

(b) Section commonly used
Area of water section 156 sq.ft.
Excavation 6.03 cu.yd. per lin.ft.

FIG. 7-3. Trapezoidal canal sections. Data for both sections:
$Q = 300$ cu ft per sec
$z = 1.5$ to 1
$n = 0.0225$ Freeboard = 2 ft
$s = 0.000134$
Slope of ground = 20 per cent
Top of embankment = 8 ft

sions approximating those commonly employed for canals of this capacity. For the indicated ground slope, 20 per cent, there will be about 5 per cent more excavation in section b than in a, but the former section will be easier to construct and maintain than the latter. For canals in flatter country the difference in excavation for the two sections will be relatively less than that indicated in the figure. As the ground slope increases, the excavation saved by using the more efficient section increases.

Energy Losses in Open Channels. As in pipes, the energy losses are of two types, those due to friction and those due to sudden changes in the direction and magnitude of the velocity, which are called minor losses. However, because this section of the Handbook deals with uniform flow, only friction losses will be discussed in this section and minor losses will be discussed in Sec. 8.

The mechanics of uniform flow can be illustrated by first considering laminar flow in wide channels. Thereafter turbulent flow will be discussed.

As shown by Eq. (3-11) of Sec. 3, the Bernoulli equation for an open channel takes on the following form:

$$z_1 + D_1 + \alpha_1 \frac{V_1{}^2}{2g} = z_2 + D_2 + \alpha_2 \frac{V_2{}^2}{2g} + h$$

where h is the energy loss between points 1 and 2 as illustrated in Fig. 7-4. For *uniform flow* the depth and velocity terms are the same at all points, so the Bernoulli equation reduces to

$$z_1 - z_2 = h \qquad (7\text{-}16)$$

thus showing that the energy loss h (Fig. 7-4) is equal to the drop in the bottom or that the energy gradient (e.g.), water surface (w.s.), and bottom are parallel.

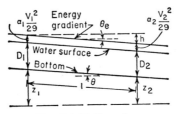

Fig. 7-4. Uniform flow.

If the energy loss per foot of length is called s, then, for any open channel,

$$s = \frac{h}{l} = \sin \theta_e \qquad (7\text{-}17)$$

where θ_e is the angle between the energy gradient and a horizontal plane and

$$h = sl \qquad (7\text{-}18)$$

The relation between the bottom slope s_0, the angle of the bottom with the horizontal θ, l, and $z_1 - z_2$ is expressed by the equations

$$s_0 = \frac{z_1 - z_2}{l \cos \theta} = \tan \theta \qquad (7\text{-}19)$$

and

$$z_1 - z_2 = s_0 l \cos \theta \qquad (7\text{-}20)$$

Then, from Eqs. (7-16) and (7-18) to (7-20), *for uniform flow only*,

$$s = s_0 \cos \theta = \sin \theta$$

When θ is very small, as is often the case for open channels, $\cos \theta \to 1$ or $\sin \theta \approx \tan \theta$ and

$$s \approx s_0$$

Again it should be emphasized that this relation applies only to uniform flow; in nonuniform flow the bottom slope has no relation to s. In conclusion it may be stated that, under all conditions, s is the energy loss per foot of length and, for open channels with very small slopes, it may also be defined as the slope of the energy gradient. For uniform flow, s is also the drop in the channel per foot of length, or $\sin \theta$, and for very small slopes, it becomes nearly equal to the slope of the channel, s_0 or $\tan \theta$.

Laminar Flow with a Free Surface. The law of laminar flow with a free surface for the case of wide rectangular channels may be developed in the same manner as for pipes.

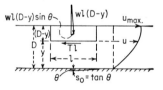

FIG. 7-5. Laminar flow in open channels.

Consider the free body of fluid shown in Fig. 7-5, having a width of 1 ft, a length l, and a height $D - y$. The summation of forces in the direction of flow gives

$$\tau l = wl(D - y) \sin \theta \qquad (7\text{-}21)$$

Replacing τ with its value from Eq. (1-3), rearranging the terms, and simplifying, the above equation becomes

$$du = \frac{w \sin \theta}{\mu} (D \, dy - y \, dy)$$

and integration gives

$$u = \frac{w \sin \theta}{\mu}\left(Dy - \frac{y^2}{2}\right) + \overset{0}{\underset{\parallel}{C}} \tag{7-22}$$

The value of C in Eq. (7-22) must be zero to satisfy the condition that $u = 0$ when $y = 0$. The maximum velocity may be obtained by letting $y = D$; then

$$u_{\max} = \frac{w \sin \theta\ D^2}{2\mu} \tag{7-23}$$

The discharge is obtained from a summation of small elements of discharge, utilizing the value of u from Eq. (7-22) as follows:

$$q = \int dq = \int u\,dy = \frac{w \sin \theta}{\mu}\int_0^D \left(Dy\,dy - \frac{y^2\,dy}{2}\right)$$

from which

$$q = \frac{w \sin \theta\ D^3}{3\mu} \tag{7-24}$$

and the average velocity is

$$V = \frac{q}{D} = \frac{w \sin \theta\ D^2}{3\mu} \tag{7-25}$$

and

$$\sin \theta = \frac{3\mu V}{wD^2} \tag{7-26}$$

Finally, the Reynolds number $R = Dv\rho/\mu$* may be introduced to give

$$\sin \theta = \frac{3V^2}{RgD} \tag{7-27}$$

From Eq. (7-17),

$$s = \frac{h}{l} = \frac{3V^2}{RgD} \tag{7-28}$$

and rearranging terms,

$$h = \frac{6}{R}\frac{l}{D}\frac{V^2}{2g} \tag{7-29}$$

---

* The Reynolds number for open channels is sometimes written with $4r$ as the length parameter, where r is the hydraulic radius. This makes the magnitudes of R correspond to those for pipes flowing full in which the length parameter is the diameter, d. Because for wide channels $r = D$, all values of R in Figs. 7-6 and 7-7 would have been four times as large if $4r$ had been used.

Letting

$$f = \frac{6}{R} \tag{7-30}$$

$$h = f \frac{l}{D} \frac{V^2}{2g} \tag{7-31}$$

In this form the equation resembles closely the Darcy-Weisbach equation for pipes [Eq. (6-19)], and Eq. (7-30) is the counterpart of the similar relationship for pipes given by Eq. (6-20). Because the Manning equation is commonly used for turbulent flow in open channels, it is of interest to relate f to n. This can be done by equating the value of s obtained from Eq. (7-31) with its value from the Manning equation [Eq. (7-35)].

$$f \frac{1}{D} \frac{V^2}{2g} = \frac{n^2 V^2}{2.208 r^{\frac{1}{3}}}$$

Because this derivation is for very wide channels, r may be replaced by D to obtain the following relationships:

$$f = \frac{2g}{2.21} \frac{n^2}{D^{\frac{1}{3}}} = 29.1 \frac{n^2}{D^{\frac{1}{3}}} \tag{7-32}$$

and

$$n = \frac{f^{\frac{1}{2}} D^{\frac{1}{6}}}{5.4} \tag{7-33}$$

Plotting $\log f$ against $\log R$ in accordance with Eq. (7-30) yields a straight line having a slope of -1 as shown in Figs. 7-6 and 7-7. Numerous tests of laminar flow in wide channels with smooth surfaces have verified Eq. (7-30).[1] However, for rough surfaces, the results follow trends parallel to that of Eq. (7-30) but with a larger value of f. Such relationships can be represented by the equation

$$f = \frac{C}{R} \tag{7-34}$$

In Fig. 7-6 the value of C from tests by Woo and Brater[1] for the rough side of masonite is 7.7, and in Fig. 7-7 tests conducted at the Waterways Experiment Station[2] on "cement" surfaces

---

[1] References to research on this topic, together with a more detailed discussion, are presented in D. C. Woo and E. F. Brater, Laminar Flow in Rough Rectangular Channels, *J. Geophys. Res.*, vol. 66, p. 4207, December, 1961.

[2] Studies of River Bed Materials and Their Movement, with Special Reference to the Lower Mississippi River, *U.S. Waterways Expt. Sta. Paper* 17, January, 1935.

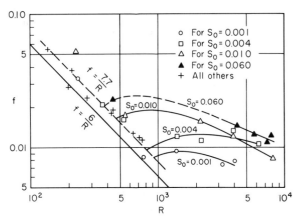

Fig. 7-6. f versus R for the rough side of masonite.

yield $C = 7.9$. Tests at the University of Michigan[1] with a surface of glued sand having an average size of 0.04 in. gave a value of C of 9.8 for slopes equal to or less than 0.003. For greater slopes, C increased consistently with s_0, reaching a value of 25.0 for a slope of 0.060. Tests at Vicksburg[1,2] with movable sand surface showed that a sand diameter of 0.0081 in. acted

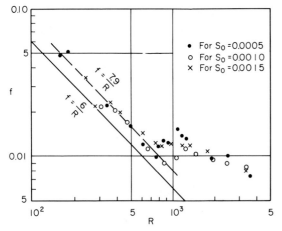

Fig. 7-7. f versus R for "cement."

[1,2] See notes on p. 7–11.

like a smooth surface ($C = 6.0$) but that C began to increase for a diameter of 0.019 in.   All the Vicksburg tests were made with relatively small slopes, so that no variation of C with slope could be detected.

Data plotted in Figs. 7-6 and 7-7 show clearly how the relationship between f and R changes when turbulence begins. It may be noted from Fig. 7-6 that the slope of the channel affects the point at which turbulence begins, there being a tendency for turbulent flow to begin at lower values of R for steeper slopes.   A review of published data[1] indicates that laminar flow ceases at values of R ranging from 400 to 900. These values appear to be consistent with those of pipes flowing full, because the depth term used in the Reynolds number is approximately equivalent to the hydraulic radius, and for a pipe flowing full, $r = d/4$.   Consequently, if values of R for pipes were based on r instead of d, they would be one-fourth as large and therefore the transition into turbulent flow would begin in about the same range of values of R as shown here.

The relationships derived and discussed here are for rectangular channels which are sufficiently wide so that the effects of the side wall will be negligible.   Based on an analytical expression for laminar flow in rectangular conduits first presented by Boussinesq,[2] it can be shown[3] that the theoretical value of C in Eq. (7-34) varies with the ratio of the width to the depth, b/D, according to the following tabulation:

b/D	C
∞	6.0
50	6.2
10	6.8
5	8.0

Laminar flow in channels other than rectangular has been investigated by Straub, Silberman, and Nelson.[4]

Turbulent Flow in Open Channels.   It is quite probable that future research and analysis will lead to the development of practical methods of determining energy losses in open channels in the transitional and fully turbulent ranges using an equation

[1] Woo and Brater, *op. cit.*

[2] M. J. Boussinesq, Memoire sur l'influence des frottements dans les mouvements réguliers des fluides, *J. Math. Pures et Appl.*, ser. II, xiii, p. 377, 1868.

[3] Woo and Brater, *op. cit.*

[4] L. G. Straub, E. Silberman, and H. C. Nelson, Open-channel Flow at Small Reynolds Numbers, *Trans. ASCE*, vol. 123, p. 685, 1958.

in the form of Eq. (7-31) and the concept of relating f to relative roughness and Reynolds number, as is done for round pipes flowing full (see pp. 6-9 to 6-12). However, the problem is exceedingly difficult for open channels because of the variety of shapes used and because relative roughness varies with depth. Furthermore, in earth canals or natural rivers the problem is further complicated when scour begins. An outline of research and writing on this topic is presented in a report of the American Society of Civil Engineers.[1] An example of the variation of f with R is provided by test data from nine large concrete-lined canals by the Bureau of Reclamation.[2] The values of R were computed from the expression $R = 4rV\rho/\mu$, and the values of f were computed from Eq. (7-31) after replacing D with $4r$. The report states that the 52 plotted test points "were chosen carefully to minimize the effects of curvature, algal growth, pier losses and all other effects except canal size." A straight line least squares fit, through a logarithmic plotting of the points, showed f varying from about 0.0148 for $R = 3 \times 10^6$ to 0.0117 for $R = 3 \times 10^7$. Although there is a scattering of the values of f about the fitted line over a range varying from 10 per cent below to 30 per cent above the line, the trend along the line is clearly evident. In this case the chief variable in the Reynolds number appears to be the hydraulic radius, and the ranges of values of Manning number n derived from these tests for various values of the hydraulic radius are shown by tabulated values in the following subsection.

The Manning Equation. Fortunately most practical problems fall in the fully turbulent range of flow at high values of the Reynolds number where the Manning equation gives satisfactory results. The historical relation of the Manning equation to the Chezy equation was discussed in Sec. 6, under Turbulent Flow in Pipes, and Selection of Energy-loss Equation and Friction Factor.

The Manning equation, as usually written in USCS units, is

$$V = \frac{1.486}{n} r^{2/3} s^{1/2} \qquad (7\text{-}35a)$$

---

[1] Task Force on Friction Factors in Open Channels, Committee on Hydromechanics of the Hydraulics Division, ASCE, Friction Factors in Open Channels, *J. Hydraulics Div.*, *ASCE*, vol. 89, March, 1963, pt. I, p. 97.

[2] Paul J. Tilp and Mansil W. Scrivner, Analysis and Description of Capacity Tests on Large Concrete-Lined Canals, *U.S. Bureau of Reclamation*, *Tech. Mem.* 661, 1964.

in which V is the velocity in feet per second, r is the hydraulic radius in feet, defined in Elements of a Cross Section, above, s is defined in Energy Losses in Open Channels, above, and the constant 1.486 was introduced to convert from the metric system. In the metric system the Manning formula is written

$$V = \frac{r^{2/3}s^{1/2}}{n} \qquad (7\text{-}35b)$$

where V is in meters per second and r is in meters. The corresponding expressions for discharge are obtained by multiplying by the cross-sectional area, a, to obtain Eq. (7-36a) for the USCS and Eq. (7-36b) for the metric system, the units of

$$Q = \frac{1.486a^{5/3}s^{1/2}}{np^{2/3}} \qquad (7\text{-}36a)$$

$$Q = \frac{a^{5/3}s^{1/2}}{np^{2/3}} \qquad (7\text{-}36b)$$

Q being ft^3/s in Eq. (7-36a) and m^3/s in Eq. (7-36b). For convenience and simplicity r was replaced by a/p in Eqs. (7-36). The use of these equations and the conversion of units are illustrated in Example 7-1.

Example 7-1. Flow is uniform in a trapezoidal channel at a depth of 5 ft. The bottom width is 200 ft, side slopes are 1:1, the bottom slope is 0.00001, and n is 0.020. Determine the discharge in cubic feet per second and cubic meters per second. Conversion factors can be obtained from Table 1-3.

$$a = 50 \times 5 + 2 \times \frac{5 \times 5}{2} = 275 \text{ ft}^3$$

or

$$a = 275 \times 0.09290 = 25.55 \text{ m}^3$$
$$p = 50 + 2 \times 1.414 \times 5 = 64.14 \text{ ft}$$

or

$$p = 64.14 \times 0.3048 = 19.55 \text{ m}$$

From Eq. (7-36a)

$$Q = \frac{1.486 \times 275^{5/3} \times 0.00001^{1/2}}{0.020 \times 64.14^{2/3}} = 171 \text{ ft}^3/s$$

or

$$Q = 171 \times 0.02832 = 4.83 \text{ m}^3/s$$

From Eq. (7-36b)

$$Q = \frac{25.55^{5/3} \times 0.00001^{1/2}}{0.020 \times 19.55^{2/3}} = 4.83 \text{ m}^3/\text{s}$$

The most common type of open-channel problem is the design situation in which channel size is required for a given Q and s. This problem must be solved by successive approximations. To avoid trial solutions and to simplify all Manning equation solutions, it is convenient to arrange the equation in such a form that dimensionless constants can be provided in tables. The procedure is to express the area in terms of D^2 and the wetted perimeter in terms of D. The development of dimensionless constants and the corresponding tables and numerical examples illustrating the use of the tables are presented for trapezoidal, circular, and parabolic channels. Rectangular and triangular channels are special cases of trapezoidal channels.

Trapezoidal Channels.   From Eq. (7-4)

$$a = \left(z + \frac{1}{x}\right) D^2 \tag{7-4}$$

in which z is the side slope (e/D) and x is the ratio of depth to the bottom width (D/b). Similarly, the wetted perimeter is written as in Eq. (7-6).

$$p = \left[\frac{1}{x} + 2(z^2 + 1)^{1/2}\right] D \tag{7-6}$$

These values are substituted in Eq. (7-36a) to obtain Eq. (7-37).

$$Q = \frac{1.486(z + 1/x)^{5/3}}{[1/x + 2(z^2 + 1)^{1/2}]^{2/3}} \frac{D^{8/3}s^{1/2}}{n} \tag{7-37}$$

and letting

$$K = \frac{1.486(z + 1/x)^{5/3}}{[1/x + 2(z^2 + 1)^{1/2}]^{2/3}} \tag{7-38}$$

the Manning equation can be written

$$Q = \frac{KD^{8/3}s^{1/2}}{n} \tag{7-39}$$

where $K = f(z, x)$; or, replacing D in Eq. (7-39) with bx from Eq. (7-3),

$$Q = \frac{Kx^{8/3}b^{8/3}s^{1/2}}{n}$$

or

$$Q = \frac{K'b^{8/3}s^{1/2}}{n} \tag{7-40}$$

where $K' = Kx^{8/3} = f_1(z, x)$.

Tabulations of data relating K and K' to z and x are presented in Tables 7-10 and 7-11, respectively. They cover all symmetrical trapezoidal channels, including rectangular and triangular channels. They permit the direct solution for D or b if the other is known, thus eliminating a solution by trial.

The computation of gradually varied flow profiles requires the solution for s in the Manning equation [Eq. (7-35)]. This solution of the Manning equation involves the term $(1/K')^2$. Consequently, a table relating $(1/K')^2$ to x and z is presented, Table 7-12. The eight-thirds and three-eighths powers of numbers may be obtained from Tables 7-19 and 7-20, respectively.

Example 7-2. Solve the problem in Example 7-1 using Eqs. (7-39) and (7-40) with Tables 7-10 and 7-11, respectively. $D/b = 5/50 = 0.10$, and from Table 7-10, $K = 14.8$. Then, using Eq. (7-39), we have

$$Q = \frac{14.8 \times 5^{8/3} \times 0.00001^{1/2}}{0.020} = 171 \text{ ft}^3/\text{s}$$

Or, from Table 7-11, $K' = 0.0318$, and Eq. (7-40) gives

$$Q = \frac{0.0318 \times 50^{8/3} \times 0.00001^{1/2}}{0.020} = 171 \text{ ft}^3/\text{s}$$

Example 7-3. What depth is required if a channel is to convey 200 ft³/s in a trapezoidal channel having a bottom width of 50 ft, side slopes of 1:1, $n = 0.020$, and a bottom slope of 0.00001? Solving Eq. (7-40) for K', we have

$$K' = \frac{Qn}{b^{8/3}s^{1/2}} = \frac{200 \times 0.020}{50^{8/3} \times 0.00001^{1/2}} = 0.0372$$

Then from Table 7-11, $D/b = D/50 = 0.11$, and $D = 5.5$ ft. When the answer is checked with Eq. (7-39), Table 7-10 yields $K = 13.42$, and

$$Q = \frac{13.42 \times 5.5^{8/3} \times 0.00001^{1/2}}{0.020} = 200 \text{ ft}^3/\text{s}$$

For *circular channels* flowing partly full (Fig. 7-2*d*), the expressions for area and wetted perimeter are given by Eqs. (7-11) and (7-12), respectively.

$$a = \left(\frac{360 - \theta}{360}\frac{\pi}{4} + \frac{\sin \theta}{8}\right)\frac{D^2}{x^2} \qquad (7\text{-}11)$$

$$p = \left(\frac{360 - \theta}{360}\right)\frac{\pi D}{x} \qquad (7\text{-}12)$$

When these values are substituted into Eq. (7-35*a*), the Manning equation again takes the form

$$Q = \frac{KD^{8/3}s^{1/2}}{n} \qquad (7\text{-}39)$$

in which

$$K = \frac{1.486[(360 - \theta)/360(\pi/4) + \frac{1}{8}\sin \theta]^{5/3}}{x^{8/3}[(360 - \theta)/360]^{2/3}} \qquad (7\text{-}41)$$

where $x = D/d$ is the ratio of depth of water to diameter of channel, and θ is the angle between the radii subtending the water surface. Since θ is a function of x, Eq. (7-41) shows that K is a function of x only. Table 7-13 contains values of K for different values of D/d.

By replacement of D with xd, the following equation is obtained for circular sections:

$$Q = \frac{K'd^{8/3}s^{1/2}}{n} \qquad (7\text{-}42)$$

where $K' + x^{8/3}K$. Therefore K' is also a function of x only. Table 7-14 contains values of K' for various values of D/d.

Example 7-4.   Determine the dimensions of a semicircular channel which will carry 100 ft³/s with a slope of 0.0001 if n is 0.013.   The channel is to have 1 ft of free board.   Then,

$$D = \frac{d}{2} - 1$$

and

$$\frac{D}{d} = 0.5 - \frac{1}{d}$$

For the first trial, assume $d = 10$ ft; then $D/d = 0.4$, and the value of K' from Table 7-14 is 0.1561.   Using Eq. (7-42), we have

$$d^{8/3} = \frac{Qn}{K's^{1/2}} = \frac{100 \times 0.013}{0.1561 \times 0.0001^{1/2}} = 833$$

and from Table 7-20, $d = 12.4$ ft. For the second trial, d is assumed to be 12.0 ft. Then $D/d = 0.417$ and $K' = 0.1683$, and solving Eq. (7-42) as above yields $d = 12.1$ ft, which checks the second assumption quite well. Then the value of D is 5.05 ft.

An independent check on the answer may now be made by means of Eq. (7-39). The value of K from Table 7-13 is 1.73, and Q is computed as follows:

$$Q = \frac{KD^{8/3}s^{1/2}}{n} = \frac{1.73 \times 75.1 \times 0.01}{0.013} = 99.9 \text{ ft}^3/\text{s}$$

which is the required capacity of the channel.

Parabolic channels have good hydraulic properties, and the cross sections of many natural rivers can be approximated by flat parabolas. The arrangement of the Manning equation in the form of Eq. (7-39) is done by substituting the expressions for area and wetted perimeter given by Eqs. (7-13) and (7-14), respectively, into Eq. (7-36).

$$a = \frac{2D^2}{3x} \tag{7-13}$$

$$p = [(16x^2 + 1)^{1/2} + \frac{1}{4x} \ln (16x^2 + 1 + 4x)] \frac{D}{2x} \tag{7-14}$$

Then

$$K = \frac{1.2}{(16x^2 + 1)^{1/2} + \dfrac{1}{4x} \ln (16x^2 = 1 + 4x)^{2/3}} \tag{7-43}$$

where $x = D/T$ is the ratio of the depth of water to the top width. Values of K are given in Table 7-15.

By replacing D with xT, the following form of the Manning equation is obtained for parabolic sections:

$$Q = \frac{K'T^{8/3}s^{1/2}}{n} \tag{7-44}$$

where $K' = x^{8/3}K$. Values of K' are given in Table 7-16.

Example 7.5. Determine the top width of a parabolic channel if it is required that the depth be 5 ft for a discharge of 100 ft^3/s. The slope of the channel is 0.0001, and n is 0.013. Derive the equation of the parabola. From Eq. (7-39) we have

$$K = \frac{Qn}{D^{8/3}s^{1/2}} = \frac{200 \times 0.013}{5^{8/3} \times 0.00001^{1/2}} = 1.78$$

Then, from Table 7-15

$$\frac{D}{T} = 0.36 = \frac{5}{T}$$

and

$$T = 13.9 \text{ ft}$$

Check, using Eq. (7-43) and Table 1-16 for K'.

$$Q = \frac{0.1168 \times 13.9^{5/3} \times 0.00001^{1/2}}{0.013} = 101 \text{ ft}^3/\text{s}$$

The general equation for a parabolic channel is $T^2/4 = kD$. Then for $T = 13.9$ and $D = 5.0$, k is 9.66, and the equation for the channel cross section becomes $T^2 = 38.64D$.

Solution of Problems by the Manning Equation. For channels of irregular shape or for forms not included in Fig. 7-2, Eqs. (7-35) and (7-36) must be used. Solutions are facilitated by the use of tables. Values of r are given in Table 7-1. Table 7-17 gives the square roots of decimal numbers, and the two-thirds powers of numbers may be obtained from Table 7-18.

The discharge of channels having any of the sectional forms shown in Fig. 7-2 can be determined from Eq. (7-39):

$$Q = \frac{KD^{5/3}s^{1/2}}{n} \tag{7-39}$$

or from the following equation:

$$Q = \frac{K'}{n} (b, d, \text{ or } T)^{5/3}s^{1/2} \tag{7-45}$$

Transposed into other forms, these formulas are, respectively,

$$D = \left(\frac{Qn}{Ks^{1/2}}\right)^{3/5} \tag{7-46}$$

$$s = \left(\frac{Qn}{KD^{5/3}}\right)^2 \tag{7-47}$$

$$K = \frac{Qn}{D^{5/3}s^{1/2}} \tag{7-48}$$

$$b, d, \text{ or } T = \left(\frac{Qn}{K's^{1/2}}\right)^{3/5} \tag{7-49}$$

$$s = \left(\frac{Qn}{K'b^{5/3}, d^{5/3}, \text{ or } T^{5/3}}\right)^2 \tag{7-50}$$

$$K' = \frac{Qn}{b^{5/3}, d^{5/3}, \text{ or } T^{5/3}s^{1/2}} \tag{7-51}$$

The above formulas provide for a simple and direct solution of problems involving discharge. They are to be solved with the aid of Tables 7-10 to 7-16. It is not necessary to determine either the area or the hydraulic radius since both are included in the discharge factor. To use these formulas, excepting (7-48) and (7-51), $x = D/b$ or D/d or D/T must be known and K or K' can then be taken from the appropriate table at the end of this section.

If discharge is the quantity sought, it can be determined from either formula (7-39) or (7-45), each formula providing an independent check on the other. If x is known or assumed, D can be obtained from formula (7-46), or if preferred, b, d, or T can be obtained from formula (7-49), the results by the two formulas checking each other. Either formula (7-47) or (7-50) will be found convenient for computing s. For determining s in rectangular and trapezoidal channels by formula (7-50), Table 7-12, giving values of $(1/K')^2$, will be most convenient. The use of this table for computations involving nonuniform flow is described on page 8-39. If the depth at which water will flow in a channel of given dimensions is required, it can best be obtained with the aid of formula (7-51) by determining K' and then from the appropriate table selecting the corresponding value of x. Then $D = xb$, xd, or xT, depending on the channel form. A method for solving for D from Eq. (7-36) by use of the bisection method and a digital computer is described in Sec. 13 and illustrated in Example 13-3. Similarly, if D is known and the other dimension unknown, it can be determined by the use of formula (7-48). Values of the eight-thirds powers and three-eighths powers of numbers are given in Tables 7-19 and 7-20, respectively.

Roughness Coefficients. Values of n to be used in the Manning equation are given in the table that follows. These values have been selected from published literature. The U.S. Bureau of Reclamation report[1] on large concrete-lined canals, described in Turbulent Flow in Open Channels, above, provides a graph showing 52 test values of n plotted against the hydraulic radius. The author has drawn envelope curves which include all but one of the 52 test points. The following

[1] Paul J. Tilp and Mansil W. Scrivner, Analysis and Description of Capacity Tests on Large Concrete-Lined Canals, *U.S. Bureau of Reclamation, Tech. Mem.* 661, 1964.

Values of n to Be Used with the Manning Equation

Surface	Best	Good	Fair	Bad
Uncoated cast-iron pipe..............	0.012	0.013	0.014	0.015
Coated cast-iron pipe................	0.011	0.012*	0.013*	
Commercial wrought-iron pipe, black...	0.012	0.013	0.014	0.015
Commercial wrought-iron pipe, galvanized	0.013	0.014	0.015	0.017
Smooth brass and glass pipe..........	0.009	0.010	0.011	0.013
Smooth lockbar and welded "OD" pipe	0.010	0.011*	0.013*	
Riveted and spiral steel pipe..........	0.013	0.015*	0.017*	
Vitrified sewer pipe..................	{ 0.010 0.011 }	0.013*	0.015	0.017
Common clay drainage tile............	0.011	0.012*	0.014*	0.017
Glazed brickwork....................	0.011	0.012	0.013*	0.015
Brick in cement mortar; brick sewers...	0.012	0.013	0.015*	0.017
Neat cement surfaces................	0.010	0.011	0.012	0.013
Cement mortar surfaces..............	0.011	0.012	0.013*	0.015
Concrete pipe.......................	0.012	0.013	0.015*	0.016
Wood stave pipe.....................	0.010	0.011	0.012	0.013
Plank Flumes:				
Planed..........................	0.010	0.012*	0.013	0.014
Unplaned........................	0.011	0.013*	0.014	0.015
With battens.....................	0.012	0.015*	0.016	
Concrete-lined channels..............	0.012	0.014*	0.016*	0.018
Cement-rubble surface................	0.017	0.020	0.025	0.030
Dry-rubble surface...................	0.025	0.030	0.033	0.035
Dressed-ashlar surface...............	0.013	0.014	0.015	0.017
Semicircular metal flumes, smooth.....	0.011	0.012	0.013	0.015
Semicircular metal flumes, corrugated..	0.0225	0.025	0.0275	0.030
Canals and Ditches:				
Earth, straight and uniform........	0.017	0.020	0.0225*	0.025
Rock cuts, smooth and uniform......	0.025	0.030	0.033*	0.035
Rock cuts, jagged and irregular......	0.035	0.040	0.045	
Winding sluggish canals............	0.0225	0.025*	0.0275	0.030
Dredged earth channels............	0.025	0.0275*	0.030	0.033
Canals with rough stony beds, weeds on earth banks.................	0.025	0.030	0.035*	0.040
Earth bottom, rubble sides.........	0.028	0.030*	0.033*	0.035
Natural Stream Channels:				
(1) Clean, straight bank, full stage, no rifts or deep pools...............	0.025	0.0275	0.030	0.033
(2) Same as (1), but some weeds and stones.......................	0.030	0.033	0.035	0.040
(3) Winding, some pools and shoals, clean..........................	0.033	0.035	0.040	0.045
(4) Same as (3), lower stages, more ineffective slope and sections......	0.040	0.045	0.050	0.055
(5) Same as (3), some weeds and stones.......................	0.035	0.040	0.045	0.050
(6) Same as (4), stony sections.......	0.045	0.050	0.055	0.060
(7) Sluggish river reaches, rather weedy or with very deep pools......	0.050	0.060	0.070	0.080
(8) Very weedy reaches.............	0.075	0.100	0.125	0.150

* Values commonly used in designing.

tabulation shows the ranges of n for three selected values of the hydraulic radius, r, as taken from these envelope curves.

	Values of n for Large *Concrete-lined Canals*
r, ft	*n*
4	0.0125–0.0152
8	0.0138–0.0161
12	0.0148–0.0171

This same report showed that values of n were increased as much as 40 per cent by algal growth during the summer season.

Values of n given in these tabulations were nearly all obtained for very large values of the Reynolds number. When the Reynolds number is small enough to approach the transition range ($rV/\nu < 15{,}000$ or $4rV/\nu < 60{,}000$), Eq. (7-31) should be used, or Eq. (7-33) may be used to compute appropriate values of n for the Manning equation.

Noneroding Velocities. Fortier and Scobey[1] pointed out that there is no sharp line of demarcation between the velocities that can no longer maintain silt in movement and those that will scour a canal bed. It is believed that there is a broad belt of velocities between these two "critical" velocities within which silt already loosened or brought in through a head gate will remain in suspension while the bed will not be scoured. In general, old and well-seasoned canals will stand much higher velocities than new ones. This is true particularly if the canal bed or the silt conveyed by the stream contains colloidal matter. Colloids, as applied to soils, give the properties of plasticity, cohesion, toughness when wet, and hardness when dry that are essential to an erosion-resisting soil.

The table that follows contains canal velocities that are recommended. The conclusions of Fortier and Scobey are:

1. The laws of hydraulics governing the movement of loose silt and detritus in open channels are only distantly related to the laws governing the scouring of a canal bed and are not directly applicable.

2. The material of seasoned canal beds is composed of particles of different sizes, and when the interstices of the larger are filled by the smaller, the mass becomes more dense, stable, and less subject to the erosive action of water.

[1] Samuel Fortier and F. C. Scobey, Permissible Canal Velocities, final Report of the Special Committee on Irrigation Hydraulics on this subject, *Trans. ASCE*, vol. 89, 1926.

3. The velocity required to ravel and scour a well-bedded canal in any material is much greater than the velocity required to maintain movement of particles of that same material before becoming bedded or that have been raveled off by higher velocities than the bed would stand.

4. Colloids in either the material of the canal bed or the water conveyed by it, or in both, tend to cement particles of clay, silt, sand, and gravel in such a way as to resist erosive effects.

5. The grading of material running from fine to coarse, coupled with the adhesion between particles brought about by colloids, makes possible high mean velocities without any appreciable scouring effect.

6. Irrigation canals may be designed for the velocity that is permissible when seasoned by age, as the demand for water grows with the age of the canal and the maximum mean velocity grows with the supply necessary to satisfy this demand.

7. Power canals are likely to be placed under peak load as soon as feasible after completion. For this reason a more conservative velocity should be chosen; otherwise scour may take place before seasoning.

Permissible Canal Velocities after Aging
Recommended in 1926 by Special Committee on Irrigation Research, ASCE

Original material excavated	Clear water, no detritus	Water transporting colloidal silts	Water transporting non-colloidal silts, sands, gravels, or rock fragments
Fine sand, non-colloidal.............	1.50	2.50	1.50
Sandy loam, non-colloidal..........	1.75	2.50	2.00
Silt loam, non-colloidal.............	2.00	3.00	2.00
Alluvial silts, non-colloidal.........	2.00	3.50	2.00
Ordinary firm loam................	2.50	3.50	2.25
Volcanic ash.....................	2.50	3.50	2.00
Fine gravel......................	2.50	5.00	3.75
Stiff clay, very colloidal............	3.75	5.00	3.00
Graded, loam to cobbles, non-colloidal.........................	3.75	5.00	5.00
Alluvial silts, colloidal..............	3.75	5.00	3.00
Graded, silt to cobbles, colloidal.....	4.00	5.50	5.00
Coarse gravel, non-colloidal........	4.00	6.00	6.50
Cobbles and shingles...............	5.00	5.50	6.50
Shales and hardpans..............	6.00	6.00	5.00

8. Canals, when new, may be operated with velocities less than the maximum permissible, by the use of check structures.

9. A slight excess of velocity is preferable to insufficient velocity. Check-drop structures will correct a slope causing erosion, but there is no method within reasonable cost by which velocities may be increased.

10. In the past, engineers have been led astray by a too close adherence to the results of experimental data on the transporting action of water on such materials as clay, silt, sand, and gravel, considered separately rather than on cohesive or mechanical combinations, and in consequence many canals have been designed and built on too flat slopes with correspondingly low velocities.

11. The growth of aquatic plants is only partly connected with velocities. Canals designed for the highest permissible velocities, from the standpoint of erosion, will be as free from plant growth as design alone can effect.

The practical difficulty that will be encountered in attempting to apply the foregoing conclusions or in selecting suitable velocities from the above table lies in properly defining the soil. Even with numerous borings and test pits, it will be difficult to determine the real character of the soil along the line of a proposed canal. This is particularly true of locations in glacial lands, where the character of soil may change at frequent intervals. Also, the definitions of soils given in the table will doubtless convey widely varying meanings to different engineers.

Criteria for scour based only on velocity neglect the fact that the shear stress on the bottom is also related to the depth. Reference to Eq. (7-21) and Fig. 7-5 will show that the expression for average shear stress in a wide rectangular channel is

$$\tau = wD \sin \theta \qquad (7\text{-}52)$$

A similar derivation for a channel of any shape yields

$$\tau = wr \sin \theta \qquad (7\text{-}53)$$

Lane[1] has taken the critical velocities given in the previous table, together with other test results, and developed criteria for noncohesive materials based on critical tractive force rather

[1] Emory W. Lane, Design of Stable Channels, *Trans. ASCE*, vol. 120, p. 1234, 1955.

than velocity. For materials having a median diameter (the size such that 50 per cent by weight is larger) greater than 5 mm, his design criterion can be expressed by the equation

$$\tau_c = 0.4d \qquad (7\text{-}54)$$

where τ_c is the limiting shear stress in pounds per square foot, and d is the particle size in inches such that 25 per cent by weight is larger. For material having a median size smaller than 5 mm, criteria are in the form of the three curves reproduced in Fig. 7-8. Curve a is for canals carrying 2 per cent or

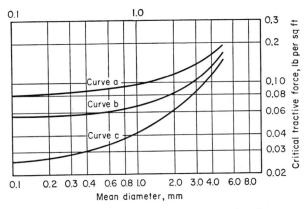

Fig. 7-8. Criteria for scour, median size less than 5 mm.

more of silt and clay two or three times per year. Curve b is for canals in which the silt and clay content reaches 0.2 per cent two or three times per year, and curve c is for clear water. Lane also presented methods of taking into account the fact that the shear stress varies from place to place in the wetted perimeter and that the sides are more vulnerable than the bottom.

Because of the rather large scatter of experimental results, and also because the greater vulnerability of the sides is compensated for to some extent by the lower shear stresses on the sides, an approximate solution for the critical tractive force for channels in which $b/D \gtreqless 2$ and $z \gtreqless 1.5$ can be obtained from the criteria given by Eq. (7-54) and Fig. 7-8 without including the refinements mentioned above. This can be illustrated by an example in which the 25 per cent size is 1 in. and the depth is 5 ft. From Eq. (7-54)

$$\tau = 0.4d = 0.4 \text{ lb per sq ft}$$

Then, from Eq. (7-52), the limiting slope is

$$\sin \theta = \frac{\tau}{wD} = \frac{0.4}{62.4 \times 5} = 0.0013$$

For this case the more refined solution given by Lane resulted in a value of 0.0011 for sin θ. For many practical cases, the approximate solution suggested here may be sufficiently accurate.

Another problem frequently encountered in designing canals is the *prevention of sedimentation* when water enters a canal with a heavy load of suspended material. Much progress is being made on this phase of flow in open channels, but the state of development does not lend itself to a condensed presentation of simple criteria.[1,2]

Air Entrainment. When water flows at high velocities, the turbulence produces a very rough water surface which tends to entrap air. The vertical components of the velocity distribute the air through the water, creating the "white water" which is associated with air entrainment. This phenomenon has been observed and studied by many hydraulic engineers, and only a representative group of references is presented here.[3-6] Detailed investigations[6] have revealed that near the bottom of a channel the water contains many small air bubbles in suspension, whereas near the top the water mixture appears as if it were predominantly air transporting globules of water.

[1] H. A. Einstein, The Bed-level Function for Sediment Transportation in Open Channel Flows, *U.S. Dept. Agr. Tech. Bull.* 1026, 1950.

[2] Carl B. Brown, "Engineering Hydraulics," chap. 12, John Wiley & Sons, Inc., New York, 1950.

[3] E. W. Lane, Entrainment of Air in Swiftly Flowing Water, *Civil Eng. (N.Y.)*, February, 1939, p. 89.

[4] G. H. Hickox, Air Entrainment on Spillway Faces, *Civil Eng. (N.Y.)*, December, 1945, p. 562.

[5] L. Standish Hall, Entrainment of Air in Flowing Water: A Symposium: Open Channel Flow at High Velocities, *Trans. ASCE*, vol. 108, p. 1394, 1943.

[6] Lorenz G. Straub and Alvin G. Anderson, Self-aerated Flow in Open Channels, *Trans. ASCE*, vol. 125, p. 456, 1960.

Because of the rapid movement of the small globules of water, it is difficult to establish the location of the surface of the mixture. An arbitrary location of the surface such that 98 or 99 per cent of the water is included is sometimes used. When the water enters a channel from a reservoir through a smooth entrance, entrainment does not occur in the central regions until the boundary layer has spread to the full depth. However, at the side walls entrainment begins sooner, because the boundary layer is exposed to the surface as soon as it begins to develop.

The water discharge in a channel with air entrainment can be expressed as follows:

$$Q = \theta_w A V \qquad (7\text{-}55)$$

where A is the total cross-sectional area of the mixture, V is the average velocity of the mixture, and θ_w is the specific gravity of the mixture.

The average velocity of the mixture can be estimated from open-channel equations like the Manning equations, using the same values of n as for ordinary flow. The value of θ_w must be known in order to solve for the area of cross section and the depth of the mixture. The value of θ_w depends on the velocity of the mixture, the depth, roughness, entrance conditions, form of the channel, the wind velocity and direction, and the fluid properties. If only water within a limited range of temperatures is considered, the effect of two important fluid properties, viscosity and surface tension, may be considered as constant. Hall[1] has shown that, for five channels which he investigated, the value of θ_w tends to vary with the Froude number, expressed as follows:

$$F = \frac{V^2}{gr_c} \qquad (7\text{-}56)$$

where r_c is the hydraulic radius that would occur if only water were flowing. All but one of the five flumes produced relationships of the following form:

$$\frac{1 - \theta_w}{\theta_w} = K \frac{V^2}{gr_c} \qquad (7\text{-}57)$$

For smooth concrete chutes a value of K of 0.006 is recommended. The value K increases with roughness. Using the same data, Douma[2] has developed a relationship which, after

[1] *Op. cit.*
[2] J. H. Douma, Discussion of Hall's paper, *op. cit.*, p. 1462.

revision to include θ_w, takes the following form:

$$(1 - \theta_w)^2 = \frac{0.002V^2}{gr} - 0.01 \qquad (7\text{-}58)$$

where r is the hydraulic radius of the mixture. Either of these expressions may be used to obtain a rough estimate regarding the degree of bulking that might be expected in reasonably straight and smooth concrete channels.

Table 7-1. For Determining Hydraulic Radius r for Trapezoidal
Channels of Various Side Slopes

Let $\dfrac{\text{depth of water}}{\text{bottom width of channel}} = \dfrac{D}{b}$ and $C_r =$ tabulated value. Then $r = C_r D$.

$\dfrac{D}{b}$	Side slopes of channel, ratio of horizontal to vertical									
	Vertical	¼–1	½–1	¾–1	1–1	1½–1	2–1	2½–1	3–1	4–1
.00	1.000	1.000	1.000	1.000	1.000	1.000	1.000	1.000	1.000	1.000
.01	.980	.982	.983	.983	.982	.980	.976	.973	.969	.961
.02	.962	.965	.967	.967	.965	.961	.955	.948	.941	.927
.03	.943	.949	.951	.951	.949	.943	.935	.926	.916	.898
.04	.926	.933	.936	.936	.934	.926	.916	.905	.894	.872
.05	.909	.918	.922	.922	.920	.911	.899	.886	.874	.850
.06	.893	.903	.908	.909	.906	.896	.883	.869	.856	.830
.07	.877	.889	.895	.896	.893	.882	.868	.853	.839	.812
.08	.862	.876	.882	.883	.881	.869	.854	.839	.823	.795
.09	.847	.863	.870	.871	.869	.857	.841	.825	.809	.781
.10	.833	.850	.858	.860	.858	.845	.829	.812	.797	.767
.11	.820	.838	.847	.849	.847	.834	.818	.801	.784	.755
.12	.806	.826	.836	.838	.836	.824	.807	.790	.773	.744
.13	.794	.814	.825	.828	.826	.814	.797	.779	.763	.734
.14	.781	.803	.815	.819	.817	.804	.787	.770	.753	.724
.15	.769	.793	.805	.809	.807	.795	.778	.761	.744	.715
.16	.758	.782	.795	.800	.799	.786	.769	.752	.736	.707
.17	.746	.772	.786	.791	.790	.778	.761	.744	.728	.700
.18	.735	.762	.777	.782	.782	.770	.753	.736	.720	.693
.19	.725	.752	.768	.774	.774	.763	.746	.729	.713	.686
.20	.714	.743	.760	.767	.766	.755	.739	.722	.706	.679
.21	.704	.734	.752	.759	.759	.748	.732	.716	.700	.674
.22	.694	.726	.744	.751	.752	.741	.726	.709	.694	.668
.23	.685	.717	.736	.744	.745	.735	.720	.704	.688	.663
.24	.676	.709	.729	.737	.739	.729	.714	.698	.683	.658
.25	.667	.701	.722	.730	.732	.723	.708	.693	.678	.653
.26	.658	.693	.715	.724	.726	.717	.703	.688	.673	.649
.27	.649	.686	.708	.717	.720	.712	.698	.683	.668	.645
.28	.641	.678	.701	.711	.714	.707	.693	.678	.664	.641
.29	.633	.671	.695	.706	.709	.702	.688	.673	.660	.637
.30	.625	.664	.688	.700	.703	.697	.683	.669	.656	.633
.31	.617	.657	.682	.694	.698	.692	.679	.665	.652	.630
.32	.610	.651	.676	.689	.693	.687	.675	.661	.648	.627
.33	.602	.644	.670	.684	.688	.683	.671	.657	.645	.624
.34	.595	.638	.665	.678	.683	.678	.667	.654	.641	.621
.35	.588	.632	.659	.673	.678	.674	.663	.650	.638	.618
.36	.581	.626	.654	.668	.674	.670	.659	.647	.635	.615
.37	.575	.620	.648	.664	.669	.666	.655	.643	.632	.612
.38	.568	.614	.643	.659	.665	.662	.652	.640	.629	.610
.39	.562	.608	.638	.654	.661	.658	.649	.637	.626	.607
.40	.556	.603	.633	.650	.657	.655	.645	.634	.623	.605
.41	.549	.598	.629	.646	.653	.652	.642	.631	.621	.603

Table 7-1. For Determining Hydraulic Radius r for Trapezoidal Channels of Various Side Slopes (*Continued*)

Let $\dfrac{\text{depth of water}}{\text{bottom width of channel}} = \dfrac{D}{b}$ and C_r = tabulated value. Then $r = C_r D$.

$\dfrac{D}{b}$	Side slopes of channel, ratio of horizontal to vertical									
	Vertical	¼–1	½–1	¾–1	1–1	1½–1	2–1	2½–1	3–1	4–1
.42	.543	.592	.624	.641	.649	.648	.639	.629	.618	.600
.43	.538	.587	.619	.637	.645	.645	.636	.626	.616	.598
.44	.532	.582	.615	.633	.641	.642	.633	.623	.613	.596
.45	.526	.577	.611	.629	.638	.639	.631	.621	.611	.594
.46	.521	.572	.606	.626	.635	.636	.628	.618	.609	.592
.47	.515	.568	.602	.622	.631	.633	.625	.616	.607	.591
.48	.510	.563	.598	.618	.628	.630	.623	.614	.605	.589
.49	.505	.558	.594	.615	.625	.627	.620	.611	.603	.587
.50	.500	.554	.590	.611	.621	.624	.618	.609	.601	.586
.51	.495	.550	.587	.608	.618	.622	.616	.607	.599	.584
.52	.490	.545	.583	.604	.615	.619	.613	.605	.597	.583
.53	.485	.541	.579	.601	.612	.617	.611	.603	.595	.581
.54	.481	.537	.576	.598	.610	.614	.609	.601	.594	.580
.55	.476	.533	.572	.595	.607	.612	.607	.600	.592	.578
.56	.472	.529	.568	.592	.604	.610	.605	.598	.590	.577
.57	.467	.525	.565	.589	.601	.607	.603	.596	.589	.576
.58	.463	.521	.562	.586	.598	.605	.601	.594	.587	.574
.59	.459	.518	.558	.583	.595	.603	.599	.593	.586	.573
.60	.455	.514	.555	.580	.593	.601	.597	.591	.584	.572
.61	.450	.510	.552	.577	.591	.599	.596	.589	.583	.571
.62	.446	.507	.549	.575	.588	.597	.594	.588	.581	.569
.63	.442	.504	.546	.572	.586	.595	.592	.586	.580	.568
.64	.439	.500	.543	.569	.584	.593	.590	.585	.579	.567
.65	.435	.497	.540	.567	.581	.591	.589	.583	.577	.566
.66	.431	.494	.537	.564	.579	.589	.587	.582	.576	.565
.67	.427	.490	.534	.562	.577	.587	.586	.580	.575	.564
.68	.424	.487	.532	.559	.575	.585	.584	.579	.574	.563
.69	.420	.484	.529	.557	.573	.583	.583	.578	.573	.562
.70	.417	.481	.526	.555	.571	.582	.581	.577	.571	.561
.71	.413	.478	.524	.552	.569	.580	.580	.575	.570	.560
.72	.410	.475	.521	.550	.567	.578	.578	.574	.569	.559
.73	.407	.472	.518	.548	.565	.577	.577	.573	.568	.558
.74	.403	.469	.516	.546	.563	.575	.576	.572	.567	.558
.75	.400	.467	.514	.544	.561	.573	.574	.570	.566	.557
.76	.397	.464	.511	.542	.559	.572	.573	.569	.565	.556
.77	.394	.461	.509	.539	.557	.570	.572	.568	.564	.555
.78	.391	.458	.507	.537	.555	.569	.570	.567	.563	.554
.79	.388	.456	.504	.535	.554	.567	.569	.566	.562	.554
.80	.385	.453	.502	.533	.552	.566	.568	.565	.561	.553
.81	.382	.450	.500	.531	.550	.565	.567	.564	.560	.552
.82	.379	.448	.498	.530	.548	.564	.566	.563	.559	.551
.83	.376	.445	.495	.528	.547	.562	.565	.562	.558	.551

Table 7-1. For Determining Hydraulic Radius r for Trapezoidal
Channels of Various Side Slopes (*Concluded*)

Let $\dfrac{\text{depth of water}}{\text{bottom width of channel}} = \dfrac{D}{b}$ and C_r = tabulated value.   Then $r = C_r D$.

$\dfrac{D}{b}$	Side slopes of channel, ratio of horizontal to vertical									
	Vertical	¼–1	½–1	¾–1	1–1	1½–1	2–1	2½–1	3–1	4–1
.84	.373	.443	.493	.526	.545	.561	.563	.561	.558	.550
.85	.370	.441	.491	.524	.544	.560	.562	.560	.557	.549
.86	.368	.438	.489	.522	.542	.558	.561	.559	.556	.549
.87	.365	.436	.487	.520	.540	.557	.560	.558	.555	.548
.88	.362	.434	.485	.519	.539	.556	.559	.558	.554	.547
.89	.360	.431	.483	.517	.537	.555	.558	.557	.554	.547
.90	.357	.429	.481	.515	.536	.554	.557	.556	.553	.546
.91	.355	.427	.479	.514	.534	.552	.556	.555	.552	.546
.92	.352	.425	.478	.512	.533	.551	.555	.554	.551	.545
.93	.350	.423	.476	.511	.532	.550	.554	.553	.551	.544
.94	.347	.420	.474	.509	.530	.549	.553	.553	.550	.544
.95	.345	.418	.472	.507	.529	.548	.553	.552	.549	.543
.96	.342	.416	.470	.506	.528	.547	.552	.551	.549	.543
.97	.340	.414	.469	.504	.526	.546	.551	.550	.548	.542
.98	.338	.412	.467	.503	.525	.545	.550	.550	.547	.542
.99	.336	.410	.465	.501	.524	.544	.549	.549	.547	.541
1.00	.333	.408	.464	.500	.522	.543	.548	.548	.546	.541
1.01	.331	.406	.462	.499	.521	.542	.547	.547	.545	.540
1.02	.329	.404	.460	.497	.520	.541	.547	.547	.545	.540
1.03	.327	.403	.459	.496	.519	.540	.546	.546	.544	.539
1.04	.325	.401	.457	.494	.518	.539	.545	.545	.544	.539
1.05	.323	.399	.456	.493	.516	.538	.544	.545	.543	.538
1.06	.321	.397	.454	.492	.515	.537	.543	.544	.543	.538
1.07	.318	.395	.452	.490	.514	.536	.543	.543	.542	.537
1.08	.316	.394	.451	.489	.513	.535	.542	.543	.541	.537
1.09	.314	.392	.449	.488	.512	.534	.541	.542	.541	.537
1.10	.312	.390	.448	.487	.511	.534	.541	.542	.540	.536
1.11	.311	.388	.446	.485	.510	.533	.540	.541	.540	.536
1.12	.309	.387	.445	.484	.509	.532	.539	.540	.539	.535
1.13	.307	.385	.444	.483	.508	.531	.539	.540	.539	.535
1.14	.305	.384	.442	.482	.507	.530	.538	.539	.538	.535
1.15	.303	.382	.441	.481	.506	.529	.537	.539	.538	.534
1.16	.301	.380	.440	.479	.505	.529	.537	.538	.537	.534
1.17	.299	.379	.438	.478	.504	.528	.536	.538	.537	.533
1.18	.298	.377	.437	.477	.503	.527	.535	.537	.536	.533
1.19	.296	.376	.436	.476	.502	.526	.535	.537	.536	.533
1.20	.294	.374	.434	.475	.501	.526	.534	.536	.536	.532
1.21	.292	.373	.433	.474	.500	.525	.533	.536	.535	.532
1.22	.291	.371	.432	.473	.499	.524	.533	.535	.535	.532
1.23	.289	.370	.431	.472	.498	.523	.532	.535	.534	.531
1.24	.287	.368	.429	.471	.497	.523	.532	.534	.534	.531
∞	.000	.121	.224	.300	.354	.416	.447	.464	.474	.485

Table 7-2. For Determining the Mean Depth D_m of a Cross Section of a Trapezoidal Channel

Let $\dfrac{\text{depth of water}}{\text{bottom width of channel}} = \dfrac{D}{b}$ and C_m = tabulated value. Then

$$D_m = C_m D.$$

$\dfrac{D}{b}$	Side slopes of channel, ratio of horizontal to vertical									
	⅛–1	¼–1	½–1	•¾–1	1–1	1½–1	2–1	2½–1	3–1	4–1
0.05	.994	.988	.976	.965	.955	.935	.917	.900	.885	.857
.1	.988	.976	.955	.935	.917	.885	.857	.833	.813	.778
.15	.982	.965	.935	.908	.885	.845	.813	.786	.763	.727
.2	.976	.955	.917	.885	.857	.813	.778	.750	.727	.692
.25	.971	.944	.900	.864	.833	.786	.750	.722	.700	.667
.3	.965	.935	.885	.845	.813	.763	.727	.700	.679	.647
.35	.960	.926	.870	.828	.794	.744	.708	.682	.661	.632
.4	.955	.917	.857	.813	.778	.727	.692	.667	.647	.619
.45	.949	.908	.845	.799	.763	.713	.679	.654	.635	.609
.5	.944	.900	.833	.786	.750	.700	.667	.643	.625	.600
.6	.935	.885	.813	.763	.727	.679	.647	.625	.609	.586
.7	.926	.870	.794	.744	.708	.661	.632	.611	.596	.576
.8	.917	.857	.778	.727	.692	.647	.619	.600	.586	.568
.9	.908	.845	.763	.713	.679	.635	.609	.591	.578	.561
1.0	.900	.833	.750	.700	.667	.625	.600	.583	.571	.556
1.1	.892	.823	.738	.689	.656	.616	.593	.577	.566	.551
1.2	.885	.813	.727	.679	.647	.609	.586	.571	.561	.547
1.3	.877	.803	.717	.669	.639	.602	.581	.567	.557	.544
1.4	.870	.794	.708	.661	.632	.596	.576	.563	.553	.541
1.5	.864	.786	.700	.654	.625	.591	.571	.559	.550	.538
1.6	.857	.778	.692	.647	.619	.586	.568	556	.547	.536
1.7	.851	.770	.685	.641	.614	.582	.564	.553	.545	.534
1.8	.845	.763	.679	.635	.609	.578	.561	.550	.542	.532
1.9	.839	.756	.672	.630	.604	.575	.558	.548	.540	.531
2.0	.833	.750	.667	.625	.600	.571	.556	.545	.538	.529

Table 7-3. For Determining the Vertical Distance $\bar{y}$ below the
Water Surface to the Center of Gravity of a Cross Section
of a Trapezoidal Channel

Let $\dfrac{\text{depth of water}}{\text{bottom width of channel}} = \dfrac{D}{b}$ and $C_{\bar{y}} =$ tabulated value. Then

$$\bar{y} = C_{\bar{y}}D.$$

$\dfrac{D}{b}$	Side slopes of channel, ratio of horizontal to vertical									
	⅛–1	¼–1	½–1	¾–1	1–1	1½–1	2–1	2½–1	3–1	4–1
0.05	.499	.498	.496	.494	.492	.488	.485	.481	.478	.472
.1	.498	.496	.492	.488	.485	.478	.472	.467	.462	.452
.15	.497	.494	.488	.483	.478	.469	.462	.455	.448	.438
.2	.496	.492	.485	.478	.472	.462	.452	.444	.438	.426
.25	.495	.490	.481	.474	.467	.455	.444	.436	.429	.417
.3	.494	.488	.478	.469	.462	.448	.438	.429	.421	.409
.35	.493	.487	.475	.465	.457	.443	.431	.422	.415	.403
.4	.492	.485	.472	.462	.452	.438	.426	.417	.409	.397
.45	.491	.483	.469	.458	.448	.433	.421	.412	.404	.393
.5	.490	.481	.467	.455	.444	.429	.417	.407	.400	.389
.6	.488	.478	.462	.448	.438	.421	.409	.400	.393	.382
.7	.487	.475	.457	.443	.431	.415	.403	.394	.387	.377
.8	.485	.472	.452	.438	.426	.409	.397	.389	.382	.373
.9	.483	.469	.448	.433	.421	.404	.393	.385	.378	.370
1.0	.481	.467	.444	.429	.417	.400	.389	.381	.375	.367
1.1	.480	.464	.441	.425	.413	.396	.385	.378	.372	.364
1.2	.478	.462	.438	.421	.409	.393	.382	.375	.370	.362
1.3	.477	.459	.434	.418	.406	.390	.380	.373	.367	.360
1.4	.475	.457	.431	.415	.403	.387	.377	.370	.365	.359
1.5	.474	.455	.429	.412	.400	.385	.375	.368	.364	.357
1.6	.472	.452	.426	.409	.397	.382	.373	.367	.362	.356
1.7	.471	.450	.423	.407	.395	.380	.371	.365	.361	.355
1.8	.469	.448	.421	.404	.393	.378	.370	.364	.359	.354
1.9	.468	.446	.419	.402	.391	.377	.368	.362	.358	.353
2.0	.467	.444	.417	.400	.389	.375	.367	.361	.357	.352

Table 7-4. For Determining the Area a of the Cross Section of a Circular Conduit Flowing Part Full

Let $\dfrac{\text{depth of water}}{\text{diameter of channel}} = \dfrac{D}{d}$ and C_a = the tabulated value.   Then $a = C_a d^2$.

$\dfrac{D}{d}$	.00	.01	.02	.03	.04	.05	.06	.07	.08	.09
.0	.0000	.0013	.0037	.0069	.0105	.0147	.0192	.0242	.0294	.0350
.1	.0409	.0470	.0534	.0600	.0668	.0739	.0811	.0885	.0961	.1039
.2	.1118	.1199	.1281	.1365	.1449	.1535	.1623	.1711	.1800	.1890
.3	.1982	.2074	.2167	.2260	.2355	.2450	.2546	.2642	.2739	.2836
.4	.2934	.3032	.3130	.3229	.3328	.3428	.3527	.3627	.3727	.3827
.5	.393	.403	.413	.423	.433	.443	.453	.462	.472	.482
.6	.492	.502	.512	.521	.531	.540	.550	.559	.569	.578
.7	.587	.596	.605	.614	.623	.632	.640	.649	.657	.666
.8	.674	.681	.689	.697	.704	.712	.719	.725	.732	.738
.9	.745	.750	.756	.761	.766	.771	.775	.779	.782	.784

Table 7-5. For Determining the Hydraulic Radius r of the Cross Section of a Circular Conduit Flowing Part Full

Let $\dfrac{\text{depth of water}}{\text{diameter of channel}} = \dfrac{D}{d}$ and C_r = the tabulated value.   Then $r = C_r d$.

$\dfrac{D}{d}$	.00	.01	.02	.03	.04	.05	.06	.07	.08	.09
.0	.000	.007	.013	.020	.026	.033	.039	.045	.051	.057
.1	.063	.070	.075	.081	.087	.093	.099	.104	.110	.115
.2	.121	.126	.131	.136	.142	.147	.152	.157	.161	.166
.3	.171	.176	.180	.185	.189	.193	.198	.202	.206	.210
.4	.214	.218	.222	.226	.229	.233	.236	.240	.243	.247
.5	.250	.253	.256	.259	.262	.265	.268	.270	.273	.275
.6	.278	.280	.282	.284	.286	.288	.290	.292	.293	.295
.7	.296	.298	.299	.300	.301	.302	.302	.303	.304	.304
.8	.304	.304	.304	.304	.304	.303	.303	.302	.301	.299
.9	.298	.296	.294	.292	.289	.286	.283	.279	.274	.267

Table 7-6. For Determining the Top Width T of the Cross Section of a Circular Channel Flowing Part Full

Let $\dfrac{\text{depth of water}}{\text{diameter of channel}} = \dfrac{D}{d}$ and C_T = tabulated value. Then $T = C_T d$.

$\dfrac{D}{d}$	.00	.01	.02	.03	.04	.05	.06	.07	.08	.09
.0	.000	.199	.280	.341	.392	.436	.475	.510	.543	.572
.1	.600	.626	.650	.673	.694	.714	.733	.751	.768	.785
.2	.800	.815	.828	.842	.854	.866	.877	.888	.898	.908
.3	.917	.925	.933	.940	.947	.954	.960	.966	.971	.975
.4	.980	.984	.987	.990	.993	.995	.997	.998	.999	1.000
.5	1.000	1.000	.999	.998	.997	.995	.993	.990	.987	.984
.6	.980	.975	.971	.966	.960	.954	.947	.940	.933	.925
.7	.917	.908	.898	.888	.877	.866	.854	.842	.828	.815
.8	.800	.785	.768	.751	.733	.714	.694	.673	.650	.626
.9	.600	.572	.543	.510	.475	.436	.392	.341	.280	.199

Table 7-7. For Determining the Mean Depth D_m* of the Cross Section of a Circular Channel Flowing Part Full

Let $\dfrac{\text{depth of water}}{\text{diameter of channel}} = \dfrac{D}{d}$ and C_m = tabulated value. Then $D_m = C_m d$.

$\dfrac{D}{d}$	.00	.01	.02	.03	.04	.05	.06	.07	.08	.09
.0	.000	.007	.013	.020	.027	.034	.040	.047	.054	.061
.1	.068	.075	.082	.089	.096	.103	.111	.118	.125	.132
.2	.140	.147	.155	.162	.170	.177	.185	.193	.200	.208
.3	.216	.224	.232	.240	.249	.257	.265	.274	.282	.291
.4	.299	.308	.317	.326	.335	.345	.354	.363	.373	.383
.5	.393	.403	.413	.423	.434	.445	.456	.467	.478	.490
.6	.502	.514	.527	.540	.553	.566	.580	.595	.610	.625
.7	.641	.657	.674	.692	.710	.730	.750	.771	.793	.817
.8	.842	.869	.897	.928	.960	.996	1.035	1.078	1.126	1.180
.9	1.241	1.311	1.393	1.492	1.613	1.768	1.977	2.282	2.792	3.940

    * D_m = area/top width is in reality the mean depth only when the circular conduit is flowing half full or less.

Table 7-8. For Determining the Vertical Distance $\bar{y}$ below the Water Surface to the Center of Gravity of a Cross Section of a Circular Channel Flowing Part Full

Let $\dfrac{\text{depth of water}}{\text{diameter of channel}} = \dfrac{D}{d}$ and $C_{\bar{y}} =$ tabulated value.   Then $\bar{y} = C_{\bar{y}}d$.

$\dfrac{D}{d}$	.00	.01	.02	.03	.04	.05	.06	.07	.08	.09
.0	.000	.004	.008	.012	.016	.020	.024	.028	.032	.036
.1	.040	.044	.049	.053	.057	.061	.065	.069	.073	.077
.2	.082	.086	.090	.094	.098	.103	.107	.111	.115	.119
.3	.124	.128	.132	.137	.141	.145	.150	.154	.158	.163
.4	.167	.172	.176	.181	.185	.189	.194	.199	.203	.208
.5	.212	.217	.221	.226	.231	.235	.240	.245	.250	.254
.6	.259	.264	.269	.274	.279	.284	.289	.294	.299	.304
.7	.309	.314	.320	.325	.330	.336	.341	.347	.352	.358
.8	.363	.369	.375	.381	.387	.393	.399	.405	.411	.418
.9	.424	.431	.438	.445	.452	.459	.466	.474	.482	.491

Table 7-9. For Determining the Hydraulic Radius r of the Cross Section of a Parabolic Channel

Let $\dfrac{\text{depth of water}}{\text{top width of section}} = \dfrac{D}{T}$ and $C_r =$ tabulated value.   Then $r = C_r D$.

$\dfrac{D}{T}$	.00	.01	.02	.03	.04	.05	.06	.07	.08	.09
.0	.667	.667	.666	.665	.664	.662	.660	.658	.656	.653
.1	.650	.646	.643	.639	.635	.631	.626	.622	.617	.612
.2	.607	.602	.597	.592	.586	.581	.575	.570	.564	.559
.3	.554	.548	.543	.537	.532	.526	.521	.516	.510	.505
.4	.500	.495	.490	.485	.480	.475	.470	.465	.460	.455
.5	.451	.446	.442	.437	.433	.428	.424	.420	.416	.412
.6	.408	.404	.400	.396	.392	.388	.385	.381	.377	.374
.7	.370	.367	.364	.360	.357	.354	.351	.348	.344	.341
.8	.338	.335	.333	.330	.327	.324	.321	.319	.316	.313
.9	.311	.308	.306	.303	.301	.298	.296	.294	.291	.289

Table 7-10. Values of K in Formula $Q = \dfrac{K}{n} D^{8/3} s^{1/2}$ for

Trapezoidal Channels

D = depth of water b = bottom width of channel

$\dfrac{D}{b}$	Side slopes of channel, ratio of horizontal to vertical									
	Vertical	¼–1	½–1	¾–1	1–1	1½–1	2–1	2½–1	3–1	4–1
.01	146.7	147.2	147.6	148.0	148.3	148.8	149.2	149.5	149.9	150.5
.02	72.4	72.9	73.4	73.7	74.0	74.5	74.9	75.3	75.6	76.3
.03	47.6	48.2	48.6	49.0	49.3	49.8	50.2	50.6	50.9	51.6
.04	35.3	35.8	36.3	36.6	36.9	37.4	37.8	38.2	38.6	39.3
.05	27.9	28.4	28.9	29.2	29.5	30.0	30.5	30.9	31.2	32.0
.06	23.0	23.5	23.9	24.3	24.6	25.1	25.5	26.0	26.3	27.1
.07	19.5	20.0	20.4	20.8	21.1	21.6	22.0	22.4	22.8	23.6
.08	16.8	17.3	17.8	18.1	18.4	18.9	13.4	19.8	20.2	21.0
.09	14.8	15.3	15.7	16.1	16.4	16.9	17.4	17.8	18.2	19.0
.10	13.2	13.7	14.1	14.4	14.8	15.3	15.7	16.2	16.6	17.4
.11	11.83	12.33	12.76	13.11	13.42	13.9	14.4	14.9	15.3	16.1
.12	10.73	11.23	11.65	12.00	12.31	12.8	13.3	13.8	14.2	15.0
.13	9.80	10.29	10.71	11.06	11.37	11.9	12.4	12.8	13.3	14.1
.14	9.00	9.49	9.91	10.26	10.57	11.1	11.6	12.0	12.5	13.4
.15	8.32	8.80	9.22	9.57	9.88	10.4	10.9	11.4	11.8	12.7
.16	7.72	8.20	8.61	8.96	9.27	9.81	10.29	10.75	11.20	12.1
.17	7.19	7.67	8.08	8.43	8.74	9.28	9.77	10.23	10.68	11.6
.18	6.73	7.20	7.61	7.96	8.27	8.81	9.30	9.76	10.21	11.1
.19	6.31	6.78	7.19	7.54	7.85	8.39	8.88	9.34	9.80	10.7
.20	5.94	6.40	6.81	7.16	7.47	8.01	8.50	8.97	9.43	10.3
.21	5.60	6.06	6.47	6.82	7.12	7.67	8.16	8.63	9.09	10.00
.22	5.30	5.76	6.16	6.51	6.82	7.36	7.86	8.33	8.79	9.70
.23	5.02	5.48	5.87	6.22	6.53	7.08	7.58	8.05	8.51	9.43
.24	4.77	5.22	5.62	5.96	6.27	6.82	7.32	7.79	8.26	9.18
.25	4.54	4.98	5.38	5.73	6.04	6.58	7.08	7.56	8.03	8.95
.26	4.32	4.77	5.16	5.51	5.82	6.37	6.87	7.35	7.81	8.74
.27	4.13	4.57	4.96	5.31	5.62	6.17	6.67	7.15	7.62	8.54
.28	3.95	4.38	4.77	5.12	5.43	5.98	6.48	6.96	7.43	8.36
.29	3.78	4.21	4.60	4.95	5.25	5.81	6.31	6.79	7.26	8.19
.30	3.62	4.05	4.44	4.78	5.09	5.64	6.15	6.63	7.10	8.04
.31	3.48	3.90	4.29	4.63	4.94	5.49	6.00	6.48	6.96	7.89
.32	3.34	3.77	4.15	4.49	4.80	5.35	5.86	6.34	6.82	7.75
.33	3.21	3.64	4.02	4.36	4.67	5.22	5.73	6.21	6.69	7.62
.34	3.09	3.51	3.89	4.23	4.54	5.10	5.60	6.09	6.56	7.50
.35	2.98	3.40	3.78	4.12	4.43	4.98	5.49	5.97	6.45	7.39
.36	2.88	3.29	3.67	4.01	4.31	4.87	5.38	5.86	6.34	7.28
.37	2.78	3.19	3.57	3.90	4.21	4.76	5.27	5.76	6.24	7.18
.38	2.68	3.09	3.47	3.81	4.11	4.67	5.17	5.66	6.14	7.09
.39	2.59	3.00	3.38	3.71	4.02	4.57	5.08	5.57	6.05	6.99
.40	2.51	2.92	3.29	3.62	3.93	4.48	4.99	5.48	5.96	6.91
.41	2.43	2.83	3.20	3.54	3.85	4.40	4.91	5.40	5.88	6.83
.42	2.36	2.76	3.13	3.46	3.77	4.32	4.83	5.32	5.80	6.75
.43	2.29	2.68	3.05	3.38	3.69	4.24	4.76	5.25	5.73	6.67
.44	2.22	2.61	2.98	3.31	3.62	4.17	4.68	5.17	5.66	6.60
.45	2.15	2.55	2.91	3.24	3.55	4.10	4.61	5.11	5.59	6.54

Table 7-10. Values of K in Formula $Q = \dfrac{K}{n} D^{8/3} s^{1/2}$ for

Trapezoidal Channels (*Continued*)

D = depth of water b = bottom width of channel

$\dfrac{D}{b}$	Side slopes of channel, ratio of horizontal to vertical									
	Ver-tical	$\frac{1}{4}$–1	$\frac{1}{2}$–1	$\frac{3}{4}$–1	1–1	$1\frac{1}{2}$–1	2–1	$2\frac{1}{2}$–1	3–1	4–1
.46	2.09	2.48	2.85	3.18	3.48	4.04	4.55	5.04	5.52	6.47
.47	2.03	2.42	2.78	3.12	3.42	3.97	4.49	4.98	5.46	6.41
.48	1.98	2.36	2.72	3.06	3.36	3.91	4.43	4.92	5.40	6.35
.49	1.92	2.31	2.67	3.00	3.30	3.85	4.37	4.86	5.34	6.29
.50	1.87	2.26	2.61	2.94	3.25	3.80	4.31	4.81	5.29	6.24
.51	1.82	2.20	2.56	2.89	3.19	3.75	4.26	4.75	5.24	6.19
.52	1.78	2.16	2.51	2.84	3.14	3.70	4.21	4.70	5.19	6.14
.53	1.73	2.11	2.46	2.79	3.09	3.65	4.16	4.65	5.14	6.09
.54	1.69	2.06	2.42	2.74	3.05	3.60	4.11	4.61	5.09	6.04
.55	1.65	2.02	2.37	2.70	3.00	3.55	4.07	4.56	5.05	6.00
.56	1.61	1.98	2.33	2.66	2.96	3.51	4.02	4.52	5.00	5.96
.57	1.57	1.94	2.29	2.61	2.92	3.47	3.98	4.48	4.96	5.92
.58	1.53	1.90	2.25	2.57	2.87	3.43	3.94	4.44	4.92	5.88
.59	1.50	1.86	2.21	2.53	2.84	3.39	3.90	4.40	4.88	5.84
.60	1.46	1.83	2.17	2.50	2.80	3.35	3.86	4.36	4.84	5.80
.61	1.43	1.79	2.14	2.46	2.76	3.31	3.83	4.32	4.81	5.76
.62	1.40	1.76	2.10	2.43	2.73	3.28	3.79	4.29	4.77	5.73
.63	1.37	1.73	2.07	2.39	2.69	3.24	3.76	4.25	4.74	5.70
.64	1.34	1.70	2.04	2.36	2.66	3.21	3.73	4.22	4.71	5.66
.65	1.31	1.67	2.01	2.33	2.63	3.18	3.69	4.19	4.68	5.63
.66	1.28	1.64	1.98	2.30	2.60	3.15	3.66	4.16	4.64	5.60
.67	1.26	1.61	1.95	2.27	2.57	3.12	3.63	4.13	4.61	5.57
.68	1.23	1.58	1.92	2.24	2.54	3.09	3.60	4.10	4.59	5.54
.69	1.21	1.56	1.89	2.21	2.51	3.06	3.58	4.07	4.56	5.51
.70	1.18	1.53	1.87	2.19	2.48	3.03	3.55	4.04	4.53	5.49
.71	1.16	1.51	1.84	2.16	2.46	3.01	3.52	4.02	4.50	5.46
.72	1.14	1.48	1.82	2.13	2.43	2.98	3.50	3.99	4.48	5.44
.73	1.12	1.46	1.79	2.11	2.41	2.96	3.47	3.97	4.45	5.41
.74	1.10	1.44	1.77	2.09	2.38	2.93	3.45	3.94	4.43	5.39
.75	1.08	1.41	1.75	2.06	2.36	2.91	3.42	3.92	4.41	5.36
.76	1.056	1.39	1.73	2.04	2.33	2.88	3.40	3.90	4.38	5.34
.77	1.037	1.37	1.70	2.02	2.31	2.86	3.38	3.87	4.36	5.32
.78	1.018	1.35	1.68	2.00	2.29	2.84	3.35	3.85	4.34	5.30
.79	1.000	1.33	1.66	1.97	2.27	2.82	3.33	3.83	4.32	5.28
.80	.982	1.31	1.64	1.95	2.25	2.80	3.31	3.81	4.30	5.26
.81	.965	1.30	1.62	1.93	2.23	2.78	3.29	3.79	4.28	5.24
.82	.949	1.28	1.60	1.92	2.21	2.76	3.27	3.77	4.26	5.22
.83	.933	1.26	1.59	1.90	2.19	2.74	3.25	3.75	4.24	5.20
.84	.917	1.24	1.57	1.88	2.17	2.72	3.23	3.73	4.22	5.18
.85	.902	1.23	1.55	1.86	2.15	2.70	3.22	3.71	4.20	5.16
.86	.887	1.21	1.53	1.84	2.14	2.68	3.20	3.70	4.18	5.14
.87	.872	1.20	1.52	1.83	2.12	2.67	3.18	3.68	4.17	5.12
.88	.858	1.18	1.50	1.81	2.10	2.65	3.16	3.66	4.15	5.11
.89	.844	1.17	1.49	1.79	2.09	2.63	3.15	3.64	4.13	5.09
.90	.831	1.15	1.47	1.78	2.07	2.62	3.13	3.63	4.12	5.08

Table 7-10. Values of K in Formula $Q = \dfrac{K}{n} D^{8/3} s^{1/2}$ for

Trapezoidal Channels (*Continued*)

D = depth of water b = bottom width of channel

$\dfrac{D}{b}$	Side slopes of channel, ratio of horizontal to vertical									
	Vertical	1/4–1	1/2–1	3/4–1	1–1	1½–1	2–1	2½–1	3–1	4–1
.91	.818	1.14	1.46	1.76	2.05	2.60	3.11	3.61	4.10	5.06
.92	.805	1.12	1.44	1.75	2.04	2.58	3.10	3.60	4.08	5.04
.93	.793	1.11	1.43	1.73	2.02	2.57	3.08	3.58	4.07	5.03
.94	.781	1.10	1.41	1.72	2.01	2.55	3.07	3.57	4.05	5.01
.95	.769	1.08	1.40	1.70	1.99	2.54	3.05	3.55	4.04	5.00
.96	.758	1.07	1.39	1.69	1.98	2.53	3.04	3.54	4.03	4.99
.97	.746	1.06	1.37	1.68	1.97	2.51	3.03	3.52	4.01	4.97
.98	.736	1.05	1.36	1.66	1.95	2.50	3.01	3.51	4.00	4.96
.99	.725	1.04	1.35	1.65	1.94	2.48	3.00	3.50	3.98	4.94
1.00	.714	1.02	1.33	1.64	1.93	2.47	2.99	3.48	3.97	4.93
1.01	.704	1.011	1.32	1.63	1.92	2.46	2.97	3.47	3.96	4.92
1.02	.694	1.000	1.31	1.61	1.90	2.45	2.96	3.46	3.95	4.91
1.03	.684	.989	1.30	1.60	1.89	2.43	2.95	3.45	3.93	4.89
1.04	.675	.979	1.29	1.59	1.88	2.42	2.94	3.43	3.92	4.88
1.05	.666	.968	1.28	1.58	1.87	2.41	2.92	3.42	3.91	4.87
1.06	.657	.958	1.27	1.57	1.86	2.40	2.91	3.41	3.90	4.86
1.07	.648	.948	1.26	1.56	1.84	2.39	2.90	3.40	3.89	4.85
1.08	.639	.939	1.25	1.55	1.83	2.38	2.89	3.39	3.88	4.84
1.09	.630	.929	1.24	1.54	1.82	2.37	2.88	3.38	3.86	4.83
1.10	.622	.920	1.23	1.53	1.81	2.36	2.87	3.37	3.85	4.81
1.11	.614	.911	1.22	1.52	1.80	2.34	2.86	3.36	3.84	4.80
1.12	.606	.902	1.21	1.51	1.79	2.33	2.85	3.35	3.83	4.79
1.13	.598	.893	1.20	1.50	1.78	2.32	2.84	3.34	3.82	4.78
1.14	.590	.884	1.19	1.49	1.77	2.31	2.83	3.33	3.81	4.77
1.15	.583	.876	1.18	1.48	1.76	2.30	2.82	3.32	3.80	4.76
1.16	.576	.868	1.17	1.47	1.75	2.30	2.81	3.31	3.79	4.75
1.17	.568	.859	1.16	1.46	1.74	2.29	2.80	3.30	3.78	4.74
1.18	.561	.851	1.15	1.45	1.74	2.28	2.79	3.29	3.77	4.74
1.19	.554	.844	1.14	1.44	1.73	2.27	2.78	3.28	3.77	4.73
1.20	.548	.836	1.14	1.43	1.72	2.26	2.77	3.27	3.76	4.72
1.21	.541	.828	1.13	1.42	1.71	2.25	2.76	3.26	3.75	4.71
1.22	.535	.821	1.12	1.42	1.70	2.24	2.75	3.25	3.74	4.70
1.23	.528	.814	1.11	1.41	1.69	2.23	2.75	3.24	3.73	4.69
1.24	.522	.807	1.10	1.40	1.68	2.22	2.74	3.23	3.72	4.68
1.25	.516	.800	1.10	1.39	1.68	2.22	2.73	3.23	3.71	4.67
1.26	.510	.793	1.09	1.38	1.67	2.21	2.72	3.22	3.71	4.67
1.27	.504	.786	1.08	1.38	1.66	2.20	2.71	3.21	3.70	4.66
1.28	.498	.779	1.08	1.37	1.65	2.19	2.70	3.20	3.69	4.65
1.29	.492	.773	1.07	1.36	1.65	2.18	2.70	3.19	3.68	4.64
1.30	.487	.767	1.06	1.35	1.64	2.18	2.69	3.19	3.67	4.64
1.31	.481	.760	1.05	1.35	1.63	2.17	2.68	3.18	3.67	4.63
1.32	.476	.754	1.05	1.34	1.62	2.16	2.67	3.17	3.66	4.62
1.33	.470	.748	1.04	1.33	1.62	2.15	2.67	3.16	3.65	4.61
1.34	.465	.742	1.04	1.33	1.61	2.15	2.66	3.16	3.65	4.61
1.35	.460	.736	1.03	1.32	1.60	2.14	2.65	3.15	3.64	4.60

Table 7-10. Values of K in Formula $Q = \dfrac{K}{n} D^{8/3} s^{1/2}$ for

Trapezoidal Channels (*Continued*)

D = depth of water b = bottom width of channel

$\dfrac{D}{b}$	Side slopes of channel, ratio of horizontal to vertical								
	Vertical	¼–1	½–1	¾–1	1–1	1½–1	2–1	2½–1	3–1	4–1
1.36	.455	.730	1.023	1.31	1.60	2.13	2.65	3.14	3.63	4.59
1.37	.450	.725	1.016	1.31	1.59	2.13	2.64	3.14	3.62	4.59
1.38	.445	.719	1.010	1.30	1.58	2.12	2.63	3.13	3.62	4.58
1.39	.441	.714	1.004	1.29	1.58	2.11	2.63	3.12	3.61	4.57
1.40	.436	.708	.998	1.29	1.57	2.11	2.62	3.12	3.60	4.57
1.41	.431	.703	.993	1.28	1.56	2.10	2.61	3.11	3.60	4.56
1.42	.427	.698	.987	1.28	1.56	2.09	2.61	3.10	3.59	4.55
1.43	.422	.692	.981	1.27	1.55	2.09	2.60	3.10	3.58	4.55
1.44	.418	.687	.976	1.26	1.55	2.08	2.59	3.09	3.58	4.54
1.45	.414	.682	.970	1.26	1.54	2.08	2.59	3.08	3.57	4.53
1.46	.409	.677	.965	1.25	1.53	2.07	2.58	3.08	3.57	4.53
1.47	.405	.672	.960	1.25	1.53	2.06	2.58	3.07	3.56	4.52
1.48	.401	.668	.954	1.24	1.52	2.06	2.57	3.07	3.56	4.52
1.49	.397	.663	.949	1.24	1.52	2.05	2.56	3.06	3.55	4.51
1.50	.393	.658	.944	1.23	1.51	2.05	2.56	3.06	3.54	4.50
1.51	.389	.654	.939	1.23	1.51	2.04	2.55	3.05	3.54	4.50
1.52	.385	.649	.934	1.22	1.50	2.04	2.55	3.04	3.53	4.49
1.53	.382	.645	.929	1.22	1.50	2.03	2.54	3.04	3.53	4.49
1.54	.378	.640	.925	1.21	1.49	2.03	2.54	3.03	3.52	4.48
1.55	.374	.636	.920	1.21	1.49	2.02	2.53	3.03	3.52	4.48
1.56	.371	.632	.915	1.20	1.48	2.02	2.53	3.02	3.51	4.47
1.57	.367	.628	.911	1.20	1.48	2.01	2.52	3.02	3.51	4.47
1.58	.364	.624	.906	1.19	1.47	2.01	2.52	3.01	3.50	4.46
1.59	.360	.620	.902	1.19	1.47	2.00	2.51	3.01	3.50	4.46
1.60	.357	.616	.897	1.18	1.46	2.00	2.51	3.00	3.49	4.45
1.61	.353	.612	.893	1.18	1.46	1.99	2.50	3.00	3.49	4.45
1.62	.350	.608	.889	1.17	1.45	1.99	2.50	2.99	3.48	4.44
1.63	.347	.604	.884	1.17	1.45	1.98	2.49	2.99	3.48	4.44
1.64	.344	.600	.880	1.16	1.44	1.98	2.49	2.98	3.47	4.43
1.65	.341	.596	.876	1.16	1.44	1.97	2.48	2.98	3.47	4.43
1.66	.337	.593	.872	1.16	1.43	1.97	2.48	2.97	3.46	4.42
1.67	.334	.589	.868	1.15	1.43	1.96	2.47	2.97	3.46	4.42
1.68	.331	.585	.864	1.15	1.42	1.96	2.47	2.96	3.45	4.41
1.69	.328	.582	.860	1.14	1.42	1.95	2.46	2.96	3.45	4.41
1.70	.326	.578	.856	1.14	1.42	1.95	2.46	2.96	3.44	4.41
1.71	.323	.575	.852	1.13	1.41	1.95	2.46	2.95	3.44	4.40
1.72	.320	.571	.849	1.13	1.41	1.94	2.45	2.95	3.44	4.40
1.73	.317	.568	.845	1.13	1.40	1.94	2.45	2.94	3.43	4.39
1.74	.314	.565	.841	1.12	1.40	1.93	2.44	2.94	3.43	4.39
1.75	.312	.561	.838	1.12	1.40	1.93	2.44	2.93	3.42	4.38
1.76	.309	.558	.834	1.12	1.39	1.92	2.43	2.93	3.42	4.38
1.77	.306	.555	.831	1.11	1.39	1.92	2.43	2.93	3.41	4.38
1.78	.304	.552	.827	1.11	1.38	1.92	2.43	2.92	3.41	4.37
1.79	.301	.549	.824	1.10	1.38	1.91	2.42	2.92	3.41	4.37
1.80	.298	.546	.820	1.10	1.38	1.91	2.42	2.91	3.40	4.36

Table 7-10. Values of K in Formula $Q = \dfrac{K}{n} D^{2/3}s^{1/2}$ for

Trapezoidal Channels (*Concluded*)

D = depth of water b = bottom width of channel

$\dfrac{D}{b}$	Side slopes of channel, ratio of horizontal to vertical									
	Ver-tical	¼–1	½–1	¾–1	1–1	1½–1	2–1	2½–1	3–1	4–1
1.81	.296	.543	.817	1.10	1.37	1.90	2 41	2.91	3.40	4.36
1.82	.293	.540	.813	1.09	1.37	1.90	2.41	2.91	3.39	4.36
1.83	.291	.537	.810	1.09	1.37	1.90	2.41	2.90	3.39	4.35
1.84	.289	.534	.807	1.09	1.36	1.89	2.40	2.90	3.39	4.35
1.85	.286	.531	.804	1.08	1.36	1.89	2.40	2.90	3.38	4.34
1.86	.284	.528	.801	1.08	1.36	1.89	2.40	2.89	3.38	4.34
1.87	.282	.525	.797	1.08	1.35	1.88	2.39	2.89	3.38	4.34
1.88	.279	.522	.794	1.07	1.35	1.88	2.39	2.88	3.37	4.33
1.89	.277	.520	.791	1.07	1.35	1.88	2.39	2.88	3.37	4.33
1.90	.275	.517	.788	1.07	1.34	1.87	2.38	2.88	3.37	4.33
1.91	.273	.514	.785	1.06	1.34	1.87	2.38	2.87	3.36	4.32
1.92	.270	.512	.782	1.06	1.34	1.87	2.38	2.87	3.36	4.32
1.93	.268	.509	.779	1.06	1.33	1.86	2.37	2.87	3.36	4.32
1.94	.266	.506	.776	1.05	1.33	1.86	2.37	2.86	3.35	4.31
1.95	.264	.504	.774	1.05	1.33	1.86	2.37	2.86	3.35	4.31
1.96	.262	.501	.771	1.05	1.32	1.85	2.36	2.86	3.35	4.31
1.97	.260	.499	.768	1.04	1.32	1.85	2.36	2.85	3.34	4.30
1.98	.258	.496	.765	1.04	1.32	1.85	2.36	2.85	3.34	4.30
1.99	.256	.494	.762	1.04	1.31	1.84	2.35	2.85	3.34	4.30
2.00	.254	.491	.760	1.04	1.31	1.84	2.35	2.84	3.33	4.29
2.01	.252	.489	.757	1.03	1.31	1.84	2.35	2.84	3.33	4.29
2.02	.250	.487	.754	1.03	1.30	1.83	2.34	2.84	3.33	4.29
2.03	.248	.484	.752	1.03	1.30	1.83	2.34	2.84	3.32	4.28
2.04	.247	.482	.749	1.02	1.30	1.83	2.34	2.83	3.32	4.28
2.05	.245	.480	.746	1.02	1.30	1.82	2.33	2.83	3.32	4.28
2.06	.243	.477	.744	1.02	1.29	1.82	2.33	2.83	3.31	4.28
2.07	.241	.475	.741	1.02	1.29	1.82	2.33	2.82	3.31	4.27
2.08	.239	.473	.739	1.01	1.29	1.82	2.33	2.82	3.31	4.27
2.09	.237	.471	.736	1.01	1.28	1.81	2.32	2.82	3.31	4.27
2.10	.236	.469	.734	1.01	1.28	1.81	2.32	2.81	3.30	4.26
2.11	.234	.466	.732	1.006	1.28	1.81	2.32	2.81	3.30	4.26
2.12	.232	.464	.729	1.004	1.28	1.81	2.31	2.81	3.30	4.26
2.13	.231	.462	.727	1.001	1.27	1.80	2.31	2.81	3.29	4.26
2.14	.229	.460	.724	.999	1.27	1.80	2.31	2.80	3.29	4.25
2.15	.227	.458	.722	.996	1.27	1.80	2.31	2.80	3.29	4.25
2.16	.226	.456	.720	.994	1.27	1.79	2.30	2.80	3.29	4.25
2.17	.224	.454	.718	.991	1.26	1.79	2.30	2.80	3.28	4.24
2.18	.223	.452	.715	.989	1.26	1.79	2.30	2.79	3.28	4.24
2.19	.221	.450	.713	.987	1.26	1.79	2.29	2.79	3.28	4.24
2.20	.219	.448	.711	.984	1.26	1.78	2.29	2.79	3.28	4.24
2.21	.218	.446	.709	.982	1.25	1.78	2.29	2.78	3.27	4.23
2.22	.216	.444	.706	.980	1.25	1.78	2.29	2.78	3.27	4.23
2.23	.215	.442	.704	.977	1.25	1.78	2.28	2.78	3.27	4.23
2.24	.213	.440	.702	.975	1.25	1.77	2.28	2.78	3.26	4.23
2.25	.212	.439	.700	.973	1.24	1.77	2.28	2.77	3.26	4.22
∞	.000	.091	.274	.500	.743	1.24	1.74	2.23	2.71	3.67

Table 7-11. Values of K' in Formula $Q = \dfrac{K'}{n} b^{8/3}s^{1/2}$ for

Trapezoidal Channels

D = depth of water b = bottom width of channel

$\dfrac{D}{b}$	Side slopes of channel, ratio of horizontal to vertical									
	Vertical	¼–1	½–1	¾–1	1–1	1½–1	2–1	2½–1	3–1	4–1
.01	.00068	.00068	.00069	.00069	.00069	.00069	.00069	.00069	.00070	.00070
.02	.00213	.00215	.00216	.00217	.00218	.00220	.00221	.00222	.00223	.00225
.03	.00414	.00419	.00423	.00426	.00428	.00433	.00436	.00439	.00443	.00449
.04	.00660	.00670	.00679	.00685	.00691	.00700	.00708	.00716	.00723	.00736
.05	.00946	.00964	.00979	.00991	.01002	.01019	.01033	.01047	.01060	.01086
.06	.0127	.0130	.0132	.0134	.0136	.0138	.0141	.0143	.0145	.0150
.07	.0162	.0166	.0170	.0173	.0175	.0180	.0183	.0187	.0190	.0197
.08	.0200	.0206	.0211	.0215	.0219	.0225	.0231	.0236	.0240	.0250
.09	.0241	.0249	.0256	.0262	.0267	.0275	.0282	.0289	.0296	.0310
.10	.0284	.0294	.0304	.0311	.0318	.0329	.0339	.0348	.0358	.0376
.11	.0329	.0343	.0354	.0364	.0373	.0387	.0400	.0413	.0424	.0448
.12	.0376	.0393	.0408	.0420	.0431	.0450	.0466	.0482	.0497	.0527
.13	.0425	.0446	.0464	.0480	.0493	.0516	.0537	.0556	.0575	.0613
.14	.0476	.0502	.0524	.0542	.0559	.0587	.0612	.0636	.0659	.0706
.15	.0528	.0559	.0585	.0608	.0627	.0662	.0692	.0721	.0749	.0805
.16	.0582	.0619	.0650	.0676	.0700	.0740	.0777	.0811	.0845	.0912
.17	.0638	.0680	.0716	.0748	.0775	.0823	.0866	.0907	.0947	.1026
.18	.0695	.0744	.0786	.0822	.0854	.0910	.0960	.1008	.1055	.1148
.19	.0753	.0809	.0857	.0899	.0936	.1001	.1059	.1115	.1169	.1277
.20	.0812	.0876	.0931	.0979	.1021	.1096	.1163	.1227	.1290	.1414
.21	.0873	.0945	.101	.106	.111	.120	.127	.135	.142	.156
.22	.0934	.1015	.109	.115	.120	.130	.139	.147	.155	.171
.23	.0997	.1087	.117	.124	.130	.141	.150	.160	.169	.187
.24	.1061	.1161	.125	.133	.140	.152	.163	.173	.184	.204
.25	.1125	.1236	.133	.142	.150	.163	.176	.188	.199	.222
.26	.119	.131	.142	.152	.160	.175	.189	.202	.215	.241
.27	.126	.139	.151	.162	.171	.188	.203	.218	.232	.260
.28	.132	.147	.160	.172	.182	.201	.217	.234	.249	.281
.29	.139	.155	.170	.182	.194	.214	.232	.250	.268	.302
.30	.146	.163	.179	.193	.205	.228	.248	.267	.287	.324
.31	.153	.172	.189	.204	.218	.242	.264	.285	.306	.347
.32	.160	.180	.199	.215	.230	.256	.281	.304	.327	.371
.33	.167	.189	.209	.227	.243	.271	.298	.323	.348	.396
.34	.174	.198	.219	.238	.256	.287	.316	.343	.370	.423
.35	.181	.207	.230	.251	.269	.303	.334	.363	.392	.450
.36	.189	.216	.241	.263	.283	.319	.353	.385	.416	.478
.37	.196	.225	.252	.275	.297	.336	.372	.406	.440	.507
.38	.203	.234	.263	.288	.312	.353	.392	.429	.465	.537
.39	.211	.244	.274	.301	.326	.371	.413	.452	.491	.568
.40	.218	.253	.286	.315	.341	.389	.434	.476	.518	.600
.41	.226	.263	.297	.328	.357	.408	.456	.501	.546	.633
.42	.233	.273	.309	.342	.373	.427	.478	.526	.574	.668
.43	.241	.283	.321	.357	.389	.447	.501	.553	.603	.703
.44	.248	.293	.334	.371	.405	.467	.525	.580	.633	.740
.45	.256	.303	.346	.386	.422	.488	.549	.607	.664	.777

Table 7-11. Values of K' in Formula $Q = \dfrac{K'}{n} b^{8/3} s^{1/2}$ for Trapezoidal Channels (*Continued*)

D = depth of water b = bottom width of channel

$\dfrac{D}{b}$	Side slopes of channel, ratio of horizontal to vertical									
	Vertical	¼–1	½–1	¾–1	1–1	1½–1	2–1	2½–1	3–1	4–1
.46	.264	.313	.359	.401	.439	.509	.574	.636	.696	.816
.47	.271	.323	.372	.416	.457	.531	.599	.665	.729	.856
.48	.279	.334	.385	.432	.474	.553	.625	.695	.763	.897
.49	.287	.344	.398	.447	.493	.575	.652	.725	.797	.939
.50	.295	.355	.412	.463	.511	.598	.679	.757	.833	.983
.51	.303	.366	.425	.480	.530	.622	.707	.789	.869	1.03
.52	.311	.377	.439	.496	.549	.646	.736	.822	.907	1.07
.53	.319	.388	.453	.513	.569	.671	.765	.856	.945	1.12
.54	.327	.399	.467	.531	.589	.696	.795	.891	.984	1.17
.55	.335	.410	.482	.548	.609	.722	.826	.926	1.025	1.22
.56	.343	.422	.497	.566	.630	.748	.857	.963	1.07	1.27
.57	.351	.433	.511	.584	.651	.775	.889	1.000	1.11	1.32
.58	.359	.445	.526	.602	.673	.802	.922	1.038	1.15	1.37
.59	.367	.456	.542	.621	.694	.830	.956	1.077	1.20	1.43
.60	.375	.468	.557	.640	.717	.858	.990	1.117	1.24	1.49
.61	.383	.480	.573	.659	.739	.887	1.02	1.16	1.29	1.54
.62	.391	.492	.588	.678	.762	.916	1.06	1.20	1.33	1.60
.63	.399	.504	.604	.698	.785	.946	1.10	1.24	1.38	1.66
.64	.408	.516	.620	.718	.809	.977	1.13	1.28	1.43	1.72
.65	.416	.529	.637	.738	.833	1.008	1.17	1.33	1.48	1.79
.66	.424	.541	.653	.759	.857	1.04	1.21	1.37	1.53	1.85
.67	.433	.553	.670	.780	.882	1.07	1.25	1.42	1.59	1.91
.68	.441	.566	.687	.801	.907	1.10	1.29	1.47	1.64	1.98
.69	.449	.579	.704	.822	.933	1.14	1.33	1.51	1.69	2.05
.70	.457	.592	.722	.844	.959	1.17	1.37	1.56	1.75	2.12
.71	.466	.604	.739	.866	.985	1.21	1.41	1.61	1.81	2.19
.72	.474	.617	.757	.889	1.012	1.24	1.46	1.66	1.86	2.26
.73	.483	.631	.775	.911	1.039	1.28	1.50	1.71	1.92	2.34
.74	.491	.644	.793	.934	1.067	1.31	1.54	1.77	1.98	2.41
.75	.499	.657	.811	.957	1.095	1.35	1.59	1.82	2.05	2.49
.76	.508	.670	.830	.981	1.12	1.39	1.63	1.87	2.11	2.57
.77	.516	.684	.849	1.005	1.15	1.43	1.68	1.93	2.17	2.65
.78	.525	.698	.868	1.029	1.18	1.46	1.73	1.99	2.24	2.73
.79	.533	.711	.887	1.053	1.21	1.50	1.78	2.04	2.30	2.81
.80	.542	.725	.906	1.078	1.24	1.54	1.83	2.10	2.37	2.90
.81	.550	.739	.925	1.10	1.27	1.58	1.88	2.16	2.44	2.98
.82	.559	.753	.945	1.13	1.30	1.62	1.93	2.22	2.51	3.07
.83	.567	.767	.965	1.15	1.33	1.67	1.98	2.28	2.58	3.16
.84	.576	.781	.985	1.18	1.36	1.71	2.03	2.34	2.65	3.25
.85	.585	.796	1.006	1.21	1.40	1.75	2.08	2.41	2.72	3.35
.86	.593	.810	1.03	1.23	1.43	1.79	2.14	2.47	2.80	3.44
.87	.602	.825	1.05	1.26	1.46	1.84	2.19	2.54	2.87	3.54
.88	.610	.839	1.07	1.29	1.49	1.88	2.25	2.60	2.95	3.63
.89	.619	.854	1.09	1.31	1.53	1.93	2.31	2.67	3.03	3.73
.90	.628	.869	1.11	1.34	1.56	1.98	2.36	2.74	3.11	3.83

Table 7-11. Values of K' in Formula $Q = \dfrac{K'}{n} b^{8/3}s^{1/2}$ for

Trapezoidal Channels (*Continued*)

D = depth of water b = bottom width of channel

$\dfrac{D}{b}$	Side slopes of channel, ratio of horizontal to vertical									
	Ver-tical	¼–1	½–1	¾–1	1–1	1½–1	2–1	2½–1	3–1	4–1
.91	.636	.884	1.13	1.37	1.60	2.02	2.42	2.81	3.19	3.93
.92	.645	.899	1.15	1.40	1.63	2.07	2.48	2.88	3.27	4.04
.93	.653	.914	1.18	1.43	1.67	2.12	2.54	2.95	3.35	4.14
.94	.662	.929	1.20	1.46	1.70	2.17	2.60	3.02	3.44	4.25
.95	.671	.944	1.22	1.49	1.74	2.22	2.66	3.10	3.52	4.36
.96	.680	.960	1.24	1.52	1.78	2.27	2.73	3.17	3.61	4.47
.97	.688	.975	1.27	1.55	1.81	2.32	2.79	3.25	3.70	4.58
.98	.697	.991	1.29	1.58	1.85	2.37	2.85	3.33	3.79	4.70
.99	.706	1.006	1.31	1.61	1.89	2.42	2.92	3.40	3.88	4.81
1.00	.714	1.022	1.33	1.64	1.93	2.47	2.99	3.48	3.97	4.93
1.01	.723	1.04	1.36	1.67	1.97	2.53	3.05	3.56	4.06	5.05
1.02	.732	1.05	1.38	1.70	2.01	2.58	3.12	3.65	4.16	5.17
1.03	.741	1.07	1.41	1.73	2.05	2.63	3.19	3.73	4.26	5.30
1.04	.749	1.09	1.43	1.77	2.09	2.69	3.26	3.81	4.35	5.42
1.05	.758	1.10	1.46	1.80	2.13	2.75	3.33	3.90	4.45	5.55
1.06	.767	1.12	1.48	1.83	2.17	2.80	3.40	3.98	4.55	5.68
1.07	.776	1.14	1.50	1.86	2.21	2.86	3.48	4.07	4.66	5.81
1.08	.784	1.15	1.53	1.90	2.25	2.92	3.55	4.16	4.76	5.94
1.09	.793	1.17	1.56	1.93	2.29	2.98	3.62	4.25	4.86	6.07
1.10	.802	1.19	1.58	1.97	2.34	3.04	3.70	4.34	4.97	6.21
1.11	.811	1.20	1.61	2.00	2.38	3.10	3.78	4.43	5.08	6.35
1.12	.820	1.22	1.63	2.04	2.42	3.16	3.85	4.53	5.19	6.49
1.13	.829	1.24	1.66	2.07	2.47	3.22	3.93	4.62	5.30	6.63
1.14	.837	1.25	1.69	2.11	2.51	3.28	4.01	4.72	5.41	6.77
1.15	.846	1.27	1.71	2.14	2.56	3.35	4.09	4.81	5.52	6.92
1.16	.855	1.29	1.74	2.18	2.61	3.41	4.17	4.91	5.63	7.06
1.17	.864	1.31	1.77	2.22	2.65	3.47	4.25	5.01	5.75	7.21
1.18	.873	1.32	1.79	2.25	2.70	3.54	4.34	5.11	5.87	7.36
1.19	.882	1.34	1.82	2.29	2.75	3.61	4.42	5.21	5.99	7.52
1.20	.891	1.36	1.85	2.33	2.79	3.67	4.51	5.32	6.11	7.67
1.21	.899	1.38	1.88	2.37	2.84	3.74	4.59	5.42	6.23	7.83
1.22	.908	1.40	1.90	2.41	2.89	3.81	4.68	5.52	6.35	7.99
1.23	.917	1.41	1.93	2.44	2.94	3.88	4.77	5.63	6.48	8.15
1.24	.926	1.43	1.96	2.48	2.99	3.95	4.86	5.74	6.61	8.31
1.25	.935	1.45	1.99	2.52	3.04	4.02	4.95	5.85	6.73	8.48
1.26	.944	1.47	2.02	2.56	3.09	4.09	5.04	5.96	6.86	8.64
1.27	.953	1.49	2.05	2.60	3.14	4.16	5.13	6.07	6.99	8.81
1.28	.962	1.51	2.08	2.64	3.19	4.23	5.22	6.18	7.13	8.98
1.29	.971	1.52	2.11	2.69	3.24	4.31	5.32	6.30	7.26	9.16
1.30	.980	1.54	2.14	2.73	3.30	4.38	5.41	6.41	7.40	9.33
1.31	.989	1.56	2.17	2.77	3.35	4.46	5.51	6.53	7.53	9.51
1.32	.997	1.58	2.20	2.81	3.40	4.53	5.61	6.65	7.67	9.69
1.33	1.006	1.60	2.23	2.85	3.46	4.61	5.71	6.77	7.81	9.87
1.34	1.015	1.62	2.26	2.90	3.51	4.69	5.81	6.89	7.96	10.05
1.35	1.024	1.64	2.29	2.94	3.57	4.77	5.91	7.01	8.10	10.24

Table 7-11. Values of K' in Formula $Q = \dfrac{K'}{n} b^{8/3} s^{1/2}$ for Trapezoidal Channels (*Continued*)

D = depth of water b = bottom width of channel

$\dfrac{D}{b}$	Vertical	¼–1	½–1	¾–1	1–1	1½–1	2–1	2½–1	3–1	4–1
					Side slopes of channel, ratio of horizontal to vertical					
1.36	1.03	1.66	2.32	2.98	3.62	4.85	6.01	7.14	8.24	10.4
1.37	1.04	1.68	2.35	3.03	3.68	4.93	6.11	7.26	8.39	10.6
1.38	1.05	1.70	2.38	3.07	3.74	5.01	6.21	7.39	8.54	10.8
1.39	1.06	1.72	2.42	3.11	3.79	5.09	6.32	7.51	8.69	11.0
1.40	1.07	1.74	2.45	3.16	3.85	5.17	6.42	7.64	8.84	11.2
1.41	1.08	1.76	2.48	3.21	3.91	5.25	6.53	7.77	8.99	11.4
1.42	1.09	1.78	2.51	3.25	3.97	5.34	6.64	7.91	9.15	11.6
1.43	1.10	1.80	2.55	3.30	4.03	5.42	6.75	8.04	9.31	11.8
1.44	1.11	1.82	2.58	3.34	4.09	5.51	6.86	8.17	9.46	12.0
1.45	1.11	1.84	2.61	3.39	4.15	5.59	6.97	8.31	9.62	12.2
1.46	1.12	1.86	2.65	3.44	4.21	5.68	7.08	8.45	9.78	12.4
1.47	1.13	1.88	2.68	3.49	4.27	5.77	7.20	8.59	9.95	12.6
1.48	1.14	1.90	2.71	3.53	4.33	5.86	7.31	8.73	10.11	12.8
1.49	1.15	1.92	2.75	3.58	4.39	5.95	7.43	8.87	10.28	13.1
1.50	1.16	1.94	2.78	3.63	4.46	6.04	7.54	9.01	10.45	13.3
1.51	1.17	1.96	2.82	3.68	4.52	6.13	7.66	9.15	10.6	13.5
1.52	1.18	1.98	2.85	3.73	4.58	6.22	7.78	9.30	10.8	13.7
1.53	1.19	2.00	2.89	3.78	4.65	6.31	7.90	9.45	11.0	14.0
1.54	1.20	2.03	2.92	3.83	4.71	6.41	8.02	9.59	11.1	14.2
1.55	1.20	2.05	2.96	3.88	4.78	6.50	8.15	9.74	11.3	14.4
1.56	1.21	2.07	3.00	3.93	4.85	6.60	8.27	9.90	11.5	14.6
1.57	1.22	2.09	3.03	3.98	4.91	6.69	8.40	10.05	11.7	14.9
1.58	1.23	2.11	3.07	4.03	4.98	6.79	8.52	10.20	11.9	15.1
1.59	1.24	2.13	3.11	4.09	5.05	6.89	8.65	10.36	12.0	15.3
1.60	1.25	2.16	3.14	4.14	5.12	6.99	8.78	10.52	12.2	15.6
1.61	1.26	2.18	3.18	4.19	5.18	7.09	8.91	10.7	12.4	15.8
1.62	1.27	2.20	3.22	4.25	5.25	7.19	9.04	10.8	12.6	16.1
1.63	1.28	2.22	3.25	4.30	5.32	7.29	9.17	11.0	12.8	16.3
1.64	1.29	2.24	3.29	4.35	5.40	7.39	9.30	11.2	13.0	16.6
1.65	1.29	2.27	3.33	4.41	5.47	7.50	9.44	11.3	13.2	16.8
1.66	1.30	2.29	3.37	4.46	5.54	7.60	9.57	11.5	13.4	17.1
1.67	1.31	2.31	3.41	4.52	5.61	7.70	9.71	11.7	13.6	17.3
1.68	1.32	2.33	3.45	4.57	5.68	7.81	9.85	11.8	13.8	17.6
1.69	1.33	2.36	3.49	4.63	5.76	7.92	9.99	12.0	14.0	17.9
1.70	1.34	2.38	3.52	4.69	5.83	8.02	10.13	12.2	14.2	18.1
1.71	1.35	2.40	3.56	4.74	5.90	8.13	10.3	12.3	14.4	18.4
1.72	1.36	2.43	3.60	4.80	5.98	8.24	10.4	12.5	14.6	18.7
1.73	1.37	2.45	3.64	4.86	6.06	8.35	10.6	12.7	14.8	18.9
1.74	1.38	2.47	3.68	4.92	6.13	8.46	10.7	12.9	15.0	19.2
1.75	1.39	2.50	3.73	4.98	6.21	8.58	10.8	13.1	15.2	19.5
1.76	1.39	2.52	3.77	5.04	6.29	8.69	11.0	13.2	15.4	19.8
1.77	1.40	2.54	3.81	5.10	6.36	8.80	11.1	13.4	15.7	20.1
1.78	1.41	2.57	3.85	5.16	6.44	8.92	11.3	13.6	15.9	20.3
1.79	1.42	2.59	3.89	5.22	6.52	9.03	11.4	13.8	16.1	20.6
1.80	1.43	2.62	3.93	5.28	6.60	9.15	11.6	14.0	16.3	20.9

Table 7-11. Values of K' in Formula $Q = \dfrac{K'}{n} b^{8/3}s^{1/2}$ for

Trapezoidal Channels (*Concluded*)

D = depth of water b = bottom width of channel

$\dfrac{D}{b}$	Side slopes of channel, ratio of horizontal to vertical									
	Ver-tical	¼–1	½–1	¾–1	1–1	1½–1	2–1	2½–1	3–1	4–1
1.81	1.44	2.64	3.97	5.34	6.68	9.27	11.7	14.2	16.5	21.2
1.82	1.45	2.66	4.02	5.40	6.76	9.39	11.9	14.4	16.8	21.5
1.83	1.46	2.69	4.06	5.46	6.84	9.51	12.1	14.5	17.0	21.8
1.84	1.47	2.71	4.10	5.52	6.93	9.63	12.2	14.7	17.2	22.1
1.85	1.48	2.74	4.15	5.59	7.01	9.75	12.4	14.9	17.5	22.4
1.86	1.49	2.76	4.19	5.65	7.09	9.87	12.5	15.1	17.7	22.7
1.87	1.49	2.79	4.23	5.71	7.18	9.99	12.7	15.3	17.9	23.0
1.88	1.50	2.81	4.28	5.78	7.26	10.12	12.9	15.5	18.2	23.3
1.89	1.51	2.84	4.32	5.84	7.34	10.24	13.0	15.7	18.4	23.6
1.90	1.52	2.86	4.36	5.91	7.43	10.37	13.2	15.9	18.6	24.0
1.91	1.53	2.89	4.41	5.97	7.52	10.5	13.4	16.1	18.9	24.3
1.92	1.54	2.91	4.45	6.04	7.60	10.6	13.5	16.3	19.1	24.6
1.93	1.55	2.94	4.50	6.10	7.69	10.8	13.7	16.6	19.4	24.9
1.94	1.56	2.96	4.55	6.17	7.78	10.9	13.9	16.8	19.6	25.3
1.95	1.57	2.99	4.59	6.24	7.87	11.0	14.0	17.0	19.9	25.6
1.96	1.58	3.02	4.64	6.31	7.96	11.1	14.2	17.2	20.1	25.9
1.97	1.59	3.04	4.68	6.37	8.05	11.3	14.4	17.4	20.4	26.2
1.98	1.60	3.07	4.73	6.44	8.14	11.4	14.6	17.6	20.6	26.6
1.99	1.60	3.09	4.78	6.51	8.23	11.5	14.7	17.8	20.9	26.9
2.00	1.61	3.12	4.82	6.58	8.32	11.7	14.9	18.1	21.2	27.3
2.01	1.62	3.15	4.87	6.65	8.41	11.8	15.1	18.3	21.4	27.6
2.02	1.63	3.17	4.92	6.72	8.50	12.0	15.3	18.5	21.7	28.0
2.03	1.64	3.20	4.97	6.79	8.60	12.1	15.5	18.7	22.0	28.3
2.04	1.65	3.23	5.01	6.86	8.69	12.2	15.6	19.0	22.2	28.7
2.05	1.66	3.25	5.06	6.93	8.79	12.4	15.8	19.2	22.5	29.0
2.06	1.67	3.28	5.11	7.00	8.88	12.5	16.0	19.4	22.8	29.4
2.07	1.68	3.31	5.16	7.08	8.98	12.7	16.2	19.7	23.0	29.7
2.08	1.69	3.33	5.21	7.15	9.08	12.8	16.4	19.9	23.3	30.1
2.09	1.70	3.36	5.26	7.22	9.17	12.9	16.6	20.1	23.6	30.5
2.10	1.70	3.39	5.31	7.30	9.27	13.1	16.8	20.4	23.9	30.8
2.11	1.71	3.42	5.36	7.37	9.37	13.2	17.0	20.6	24.2	31.2
2.12	1.72	3.44	5.41	7.44	9.47	13.4	17.2	20.8	24.5	31.6
2.13	1.73	3.47	5.46	7.52	9.57	13.5	17.4	21.1	24.7	32.0
2.14	1.74	3.50	5.51	7.60	9.67	13.7	17.6	21.3	25.0	32.3
2.15	1.75	3.53	5.56	7.67	9.77	13.8	17.8	21.6	25.3	32.7
2.16	1.76	3.56	5.61	7.75	9.87	14.0	18.0	21.8	25.6	33.1
2.17	1.77	3.58	5.66	7.82	9.97	14.1	18.2	22.1	25.9	33.5
2.18	1.78	3.61	5.72	7.90	10.08	14.3	18.4	22.3	26.2	33.9
2.19	1.79	3.64	5.77	7.98	10.18	14.5	18.6	22.6	26.5	34.3
2.20	1.80	3.67	5.82	8.06	10.28	14.6	18.8	22.8	26.8	34.7
2.21	1.81	3.70	5.87	8.14	10.4	14.8	19.0	23.1	27.1	35.1
2.22	1.81	3.73	5.93	8.22	10.5	14.9	19.2	23.3	27.4	35.5
2.23	1.82	3.75	5.98	8.29	10.6	15.1	19.4	23.6	27.7	35.9
2.24	1.83	3.78	6.03	8.37	10.7	15.2	19.6	23.9	28.0	36.3
2.25	1.84	3.81	6.09	**8.46**	10.8	15.4	19.8	24.1	28.4	36.7

Table 7-12. Values of $(1/K')^2$ in Formula $s = (Qn/K'b^{8/3})^2$ for Trapezoidal Channels

D = depth of water b = bottom width of channel

$\dfrac{D*}{b}$	Side slopes of channel, ratio of horizontal to vertical				
	Vertical	½–1	1–1	2–1	3–1
.001	4,540,000,000	4,530,000,000	4,530,000,000	4,530,000,000	4,520,000,000
.002	452,000,000	451,000,000	450,000,000	449,000,000	448,000,000
.003	117,000,000	117,000,000	116,000,000	116,000,000	116,000,000
.004	45,100,000	44,800,000	44,700,000	44,400,000	44,300,000
.005	21,500,000	21,300,000	21,200,000	21,100,000	21,000,000
.006	11,700,000	11,600,000	11,600,000	11,500,000	11,400,000
.007	7,030,000	6,960,000	6,920,000	6,870,000	6,820,000
.008	4,520,000	4,470,000	4,440,000	4,400,000	4,360,000
.009	3,060,000	3,020,000	3,000,000	2,970,000	2,940,000
.010	2,160,000	2,130,000	2,110,000	2,090,000	2,070,000
.011	1,570,000	1,550,000	1,540,000	1,520,000	1,500,000
.012	1,180,000	1,160,000	1,150,000	1,130,000	1,120,000
.013	907,000	891,000	881,000	868,000	857,000
.014	710,000	697,000	688,000	677,000	669,000
.015	566,000	555,000	547,000	538,000	530,000
.016	458,000	448,000	441,000	433,000	427,000
.017	375,000	366,000	361,000	354,000	348,000
.018	311,000	303,000	298,000	292,000	287,000
.019	260,000	253,000	249,000	244,000	239,000
.020	220,000	214,000	210,000	205,000	201,000
.021	187,000	182,000	179,000	174,000	171,000
.022	161,000	156,000	153,000	149,000	146,000
.023	139,000	135,000	132,000	128,000	126,000
.024	121,000	117,000	115,000	111,000	109,000
.025	106,000	102,000	100,000	97,000	94,700

* The small values of D/b given above can occur only in wide channels carrying relatively small depths of water. For this condition there is a wide variation in the tabulated values of $(1/K)^2$, and interpolations for intermediate values of D/b are not practicable. To avoid such interpolations, it will be simpler to make computations for a channel of greater or less width which for the given depth will correspond to the tabulated value of D/b nearest to the actual value, the discharge also being so increased or decreased that the discharge per unit width will remain unchanged.

For example, if $Q = 600$, $D = 1.38$, and $b = 425$, then $D/b = 0.00325$. In this case use $b = 1.38/0.003 = 460$ and $Q = 600 \times {}^{460}\!/_{425} = 649$. Results by this method will be practically the same as would be obtained by using actual values of Q and $(1/K')^2$.

Table 7-12. Values of $(1/K')^2$ in Formula $s = (Qn/K'b^{8/3})^2$ for Trapezoidal Channels (*Continued*)

D = depth of water b = bottom width of channel

$\dfrac{D}{b}$	Side slopes of channel, ratio of horizontal to vertical									
	Vertical	¼–1	½–1	¾–1	1–1	1½–1	2–1	2½–1	3–1	4–1
.026	93,100	91,300	89,800	88,700	87,800	86,300	85,100	84,000	82,900	81,000
.027	82,300	80,600	79,300	78,300	77,400	76,000	74,900	73,900	73,000	71,200
.028	73,100	71,500	70,300	69,400	68,600	67,300	66,300	65,400	64,500	62,900
.029	65,200	63,700	62,600	61,800	61,000	59,900	58,900	58,100	57,300	55,800
.030	58,300	57,000	56,000	55,200	54,500	53,500	52,600	51,800	51,100	49,700
.031	52,400	51,200	50,300	49,500	48,900	47,900	47,100	46,400	45,700	44,400
.032	47,300	46,200	45,300	44,600	44,000	43,100	42,300	41,600	41,000	39,800
.033	42,800	41,700	40,900	40,200	39,700	38,900	38,100	37,500	36,900	35,800
.034	38,800	37,800	37,100	36,500	36,000	35,200	34,500	33,900	33,400	32,300
.035	35,300	34,400	33,700	33,100	32,700	31,900	31,300	30,700	30,200	29,300
.036	32,300	31,400	30,700	30,200	29,700	29,000	28,400	27,900	27,500	26,500
.037	29,500	28,700	28,100	27,600	27,100	26,500	25,900	25,500	25,000	24,200
.038	27,100	26,300	25,700	25,200	24,800	24,200	23,700	23,300	22,800	22,000
.039	24,900	24,200	23,600	23,100	22,800	22,200	21,700	21,300	20,900	20,100
.040	22,900	22,200	21,700	21,300	20,900	20,400	19,900	19,500	19,200	18,400
.041	21,200	20,500	20,000	19,600	19,300	18,800	18,300	18,000	17,600	16,900
.042	19,600	19,000	18,500	18,100	17,800	17,300	16,900	16,500	16,200	15,600
.043	18,100	17,600	17,100	16,800	16,500	16,000	15,600	15,300	15,000	14,400
.044	16,900	16,300	15,900	15,500	15,300	14,800	14,400	14,100	13,800	13,300
.045	15,700	15,200	14,700	14,400	14,200	13,700	13,400	13,100	12,800	12,300
.046	14,600	14,100	13,700	13,400	13,150	12,760	12,430	12,130	11,860	11,350
.047	13,600	13,200	12,800	12,500	12,250	11,870	11,550	11,280	11,020	10,530
.048	12,700	12,300	11,900	11,600	11,420	11,060	10,760	10,490	10,250	9,790
.049	11,900	11,500	11,100	10,900	10,660	10,320	10,030	9,780	9,540	9,110
.050	11,200	10,800	10,400	10,200	9,970	9,640	9,370	9,130	8,900	8,490
.051	10,480	10,080	9,780	9,530	9,330	9,020	8,760	8,530	8,310	7,920
.052	9,850	9,470	9,170	8,940	8,750	8,450	8,200	7,980	7,780	7,400
.053	9,260	8,900	8,620	8,390	8,210	7,920	7,690	7,480	7,280	6,920
.054	8,720	8,380	8,110	7,890	7,720	7,440	7,200	7,010	6,820	6,480
.055	8,230	7,890	7,630	7,430	7,260	6,990	6,780	6,580	6,410	6,070
.056	7,760	7,440	7,190	7,000	6,840	6,580	6,370	6,190	6,020	5,700
.057	7,340	7,030	6,790	6,600	6,450	6,200	6,000	5,820	5,660	5,360
.058	6,940	6,640	6,410	6,230	6,080	5,850	5,660	5,490	5,330	5,040
.059	6,570	6,290	6,060	5,890	5,750	5,520	5,340	5,170	5,020	4,740
.060	6,230	5,950	5,740	5,570	5,440	5,220	5,040	4,880	4,740	4,470
.061	5,910	5,640	5,440	5,280	5,140	4,930	4,760	4,610	4,470	4,210
.062	5,610	5,350	5,160	5,000	4,870	4,670	4,510	4,360	4,230	3,980
.063	5,330	5,080	4,890	4,740	4,620	4,430	4,270	4,130	4,000	3,760
.064	5,070	4,830	4,650	4,500	4,380	4,200	4,040	3,910	3,780	3,550
.065	4,830	4,600	4,420	4,280	4,160	3,980	3,830	3,700	3,580	3,360
.066	4,600	4,380	4,200	4,070	3,960	3,780	3,640	3,510	3,400	3,190
.067	4,380	4,170	4,000	3,870	3,760	3,600	3,460	3,340	3,220	3,020
.068	4,180	3,970	3,810	3,690	3,580	3,420	3,290	3,170	3,060	2,860
.069	3,990	3,790	3,630	3,510	3,410	3,250	3,130	3,010	2,910	2,720
.070	3,820	3,620	3,470	3,350	3,250	3,100	2,980	2,870	2,770	2,580

Table 7-12. Values of $(1/K')^2$ in Formula $s = (Qn/K'b^{8/3})^2$ for
Trapezoidal Channels (*Continued*)

D = depth of water b = bottom width of channel

$\dfrac{D}{b}$	Side slopes of channel, ratio of horizontal to vertical									
	Vertical	¼–1	½–1	¾–1	1–1	1½–1	2–1	2½–1	3–1	4–1
.071	3,650	3,460	3,310	3,200	3,100	2,960	2,840	2,730	2,630	2,460
.072	3,490	3,300	3,160	3,050	2,960	2,820	2,700	2,600	2,510	2,340
.073	3,340	3,160	3,020	2,920	2,830	2,690	2,580	2,480	2,390	2,220
.074	3,200	3,030	2,890	2,790	2,700	2,570	2,460	2,360	2,280	2,120
.075	3,070	2,900	2,770	2,670	2,590	2,450	2,350	2,260	2,170	2,020
.076	2,940	2,780	2,650	2,550	2,470	2,350	2,240	2,150	2,070	1,920
.077	2,820	2,660	2,540	2,450	2,370	2,250	2,150	2,060	1,980	1,840
.078	2,710	2,550	2,440	2,340	2,270	2,150	2,050	1,970	1,890	1,750
.079	2,600	2,450	2,340	2,250	2,170	2,060	1,970	1,880	1,810	1,670
.080	2,500	2,360	2,240	2,160	2,080	1,970	1,880	1,800	1,730	1,600
.081	2,410	2,260	2,150	2,070	2,000	1,890	1,800	1,730	1,660	1,530
.082	2,310	2,180	2,070	1,990	1,920	1,810	1,730	1,650	1,590	1,460
.083	2,230	2,090	1,990	1,910	1,840	1,740	1,660	1,580	1,520	1,400
.084	2,150	2,010	1,910	1,830	1,770	1,670	1,590	1,520	1,460	1,340
.085	2,070	1,940	1,840	1,760	1,700	1,610	1,530	1,460	1,400	1,280
.086	1,990	1,870	1,770	1,700	1,640	1,540	1,470	1,400	1,340	1,230
.087	1,920	1,800	1,710	1,630	1,580	1,480	1,410	1,340	1,290	1,180
.088	1,850	1,740	1,640	1,570	1,520	1,430	1,350	1,290	1,230	1,130
.089	1,790	1,670	1,590	1,520	1,460	1,370	1,300	1,240	1,190	1,090
.090	1,730	1,620	1,530	1,460	1,410	1,320	1,250	1,190	1,140	1,040
.091	1,670	1,560	1,470	1,410	1,360	1,270	1,210	1,148	1,096	1,001
.092	1,610	1,510	1,420	1,360	1,310	1,230	1,160	1,105	1,054	962
.093	1,560	1,450	1,370	1,310	1,260	1,180	1,120	1,064	1,014	925
.094	1,510	1,410	1,330	1,270	1,220	1,140	1,080	1,024	976	889
.095	1,460	1,360	1,280	1,220	1,170	1,100	1,040	987	940	856
.096	1,410	1,310	1,240	1,180	1,134	1,061	1,002	951	905	823
.097	1,370	1,270	1,200	1,140	1,096	1,024	967	917	872	793
.098	1,320	1,230	1,160	1,100	1,059	989	933	885	841	763
.099	1,280	1,190	1,120	1,070	1,024	955	901	853	811	735
.100	1,240	1,150	1,090	1,030	990	923	870	824	782	709
.101	1,210	1,118	1,051	999	957	892	840	795	755	683
.102	1,170	1,083	1,018	967	926	863	812	768	728	659
.103	1,130	1,050	986	936	897	834	785	742	703	635
.104	1,100	1,018	955	907	868	807	759	717	679	613
.105	1,070	988	926	879	841	781	734	693	656	592
.106	1,038	958	898	852	815	756	710	670	634	571
.107	1,008	930	871	826	789	732	687	648	613	552
.108	980	903	845	801	765	709	665	627	593	533
.109	952	877	820	777	742	687	644	607	574	515
.110	926	852	796	754	720	666	624	588	555	498
.111	900	828	773	732	698	646	605	569	537	482
.112	876	805	751	710	677	626	586	551	520	466
.113	852	782	730	690	658	608	568	534	504	451
.114	829	761	709	670	639	590	551	517	488	436
.115	807	740	689	651	620	572	534	501	472	422

Table 7-12. Values of $(1/K')^2$ in Formula $s = (Qn/K'b^{8/3})^2$ for Trapezoidal Channels (*Continued*)

D = depth of water $\quad$ b = bottom width of channel

$\dfrac{D}{b}$	Side slopes of channel, ratio of horizontal to vertical									
	Ver-tical	¼–1	½–1	¾–1	1–1	1½–1	2–1	2½–1	3–1	4–1
.116	786	720	670	633	602	555	518	486	458	409
.117	765	701	652	615	585	539	503	472	444	396
.118	745	682	634	598	569	524	488	457	430	383
.119	726	664	617	581	553	509	474	444	417	371
.120	708	647	601	566	538	494	460	431	405	360
.121	690	630	585	550	523	480	447	418	393	349
.122	673	614	569	536	509	467	434	406	381	338
.123	656	598	554	521	495	454	422	394	370	328
.124	640	583	540	508	482	441	410	383	359	318
.125	624	568	526	494	469	429	398	372	349	309
.126	609	554	513	481	457	418	387	362	339	300
.127	595	540	500	469	445	407	377	351	329	291
.128	581	527	487	457	433	396	367	342	320	282
.129	567	514	475	445	422	385	357	332	311	274
.130	554	502	464	434	411	375	347	323	302	266
.131	541	490	452	423	401	365	338	314	294	259
.132	528	478	441	413	391	356	329	306	286	251
.133	516	467	431	403	381	347	320	298	278	244
.134	505	456	420	393	371	338	312	290	270	237
.135	493	446	410	383	362	329	304	282	263	231
.136	482	435	401	374	353	321	296	275	256	224
.137	472	425	391	365	345	313	288	267	249	218
.138	461	416	382	357	336	305	281	260	243	212
.139	451	406	373	348	328	298	274	254	236	206
.140	442	397	365	340	320	290	267	247	230	201
.141	432	389	356	332	313	283	260	241	224	195
.142	423	380	348	324	305	276	254	235	218	190
.143	414	372	341	317	298	270	248	229	213	185
.144	405	364	333	310	291	263	242	223	207	180
.145	397	356	326	303	285	257	236	218	202	176
.146	389	348	318	296	278	251	230	212	197	171
.147	381	341	311	289	272	245	224	207	192	167
.148	373	334	305	283	266	239	219	202	187	162
.149	366	327	298	277	260	234	214	197	183	158
.150	358	320	292	271	254	228	209	192	178	154
.151	351	313	286	265	248	223	204	188	174	150
.152	344	307	280	259	243	218	199	183	170	147
.153	337	301	274	253	238	213	195	179	165	143
.154	331	295	268	248	232	208	190	175	162	139
.155	324	289	262	243	227	204	186	171	158	136
.156	318	283	257	238	222	199	182	167	154	133
.157	312	277	252	233	218	195	177	163	150	129
.158	306	272	247	228	213	191	173	159	147	126
.159	301	267	242	223	209	187	170	155	143	123
.160	295	261	237	219	204	183	166	152	140	120

Table 7-12. Values of $(1/K')^2$ in Formula $s = (Qn/K'b^{8/3})^2$ for Trapezoidal Channels (*Continued*)

D = depth of water b = bottom width of channel

$\dfrac{D}{b}$	Side slopes of channel, ratio of horizontal to vertical									
	Ver-tical	¼–1	½–1	¾–1	1–1	1½–1	2–1	2½–1	3–1	4–1
.161	289	256	232	214	200	179	162	148	137	117
.162	284	251	228	210	196	175	159	145	134	115
.163	279	247	223	206	192	171	155	142	131	112
.164	274	242	219	201	188	167	152	139	128	109
.165	269	237	214	197	184	164	148	136	125	107
.166	264	233	210	194	180	160	145	133	122	104.2
.167	259	229	206	190	177	157	142	130	119	101.8
.168	255	224	202	186	173	154	139	127	117	99.4
.169	250	220	199	182	170	151	136	124	114	97.2
.170	246	216	195	179	166	148	133	122	111	95.0
.171	242	212	191	175	163	145	131	119	109.1	92.8
.172	237	208	188	172	160	142	128	116	106.7	90.7
.173	233	205	184	169	157	139	125	114	104.4	88.7
.174	229	201	181	166	154	136	123	112	102.1	86.7
.175	225	197	177	162	151	133	120	109	99.9	84.8
.176	222	194	174	159	148	131	118	106.9	97.8	82.9
.177	218	191	171	156	145	128	115	104.7	95.7	81.1
.178	214	187	168	154	142	126	113	102.6	93.7	79.3
.179	211	184	165	151	140	123	111	100.4	91.7	77.6
.180	207	181	162	148	137	121	108	98.4	89.8	75.9
.181	204	178	159	145	135	118	106.3	96.4	88.0	74.3
.182	201	175	156	143	132	116	104.2	94.4	86.1	72.7
.183	197	172	154	140	130	114	102.1	92.5	84.4	71.1
.184	194	169	151	138	127	112	100.1	90.7	82.6	69.6
.185	191	166	148	135	125	110	98.2	88.9	81.0	68.1
.186	188	163	146	133	123	107.6	96.3	87.1	79.3	66.7
.187	185	161	143	130	120	105.6	94.4	85.4	77.7	65.3
.188	182	158	141	128	118	103.6	92.6	83.7	76.1	63.9
.189	179	155	138	126	116	101.7	90.8	82.0	74.6	62.6
.190	176	153	136	124	114	99.8	89.1	80.4	73.1	61.3
.191	174	150	134	122	112	98.0	87.4	78.9	71.7	60.1
.192	171	148	132	119	110	96.2	85.8	77.4	70.3	58.8
.193	168	146	129	117	108	94.5	84.2	75.9	68.9	57.6
.194	166	143	127	115	106	92.7	82.6	74.4	67.5	56.5
.195	163	141	125	113	104	91.1	81.1	73.0	66.2	55.3
.196	161	139	123	112	102.7	89.4	79.6	71.6	64.9	54.2
.197	159	137	121	110	100.9	87.8	78.1	70.3	63.7	53.1
.198	156	134	119	108	99.2	86.3	76.7	68.9	62.5	52.1
.199	154	132	117	106	97.5	84.8	75.3	67.7	61.3	51.0
.200	152	130	115	104	95.8	83.3	73.9	66.4	60.1	50.0
.201	149	128	113	102.6	94.2	81.8	72.6	65.2	59.0	49.0
.202	147	126	112	100.9	92.6	80.4	71.3	64.0	57.8	48.1
.203	145	124	110	99.3	91.1	79.0	70.0	62.8	56.8	47.1
.204	143	123	108	97.7	89.6	77.6	68.8	61.6	55.7	46.2
.205	141	121	107	96.1	88.1	76.3	67.5	60.5	54.7	45.3

Table 7-12. Values of $(1/K')^2$ in Formula $s = (Qn/K'b^{8/3})^2$ for Trapezoidal Channels (*Continued*)

D = depth of water b = bottom width of channel

$\dfrac{D}{b}$	Side slopes of channel, ratio of horizontal to vertical									
	Vertical	¼–1	½–1	¾–1	1–1	1½–1	2–1	2½–1	3–1	4–1
.206	139	119	104.8	94.5	86.7	75.0	66.3	59.4	53.6	44.4
.207	137	117	103.2	93.0	85.2	73.7	65.2	58.3	52.6	43.6
.208	135	115	101.6	91.6	83.8	72.4	64.0	57.3	51.7	42.8
.209	133	114	100.1	90.1	82.5	71.2	62.9	56.3	50.7	42.0
.210	131	112	98.5	88.7	81.1	70.0	61.8	55.3	49.8	41.2
.211	129	110	97.0	87.3	79.8	68.8	60.7	54.3	48.9	40.4
.212	128	109	95.6	85.9	78.6	67.7	59.7	53.3	48.0	39.6
.213	126	107	94.1	84.6	77.3	66.6	58.7	52.4	47.1	38.9
.214	124	106	92.7	83.3	76.1	65.5	57.7	51.5	46.3	38.2
.215	123	104	91.3	82.0	74.9	64.4	56.7	50.6	45.5	37.4
.216	121	102.7	90.0	80.7	73.7	63.3	55.7	49.7	44.7	36.8
.217	119	101.3	88.7	79.5	72.5	62.3	54.8	48.8	43.9	36.1
.218	118	99.8	87.3	78.3	71.4	61.3	53.9	48.0	43.1	35.4
.219	116	98.4	86.1	77.1	70.3	60.3	53.0	47.1	42.3	34.8
.220	115	97.0	84.8	76.0	69.2	59.3	52.1	46.3	41.6	34.1
.221	113	95.7	83.6	74.8	68.1	58.4	51.2	45.6	40.9	33.5
.222	112	94.4	82.4	73.7	67.1	57.4	50.4	44.8	40.2	32.9
.223	110	93.1	81.2	72.6	66.1	56.5	49.5	44.0	39.5	32.3
.224	109	91.8	80.0	71.5	65.1	55.6	48.7	43.3	38.8	31.7
.225	107	90.5	78.9	70.5	64.1	54.7	47.9	42.6	38.1	31.2
.226	106	89.3	77.8	69.4	63.1	53.9	47.2	41.8	37.5	30.6
.227	105	88.1	76.7	68.4	62.2	53.0	46.4	41.1	36.8	30.1
.228	103	86.9	75.6	67.4	61.2	52.2	45.6	40.5	36.2	29.5
.229	102	85.7	74.5	66.5	60.3	51.4	44.9	39.8	35.6	29.0
.230	101	84.6	73.5	65.5	59.4	50.6	44.2	39.1	35.0	28.5
.231	99.4	83.5	72.5	64.6	58.6	49.8	43.5	38.5	34.4	28.0
.232	98.1	82.4	71.5	63.6	57.7	49.1	42.8	37.9	33.8	27.5
.233	96.9	81.3	70.5	62.7	56.8	48.3	42.1	37.2	33.3	27.1
.234	95.7	80.2	69.5	61.8	56.0	47.6	41.4	36.6	32.7	26.6
.235	94.5	79.2	68.6	61.0	55.2	46.8	40.8	36.1	32.2	26.1
.236	93.4	78.1	67.6	60.1	54.4	46.1	40.2	35.5	31.6	25.7
.237	92.2	77.1	66.7	59.3	53.6	45.4	39.5	34.9	31.1	25.2
.238	91.1	76.1	65.8	58.4	52.9	44.8	38.9	34.3	30.6	24.8
.239	90.0	75.1	64.9	57.6	52.1	44.1	38.3	33.8	30.1	24.4
.240	88.9	74.2	64.1	56.8	51.3	43.4	37.7	33.3	29.6	24.0
.241	87.8	73.2	63.2	56.0	50.6	42.8	37.1	32.7	29.1	23.6
.242	86.8	72.3	62.4	55.3	49.9	42.1	36.6	32.2	28.7	23.2
.243	85.8	71.4	61.5	54.5	49.2	41.5	36.0	31.7	28.2	22.8
.244	84.8	70.5	60.7	53.8	48.5	40.9	35.5	31.2	27.8	22.4
.245	83.8	69.6	59.9	53.0	47.8	40.3	34.9	30.7	27.3	22.0
.246	82.8	68.8	59.2	52.3	47.2	39.7	34.4	30.3	26.9	21.7
.247	81.8	67.9	58.4	51.6	46.5	39.2	33.9	29.8	26.5	21.3
.248	80.9	67.1	57.6	50.9	45.9	38.6	33.4	29.3	26.0	21.0
.249	79.9	66.2	56.9	50.2	45.2	38.0	32.9	28.9	25.6	20.6
.250	79.0	65.4	56.2	49.6	44.6	37.5	32.4	28.4	25.2	20.3

Table 7-12. Values of $(1/K')^2$ in Formula $s = (Qn/K'b^{8/3})^2$ for
Trapezoidal Channels (*Continued*)

D = depth of water b = bottom width of channel

$\dfrac{D}{b}$	Side slopes of channel, ratio of horizontal to vertical									
	Vertical	¼–1	½–1	¾–1	1–1	1½–1	2–1	2½–1	3–1	4–1
.251	78.1	64.6	55.4	48.9	44.0	37.0	31.9	28.0	24.8	20.0
.252	77.2	63.8	54.7	48.3	43.4	36.4	31.4	27.6	24.4	19.6
.253	76.3	63.1	54.0	47.6	42.8	35.9	31.0	27.2	24.1	19.3
.254	75.5	62.3	53.4	47.0	42.2	35.4	30.5	26.7	23.7	19.0
.255	74.6	61.6	52.7	46.4	41.7	34.9	30.1	26.3	23.3	18.7
.256	73.8	60.8	52.0	45.8	41.1	34.4	29.6	25.9	23.0	18.4
.257	72.9	60.1	51.4	45.2	40.6	33.9	29.2	25.6	22.6	18.1
.258	72.1	59.4	50.7	44.6	40.0	33.5	28.8	25.2	22.3	17.8
.259	71.3	58.7	50.1	44.0	39.5	33.0	28.4	24.8	21.9	17.5
.260	70.6	58.0	49.5	43.5	39.0	32.5	28.0	24.4	21.6	17.3
.261	69.8	57.3	48.9	42.9	38.5	32.1	27.6	24.1	21.3	17.0
.262	69.0	56.6	48.3	42.4	37.9	31.6	27.2	23.7	21.0	16.7
.263	68.3	56.0	47.7	41.8	37.5	31.2	26.8	23.4	20.6	16.5
.264	67.5	55.3	47.1	41.3	37.0	30.8	26.4	23.0	20.3	16.2
.265	66.8	54.7	46.5	40.8	36.5	30.4	26.0	22.7	20.0	16.0
.266	66.1	54.1	46.0	40.3	36.0	29.9	25.7	22.4	19.7	15.7
.267	65.4	53.5	45.4	39.8	35.5	29.5	25.3	22.0	19.4	15.5
.268	64.7	52.8	44.9	39.3	35.1	29.1	24.9	21.7	19.1	15.2
.269	64.0	52.2	44.3	38.8	34.6	28.8	24.6	21.4	18.9	15.0
.270	63.3	51.7	43.8	38.3	34.2	28.4	24.3	21.1	18.6	14.8
.271	62.6	51.1	43.3	37.8	33.8	28.0	23.9	20.8	18.3	14.5
.272	62.0	50.5	42.8	37.4	33.3	27.6	23.6	20.5	18.1	14.3
.273	61.3	49.9	42.3	36.9	32.9	27.3	23.3	20.2	17.8	14.1
.274	60.7	49.4	41.8	36.5	32.5	26.9	23.0	19.9	17.5	13.9
.275	60.1	48.8	41.3	36.0	32.1	26.5	22.6	19.7	17.3	13.7
.276	59.4	48.3	40.8	35.6	31.7	26.2	22.3	19.4	17.0	13.5
.277	58.8	47.8	40.3	35.1	31.3	25.8	22.0	19.1	16.8	13.3
.278	58.2	47.2	39.9	34.7	30.9	25.5	21.7	18.8	16.5	13.1
.279	57.6	46.7	39.4	34.3	30.5	25.2	21.4	18.6	16.3	12.9
.280	57.1	46.2	39.0	33.9	30.1	24.8	21.1	18.3	16.1	12.7
.281	56.5·	45.7	38.5	33.5	29.8	24.5	20.9	18.1	15.8	12.5
.282	55.9	45.2	38.1	33.1	29.4	24.2	20.6	17.8	15.6	12.3
.283	55.3	44.7	37.6	32.7	29.0	23.9	20.3	17.6	15.4	12.2
.284	54.8	44.2	37.2	32.3	28.7	23.6	20.0	17.3	15.2	12.0
.285	54.2	43.8	36.8	31.9	28.3	23.3	19.8	17.1	15.0	11.8
.286	53.7	43.3	36.4	31.6	28.0	23.0	19.5	16.9	14.8	11.6
.287	53.2	42.8	36.0	31.2	27.7	22.7	19.3	16.6	14.6	11.5
.288	52.7	42.4	35.6	30.8	27.3	22.4	19.0	16.4	14.4	11.3
.289	52.1	41.9	35.2	30.5	27.0	22.1	18.8	16.2	14.2	11.1
.290	51.6	41.5	34.8	30.1	26.7	21.9	18.5	16.0	14.0	11.0
.291	51.1	41.1	34.4	29.8	26.4	21.6	18.3	15.8	13.8	10.8
.292	50.6	40.6	34.0	29.4	26.0	21.3	18.0	15.5	13.6	10.7
.293	50.1	40.2	33.6	29.1	25.7	21.0	17.8	15.3	13.4	10.5
.294	49.7	39.8	33.3	28.8	25.4	20.8	17.6	15.1	13.2	10.4
.295	49.2	39.4	32.9	28.4	25.1	20.5	17.3	14.9	13.0	10.2

Table 7-12. Values of $(1/K')^2$ in Formula $s = (Qn/K'b^{8/3})^2$ for
Trapezoidal Channels (*Continued*)

D = depth of water b = bottom width of channel

$\dfrac{D}{b}$	Side slopes of channel, ratio of horizontal to vertical									
	Ver-tical	¼–1	½–1	¾–1	1–1	1½–1	2–1	2½–1	3–1	4–1
.296	48.7	39.0	32.6	28.1	24.8	20.3	17.1	14.7	12.9	10.07
.297	48.2	38.6	32.2	27.8	24.6	20.0	16.9	14.5	12.7	9.93
.298	47.8	38.2	31.9	27.5	24.3	19.8	16.7	14.4	12.5	9.79
.299	47.3	37.8	31.5	27.2	24.0	19.5	16.5	14.2	12.3	9.65
.300	46.9	37.4	31.2	26.9	23.7	19.3	16.3	14.0	12.2	9.52
.301	46.4	37.0	30.8	26.6	23.4	19.1	16.1	13.8	12.0	9.39
.302	46.0	36.7	30.5	26.3	23.2	18.8	15.9	13.6	11.9	9.26
.303	45.6	36.3	30.2	26.0	22.9	18.6	15.7	13.4	11.7	9.13
.304	45.2	35.9	29.9	25.7	22.6	18.4	15.5	13.3	11.5	9.00
.305	44.7	35.6	29.6	25.4	22.4	18.2	15.3	13.1	11.4	8.88
.306	44.3	35.2	29.2	25.1	22.1	17.9	15.1	12.9	11.2	8.76
.307	43.9	34.9	28.9	24.8	21.9	17.7	14.9	12.8	11.1	8.64
.308	43.5	34.5	28.6	24.6	21.6	17.5	14.7	12.6	11.0	8.52
.309	43.1	34.2	28.3	24.3	21.4	17.3	14.5	12.4	10.8	8.40
.310	42.7	33.8	28.0	24.0	21.1	17.1	14.3	12.3	10.7	8.29
.311	42.3	33.5	27.7	23.8	20.9	16.9	14.2	12.1	10.5	8.18
.312	42.0	33.2	27.5	23.5	20.7	16.7	14.0	12.0	10.4	8.07
.313	41.6	32.9	27.2	23.3	20.4	16.5	13.8	11.8	10.3	7.96
.314	41.2	32.5	26.9	23.0	20.2	16.3	13.7	11.7	10.1	7.85
.315	40.8	32.2	26.6	22.8	20.0	16.1	13.5	11.5	10.0	7.75
.316	40.5	31.9	26.4	22.5	19.8	15.9	13.3	11.4	9.87	7.65
.317	40.1	31.6	26.1	22.3	19.5	15.8	13.2	11.2	9.74	7.54
.318	39.8	31.3	25.8	22.1	19.3	15.6	13.0	11.1	9.62	7.44
.319	39.4	31.0	25.6	21.8	19.1	15.4	12.9	11.0	9.50	7.35
.320	39.1	30.7	25.3	21.6	18.9	15.2	12.7	10.8	9.38	7.25
.321	38.7	30.4	25.0	21.4	18.7	15.0	12.5	10.7	9.26	7.15
.322	38.4	30.1	24.8	21.1	18.5	14.9	12.4	10.6	9.14	7.06
.323	38.1	29.9	24.5	20.9	18.3	14.7	12.2	10.4	9.03	6.97
.324	37.7	29.6	24.3	20.7	18.1	14.5	12.1	10.3	8.91	6.88
.325	37.4	29.3	24.1	20.5	17.9	14.4	12.0	10.2	8.80	6.79
.326	37.1	29.0	23.8	20.3	17.7	14.2	11.8	10.06	8.69	6.70
.327	36.8	28.8	23.6	20.1	17.5	14.0	11.7	9.94	8.58	6.61
.328	36.5	28.5	23.4	19.9	17.3	13.9	11.5	9.82	8.48	6.53
.329	36.1	28.2	23.1	19.7	17.2	13.7	11.4	9.70	8.37	6.44
.330	35.8	28.0	22.9	19.5	17.0	13.6	11.3	9.58	8.27	6.36
.331	35.5	27.7	22.7	19.3	16.8	13.4	11.1	9.47	8.17	6.28
.332	35.2	27.5	22.5	19.1	16.6	13.3	11.0	9.35	8.07	6.20
.333	34.9	27.2	22.2	18.9	16.4	13.1	10.9	9.24	7.97	6.12
.334	34.7	27.0	22.0	18.7	16.3	13.0	10.8	9.13	7.87	6.04
.335	34.4	26.7	21.8	18.5	16.1	12.8	10.6	9.02	7.78	5.97
.336	34.1	26.5	21.6	18.3	15.9	12.7	10.5	8.92	7.68	5.89
.337	33.8	26.2	21.4	18.1	15.8	12.6	10.4	8.81	7.59	5.82
.338	33.5	26.0	21.2	17.9	15.6	12.4	10.3	8.71	7.50	5.74
.339	33.2	25.8	21.0	17.8	15.4	12.3	10.2	8.61	7.41	5.67
.340	33.0	25.5	20.8	17.6	15.3	12.1	10.0	8.51	7.32	5.60

Table 7-12. Values of $(1/K')^2$ in Formula $s = (Qn/K'b^{\frac{8}{3}})^2$ for
Trapezoidal Channels (*Continued*)

D = depth of water b = bottom width of channel

$\dfrac{D}{b}$	Side slopes of channel, ratio of horizontal to vertical									
	Vertical	¼–1	½–1	¾–1	1–1	1½–1	2–1	2½–1	3–1	4–1
.341	32.7	25.3	20.6	17.4	15.1	12.0	9.93	8.41	7.23	5.53
.342	32.4	25.1	20.4	17.2	15.0	11.9	9.82	8.31	7.14	5.46
.343	32.2	24.9	20.2	17.1	14.8	11.8	9.71	8.21	7.06	5.39
.344	31.9	24.6	20.0	16.9	14.7	11.6	9.60	8.12	6.97	5.33
.345	31.7	24.4	19.8	16.7	14.5	11.5	9.49	8.02	6.89	5.26
.346	31.4	24.2	19.6	16.6	14.4	11.4	9.39	7.93	6.81	5.20
.347	31.1	24.0	19.5	16.4	14.2	11.3	9.28	7.84	6.73	5.13
.348	30.9	23.8	19.3	16.2	14.1	11.1	9.18	7.75	6.65	5.07
.349	30.7	23.6	19.1	16.1	13.9	11.0	9.08	7.66	6.57	5.01
.350	30.4	23.4	18.9	15.9	13.8	10.9	8.98	7.57	6.49	4.95
.351	30.2	23.2	18.7	15.8	13.7	10.8	8.88	7.49	6.42	4.89
.352	29.9	23.0	18.6	15.6	13.5	10.7	8.78	7.40	6.34	4.83
.353	29.7	22.8	18.4	15.5	13.4	10.6	8.68	7.32	6.27	4.77
.354	29.5	22.6	18.2	15.3	13.3	10.4	8.59	7.23	6.20	4.71
.355	29.2	22.4	18.1	15.2	13.1	10.3	8.49	7.15	6.13	4.66
.356	29.0	22.2	17.9	15.0	13.0	10.23	8.40	7.07	6.05	4.60
.357	28.8	22.0	17.7	14.9	12.9	10.12	8.31	6.99	5.98	4.54
.358	28.6	21.8	17.6	14.8	12.7	10.02	8.22	6.91	5.92	4.49
.359	28.3	21.6	17.4	14.6	12.6	9.91	8.13	6.84	5.85	4.44
.360	28.1	21.5	17.3	14.5	12.5	9.81	8.04	6.76	5.78	4.38
.361	27.9	21.3	17.1	14.3	12.4	9.71	7.96	6.69	5.72	4.33
.362	27.7	21.1	17.0	14.2	12.2	9.61	7.87	6.61	5.65	4.28
.363	27.5	20.9	16.8	14.1	12.1	9.51	7.79	6.54	5.59	4.23
.364	27.3	20.8	16.7	13.9	12.0	9.41	7.70	6.47	5.52	4.18
.365	27.1	20.6	16.5	13.8	11.9	9.32	7.62	6.39	5.46	4.13
.366	26.9	20.4	16.4	13.7	11.8	9.22	7.54	6.32	5.40	4.08
.367	26.7	20.2	16.2	13.6	11.7	9.13	7.46	6.25	5.34	4.03
.368	26.5	20.1	16.1	13.4	11.6	9.03	7.38	6.19	5.28	3.99
.369	26.3	19.9	15.9	13.3	11.4	8.94	7.30	6.12	5.22	3.94
.370	26.1	19.7	15.8	13.2	11.3	8.85	7.22	6.05	5.16	3.90
.371	25.9	19.6	15.7	13.1	11.2	8.76	7.15	5.99	5.10	3.85
.372	25.7	19.4	15.5	12.9	11.1	8.67	7.07	5.92	5.05	3.81
.373	25.5	19.3	15.4	12.8	11.0	8.59	7.00	5.86	4.99	3.76
.374	25.3	19.1	15.3	12.7	10.9	8.50	6.93	5.79	4.93	3.72
.375	25.1	19.0	15.1	12.6	10.8	8.42	6.85	5.73	4.88	3.68
.376	24.9	18.8	15.0	12.5	10.7	8.33	6.78	5.67	4.83	3.63
.377	24.7	18.7	14.9	12.4	10.6	8.25	6.71	5.61	4.77	3.59
.378	24.6	18.5	14.7	12.3	10.5	8.17	6.64	5.55	4.72	3.55
.379	24.4	18.4	14.6	12.1	10.4	8.09	6.57	5.49	4.67	3.51
.380	24.2	18.2	14.5	12.0	10.3	8.01	6.51	5.43	4.62	3.47
.381	24.0	18.1	14.4	11.9	10.21	7.93	6.44	5.37	4.57	3.43
.382	23.9	17.9	14.2	11.8	10.11	7.85	6.37	5.32	4.52	3.39
.383	23.7	17.8	14.1	11.7	10.02	7.77	6.31	5.26	4.47	3.35
.384	23.5	17.6	14.0	11.6	9.93	7.70	6.24	5.21	4.42	3.32
.385	23.4	17.5	13.9	11.5	9.84	7.62	6.18	5.15	4.37	3.28

Table 7-12. Values of $(1/K')^2$ in Formula $s = (Qn/K'b^{8/3})^2$ for
Trapezoidal Channels (*Continued*)

D = depth of water b = bottom width of channel

$\dfrac{D}{b}$	Vertical	$\frac{1}{4}$-1	$\frac{1}{2}$-1	$\frac{3}{4}$-1	1-1	$1\frac{1}{2}$-1	2-1	$2\frac{1}{2}$-1	3-1	4-1
					Side slopes of channel, ratio of horizontal to vertical					
.386	23.2	17.4	13.8	11.4	9.75	7.55	6.12	5.10	4.33	3.24
.387	23.0	17.2	13.7	11.3	9.66	7.47	6.06	5.04	4.28	3.21
.388	22.9	17.1	13.5	11.2	9.57	7.40	5.99	4.99	4.23	3.17
.389	22.7	17.0	13.4	11.1	9.48	7.33	5.93	4.94	4.19	3.14
.390	22.5	16.8	13.3	11.0	9.39	7.26	5.87	4.89	4.14	3.10
.391	22.4	16.7	13.2	10.9	9.31	7.19	5.81	4.84	4.10	3.07
.392	22.2	16.6	13.1	10.8	9.22	7.12	5.76	4.79	4.06	3.03
.393	22.1	16.4	13.0	10.7	9.14	7.05	5.70	4.74	4.01	3.00
.394	21.9	16.3	12.9	10.6	9.06	6.98	5.64	4.69	3.97	2.97
.395	21.8	16.2	12.8	10.5	8.98	6.91	5.59	4.64	3.93	2.93
.396	21.6	16.1	12.7	10.4	8.90	6.85	5.53	4.59	3.89	2.90
.397	21.5	15.9	12.6	10.4	8.82	6.78	5.47	4.54	3.85	2.87
.398	21.3	15.8	12.5	10.3	8.74	6.72	5.42	4.50	3.81	2.84
.399	21.2	15.7	12.4	10.2	8.66	6.66	5.37	4.45	3.77	2.81
.400	21.0	15.6	12.3	10.1	8.58	6.59	5.31	4.41	3.73	2.78
.401	20.9	15.5	12.2	10.01	8.50	6.53	5.26	4.36	3.69	2.75
.402	20.7	15.3	12.1	9.92	8.43	6.47	5.21	4.32	3.65	2.72
.403	20.6	15.2	12.0	9.84	8.35	6.41	5.16	4.27	3.61	2.69
.404	20.5	15.1	11.9	9.75	8.28	6.35	5.11	4.23	3.57	2.66
.405	20.3	15.0	11.8	9.67	8.21	6.29	5.06	4.19	3.54	2.63
.406	20.2	14.9	11.7	9.59	8.14	6.23	5.01	4.15	3.50	2.60
.407	20.1	14.8	11.6	9.51	8.06	6.17	4.96	4.11	3.47	2.57
.408	19.9	14.7	11.5	9.43	7.99	6.11	4.91	4.06	3.43	2.55
.409	19.8	14.6	11.4	9.35	7.92	6.06	4.87	4.02	3.39	2.52
.410	19.7	14.5	11.3	9.27	7.85	6.00	4.82	3.98	3.36	2.49
.411	19.5	14.4	11.2	9.19	7.79	5.95	4.77	3.94	3.33	2.47
.412	19.4	14.2	11.1	9.12	7.72	5.89	4.73	3.90	3.29	2.44
.413	19.3	14.1	11.0	9.04	7.65	5.84	4.68	3.87	3.26	2.41
.414	19.1	14.0	11.0	8.97	7.59	5.78	4.64	3.83	3.23	2.39
.415	19.0	13.9	10.9	8.89	7.52	5.73	4.59	3.79	3.19	2.36
.416	18.9	13.8	10.8	8.82	7.46	5.68	4.55	3.75	3.16	2.34
.417	18.8	13.7	10.7	8.75	7.39	5.63	4.50	3.72	3.13	2.32
.418	18.6	13.6	10.6	8.67	7.33	5.58	4.46	3.68	3.10	2.29
.419	18.5	13.5	10.5	8.60	7.27	5.53	4.42	3.64	3.07	2.27
.420	18.4	13.4	10.5	8.53	7.20	5.48	4.38	3.61	3.04	2.24
.421	18.3	13.3	10.4	8.46	7.14	5.43	4.34	3.57	3.01	2.22
.422	18.2	13.2	10.3	8.39	7.08	5.38	4.30	3.54	2.98	2.20
.423	18.0	13.2	10.2	8.32	7.02	5.33	4.26	3.50	2.95	2.17
.424	17.9	13.1	10.1	8.26	6.96	5.28	4.22	3.47	2.92	2.15
.425	17.8	13.0	10.1	8.19	6.90	5.23	4.18	3.44	2.89	2.13
.426	17.7	12.9	9.98	8.12	6.85	5.19	4.14	3.40	2.86	2.11
.427	17.6	12.8	9.91	8.06	6.79	5.14	4.10	3.37	2.83	2.09
.428	17.5	12.7	9.83	7.99	6.73	5.09	4.06	3.34	2.80	2.06
.429	17.4	12.6	9.76	7.93	6.67	5.05	4.02	3.31	2.77	2.04
.430	17.3	12.5	9.68	7.87	6.62	5.00	3.99	3.27	2.75	2.02

Table 7-12. Values of $(1/K')^2$ in Formula $s = (Qn/K'b^{8/3})^2$ for Trapezoidal Channels (*Continued*)

D = depth of water b = bottom width of channel

$\dfrac{D}{b}$	Side slopes of channel, ratio of horizontal to vertical									
	Ver-tical	$\frac{1}{4}$–1	$\frac{1}{2}$–1	$\frac{3}{4}$–1	1–1	$1\frac{1}{2}$–1	2–1	$2\frac{1}{2}$–1	3–1	4–1
.431	17.2	12.4	9.61	7.80	6.56	4.96	3.95	3.24	2.72	2.00
.432	17.0	12.3	9.54	7.74	6.51	4.92	3.91	3.21	2.69	1.98
.433	16.9	12.3	9.46	7.68	6.45	4.87	3.88	3.18	2.67	1.96
.434	16.8	12.2	9.39	7.62	6.40	4.83	3.84	3.15	2.64	1.94
.435	16.7	12.1	9.32	7.56	6.35	4.79	3.81	3.12	2.62	1.92
.436	16.6	12.0	9.25	7.50	6.30	4.75	3.77	3.09	2.59	1.90
.437	16.5	11.9	9.18	7.44	6.24	4.70	3.74	3.06	2.57	1.88
.438	16.4	11.8	9.11	7.38	6.19	4.66	3.70	3.03	2.54	1.87
.439	16.3	11.8	9.05	7.32	6.14	4.62	3.67	3.01	2.52	1.85
.440	16.2	11.7	8.98	7.27	6.09	4.58	3.64	2.98	2.49	1.83
.441	16.1	11.6	8.91	7.21	6.04	4.54	3.60	2.95	2.47	1.81
.442	16.0	11.5	8.85	7.15	5.99	4.50	3.57	2.92	2.44	1.79
.443	15.9	11.4	8.78	7.10	5.94	4.46	3.54	2.89	2.42	1.77
.444	15.8	11.4	8.72	7.04	5.90	4.43	3.51	2.87	2.40	1.76
.445	15.7	11.3	8.65	6.99	5.85	4.39	3.47	2.84	2.38	1.74
.446	15.6	11.2	8.59	6.93	5.80	4.35	3.44	2.81	2.35	1.72
.447	15.5	11.1	8.53	6.88	5.75	4.31	3.41	2.79	2.33	1.70
.448	15.4	11.1	8.47	6.83	5.71	4.27	3.38	2.76	2.31	1.69
.449	15.4	11.0	8.40	6.77	5.66	4.24	3.35	2.74	2.29	1.67
.450	15.3	10.9	8.34	6.72	5.62	4.20	3.32	2.71	2.26	1.66
.451	15.2	10.8	8.28	6.67	5.57	4.17	3.29	2.69	2.24	1.64
.452	15.1	10.8	8.22	6.62	5.53	4.13	3.26	2.66	2.22	1.62
.453	15.0	10.7	8.16	6.57	5.48	4.10	3.23	2.64	2.20	1.61
.454	14.9	10.6	8.10	6.52	5.44	4.06	3.21	2.61	2.18	1.59
.455	14.8	10.5	8.05	6.47	5.40	4.03	3.18	2.59	2.16	1.58
.456	14.7	10.5	7.99	6.42	5.35	3.99	3.15	2.57	2.14	1.56
.457	14.6	10.4	7.93	6.37	5.31	3.96	3.12	2.54	2.12	1.55
.458	14.6	10.3	7.87	6.32	5.27	3.93	3.09	2.52	2.10	1.53
.459	14.5	10.3	7.82	6.27	5.23	3.89	3.07	2.50	2.08	1.52
.460	14.4	10.2	7.76	6.23	5.19	3.86	3.04	2.48	2.06	1.50
.461	14.3	10.14	7.71	6.18	5.15	3.83	3.01	2.45	2.04	1.49
.462	14.2	10.07	7.65	6.13	5.11	3.80	2.99	2.43	2.02	1.47
.463	14.1	10.01	7.60	6.09	5.07	3.77	2.96	2.41	2.01	1.46
.464	14.1	9.94	7.55	6.04	5.03	3.73	2.94	2.39	1.99	1.44
.465	14.0	9.87	7.49	6.00	4.99	3.70	2.91	2.37	1.97	1.43
.466	13.9	9.81	7.44	5.95	4.95	3.67	2.88	2.35	1.95	1.42
.467	13.8	9.75	7.39	5.91	4.91	3.64	2.86	2.32	1.93	1.40
.468	13.7	9.68	7.34	5.86	4.87	3.61	2.84	2.30	1.92	1.39
.469	13.7	9.62	7.28	5.82	4.83	3.58	2.81	2.28	1.90	1.38
.470	13.6	9.56	7.23	5.78	4.80	3.55	2.79	2.26	1.88	1.36
.471	13.5	9.50	7.18	5.74	4.76	3.52	2.76	2.24	1.86	1.35
.472	13.4	9.44	7.13	5.69	4.72	3.49	2.74	2.22	1.85	1.34
.473	13.3	9.38	7.08	5.65	4.69	3.47	2.72	2.20	1.83	1.33
.474	13.3	9.32	7.04	5.61	4.65	3.44	2.69	2.18	1.81	1.31
.475	13.2	9.26	6.99	5.57	4.62	3.41	2.67	2.16	1.80	1.30

Table 7-12. Values of $(1/K')^2$ in Formula $s = (Qn/K'b^{8/3})^2$ for Trapezoidal Channels (*Continued*)

D = depth of water b = bottom width of channel

$\dfrac{D}{b}$	Side slopes of channel, ratio of horizontal to vertical									
	Ver-tical	¼–1	½–1	¾–1	1–1	1½–1	2–1	2½–1	3–1	4–1
.476	13.1	9.20	6.94	5.53	4.58	3.38	2.65	2.15	1.78	1.29
.477	13.0	9.14	6.89	5.49	4.54	3.35	2.63	2.13	1.77	1.28
.478	13.0	9.08	6.84	5.45	4.51	3.33	2.60	2.11	1.75	1.27
.479	12.9	9.03	6.80	5.41	4.48	3.30	2.58	2.09	1.73	1.25
.480	12.8	8.97	6.75	5.37	4.44	3.27	2.56	2.07	1.72	1.24
.481	12.8	8.91	6.70	5.33	4.41	3.25	2.54	2.05	1.70	1.23
.482	12.7	8.86	6.66	5.29	4.38	3.22	2.52	2.04	1.69	1.22
.483	12.6	8.80	6.61	5.25	4.34	3.20	2.50	2.02	1.67	1.21
.484	12.5	8.75	6.57	5.22	4.31	3.17	2.47	2.00	1.66	1.20
.485	12.5	8.69	6.52	5.18	4.28	3.14	2.45	1.98	1.64	1.19
.486	12.4	8.64	6.48	5.14	4.24	3.12	2.43	1.97	1.63	1.18
.487	12.3	8.59	6.44	5.10	4.21	3.09	2.41	1.95	1.61	1.16
.488	12.3	8.53	6.39	5.07	4.18	3.07	2.39	1.93	1.60	1.15
.489	12.2	8.48	6.35	5.03	4.15	3.05	2.37	1.92	1.59	1.14
.490	12.1	8.43	6.31	5.00	4.12	3.02	2.35	1.90	1.57	1.13
.491	12.1	8.38	6.27	4.96	4.09	3.00	2.33	1.88	1.56	1.12
.492	12.0	8.32	6.22	4.93	4.06	2.97	2.32	1.87	1.54	1.11
.493	11.9	8.27	6.18	4.89	4.03	2.95	2.30	1.85	1.53	1.10
.494	11.9	8.22	6.14	4.86	4.00	2.93	2.28	1.84	1.52	1.09
.495	11.8	8.17	6.10	4.82	3.97	2.90	2.26	1.82	1.51	1.08
.496	11.8	8.12	6.06	4.79	3.94	2.88	2.24	1.81	1.49	1.07
.497	11.7	8.07	6.02	4.75	3.91	2.86	2.22	1.79	1.48	1.06
.498	11.6	8.02	5.98	4.72	3.88	2.84	2.20	1.78	1.47	1.05
.499	11.6	7.98	5.94	4.69	3.85	2.81	2.19	1.76	1.45	1.04
.500	11.5	7.93	5.90	4.66	3.83	2.79	2.17	1.75	1.44	1.04
.501	11.4	7.88	5.86	4.62	3.80	2.77	2.15	1.73	1.43	1.026
.502	11.4	7.83	5.82	4.59	3.77	2.75	2.13	1.72	1.42	1.017
.503	11.3	7.78	5.79	4.56	3.74	2.73	2.12	1.70	1.40	1.008
.504	11.3	7.74	5.75	4.53	3.72	2.71	2.10	1.69	1.39	.999
.505	11.2	7.69	5.71	4.50	3.69	2.69	2.08	1.67	1.38	.990
.506	11.1	7.65	5.67	4.46	3.66	2.67	2.06	1.66	1.37	.981
.507	11.1	7.60	5.64	4.43	3.64	2.65	2.05	1.65	1.36	.973
.508	11.0	7.55	5.60	4.40	3.61	2.62	2.03	1.63	1.35	.964
.509	11.0	7.51	5.56	4.37	3.58	2.60	2.02	1.62	1.33	.956
.510	10.9	7.47	5.53	4.34	3.56	2.58	2.00	1.61	1.32	.947
.511	10.9	7.42	5.49	4.31	3.53	2.57	1.98	1.59	1.31	.939
.512	10.8	7.38	5.46	4.28	3.51	2.55	1.97	1.58	1.30	.931
.513	10.7	7.33	5.42	4.25	3.48	2.53	1.95	1.57	1.29	.923
.514	10.7	7.29	5.39	4.23	3.46	2.51	1.94	1.55	1.28	.915
.515	10.6	7.25	5.35	4.20	3.43	2.49	1.92	1.54	1.27	.907
.516	10.6	7.21	5.32	4.17	3.41	2.47	1.91	1.53	1.26	.899
.517	10.5	7.16	5.28	4.14	3.38	2.45	1.89	1.52	1.25	.891
.518	10.5	7.12	5.25	4.11	3.36	2.43	1.88	1.50	1.24	.883
.519	10.4	7.08	5.22	4.08	3.34	2.41	1.86	1.49	1.23	.876
.520	10.4	7.04	5.18	4.06	3.31	2.40	1.85	1.48	1.22	.868

Table 7-12. Values of $(1/K')^2$ in Formula $s = (Qn/K'b^{8/3})^2$ for
Trapezoidal Channels (*Continued*)

D = depth of water b = bottom width of channel

$\dfrac{D}{b}$	Side slopes of channel, ratio of horizontal to vertical									
	Vertical	1/4–1	1/2–1	3/4–1	1–1	1½–1	2–1	2½–1	3–1	4–1
.52	10.36	7.04	5.18	4.06	3.31	2.40	1.85	1.48	1.216	.868
.53	9.85	6.65	4.87	3.79	3.09	2.22	1.71	1.36	1.119	.797
.54	9.38	6.28	4.58	3.55	2.88	2.06	1.58	1.26	1.032	.732
.55	8.93	5.94	4.31	3.33	2.69	1.92	1.47	1.17	.953	.674
.56	8.52	5.62	4.06	3.12	2.52	1.79	1.36	1.079	.880	.621
.57	8.13	5.33	3.82	2.93	2.36	1.67	1.26	1.000	.814	.573
.58	7.77	5.06	3.61	2.76	2.21	1.56	1.18	.928	.754	.529
.59	7.43	4.80	3.41	2.60	2.07	1.45	1.10	.862	.700	.489
.60	7.11	4.56	3.22	2.44	1.95	1.36	1.02	.802	.650	.453
.61	6.81	4.34	3.05	2.30	1.83	1.272	.953	.747	.604	.420
.62	6.53	4.13	2.89	2.17	1.72	1.191	.890	.696	.562	.390
.63	6.27	3.94	2.74	2.05	1.62	1.117	.832	.649	.523	.362
.64	6.02	3.75	2.60	1.94	1.53	1.048	.779	.606	.488	.337
.65	5.78	3.58	2.47	1.83	1.44	.985	.729	.567	.455	.314
.66	5.56	3.42	2.34	1.74	1.36	.926	.684	.530	.425	.292
.67	5.35	3.27	2.23	1.64	1.28	.871	.642	.497	.397	.273
.68	5.15	3.12	2.12	1.56	1.21	.820	.603	.465	.372	.255
.69	4.96	2.99	2.02	1.48	1.15	.773	.566	.436	.348	.238
.70	4.78	2.86	1.92	1.40	1.09	.729	.532	.410	.326	.223
.71	4.61	2.74	1.83	1.33	1.030	.688	.501	.385	.306	.208
.72	4.45	2.62	1.75	1.27	.976	.649	.472	.362	.288	.195
.73	4.29	2.52	1.67	1.20	.926	.613	.445	.340	.270	.183
.74	4.15	2.41	1.59	1.15	.879	.580	.420	.321	.254	.172
.75	4.01	2.32	1.52	1.09	.835	.549	.396	.302	.239	.161
.76	3.88	2.22	1.45	1.039	.793	.520	.374	.285	.225	.152
.77	3.75	2.14	1.39	.991	.754	.492	.354	.269	.212	.143
.78	3.63	2.05	1.33	.945	.717	.467	.334	.254	.200	.134
.79	3.52	1.98	1.27	.901	.683	.443	.316	.240	.189	.126
.80	3.41	1.90	1.22	.861	.650	.420	.300	.227	.178	.119
.81	3.30	1.83	1.168	.822	.619	.399	.284	.214	.168	.1123
.82	3.20	1.76	1.119	.785	.590	.379	.269	.203	.159	.1059
.83	3.11	1.70	1.074	.751	.563	.360	.255	.192	.150	.1000
.84	3.01	1.64	1.030	.718	.537	.343	.242	.182	.142	.0945
.85	2.93	1.58	.989	.687	.513	.326	.230	.173	.135	.0894
.86	2.84	1.53	.950	.658	.490	.310	.219	.164	.128	.0845
.87	2.76	1.47	.913	.630	.468	.296	.208	.155	.121	.0800
.88	2.68	1.42	.877	.604	.447	.282	.198	.148	.115	.0758
.89	2.61	1.37	.843	.579	.428	.269	.188	.140	.109	.0718
.90	2.54	1.33	.811	.555	.409	.256	.179	.133	.104	.0681
.91	2.47	1.28	.781	.532	.392	.245	.170	.127	.0984	.0646
.92	2.40	1.24	.751	.511	.375	.234	.162	.121	.0935	.0613
.93	2.34	1.20	.724	.491	.360	.223	.155	.115	.0890	.0582
.94	2.28	1.16	.697	.471	.345	.213	.148	.109	.0846	.0553
.95	2.22	1.12	.672	.453	.330	.204	.141	.104	.0806	.0526

Table 7-12. Values of $(1/K')^2$ in Formula $s = (Qn/K'b^{8/3})^2$ for Trapezoidal Channels (*Continued*)

D = depth of water b = bottom width of channel

$\dfrac{D}{b}$	Side slopes of channel, ratio of horizontal to vertical									
	Ver-tical	¼–1	½–1	¾–1	1–1	1½–1	2–1	2½–1	3–1	4–1
.96	2.17	1.086	.648	.435	.317	.195	.135	.0993	.0767	.0500
.97	2.11	1.052	.624	.418	.304	.186	.128	.0947	.0731	.0476
.98	2.06	1.019	.603	.402	.292	.178	.123	.0904	.0697	.0453
.99	2.01	.987	.581	.387	.280	.171	.117	.0863	.0665	.0432
1.00	1.96	.957	.561	.373	.269	.164	.112	.0824	.0634	.0411
1.01	1.91	.928	.542	.359	.259	.157	.1073	.0787	.0605	.0392
1.02	1.87	.900	.523	.345	.249	.150	.1026	.0752	.0578	.0374
1.03	1.82	.873	.505	.333	.239	.144	.0983	.0719	.0552	.0357
1.04	1.78	.847	.488	.321	.230	.138	.0941	.0688	.0528	.0340
1.05	1.74	.822	.472	.309	.221	.133	.0901	.0658	.0504	.0325
1.06	1.70	.798	.457	.298	.213	.127	.0864	.0630	.0482	.0310
1.07	1.66	.775	.442	.288	.205	.122	.0828	.0603	.0461	.0297
1.08	1.62	.753	.427	.277	.197	.117	.0794	.0578	.0442	.0284
1.09	1.59	.732	.413	.268	.190	.113	.0762	.0554	.0423	.0271
1.10	1.55	.711	.400	.259	.183	.108	.0731	.0531	.0405	.0259
1.11	1.52	.691	.387	.250	.176	.1043	.0702	.0509	.0388	.0248
1.12	1.49	.672	.375	.241	.170	.1003	.0674	.0488	.0372	.0238
1.13	1.46	.654	.363	.233	.164	.0965	.0647	.0469	.0357	.0228
1.14	1.43	.636	.352	.225	.158	.0928	.0622	.0450	.0342	.0218
1.15	1.40	.619	.341	.218	.153	.0893	.0598	.0432	.0328	.0209
1.16	1.37	.602	.331	.210	.147	.0860	.0575	.0415	.0315	.0200
1.17	1.34	.586	.321	.203	.142	.0829	.0553	.0398	.0302	.0192
1.18	1.31	.571	.311	.197	.137	.0798	.0532	.0383	.0290	.0184
1.19	1.29	.556	.302	.190	.133	.0769	.0512	.0368	.0279	.0177
1.20	1.26	.541	.293	.184	.128	.0741	.0492	.0354	.0268	.0170
1.21	1.24	.527	.284	.178	.124	.0715	.0474	.0340	.0258	.0163
1.22	1.21	.514	.276	.173	.120	.0689	.0457	.0328	.0248	.0157
1.23	1.19	.501	.268	.167	.116	.0665	.0440	.0315	.0238	.0151
1.24	1.17	.488	.260	.162	.112	.0642	.0424	.0304	.0229	.0145
1.25	1.14	.476	.253	.157	.108	.0619	.0409	.0292	.0221	.0139
1.26	1.12	.464	.245	.152	.1047	.0598	.0394	.0282	.0212	.0134
1.27	1.10	.452	.238	.148	.1014	.0577	.0380	.0271	.0204	.0129
1.28	1.08	.441	.232	.143	.0981	.0558	.0366	.0261	.0197	.0124
1.29	1.06	.430	.225	.139	.0950	.0539	.0354	.0252	.0190	.0119
1.30	1.04	.420	.219	.135	.0920	.0521	.0341	.0243	.0183	.0115
1.31	1.023	.410	.213	.131	.0891	.0503	.0329	.0234	.0176	.01106
1.32	1.005	.400	.207	.127	.0863	.0487	.0318	.0226	.0170	.01065
1.33	.987	.391	.201	.123	.0836	.0471	.0307	.0218	.0164	.01027
1.34	.970	.381	.196	.119	.0810	.0455	.0297	.0211	.0158	.00990
1.35	.953	.372	.191	.116	.0786	.0440	.0287	.0203	.0152	.00954
1.36	.937	.364	.186	.112	.0762	.0426	.0277	.0196	.0147	.00920
1.37	.921	.355	.181	.109	.0739	.0412	.0268	.0190	.0142	.00887
1.38	.905	.347	.176	.106	.0716	.0399	.0259	.0183	.0137	.00856
1.39	.890	.339	.171	.103	.0695	.0386	.0250	.0177	.0132	.00826
1.40	.875	.331	.167	.100	.0674	.0374	.0242	.0171	.0128	.00797

Table 7-12. Values of $(1/K')^2$ in Formula $s = (Qn/K'b^{8/3})^2$ for Trapezoidal Channels (*Continued*)

D = depth of water　　b = bottom width of channel

$\dfrac{D}{b}$	Side slopes of channel, ratio of horizontal to vertical									
	Ver-tical	¼–1	½–1	¾–1	1–1	1½–1	2–1	2½–1	3–1	4–1
1.41	.860	.324	.162	.0973	.0654	.0362	.0234	.0165	.0124	.00770
1.42	.846	.317	.158	.0946	.0635	.0351	.0227	.0160	.0119	.00743
1.43	.832	.310	.154	.0920	.0617	.0340	.0220	.0155	.0115	.00718
1.44	.819	.303	.150	.0894	.0599	.0330	.0213	.0150	.0112	.00694
1.45	.806	.296	.146	.0870	.0581	.0320	.0206	.0145	.0108	.00670
1.46	.793	.290	.143	.0846	.0565	.0310	.0199	.0140	.01044	.00648
1.47	.780	.283	.139	.0823	.0549	.0301	.0193	.0136	.01010	.00626
1.48	.768	.277	.136	.0801	.0533	.0292	.0187	.0131	.00978	.00606
1.49	.756	.271	.132	.0779	.0518	.0283	.0181	.0127	.00946	.00586
1.50	.744	.265	.129	.0759	.0503	.0274	.0176	.0123	.00916	.00567
1.51	.733	.260	.126	.0739	.0489	.0266	.0170	.0119	.00887	.00549
1.52	.722	.254	.123	.0719	.0476	.0258	.0165	.0116	.00859	.00531
1.53	.711	.249	.120	.0700	.0463	.0251	.0160	.0112	.00832	.00514
1.54	.700	.244	.117	.0682	.0450	.0244	.0155	.0109	.00806	.00497
1.55	.690	.239	.114	.0664	.0438	.0237	.0151	.0105	.00781	.00482
1.56	.679	.234	.111	.0647	.0426	.0230	.0146	.01021	.00756	.00467
1.57	.669	.229	.109	.0630	.0414	.0223	.0142	.00990	.00734	.00452
1.58	.660	.224	.106	.0614	.0403	.0217	.0138	.00961	.00712	.00438
1.59	.650	.220	.104	.0599	.0392	.0211	.0134	.00932	.00690	.00424
1.60	.641	.215	.101	.0584	.0382	.0205	.0130	.00904	.00669	.00411
1.61	.631	.211	.0989	.0569	.0372	.0199	.0126	.00878	.00649	.00399
1.62	.622	.207	.0966	.0555	.0362	.0194	.0122	.00852	.00630	.00387
1.63	.614	.203	.0944	.0541	.0353	.0188	.0119	.00827	.00611	.00375
1.64	.605	.199	.0923	.0527	.0344	.0183	.0116	.00803	.00593	.00364
1.65	.597	.195	.0902	.0514	.0335	.0178	.0112	.00780	.00576	.00353
1.66	.588	.191	.0881	.0502	.0326	.0173	.01091	.00758	.00559	.00342
1.67	.580	.187	.0861	.0490	.0318	.0168	.01061	.00736	.00543	.00332
1.68	.572	.183	.0842	.0478	.0310	.0164	.01031	.00715	.00527	.00323
1.69	.564	.180	.0823	.0466	.0302	.0160	.01003	.00695	.00512	.00313
1.70	.557	.176	.0805	.0455	.0294	.0155	.00975	.00675	.00498	.00304
1.71	.549	.173	.0787	.0444	.0287	.0151	.00949	.00656	.00483	.00295
1.72	.542	.170	.0770	.0434	.0280	.0147	.00923	.00638	.00470	.00287
1.73	.535	.167	.0753	.0423	.0273	.0143	.00898	.00621	.00457	.00279
1.74	.528	.163	.0736	.0413	.0266	.0140	.00874	.00604	.00444	.00271
1.75	.521	.160	.0721	.0404	.0259	.0136	.00850	.00587	.00432	.00263
1.76	.514	.157	.0705	.0394	.0253	.0132	.00827	.00571	.00420	.00256
1.77	.508	.154	.0690	.0385	.0247	.0129	.00805	.00556	.00408	.00249
1.78	.501	.152	.0675	.0376	.0241	.0126	.00784	.00541	.00397	.00242
1.79	.495	.149	.0661	.0368	.0235	.0123	.00764	.00526	.00386	.00235
1.80	.488	.146	.0647	.0359	.0230	.0119	.00744	.00512	.00376	.00228
1.81	.482	.143	.0633	.0351	.0224	.0116	.00724	.00498	.00366	.00222
1.82	.476	.141	.0620	.0343	.0219	.0113	.00706	.00485	.00356	.00216
1.83	.470	.138	.0607	.0335	.0214	.0111	.00687	.00473	.00346	.00210
1.84	.464	.136	.0594	.0328	.0208	.0108	.00670	.00460	.00337	.00205
1.85	.459	.133	.0582	.0320	.0204	.0105	.00653	.00448	.00328	.00199

Table 7-12. Values of $(1/K')^2$ in Formula $s = (Qn/K'b^{8/3})^2$ for Trapezoidal Channels (*Concluded*)

D = depth of water b = bottom width of channel

$\dfrac{D}{b}$	Side slopes of channel, ratio of horizontal to vertical									
	Vertical	¼–1	½–1	¾–1	1–1	1½–1	2–1	2½–1	3–1	4–1
1.86	.453	.131	.0570	.0313	.0199	.01026	.00636	.00437	.00320	.00194
1.87	.448	.129	.0558	.0306	.0194	.01001	.00620	.00425	.00311	.00189
1.88	.442	.126	.0547	.0300	.0190	.00977	.00605	.00415	.00303	.00184
1.89	.437	.124	.0536	.0293	.0185	.00953	.00589	.00404	.00295	.00179
1.90	.432	.122	.0525	.0287	.0181	.00930	.00575	.00394	.00288	.00174
1.91	.426	.120	.0514	.0280	.0177	.00908	.00560	.00384	.00280	.00170
1.92	.421	.118	.0504	.0274	.0173	.00886	.00547	.00374	.00273	.00165
1.93	.417	.116	.0494	.0268	.0169	.00865	.00533	.00365	.00266	.00161
1.94	.412	.114	.0484	.0263	.0165	.00844	.00520	.00356	.00260	.00157
1.95	.407	.112	.0474	.0257	.0162	.00824	.00508	.00347	.00253	.00153
1.96	.402	.110	.0465	.0252	.0158	.00805	.00495	.00338	.00247	.00149
1.97	.398	.108	.0456	.0246	.0154	.00786	.00483	.00330	.00241	.00145
1.98	.393	.106	.0447	.0241	.0151	.00768	.00472	.00322	.00235	.00142
1.99	.389	.104	.0438	.0236	.0148	.00750	.00460	.00314	.00229	.00138
2.00	.384	.103	.0430	.0231	.0144	.00733	.00450	.00306	.00223	.00135
2.01	.380	.1010	.0422	.0226	.0141	.00716	.00439	.00299	.00218	.00131
2.02	.376	.0993	.0413	.0221	.0138	.00699	.00429	.00292	.00213	.00128
2.03	.371	.0977	.0406	.0217	.0135	.00683	.00418	.00285	.00207	.00125
2.04	.367	.0961	.0398	.0212	.0132	.00668	.00409	.00278	.00202	.00122
2.05	.363	.0945	.0390	.0208	.0130	.00653	.00399	.00272	.00198	.00119
2.06	.359	.0929	.0383	.0204	.0127	.00638	.00390	.00265	.00193	.00116
2.07	.355	.0914	.0376	.0200	.0124	.00624	.00381	.00259	.00188	.00113
2.08	.352	.0900	.0369	.0196	.0121	.00610	.00372	.00253	.00184	.00110
2.09	.348	.0885	.0362	.0192	.0119	.00596	.00364	.00247	.00180	.00108
2.10	.344	.0871	.0355	.0188	.0116	.00583	.00355	.00241	.00175	.00105
2.11	.340	.0857	.0348	.0184	.0114	.00570	.00347	.00236	.00171	.00103
2.12	.337	.0843	.0342	.0180	.0112	.00558	.00340	.00230	.00167	.00100
2.13	.333	.0830	.0336	.0177	.0109	.00546	.00332	.00225	.00163	.00098
2.14	.330	.0817	.0329	.0173	.0107	.00534	.00325	.00220	.00160	.00096
2.15	.326	.0804	.0323	.0170	.0105	.00522	.00317	.00215	.00156	.00093
2.16	.323	.0791	.0318	.0167	.01026	.00511	.00310	.00210	.00152	.00091
2.17	.320	.0779	.0312	.0163	.01005	.00500	.00303	.00205	.00149	.00089
2.18	.316	.0767	.0306	.0160	.00985	.00489	.00297	.00201	.00146	.00087
2.19	.313	.0755	.0301	.0157	.00965	.00479	.00290	.00196	.00142	.00083
2.20	.310	.0743	.0295	.0154	.00945	.00469	.00284	.00192	.00139	.00083
2.21	.307	.0732	.0290	.0151	.00926	.00459	.00278	.00188	.00136	.00081
2.22	.304	.0720	.0285	.0148	.00908	.00449	.00272	.00184	.00133	.00079
2.23	.301	.0709	.0280	.0145	.00890	.00440	.00266	.00180	.00130	.00078
2.24	.298	.0698	.0275	.0143	.00872	.00431	.00260	.00176	.00127	.00076
2.25	.295	.0688	.0270	.0140	.00855	.00422	.00255	.00172	.00124	.00074
2.26	.292	.0678	.0265	.0137	.00838	.00413	.00249	.00168	.00122	.00073
2.27	.289	.0667	.0261	.0135	.00822	.00404	.00244	.00165	.00119	.00071
2.28	.286	.0657	.0256	.0132	.00805	.00396	.00239	.00161	.00116	.00069
2.29	.283	.0647	.0252	.0130	.00790	.00388	.00234	.00158	.00114	.00068
2.30	.280	.0638	.0247	.0127	.00774	.00380	.00229	.00154	.00111	.00066

Table 7-13. Values of K for Circular Channels in the Formula

$$Q = \frac{K}{n} D^{8/3} s^{1/2}$$

D = depth of water d = diameter of channel

$\dfrac{D}{d}$	.00	.01	.02	.03	.04	.05	.06	.07	.08	.09
.0		15.02	10.56	8.57	7.38	6.55	5.95	5.47	5.08	4.76
.1	4.49	4.25	4.04	3.86	3.69	3.54	3.41	3.28	3.17	3.06
.2	2.96	2.87	2.79	2.71	2.63	2.56	2.49	2.42	2.36	2.30
.3	2.25	2.20	2.14	2.09	2.05	2.00	1.96	1.92	1.87	1.84
.4	1.80	1.76	1.72	1.69	1.66	1.62	1.59	1.56	1.53	1.50
.5	1.470	1.442	1.415	1.388	1.362	1.336	1.311	1.286	1.262	1.238
.6	1.215	1.192	1.170	1.148	1.126	1.105	1.084	1.064	1.043	1.023
.7	1.004	.984	.965	.947	.928	.910	.891	.874	.856	.838
.8	.821	.804	.787	.770	.753	.736	.720	.703	.687	.670
.9	.654	.637	.621	.604	.588	.571	.553	.535	.516	.496
1.0	.463									

Table 7-14. Values of K' for Circular Channels in the Formula

$$Q = \frac{K'}{n} d^{8/3} s^{1/2}$$

D = depth of water d = diameter of channel

$\dfrac{D}{d}$	.00	.01	.02	.03	.04	.05	.06	.07	.08	.09
.0		.00007	.00031	.00074	.00138	.00222	.00328	.00455	.00604	.00775
.1	.00967	.0118	.0142	.0167	.0195	.0225	.0257	.0291	.0327	.0366
.2	.0406	.0448	.0492	.0537	.0585	.0634	.0686	.0738	.0793	.0849
.3	.0907	.0966	.1027	.1089	.1153	.1218	.1284	.1352	.1420	.1490
.4	.1561	.1633	.1705	.1779	.1854	.1929	.2005	.2082	.2160	.2238
.5	.232	.239	.247	.255	.263	.271	.279	.287	.295	.303
.6	.311	.319	.327	.335	.343	.350	.358	.366	.373	.380
.7	.388	.395	.402	.409	.416	.422	.429	.435	.441	.447
.8	.453	.458	.463	.468	.473	.477	.481	.485	.488	.491
.9	.494	.496	.497	.498	.498	.498	.496	.494	.489	.483
1.0	.463									

Table 7-15. Values of K for Parabolic Channels in the Formula

$$Q = \frac{K}{n} D^{2/3} s^{1/2}$$

D = depth of water T = top width of channel

$\dfrac{D}{T}$	.00	.01	.02	.03	.04	.05	.06	.07	.08	.09
.0		75.59	37.77	25.16	18.85	15.05	12.52	10.71	9.35	8.28
.1	7.43	6.73	6.15	5.65	5.23	4.86	4.53	4.24	3.99	3.76
.2	3.55	3.36	3.19	3.04	2.89	2.76	2.64	2.52	2.42	2.32
.3	2.226	2.140	2.059	1.984	1.912	1.845	1.782	1.722	1.665	1.611
.4	1.560	1.511	1.465	1.421	1.379	1.339	1.301	1.265	1.230	1.197
.5	1.165	1.134	1.105	1.077	1.050	1.024	.999	.975	.952	.929
.6	.908	.887	.867	.848	.829	.811	.794	.777	.761	.745
.7	.730	.715	.701	.687	.674	.661	.648	.636	.624	.613
.8	.601	.590	.580	.570	.560	.550	.540	.531	.522	.514
.9	.505	.497	.489	.481	.473	.466	.458	.451	.444	.438
1.0	.431									

Table 7-16. Values of K' for Parabolic Channels in the Formula

$$Q = \frac{K'}{n} T^{2/3} s^{1/2}$$

D = depth of water T = top width of channel

$\dfrac{D}{T}$	.00	.01	.02	.03	.04	.05	.06	.07	.08	.09
.0		.00035	.00111	.00219	.00353	.00511	.00691	.00891	.01110	.01347
.1	.0160	.0187	.0215	.0245	.0276	.0308	.0342	.0376	.0412	.0448
.2	.0486	.0524	.0563	.0603	.0643	.0684	.0726	.0768	.0811	.0854
.3	.0898	.0942	.0987	.1032	.1077	.1123	.1168	.1215	.1261	.1308
.4	.1355	.1402	.1450	.1497	.1545	.1593	.1641	.1689	.1737	.1786
.5	.183	.188	.193	.198	.203	.208	.213	.218	.223	.228
.6	.232	.237	.242	.247	.252	.257	.262	.267	.272	.277
.7	.282	.287	.292	.297	.302	.307	.312	.317	.322	.327
.8	.332	.337	.342	.347	.352	.357	.361	.366	.371	.376
.9	.381	.386	.391	.396	.401	.406	.411	.416	.421	.426
1.0	.431									

Table 7-17. Square Roots of Decimal Numbers

Number	.--0	.--1	.--2	.--3	.--4	.--5	.--6	.--7	.--8	.--9
.00001	.003162	.003317	.003464	.003606	.003742	.003873	.004000	.004123	.004243	.004359
.00002	.004472	.004583	.004690	.004796	.004899	.005000	.005099	.005196	.005292	.005385
.00003	.005477	.005568	.005657	.005745	.005831	.005916	.006000	.006083	.006164	.006245
.00004	.006325	.006403	.006481	.006557	.006633	.006708	.006782	.006856	.006928	.007000
.00005	.007071	.007141	.007211	.007280	.007348	.007416	.007483	.007550	.007616	.007681
.00006	.007746	.007810	.007874	.007937	.008000	.008062	.008124	.008185	.008246	.008307
.00007	.008367	.008426	.008485	.008544	.008602	.008660	.008718	.008775	.008832	.008888
.00008	.008944	.009000	.009055	.009110	.009165	.009220	.009274	.009327	.009381	.009434
.00009	.009487	.009539	.009592	.009644	.009695	.009747	.009798	.009849	.009899	.009950
.00010	.010000	.010050	.010100	.010149	.010198	.010247	.010296	.010344	.010392	.010440
.0001	.01000	.01049	.01095	.01140	.01183	.01225	.01265	.01304	.01342	.01378
.0002	.01414	.01449	.01483	.01517	.01549	.01581	.01612	.01643	.01673	.01703
.0003	.01732	.01761	.01789	.01817	.01844	.01871	.01897	.01924	.01949	.01975
.0004	.02000	.02025	.02049	.02074	.02098	.02121	.02145	.02168	.02191	.02214
.0005	.02236	.02258	.02280	.02302	.02324	.02345	.02366	.02387	.02408	.02429
.0006	.02449	.02470	.02490	.02510	.02530	.02550	.02569	.02588	.02608	.02627
.0007	.02646	.02665	.02683	.02702	.02720	.02739	.02757	.02775	.02793	.02811
.0008	.02828	.02846	.02864	.02881	.02898	.02915	.02933	.02950	.02966	.02983
.0009	.03000	.03017	.03033	.03050	.03066	.03082	.03098	.03114	.03130	.03146
.0010	.03162	.03178	.03194	.03209	.03225	.03240	.03256	.03271	.03286	.03302
.001	.03162	.03317	.03464	.03606	.03742	.03873	.04000	.04123	.04243	.04359
.002	.04472	.04583	.04690	.04796	.04899	.05000	.05099	.05196	.05292	.05385
.003	.05477	.05568	.05657	.05745	.05831	.05916	.06000	.06083	.06164	.06245
.004	.06325	.06403	.06481	.06557	.06633	.06708	.06782	.06856	.06928	.07000
.005	.07071	.07141	.07211	.07280	.07348	.07416	.07483	.07550	.07616	.07681
.006	.07746	.07810	.07874	.07937	.08000	.08062	.08124	.08185	.08246	.08307
.007	.08367	.08426	.08485	.08544	.08602	.08660	.08718	.08775	.08832	.08888
.008	.08944	.09000	.09055	.09110	.09165	.09220	.09274	.09327	.09381	.09434
.009	.09487	.09539	.09592	.09644	.09695	.09747	.09798	.09849	.09899	.09950
.010	.10000	.10050	.10100	.10149	.10198	.10247	.10296	.10344	.10392	.10440
.01	.1000	.1049	.1095	.1140	.1183	.1225	.1265	.1304	.1342	.1378
.02	.1414	.1449	.1483	.1517	.1549	.1581	.1612	.1643	.1673	.1703
.03	.1732	.1761	.1789	.1817	.1844	.1871	.1897	.1924	.1949	.1975
.04	.2000	.2025	.2049	.2074	.2098	.2121	.2145	.2168	.2191	.2214
.05	.2236	.2258	.2280	.2302	.2324	.2345	.2366	.2387	.2408	.2429
.06	.2449	.2470	.2490	.2510	.2530	.2550	.2569	.2588	.2608	.2627
.07	.2646	.2665	.2683	.2702	.2720	.2739	.2757	.2775	.2793	.2811
.08	.2828	.2846	.2864	.2881	.2898	.2915	.2933	.2950	.2966	.2983
.09	.3000	.3017	.3033	.3050	.3066	.3082	.3098	.3114	.3130	.3146
.10	.3162	.3178	.3194	.3209	.3225	.3240	.3256	.3271	.3286	.3302

Table 7-18. Two-thirds Powers of Numbers

Number	.00	.01	.02	.03	.04	.05	.06	.07	.08	.09
.0	.000	.046	.074	.097	.117	.136	.153	.170	.186	.201
.1	.215	.229	.243	.256	.269	.282	.295	.307	.319	.331
.2	.342	.353	.364	.375	.386	.397	.407	.418	.428	.438
.3	.448	.458	. 468	.477	.487	.497	.506	.515	.525	.534
.4	.543	.552	.561	.570	.578	.587	.596	.604	.613	.622
.5	.630	.638	.647	.655	.663	.671	.679	.687	.695	.703
.6	.711	.719	.727	.735	.743	.750	.758	.765	.773	.781
.7	.788	.796	.803	.811	.818	.825	.832	.840	.847	.855
.8	.862	.869	.876	.883	.890	.897	.904	.911	.918	.925
.9	.932	.939	.946	.953	.960	.966	.973	.980	.987	.993
1.0	1.000	1.007	1.013	1.020	1.027	1.033	1.040	1.046	1.053	1.059
1.1	1.065	1.072	1.078	1.085	1.091	1.097	1.104	1.110	1.117	1.123
1.2	1.129	1.136	1.142	1.148	1.154	1.160	1.167	1.173	1.179	1.185
1.3	1.191	1.197	1.203	1.209	1.215	1.221	1.227	1.233	1.239	1.245
1.4	1.251	1.257	1.263	1.269	1.275	1.281	1.287	1.293	1.299	1.305
1.5	1.310	1.316	1.322	1.328	1.334	1.339	1.345	1.351	1.357	1.362
1.6	1.368	1.374	1.379	1.385	1.391	1.396	1.402	1.408	1.413	1.419
1.7	1.424	1.430	1.436	1.441	1.447	1.452	1.458	1.463	1.469	1.474
1.8	1.480	1.485	1.491	1.496	1.502	1.507	1.513	1.518	1.523	1.529
1.9	1.534	1.539	1.545	1.550	1.556	1.561	1.566	1.571	1.577	1.582
2.0	1.587	1.593	1.598	1.603	1.608	1.613	1.619	1.624	1.629	1.634
2.1	1.639	1.645	1.650	1.655	1.660	1.665	1.671	1.676	1.681	1.686
2.2	1.691	1.697	1.702	1.707	1.712	1.717	1.722	1.727	1.732	1.737
2.3	1.742	1.747	1.752	1.757	1.762	1.767	1.772	1.777	1.782	1.787
2.4	1.792	1.797	1.802	1.807	1.812	1.817	1.822	1.827	1.832	1.837
2.5	1.842	1.847	1.852	1.857	1.862	1.867	1.871	1.876	1.881	1.886
2.6	1.891	1.896	1.900	1.905	1.910	1.915	1.920	1.925	1.929	1.934
2.7	1.939	1.944	1.949	1.953	1.958	1.963	1.968	1.972	1.977	1.982
2.8	1.987	1.992	1.996	2.001	2.006	2.010	2.015	2.020	2.024	2.029
2.9	2.034	2.038	2.043	2.048	2.052	2.057	2.062	2.066	2.071	2.075
3.0	2.080	2.085	2.089	2.094	2.099	2.103	2.108	2.112	2.117	2.122
3.1	2.126	2.131	2.135	2.140	2.144	2.149	2.153	2.158	2.163	2.167
3.2	2.172	2.176	2.180	2.185	2.190	2.194	2.199	2.203	2.208	2.212
3.3	2.217	2.221	2.226	2.230	2.234	2.239	2.243	2.248	2.252	2.257
3.4	2.261	2.265	2.270	2.274	2.279	2.283	2.288	2.292	2.296	2.301
3.5	2.305	2.310	2.314	2.318	2.323	2.327	2.331	2.336	2.340	2.345
3.6	2.349	2.353	2.358	2.362	2.366	2.371	2.375	2.379	2.384	2.388
3.7	2.392	2.397	2.401	2.405	2.409	2.414	2.418	2.422	2.427	2.431
3.8	2.435	2.439	2.444	2.448	2.452	2.457	2.461	2.465	2.469	2.474
3.9	2.478	2.482	2.486	2.490	2.495	2.499	2.503	2.507	2.511	2.516
4.0	2.520	2.524	2.528	2.532	2.537	2.541	2.545	2.549	2.553	2.558
4.1	2.562	2.566	2.570	2.574	2.579	2.583	2.587	2.591	2.595	2.599
4.2	2.603	2.607	2.611	2.616	2.620	2.624	2.628	2.632	2.636	2.640
4.3	2.644	2.648	2.653	2.657	2.661	2.665	2.669	2.673	2.677	2.681
4.4	2.685	2.689	2.693	2.698	2.702	2.706	2.710	2.714	2.718	2.722
4.5	2.726	2.730	2.734	2.738	2.742	2.746	2.750	2.754	2.758	2.762
4.6	2.766	2.770	2.774	2.778	2.782	2.786	2.790	2.794	2.798	2.802
4.7	2.806	2.810	2.814	2.818	2.822	2.826	2.830	2.834	2.838	2.842
4.8	2.846	2.850	2.854	2.858	2.862	2.865	2.869	2.873	2.877	2.881
4.9	2.885	2.889	2.893	2.897	2.901	2.904	2.908	2.912	2.916	2.920

Table 7-18. Two-thirds Powers of Numbers (*Continued*)

Number	.0	.1	.2	.3	.4	.5	.6	.7	.8	.9
5	2.924	2.963	3.001	3.040	3.078	3.116	3.154	3.191	3.228	3.265
6	3.302	3.339	3.375	3.411	3.447	3.483	3.519	3.554	3.589	3.624
7	3.659	3.694	3.729	3.763	3.797	3.832	3.866	3.899	3.933	3.967
8	4.000	4.033	4.066	4.099	4.132	4.165	4.198	4.230	4.262	4.295
9	4.327	4.359	4.391	4.422	4.454	4.486	4.517	4.548	4.580	4.611
10	4.642	4.672	4.703	4.734	4.765	4.795	4.825	4.856	4.886	4.916
11	4.946	4.976	5.006	5.036	5.065	5.095	5.124	5.154	5.183	5.212
12	5.241	5.271	5.300	5.329	5.357	5.386	5.415	5.443	5.472	5.500
13	5.529	5.557	5.585	5.614	5.642	5.670	5.698	5.725	5.753	5.781
14	5.809	5.836	5.864	5.892	5.919	5.946	5.974	6.001	6.028	6.055
15	6.082	6.109	6.136	6.163	6.190	6.217	6.243	6.270	6.297	6.323
16	6.350	6.376	6.402	6.429	6.455	6.481	6.507	6.533	6.560	6.586
17	6.611	6.637	6.663	6.689	6.715	6.740	6.766	6.792	6.817	6.843
18	6.868	6.894	6.919	6.944	6.970	6.995	7.020	7.045	7.070	7.095
19	7.120	7.145	7.170	7.195	7.220	7.245	7.270	7.294	7.319	7.343
20	7.368	7.393	7.417	7.442	7.466	7.490	7.515	7.539	7.563	7.587
21	7.612	7.636	7.660	7.684	7.708	7.732	7.756	7.780	7.804	7.828
22	7.851	7.875	7.899	7.923	7.946	7.970	7.994	8.017	8.041	8.064
23	8.088	8.111	8.134	8.158	8.181	8.204	8.228	8.251	8.274	8.297
24	8.320	8.343	8.366	8.390	8.413	8.436	8.458	8.481	8.504	8.527
25	8.550	8.573	8.595	8.618	8.641	8.664	8.686	8.709	8.731	8.754
26	8.776	8.799	8.821	8.844	8.866	8.889	8.911	8.933	8.956	8.978
27	9.000	9.022	9.044	9.067	9.089	9.111	9.133	9.155	9.177	9.199
28	9.221	9.243	9.265	9.287	9.308	9.330	9.352	9.374	9.396	9.417
29	9.439	9.461	9.482	9.504	9.526	9.547	9.569	9.590	9.612	9.633
30	9.655									

Table 7-19. Eight-thirds Powers of Numbers

Number	.00	.01	.02	.03	.04	.05	.06	.07	.08	.09
.1	.002	.003	.004	.004	.005	.006	.008	.009	.010	.012
.2	.014	.016	.018	.020	.022	.025	.028	.030	.034	.037
.3	.040	.044	.048	.052	.056	.061	.066	.071	.076	.081
.4	.087	.093	.099	.105	.112	.119	.126	.134	.141	.149
.5	.157	.166	.175	.184	.193	.203	.213	.223	.234	.245
.6	.256	.268	.279	.292	.304	.317	.330	.344	.358	.372
.7	.386	.401	.416	.432	.448	.464	.481	.498	.516	.533
.8	.552	.570	.589	.608	.628	.648	.669	.690	.711	.733
.9	.755	.778	.801	.824	.848	.872	.897	.922	.948	.973
1.0	1.000	1.027	1.054	1.082	1.110	1.139	1.168	1.198	1.228	1.258
1.1	1.29	1.32	1.35	1.39	1.42	1.45	1.49	1.52	1.55	1.59
1.2	1.63	1.66	1.70	1.74	1.77	1.81	1.85	1.89	1.93	1.97
1.3	2.01	2.05	2.10	2.14	2.18	2.23	2.27	2.32	2.36	2.41
1.4	2.45	2.50	2.55	2.60	2.64	2.69	2.74	2.79	2.84	2.90
1.5	2.95	3.00	3.05	3.11	3.16	3.22	3.27	3.33	3.39	3.44
1.6	3.50	3.56	3.62	3.68	3.74	3.80	3.86	3.93	3.99	4.05
1.7	4.12	4.18	4.25	4.31	4.38	4.45	4.51	4.58	4.65	4.72
1.8	4.79	4.87	4.94	5.01	5.08	5.16	5.23	5.31	5.39	5.46
1.9	5.54	5.62	5.69	5.77	5.85	5.93	6.02	6.10	6.18	6.26
2.0	6.35	6.43	6.52	6.61	6.69	6.78	6 87	6.96	7.05	7.14
2.1	7.23	7.32	7.42	7.51	7.60	7.70	7.80	7.89	7.99	8.09
2.2	8.19	8.29	8.39	8.49	8.59	8.69	8.80	8.90	9.00	9.11
2.3	9.22	9.32	9.43	9.54	9.65	9.76	9.87	9.98	10.10	10.21
2.4	10.33	10.44	10.56	10.67	10.79	10.91	11.03	11.15	11.27	11.39
2.5	11.51	11.64	11.76	11.88	12.01	12.14	12.26	12.39	12.52	12.65
2.6	12.8	12.9	13.0	13.2	13.3	13.4	13.6	13.7	13.9	14.0
2.7	14.1	14.3	14.4	14.6	14.7	14.8	15.0	15.1	15.3	15.4
2.8	15.6	15.7	15.9	16.0	16.2	16.3	16.5	16.6	16.8	16.9
2.9	17.1	17.3	17.4	17.6	17.7	17.9	18.1	18.2	18.4	18.6
3.0	18.7	18.9	19.1	19.2	19.4	19.6	19.7	19.9	20.1	20.3
3.1	20.4	20.6	20.8	21.0	21.1	21.3	21.5	21.7	21.9	22.1
3.2	22.2	22.4	22.6	22.8	23.0	23.2	23.4	23.6	23.7	23.9
3.3	24.1	24.3	24.5	24.7	24.9	25.1	25.3	25.5	25.7	25.9
3.4	26.1	26.3	26.6	26.8	27.0	27.2	27.4	27.6	27.8	28.0
3.5	28.2	28.5	28.7	28.9	29.1	29.3	29.5	29.8	30.0	30.2
3.6	30.4	30.7	30.9	31.1	31.4	31.6	31.8	32.0	32.3	32.5
3.7	32.7	33.0	33.2	33.5	33.7	33.9	34.2	34.4	34.7	34.9
3.8	35.2	35.4	35.7	35.9	36.2	36.4	36.7	36.9	37.2	37.4
3.9	37.7	37.9	38.2	38.5	38.7	39.0	39.3	39.5	39.8	40.0
4.0	40.3	40.6	40.9	41.1	41.4	41.7	42.0	42.2	42.5	42.8
4.1	43.1	43.3	43.6	43.9	44.2	44.5	44.8	45.1	45.3	45.6
4.2	45.9	46.2	46.5	46.8	47.1	47.4	47.7	48.0	48.3	48.6
4.3	48.9	49.2	49.5	49.8	50.1	50.4	50.7	51.0	51.4	51.7
4.4	52.0	52.3	52.6	52.9	53.3	53.6	53.9	54.2	54.5	54.9
4.5	55.2	55.5	55.9	56.2	56.5	56.8	57.2	57.5	57.9	58.2
4.6	58.5	58.9	59.2	59.5	59.9	60.2	60.6	60.9	61.3	61.6
4.7	62.0	62.3	62.7	63.0	63.4	63.8	64.1	64.5	64.8	65.2
4.8	65.6	65.9	66.3	66.7	67.0	67.4	67.8	68.1	68.5	68.9
4.9	69.3	69.6	70.0	70.4	70.8	71.2	71.6	71.9	72.3	72.7
5.0	73.1	73.5	73.9	74.3	74.7	75.1	75.5	75.9	76.3	76.7

Table 7-19. Eight-thirds Powers of Numbers (*Continued*)

Number	.00	.01	.02	.03	.04	.05	.06	.07	.08	.09
5.1	77.1	77.5	77.9	78.3	78.7	79.1	79.5	79.9	80.3	80.7
5.2	81.2	81.6	82.0	82.4	82.8	83.3	83.7	84.1	84.5	85.0
5.3	85.4	85.8	86.3	86.7	87.1	87.6	88.0	88.4	88.9	89.3
5.4	89.8	90.2	90.6	91.1	91.5	92.0	92.4	92.9	93.3	93.8
5.5	94.3	94.7	95.2	95.6	96.1	96.6	97.0	97.5	98.0	98.4
5.6	98.9	99.4	99.8	100	101	101	102	102	103	103
5.7	104	104	105	105	106	106	107	107	108	108
5.8	109	109	110	110	111	111	112	112	113	113
5.9	114	114	115	116	116	116	117	117	118	118
6.0	119	119	120	120	121	122	122	123	123	124
6.1	124	125	125	126	126	127	128	128	129	129
6.2	130	130	131	131	132	133	133	134	134	135
6.3	135	136	137	137	138	138	139	139	140	141
6.4	141	142	142	143	144	144	145	145	146	147
6.5	147	148	148	149	150	150	151	151	152	153
6.6	153	154	155	155	156	156	157	158	158	159
6.7	160	160	161	161	162	163	163	164	165	165
6.8	166	167	167	168	169	169	170	171	171	172
6.9	173	173	174	175	175	176	177	177	178	179
7.0	179	180	181	181	182	183	183	184	185	186
7.1	186	187	188	188	189	190	190	191	192	193
7.2	193	194	195	195	196	197	198	198	199	200
7.3	201	201	202	203	203	204	205	206	206	207
7.4	208	209	209	210	211	212	212	213	214	215
7.5	216	216	217	218	219	219	220	221	222	222
7.6	223	224	225	226	226	227	228	229	230	230
7.7	231	232	233	234	234	235	236	237	238	238
7.8	239	240	241	242	243	243	244	245	246	247
7.9	248	248	249	250	251	252	253	253	254	255
8.0	256	257	258	259	259	260	261	262	263	264
8.1	265	265	266	267	268	269	270	271	272	273
8.2	273	274	275	276	277	278	279	280	281	282
8.3	282	283	284	285	286	287	288	289	290	291
8.4	292	293	293	294	295	296	297	298	299	300
8.5	301	302	303	304	305	306	307	308	309	309
8.6	310	311	312	313	314	315	316	317	318	319
8.7	320	321	322	323	324	325	326	327	328	329
8.8	330	331	332	333	334	335	336	337	338	339
8.9	340	341	342	343	344	345	346	347	348	349
9 0	350	352	353	354	355	356	357	358	359	360
9.1	361	362	363	364	365	366	367	368	369	371
9.2	372	373	374	375	376	377	378	379	380	381
9.3	382	384	385	386	387	388	389	390	391	392
9.4	394	395	396	397	398	399	400	401	403	404
9.5	405	406	407	408	409	411	412	413	414	415
9.6	416	417	419	420	421	422	423	424	426	427
9.7	428	429	430	431	433	434	435	436	437	439
9.8	440	441	442	443	445	446	447	448	449	451
9.9	452	453	454	456	457	458	459	460	462	463
10.0	464	465	467	468	469	470	472	473	474	475

Table 7-19. Eight-thirds Powers of Numbers (*Continued*)

Number	.00	.01	.02	.03	.04	.05	.06	.07	.08	.09
10.1	477	478	479	480	482	483	484	485	487	488
10.2	489	491	492	493	494	496	497	498	500	501
10.3	502	504	505	506	507	509	510	511	513	514
10.4	515	517	518	519	521	522	523	525	526	527
10.5	529	530	531	533	534	535	537	538	539	541
10.6	542	544	545	546	548	549	550	552	553	555
10.7	556	557	559	560	561	563	564	566	567	568
10.8	570	571	573	574	576	577	578	580	581	583
10.9	584	586	587	588	590	591	593	594	596	597
11.0	598	600	601	603	604	606	607	609	610	612
11.1	613	615	616	618	619	620	622	623	625	626
11.2	628	629	631	632	634	635	637	638	640	641
11.3	643	645	646	648	649	651	652	654	655	657
11.4	658	660	661	663	664	666	668	669	671	672
11.5	674	675	677	678	680	682	683	685	686	688
11.6	690	691	693	694	696	697	699	701	702	704
11.7	705	707	709	710	712	714	715	717	718	720
11.8	722	723	725	727	728	730	732	733	735	736
11.9	738	740	741	743	745	746	748	750	751	753
12.0	755	756	758	760	762	763	765	767	768	770
12.1	772	773	775	777	778	780	782	784	785	787
12.2	789	791	792	794	796	797	799	801	803	804
12.3	806	808	810	811	813	815	817	818	820	822
12.4	824	826	827	829	831	833	834	836	838	840
12.5	842	843	845	847	849	851	852	854	856	858
12.6	860	861	863	865	867	869	871	872	874	876
12.7	878	880	882	884	885	887	889	891	893	895
12.8	897	898	900	902	904	906	908	910	912	913
12.9	915	917	919	921	923	925	927	929	931	932
13.0	934	936	938	940	942	944	946	948	950	952
13.1	954	956	958	959	961	963	965	967	969	971
13.2	973	975	977	979	981	983	985	987	989	991
13.3	993	995	997	999	1001	1003	1005	1007	1009	1011
13.4	1013	1015	1017	1019	1021	1023	1025	1027	1029	1031
13.5	1033	1035	1037	1039	1041	1044	1046	1048	1050	1052
13.6	1050	1060	1060	1060	1060	1060	1070	1070	1070	1070
13.7	1070	1080	1080	1080	1080	1090	1090	1090	1090	1090
13.8	1100	1100	1100	1100	1100	1110	1110	1110	1110	1110
13.9	1120	1120	1120	1120	1130	1130	1130	1130	1130	1140
14.0	1140	1140	1140	1150	1150	1150	1150	1150	1160	1160
14.1	1160	1160	1160	1170	1170	1170	1170	1180	1180	1180
14.2	1180	1180	1190	1190	1190	1190	1200	1200	1200	1200
14.3	1200	1210	1210	1210	1210	1220	1220	1220	1220	1230
14.4	1230	1230	1230	1230	1240	1240	1240	1240	1250	1250
14.5	1250	1250	1250	1260	1260	1260	1260	1270	1270	1270
14.6	1270	1280	1280	1280	1280	1280	1290	1290	1290	1290
14.7	1300	1300	1300	1300	1310	1310	1310	1310	1320	1320
14.8	1320	1320	1330	1330	1330	1330	1330	1340	1340	1340
14.9	1340	1350	1350	1350	1350	1360	1360	1360	1360	1370
15.0	1370	1370	1370	1380	1380	1380	1380	1390	1390	1390

Table 7-19. Eight-thirds Powers of Numbers (*Concluded*)

Num-ber	.0	.1	.2	.3	.4	.5	.6	.7	.8	.9
15	1370	1390	1420	1440	1470	1490	1520	1550	1570	1600
16	1630	1650	1680	1710	1740	1760	1790	1820	1850	1880
17	1910	1940	1970	2000	2030	2060	2100	2130	2160	2190
18	2230	2260	2290	2330	2360	2390	2430	2460	2500	2530
19	2570	2610	2640	2680	2720	2750	2790	2830	2870	2910
20	2950	2990	3030	3070	3110	3150	3190	3230	3270	3310
21	3360	3400	3440	3490	3530	3570	3620	3660	3710	3750
22	3800	3850	3890	3940	3990	4030	4080	4130	4180	4230
23	4280	4330	4380	4430	4480	4530	4580	4630	4690	4740
24	4790	4850	4900	4950	5010	5060	5120	5170	5230	5290
25	5340	5400	5460	5520	5570	5630	5690	5750	5810	5870
26	5930	5990	6060	6120	6180	6240	6300	6370	6430	6500
27	6560	6630	6690	6760	6820	6890	6960	7020	7090	7160
28	7230	7300	7370	7440	7510	7580	7650	7720	7790	7870
29	7940	8010	8090	8160	8230	8310	8380	8460	8540	8610
30	8690	8770	8840	8920	9000	9080	9160	9240	9320	9400
31	9480	9570	9650	9730	9810	9900	9980	10070	10150	10240
32	10320	10410	10490	10580	10670	10760	10850	10930	11020	11110
33	11200	11290	11390	11480	11570	11660	11760	11850	11940	12040
34	12130	12230	12320	12420	12520	12610	12710	12810	12910	13010
35	13110									

Table 7-20. Three-eighths Powers of Numbers

Number	0	1	2	3	4	5	6	7	8	9
0	0.00	1.00	1.30	1.51	1.68	1.83	1.96	2.07	2.18	2.28
10	2.37	2.46	2.54	2.62	2.69	2.76	2.83	2.89	2.96	3.02
20	3.08	3.13	3.19	3.24	3.29	3.34	3.39	3.44	3.49	3.54
30	3.58	3.62	3.67	3.71	3.75	3.79	3.83	3.87	3.91	3.95
40	3.99	4.03	4.06	4.10	4.13	4.17	4.20	4.24	4.27	4.30
50	4.34	4.37	4.40	4.43	4.46	4.49	4.52	4.55	4.58	4.61
6C	4.64	4.67	4.70	4.73	4.76	4.78	4.81	4.84	4.87	4.89
70	4.92	4.95	4.97	5.00	5.02	5.05	5.07	5.10	5.12	5.15
80	5.17	5.20	5.22	5.24	5.27	5.29	5.31	5.34	5.36	5.38
90	5.41	5.43	5.45	5.47	5.49	5.52	5.54	5.56	5.58	5.60

Number	0	10	20	30	40	50	60	70	80	90
100	5.62	5.83	6.02	6.20	6.38	6.55	6.71	6.86	7.01	7.15
200	7.29	7.43	7.56	7.69	7.81	7.93	8.05	8.16	8.27	8.38
300	8.49	8.60	8.70	8.80	8.90	9.00	9.09	9.18	9.28	9.37
400	9.46	9.55	9.63	9.72	9.80	9.88	9.97	10.05	10.13	10.21
500	10.28	10.36	10.44	10.51	10.58	10.66	10.73	10.80	10.87	10.94
600	11.01	11.08	11.15	11.21	11.28	11.35	11.41	11.48	11.54	11.60
700	11.67	11.73	11.79	11.85	11.91	11.97	12.03	12.09	12.15	12.21
800	12.26	12.32	12.38	12.44	12.49	12.55	12.60	12.66	12.71	12.77
900	12.82	12.87	12.92	12.98	13.03	13.08	13.13	13.18	13.23	13.29

Number	0	100	200	300	400	500	600	700	800	900
1,000	13.34	13.82	14.28	14.71	15.13	15.59	15.91	16.27	16.62	16.96
2,000	17.29	17.61	17.92	18.22	18.52	18.80	19.08	19.35	19.62	19.88
3,000	20.13	20.38	20.63	20.87	21.10	21.33	21.56	21.78	22.00	22.22
4,000	22.43	22.64	22.84	23.04	23.24	23.44	23.63	23.83	24.01	24.20
5,000	24.38	24.57	24.75	24.92	25.10	25.27	25.44	25.61	25.78	25.95
6,000	26.11	26.27	26.43	26.59	26.75	26.90	27.05	27.21	27.36	27.51
7,000	27.66	27.81	27.96	28.10	28.25	28.39	28.53	28.67	28.81	28.95
8,000	29.08	29.22	29.36	29.49	29.62	29.75	29.88	30.01	30.14	30.27
9,000	30.40	30.52	30.65	30.77	30.90	31.02	31.14	31.26	31.38	31.50

Table 7-20. Three-eighths Powers of Numbers (*Concluded*)

Number	0	1,000	2,000	3,000	4,000	5,000	6,000	7,000	8,000	9,000
10,000	31.62	32.77	33.86	34.89	35.88	36.82	37.72	38.58	39.42	40.23
20,000	41.01	41.77	42.50	43.22	43.91	44.59	45.25	45.89	46.52	47.14
30,000	47.74	48.33	48.91	49.48	50.04	50.59	51.12	51.65	52.17	52.68
40,000	53.18	53.68	54.16	54.65	55.12	55.58	56.04	56.50	56.95	57.39
50,000	57.82	58.26	58.68	59.10	59.52	59.93	60.33	60.74	61.13	61.53
60,000	61.92	62.30	62.68	63.06	63.43	63.80	64.17	64.53	64.89	65.25
70,000	65.60	65.95	66.30	66.64	66.98	67.32	67.66	67.99	68.32	68.64
80,000	68.97	69.29	69.61	69.93	70.24	70.56	70.87	71.17	71.48	71.78
90,000	72.08	72.38	72.68	72.98	73.27	73.56	73.85	74.14	74.42	74.71

Number	0	10,000	20,000	30,000	40,000	50,000	60,000	70,000	80,000	90,000
100,000	74.99	77.72	80.30	82.74	85.07	87.30	89.44	91.50	93.48	95.40
200,000	97.25	99.05	100.8	102.5	104.1	105.7	107.3	108.8	110.3	111.8
300,000	113.2	114.6	116.0	117.3	118.6	120.0	121.2	122.5	123.7	124.9
400,000	126.1	127.3	128.4	129.6	130.7	131.8	132.9	134.0	135.0	136.1
500,000	137.1	138.1	139.1	140.1	141.1	142.1	143.1	144.0	145.0	145.9

SECTION 8

OPEN CHANNELS WITH NONUNIFORM FLOW

This section deals with the action of water in open channels under special conditions which are usually associated with sudden or gradual changes in the cross-sectional area of the stream. The terms *rapidly varied flow* and *gradually varied flow* are used to describe these two types of nonuniform flow. The first part of the section is devoted to a discussion of the principles of rapidly varied flow. The effect of constrictions and enlargements on the water-surface profile are described. The principles of flow at critical depth are developed, and expressions for flow at critical depth are derived for all shapes of channel cross sections. The basic equations are arranged in terms of dimensionless quantities to permit the development of tables for the solution of critical-depth problems. Critical-depth meters and other examples of flow at critical depth are discussed. The principles of the hydraulic jump are derived, and methods of designing transition sections are described.

The second portion of the section deals with gradually varied flow. The general differential equations of gradually varied flow are derived, and the generalized water-surface profiles are presented. Methods of computing water-surface profiles under all conditions are described. Procedures for locating the position of a hydraulic jump and methods of solving such special problems as flow in short channels, flow in chutes, and flow down very steep spillways are presented.

Velocity head, which appears in many of the equations presented in this section, is assumed to be $V^2/2g$; that is, α [Eq. (3-11)] is assumed to be unity. The approximation thus introduced will not ordinarily be of importance, but it should be kept in mind because in some cases it may be necessary to modify expressions to include an estimated value of α.

Rapidly Varied Flow

The principles of rapidly varied flow may be derived by considering the specific energy of the water flowing in an open channel. The general Bernoulli constant for an open channel is

$$H = z + D + \frac{V^2}{2g} \tag{8-1}$$

in which H is the energy of the fluid in foot-pounds per pound with respect to an arbitrarily chosen datum plane as illustrated in Fig. 8-1. The specific energy H_e is obtained by letting the datum plane pass through the bottom of the channel. Thus z in Eq. (8-1) becomes zero, and the expression for specific energy is as shown by the equation

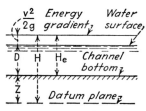

FIG. 8-1. Energy of open-channel flow.

$$H_e = D + \frac{V^2}{2g} \tag{8-2}$$

If the value of V from the equation

$$Q = aV \tag{8-3}$$

is substituted into Eq. (8-2), the following equation for specific energy is obtained:

$$H_e = D + \frac{Q^2}{2ga^2} \tag{8-4}$$

For the special case of discharge in a rectangular channel

$$a = bD \tag{8-5}$$

and

$$Q = bDV \tag{8-6}$$

If the discharge per foot of width Q/b is designated by q, the insertion of Eqs. (8-5) and (8-6) in Eq. (8-4) yields the following expression for specific energy in a rectangular channel:

$$H_e = D + \frac{q^2}{2gD^2} \tag{8-7}$$

This equation, or the general expression Eq. (8-4), may be used to show what happens when a channel cross section changes rapidly. For the sake of simplicity, the discussion will be based on the case of flow in a rectangular channel where Eq. (8-7) will apply. The equation may be studied from two points of view, first, by keeping the discharge constant while H_e and D are permitted to vary, and second, by holding H_e constant while D and q are the variables.

Constant-discharge Relations. If the value of q is taken as a constant, Eq. (8-7) will yield three values of D for each value of H_e. One of the values will be negative, so that only two of the values have practical significance. Figure 8-2a was obtained by taking q as 2 sec-ft per ft of width and solving for various values of D and H_e. It may be seen that there are two values of D for each value of H_e, except at the point of

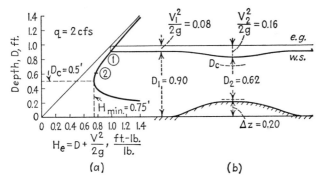

FIG. 8-2. Relationship between specific energy and depth for constant discharge in rectangular channels.

minimum energy H_m, where there is only a single value. This particular depth is called *critical depth* D_c and has great significance in the solution of many nonuniform flow problems.

The usefulness of graphs of Eq. (8-7), such as the one shown in Fig. 8-2a, in solving problems where there is a sudden change of bottom elevation is illustrated by the example shown in Fig. 8-2b. In this example it was assumed that the depth of water was 0.9 ft and that the bottom was raised 0.2 ft for a short distance. At the original depth, corresponding to point 1 in Fig. 8-2a, flow occurred with a specific energy of 0.98 ft-lb per lb. Raising the bottom 0.2 ft changes the specific energy to 0.78, which corresponds to point 2 in Fig. 8-2a. The depth at this point is 0.62 ft, and the water-surface profile will be as shown in Fig. 8-2b. In this example it was assumed that there was no energy loss due to the constriction.

The maximum distance that the bottom of this channel could be raised, with the original depth of 0.9 ft, without causing backwater is the one which will reduce the value of H_e to H_m, 0.75 ft in this case. The depth would then be D_c. This condition is shown by the broken lines in Fig. 8-2b. Any larger rise would attempt to reduce the specific energy to a value less than 0.75, and the curve of Fig. 8-2a shows that a discharge of 2 sec-ft per ft of width cannot flow with H_e less than 0.75. Consequently, the water would have to become deeper upstream in order to raise the energy gradient farther above the channel bottom, or, in other words, to increase the specific energy with which the water approaches the constriction. The problem of lowering the channel bottom over a short distance may be solved in a similar manner.

Constant-energy Relations. If the value of H_e in Eq. (8-7) is taken as constant, there will be two positive values of D for each value of q, as shown in Fig. 8-3a. The curve shown in the figure was obtained by taking the value of H_e as 3.0 ft-lb per lb and computing corresponding values of D and q from Eq. (8-7). Again, as in the case of Fig. 8-2a, there is a unique value of D, which in Fig. 8-3a occurs at the point of maximum discharge. This depth is the critical depth D_c.

The application of Fig. 8-3a to a channel constriction problem is illustrated by the example shown in Fig. 8-3b. The discharge in a rectangular channel 4 ft wide was assumed to be 10 sec-ft per ft of width, corresponding to point 1 in Fig. 8-3a. The width was assumed to be changed to 3 ft for a short distance, thus increasing the discharge per foot of width to 13.3 sec-ft at the constriction. This value of q, point 2 in Fig. 8-3a, corresponds to a depth of 2.59 ft. The water-surface profile will then be as shown in Fig. 8-3b.

The minimum width to which the channel may be constricted without causing backwater will be the width which will cause the maximum discharge to occur, 2.49 ft in this case, and the depth at the constriction will then be critical depth. This condition is illustrated by the broken lines in Fig. 8-3b. The graph of Eq. (8-7), Fig. 8-3a, shows that the discharge per foot of width cannot exceed 16.08 sec-ft with a specific energy of 3 ft-lb per lb. If, then, the width of the constriction is made less than 2.49 ft, thus increasing the value of q above 16.08, the water must become deeper upstream from the constriction in order to gain the additional energy required for this larger discharge. The case of an expansion in the channel may be solved in a similar manner with the aid of Fig. 8-3a. Had the original depth been less than D_c, the water surface would have risen in passing through the constriction (see Sec. 9).

Analytical Solutions of Constriction Problems. The problem of determining the depth of water in a constriction may also be

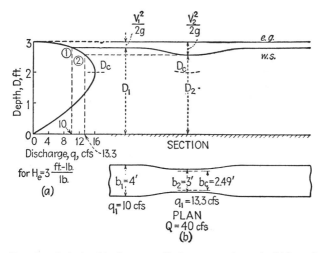

FIG. 8-3. Relationship between discharge per foot of width and depth for constant specific energy in rectangular channels.

solved without the aid of curves by writing the Bernoulli equation from a point above the constriction to the constriction. It is well to keep in mind, however, the general nature of the curves (Figs. 8-2a and 8-3a) when solving such problems because there are always two possible answers for the depth in the constriction. The correct one can be determined only by knowing in advance whether the depth will be greater or less than D_c. In the general case, the bottom may be raised or lowered, the width may be increased or decreased, and the energy loss must be included.

The Bernoulli equation written with reference to the symbols used in either Fig. 8-2b or 8-3b is shown as Eq. (8-8).

$$\frac{V_1^2}{2g} + D_1 = \frac{V_2^2}{2g} + D_2 + \Delta z + h_l \qquad (8\text{-}8)$$

The value of the energy loss h_l may be determined in the manner which will be described under Minor Losses. The unknowns are V_2 and D_2, but V_2 may be related to Q, b_2, and D_2 by the use of Eq. (8-6), thus making D_2 the only unknown quantity. Arranged in this fashion, Eq. (8-8) may be solved by successive approximations.

Tables for Solving Constriction Problems. Tables 8-1 to 8-3 were prepared to aid in the construction of curves such as those shown in Figs. 8-2a and 8-3a. By introducing $x = D/H_e$, Eq. (8-7) may be written

$$x^2 - x^3 = \frac{q^2}{2gH_e^3} \qquad (8\text{-}9)$$

It should be kept in mind that Eqs. (8-7) and (8-9) apply only to rectangular channels. Table 8-1 gives values of x as a function of $q^2/2gH_e^3$. When q is constant, values of D corresponding to various values of H_e may be obtained. When H_e is constant, values of D corresponding to various values of q may be obtained.

A similar derivation for triangular channels may be made as follows. Letting z be the side slope (Fig. 8-5), the expression for the area becomes

$$a = zD^2 \qquad (8\text{-}10)$$

This value of a may be inserted into Eq. (8-4), again letting $x = D/H_e$, to obtain the following expression:

$$x^4 - x^5 = \frac{Q^2}{2gz^2H_e^5} \qquad (8\text{-}11)$$

Table 8-2 gives x as a function of $Q^2/2gz^2H_e^5$ for triangular channels.

For trapezoidal channels the expression for area is

$$a = D(b + zD) \qquad (8\text{-}12)$$

where b is the bottom width, and z is the side slope (Fig. 8-7). The value of a from Eq. (8-12) and the value of D from

$$x = \frac{D}{H_e}$$

may be introduced into Eq. (8-4) to give

$$\left[1 + \left(\frac{zH_e}{b} \right) x \right]^2 (x^2 - x^3) = \frac{Q^2}{2gb^2H_e^3} \tag{8-13}$$

It may be seen from Eq. (8-13) that x is a function of zH_e/b and $Q^2/2gb^2H_e^3$. Table 8-3 gives values of x for various values of these two variables.

Critical Depth—General Case. The expressions for flow at critical depth may be derived by setting $dH_e/dD = 0$, as suggested by Fig. 8-2a, or by setting $dq/dD = 0$, as suggested by Fig. 8-3a. The first-mentioned procedure will be used here to obtain general expressions for flow at critical depth which are applicable to channels of any shape. The value of dH_e/dD will be obtained from Eq. (8-4).

$$H_e = D + \frac{Q^2}{2ga^2} \tag{8-4}$$

The area of any cross section may be expressed as a function of the depth, as follows:

$$a = f(D) \tag{8-14}$$

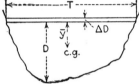

Fig. 8-4. Channel cross section.

Replacing a in Eq. (8-4) with $f(D)$ and differentiating,

$$dH_e = dD - \frac{Q^2 f'(D)}{gf^3(D)} \tag{8-15}$$

From Eq. (8-14) we have

$$f'(D) = da \tag{8-16}$$

and from Fig. 8-4 it may be seen that

$$da = T dD \tag{8-17}$$

By replacing $f(D)$ with a and $f'(D)$ with $T dD$, the following value of dH_e/dD is obtained from Eq. (8-15):

$$\frac{dH_e}{dD} = 1 - \frac{TQ^2}{ga^3} \tag{8-18}$$

The following general expression for flow at critical depth is obtained by setting the right side of Eq. (8-18) equal to zero:

$$\frac{Q^2}{g} = \frac{a^3}{T} \tag{8-19}$$

Equation (8-19) must be satisfied, no matter what the shape of the channel, when flow is at critical depth.

Other useful general expressions for flow at critical depth may be obtained by introducing the mean depth D_m, as defined by the equation

$$D_m = \frac{a}{T} \qquad (8\text{-}20)$$

The following critical-depth equations may be derived from Eq. (8-17) by substituting values from Eqs. (8-2), (8-3), and (8-20), keeping in mind that when $D = D_c$, $H_e = H_m$, where H_m is the minimum specific energy:

$$Q = a \sqrt{gD_m} \qquad (8\text{-}21)$$

$$D_m = \frac{Q^2}{ga^2} \qquad (8\text{-}22)$$

$$H_m = D_c + \frac{D_m}{2} \qquad (8\text{-}23)$$

$$V_c = \sqrt{gD_m} \qquad (8\text{-}24)$$

$$D_m = \frac{V_c{}^2}{g} \qquad (8\text{-}25)$$

$$\frac{V_c{}^2}{gD_m} = 1 \qquad (8\text{-}26)$$

The critical-depth equations for particular shapes of channels may be derived from these general equations, Eqs. (8-19) to (8-26), or by direct application of the basic principles. The equations for flow at critical depth in rectangular, triangular, parabolic, trapezoidal, and circular channels are derived on the following pages.

Critical Depth in Rectangular Channels. In channels of rectangular cross section, the depth D_c is equal to the mean depth D_m, the bottom width b is equal to the top width T, and when the discharge is taken as the discharge per foot of width q, both b and T are equal to unity. By making appropriate substitutions, Eqs. (8-24) and (8-25) become

$$V_c = \sqrt{gD_c} \qquad (8\text{-}27)$$

and

$$D_c = \frac{V_c{}^2}{g} \qquad (8\text{-}28)$$

Equation (8-21) yields the following expressions for discharge in rectangular channels:

$$Q = \sqrt{g}\, bD_c{}^{3/2} \qquad (8\text{-}29)$$

$$q = \sqrt{g}\, D_c{}^{3/2} \qquad (8\text{-}30)$$

and Eq. (8-22) becomes

$$D_c = \sqrt[3]{\frac{q^2}{g}} \qquad (8\text{-}31)$$

From Eq. (8-23)

$$H_m = \tfrac{3}{2}D_c \qquad (8\text{-}32)$$

and

$$D_c = \tfrac{2}{3}H_m \qquad (8\text{-}33)$$

If the value of D_c from Eq. (8-33) is substituted in Eq. (8-30), the following expression for discharge per foot of width is obtained:

$$q = \sqrt{g}\,(\tfrac{2}{3})^{3\!/\!2}H_m{}^{3\!/\!2} \qquad (8\text{-}34)$$

With the value of g taken as 32.16, Eq. (8-34) becomes

$$q = 3.087 H_m{}^{3\!/\!2} \qquad (8\text{-}35)$$

Critical Depth in Triangular Channels. For the triangular section shown in Fig. 8-5, the maximum depth is D_c, and the mean depth D_m is equal to $\tfrac{1}{2}D_c$. From Eqs. (8-24) and (8-25),

$$V_c = \sqrt{\frac{gD_c}{2}} \qquad (8\text{-}36)$$

and

$$D_c = \frac{2V_c{}^2}{g} \qquad (8\text{-}37)$$

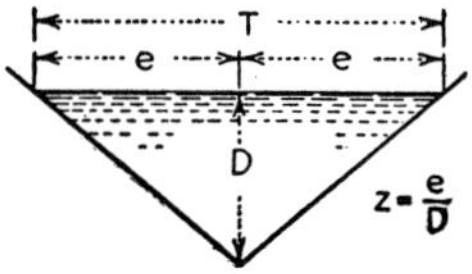

FIG. 8-5. Triangle channel.

As shown in Fig. 8-5, z is the slope of the sides of the channel, expressed as the ratio of horizontal to vertical, and for symmetrical sections it is $\tfrac{1}{2}T/D_c$. The area is $a = zD_c{}^2$. Substituting in Eqs. (8-21) and (8-22),

$$Q = \sqrt{\frac{g}{2}}\,zD_c{}^{5\!/\!2} \qquad (8\text{-}38)$$

or for $g = 32.16$, Eq. (8-38) becomes

$$Q = 4.01zD_c{}^{5\!/\!2} \qquad (8\text{-}39)$$

and

$$D_c = \sqrt[5]{\frac{2Q^2}{gz^2}} \qquad (8\text{-}40)$$

From Eq. (8-23),

$$H_m = \tfrac{5}{4}D_c \qquad (8\text{-}41)$$

and

$$D_c = \tfrac{4}{5}H_m \qquad (8\text{-}42)$$

Substituting this value of D_c in Eq. (8-38),

$$Q = \sqrt{\frac{g}{2}}\left(\frac{4}{5}\right)^{5\!/\!2} z H_m{}^{5\!/\!2} \qquad (8\text{-}43)$$

or, for $g = 32.16$,

$$Q = 2.295 z H_m{}^{5\!/\!2} \qquad (8\text{-}44)$$

Critical Depth in Parabolic Channels. It is convenient to define the parabolic channel (Fig. 8-6) in terms of the top width T and the depth D_c. The area $a = \tfrac{2}{3}D_c T$, and the mean depth $D_m = \tfrac{2}{3}D_c$. Substituting in Eqs. (8-24) and (8-25),

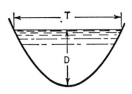

$$V_c = \sqrt{\tfrac{2}{3}g D_c} \qquad (8\text{-}45)$$

and

$$D_c = \frac{3}{2}\frac{V_c{}^2}{g} \qquad (8\text{-}46)$$

Fig. 8-6. Parabolic channel.

Also substituting in Eqs. (8-21) and (8-22),

$$Q = \sqrt{\frac{8g}{27}}\, T D_c{}^{3\!/\!2} \qquad (8\text{-}47)$$

or for $g = 32.16$,

$$Q = 3.087 T D_c{}^{3\!/\!2} \qquad (8\text{-}48)$$

and

$$D_c = \frac{3}{2}\sqrt[3]{\frac{Q^2}{gT^2}} \qquad (8\text{-}49)$$

From Eq. (8-23),

$$H_m = \tfrac{4}{3}D_c \qquad (8\text{-}50)$$

and

$$D_c = \tfrac{3}{4}H_m \qquad (8\text{-}51)$$

Substituting this value of D_c in Eq. (8-47),

$$Q = \sqrt{\frac{8g}{27}}\left(\frac{3}{4}\right)^{3\!/\!2} T H_m{}^{3\!/\!2} \qquad (8\text{-}52)$$

or, for $g = 32.16$,

$$Q = 2.005 T H_m{}^{3\!/\!2} \qquad (8\text{-}53)$$

Critical Depth in Trapezoidal Sections. The trapezoidal section shown in Fig. 8-7 has a depth D_c and a bottom width b. The slope of the sides, horizontal divided by vertical, is z.

Expressing the mean depth D_m of Eqs. (8-24) and (8-25) in terms of channel dimensions, the following relations between critical depth D_c and average velocity V_c are obtained:

$$V_c = \sqrt{\frac{b + zD_c}{b + 2zD_c} gD_c} \qquad (8\text{-}54)$$

and

$$D_c = \frac{V_c{}^2}{g} - \frac{b}{2z} + \sqrt{\frac{V_c{}^4}{g^2} + \frac{b^2}{4z^2}} \qquad (8\text{-}55)$$

With mean depth D_m and the area a expressed in terms of channel dimensions, Eq. (8-21) yields the following expression for discharge at critical depth in a trapezoidal channel:

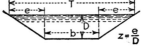

$$Q = \sqrt{g\,\frac{(b + zD_c)^3}{b + 2zD_c}} \; D_c{}^{3\!/\!2} \quad (8\text{-}56) \qquad \text{Fig. 8-7. Trapezoidal channel.}$$

The following expressions may be derived from Eq. (8-23):

$$H_m = \frac{3b + 5zD_c}{2b + 4zD_c} D_c \qquad (8\text{-}57)$$

and

$$D_c = \frac{4zH_m - 3b + \sqrt{16z^2H_m{}^2 + 16zH_mb + 9b^2}}{10z} \qquad (8\text{-}58)$$

Tables have been prepared to aid in the solution of the expressions for flow at critical depth in trapezoidal channels. Preparation of these tables required that the above equations be simplified by introducing dimensionless ratios. Let y be the ratio of the critical depth to the bottom width, as shown in the following equation:

$$y = \frac{D_c}{b} \qquad (8\text{-}59)$$

By substituting the value of b from Eq. (8-59) in Eq. (8-56), the following expression is obtained:

$$Q = \frac{(1/y + z)^{3\!/\!2}}{(1/y + 2z)^{1\!/\!2}} \; g^{1\!/\!2} D_c{}^{5\!/\!2} \qquad (8\text{-}60)$$

Equation (8-60) may be written as follows:

$$Q = K_c D_c{}^{5\!/\!2} \qquad (8\text{-}61)$$

where K_c is a function of z and y. Values of K_c are tabulated in Table 8-4. If the value of D_c from Eq. (8-59) is substituted in Eq. (8-61),

$$Q = K_c y^{5/2} b^{5/2} \tag{8-62}$$

or letting $K_c' = K_c y^{5/2}$,

$$Q = K_c' b^{5/2} \tag{8-63}$$

where K_c' is also a function of z and y. Values of K_c' are tabulated in Table 8-5. Equations (8-61) and (8-63) may also be written

$$K_c = \frac{Q}{D_c^{5/2}} \tag{8-64}$$

and

$$K_c' = \frac{Q}{b^{5/2}} \tag{8-65}$$

If it is required to obtain the critical depth corresponding to a given discharge in a trapezoidal channel of known bottom width and side slopes, K_c' can be computed from Eq. (8-65), and the value of D_c/b corresponding to this K_c' can be selected from Table 8-5. This value multiplied by b gives D_c. Similarly, if b is the only unknown, it can be obtained with the aid of Eq. (8-64) and Table 8-4. A solution for D_c using Newton's method and a digital computer is described in Sec. 13 and demonstrated in Example 13-4.

Equation (8-60) may also be written in the form

$$Q = \frac{(1 + zy)^{3/2}}{(1 + 2zy)^{1/2}} g^{1/2} b D_c^{3/2} \tag{8-66}$$

Equation (8-66) may be written

$$Q = c_1 b D_c^{3/2} \tag{8-67}$$

where c_1 is a function of the dimensionless product zy. Values of c_1 for various values of zy are tabulated in Table 8-6. This table covers a wider range of conditions than Tables 8-4 and 8-5.

If another ratio is introduced, namely, that of minimum specific energy H_m to bottom width b as shown by the equation

$$x = \frac{H_m}{b} \tag{8-68}$$

Eqs. (8-56) and (8-58) may be combined in the following form:

$$Q = c_2 b H_m^{3/2} \tag{8-69}$$

In the above expression, c_2 is a function of the dimensionless product zx. Values of c_2 corresponding to various values of zx are given in Table 8-7.

Equation (8-58) may be rearranged to show that $D_c = cH_m$, where c is a function of H_m/b and z. This relationship was utilized to prepare Table 8-8, from which values of D_c may be obtained when values H_m are known.

Critical Depth in Circular Channels. By referring to Fig. 8-8, the following expressions for the area, top width, and depth of a circular channel may be obtained:

$$a = \frac{d^2}{4}(\theta_r - \tfrac{1}{2}\sin 2\theta) \quad (8\text{-}70)$$

$$T = d \sin \theta \quad (8\text{-}71)$$

and

$$D_c = \frac{d}{2}(1 - \cos \theta) \quad (8\text{-}72)$$

where θ is in degrees and θ_r is in radians. Solutions of Eqs. (8-70) and (8-71) may

FIG. 8-8. Circular channel.

be obtained from Tables 7-4 and 7-6, respectively. Values of a, T, and D_c from Eqs. (8-70) to (8-72) may be substituted in Eq. (8-19) to obtain the following expression:

$$Q = \frac{2^{5/2}g^{1/2}(\theta_r - \tfrac{1}{2}\sin 2\theta)^{3/2}}{8(\sin \theta)^{1/2}(1 - \cos \theta)^{5/2}} D_c^{5/2} \quad (8\text{-}73)$$

Equation (8-73) may be written

$$Q = K_c D_c^{5/2} \quad (8\text{-}74)$$

It may be seen from an examination of Eq. (8-73) that K_c is a function of θ and from Eq. (8-72) that θ is a function of D_c/d. Therefore values of K_c may be tabulated as functions of D_c/d. This is done in Table 8-9. Using the relationship between D_c and d shown by Eq. (8-72), the discharge at critical depth may be expressed in terms of the diameter as follows:

$$Q = K_c' d^{5/2} \quad (8\text{-}75)$$

K_c' is also a function of D_c/d. Values of K_c' are tabulated in Table 8-10.

Equations (8-70), (8-72), and (8-4) may be combined to show that

$$D_o = cH_m \quad (8\text{-}76)$$

where c is a function of H_m/d. Values of c may be determined from Table 8-11.

Because there is a particular value of H_m for each value of D_c, as shown by Eq. (8-76), K_c' in Eq. (8-75) may also be expressed as a function of H_m/d. Values of K_c' corresponding to various values of H_m/d are given in Table 8-12. Problems involving the determination of D_c when Q or H_m is known, or the determination of Q when D_c or H_m is known, may be solved by means of Eqs. (8-74) to (8-76) with the aid of the corresponding tables described above.

Critical-depth Meters. One of the most ideal methods of measuring the discharge in open channels is by means of constriction built for the purpose of causing critical depth to occur. This device, known as a critical-depth meter or a control meter, has the advantage over a weir in that it requires no stilling basin, is practically invulnerable to damage by floating debris, and does not require calibration.

Critical-depth meters may be made by constricting the width of the channel, by raising the bottom, or by doing both. The principles involved were fully set forth earlier in this section on pages 8-2 to 8-7, where it was shown that raising the bottom a certain amount or constricting the width beyond a particular point causes backwater upstream from the constriction and critical depth in the constriction. The most important consideration in the design is that the throat be level, uniform in cross section, and of sufficient length to ensure critical depth will occur in this section. A throat length only two or three times D_c is usually enough unless the meter ends in a fall or a very steep slope, in which case the throat length should be longer (see The Fall, p. 8-18).

It is impossible to measure critical depth itself, because its exact location is not known and because the water surface is often wavy at that location. For these reasons the gage is located a short distance upstream from the throat, as shown in Fig. 8-9. The nearer the gage is located to the throat, the smaller will be the energy loss between the gage and the location of critical depth. The energy loss may be estimated on the basis of the material presented for transitions (p. 8-31). Equation (8-77) is the Bernoulli equation, written from the gage location, point 1, to the location of critical depth, point c.

$$D_1 + \frac{V_1^2}{2g} = z + D_c + \frac{V_c^2}{2g} + h_l \qquad (8\text{-}77)$$

Replacing $(D_c + V_c^2/2g)$ with H_m, and h_l with its value from page 8-31, $\frac{1}{10}(V_c^2/2g - V_1^2/2g)$, Eq. (8-77) may be written

$$D_1 + \frac{V_1^2}{2g} = z + H_m + \frac{1}{10}\left(\frac{V_c^2}{2g} - \frac{V_1^2}{2g}\right) \qquad (8\text{-}78)$$

For rectangular channels, Eq. (8-78) may be simplified by making use of the relation $V_c^2/2g = H_m/3$ to give the following expression:

$$D_1 + 1.1\frac{V_1^2}{2g} = z + 1.03H_m \qquad (8\text{-}79)$$

Because z is known and D_1 is measured by the gage, the only unknowns in Eq. (8-79) are $V_1^2/2g$ and H_m. The value of $V_1^2/2g$ is usually small in comparison with the other terms.

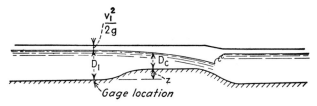

FIG. 8-9. Critical-depth meter.

Therefore, as a first approximation, H_m may be determined from Eq. (8-79) by letting $V_1 = 0$. The approximate discharge may then be determined from Eq. (8-35). The correct discharge is then determined by successive approximations.

For channels other than rectangular the transformation from Eq. (8-78) to an equation similar to Eq. (8-79) will require the use of the appropriate relationship for that particular type of channel. The corresponding expression for discharge in terms of H_m must be used in place of Eq. (8-35).

In many cases the energy loss is so small that it may be neglected. If a critical-depth meter is operating properly, a hydraulic jump will occur below the meter when the original depth is greater than D_c and the jump will occur upstream from the meter if the original depth is less than critical.

Critical Slope. Uniform flow at critical depth will occur when the grade or slope of the channel is just equal to the loss of head per foot resulting from flow at this depth. In any channel for any given discharge there is one grade that will maintain uniform flow at critical depth. This is termed the *critical slope.* For any grade flatter or steeper than critical slope the depth of flow will be, respectively, greater or less than critical depth.

In cases where nonuniform (accelerated) flow passes through the critical stage, critical depth will occur at the section at which the energy gradient has critical slope. Examples of flow passing through critical stage are contained in the following pages.

From the Chezy formula (Sec. 6), the discharge at critical depth is $Q = ac \sqrt{rs_c}$, a being the cross-sectional area, r the hydraulic radius, s_c the critical slope, and c the Chezy coefficient. Equating this value of Q to the value in the critical depth criterion [Eq. (8-19)] and reducing,

$$s_c = \frac{gD_m}{c^2 r} \tag{8-80}$$

In this formula D_m is the area divided by the top width or the mean depth. In a channel that is relatively wide for its depth, $D_m = r$ (approximately), and Eq. (8-80) reduces to

$$s_c = \frac{g}{c^2} \tag{8-81}$$

Substituting $c = (1.486/n)r^{1/6}$, as given by the Manning formula [Eq. (6-25)], and writing $g = 32.16$, the above formulas become, respectively,

$$s_c = \frac{14.56 n^2 D_m}{r^{4/3}} \tag{8-82}$$

and

$$s_c = \frac{14.56 n^2}{D_m^{1/3}} \tag{8-83}$$

Values of the coefficient of roughness n are contained in the table in Sec. 7 in the subsection on Roughness Coefficients. Since s_c varies as the square of this coefficient, errors made in estimating its value are magnified, and slopes computed by the above formulas are apt to show considerable variance from actual conditions.

When flow is at or near critical stage, considerable change in depth may occur without material change in the energy content of the stream. Flow in this region is therefore quite unstable, and a slight disturbance will frequently produce excessive wave action or set up pronounced oscillations of the water surface.

Channel Entrance. The entrance to a channel must be designed so that the size of the channel at the entrance will produce the required discharge in accordance with the limitations on head in the reservoir and the desired depth in the channel. Writing the Bernoulli equation from the reservoir gives this expression, the symbols being defined in Fig. 8-10b.

$$D_r + \frac{V_r^2}{2g} = D_e + \frac{V_e^2}{2g} + h_e \qquad (8\text{-}84)$$

The kinetic-energy term for the reservoir, $V_r^2/2g$, is usually negligible. If the minor loss at the entrance is also neglected, Eq. (8-84) can be written as follows:

$$D_r = D_e + \frac{V_e^2}{2g} \qquad (8\text{-}85)$$

This is the relationship expressed by Eq. (8-2), D_r being the specific energy with which the water enters the channel. The

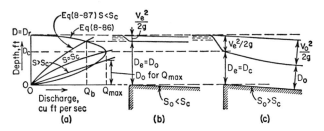

Fig. 8-10. Channel entrance.

relationship can also be written in the form of Eq. (8-4) as follows:

$$D_r = D_e + \frac{Q^2}{2ga^2} \qquad (8\text{-}86)$$

Since a is a function of D, this equation can be plotted using Q and D as the variables as illustrated in Fig. 8-10a.

For a channel having $s_0 < s_c$, water must enter the channel at the uniform flow depth ($D_e = D_0$) because, as shown on pp. 8-36 to 8-39, for subcritical flow, no water surface can exist in which the water surface approaches the uniform flow depth from a smaller or larger depth. Consequently, for a given shape of channel and a given D_r, the discharge into the channel and the depth at the entrance must satisfy Eq. (8-86) as well as the Manning equation [Eq. (8-87/88)].

$$Q = \frac{K'b^{8/3}s^{1/2}}{n} \qquad (8\text{-}87/88)$$

In each equation the only unknowns are depth and discharge, depth being one of the variables controlling K' in Eq. (8-87/88). For a given value of b, n, and s_0, the simultaneous solution of Eqs. (8-86) and (8-87/88) would yield D_e or D_0 and Q. This solution is accomplished graphically in Fig. 8-10a by plotting Eq. (8-87/88) and noting where it crosses graph of Eq. (8-86). The corresponding discharge is noted as Q_b, and the corresponding value of D_0 is plotted in Fig. 8-10b. As channel slope is increased, lines resulting from Eq. (8-87/88) will cut the curve of Eq. (8-86) at larger discharges until $s_0 = s_c$, when the crossing of the two curves will be at Q_{max}, as shown in Fig. 8-10a.

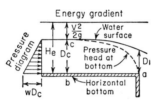

When $s_0 > s_c$ the discharge is equal to Q_{max} and the intersection of the two curves no longer has any physical meaning. However, the value of D from the curve of Eq. (8-87/88)

FIG. 8-11. Pressures upstream from fall.

at Q_{max} gives uniform flow depth as illustrated in Fig. 8-10a and c. The water surface in the channel (Fig. 8-10c) is concave upward, the depth varying from D_c at the entrance to D_0. This is known as an S_2 curve (p. 8-38).

When an *increase in slope* occurs in a channel in which flow is subcritical, the analysis follows the same pattern as that for a channel entrance. When the downstream slope is increased to a value less than s_c, the water enters the steeper channel at D_0 for that channel. If the slope in the steeper channel is increased to a value greater than s_c, water will enter the steeper channel at D_c.

The Fall. The reach of channel illustrated in Fig. 8-11 has a grade less than critical slope and terminates in a fall which discharges freely into the air. Critical depth D_c occurs at section b, a short distance upstream from the rim a where the depth is D_1. The depth gradually increases upstream from b, and between b and the rim there is a pronounced drop in water surface, or *drop-down curve*. The fall possesses interesting hydraulic characteristics which will be briefly discussed.

In an experimental investigation by O'Brien[1] of a fall at the end of a channel of rectangular cross section having a horizontal bottom, the form assumed by the drop-down curve was determined and hydrostatic pressures were measured within the nappe and on the bottom of the channel. Since contraction continues a short distance beyond the end of the channel, there is, theoretically, a slight hydrostatic pressure within the nappe continuing as far as the vena contracta. Actually, however, as proved by the measurements, the pressures at all depths in section a are very nearly atmospheric. O'Brien found pressure heads on the bottom of the channel to vary from zero at the end section to the full depth of water approximately $3D_1$ (or $2D_c$) upstream from the rim, about as indicated by the line ac (Fig. 8-11).

Considering the pressure head at section a to be zero, there are left only velocity head and head of elevation. The head due to pressure and part of the elevation head at b has been converted into velocity head at a. D_1 must therefore be less than D_c. The depth at b, where full hydrostatic pressure exists, cannot in theory be less than critical depth since this is the depth of minimum energy and any decrease below this depth would require the addition of energy from an outside source. Because of the instability of flow at this stage, however, depths less than critical may extend some distance back from the drop-down curve, and if waves form on the surface, there may be three or more sections where critical depth occurs. O'Brien found critical depth to be approximately $11.6D_c$ upstream from the rim of the fall. Any increase in the grade of the channel (between zero and critical slope) will cause a corresponding increase in the slope of the energy gradient, and thus it tends to move the position of critical depth farther back from the rim of the fall.

An estimate of the relation between D_c and D_1 can be made for a rectangular channel with a horizontal bottom by writing the Bernoulli equation from b to a. Because of the absence of hydrostatic pressure, the potential energy term is taken as $D_1/2$ at point a. Then, by making use of Eq. (8-30), the following relation is obtained:

[1] M. P. O'Brien, Analyzing Hydraulic Models for Effects of Distortion, *Eng. News-Rec.*, Sept. 15, 1932.

$$D_1 = 0.655D_c \qquad (8\text{-}89)$$

Assuming atmospheric pressure and equal velocities throughout section a (Fig. 8-11) from the momentum equation between sections b and a, after making proper substitutions and reductions, $D_1 = \frac{2}{3}D_c$ is obtained. From his experiments, O'Brien obtained the relation $D_1 = 0.643D_c$.

The Hydraulic Jump. When conditions are such that the depth in an open channel must increase from a depth less than D_c to one greater than D_c, the water must pass through a hydraulic jump unless special provisions are made (p. 8-35). The location of the jump must be such that the rate of change in momentum is equal to the sum of the forces in the direction of flow. The problem of the jump will be presented in its most general form, after which simplifying assumptions will be made. With reference to Fig. 8-12, the momentum equation is

$$P_2 - W \sin\theta - P_1 + F_{\tau b} + F_{\tau a} = \frac{Qw}{g}\,(\beta_1 V_1 - \beta_2 V_2) \quad (8\text{-}90)$$

where β is the momentum correction coefficient (p. 3-12), W is the weight of the water in the jump, $F_{\tau b}$ and $F_{\tau a}$ are shear forces due to the channel walls and the air, respectively, and

other symbols are identified in Fig. 8-12. The values of P_1 and P_2 are

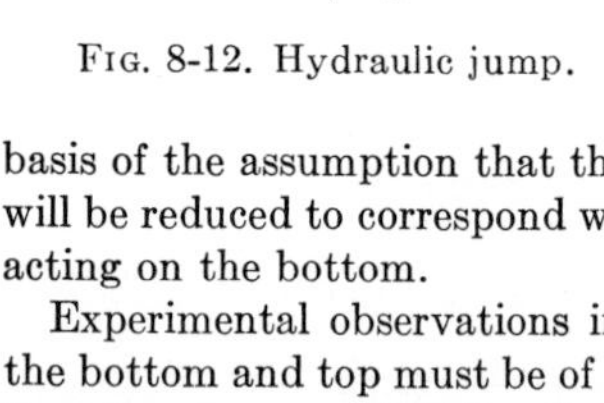

$$P_1 = wa_1\bar{y}_1 \cos\theta \quad (8\text{-}91)$$

and

$$P_2 = wa_2\bar{y}_2 \cos\theta \quad (8\text{-}92)$$

Fig. 8-12. Hydraulic jump.

The $\cos\theta$ terms in the above expressions are inserted on the basis of the assumption that the pressures throughout the fluid will be reduced to correspond with the component of the weight acting on the bottom.

Experimental observations indicate that the shear forces on the bottom and top must be of little importance compared with the other terms. Omitting the shear-force terms, assuming the β factors are unity, and including values of P_1 and P_2 from Eqs. (8-91) and (8-92), respectively, Eq. (8-90) becomes

$$wa_2\bar{y}_2 \cos\theta - W \sin\theta - wa_1\bar{y}_1 \cos\theta = \frac{Qw}{g}\,(V_1 - V_2) \quad (8\text{-}93)$$

The Hydraulic Jump for Small Slopes. When the slope is small, $\cos \theta \approx 1$, $\sin \theta \approx 0$, and Eq. (8-93) becomes

$$wa_2\bar{y}_2 - wa_1\bar{y}_1 = \frac{Qw}{g}(V_1 - V_2) \tag{8-94}$$

Equation (8-94) can be arranged in the following form:

$$\frac{QwV_1}{g} + wa_1\bar{y}_1 = \frac{QwV_2}{g} + wa_2\bar{y}_2 \tag{8-95}$$

Dividing through by w and substituting a_1V_1 for Q and a_1V_1/a_2 for V_2, there follows, after algebraic transformation,

$$V_1{}^2 = g\,\frac{a_2\bar{y}_2 - a_1\bar{y}_1}{a_1(1 - a_1/a_2)} \tag{8-96}$$

or, expressed in terms of discharge, Eq. (8-96) becomes

$$Q^2 = g\,\frac{a_2\bar{y}_2 - a_1\bar{y}_1}{1/a_1 - 1/a_2} \tag{8-97}$$

Values of $\bar{y}$ for trapezoidal and circular sections, respectively, can be obtained with the aid of Tables 7-3 and **7-8**.

Within the limits of error introduced by ignoring all external forces except P_1 and P_2, hydraulic jump must occur in conformity to the law expressed by the above equations. Equations (8-95), (8-96), and (8-97) differ from each other only in symbols and arrangement. They are the basis of all the more specialized hydraulic-jump formulas (p. 8-23).

Force Equation. An examination of Eq. (8-95) indicates that for a given discharge in any channel, if water flows at a given depth, there will always be another depth such that the sum of force due to velocity plus hydrostatic pressure at respective cross sections will be the same. If the sum of these forces is designated by the symbol F_m, Eq. (8-95) can be expressed in the general form

$$\frac{F_m}{w} = \frac{Q}{g}\,V + a\bar{y} \tag{8-98a}$$

where Q, V, a, and $\bar{y}$ are, respectively, discharge, mean velocity, area of cross section, and depth to center of gravity of cross section. Since $V = Q/a$, Eq. (8-98a) can also be written

$$\frac{F_m}{w} = \frac{Q^2}{ga} + a\bar{y} \tag{8-98b}$$

Curve b, Fig. 8-13, is a graph of Eq. (8-98a) or (8-98b) for a trapezoidal channel when Q has a constant value of 200. Curve a is a graph of the energy equation (8-1) or (8-2) for the same section and discharge. Curves a and b are similar in that they have conjugate depths for corresponding values of H_e and F_m/w, respectively; also, each curve has a minimum point. If a hydraulic jump occurs in this channel, it is from the lesser to the greater of the conjugate depths indicated on curve b.

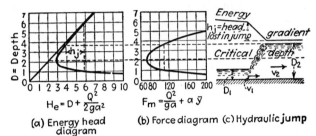

(a) Energy head diagram

(b) Force diagram (c) Hydraulic jump

$H_e = D + \dfrac{Q^2}{2ga^2}$ $F_m = \dfrac{Q^2}{ga} + a\,\bar{y}$

Fig. 8-13. Conditions producing hydraulic jump.

Mathematical proof that critical depth is the depth of minimum force (Fig. 8-13b) follows. Since a and $a\bar{y}$ are functions of D, Eq. (8-98b) can be written

$$\frac{F_m}{w} = \frac{1}{f(D)} \frac{Q^2}{g} + \phi(D) \qquad (8\text{-}99)$$

An expression for minimum F_m is obtained by differentiating Eq. (8-99) with respect to D and equating to zero. Then

$$d(F_m/w) = -\frac{f'(D)}{f^2(D)} \frac{Q^2}{g} + \phi'(D) = 0 \qquad (8\text{-}100)$$

In Eq. (8-100), $f(D) = a$ and, as in Eq. (8-15), $f'(D) = TdD$. The value of the term $\phi'D$, which is the first derivative of the statical moment $a\bar{y}$, can be determined by examining Fig. 8-4. If the depth D is increased by the increment ΔD, there follows

$$\Delta(a\bar{y}) = (\bar{y} + \Delta D)a + T\frac{\overline{\Delta D^2}}{2} - a\bar{y} \qquad (8\text{-}101)$$

or in the limit, after dropping the infinitesimal of the second order and reducing,

$$d(a\bar{y}) = \phi'(D) = adD \qquad (8\text{-}102)$$

Equation (8-100) can thus be reduced to

$$\frac{a^3}{T} = \frac{Q^2}{g} \tag{8-19}$$

which is also the criterion for critical depth for the energy curve (Fig. 8-13a).

Hydraulic-jump Computations. The drawings shown in Fig. 8-13 are to scale and based on a trapezoidal channel having a bottom width of 10 ft, side slopes of $1\frac{1}{2}$ horizontal to 1 vertical, and carrying a discharge of 200 sec-ft. A jump from a depth of 1 ft is illustrated in c. The depth after jump is approximately 3.6 ft, as shown by curve b at the point vertically above the 1-ft depth. The head lost in the jump is about 2 ft, as indicated by h_j on a and c. The jump is always to a depth of lesser energy and always passes through the critical depth.

In problems involving a hydraulic jump, the variable quantities are the discharge Q and the depths before and after the jump, respectively, D_1 and D_2. If Q is the quantity sought, it is given by a direct solution of Eq. (8-97). If either D_1 or D_2 is required, it can be scaled from a force diagram similar to Fig. 8-13b. The use of this diagram is particularly advantageous when a number of different depths at the same discharge are required. Values of D_1 and D_2 can also be obtained by trial solutions of Eq. (8-97).

Hydraulic Jump in Trapezoidal Channels. For trapezoidal channels with slopes sufficiently small so that Eq. (8-95) will apply, it is possible to arrange the equation into a dimensionless form which permits solution by means of a table. The following dimensionless ratios and equations are used. Reference should be made to Figs. 8-7 and 7-2a.

$$z = \frac{e}{D} \tag{8-103}$$

$$x_1 = \frac{D_1}{H_1} \tag{8-104}$$

$$x_2 = \frac{D_2}{H_1} \tag{8-105}$$

Then

$$a_1 = bD_1 + zD_1{}^2 = bx_1H_1\left(1 + \frac{zH_1x_1}{b}\right) \tag{8-106}$$

and

$$a_2 = bD_2 + zD_2{}^2 = bx_2H_1\left(1 + \frac{zH_1x_2}{b}\right) \tag{8-107}$$

The values of $\bar{y}$ become

$$\bar{y}_1 = x_1 H_1 \frac{\dfrac{1}{2} + \dfrac{1}{3} \dfrac{zH_1}{b} x_1}{1 + \dfrac{zH_1}{b} x_1} \tag{8-108}$$

and

$$\bar{y}_2 = x_2 H_1 \frac{\dfrac{1}{2} + \dfrac{1}{3} \dfrac{zH_1}{b} x_2}{1 + \dfrac{zH_1}{b} x_2} \tag{8-109}$$

Then, making use of Eq. (8-11), it can be shown that

$$x_2 = f\left(x_1, \frac{H_1}{b}\right) \tag{8-110}$$

Numerical values of $x_2 = D_2/H_1$ have been tabulated for various values of $x_1 = D_1/H_1$ and zH_1/b in Table 8-13.

The use of this table will be illustrated by application to the numerical example given in Fig. 8-13.   If $D_1 = 1.0$ and $z = 1.5$, then

$$V_1 = \frac{Q}{a_1} = \frac{200}{11.5} = 17.4 \text{ ft per sec}$$

and

$$H_1 = D_1 + \frac{V_1{}^2}{2g} = 1 + 4.7 = 5.7 \text{ ft}$$

Then

$$\frac{z_1 H_1}{b} = \frac{1.5 \times 5.7}{10} = 0.855$$

The value of x_1 is

$$x_1 = \frac{D_1}{H_1} = \frac{1}{5.7} = 0.175$$

Then, from Table 8-13,

$$x_2 = \frac{D_2}{H_1} = 0.64$$

and

$$D_2 = 0.64 \times 5.7 = 3.65$$

This value can be checked by means of Eq. (8-97).

Hydraulic Jump in Rectangular Channels.   For rectangular channels of small slope the jump equations can be greatly simplified.   A derivation similar to the one for the general case but using $q = Q/b$ in place of Q and noting that $P = wD^2/2$ yields the following equations:

$$D_2 = \frac{-D_1}{2} + \sqrt{\frac{2V_1{}^2 D_1}{g} + \frac{D_1{}^2}{4}} \qquad (8\text{-}111)$$

and

$$D_1 = \frac{-D_2}{2} + \sqrt{\frac{2V_2{}^2 D_2}{g} + \frac{D_2{}^2}{4}} \qquad (8\text{-}112)$$

By dividing Eq. (8-111) by D_2 and introducing the Froude number ($F_1 = V_1/\sqrt{gD_1}$), Eq. (8-111) can be changed to the following form:

$$\frac{D_2}{D_1} = -\frac{1}{2} + \sqrt{2F_1{}^2 + \frac{1}{4}} \qquad (8\text{-}113)$$

Similar substitutes in Eq. (8-112) yield

$$\frac{D_1}{D_2} = -\frac{1}{2} + \sqrt{2F_2{}^2 + \frac{1}{4}} \qquad (8\text{-}114)$$

Values of D_2 corresponding to various values of D_1 and V_1 are given in Table 8-14.

Hydraulic Jump in Sloping Channels. When the slope is steep, the simplifying assumptions made in Eqs. (8-94) to (8-114) do not apply, and Eq. (8-93) should be used. If Eq. (8-93) is divided by the specific weight of the fluid, w, the weight term becomes $W \sin \theta/w$. Noting that W/w is the volume of the liquid in the jump, it can be expressed as follows:

$$\frac{W \sin \theta}{w} = C \frac{a_1 + a_2}{2} L \sin \theta \qquad (8\text{-}115)$$

where L is the length of the jump, and C is a factor which takes into consideration the fact that the water surface may not be a plane surface. Then Eq. (8-93) becomes

$$a_2 \bar{y}_2 \cos \theta - C \frac{a_1 + a_2}{2} L \sin \theta - a_1 \bar{y}_1 \cos \theta$$
$$= \frac{Q}{g} (V_1 - V_2) \quad (8\text{-}116)$$

Letting $V_1 = Q/a_1$ and $V_2 = Q/a_2$, Eq. (8-116) can be changed to

$$Q^2 = \frac{g \left[(a_2 \bar{y}_2 - a_1 \bar{y}_1) \cos \theta - C \dfrac{a_1 + a_2}{2} L \sin \theta \right]}{1/a_1 - 1/a_2} \qquad (8\text{-}117)$$

or, for rectangular channels,

$$Q^2 = \frac{g\left[\frac{1}{2}(D_2{}^2 - D_1{}^2)\cos\theta - \frac{C(D_1 + D_2)}{2}L\sin\theta\right]}{1/D_1 - 1/D_2} \quad (8\text{-}118)$$

The U.S. Bureau of Reclamation[1] has published information on the depth after the jump in sloping channels $(D_{2\theta})$ based on their own tests together with those of other investigators.[2,3]

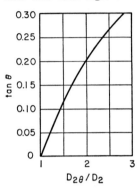

They found that the downstream depth $D_{2\theta}$ exceeded that computed for channels of small slope D_2, as obtained from Eq. (8-111) or (8-113), by an amount which varied with the slope of the bottom, tan θ. This curve is reproduced in Fig. 8-14. In order to use this curve, D_2 would be computed from Eq. (8-111) or (8-113) or obtained from Table 8-14, and then the downstream depth for a particular value of tan θ would be computed by using the value of $D_{2\theta}/D_2$ from Fig. 8-14. This method applies only for cases in which the entire jump occurs on one bottom slope. It is probable that Fig. 8-14 would also serve as a rough approximation for channels other than rectangular.

Fig. 8-14. Depth after jump in sloping channels.

Length of Jump. The U.S. Bureau of Reclamation[4] has published curves showing the length of the jump in terms of the depth after the jump, $L/D_{2\theta}$, as a function of F_1, for various values of bottom slope, tan θ. The maximum length of the jump occurs when F_1 is approximately 6.0. Maximum lengths for each value of tan θ are given in the following tabulation:

[1] Hydraulic Design of Stilling Basin and Bucket Energy Dissipators, *U.S. Bur. Reclamation Eng. Monograph* 25, 1958.

[2] Carl E. Kindsvater, The Hydraulic Jump in Sloping Channels, *Trans. ASCE*, vol. 109, p. 1107, 1944, with discussion by G. H. Hickox.

[3] B. A. Bakhmeteff and A. E. Mutzke, The Hydraulic Jump in Sloped Channels, *Trans. ASME*, vol. 60, p. 60, 1938.

[4] Hydraulic Design of Stilling Basin and Bucket Energy Dissipators, *U.S. Bur. Reclamation Eng. Monograph* 25, 1958.

tan θ	$L/D_{2\theta}$
0	6.15
0.05	5.20
0.10	4.40
0.15	3.85
0.20	3.40
0.25	3.00

For practical purposes these values may be used for $F_1 \gtreqless 4$. The length decreases when $F < 4$. For example, when $F_1 = 3$, values of $L/D_{2\theta}$ are approximately 10 per cent smaller than the tabulated values.

Position of Jump. Hydraulic jumps can occur only when water flowing below critical stage enters a channel in which flow is normally above critical stage and where all the requirements expressed by the force equation (8-95) and illustrated

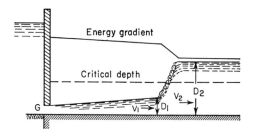

Fɪɢ. 8-15. Hydraulic jump downstream from gate.

in Fig. 8-13 can be fulfilled. In passing through the jump, the flow may change abruptly from nonuniform to uniform or from uniform to nonuniform, or it may be nonuniform both before and after the jump. The method of determining the position of the jump for each of these three conditions is discussed below.

A case where nonuniform flow becomes uniform after the jump is illustrated by Fig. 8-15. A given discharge Q enters a canal of uniform cross section through the gate G at less than critical stage, the grade of the canal being less than critical slope and the uniform flow depth D_2 being less than the upper conjugate depth corresponding to that at which water enters the canal. As the canal grade is not sufficient to compensate for loss of head due to friction, the water increases in depth in an M_3 curve as it passes downstream from G, and its surface slopes upward. A jump will occur at the section where the depth D_1 becomes the lower conjugate depth corresponding to D_2. Since D_2 and Q are known, D_1 can be computed from formula (8-112) for rectangular channels and from (8-97) for other channels. With the velocity and depth at G known, the distance downstream from the gate to the section of depth D_1, where the jump occurs, can be obtained from Eq. (8-135a). If the velocity change is not too great, computations may be made for the single reach; otherwise the distance should be divided into two or more reaches. For the case where the uniform flow depth D_2 is greater than the upper conjugate depth, the jump will drown out the jet and move up to the gate. The solution of the problem under such conditions is described on page 4-13. Another example of change from nonuniform to uniform flow, illustrated in Fig. 8-26, is that of a jump on the apron of an overflow dam when the apron is approximately parallel to the surface of the tail water.

Uniform flow changes abruptly in a hydraulic jump to nonuniform flow when a channel having a grade steeper than critical slope (Fig. 8-21) encounters backwater. In this case, by a method corresponding to that described above for computing D_1, if D_2 and Q are known, D_2 can be computed from formula (8-111) for rectangular channels and from formula (8-97) for other channels; the distance upstream from the dam to the section of depth D_2, where the jump occurs, can be obtained from Eq. (8-135a).

An example of nonuniform flow occurring both before and after a jump is afforded by the overflow dam illustrated in Fig. 8-16. The slope of the apron is insufficient to provide for loss of head due to friction before the jump, but it is more than sufficient after the jump. In both cases, therefore, the depths increase with the distance downstream and flow is nonuniform. To determine the position of the jump, the discharge Q must be known, and data must be available for determining the profile of water surface in the higher stage projected some distance upstream from the place where the jump will occur. The water surface in the lower stage must be computed downstream from a known depth, as from the toe of the dam, to a place beyond the position of the jump. Trial values of D_2 should be computed for three sections a, b, and c, which will locate three points a', b', and c' to which the water must jump at the respective sections. One of the points should be on the opposite side of the jump from the other two, and preferably, the middle point should be near the jump. The intersection of the line $a'b'c'$ with the higher water-surface profile gives the position of the jump. Figure 8-24d shows another example of nonuniform flow occurring both before and after the jump.

When several determinations of depth after jump in a channel are required for the same discharge, as in the last case above, it may be less laborious to obtain them from a graph of the momentum-pressure diagram (Fig. 8-13) than from a solution of Eq. (8-97). For rectangular channels, or for channels that are wide in comparison with the depth, Table 8-14 gives depths

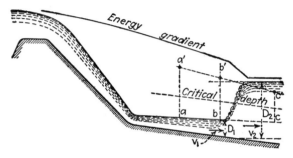

Fig. 8-16. Hydraulic jump on sloping apron of dam.

after jump, and for trapezoidal channels approximate values can be taken from Table 8-13.

Minor Losses. The losses which are caused by rapid local changes in magnitude or direction of velocity are called minor losses. (For minor losses in pipes, see p. 6-18.) Such losses would occur at bends, contractions, enlargements, or obstructions in channels.

Channel Bends. When a fluid flows around a bend the centrifugal force tends to develop a water surface which is higher at the outside of the channel. If the velocity in the channel were everywhere equal to the average velocity V, the amount that the water surface would rise at the outside wall and the amount that it would fall at the inner wall would be given approximately for *subcritical flow* by the following equation:

$$D = \frac{V^2 b}{2gr_c} \tag{8-119}$$

where V is the average velocity, b is the width of the channel, and r_c is the radius of curvature of the center line. This equation is derived by noting that the water surface will be perpendicular to the resultant of the radial and gravitational forces on a particle of fluid. However, because the radial force is proportional to the square of the velocity, this force will be greatest on the high-velocity water near the center of the channel, thus developing crosscurrents, eddies, and spiral motion. Also, there may be a tendency toward separation along the inner wall. Furthermore, for supercritical flow, a standing-wave pattern complicates the flow pattern. Supercritical flow in bends is discussed in Sec. 9, p. 9-16.

Information on losses at bends in rectangular channels has been presented by various investigators. Yen and Howe[1] reported that K_b in the following expression was 0.38 for a 90° bend having a radius of curvature of 5 ft and a width of 11 in.

$$h_b = K_b \frac{V^2}{2g} \tag{8-120}$$

Shukry[2] reported test results in which the variables were the angle through which the water was turned, θ, the ratio of the radius of curvature to the width, r_c/b, the ratio of the depth to the width, D/b, and the Reynolds number. He used the Reynolds number in the following form:

$$R = \frac{rV}{\nu} \tag{8-121}$$

where r is the hydraulic radius. These tests indicate that K_b is affected very little by D/b except when r_c/b is very small. When $\theta \lesseqgtr 45°$, the loss is negligible. The loss increases as θ is increased from 45 to 90°, and for values of θ ranging from 90 to 180° the loss is about constant. When $r_c/b \gtreqless 3.0$, losses were found to be negligible. (It should be noted that this does not agree with the results of Yen and Howe previously reported.) For values of $r_c/b < 3$, values of K_b are given in the following tabulation for $R = 31,500$. Also shown are experimental values of K_b for various values of R, with $r_c/b = 1.0$.

[1] C. H. Yen and J. W. Howe, Effects of Channel Shape on Losses in a Canal Bend, *Civil Eng.* (*N.Y.*), January, 1942, p. 28.

[2] Alumed Shukry, Flow around Bends in an Open Flume, *Trans. ASCE*, vol. 115, p. 751, 1950.

Bend loss coefficients*			
$R = 31,500$		$r_c/b = 1.0$	
r_c/b	K_b	R	K_b
2.5	0.02	1×10^4	0.59
2.0	0.07	3×10^4	0.27
1.5	0.12	5×10^4	0.25
1.0	0.25	7×10^4	0.35

* Alumed Shukry, Flow around Bends in an Open Flume, *Trans. ASCE*, vol. 115, p. 751, 1950.

Tests on large canals[1] showed that losses due to bends could be estimated from the following equation in which $(\Sigma\Delta°)$ is the summation of deflection angles in the reach.

$$h_b = 0.001(\Sigma\Delta°)\frac{V^2}{2g}$$

In sinuous natural rivers, the bend losses are included in the friction losses.

Contractions and Enlargements. The energy losses for contractions have been expressed by Hinds[2] in terms of the difference in kinetic energy at the two ends as follows:

$$h_c = K_c\left(\frac{V_2^2}{2g} - \frac{V_1^2}{2g}\right) \tag{8-122}$$

and for enlargements

$$h_e = K_e\left(\frac{V_1^2}{2g} - \frac{V_2^2}{2g}\right) \tag{8-123}$$

Values of K_c and K_e are given in the following table.   Addi-

Form of transition	K_c	K_e
Sudden change in area, sharp corners.....	0.5	1.0
"Well-designed":		
Best..................................	0.05	0.10
Design value........................	0.10	0.20

[1] Paul J. Tilp and Mansil W. Scrivner, Analyses and Descriptions of Capacity Tests on Large Concrete Lined Canals, *U.S. Bureau of Reclamation Tech. Mem.* 661, 1964.

[2] Julian Hinds, The Hydraulic Design of Flume and Siphon Transitions, *Trans. ASCE*, vol. 92, 1928.

tional information on entrance losses is given on page 4-26. A "well-designed" transition is one in which all plane surfaces are connected by tangent curves and a straight line connecting flow lines at the two ends does not make an angle greater than $12\frac{1}{2}°$ with the axis of the channel.

Contracting and enlarging sections are used at channel entrances or to form *transitions* between channels of different size. Hinds has summarized the art of designing transitions for subcritical flow as practiced by the U.S. Bureau of Reclamation as follows (transitions with supercritical flow are discussed in Sec. 9, pp. 9-1–9-26):

1. Sufficient fall must be allowed at all inlet structures to accelerate the flow and to overcome frictional and entrance losses.

2. The theoretical recovery at an outlet structure is reduced by frictional and outlet losses.

3. At open-channel outlets a small factor of safety may be obtained by setting the transition for less than its maximum recovering capacity, but erosion below the structure may be slightly increased.

4. At siphon outlets a small factor of safety may be obtained and erosion avoided by setting the transition for more than its assumed recovering capacity

5. Simple designs may be prepared by adapting the details of previous designs, known to be satisfactory, if proper allowance is made for loss of head.

6. Important structures, where velocities are high, must be carefully designed to conform to a smooth theoretical water surface.   Sharp angles must be avoided.

7. Horizontal curvature in the conduit above an outlet appears to reduce its efficiency and to produce objectionable cutting velocities in the canal below.

8. K_c [formula (8-122)] for a well-designed inlet is likely to be less than 0.05.   A value of 0.1 is safe for use in designing.

9. K_e [formula (8-123)] for a well-designed outlet is likely to be less than 0.1, unless the conduit above the structure is curved.   A value of 0.2 is safe for use in designing.

10. No definite data as to the best form of water-surface profile, best form of structure, or most efficient length of transition are available.

11. Special care is required where the critical depth is approached or where the hydraulic jump is involved.

12. The disturbances often observed in long, uncontrolled siphons, at part capacity, are not caused by entrained air but by the hydraulic jump in the pipe.

Losses at Obstructions. Water passing through a constriction in an open channel at *subcritical velocity* decreases in depth as shown in Fig. 8-3. The depth downstream from the constriction must be the uniform flow depth or normal depth for this discharge because no other water-surface profile can exist (pp. 8-36–8-39). The Bernoulli equation, written from a point

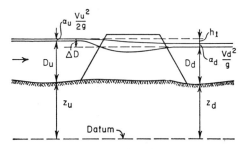

FIG. 8-17. Flow past obstructions.

just upstream from the obstruction to a point just downstream, is

$$z_u + D_u + \alpha_u \frac{V_u^2}{2g} = z_d + D_d + \alpha_d \frac{V_d^2}{2g} + h_l \quad (8\text{-}124)$$

The symbols used in Eq. (8-124) are defined in Fig. 8-17. The amount of backwater caused by the obstruction, D, can then be obtained from Eq. (8-124), using Fig. 8-17 as a reference.

$$\Delta D = (z_u + D_u) - (z_d + D_d) = \alpha_d \frac{V_d^2}{2g} - \alpha_u \frac{V_u^2}{2g} + h_l \quad (8\text{-}125)$$

The losses at obstructions in open channels consist of the loss due to a constriction and enlargement and, if the obstruction has considerable length in the direction of flow, of a friction loss. Usually, the principal loss is that due to the enlargement at the downstream end of the obstruction because losses are invariably larger when velocities are decreased than when flow is speeded up. This is illustrated by the coefficients for losses in the previous subsection, the coefficients for enlargements being twice those for contractions under similar conditions.

Energy losses at piers can be reduced to a minimum by rounding the upstream corners and tapering, or "streamlining," the downstream end. The losses could be estimated by treating them as combinations of constriction and enlargements and using the coefficients given in the previous subsection.

Flow through bridge openings has been investigated by means of model studies.[1] The results are presented in a series of curves which are useful in designing bridge openings. The procedure for expressing the losses is based on the following equation:

$$h_l = K_b \frac{V_n{}^2}{2g} \tag{8-126}$$

where h_l is the total loss, K_b is the loss coefficient, and V_n is the average velocity that would occur in the bridge opening if

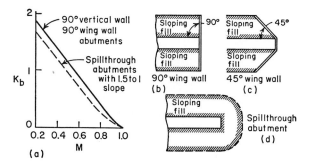

Fig. 8-18. Losses at bridge piers.

the entire discharge were to pass through the bridge opening at the normal depth in the river for this discharge. Values of K_b are related to the bridge-opening ratio M. The value of M is obtained by dividing the portion of discharge that would normally flow through the bridge opening if no piers were present by the total discharge. Reproduced in Fig. 8-18 are two curves relating K_b to M. One curve applies to abutments with vertical walls and 90° corners, as well as to abutments with sloped embankments on the upstream and downstream sides held in place at the ends by wing walls making an angle of 90° with the piers as illustrated in Fig. 8-18b. For wing walls

[1] Joseph N. Bradley, Hydraulics of Bridge Waterways, *U.S. Bur. Public Roads, Div. Hydraulic Res., Hydraulic Design Ser.* 1, 1960.

having angles other than 90°, as shown in Fig. 8-18c, the values of K_b are smaller than those shown in the graph, the reduction being, on the average, about 12 per cent for a wing-wall angle of 30° and approximately 30 per cent for angles of 45 and 60°.

The second curve applies to piers, referred to as spill-through abutments, which have the sloped embankment extending around the ends of the piers as illustrated in Fig. 8-18d. The curve shown is for an embankment slope of 1.5:1, horizontal to vertical. Values of K_b for an embankment slope of 2:1 are from 5 to 10 per cent larger than those shown, and for a 1:1

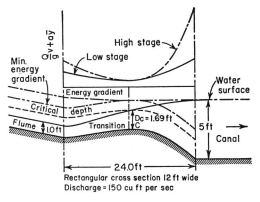

Fig. 8-19. Transition through critical depth to higher stage without jump.

slope, the values are 4 to 9 per cent lower than those shown by the curve.

The Bureau of Public Roads publication[1] also provided coefficients, ΔK, to be added to K_b to take care of minor effects on the losses at the bridge opening. One such coefficient takes care of the increase in loss which occurs when the bridge opening is not in the center of the river. Another includes the additional losses caused by obstructions in the opening. A third one introduces the effect of having the bridge cross the river at an angle differing from 90°.

Transition through Critical Depth without Jump. If water flowing at less than critical depth enters a channel having less than critical slope, change to a higher stage will normally occur

[1] *Ibid.*, p. 3.

in a jump (p. 8-20) unless special means are provided for making velocity changes gradually.   A transition designed to prevent a jump, for the specific data indicated, is illustrated in Fig. 8-19. The raised bottom has a smooth surface, the elevation at the crest C being such that the minimum energy gradient is tangent to the energy gradient of the stream.   For this condition a jump is impossible.   A similar design could be prepared for channels having other sectional forms.

In Fig. 8-19 lower-stage flow is indicated up to section C where critical depth occurs and then follows higher-stage flow.   On both sides of C the other stages which could be computed are not shown.   The force curves $[QV/g + a\bar{y}]$ (see p. 8-21) for the two stages of flow are tangent to each other.   If the crest C is lower than that indicated in the figure, the curves will intersect to the right of C at the section where a jump will occur.   If the crest is higher than that indicated, backwater will be produced, and there will be a jump to the left of C.   The water-surface profile in the transition can be computed in short reaches by the method described on page 8-3.   Energy losses may be estimated using Eqs. (8-122) and (8-123).

Gradually Varied Flow

This phase of nonuniform flow deals with the case where the area of the stream cross section changes so slowly that the energy losses can be computed for various reaches in the same manner as for uniform flow.

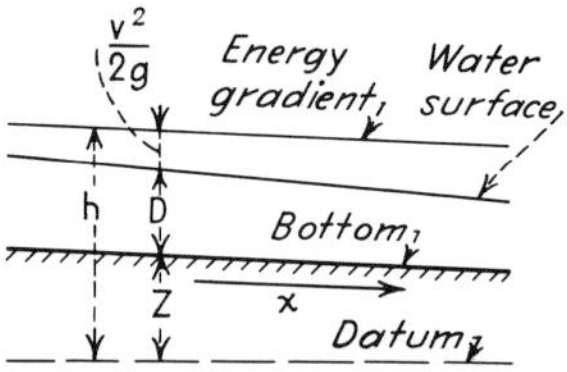

FIG. 8-20. Energy relationships for open-channel flow.

Equations of Gradually Varied Flow and Generalized Profiles. Before discussing the methods of computing water-surface profiles for specific conditions, the differential equation giving the rate of change of depth with respect to distance along the channel will be derived.   This equation is useful in developing an understanding of the various types of profiles which may occur. With reference to Fig. 8-20, the total energy per pound of fluid is

$$h = z + D + \frac{V^2}{2g} \qquad (8\text{-}127)$$

If this equation is differentiated with respect to x, the distance along the channel, the following expression is obtained:

$$\frac{dH}{dx} = \frac{dz}{dx} + \frac{dD}{dx} + \frac{d(V^2/2g)}{dx} \tag{8-128}$$

For the particular case of a rectangular channel the differentiation of the last term may be carried out as follows:

$$\frac{d(V^2/2g)}{dx} = \frac{d(q^2/2gD^2)}{dx} = \frac{-2q^2}{2gD^3}\frac{dD}{dx} = \frac{-V^2}{gD}\frac{dD}{dx}$$

Also, by designating the slope of the bottom, $\tan \theta$, as $-s_o$ (θ being the angle between the bottom and horizontal),

$$\frac{dz}{dx} = \sin \theta = -s_o \cos \theta$$

Then, if the energy loss per unit of length, dh/dx, is designated as $-s$ and if $\cos \theta$ is taken as unity, Eq. (8-128) can be written

$$-s = -s_o + \frac{dD}{dx} - \frac{V^2}{gD}\frac{dD}{dx} \tag{8-129}$$

In Eq. (8-129), s is the slope of the energy gradient and s_o is the slope of the bottom.   The value of s is always positive, and s_o is positive when the channel slopes down in the direction of flow and negative for the opposite condition.   Solving for dD/dx from Eq. (8-129),

$$\frac{dD}{dx} = \frac{s_o - s}{1 - V^2/gD} \tag{8-130}$$

Equation (8-130) gives the rate of change of depth along a rectangular channel under all conditions.   Numerical values may be obtained by solving for s from the Manning formula [Eq. (7-50)].   When dD/dx is positive, the depth is increasing in the downstream direction, and when dD/dx is negative, the depth is decreasing.   When flow is uniform, $s = s_o$, and dD/dx becomes zero.   A careful study of Eq. (8-130) will show that there are 12 possible regimes of flow, depending on the relation of the depth to the uniform flow depth D_o and to the critical depth D_c. For each regime there is possible only one type of water-surface profile.   These are summarized in Fig. 8-21.   The scheme of identifying these curves is based on that used by Bakhmeteff.[1]

[1] B. A. Bakhmeteff, "Hydraulics of Open Channels," McGraw-Hill Book Company, Inc., New York, 1932.

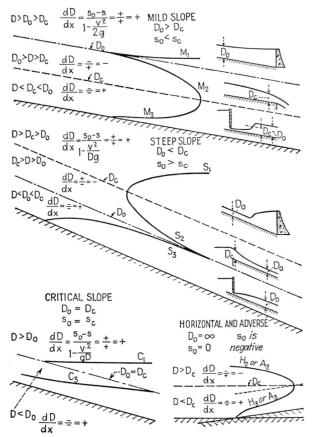

Fig. 8-21. Water-surface profiles for gradually varied flow in open channels.

These curves provide a check on profile computations, because in any regime the computed profile must be concave up or down and the depth must increase or decrease as shown by the curves.

If a derivation similar to that leading to Eq. (8-130) is carried out for the general case, the following equation is obtained:

$$\frac{dD}{dx} = \frac{s_o - s}{1 - Q^2 T / g a^3} \tag{8-131}$$

In the above equation, T is the top width, a is the area, and the other quantities are defined as for Eq. (8-130). Equation (8-131) may be used to determine the rate of change of depth with respect to distance along the bottom for channels of any cross section.

If the width of the channel varies at a known rate (dT/dx), a similar derivation will yield Eq. (8-132) for rectangular channels and Eq. (8-133) for trapezoidal channels.

$$\frac{dD}{dx} = \frac{s_o - s + \frac{V^2}{gT}\frac{dT}{dx}}{1 - \frac{V^2}{gD}} \quad (8\text{-}132)$$

$$\frac{dD}{dx} = \frac{s_o - s + \frac{Q^2D}{ga^3}\frac{dT}{dx}}{1 - \frac{Q^2T}{ga^3}} \quad (8\text{-}133)$$

As for the case of dD/dx, dT/dx is positive when the width of the channel is increasing in the downstream direction. Equations (8-132) and (8-133) will be found useful in determining whether the depth is increasing or decreasing in channels of varying width.

Methods of Computing Water-surface Profiles. Retarded and accelerated flow are illustrated, respectively, by Fig. 8-22a

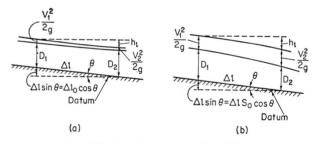

FIG. 8-22. Retarded and accelerated flow.

and b. The same analysis applies to each. It is customary to divide the channel into reaches and proceed consecutively with computations for adjoining reaches, either upstream or downstream. The length of reach between sections 1 and 2 is Δl, and the slope of the bottom of the channel is s_o. The loss of head in the reach is H_l, the drop in the energy gradient, and the average loss of head per foot is $H_l/\Delta l = s_{av}$. Velocities at the upstream and downstream ends of the reach, respectively, are V_1 and V_2, and the corresponding depths are D_1 and D_2. If the datum is the bottom of the channel at the downstream section, from Bernoulli's theorem

$$\frac{V_1{}^2}{2g} + D_1 + s_o\, \Delta l \cos \theta = \frac{V_2{}^2}{2g} + D_2 + h_l \qquad (8\text{-}134)$$

or writing $h_l = s_{av}\, \Delta l$ letting $\cos \theta$ be unity, and transposing,

$$\Delta l = \frac{\dfrac{V_2{}^2}{2g} + D_2 - \dfrac{V_1{}^2}{2g} - D_1}{s_o - s_{av}} \qquad (8\text{-}135a)$$

From the above equation it appears that the length of reach is equal to the difference in energy heads at the two sections divided by the difference in slope between the channel bottom and the energy gradient; or expressed in symbols,

$$\Delta l = \frac{H_2 - H_1}{s_o - s_{av}} \qquad (8\text{-}135b)$$

The numerator and denominator of this fraction will always be of the same sign.

The value of s_{av} in formula (8-135a) can be determined by the Manning formula, for the average velocity in the reach or for the average depth. Either is an approximation, but the error decreases with the difference in velocities at the two end sections and can be kept within any desired limits by selecting proper lengths of reaches. No general rule can be applied to all conditions, but ordinarily, velocity changes should not exceed 10 to 20 per cent. The Manning formula in the general form for computing s [formula (7-35)] is

$$s = \frac{n^2 V^2}{2.2082 r^{4/3}} \qquad (8\text{-}136)$$

where n is the coefficient of roughness, and r the hydraulic radius. Formula (8-136) should be employed only for irregular channels and in other cases where the more usable formulas (8-137) and (8-138), which are given below, cannot be applied.

In the following modified forms of the Manning formula, the discharge is Q and the maximum depth of water is D. Formula (7-47), which can be applied to any of the simple forms of channel sections shown in Fig. 7-2, is

$$s_{\mathrm{av}} = \left(\frac{Qn}{K D_{\mathrm{av}}^{\frac{5}{3}}} \right)^2 \qquad (8\text{-}137)$$

The use of this formula and the accompanying tables for determining the factor K are described on page 7-20. For rectangular or trapezoidal channels, formula (7-50), written

$$s_{\mathrm{av}} = \left(\frac{Qn}{K' b^{\frac{5}{3}}} \right)^2 \qquad (8\text{-}138)$$

is in the form most convenient for general use. In this formula b is the bottom width and K' is a factor varying with D/b which is contained in Table 7-11. Values of $(1/K')^2$ are given in Table 7-12. Formula (8-138) is particularly convenient in channels of uniform cross section where a number of computations involving nonuniform flow are to be made at the same discharge. The quantity $(Qn/b^{\frac{5}{3}})^2$ is then constant and need be computed but once, and the value $(1/K')^2$ multiplied by this quantity gives s.

Formula (8-135a) provides for the direct determination of the water-surface profile in all cases of nonuniform flow where the channel has a constant cross section. In such cases, if s_o, n, Q, and the depth at either end of the reach are known, the distance l to any other assumed depth upstream or downstream for either accelerated or retarded flow can be computed. For rectangular or trapezoidal channels formula (8-138) should be used for determining s, assuming $D = \frac{1}{2}(D_1 + D_2)$. If the channel does not have a constant cross section and in all cases where the length of reach is specified, trial solutions of Eq. (8-134) or (8-135) will be necessary.

Example 8-1. The depth at the upstream side of a gate in a trapezoidal concrete channel is 8 ft, as shown in Fig. 8-23. The channel has a bottom width of 8 ft and side slopes of 1:1. The bottom slope is 0.03. Flow in the channel is uniform upstream from the influence of the gate. The discharge is 200 cu ft per sec. The problem is to determine the water-surface profile upstream from the gate.

The uniform flow depth is first computed, using the Manning equation in the following form, assuming n is 0.011 (Sec. 7, pp. 7-20–7-21):

$$Q = \frac{K' b^{\frac{5}{3}} s^{\frac{1}{2}}}{n} \qquad (8\text{-}139)$$

or

$$K' = \frac{Qn}{b^{8/3}s^{1/2}} = \frac{200 \times 0.011}{8^{8/3}(0.03)^{1/2}} = 0.0496$$

The value of $8^{8/3}$ may be obtained from Table 7-19. From Table 7-11, the value of D_0/b for this K' is 0.13, and then the uniform flow depth is

$$D_0 = 8 \times 0.13 = 1.04 \text{ ft}$$

The value of critical depth is obtained by means of Eq. (8-63),

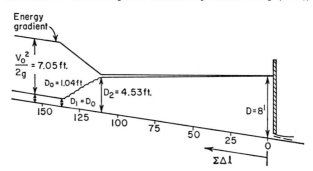

Fig. 8-23. Gradually varied flow profile, Example 8-1.

together with Table 8-5.

$$Q = K_c' b^{5/2} \qquad (8\text{-}63)$$

or

$$K_c' = \frac{Q}{b^{5/2}} = \frac{200}{8^{5/2}} = 1.105$$

Then, from Table 8-5, $D_c/b = 0.302$ and

$$D_c = 8 \times 0.302 = 2.42 \text{ ft}$$

Because $D_c > D_0$, the bottom slope is greater than the critical slope and uniform flow must change abruptly through a hydraulic jump to an s_1 curve (p. 8-36) as illustrated in Fig. 8-21.

The depth after the jump may be determined by means of Table 8-13. The specific energy before the jump H_1 is obtained as follows:

$$V_0 = \frac{Q}{a} = \frac{200}{8 \times 1.04 + (1.04)^2} = 21.3 \text{ ft per sec}$$

and

$$H_1 = D_0 + \frac{V_0{}^2}{2g} = 1.04 + 7.05 = 8.09 \text{ ft}$$

Then

$$\frac{zH_1}{b} = \frac{1 \times 8.09}{8} = 1.01$$

and $D_1/H_1 = 1.04/8.09 = 0.129$.

Then interpolation in Table 8-13 yields $D_2/H_1 = 0.56$ and $D_2 = 0.56 \times 8.09 = 4.53$ ft.

The gradually varied flow profile may be computed starting from either end. In this case the computations are started at the gate. The arrangement of the computations illustrated in the following table helps to eliminate errors. The water-surface profile is determined by computing the lengths of reaches between depths varying in increments of 1 ft until the final reach, where the change is 0.47 ft.

A consideration of the terms in Eqs. (8-135a) and (8-135b), along with the column headings in the following table, show the

$$\Delta l = \frac{\left(D_2 + \frac{V_2{}^2}{2g}\right) - \left(D_1 + \frac{V_1{}^2}{2g}\right)}{s_0 - s_{\text{av}}} = \frac{H_2 - H_1}{s_0 - s_{\text{av}}} \quad (8\text{-}135)$$

order of computations for successive values of Δl. The value of D and other values applying to the ends of reaches are placed together on horizontal lines, whereas values of D_{av} and other quantities applying to an entire reach are placed on a horizontal line between the lines which apply to the ends of that reach. Values of s_{av} are computed from the Manning equation in the form of Eq. (8-136),[1] and values of $(1/K')^2$ are obtained from Table 7-12.

$$s_{\text{av}} = \left(\frac{Qn}{b^{5/3}}\right)^2 \left(\frac{1}{K'}\right)^2 \quad (8\text{-}136)$$

All terms on the right side of Eq. (8-136) remain the same for each reach except $(1/K')^2$. Therefore the equation can be arranged as follows:

$$s_{\text{av}} = \left(\frac{Qn}{b^{5/3}}\right)^2 \left(\frac{1}{K'}\right)^2 = \left(\frac{200 \times 0.011}{8^{5/3}}\right)^2 \left(\frac{1}{K'}\right)^2$$
$$= 0.0000738 \left(\frac{1}{K'}\right)^2$$

[1] See the derivation of this equation in The Manning Equation, Sec. 7.

Example 8-1

D	a	V	$\dfrac{V^2}{2g}$	H	$H_2 - H_1$	D_{av}	$\dfrac{D_{av}}{b}$	$\left(\dfrac{1}{K'}\right)^2$	s_{av}	$s_0 - s_{av}$	Δl	$\Sigma\,\Delta l$
8	128	1.6	.04	8.04								
...	...	...	...	...	.98	7.5	.94	.345	.0000255	.0300	32.7	32.7
7	105	1.9	.06	7.06								
...	...	...	...	...	.97	6.5	.81	.619	.0000456	.0300	32.3	65.0
6	84	2.4	.09	6.09								
...	...	...	...	...	.94	5.5	.69	1.15	.0000850	.0299	31.4	96.4
5	65	3.1	.15	5.15								
...	...	...	...	...	.43	4.8	.60	1.95	.000144	.0299	14.4	110.8
4.53	56.7	3.5	.19	4.72	...	...	...	...	...	...	...	

The computed profile as represented by values of D and Δl in the table is plotted in Fig. 8-23. This same problem is solved by numerical integration using the digital computer in Example 13-5.

Short Channels. Four examples of nonuniform flow in short channels receiving water from a reservoir are illustrated in Fig. 8-24a to c. The first two channels have grades less, and

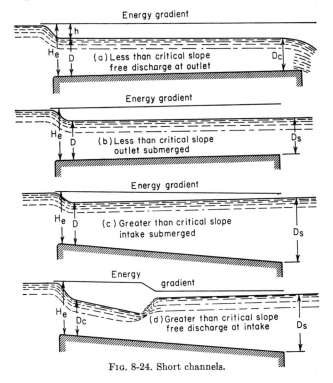

FIG. 8-24. Short channels.

the last two have grades greater, than critical slope.   Channel a terminates in a fall and thus has free discharge at the outlet. Channels b to d discharge into another reservoir, and the depth of submergence at each outlet is D_s.

Critical depth D_c occurs slightly upstream from the outlet of channel a (p. 8-18), and the relation of depth at the intake D to discharge is expressed by formula (8-86). To determine the discharge of the channel, assume the discharge and compute the corresponding depths of water D_c and D. Then, applying the principles of nonuniform flow described in the preceding pages and using formula (8-135), determine the length of channel corresponding to these two depths. Continue trial solutions for other assumed discharges. If assumed discharge is plotted against computed length, the intersection of the resulting curve with the given length of channel will be the discharge sought.

If the submergence D_s of channel b is less than critical depth, it will have no influence on the flow of the channel and discharge will be determined the same as for channel a. If the submergence is greater than critical depth, in making discharge computations, the outlet depth D_s will be constant, and only the intake depth D will vary with the discharge. The method of computing discharge for channel b will otherwise be the same as that described above for channel a.

Examples c and d represent the same channel with its outlet subjected to different depths of submergence. Since the grade is steeper than critical slope, critical depth D_c will occur at the intake if there is no interference from backwater. In channel c, because of backwater, depth at the intake is increased from D_c to D and discharge occurs in accordance with the same principles that apply to channel b. In example d, backwater is not sufficient to affect conditions at the intake. Discharge is at critical depth, and a hydraulic jump occurs in the channel. For the condition shown in the figure, the discharge will not be affected by reducing the depth of submergence D_s or by increasing it up to the point that there is still some acceleration beyond the section where critical depth occurs. The presence of a jump downstream from the intake is evidence that discharge is occurring at critical depth.

Chutes. A channel with a steep slope that is used to convey water from a higher to a lower elevation is termed a *chute*. As illustrated in Fig. 8-25, water is received by a channel of uniform cross section through a rounded entrance at critical depth from another channel, the velocity accelerating and gradually approaching uniform flow in the lower reaches. Beginning at the entrance, distances to assumed depths of water at the ends of successive reaches can be computed by Eq. (8-135). The depth at uniform flow can be obtained from Eq. (8-139) and Table 7-11.

In designing a chute, it is usually required to determine the dimensions that will provide for a given discharge. Since flow is accelerated, the cross section of the channel should be gradually reduced to correspond to the reducing cross section of the stream. Before proceeding with computations, it will be necessary to know the form of channel that is to be designed and to

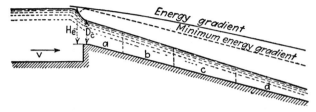

Fig. 8-25. Chute.

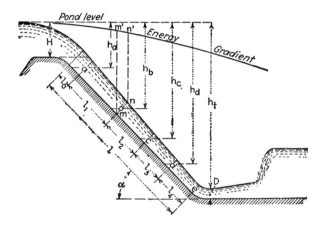

Fig. 8-26. Flow over spillway of dam.

assume, at least tentatively, a relation between the depth of water and some linear dimension of the cross section. It may, for example, be decided to give D/b a constant value or to use a constant depth and gradually reduce the width. With the relation of D to b decided upon, the entrance dimensions should be first computed, and then, using Eq. (8-135), the respective distances downstream should be determined to cross sections

of successively smaller cross-sectional area.   Formulas (8-61)
and (8-63) will be helpful in computing entrance dimensions for
trapezoidal channels.

Flow over Very Steep Inclines.   Equation (8-135) cannot be
adapted readily to very steep slopes like the one illustrated in
Fig. 8-26.   This is because (p. 8-39) heads are measured vertically and the normal cross section, perpendicular to the direction
of flow, is inclined.   Points at different elevations in the cross
section then contain different amounts of energy, and it is not
practicable to write Bernoulli's equation in the usual manner.
For example, for section b (Fig. 8-26), the energy content of
a point m on the bottom is relatively more than that of a point
n on the surface by the amount of drop between m' and n',
the projections of the respective points on the energy gradient.
The variation in energy of intermediate points in the cross
section is indicated by the slope of the energy gradient.   The
solution for such problems may be obtained by writing the
Bernoulli equation from the reservoir to the centers of the
selected cross sections, ignoring the hydrostatic pressure.   For
example, for section c the equation becomes $h_c = V_c^2/2g + \Sigma h_l$
which reduces to $V_c = \sqrt{2g(h_c - \Sigma h_l)}$.   The term Σh_l is the
sum of the energy losses for the selected reaches from the crest
to the selected section determined for individual reaches by
means of Eq. (8-139).   The final application of the Bernoulli
equation to point D will again include the depth term, and the
equation for velocity at D becomes $V_D = \sqrt{2g(h_t - \Sigma h_l)}$.

Table 8-1. Depths of Equal Energy for Rectangular Cross Sections Expressed in Terms of Energy Head

If x = tabulated value, $D = xH_e$.

$\dfrac{q^2}{2gH_e{}^3}$	.000	.001	.002	.003	.004	.005	.006	.007	.008	.009
.00	.000 1.000	.032 .999	.046 .998	.056 .997	.065 .996	.073 .995	.081 .994	.088 .993	.094 .992	.100 .991
.01	.106 .990	.111 .989	.117 .988	.122 .987	.127 .986	.131 .984	.136 .983	.141 .982	.145 .981	.150 .980
.02	.154 .979	.158 .978	.162 .977	.166 .976	.170 .975	.174 .974	.178 .973	.182 .971	.185 .970	.189 .969
.03	.193 .968	.196 .967	.200 .966	.204 .965	.207 .963	.211 .962	.214 .961	.217 .960	.221 .959	.224 .957
.04	.228 .956	.231 .955	.234 .954	.237 .953	.241 .951	.244 .950	.247 .949	.250 .948	.254 .946	.257 .945
.05	.260 .944	.263 .943	.266 .941	.269 .940	.272 .939	.276 .937	.279 .936	.282 .935	.285 .933	.288 .932
.06	.291 .931	.294 .929	.297 .928	.300 .927	.303 .925	.306 .924	.309 .922	.312 .921	.315 .920	.318 .918
.07	.321 .917	.324 .915	.327 .914	.330 .912	.333 .911	.336 .909	.339 .908	.342 .906	.345 .905	.348 .903
.08	.351 .902	.354 .900	.357 .898	.360 .897	.363 .895	.366 .894	.369 .892	.372 .890	.375 .889	.378 .887
.09	.381 .885	.385 .883	.388 .882	.391 .880	.394 .878	.397 .876	.400 .874	.403 .873	.406 .871	.409 .869
.10	.413 .867	.416 .865	.419 .863	.422 .861	.425 .859	.429 .857	.432 .855	.435 .853	.439 .851	.442 .849
.11	.445 .846	.449 .844	.452 .842	.456 .840	.459 .837	.463 .835	.466 .833	.470 .830	.473 .828	.477 .825
.12	.481 .823	.484 .820	.488 .817	.492 .815	.496 .812	.500 .809	.504 .806	.508 .803	.512 .800	.517 .797
.13	.521 .794	.525 .790	.530 .787	.535 .783	.539 .779	.544 .775	.549 .771	.555 .767	.560 .763	.566 .758
.14	.572 .753	.578 .748	.585 .742	.592 .736	.600 .729	.609 .721	.619 .712	.632 .700	.654 .679	⅔ at .14815

8-50 HANDBOOK OF HYDRAULICS

Table 8-2. Depths of Equal Energy for Triangular Sections

If x = tabulated value, $D = xH_e$.

$\dfrac{Q^2}{2gz^2H_e^5}$	x	$\dfrac{Q^2}{2gz^2H_e^5}$	x	$\dfrac{Q^2}{2gz^2H_e^5}$	x	$\dfrac{Q^2}{2gz^2H_e^5}$	x	$\dfrac{Q^2}{2gz^2H_e^5}$	x
.000	.000 1.000	.017	.412 .982	.034	.514 .960	.051	.596 .932	.068	.678 .893
.001	.184 .999	.018	.420 .981	.035	.520 .958	.052	.601 .931	.069	.683 .890
.002	.225 .998	.019	.427 .979	.036	.525 .957	.053	.605 .929	.070	.689 .887
.003	.252 .997	.020	.433 .978	.037	.530 .956	.054	.610 .927	.071	.694 .883
.004	.272 .996	.021	.440 .977	.038	.535 .954	.055	.614 .925	.072	.700 .880
.005	.290 .995	.022	.446 .976	.039	.539 .953	.056	.619 .923	.073	.706 .876
.006	.305 .994	.023	.453 .974	.040	.544 .951	.057	.624 .921	.074	.712 .872
.007	.318 .993	.024	.459 .973	.041	.549 .950	.058	.629 .918	.075	.718 .868
.008	.331 .992	.025	.465 .972	.042	.554 .948	.059	.633 .916	.076	.725 .863
.009	.342 .991	.026	.471 .971	.043	.559 .946	.060	.638 .914	.077	.733 .858
.010	.352 .990	.027	.476 .969	.044	.563 .945	.061	.643 .912	.078	.740 .852
.011	.362 .988	.028	.482 .968	.045	.568 .943	.062	.648 .909	.079	.749 .845
.012	.372 .987	.029	.488 .967	.046	.573 .941	.063	.653 .907	.080	.759 .837
.013	.381 .986	.030	.493 .965	.047	.578 .940	.064	.657 .904	.081	.773 .825
.014	.389 .985	.031	.499 .964	.048	.582 .938	.065	.662 .902	.0819	.800 .800
.015	.397 .984	.032	.504 .963	.049	.587 .936	.066	.667 .899		
.016	.405 .983	.033	.509 .961	.050	.591 .934	.067	.673 .896		

Table 8-3. Depths of Equal Energy for Trapezoidal Cross Sections Expressed in Terms of Energy Head

If x = tabulated value, $D = xH_e$.

$$K = Q^2/2gH_e{}^3b^2 \qquad y = zH_e/b$$

y = 0.0		y = 0.1		y = 0.2		y = 0.3		y = 0.4		y = 0.5		y = 0.6	
K	x	K	x	K	x	K	x	K	x	K	x	K	x
.005	.07/.99	.01	.10/.99	.01	.10/.99	.01	.10/.99	.01	.10/.99	.01	.10/1.00	.01	.10/1.00
.01	.11/.99	.02	.15/.98	.02	.15/.99	.02	.15/.99	.02	.14/.99	.02	.14/.99	.02	.14/.99
.015	.13/.98	.03	.19/.97	.03	.19/.98	.03	.18/.98	.03	.18/.98	.03	.18/.99	.03	.17/.99
.02	.15/.98	.04	.22/.96	.04	.22/.97	.04	.21/.97	.04	.21/.98	.04	.20/.98	.04	.20/.98
.03	.19/.97	.05	.25/.95	.05	.25/.96	.05	.24/.97	.05	.23/.97	.05	.23/.98	.06	.25/.97
.04	.23/.96	.06	.28/.94	.06	.27/.95	.06	.26/.96	.06	.26/.97	.06	.25/.97	.08	.29/.97
.05	.26/.94	.07	.31/.93	.07	.30/.94	.07	.29/.95	.07	.28/.96	.08	.29/.96	.10	.32/.96
.06	.29/.93	.08	.34/.92	.08	.32/.93	.08	.31/.95	.08	.30/.95	.10	.33/.95	.12	.36/.95
.07	.32/.92	.09	.36/.91	.09	.35/.92	.10	.36/.93	.10	.34/.94	.12	.37/.94	.14	.39/.93
.08	.35/.90	.10	.39/.89	.10	.37/.91	.12	.40/.91	.12	.38/.93	.14	.40/.92	.16	.42/.92
.09	.38/.88	.11	.42/.88	.12	.42/.89	.14	.44/.89	.14	.42/.91	.16	.44/.91	.18	.45/.91
.10	.41/.87	.12	.45/.86	.14	.47/.86	.16	.48/.87	.16	.46/.89	.18	.47/.89	.20	.48/.89
.11	.44/.85	.13	.48/.84	.15	.50/.85	.17	.51/.85	.18	.50/.87	.20	.51/.87	.22	.51/.88
.12	.48/.82	.14	.51/.82	.16	.53/.83	.18	.54/.84	.20	.54/.84	.22	.55/.85	.24	.55/.86
.13	.52/.79	.15	.55/.79	.17	.56/.81	.19	.57/.81	.22	.59/.81	.24	.59/.82	.26	.59/.83
.14	.57/.75	.16	.59/.76	.18	.60/.78	.20	.60/.79	.23	.63/.78	.25	.62/.80	.28	.63/.80
.145	.61/.72	.165	.62/.73	.19	.66/.72	.21	.64/.75	.24	.69/.73	.26	.65/.78	.29	.66/.77
.148	.67/.67	.169	.68/.68	.191	.69/.69	.215	.70/.70	.241	.71/.71	.269	.72/.72	.298	.72/.72

Table 8-3. Depths of Equal Energy for Trapezoidal Cross Sections Expressed in Terms of Energy Head (*Continued*)

If x = tabulated value, $D = xH_e$.

$K = Q^2/2gH_e{}^3b^2$ $y = zH_e/b$

$y = 0.7$		$y = 0.8$		$y = 0.9$		$y = 1$		$y = 2$		$y = 3$		$y = 4$	
K	x	K	x	K	x	K	x	K	x	K	x	K	x
.01	.10 / 1.00	.01	.10 / 1.00	.01	.10 / 1.00	.01	.10 / 1.00	.01	.09 / 1.00	.01	.08 / 1.00	.01	.08 / 1.00
.02	.14 / .99	.02	.14 / .99	.02	.14 / .99	.02	.13 / .99	.05	.18 / .99	.05	.16 / 1.00	.05	.15 / 1.00
.04	.20 / .99	.04	.19 / .99	.04	.19 / .99	.04	.19 / .99	.10	.24 / .99	.10	.22 / .99	.10	.20 / 1.00
.06	.24 / .98	.06	.24 / .98	.06	.23 / .98	.06	.23 / .98	.15	.29 / .98	.20	.29 / .99	.20	.26 / .99
.08	.28 / .97	.08	.27 / .97	.08	.27 / .97	.09	.28 / .98	.20	.33 / .98	.30	.33 / .98	.30	.30 / .99
.10	.31 / .96	.10	.30 / .97	.10	.30 / .97	.12	.32 / .97	.25	.36 / .97	.40	.38 / .97	.40	.33 / .98
.12	.34 / .95	.12	.33 / .96	.12	.33 / .96	.15	.36 / .96	.30	.39 / .96	.50	.41 / .96	.60	.39 / .97
.14	.37 / .94	.15	.38 / .95	.15	.37 / .95	.18	.39 / .95	.35	.42 / .95	.60	.45 / .96	.80	.43 / .96
.16	.40 / .93	.18	.42 / .93	.18	.40 / .94	.21	.42 / .94	.40	.45 / .95	.70	.48 / .95	1.0	.48 / .95
.18	.43 / .92	.21	.45 / .92	.21	.44 / .93	.24	.46 / .92	.45	.47 / .94	.80	.51 / .94	1.2	.51 / .94
.20	.46 / .91	.24	.49 / .90	.24	.47 / .91	.27	.49 / .91	.50	.50 / .93	.90	.53 / .93	1.4	.55 / .93
.22	.49 / .90	.26	.52 / .89	.27	.51 / .90	.30	.52 / .90	.60	.55 / .91	1.0	.56 / .92	1.6	.59 / .91
.24	.52 / .88	.28	.55 / .87	.30	.55 / .88	.33	.55 / .88	.65	.58 / .90	1.1	.59 / .91	1.8	.63 / .89
.26	.55 / .87	.30	.58 / .86	.33	.58 / .86	.36	.59 / .86	.70	.60 / .88	1.2	.62 / .89	1.9	.65 / .88
.28	.58 / .85	.32	.61 / .84	.36	.63 / .83	.38	.62 / .84	.75	.63 / .87	1.3	.65 / .87	2.0	.67 / .87
.30	.62 / .82	.34	.65 / .81	.38	.67 / .80	.40	.65 / .82	.80	.66 / .85	1.4	.69 / .84	2.1	.69 / .85
.32	.67 / .78	.36	.71 / .75	.39	.70 / .77	.42	.69 / .79	.85	.70 / .81	1.45	.72 / .82	2.2	.73 / .82
.329	.73 / .73	.361	.73 / .73	.395	.74 / .74	.431	.74 / .74	.880	.76 / .76	1.49	.77 / .77	2.27	.78 / .78

Table 8-3. Depths of Equal Energy for Trapezoidal Cross Sections Expressed in Terms of Energy Head (*Concluded*)

If x = tabulated value, $D = xH_e$.

$$K = Q^2/2gH_e{}^3b^2 \qquad y = zH_e/b$$

$y=5$ K	$y=5$ x	$y=6$ K	$y=6$ x	$y=7$ K	$y=7$ x	$y=8$ K	$y=8$ x	$y=9$ K	$y=9$ x	$y=10$ K	$y=10$ x	$y=11$ K	$y=11$ x
.01	.08 / 1.00	.01	.07 / 1.00	.01	.07 / 1.00	.01	.07 / 1.00	.01	.06 / 1.00	.01	.06 / 1.00	.01	.06 / 1.00
.05	.4 / 1.00	.05	.13 / 1.00	.05	.13 / 1.00	.05	.12 / 1.00	.05	.12 / 1.00	.05	.11 / 1.00	.05	.11 / 1.00
.10	.18 / 1.00	.10	.17 / 1.00	.20	.21 / 1.00	.25	.21 / 1.00	.25	.20 / 1.00	.25	.19 / 1.00	.25	.18 / 1.00
.20	.23 / .99	.30	.25 / .99	.40	.26 / .99	.50	.26 / .99	.50	.25 / .99	.50	.24 / 1.00	.50	.23 / 1.00
.40	.30 / .99	.60	.32 / .99	.80	.33 / .99	1.0	.33 / .99	1.0	.31 / .99	1.0	.30 / .99	1.0	.29 / .99
.60	.35 / .98	.90	.37 / .98	1.2	.38 / .98	1.5	.38 / .98	1.5	.36 / .98	1.5	.34 / .99	1.5	.33 / .99
.80	.39 / .98	1.2	.41 / .97	1.6	.42 / .97	2.0	.42 / .97	2.0	.40 / .98	2.0	.38 / .98	2.0	.36 / .99
1.0	.42 / .97	1.5	.45 / .96	2.0	.46 / .96	2.5	.46 / .96	2.5	.43 / .97	2.5	.41 / .98	3.0	.41 / .98
1.2	.45 / .96	1.8	.48 / .96	2.4	.49 / .96	3.0	.49 / .96	3.0	.46 / .96	3.0	.43 / .97	4.0	.45 / .97
1.5	.50 / .95	2.1	.51 / .95	2.8	.52 / .95	3.5	.52 / .95	4.0	.51 / .95	4.0	.48 / .96	5.0	.49 / .96
1.8	.54 / .94	2.4	.54 / .94	3.2	.55 / .94	4.0	.55 / .94	5.0	.56 / .94	5.0	.52 / .95	6.0	.52 / .95
2.1	.57 / .92	2.7	.57 / .93	3.6	.58 / .92	4.5	.58 / .93	6.0	.60 / .92	6.0	.56 / .94	7.0	.56 / .94
2.4	.61 / .90	3.0	.60 / .91	4.0	.61 / .91	5.0	.61 / .91	6.5	.63 / .91	7.0	.60 / .92	8.0	.59 / .92
2.6	.64 / .89	3.3	.63 / .90	4.4	.64 / .90	5.5	.64 / .90	7.0	.65 / .89	8.0	.64 / .90	9.0	.62 / .91
2.8	.67 / .87	3.6	.66 / .88	4.8	.67 / .88	6.0	.67 / .88	7.5	.68 / .88	9.0	.68 / .88	10.0	.66 / .89
3.0	.70 / .85	3.9	.69 / .86	5.2	.71 / .85	6.5	.71 / .85	8.0	.71 / .86	9.5	.71 / .86	11.0	.70 / .87
3.2	.76 / .80	4.2	.74 / .83	5.5	.75 / .82	7.0	.77 / .80	8.5	.75 / .82	10.0	.74 / .84	12.0	.75 / .83
3.21	.78 / .78	4.32	.78 / .78	5.59	.79 / .79	7.02	.79 / .79	8.61	.79 / .79	10.4	.79 / .79	12.3	.79 / .79

Table 8-4. Values of K_c in the Formula $Q = K_c D_c^{5/2}$ for Trapezoidal Channels

Q = discharge D_c = critical depth b = bottom width of channel

$\dfrac{D_c}{b}$	Side slopes of channel, ratio of horizontal to vertical									
	Vertical	1/4–1	1/2–1	3/4–1	1–1	1 1/2–1	2–1	2 1/2–1	3–1	4–1
.01	567.	568.	569.	569.	570.	571.	573.	574.	576.	579.
.02	284.	284.	285.	286.	286.	288.	289.	291.	292.	295.
.03	189.	190.	190.	191.	192.	193.	195.	196.	198.	201.
.04	142.	142.	143.	144.	145.	146.	148.	149.	151.	154.
.05	113.	114.	115.	116.	116.	118.	119.	121.	123.	126.
.06	94.5	95.2	96.0	96.8	97.5	99.0	100.6	102.2	103.9	107.3
.07	81.0	81.7	82.5	83.2	84.0	85.5	87.2	88.8	90.5	93.9
.08	70.9	71.6	72.3	73.1	73.9	75.5	77.1	78.8	80.5	83.9
.09	63.0	63.7	64.5	65.2	66.0	67.6	69.3	70.9	72.7	76.2
.10	56.7	57.4	58.2	58.9	59.7	61.3	63.0	64.7	66.5	70.0
.11	51.6	52.3	53.0	53.8	54.6	56.2	57.9	59.6	61.4	65.0
.12	47.3	48.0	48.7	49.5	50.3	51.9	53.6	55.4	57.2	60.8
.13	43.6	44.3	45.1	45.9	46.7	48.3	50.0	51.8	53.6	57.2
.14	40.5	41.2	42.0	42.8	43.6	45.2	47.0	48.7	50.5	54.2
.15	37.8	38.5	39.3	40.1	40.9	42.6	44.3	46.1	47.9	51.6
.16	35.44	36.17	36.94	37.73	38.54	40.23	41.97	43.76	45.58	49.30
.17	33.36	34.09	34.86	35.65	36.47	38.17	39.92	41.72	43.55	47.28
.18	31.51	32.24	33.01	33.81	34.63	36.34	38.10	39.91	41.75	45.50
.19	29.85	30.58	31.35	32.15	32.98	34.70	36.47	38.29	40.14	43.90
.20	28.35	29.09	29.86	30.67	31.50	33.23	35.01	36.83	38.69	42.47
.21	27.00	27.74	28.52	29.33	30.16	31.90	33.69	35.52	37.38	41.17
.22	25.78	26.51	27.29	28.11	28.95	30.69	32.49	34.33	36.20	40.00
.23	24.66	25.39	26.18	26.99	27.84	29.59	31.39	33.24	35.11	38.92
.24	23.63	24.37	25.15	25.97	26.82	28.58	30.39	32.24	34.12	37.94
.25	22.68	23.42	24.21	25.03	25.88	27.65	29.47	31.33	33.21	37.04
.26	21.81	22.55	23.34	24.17	25.02	26.79	28.62	30.48	32.37	36.21
.27	21.00	21.74	22.54	23.37	24.22	26.00	27.83	29.70	31.60	35.44
.28	20.25	21.00	21.79	22.62	23.48	25.27	27.10	28.98	30.88	34.73
.29	19.55	20.30	21.09	21.93	22.79	24.58	26.43	28.30	30.21	34.07
.30	18.90	19.65	20.45	21.28	22.15	23.95	25.79	27.68	29.59	33.45
.31	18.29	19.04	19.84	20.68	21.55	23.35	25.20	27.09	29.00	32.88
.32	17.72	18.47	19.27	20.11	20.99	22.79	24.65	26.54	28.46	32.34
.33	17.18	17.93	18.74	19.58	20.46	22.27	24.13	26.03	27.95	31.83
.34	16.68	17.43	18.23	19.08	19.96	21.78	23.64	25.54	27.46	31.35
.35	16.20	16.95	17.76	18.61	19.49	21.31	23.18	25.09	27.01	30.90
.36	15.75	16.50	17.31	18.17	19.05	20.87	22.75	24.66	26.58	30.48
.37	15.33	16.08	16.89	17.75	18.63	20.46	22.34	24.25	26.18	30.08
.38	14.92	15.68	16.49	17.35	18.24	20.07	21.95	23.86	25.80	29.70
.39	14.54	15.29	16.11	16.96	17.86	19.70	21.58	23.50	25.43	29.34
.40	14.18	14.93	15.75	16.61	17.50	19.35	21.23	23.15	25.09	29.00
.41	13.83	14.59	15.41	16.27	17.17	19.01	20.90	22.82	24.76	28.68
.42	13.50	14.26	15.08	15.95	16.84	18.69	20.59	22.51	24.45	28.37
.43	13.19	13.94	14.77	15.64	16.54	18.39	20.29	22.21	24.15	28.08
.44	12.89	13 65	14.47	15.34	16.24	18.10	20.00	21.93	23.87	27.80
.45	12.60	13.36	14.19	15.06	15.96	17.82	19.72	21.65	23.60	27.53

Table 8-4. Values of K_c in the Formula $Q = K_c D_c^{5/2}$ for Trapezoidal Channels (*Concluded*)

Q = discharge D_c = critical depth b = bottom width of channel

$\dfrac{D_c}{b}$	Side slopes of channel, ratio of horizontal to vertical									
	Vertical	¼–1	½–1	¾–1	1–1	1½–1	2–1	2½–1	3–1	4–1
.46	12.33	13.09	13.92	14.79	15.70	17.56	19.46	21.39	23.34	27.27
.47	12.07	12.83	13.66	14.53	15.44	17.30	19.21	21.15	23.10	27.03
.48	11.81	12.58	13.41	14.29	15.19	17.06	18.97	20.91	22.86	26.80
.49	11.57	12.34	13.17	14.05	14.96	16.83	18.74	20.68	22.63	26.57
.50	11.34	12.10	12.94	13.82	14.73	16.61	18.52	20.46	22.42	26.36
.51	11.12	11.88	12.72	13.61	14.52	16.39	18.31	20.25	22.21	26.15
.52	10.91	11.67	12.51	13.40	14.31	16.19	18.11	20.05	22.01	25.95
.53	10.70	11.47	12.31	13.19	14.11	15.99	17.91	19.86	21.81	25.76
.54	10.50	11.27	12.11	13.00	13.92	15.80	17.72	19.67	21.63	25.58
.55	10.31	11.08	11.92	12.81	13.73	15.62	17.54	19.49	21.45	25.40
.56	10.13	10.89	11.74	12.63	13.55	15.44	17.37	19.32	21.28	25.23
.57	9.95	10.72	11.57	12.46	13.38	15.27	17.20	19.15	21.11	25.06
.58	9.78	10.55	11.40	12.29	13.21	15.11	17.04	18.99	20.95	24.91
.59	9.61	10.38	11.23	12.13	13.05	14.95	16.88	18.83	20.80	24.75
.60	9.45	10.22	11.08	11.97	12.90	14.79	16.73	18.68	20.65	24.60
.61	9.30	10.07	10.92	11.82	12.75	14.64	16.58	18.53	20.50	24.46
.62	9.15	9.92	10.78	11.67	12.60	14.50	16.44	18.39	20.36	24.32
.63	9.00	9.78	10.63	11.53	12.46	14.36	16.30	18.26	20.23	24.19
.64	8.86	9.64	10.49	11.40	12.32	14.23	16.17	18.13	20.10	24.06
.65	8.72	9.50	10.36	11.26	12.19	14.10	16.04	18.00	19.97	23.93
.66	8.59	9.37	10.23	11.13	12.07	13.97	15.91	17.87	19.85	23.81
.67	8.46	9.24	10.10	11.01	11.94	13.85	15.79	17.75	19.73	23.69
.68	8.34	9.12	9.98	10.89	11.82	13.73	15.68	17.64	19.61	23.58
.69	8.22	9.00	9.86	10.77	11.70	13.62	15.56	17.53	19.50	23.47
.70	8.10	8.88	9.75	10.66	11.59	13.51	15.45	17.42	19.39	23.36
.71	7.99	8.77	9.63	10.54	11.48	13.40	15.34	17.31	19.28	23.25
.72	7.88	8.66	9.52	10.44	11.37	13.29	15.24	17.21	19.18	23.15
.73	7.77	8.55	9.42	10.33	11.27	13.19	15.14	17.11	19.08	23.05
.74	7.66	8.45	9.32	10.23	11.17	13.09	15.04	17.01	18.99	22.96
.75	7.56	8.34	9.22	10.13	11.07	12.99	14.94	16.91	18.89	22.86
.76	7.46	8.25	9.12	10.03	10.98	12.90	14.85	16.82	18.80	22.77
.77	7.36	8.15	9.02	9.94	10.88	12.81	14.76	16.73	18.71	22.68
.78	7.27	8.06	8.93	9.85	10.79	12.72	14.67	16.64	18.62	22.60
.79	7.18	7.96	8.84	9.76	10.70	12.63	14.59	16.56	18.54	22.51
.80	7.09	7.88	8.75	9.67	10.62	12.54	14.50	16.47	18.45	22.43
.82	6.92	7.70	8.58	9.51	10.45	12.38	14.34	16.31	18.29	22.27
.84	6.75	7.54	8.42	9.35	10.29	12.23	14.19	16.16	18.14	22.12
.86	6.59	7.39	8.27	9.19	10.14	12.08	14.04	16.01	18.00	21.98
.88	6.44	7.24	8.12	9.05	10.00	11.94	13.90	15.87	17.86	21.84
.90	6.30	7.09	7.98	8.91	9.86	11.80	13.76	15.74	17.73	21.71
.92	6.16	6.96	7.85	8.78	9.73	11.67	13.64	15.62	17.60	21.58
.94	6.03	6.83	7.72	8.65	9.61	11.55	13.52	15.49	17.48	21.46
.96	5.91	6.70	7.60	8.53	9.49	11.43	13.40	15.38	17.36	21.35
.98	5.79	6.59	7.48	8.41	9.37	11.32	13.29	15.27	17.25	21.24
1.00	5.67	6.47	7.37	8.30	9.26	11.21	13.18	15.16	17.15	21.13

Table 8-5. Values of K'_c in the Formula $Q = K'_c b^{5/2}$ for Trapezoidal Channels

Q = discharge D_c = critical depth b = bottom width of channel

$\dfrac{D_c}{b}$	Side slopes of channel, ratio of horizontal to vertical									
	Vertical	$\frac{1}{4}$–1	$\frac{1}{2}$–1	$\frac{3}{4}$–1	1–1	$1\frac{1}{2}$–1	2–1	$2\frac{1}{2}$–1	3–1	4–1
.01	.0057	.0057	.0057	.0057	.0057	.0057	.0057	.0057	.0058	.0058
.02	.0160	.0161	.0161	.0162	.0162	.0163	.0164	.0165	.0165	.0167
.03	.0295	.0296	.0297	.0298	.0299	.0302	.0304	.0306	.0309	.0314
.04	.0454	.0456	.0458	.0461	.0463	.0468	.0473	.0478	.0483	.0493
.05	.0634	.0638	.0642	.0646	.0650	.0659	.0668	.0677	.0686	.0704
.06	.0833	.0840	.0846	.0853	.0859	.0873	.0887	.0902	.0916	.0946
.07	.1050	.1060	.1069	.1079	.1089	.1109	.1130	.1151	.1173	.1218
.08	.1283	.1296	.1310	.1323	.1337	.1366	.1395	.1426	.1456	.1520
.09	.1531	.1549	.1567	.1585	.1604	.1643	.1683	.1724	.1766	.1852
.10	.1793	.1816	.1840	.1864	.1889	.1940	.1992	.2046	.2101	.2214
.11	.2069	.2098	.2128	.2159	.2191	.2256	.2323	.2392	.2463	.2607
.12	.2357	.2394	.2431	.2470	.2509	.2591	.2676	.2762	.2851	.3032
.13	.2658	.2702	.2748	.2796	.2844	.2945	.3049	.3156	.3265	.3488
.14	.2971	.3024	.3079	.3137	.3196	.3318	.3444	.3574	.3706	.3975
.15	.3295	.3358	.3424	.3493	.3563	.3710	.3861	.4015	.4173	.4495
.16	.363	.370	.378	.386	.395	.412	.430	.448	.467	505
.17	.397	.406	.415	.425	.435	.455	.476	.497	.519	.563
.18	.433	.443	.454	.465	.476	.499	.524	.549	.574	.625
.19	.470	.481	.493	.506	.519	.546	.574	.603	.632	.691
.20	.507	.520	.534	.549	.564	.594	.626	.659	.692	.760
.21	.546	.561	.576	.593	.610	.645	.681	.718	.755	.832
.22	.585	.602	.620	.638	.657	.697	.737	.779	.822	.908
.23	.626	.644	.664	.685	.706	.751	.796	.843	.891	.988
.24	.667	.688	.710	.733	.757	.806	.858	.910	.963	1.071
.25	.709	.732	.757	.782	.809	.864	.921	.979	1.038	1.158
.26	.752	.777	.805	.833	.862	.923	.986	1.051	1.116	1.248
.27	.796	.824	.854	.885	.918	.985	1.054	1.125	1.197	1.343
.28	.840	.871	.904	.938	.974	1.048	1.124	1.202	1.281	1.441
.29	.886	.919	.955	.993	1.032	1.113	1.197	1.283	1.368	1.543
.30	.932	.969	1.008	1.049	1.092	1.180	1.272	1.365	1.458	1.649
.31	.979	1.019	1.062	1.107	1.153	1.249	1.349	1.450	1.552	1.759
.32	1.027	1.070	1.116	1.165	1.216	1.320	1.428	1.537	1.648	1.873
.33	1.075	1.122	1.172	1.225	1.280	1.393	1.510	1.628	1.748	1.991
.34	1.124	1.175	1.229	1.286	1.345	1.468	1.594	1.722	1.851	2.113
.35	1.174	1.229	1.287	1.349	1.413	1.545	1.680	1.818	1.958	2.240
.36	1.225	1.283	1.346	1.413	1.481	1.623	1.769	1.917	2.067	2.370
.37	1.276	1.339	1.407	1.478	1.552	1.704	1.860	2.019	2.180	2.505
.38	1.328	1.395	1.468	1.544	1.623	1.786	1.954	2.124	2.296	2.644
.39	1.381	1.453	1.530	1.612	1.697	1.871	2.050	2.232	2.416	2.787
.40	1.435	1.511	1.594	1.681	1.771	1.958	2.149	2.343	2.539	2.935
.41	1.489	1.570	1.658	1.752	1.848	2.046	2.250	2.457	2.665	3.087
.42	1.544	1.630	1.724	1.823	1.926	2.137	2.353	2.573	2.795	3.243
.43	1.599	1.691	1.791	1.896	2.005	2.229	2.460	2.693	2.929	3.404
.44	1.655	1.752	1.859	1.970	2.086	2.324	2.568	2.816	3.066	3.570
.45	1.712	1.815	1.928	2.046	2.168	2.421	2.679	2.942	3.206	3.740

Table 8-5. Values of K_c' in the Formula $Q = K_c' b^{5/2}$ for Trapezoidal Channels (*Concluded*)

Q = discharge D_c = critical depth b = bottom width of channel

$\dfrac{D_c}{b}$	Side slopes of channel, ratio of horizontal to vertical									
	Vertical	¼–1	½–1	¾–1	1–1	1½–1	2–1	2½–1	3–1	4–1
.46	1.769	1.878	1.997	2.123	2.253	2.520	2.793	3.070	3.35	3.91
.47	1.827	1.942	2.068	2.201	2.338	2.620	2.909	3.202	3.50	4.09
.48	1.886	2.007	2.141	2.281	2.425	2.723	3.028	3.337	3.65	4.28
.49	1.945	2.073	2.214	2.362	2.514	2.828	3.150	3.476	3.80	4.47
.50	2.005	2.140	2.288	2.444	2.605	2.936	3.274	3.617	3.96	4.66
.51	2.065	2.207	2.363	2.527	2.697	3.045	3.401	3.76	4.13	4.86
.52	2.127	2.276	2.440	2.612	2.790	3.156	3.530	3.91	4.29	5.06
.53	2.188	2.345	2.517	2.698	2.885	3.270	3.663	4.06	4.46	5.27
.54	2.250	2.415	2.595	2.786	2.982	3.385	3.798	4.21	4.63	5.48
.55	2.313	2.485	2.675	2.874	3.080	3.503	3.935	4.37	4.81	5.70
.56	2.377	2.557	2.755	2.965	3.180	3.62	4.08	4.53	4.99	5.92
.57	2.441	2.629	2.837	3.056	3.282	3.75	4.22	4.70	5.18	6.15
.58	2.505	2.702	2.920	3.149	3.385	3.87	4.36	4.86	5.37	6.38
.59	2.570	2.776	3.004	3.243	3.490	4.00	4.51	5.03	5.56	6.62
.60	2.636	2.851	3.088	3.339	3.596	4.13	4.66	5.21	5.76	6.86
.61	2.702	2.926	3.174	3.44	3.70	4.26	4.82	5.39	5.96	7.11
.62	2.769	3.002	3.261	3.53	3.81	4.39	4.98	5.57	6.16	7.36
.63	2.836	3.079	3.349	3.63	3.93	4.52	5.14	5.75	6.37	7.62
.64	2.904	3.157	3.438	3.73	4.04	4.66	5.30	5.94	6.59	7.88
.65	2.972	3.236	3.529	3.84	4.15	4.80	5.46	6.13	6.80	8.15
.66	3.041	3.315	3.62	3.94	4.27	4.94	5.63	6.33	7.02	8.43
.67	3.110	3.396	3.71	4.05	4.39	5.09	5.80	6.52	7.25	8.71
.68	3.180	3.477	3.81	4.15	4.51	5.24	5.98	6.73	7.48	8.99
.69	3.250	3.558	3.90	4.26	4.63	5.39	6.15	6.93	7.71	9.28
.70	3.321	3.641	4.00	4.37	4.75	5.54	6.33	7.14	7.95	9.58
.71	3.39	3.72	4.09	4.48	4.88	5.69	6.52	7.35	8.19	9.88
.72	3.46	3.81	4.19	4.59	5.00	5.85	6.70	7.57	8.44	10.18
.73	3.54	3.89	4.29	4.70	5.13	6.01	6.89	7.79	8.69	10.50
.74	3.61	3.98	4.39	4.82	5.26	6.17	7.08	8.01	8.94	10.81
.75	3.68	4.06	4.49	4.94	5.39	6.33	7.28	8.24	9.20	11.14
.76	3.76	4.15	4.59	5.05	5.53	6.50	7.48	8.47	9.47	11.47
.77	3.83	4.24	4.69	5.17	5.66	6.66	7.68	8.70	9.73	11.80
.78	3.91	4.33	4.80	5.29	5.80	6.83	7.88	8.94	10.01	12.14
.79	3.98	4.42	4.90	5.41	5.94	7.01	8.09	9.18	10.28	12.49
.80	4.06	4.51	5.01	5.54	6.08	7.18	8.30	9.43	10.56	12.84
.82	4.21	4.69	5.23	5.79	6.36	7.54	8.73	9.93	11.14	13.56
.84	4.37	4.88	5.45	6.04	6.66	7.91	9.17	10.45	11.73	14.31
.86	4.52	5.07	5.67	6.31	6.96	8.28	9.63	10.98	12.34	15.07
.88	4.68	5.26	5.90	6.57	7.26	8.67	10.10	11.53	12.97	15.87
.90	4.84	5.45	6.13	6.85	7.58	9.07	10.58	12.10	13.62	16.68
.92	5.00	5.65	6.37	7.13	7.90	9.48	11.07	12.68	14.29	17.52
.94	5.17	5.85	6.61	7.41	8.23	9.89	11.58	13.27	14.97	18.39
.96	5.33	6.05	6.86	7.70	8.57	10.32	12.10	13.89	15.68	19.28
.98	5.50	6.26	7.11	8.00	8.91	10.76	12.63	14.51	16.40	20.19
1.00	5.67	6.47	7.37	8.30	9.26	11.21	13.18	15.16	17.15	21.13

Table 8-6. For Determining the Discharge Q of a Trapezoidal
Channel When Flow Is at Critical Depth

Let z = side slopes of channel expressed as ratio of horizontal to vertical; also
let $\dfrac{\text{depth of water}}{\text{bottom width of channel}} = \dfrac{D_c}{b}$. The table gives values of c_1 correspond-

ing to different values of $\dfrac{D_c z}{b}$ in the formula $Q = c_1 b D_c{}^{3/2}$.

$\dfrac{D_c z}{b}$	.00	.01	.02	.03	.04	.05	.06	.07	.08	.09
.0	5.67	5.70	5.73	5.76	5.79	5.82	5.85	5.88	5.91	5.94
.1	5.97	6.00	6.04	6.07	6.10	6.13	6.17	6.20	6.23	6.27
.2	6.30	6.33	6.37	6.40	6.44	6.47	6.51	6.54	6.58	6.61
.3	6.65	6.68	6.72	6.75	6.79	6.82	6.86	6.89	6.93	6.97
.4	7.00	7.04	7.07	7.11	7.15	7.18	7.22	7.26	7.29	7.33
.5	7.37	7.40	7.44	7.48	7.51	7.55	7.59	7.63	7.66	7.70
.6	7.74	7.78	7.81	7.85	7.89	7.93	7.96	8.00	8.04	8.08
.7	8.11	8.15	8.19	8.23	8.27	8.30	8.34	8.38	8.42	8.46
.8	8.49	8.53	8.57	8.61	8.65	8.68	8.72	8.76	8.80	8.84
.9	8.88	8.91	8.95	8.99	9.03	9.07	9.11	9.15	9.18	9.22
1.0	9.26	9.30	9.34	9.38	9.42	9.45	9.49	9.53	9.57	9.61
1.1	9.65	9.69	9.72	9.76	9.80	9.84	9.88	9.92	9.96	10.00
1.2	10.04	10.07	10.11	10.15	10.19	10.23	10.27	10.31	10.35	10.39
1.3	10.43	10.46	10.50	10.54	10.58	10.62	10.66	10.70	10.74	10.78
1.4	10.82	10.86	10.89	10.93	10.97	11.01	11.05	11.09	11.13	11.17
1.5	11.21	11.25	11.29	11.33	11.37	11.40	11.44	11.48	11.52	11.56
1.6	11.60	11.64	11.68	11.72	11.76	11.80	11.84	11.88	11.92	11.95
1.7	11.99	12.03	12.07	12.11	12.15	12.19	12.23	12.27	12.31	12.35
1.8	12.39	12.43	12.47	12.51	12.55	12.59	12.63	12.66	12.70	12.74
1.9	12.78	12.82	12.86	12.90	12.94	12.98	13.02	13.06	13.10	13.14
2.0	13.18	13.22	13.26	13.30	13.34	13.38	13.42	13.46	13.49	13.53
2.1	13.57	13.61	13.65	13.69	13.73	13.77	13.81	13.85	13.89	13.93
2.2	13.97	14.01	14.05	14.09	14.13	14.17	14.21	14.25	14.29	14.33
2.3	14.37	14.41	14.45	14.48	14.52	14.56	14.60	14.64	14.68	14.72
2.4	14.76	14.80	14.84	14.88	14.92	14.96	15.00	15.04	15.08	15.12
2.5	15.16	15.20	15.24	15.28	15.32	15.36	15.40	15.44	15.48	15.52
2.6	15.56	15.60	15.64	15.68	15.72	15.76	15.80	15.83	15.87	15.91
2.7	15.95	15.99	16.03	16.07	16.11	16.15	16.19	16.23	16.27	16.31
2.8	16.35	16.39	16.43	16.47	16.51	16.55	16.59	16.63	16.67	16.71
2.9	16.75	16.79	16.83	16.87	16.91	16.95	16.99	17.03	17.07	17.11
3.0	17.15	17.19	17.23	17.27	17.31	17.35	17.39	17.43	17.47	17.51
3.1	17.55	17.59	17.63	17.67	17.70	17.74	17.78	17.82	17.86	17.90
3.2	17.94	17.98	18.02	18.06	18.10	18.14	18.18	18.22	18.26	18.30
3.3	18.34	18.38	18.42	18.46	18.50	18.54	18.58	18.62	18.66	18.70
3.4	18.74	18.78	18.82	18.86	18.90	18.94	18.98	19.02	19.06	19.10
3.5	19.14	19.18	19.22	19.26	19.30	19.34	19.38	19.42	19.46	19.50
3.6	19.54	19.58	19.62	19.66	19.70	19.74	19.78	19.82	19.86	19.90
3.7	19.94	19.98	20.02	20.06	20.10	20.14	20.18	20.22	20.26	20.30
3.8	20.34	20.38	20.42	20.46	20.50	20.54	20.58	20.62	20.66	20.70
3.9	20.74	20.78	20.82	20.86	20.89	20.93	20.97	21.01	21.05	21.09

Table 8-7. For Determining the Discharge Q of a Trapezoidal Channel When Flow Is at Critical Depth

Let z = side slopes of channel expressed as a ratio of horizontal to vertical, let H_m = energy head, and let b = bottom width of channel. The table gives values of c_2 corresponding to different values of $H_m z/b$ in the formula

$$Q = c_2 b H_m^{3/2}.$$

$\frac{H_m z}{b}$	.00	.01	.02	.03	.04	.05	.06	.07	.08	.09
.0	3.09	3.11	3.13	3.15	3.17	3.19	3.21	3.23	3.25	3.27
.1	3.29	3.32	3.34	3.36	3.38	3.40	3.42	3.44	3.46	3.49
.2	3.51	3.53	3.55	3.57	3.59	3.61	3.63	3.66	3.68	3.70
.3	3.72	3.74	3.76	3.79	3.81	3.83	3.85	3.87	3.89	3.92
.4	3.94	3.96	3.98	4.00	4.02	4.05	4.07	4.09	4.11	4.13
.5	4.16	4.18	4.20	4.22	4.24	4.27	4.29	4.31	4.33	4.35
.6	4.38	4.40	4.42	4.44	4.46	4.49	4.51	4.53	4.55	4.57
.7	4.60	4.62	4.64	4.66	4.69	4.71	4.73	4.75	4.77	4.80
.8	4.82	4.84	4.86	4.89	4.91	4.93	4.95	4.97	5.00	5.02
.9	5.04	5.06	5.09	5.11	5.13	5.15	5.18	5.20	5.22	5.24
1.0	5.27	5.29	5.31	5.33	5.36	5.38	5.40	5.42	5.44	5.47
1.1	5.49	5.51	5.53	5.56	5.58	5.60	5.62	5.65	5.67	5.69
1.2	5.71	5.74	5.76	5.78	5.80	5.83	5.85	5.87	5.89	5.92
1.3	5.94	5.96	5.98	6.01	6.03	6.05	6.07	6.10	6.12	6.14
1.4	6.17	6.19	6.21	6.23	6.26	6.28	6.30	6.32	6.35	6.37
1.5	6.39	6.41	6.44	6.46	6.48	6.50	6.53	6.55	6.57	6.59
1.6	6.62	6.64	6.66	6.69	6.71	6.73	6.75	6.78	6.80	6.82
1.7	6.84	6.87	6.89	6.91	6.93	6.96	6.98	7.00	7.03	7.05
1.8	7.07	7.09	7.12	7.14	7.16	7.18	7.21	7.23	7.25	7.28
1.9	7.30	7.32	7.34	7.37	7.39	7.41	7.43	7.46	7.48	7.50
2.0	7.52	7.55	7.57	7.59	7.62	7.64	7.66	7.68	7.71	7.73
2.1	7.75	7.77	7.80	7.82	7.84	7.87	7.89	7.91	7.93	7.96
2.2	7.98	8.00	8.02	8.05	8.07	8.09	8.12	8.14	8.16	8.18
2.3	8.21	8.23	8.25	8.28	8.30	8.32	8.34	8.37	8.39	8.41
2.4	8.43	8.46	8.48	8.50	8.53	8.55	8.57	8.59	8.62	8.64
2.5	8.66	8.69	8.71	8.73	8.75	8.78	8.80	8.82	8.85	8.87
2.6	8.89	8.91	8.94	8.96	8.98	9.00	9.03	9.05	9.07	9.10
2.7	9.12	9.14	9.16	9.19	9.21	9.23	9.26	9.28	9.30	9.32
2.8	9.35	9.37	9.39	9.42	9.44	9.46	9.48	9.51	9.53	9.55
2.9	9.57	9.60	9.62	9.64	9.67	9.69	9.71	9.73	9.76	9.78
3.0	9.80	9.83	9.85	9.87	9.89	9.92	9.94	9.96	9.99	10.01
3.1	10.03	10.05	10.08	10.10	10.12	10.15	10.17	10.19	10.21	10.24
3.2	10.26	10.28	10.31	10.33	10.35	10.37	10.40	10.42	10.44	10.47
3.3	10.49	10.51	10.53	10.56	10.58	10.60	10.63	10.65	10.67	10.69
3.4	10.72	10.74	10.76	10.79	10.81	10.83	10.85	10.88	10.90	10.92
3.5	10.95	10.97	10.99	11.01	11.04	11.06	11.08	11.11	11.13	11.15
3.6	11.17	11.20	11.22	11.24	11.27	11.29	11.31	11.33	11.36	11.38
3.7	11.40	11.43	11.45	11.47	11.49	11.52	11.54	11.56	11.59	11.61
3.8	11.63	11.65	11.68	11.70	11.72	11.75	11.77	11.79	11.81	11.84
3.9	11.86	11.88	11.91	11.93	11.95	11.97	12.00	12.02	12.04	12.07

Table 8-8. Critical Depth for Trapezoidal Sections

Let H_m = energy head and b = bottom width of channel. If c = tabulated value, $D_c = cH_m$.

$\dfrac{H_m}{b}$	Side slopes of channel, ratio of horizontal to vertical									
	Vertical	¼–1	½–1	¾–1	1–1	1½–1	2–1	2½–1	3–1	4–1
.00		.667	.667	.667	.667	.667	.667	.667	.667	.667
.01	.667	.667	.667	.668	.668	.669	.670	.670	.671	.672
.02	.667	.667	.668	.669	.670	.671	.672	.674	.675	.678
.03	.667	.668	.669	.670	.671	.673	.675	.677	.679	.683
.04	.667	.668	.670	.671	.672	.675	.677	.680	.683	.687
.05	.667	.668	.670	.672	.674	.677	.680	.683	.686	.692
.06	.667	.669	.671	.673	.675	.679	.683	.686	.690	.696
.07	.667	.669	.672	.674	.676	.681	.685	.689	.693	.699
.08	.667	.670	.672	.675	.678	.683	.687	.692	.696	.703
.09	.667	.670	.673	.676	.679	.684	.690	.695	.698	.706
.10	.667	.670	.674	.677	.680	.686	.692	.697	.701	.709
.12	.667	.671	.675	.679	.684	.690	.696	.701	.706	.715
.14	.667	.672	.676	.681	.686	.693	.699	.705	.711	.720
.16	.667	.672	.678	.683	.687	.696	.703	.709	.715	.725
.18	.667	.673	.679	.684	.690	.698	.706	.713	.719	.729
.20	.667	.674	.680	.686	.692	.701	.709	.717	.723	.733
.22	.667	.674	.681	.688	.694	.704	.712	.720	.726	.736
.24	.667	.675	.683	.689	.696	.706	.715	.723	.729	.739
.26	.667	.676	.684	.691	.698	.709	.718	.725	.732	.742
.28	.667	.676	.685	.693	.699	.711	.720	.728	.734	.744
.30	.667	.677	.686	.694	.701	.713	.723	.730	.737	.747
.32	.667	.678	.687	.696	.703	.715	.725	.733	.739	.749
.34	.667	.678	.689	.697	.705	.717	.727	.735	.741	.751
.36	.667	.679	.690	.699	.706	.719	.729	.737	.743	.752
.38	.667	.680	.691	.700	.708	.721	.731	.738	.745	.754
.40	.667	.680	.692	.701	.709	.723	.733	.740	.747	.756
.42	.667	.681	.693	.703	.711	.725	.734	.742	.748	.757
.44	.667	.681	.694	.704	.712	.727	.736	.744	.750	.759
.46	.667	.682	.695	.705	.714	.728	.737	.745	.751	.760
.48	.667	.683	.696	.706	.715	.729	.739	.747	.752	.761
.5	.667	.683	.697	.708	.717	.730	.740	.748	.754	.762
.6	.667	.686	.701	.713	.723	.737	.747	.754	.759	.767
.7	.667	.688	.706	.718	.728	.742	.752	.758	.764	.771
.8	.667	.692	.709	.723	.732	.746	.756	.762	.767	.774
.9	.667	.694	.713	.727	.737	.750	.759	.766	.770	.776
1.0	.667	.697	.717	.730	.740	.754	.762	.768	.773	.778
1.2	.667	.701	.723	.737	.747	.759	.767	.772	.776	.782
1.4	.667	.706	.729	.742	.752	.764	.771	.776	.779	.784
1.6	.667	.709	.733	.747	.756	.767	.774	.778	.781	.786
1.8	.667	.713	.737	.750	.759	.770	.776	.781	.783	.787
2	.667	.717	.740	.754	.762	.773	.778	.782	.785	.788
3	.667	.730	.753	.766	.773	.781	.785	.787	.790	.792
4	.667	.740	.762	.773	.778	.785	.788	.790	.792	.794
5	.667	.748	.768	.777	.782	.788	.791	.792	.794	.795
10	.667	.768	.782	.788	.791	.794	.795	.796	.797	.798
∞		.800	.800	.800	.800	.800	.800	.800	.800	.800

Table 8-9. For Determining the Discharge Q of a Circular Channel Flowing Part Full When Flow Is at Critical Depth

Let $\dfrac{\text{depth of water}}{\text{diameter of channel}} = \dfrac{D_c}{d}$ and K_c the tabulated value. Then $Q = K_c D_c^{5/2}$.

$\dfrac{D_c}{d}$	.00	.01	.02	.03	.04	.05	.06	.07	.08	.09
.0		61.59	43.49	35.43	30.62	27.33	24.90	22.98	21.48	20.21
.1	19.13	18.20	17.39	16.68	16.04	15.46	14.94	14.46	14.03	13.63
.2	13.25	12.91	12.59	12.28	12.00	11.73	11.48	11.24	11.02	10.80
.3	10.60	10.41	10.22	10.05	9.88	9.71	9.56	9.41	9.27	9.13
.4	9.00	8.87	8.74	8.63	8.51	8.40	8.29	8.19	8.09	7.99
.5	7.89	7.80	7.71	7.63	7.54	7.46	7.38	7.31	7.23	7.16
.6	7.09	7.02	6.96	6.89	6.83	6.77	6.71	6.66	6.60	6.55
.7	6.50	6.45	6.41	6.36	6.32	6.28	6.25	6.21	6.18	6.15
.8	6.12	6.10	6.08	6.06	6.05	6.05	6.05	6.05	6.06	6.09
.9	6.12	6.17	6.23	6.32	6.44	6.61	6.84	7.20	7.79	9.05

Table 8-10. For Determining the Discharge Q of a Circular Channel Flowing Part Full When Flow Is at Critical Depth

Let $\dfrac{\text{depth of water}}{\text{diameter of channel}} = \dfrac{D_c}{d}$ and let $K_c' =$ tabulated value.
Then $Q = K_c' d^{5/2}$.

$\dfrac{D_c}{d}$	.00	.01	.02	.03	.04	.05	.06	.07	.08	.09
.0		.0006	.0025	.0055	.0098	.0153	.0220	.0298	.0389	.0491
.1	.0605	.0731	.0868	.1016	.1176	.1347	.1530	.1724	.1928	.2144
.2	.2371	.2609	.2857	.3116	.3386	.3666	.3957	.4259	.4571	.4893
.3	.523	.557	.592	.628	.666	.704	.743	.784	.825	.867
.4	.910	.955	1.000	1.046	1.093	1.141	1.190	1.240	1.291	1.343
.5	1.396	1.449	1.504	1.560	1.616	1.674	1.733	1.792	1.853	1.915
.6	1.977	2.041	2.106	2.172	2.239	2.307	2.376	2.446	2.518	2.591
.7	2.666	2.741	2.819	2.898	2.978	3.061	3.145	3.231	3.320	3.411
.8	3.505	3.602	3.702	3.806	3.914	4.028	4.147	4.272	4.406	4.549
.9	4.70	4.87	5.06	5.27	5.52	5.81	6.18	6.67	7.41	8.83

Table 8-11. Critical Depth for Circular Sections

Let H_m = energy head and d = diameter of channel.   If c = tabulated value,
$$D_c = cH_m.$$

$\dfrac{H_m}{d}$	.00	.01	.02	.03	.04	.05	.06	.07	.08	.09
.0	.750	.750	.750	.749	.749	.749	.748	.748	.748	.747
.1	.747	.747	.746	.746	.746	.745	.745	.745	.744	.744
.2	.744	.743	.743	.743	.742	.742	.741	.741	.741	.740
.3	.740	.740	.739	.739	.738	.738	.737	.737	.736	.736
.4	.736	.735	.735	.734	.734	.733	.733	.732	.732	.731
.5	.730	.730	.729	.729	.728	.728	.727	.727	.726	.725
.6	.725	.724	.723	.723	.722	.721	.721	.720	.719	.719
.7	.718	.717	.716	.716	.715	.714	.713	.712	.711	.711
.8	.710	.709	.708	.707	.706	.705	.704	.703	.702	.701
.9	.700	.699	.698	.697	.696	.695	.693	.692	.691	.690
1.0	.689	.687	.686	.685	.683	.682	.681	.679	.678	.677
1.1	.675	.673	.672	.670	.669	.667	.665	.664	.662	.660
1.2	.659	.657	.655	.654	.652	.650	.648	.646	.644	.642
1.3	.640	.638	.636	.634	.632	.630	.628	.626	.624	.622
1.4	.620	.617	.615	.613	.610	.608	.606	.604	.601	.599
1.5	.596	.594	.592	.589	.587	.585	.582	.580	.578	.575
1.6	.573	.571	.568	.566	.564	.561	.559	.556	.554	.551
1.7	.549	.547	.545	.542	.540	.538	.535	.533	.531	.528
1.8	.526	.524	.521	.519	.517	.514	.512	.510	.508	.506
1.9	.503	.501	.499	.497	.495	.492	.490	.488	.486	.484
2.0	.482	.480	.478	.476	.474	.472	.470	.468	.466	.464

Table 8-12. For Determining the Discharge Q of a Circular Channel Flowing Part Full When Flow Is at Critical Depth

Let $\dfrac{\text{energy head}}{\text{diameter of channel}} = \dfrac{H_m}{d}$ and let $K_c' =$ tabulated value. Then

$$Q = K_c' d^{5/2}.$$

$\dfrac{H_m}{d}$	.00	.01	.02	.03	.04	.05	.06	.07	.08	.09
.0	.0000	.0004	.0014	.0031	.0056	.0086	.0123	.0167	.0219	.0275
.1	.0339	.0409	.0486	.0571	.0660	.0755	.0858	.0965	.1079	.1199
.2	.1326	.1458	.1595	.1739	.1889	.2045	.2206	.2372	.2545	.2723
.3	.291	.310	.329	.349	.370	.391	.412	.434	.457	.480
.4	.503	.527	.552	.577	.602	.628	.654	.681	.708	.736
.5	.764	.793	.822	.851	.881	.911	.942	.973	1.004	1.036
.6	1.068	1.101	1.134	1.167	1.200	1.234	1.268	1.303	1.338	1.373
.7	1.409	1.445	1.481	1.517	1.554	1.591	1.628	1.665	1.703	1.741
.8	1.779	1.818	1.856	1.895	1.934	1.973	2.012	2.052	2.092	2.132
.9	2.172	2.212	2.253	2.294	2.334	2.375	2.416	2.457	2.498	2.540
1.0	2.581	2.623	2.664	2.706	2.748	2.789	2.831	2.873	2.915	2.957
1.1	2.999	3.041	3.083	3.124	3.166	3.208	3.250	3.292	3.334	3.376
1.2	3.42	3.46	3.50	3.54	3.58	3.62	3.67	3.71	3.75	3.79
1.3	3.83	3.87	3.91	3.95	3.99	4.03	4.08	4.12	4.16	4.20
1.4	4.24	4.28	4.31	4.35	4.39	4.43	4.47	4.51	4.55	4.59
1.5	4.62	4.66	4.70	4.74	4.78	4.81	4.85	4.89	4.93	4.96
1.6	5.00	5.04	5.07	5.11	5.14	5.18	5.21	5.25	5.29	5.32
1.7	5.36	5.39	5.43	5.46	5.50	5.53	5.56	5.60	5.63	5.67
1.8	5.70	5.73	5.77	5.80	5.83	5.86	5.90	5.93	5.96	5.99
1.9	6.03	6.06	6.09	6.12	6.15	6.18	6.22	6.25	6.28	6.31
2.0	6.34	6.37	6.40	6.43	6.46	6.49	6.52	6.55	6.58	6.61

Table 8-13. Higher Stage of Equal Energy and Hydraulic Jump for Trapezoidal Channels

D_1 = depth before jump; z = side slope of channel, horizontal to vertical; H_1 = energy head before jump; b = bottom width of channel. Figures in top row multiplied by H_1 give higher stage of equal energy. Figures in bottom row multiplied by H_1 give depth after jump. First column is for rectangular channels. Last column is for triangular channels

$\dfrac{D_1}{H_1}$	$\dfrac{zH_1}{b}$												
	0	0.1	0.2	0.3	0.4	0.5	0.6	0.7	0.8	0.9	1.0	10	∞
.05	.99	.99											
	.41	.41	.40	.39	.39	.38	.38	.37	.37	.36	.36	.31	.24
.10	.99	.99	.99	.99	.99								
	.56	.55	.55	.54	.53	.53	.52	.52	.51	.51	.50	.42	.37
.15	.98	.98	.99	.99	.99	.99	.99	.99	.99	.99	.99		
	.65	.64	.64	.63	.62	.62	.61	.61	.61	.60	.60	.52	.48
.20	.97	.97	.98	.98	.98	.98	.99	.99	.99	.98	.99		
	.71	.70	.70	.69	.69	.69	.68	.68	.68	.67	.67	.60	.56
.25	.95	.95	.96	.97	.97	.97	.98	.98	.98	.98	.98	.99	
	.75	.75	.74	.74	.74	.73	.73	.73	.73	.73	.72	.66	.63
.30	.92	.93	.94	.95	.95	.96	.97	.97	.97	.97	.97	.99	
	.78	.78	.78	.78	.77	.77	.77	.77	.77	.77	.77	.72	.69
.35	.90	.91	.92	.93	.94	.94	.95	.95	.95	.95	.96	.98	.99
	.79	.80	.80	.80	.80	.80	.80	.80	.80	.80	.80	.76	.75
.40	.87	.89	.90	.91	.92	.92	.93	.93	.93	.94	.95	.98	.99
	.80	.80	.81	.81	.81	.82	.82	.82	.82	.82	.82	.80	.79
.45	.84	.86	.87	.88	.89	.90	.91	.91	.92	.92	.93	.97	.98
	.80	.80	.81	.82	.82	.83	.83	.83	.83	.83	.83	.84	.83
.50	.81	.83	.85	.86	.87	.87	.88	.89	.90	.90	.91	.96	.97
	.78	.79	.80	.80	.81	.82	.83	.83	.83	.84	.84	.86	.85
.55	.77	.79	.81	.82	.83	.85	.86	.87	.87	.88	.88	.94	.95
	.76	.77	.78	.79	.80	.81	.82	.83	.83	.83	.84	.87	.87
.60	.73	.75	.77	.79	.80	.82	.82	.83	.84	.85	.85	.92	.93
	.73	.74	.76	.77	.79	.80	.81	.81	.82	.82	.83	.87	.88
.65	.69	.71	.73	.74	.76	.78	.79	.80	.81	.81	.82	.89	.91
	.69	.71	.73	.74	.76	.77	.78	.79	.80	.80	.81	.87	.88
.70	...	...	...	...	.72	.73	.74	.75	.76	.77	.78	.86	.88
	...	...	...	...	.72	.73	.74	.75	.76	.77	.78	.85	.87
.75	...	...	...	...	...	...	...	...	...	...	...	.83	.85
	...	...	...	...	...	...	...	...	...	...	...	.83	.84
D_c	.67	.68	.69	.70	.71	.72	.72	.73	.73	.74	.74	.79	.80

Table 8-14. Depth after Hydraulic Jump for Rectangular Cross Sections

D_1	V_1									
	5	6	7	8	9	10	11	12	13	14
.1	.35	.43	.50	.58	.66	.74	.82	.90	.98	1.06
.2	.47	.58	.69	.80	.91	1.02	1.13	1.24	1.35	1.46
.3	.55	.68	.82	.95	1.09	1.22	1.36	1.50	1.63	1.77
.4	.61	.77	.92	1.08	1.23	1.39	1.55	1.70	1.86	2.02
.5	.67	.84	1.01	1.18	1.36	1.53	1.71	1.88	2.06	2.23
.6	.71	.90	1.09	1.27	1.46	1.66	1.85	2.04	2.23	2.42
.7	.75	.95	1.15	1.36	1.56	1.77	1.97	2.18	2.38	2.59
.8	.79	1.00	1.21	1.43	1.65	1.87	2.09	2.31	2.53	2.75
.9	...	1.04	1.27	1.50	1.73	1.96	2.19	2.42	2.66	2.89
1.0	...	1.08	1.32	1.56	1.80	2.04	2.29	2.53	2.78	3.03
1.1	...	1.12	1.37	1.62	1.87	2.12	2.38	2.63	2.89	3.15
1.2	...	...	1.41	1.67	1.93	2.20	2.46	2.73	3.00	3.27
1.3	...	...	1.45	1.72	1.99	2.27	2.54	2.82	3.10	3.38
1.4	...	...	1.48	1.76	2.05	2.33	2.62	2.91	3.20	3.49
1.5	...	...	1.52	1.81	2.10	2.40	2.69	2.99	3.29	3.59
1.6	...	....	....	1.85	2.15	2.46	2.76	3.07	3.38	3.69
1.7	...	....	....	1.89	2.20	2.51	2.83	3.14	3.46	3.78
1.8	...	....	....	1.93	2.25	2.57	2.89	3.21	3.54	3.87
1.9	...	....	....	1.96	2.29	2.62	2.95	3.28	3.62	3.96
2.0	...	....	....	2.00	2.33	2.67	3.01	3.35	3.69	4.04
2.1	...	....	....	....	2.37	2.72	3.07	3.42	3.77	4.12
2.2	...	....	....	....	2.41	2.76	3.12	3.48	3.84	4.19
2.3	....	....	....	....	2.45	2.81	3.17	3.54	3.90	4.27
2.4	...	....	....	....	2.48	2.85	3.22	3.60	3.97	4.34
2.5	...	....	....	....	2.52	2.89	3.27	3.65	4.03	4.41
2.6	...	....	....	....	....	2.93	3.32	3.71	4.09	4.48
2.7	...	....	....	....	....	2.97	3.37	3.76	4.15	4.54
2.8	...	....	....	....	....	3.01	3.41	3.81	4.21	4.61
2.9	...	....	....	....	....	3.04	3.45	3.86	4.26	4.67
3.0	...	....	....	....	....	3.08	3.49	3.90	4.31	4.73
3.1	...	....	....	....	....	3.11	3.53	3.95	4.37	4.79
3.2	...	....	....	....	....	....	3.57	3.99	4.42	4.85
3.3	...	....	....	....	....	....	3.61	4.04	4.47	4.91
3.4	...	....	....	....	....	....	3.65	4.08	4.52	4.96
3.5	...	....	....	....	....	....	3.68	4.12	4.57	5.01
3.6	...	....	....	....	....	....	3.72	4.16	4.61	5.07
3.7	...	....	....	....	....	....	3.75	4.20	4.66	5.12
3.8	...	....	....	....	....	....	3.79	4.24	4.70	5.17
3.9	...	....	....	....	....	....	....	4.28	4.75	5.22
4.0	...	....	....	....	....	....	....	4.32	4.79	5.27
4.1	...	....	....	....	....	....	....	4.35	4.83	5.31
4.2	...	....	....	....	....	....	....	4.39	4.87	5.36
4.3	...	....	....	....	....	....	....	4.43	4.91	5.41
4.4	...	....	....	....	....	....	....	4.46	4.95	5.45
4.5	...	....	....	....	....	....	....	4.50	4.99	5.50
4.6	...	....	....	....	....	....	....	....	5.03	5.54
4.7	...	....	....	....	....	....	....	....	5.07	5.58
4.8	...	....	....	....	....	....	....	....	5.11	5.62
4.9	...	....	....	....	....	....	....	....	5.14	5.66
5.0	...	....	....	....	....	....	....	....	5.18	5.70

Table 8-14. Depth after Hydraulic Jump for Rectangular
Cross Sections (*Concluded*)

D_1	V_1									
	15	20	25	30	35	40	45	50	55	60
.1	1.13	1.53								
.2	1.58	2.13	2.69							
.3	1.90	2.59	3.27							
.4	2.17	2.96	3.75	4.54						
.5	2.41	3.29	4.17	5.05						
.6	2.61	3.58	4.54	5.50						
.7	2.80	3.84	4.88	5.92	6.96					
.8	2.97	4.08	5.19	6.30	7.41					
.9	3.13	4.31	5.48	6.66	7.84					
1.0	3.27	4.51	5.75	7.00	8.24	9.49	10.73	11.98	13.23	14.47
1.1	3.41	4.71	6.01	7.32	8.62	9.93	11.23	12.54	13.85	15.15
1.2	3.55	4.90	6.25	7.62	8.98	10.34	11.71	13.07	14.44	15.80
1.3	3.67	5.07	6.48	7.90	9.32	10.74	12.16	13.58	15.00	16.42
1.4	3.79	5.24	6.71	8.18	9.65	11.12	12.60	14.07	15.54	17.02
1.5	3.90	5.40	6.92	8.44	9.97	11.49	13.01	14.54	16.06	17.59
1.6	4.00	5.56	7.13	8.70	10.27	11.84	13.42	14.99	16.57	18.14
1.7	4.10	5.71	7.32	8.94	10.56	12.18	13.81	15.43	17.05	18.68
1.8	4.20	5.85	7.51	9.18	10.84	12.51	14.18	15.85	17.52	19.19
1.9	4.29	5.99	7.70	9.41	11.12	12.83	14.55	16.26	17.98	19.70
2.0	4.38	6.12	7.87	9.63	11.38	13.14	14.90	16.66	18.42	20.18
2.1	4.47	6.25	8.04	9.84	11.64	13.45	15.25	17.05	18.85	20.66
2.2	4.56	6.38	8.21	10.05	11.89	13.74	15.58	17.43	19.27	21.12
2.3	4.64	6.50	8.38	10.26	12.14	14.02	15.91	17.80	19.68	21.57
2.4	4.72	6.62	8.53	10.45	12.38	14.30	16.23	18.15	20.08	22.01
2.5	4.80	6.73	8.69	10.65	12.61	14.57	16.54	18.50	20.47	22.44
2.6	4.87	6.85	8.84	10.83	12.83	14.84	16.84	18.85	20.85	22.86
2.7	4.94	6.96	8.98	11.02	13.05	15.10	17.14	19.18	21.23	23.27
2.8	5.01	7.06	9.13	11.20	13.27	15.35	17.43	19.51	21.59	23.67
2.9	5.08	7.17	9.27	11.37	13.48	15.60	17.72	19.83	21.95	24.07
3.0	5.15	7.27	9.40	11.54	13.69	15.84	18.00	20.15	22.30	24.46
3.1	5.22	7.37	9.54	11.72	13.90	16.08	18.27	20.46	22.65	24.84
3.2	5.28	7.47	9.67	11.88	14.10	16.32	18.54	20.76	22.99	25.22
3.3	5.34	7.56	9.80	12.04	14.29	16.55	18.80	21.06	23.32	25.58
3.4	5.41	7.65	9.92	12.20	14.48	16.77	19.06	21.35	23.65	25.94
3.5	5.47	7.74	10.04	12.35	14.67	16.99	19.32	21.64	23.97	26.30
3.6	5.53	7.83	10.17	12.51	14.86	17.21	19.57	21.93	24.29	26.65
3.7	5.58	7.92	10.28	12.66	15.04	17.43	19.82	22.21	24.60	26.99
3.8	5.64	8.01	10.40	12.81	15.22	17.64	20.06	22.48	24.90	27.33
3.9	5.69	8.09	10.52	12.96	15.40	17.85	20.30	22.75	25.20	27.66
4.0	5.75	8.17	10.63	13.10	15.57	18.05	20.53	23.02	25.50	27.99
4.1	5.80	8.26	10.74	13.24	15.74	18.25	20.76	23.28	25.80	28.31
4.2	5.85	8.34	10.85	13.38	15.91	18.45	20.99	23.54	26.09	28.64
4.3	5.90	8.41	10.96	13.51	16.07	18.65	21.22	23.79	26.37	28.95
4.4	5.95	8.49	11.06	13.65	16.24	18.84	21.44	24.05	26.65	29.26
4.5	6.00	8.57	11.17	13.78	16.40	19.03	21.66	24.30	26.93	29.57
4.6	6.05	8.64	11.27	13.91	16.56	19.22	21.88	24.54	27.21	29.87
4.7	6.10	8.72	11.37	14.04	16.72	19.41	22.09	24.78	27.48	30.17
4.8	6.15	8.79	11.47	14.17	16.87	19.59	22.30	25.02	27.75	30.47
4.9	6.19	8.86	11.57	14.30	17.03	19.77	22.51	25.26	28.01	30.76
5.0	6.24	8.93	11.66	14.42	17.18	19.95	22.72	25.49	28.27	31.05

SECTION 9

HIGH - VELOCITY TRANSITIONS

When water flows at supercritical velocities $(D < D_c)$ a change in alignment of the walls of a channel creates standing-wave patterns which must be taken into consideration in the design of a channel. When the change in alignment turns the water toward the center of the channel, as in a constriction or at the outside wall of a bend, the waves create depths which are considerably in excess of those that would be expected under subcritical conditions. Changes in alignment which permit the water to turn away from the center of a channel create negative waves, or depressions. The principles involved, as well as the results of laboratory verifications, have been set forth in a symposium.[1]

Straight-walled Constrictions. The analytical and experimental study of channel constrictions indicated that straight-walled constrictions are more satisfactory than the smoothly curved transitions used for subcritical flow (p. 8-31).

The effect of a change in wall alignment toward the center line of the original channel is illustrated in Fig. 9-1. The original velocity, depth, and Froude number are V_1, D_1, and F_1, respectively. The wall is turned through an angle θ, which causes the fluid to turn through the same angle and flow at a new velocity V_2 with a depth D_2 and a Froude number F_2. The changes in depth and velocity occur along a wavefront bd oriented at the angle β with respect to the original direction of flow. A change in momentum normal to the wave occurs at the wave, the velocity components normal to the wave being

[1] High Velocity Flow in Open Channels: A Symposium, *Trans. ASCE*, vol. 116, p. 265, 1951. Arthur T. Ippen, Mechanics of Supercritical Flow; Robert T. Knapp, Design of Channel Curves for Supercritical Flow; Arthur T. Ippen and John H. Dawson, Design of Channel Contractions; Hunter Rouse, B. V. Bhoota, and En-Yun Hsu, Design of Channel Expansions.

reduced from V_{n1} to V_{n2}. It is assumed that the velocity components parallel to the wave, V_p, are not changed, so that

$$V_{p1} = V_{p2} \qquad (9\text{-}1)$$

Continuity requires that

$$q_{n1} = q_{n2} \qquad (9\text{-}2)$$

or

$$D_1 V_{n1} = D_2 V_{n2} \qquad (9\text{-}3)$$

Assuming that the applied force is due only to the difference in hydrostatic pressures, then a derivation identical with that

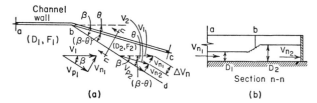

Fig. 9-1. Straight-walled constrictions, large changes in direction.

for the hydraulic jump (pp. 8-21, 8-25) yields the following expression:

$$Vn_1 = \sqrt{gD_1} \ \sqrt{\frac{D_2}{2D_1}\left(\frac{D_2}{D_1} + 1\right)} \qquad (9\text{-}4)$$

From Fig. 9-1a it may be seen that

$$\sin \beta = \frac{V_{n1}}{V_1} \qquad (9\text{-}5)$$

By inserting the value of Vn_1 from Eq. (9-4) and replacing $V_1/\sqrt{gD_1}$ with F_1, the following relationship is obtained:

$$\sin \beta = \frac{1}{F_1} \ \sqrt{\frac{D_2}{2D_1}\left(\frac{D_2}{D_1} + 1\right)} \qquad (9\text{-}6)$$

For small waves, in which $D_2 \to D_1$, Eq. (9-6) reduces to the following approximate relation between β and F_1:

$$\sin \beta = \frac{1}{F_1} \qquad (9\text{-}7)$$

Equation (9-7) is useful for determining the location of the disturbance line for very small channel irregularities, but its principal value is for curved walls or for enlarging sections, as will be shown later.

Equation (9-6) may be solved for D_2/D_1 to obtain the following expression:

$$\frac{D_2}{D_1} = \frac{\sqrt{1 + 8F_1^2 \sin^2 \beta} - 1}{2} \tag{9-8}$$

Values D_2/D_1 obtained from this equation are plotted against β for various values of F_1 in the upper right quadrant of Fig. 9-2.

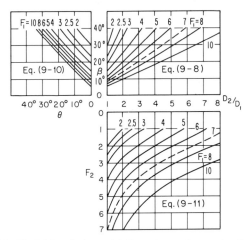

FIG. 9-2. Straight-walled constrictions, large changes in direction.

Trigonometric relationships for the vector triangles shown in Fig. 9-1a lead to the following expression for θ:

$$\tan \theta = \frac{(1 - D_1/D_2) \tan \beta}{1 + D_1/D_2 \tan^2 \beta} \tag{9-9}$$

If the value of D_2/D_1 from Eq. (9-8) is substituted in Eq. (9-9), the following expression involving β, F_1, and θ is obtained:

$$\tan \theta = \frac{(\sqrt{1 + 8F_1^2 \sin^2 \beta} - 3) \tan \beta}{2 \tan^2 \beta + \sqrt{1 + 8F_1^2 \sin^2 \beta} - 1} \tag{9-10}$$

This equation can be solved graphically by plotting θ against β for various values of F_1 as shown in the upper left quadrant of **Fig. 9-2.**

In order to determine the effects at a second change in direction, it is necessary to compute the value of F_2. Solution for F_2 may be accomplished by means of the following relationship derived from the velocity vector triangles of Fig. 9-1a:

$$V_{p1}{}^2 = V_1{}^2 - V_{n1}{}^2 = V_{p2}{}^2 = V_2{}^2 - V_{n2}{}^2$$

Then, making use of Eqs. (9-3) and (9-4) and inserting the Froude numbers, the following expression is obtained:

$$F_2{}^2 = \frac{D_1}{D_2}\left[F_1{}^2 - \frac{1}{2}\frac{D_1}{D_2}\left(\frac{D_2}{D_1} - 1\right)\left(\frac{D_2}{D_1} + 1\right)^2 \right] \quad (9\text{-}11)$$

This equation was used to derive values for the curves of F_2 versus D_2/D_1 shown in the lower right quadrant of Fig. 9-2. The curves are presented in the manner used by Ippen.[1]

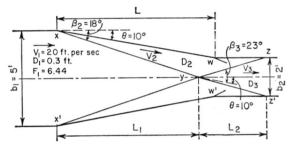

Fig. 9-3. Examples 9-1 and 9-2.

The application of these equations will be illustrated by means of a numerical problem.

Example 9-1. Water is flowing at a depth of 0.3 ft and a velocity of 20 ft per sec in a rectangular channel 5 ft wide. Determine the wave pattern and water depths if this channel is constricted by symmetrical straight walls to a width of 2.0 ft with θ taken as 10° (Fig. 9-3).

$$F_1 = \frac{V_1}{\sqrt{gD_1}} = 6.44$$

From Fig. 9-2, $\beta_2 = 18°$, $D_2/D_1 = 2.35$, and $F_2 = 4.05$ and $D_2 = 0.72$ ft.

As the water moves in the regions where the depth is D_2, it

[1] *Ibid.*

approaches the center from each side at an angle of 10°. At the center line it may be assumed that the velocity is again deflected through 10° ($\theta_2 = 10°$) and that the water again flows parallel to the center line. Then new standing waves yz and yz' are developed. The angle β_3 and the depth D_3 can be obtained from Fig. 9-2 by letting D_2 be D_1 and D_3 be D_2. Then $\beta_3 = 23°$, $F_3 = 2.85$, $D_3/D_2 = 1.8$, and $D_3 = 1.3$ ft. Following this second change in direction and depth, no further reflection will occur if $(L_1 + L_2) > L$. Investigation of this phase of the example will be continued after the following derivations.

A consideration of the geometry of Fig. 9-3 yields the following relationship involving dimensions of the plan of the constriction and the wave pattern:

$$L = \frac{b_1 - b_2}{2 \tan \theta} \tag{9-12}$$

$$L_1 = \frac{b_1}{2 \tan \beta_2} \tag{9-13}$$

$$L_2 = \frac{b_2}{2 \tan (\beta_3 - \theta)} \tag{9-14}$$

If $(L_2 + L_1) < L$, the point z would be upstream from the end of the transition, w, and another increase in depth would be created. Such a design is usually avoided. It should be noted that the equations developed in this section would not be valid if the downstream conditions were such that subcritical flow would occur ($F < 1$). Under such conditions flow in the constriction would be affected by a downstream control.

Example 9-1 (*continued*)
From Eq. (9-12):

$$L = \frac{5 - 2}{2 \times 0.1763} = 8.5 \text{ ft}$$

From Eq. (9-13):

$$L_1 = \frac{5}{2 \times 0.325} = 7.7 \text{ ft}$$

From Eq. (9-14):

$$L_2 = \frac{2}{2 \times 0.231} = 4.3 \text{ ft}$$

Thus $L_1 + L_2 = 12.0$, which is greater than L, and therefore D_3 would be the highest depth encountered. The depth D_3 will occur only in the region near the center line (Fig. 9-3), because negative waves will emanate from w and w', causing a decrease in depth.   Negative waves will be discussed in the following paragraphs.

Enlargements and Curved-wall Constrictions. In channel enlargements and in curved-wall constrictions, the change in direction takes place gradually instead of in one relatively steep standing wave (as for straight-wall constrictions) and the resulting wave configuration may be determined by considering the total change in fluid direction, θ, to be made up of many small angles, $\Delta\theta$. The following equations are based on Ippen's work.[1] For very small directional changes it has already been shown that Eq. (9-7) may be used to present the relationship between β and F_1.

$$\sin \beta = \frac{1}{F_1} \qquad (9\text{-}7)$$

Referring to the velocity vector triangles of Fig. 9-1a and assuming that θ is such a small angle, $d\theta$, that

$$\sin (90 + \beta - d\theta) = \sin (90 + \beta)$$

application of the law of sines yields the following relationship:

$$dV_n = \frac{-V\,d\theta}{\cos \beta} \qquad (9\text{-}15)$$

Application of the momentum relationship for very small changes in depth, dD, yields

$$-dV_n = \frac{g\,dD}{V_n} \qquad (9\text{-}16)$$

Then, from Eqs. (9-15) and (9-16),

$$\frac{dD}{d\theta} = \frac{V^2}{g} \tan \beta \qquad (9\text{-}17)$$

The specific energy H is defined as follows:

$$H = D + \frac{V^2}{2g} \qquad (9\text{-}18)$$

from which

$$V = \sqrt{2g(H - D)} \qquad (9\text{-}19)$$

or

$$\frac{H}{D} = 1 + F^2 \qquad (9\text{-}20)$$

[1] *Ibid.*

In the case of very small angles, Eq. (9-4) reduces to

$$V_n = \sqrt{gD} \qquad (9\text{-}21)$$

The vector triangles (Fig. 9-1a) yield the following relationship:

$$V_p = \sqrt{V^2 - V_n{}^2} \qquad (9\text{-}22)$$

and

$$\tan \beta = \frac{V_n}{V_p} \qquad (9\text{-}23)$$

Assuming that the specific energy H will be constant, Eqs. (9-17) to (9-23) can be combined to yield the following expression:

$$\frac{dD}{d\theta} = \frac{2H \sqrt{(D/2H)(1 - D/H)}}{\sqrt{1 - \tfrac{3}{2}(D/H)}} \qquad (9\text{-}24)$$

and upon integration

$$\theta + \theta_1 = \sqrt{3} \tan^{-1} \sqrt{\frac{D/\tfrac{2}{3}H}{1 - D/\tfrac{2}{3}H}} - \tan^{-1} \frac{1}{\sqrt{3}} \sqrt{\frac{D/\tfrac{2}{3}H}{1 - D/\tfrac{2}{3}H}} \qquad (9\text{-}25)$$

Equation (9-25) can also be stated in terms of F, using Eq. (9-20) as follows:

$$\theta + \theta_1 = \sqrt{3} \tan^{-1} \sqrt{\frac{3}{F^2 - 1}} - \tan^{-1} \sqrt{\frac{1}{F^2 - 1}} \qquad (9\text{-}26)$$

In these equations θ may be considered as $\Sigma(\Delta\theta)$ for any location. θ_1 may be evaluated by means of Eq. (9-25) or (9-26) for the original conditions, in which case $\theta = 0$, $V = V_1$, and $F = F_1 = V_1/\sqrt{gD_1}$. Values of $\theta + \theta_1$ for various values of D/H as obtained from Eq. (9-25) are plotted in Fig. 9-4. Also shown in Fig. 9-4 is a curve of F versus D/H, determined from Eq. (9-20).

Equations (9-25) and (9-26) are not intended to be used for abrupt straight-walled constrictions, because, by neglecting energy losses, the results cannot be expected to be as accurate as the use of the curves of Fig. 9-2. Yet, for angles as small as 10°, the differences in computed values of D_2 and F_2 are negligible and the straight-walled constriction shown in Fig. 9-3 will be used as the first illustration (Example 9-2) of the application of Eqs. (9-25) and (9-26). Example 9-3 illustrates the use of Eqs. (9-25) and (9-26) in the solution of a nonsymmetrical straight-walled constriction.

Example 9-2. Data are the same as in Example 9-1.

$$F_1 = 6.44 \qquad D_1 = 0.3' \qquad \theta = 10°$$

From Fig. 9-4, θ_1 is determined by entering at $F_1 = 6.44$, locating $D_1/H = 0.045$ and $\theta + \theta_1 = 17.20$. Then, when

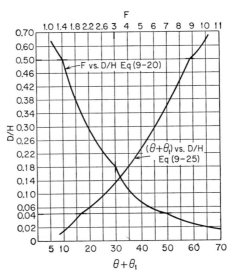

Fig. 9-4. D/H versus F and $\theta + \theta_1$ from Eqs. (9-20) and (9-25) respectively. (Note the changes in scale.)

$\theta = 10°$, $\theta + \theta_1 = 27.2°$ and from the curves $D_2/H = 0.11$ and $F_2 = 4.0$. Then $D_2 = 0.11/0.045 \times 0.30 = 0.73$ ft. As the water deflects through another 10° at the center line,

$$\theta + \theta_1 = 37.2°$$

and from the curves $D_3/H = 0.202$ and

$$D_3 = 0.202/0.11 \times 0.73 = 1.34 \text{ ft}$$

Although these values agree closely with those obtained in the previous example from Fig. 9-2, it should be noted that β must still be obtained from Eq. (9-8) or Fig. 9-2.

Example 9-3. Shown in Fig. 9-5*b* is a rectangular channel in which $F_1 = 4.0$, $V_1 = 25$ ft per sec, and $D_1 = 1.21$ ft. The left side, looking downstream, converges at an angle $\Delta\theta_{L1}$ of 4°, and the right side at an angle $\Delta\theta_{R1}$ of 2°. The problem is to determine the locations of the standing waves LC, RC, CL', and CR' and the water depths and velocities. Conditions after the first changes in direction, in the regions LCL' and RCR', could be determined from Fig. 9-2 as in Example 9-1; however, Eq. (9-25) and Fig. 9-4 will be used in this example.

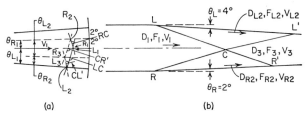

FIG. 9-5. Examples 9-3 and 9-5.

Entering Fig. 9-4 with $F_1 = 4.0$, then $D_1/H = 0.111$ and $\theta_1 = 27.2°$. Then $\Delta\theta_{L1} + \theta_1 = 31.2°$ and $\Delta\theta_{R1} + \theta_1 = 29.2°$. The corresponding values of the parameters as obtained from Fig. 9-4 are:

$$\frac{D_{L2}}{H} = 0.144 \qquad\qquad \frac{D_{R2}}{H} = 0.127$$

$$F_{L2} = 3.41 \qquad\qquad F_{R2} = 3.70$$

and

$$D_{L2} = \frac{0.144}{0.111} \times 1.21 \qquad D_{R2} = \frac{0.127}{0.111} \times 1.21$$

$$= 1.57 \text{ ft} \qquad\qquad = 1.38 \text{ ft}$$

After the waters from the two sides converge in the region downstream from $L'CR'$, a common velocity V_3, depth D_3, and Froude number F_3 must be attained. Since V_{L2} and V_{R2} differ in direction by $\Delta\theta_{L1} + \Delta\theta_{R1} = 6°$, it is apparent that the $\Delta\theta_{L2} + \Delta\theta_{R2}$ must also be 6°. Knowing this, the solution for D_3 and V_3 could be obtained from Fig. 9-2, by successive approximation. However, a consideration of Eq. (9-25), as plotted in Fig. 9-4, shows that a common depth and Froude number can be achieved only if

$$\Delta\theta_{L1} + \Delta\theta_{L2} + \theta_1 = \Delta\theta_{R1} + \Delta\theta_{R2} + \theta_1$$

or therefore $\Delta\theta_{L1} + \Delta\theta_{L2} = \Delta\theta_{R1} + \Delta\theta_{R2}$. Since $\Delta\theta_{L1}$ and $\Delta\theta_{R1}$ are 4° and 2°, respectively, it follows that $\Delta\theta_{L2} = 2°$ and $\Delta\theta_{R2} = 4°$. Then, knowing that $\Delta\theta_{L1} + \Delta\theta_{L2} + \theta_1 = 33.2°$, the following values may be obtained from Fig. 9-4:

$$\frac{D_3}{H} = 0.163 \qquad D_3 = \frac{0.163}{0.111} \times 1.21 = 1.78 \text{ ft}$$

and

$$F_3 = 3.2$$

V_3 can be obtained as follows:

$$F_3 = \frac{V_3}{\sqrt{gD_3}} = \frac{V_3}{\sqrt{32.3 \times 1.78}} = 3.2$$

and

$$V_3 = 24.2 \text{ ft per sec}$$

One of the most important applications of Eqs. (9-25) and (9-26) is in the computation of depths in an *enlarging section*. The method will be illustrated for the enlargement shown in Fig. 9-6. This example is one of those tested and reported by Ippen and Harleman.[1]

Example 9-4. A channel section is enlarged by a straight wall at an angle of 15°. $F_1 = 2.94$. The problem is to determine lines of equal depth, and thus establish the water-surface form. The assumption is made that the velocity will ultimately turn through the total 15° and that flow near the wall will turn without separation. The computations which are shown in the following table are carried forward in five uniform angular increments, $\Delta\theta$, of 3°. The value of θ_1 is found to be 35.7, from Fig. 9-4.

The water crosses the line $D_n/D_1 = 1.0$ with a velocity V_1. In the space between $D_n/D_1 = 1.0$ and $D_n/D_1 = D_2/D_1 = 0.84$, the velocity changes its magnitude to V_2 and its direction through $\Delta\theta = 3°$. At each line of D_n/D_1, the summation of

[1] Arthur T. Ippen and R. F. Harleman, Verification of Theory for Oblique Standing Waves, *Trans. ASCE*, vol. 121, p. 678, 1956.

angular increments is called $\Sigma_n \Delta\theta$. The subscripts n are given in column 1 of the following table. Values of F_n and D_n/H (columns 4 and 9) are read from Fig. 9-4, and values of β are computed from Eq. (9-7). Each β_n is the angle between the imaginary small wave, or line of constant D_n/D_1, and the velocity vector approaching that line, V_n, and since the angle between V_n and the original velocity V_1 is $\Sigma_n \Delta\theta$, the angle between lines of D_n/D_1 and V_1 is $\beta_n - \Sigma_n \Delta\theta$. This is illustrated in Fig. 9-6. Values of $\beta_n - \Sigma_n \Delta\theta$ are shown in column 8.

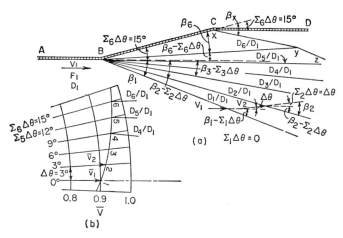

FIG. 9-6. Straight-walled enlargement, Examples 9-4 and 9-6.

These values provide a convenient method of locating the lines of equal depth. It follows also from the diagram that the angle between the new wall direction BC and any constant depth line D_n/D_1 is $\Sigma_6 \Delta\theta + (\beta_n - \Sigma_n \Delta\theta)$. This is of particular interest for the final line (D_6/D_1 in this case), beyond which no further changes in depth or velocity occur, because its angle with the new wall direction is then simply equal to β_6. Therefore the values of β_6, D_6, and F_6 can be computed without determining the intermediate conditions if this is all the information needed. The values of β and D_n/D_1 computed in this example differ by approximately 10 per cent from measured values.[1]

[1] *Ibid.*

(1)	(2)	(3)	(4)	(5)	(6)	(7)	(8)	(9)	(10)
n	$\theta + \theta_1$	$\Delta\theta$	F_n	$1/F_n$	β_n	$\Sigma_n \, \Delta\theta$	$\beta_n - \Sigma_n \, \Delta\theta$	D_n/H	D_n/D_1
1	35.7		2.94	.340	19°50′	0	19°50′	.187	1.0
		3							
2	32.7		3.30	.303	17°40′	3	14°40′	.158	.84
		3							
3	29.7		3.65	.274	15°50′	6	9°50′	.130	.70
		3							
4	26.7		4.15	.241	14°00′	9	5°00′	.106	.57
		3							
5	23.7		4.70	.213	12°20′	12	0°20′	.084	.45
		3							
6	20.7		5.38	.186	10°40′	15	−4°20′	.065	.35

In this example no consideration has so far been given to possible effects from the opposite wall. If an enlargement also occurred on the opposite side of the channel, the disturbance lines would cross, or if the other side continued in its original direction, some of the disturbance lines shown in Fig. 9-6 would reflect from this opposite wall and cross other disturbance lines. This situation is much more complex than the case of a single symmetrical crossing of an abrupt wave which was solved in the previous example (p. 9-8). A method of solving such complex problems using characteristic curves will be presented in the following section. At point C, where the wall resumes its original direction, an abrupt positive wave xy is formed in the same manner as previously discussed.

The Method of Characteristics. Another method of solving problems in which the disturbances may be treated as a series of small waves, which is particularly useful for complex wave systems, is known as the method of characteristics. The equations are derived as follows. Equation (9-18) may be rearranged in the following form:

$$1 = \frac{D}{H} + \frac{V^2}{2gH} \qquad (9\text{-}27)$$

If $V/\sqrt{2gH}$ is replaced by $\bar{V}$, Eq. (9-27) can be written as follows:

$$\frac{D}{H} = 1 - \bar{V}^2 \qquad (9\text{-}28)$$

or

$$\bar{V} = \sqrt{1 - \frac{D}{H}} \tag{9-29}$$

Substitution of the value for D/H from Eq. (9-28) in Eq. (9-25) yields the following equation for θ:

$$\theta + \theta_1 = \sqrt{3} \tan^{-1} \sqrt{\frac{1 - \bar{V}^2}{\bar{V}^2 - \frac{1}{3}}} - \tan^{-1} \frac{1}{\sqrt{3}} \sqrt{\frac{1 - \bar{V}^2}{\bar{V}^2 - \frac{1}{3}}} \tag{9-30}$$

Corresponding values of $\bar{V}$ and D/H obtained from Eq. (9-28) or (9-29) are plotted in Fig. 9-7. Shown in the same figure is a curve of $\bar{V}$ versus $(\theta + \theta_1)$ as obtained from Eq. (9-30).

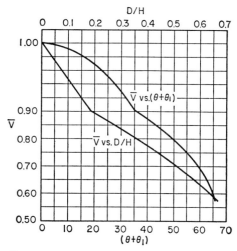

FIG. 9-7. $\bar{V}$ versus D/H and $\theta + \theta_1$ from Eqs. (9-28) and (9-30), respectively. (Note the change in the vertical scale.)

When $\bar{V}$ and $(\theta + \theta_1)$ are plotted on polar coordinates, Eq. (9-30) represents a family of curves such as those shown in Fig. 9-8. These curves are called characteristic curves, perhaps because $\bar{V}$ has the same characteristics as velocity, in that values of $\dot{V}$ plotted on Fig. 9-8 have the same direction as the actual velocity and a length that is proportional to the length of the velocity vector.   The use of Eq. (9-30) in this graphical form provides a convenient tool for solving problems in which many small changes in direction are involved.   As an illustration, the problem shown in Fig. 9-5, previously solved in Example 9-3 by other methods, will now be solved by this method.

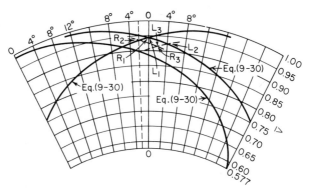

Fig. 9-8. $\bar{V}$ versus $(\theta + \theta_1)$ from Eq. (9-30), using polar coordinates.

Example 9-5.   The problem is to determine the depths, velocities, and wave pattern for the unsymmetrical straight-walled constriction shown in Fig. 9-5*b*.   The initial conditions are as follows:

$$V_1 = 25 \text{ ft per sec} \qquad F = 4.0 \qquad D_1 = 1.21 \text{ ft}$$

D_1/H may be read from Fig. 9-4, knowing θ_1 from Example 9-3, or computed as follows:

$$\frac{V_1{}^2}{2g} = 9.70 \qquad H_1 = D_1 + \frac{V_1{}^2}{2g} = 1.21 + 9.70 = 10.91$$

$$\frac{D_1}{H} = 1.21/10.91 = 0.111$$

From Fig. 9-7,

$$\bar{V}_1 = 0.943$$

The direction of the initial velocity V_1 or $\bar{V}_1$ is taken as the $0°$ line in Fig. 9-8, and the end of the vector $\bar{V}$ is located at the point designated as R_1 and L_1, because this point represents the initial condition for both the left and right deflections.   Noting that Eq. (9-30) must be satisfied for the initial conditions as

well as after the first deflections from each side, curves of Eq.
(9-30) are plotted in both directions through point L_1R_1.   The
curve L_1L_2 gives the change in magnitude and direction of $\bar{V}$
as the water is deflected 4° at the left side.   After the deflection, the direction of flow is along the ray through L_2, and
the value of $\bar{V}_{L2}$, read at L_2, is 0.925.   Then, from Fig. 9-7,
$D_{L2}/H = 0.148$ and $D_{L2} = 0.148 \times 10.91 = 1.62$ ft, and from
Fig. 9-4, $F_{L2} = 3.4$.   Similarly, R_2 represents conditions after
the deflection of 2° from the right wall.   The corresponding
values for the right side are $\bar{V}_{R2} = 0.935$, $D_{R2}/H = 0.126$,
$D_{R2} = 1.37$ ft, and $F_{R2} = 3.7$.

The orientation of the standing waves on the left side, LC in
Fig. 9-5b, must be perpendicular to the segment of the characteristic curve L_1L_2.   This is because L_1L_2 has the same direction as the vector difference between V_1 and V_{L2}, and therefore
this is the component of velocity normal to the standing wave
which has been designated as V_n in the derivation of the equations.   A portion of Fig. 9-8 has been reproduced in Fig. 9-5a,
in which the line LC is drawn perpendicular to L_1L_2 and serves
to establish the direction of LC in Fig. 9-5b.   Correspondingly,
the line RC, perpendicular to R_1R_2 (Fig. 9-5a), establishes the
direction of the standing wave RC in Fig. 9-5.

Until this point in the solution of the problem the use of the
characteristic curves has provided little advantage over the
methods previously used to solve this problem.   However, in
determining the conditions downstream from LCR there is an
advantage in this graphical procedure in that a direct solution
(without successive approximation) can be made.   This is done
in Figs. 9-8 and 9-5a by noting that, after the waters from the
two sides converge beyond LCR, there will be a common value
of $\bar{V}(\bar{V}_3)$ and that the relation between the new angle $(\theta_3 + \theta_1)$
and $\bar{V}_3$ must be in accordance with Eq. (9-30).   Consequently,
curves of Eq. (9-30) (L_2L_3 and R_2R_3) are plotted through L_2
and R_2, respectively.   These curves cross at point L_3R_3.   This
point gives the value of $\bar{V}_3$, as well as the angle θ_{L2} through
which the waters from the left side are deflected to the left and
the angle θ_{R2} through which the waters from the right are
deflected back to the right.   Furthermore, the orientation of
the standing waves CL' and CR' can be determined from lines
perpendicular to L_2L_3 and R_2R_3, respectively, as shown in Fig.
9-5a.   Numerical values of D_3, V_3, and F_3 are obtained as follows. $\bar{V}_3$, from Fig. 9-8 or 9-5a, is 0.916.   Then, from Fig. 9-7,

$$\frac{D_3}{H} = 0.16 \qquad \text{or} \qquad D_3 = 0.16 \times 10.91 = 1.75$$

From Fig. 9-4,

$$F_3 = 3.24$$

Finally,

$$\bar{V}_3 = \frac{V_3}{\sqrt{2gh}} = 0.916 = \frac{V_3}{\sqrt{64.4 \times 10.91}} = \frac{V_3}{26.5}$$

and

$$V_3 = 24.3 \text{ ft per sec}$$

V_3 might also be obtained from F_3. Additional reflections would be handled in the same manner.

Example 9-6.   Another illustration of the use of this method is presented for the expanding channel (Example 9-4) shown in Fig. 9-6.   The problem here is to determine the flow directions and lines of uniform depth.   In Fig. 9-6b is shown a graph of $\bar{V}$ versus $(\theta + \theta_1)$ as plotted from Eq. (9-30).   The graph was laid out so that the ray for 0^0 is parallel to the center line of the original channel, and rays were laid out at $3°$ angles so that a total deflection of $15°$ may be illustrated.   Knowing $F_1 = 2.94$, $\bar{V}$ and D_1/H were determined from Figs. 9-7 and 9-4 as 0.902 and 0.187, respectively.   The curve of Eq. (9-30) was so located in Fig. 9-6b that, at 0^0, $\bar{V}$ has the value of 0.902.   Then the values of $\bar{V}$ may be read for all deflection angles, and the corresponding values of D/H may be obtained from Fig. 9-7. Values of any D can then be computed, knowing D_1/H and D_1. The computations are not shown because they are the same as those in the table on page 9-12.   The direction of the various lines of constant D/H could be taken from the graph as illustrated in the figure.   When the channel wall abruptly resumes its original direction, a positive wave xyz is developed as shown in Fig. 9-6a.   The angles β_x and β_y were determined from Fig. 9-2.   The depth downstream from xyz is equal to the original depth D_1.

High-velocity Flow at Channel Bends.   As water enters a bend in a channel at supercritical velocity, it undergoes a continuous change in direction which can be analyzed in the manner described in the previous section.   At the outer wall a standing positive wave is developed along AM, in Fig. 9-9a, whereas a decrease in depth occurs along $A'M'$.   The growth of the waves is interrupted at M and M' because at these locations waves have crossed the channel.   Downstream from M

the wave height decreases because of the negative wave emanating from A'. This decrease continues to N, where the reflected positive wave again begins to build up the wave height. At N the water depth is approximately the same as A. The distance from A to N is one wavelength L, and the distance from A to the crest of the wave at M is one-half wavelength. The elevation of the water surface at M is a critical design criterion.

If it is assumed that the initial wave orientation, given by β_0, extends across the channel from A' to C as a straight line, then the distance AC is approximately equal to AM. The angle θ_0 is the angular change required to develop the maximum

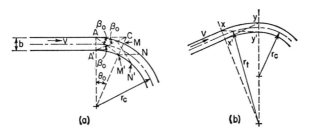

Fig. 9-9. Channel bend, Example 9-7.

water-surface elevation. The geometry of Fig. 9-9a leads to the following approximate relationships, using symbols defined in the figure:

$$\tan \beta_0 = \frac{b}{AC} \tag{9-31}$$

or

$$\frac{L}{2} = AC = \frac{b}{\tan \beta_0} \tag{9-32}$$

and

$$\tan \theta_0 = \frac{AC}{r_c + b/2} \tag{9-33}$$

Inserting the value of AC from Eq. (9-32) in Eq. (9-33) yields the following expression for $\tan \theta_0$:

$$\tan \theta_0 = \frac{b}{(r_c + b/2) \tan \beta_0} \tag{9-34}$$

With θ_0 determined from Eq. (9-34), the depth at the wave crest M can be readily evaluated by means of Eqs. (9-20) and (9-25), using Fig. 9-4 for convenience.

It was observed by Knapp[1] that the increase in elevation of the water surface above the uniform flow depth D_0 at wave crests such as M was approximately given by the following expression:

$$\Delta D_M = \frac{V^2 b}{g r_c} \qquad (9\text{-}35)$$

where V is the average velocity in the channel. It may be noted that this is twice the increase in depth caused by centrifugal force, as developed on page 8-29. Thus the water surface along the outer wall during supercritical flow may be visualized as a series of undulations above and below the surface that would occur because of centrifugal force alone, the depth at the troughs being D_0 and at crests

$$D_M = D_0 + \frac{V^2 b}{g r_c} \qquad (9\text{-}36)$$

The determinations of the depth at a wave crest such as M will be illustrated by the following example, which is one for which observed values were reported by Knapp.

Example 9-7.   The discharge in a rectangular channel 1.5 ft wide is 3.50 cu ft per sec, the uniform flow depth is 0.194 ft, and the average velocity is 12 ft per sec. The radius of the bend is 50 ft. The problem is to determine the location of the first wave crest and the depth at that location.

$$F_1 = V_1 / \sqrt{g D_1} = 4.8$$

From Eq. (9-7),

$$\sin \beta_0 = \frac{1}{F_1} = 0.208$$

and

$$\beta_0 = 12°$$

Then, from Eq. (9-34),

$$\tan \theta_0 = \frac{1.5}{(50 + 0.75)0.2125} = 0.139$$

and

$$\theta_0 = 8°$$

The observed value[2] of θ_0 was 7.75°.

The distance from the beginning of the bend to the wave

---

[1] High Velocity Flow in Open Channels: A Symposium, *loc. cit.*
[2] *Ibid.*

crest (AM in Fig. 9-9) is, from Eq. (9-32),

$$AM \approx AC = 1.5/0.2125 = 7 \text{ ft}$$

The depth at M will first be computed by means of Eqs. (9-20) and (9-25), using Fig. 9-4. Values of D_1/H and θ_1 are determined to be 0.08 and 23.0°, respectively. Knowing $\theta_0 = 8°$, ($\theta + \theta_1$) is 31.0°, and from Fig. 9-4, $D_M/H = 0.143$. Then

$$D_M = \frac{D_M/H}{D_1/H} D_1 = 0.143/0.08 \times 0.194 = 0.35 \text{ ft}$$

Using Eq. (9-36),

$$D_M = 0.194 + \frac{12^2 \times 1.5}{32.2 \times 50}$$
$$= 0.194 + 0.134$$
$$= 0.33 \text{ ft}$$

The observed value[1] of D_M for this example was 0.32 ft.

Several methods of reducing the height of the wave crests at the outside of a bend have been suggested. One method is to begin the bend with a transition section, xy in Fig. 9-9b, in which the radius of curvature is larger than that of the bend and the length such that at the end of the transition yy' the negative wave from x' will begin to reduce the depth on the outside at the same time that the increased curvature, beyond yy', would tend to increase the depth. If the increase or decrease in depth due to the transition is made just half as much as that due to the bend itself, the two effects will tend to nullify each other beyond yy' and the total increase in depth will be reduced by approximately half.

This can be accomplished by either a spiral or circular transition. The use of a circular transition will be described here. It may be seen from Eq. (9-35) that the maximum increase in depth is inversely proportional to the radius of curvature. Therefore, in order to cause an increase in depth at y of one-half of this amount, the radius of the transition section, r_t, should be $2r_c$. The distance xy can then be computed from Eq. (9-32) and the angle θ_t from Eq. (9-34), using r_t in place of r_c.

Other methods of reducing the height of the waves are banking the channel and the use of diagonal sills. Sills are subject to the possibility of erosion or sedimentation and may cause cavitation at very high velocities. Nevertheless, under labora-

[1] *Ibid.*

tory conditions, satisfactory results have been obtained by the use of sills.   If the channel is banked at the angle that the water surface would assume because of the centrifugal force, there will be no increase or decrease in depth along the walls.   However, it is necessary to begin the curvature of the bend gradually in a transition so that the maximum curvature of the bend is reached at the same time that the curvature of the channel attains its full banking angle.

SECTION 10

WAVE MOTION AND FORCES

This section is devoted to a discussion of surface-water waves. The first part will deal with oscillatory waves, and the second part, with translatory waves. The propagation of a change in surface configuration, which is the visible manifestation of water-wave motion, is accompanied by the transmission of energy, pressure changes, and velocity changes. The forward motion of the water is very small for oscillatory waves, particularly in deep water. However, in shallow water a considerable volume of water is transported, with the result that currents are created as the waves approach a shoreline. As the name implies, translatory waves are characterized by a transverse displacement of water. The characteristics of the wave motion and currents near shore establish the design criteria for harbors and, along with the wind, constitute the dominant factors in all shore processes. The forces resulting from wave motion must be evaluated for the design of marine structures. The increasing use of offshore structures, together with man's greater need for shore areas, both for industry and for recreation, indicates that there will be an ever-increasing need for an understanding of the mechanics of wave motion.

Water waves may be generated by any disturbance which affects the local velocity, surface elevation, or pressure. In nature, waves are most commonly generated by the action of the wind. Other natural phenomena which create waves are tides, seismic disturbances, and barometric-pressure fluctuations. Waves may be generated artificially by the opening or closing of a gate, the breaking of a dam, or, in the laboratory, by means of plungers designed for the purpose.

Once wave motion has been started, it is controlled primarily by gravitational forces, although short waves of low amplitude are influenced by surface tension. The principal role of viscosity is in the gradual damping of waves. Elasticity plays no part in water-wave motion.

Oscillatory Waves

One of the earliest investigations of oscillatory-wave motion was made by Gerstner.[1],* His investigation resulted in equations[2,3] which closely describe wave motion.[4] However, because he did not include the assumption of irrotational flow, his equations have not been applied as much as those of Airy and Stokes. In 1845, Airy[5] presented a theory for oscillatory waves of small amplitude, and in 1847, Stokes[6] developed an approximate solution for waves of finite amplitude. The convergence of Stokes' series was proved by Levi-Cevita[7] for large depths and by Struik[8] for small depths. The solutions of Airy and Stokes are based on the assumption that the form of the oscillatory wave is sinusoidal. The simplifying assumption included in Airy's derivation was that the velocity-squared term in Bernoulli's equation could be neglected and the slope of the water surface is very small.

Both the Stokes and Airy equations describe wave motion well enough for practical purposes. The Stokes equations give results which differ from the Airy results for small depths and large wave heights. Although the Stokes equations can be expected to give better results from a theoretical point of view, the available test results indicate that, for engineering purposes, the Airy equations give results which are as dependable as those obtained from the Stokes equations. The exceedingly complex form of the Stokes equations makes them unsuitable for use in many cases. However, tables presented by Skjelbreia[9] greatly simplify their solution. This study also provides the best available reference for all the Stokes wave equations. The equations presented here are those resulting from the simplifying assumption of Airy, except where it is noted otherwise.

Oscillatory waves are so called because water particles oscillate in circular or elliptical paths, the forward motion visible to the eye being primarily that of the waveform. The simplified equations describe oscillations in closed orbits, whereas the Stokes equations provide for open orbits and a small amount of forward motion of the fluid, which is called mass transport.

---

* In this section all numbered references are given in the Bibliography at the end of the section.

Surface Form. According to the Airy equations, the surface form of oscillatory waves is that of the simple sine curve as described by the following equation:

$$y = \frac{H}{2} \cos \theta \tag{10-1}$$

where y is the vertical coordinate of the water surface with respect to the still-water level (SWL), H is the wave height, and the phase angle θ is defined by the equation

$$\theta = 2\pi \left(\frac{x}{L} - \frac{t}{T} \right) \tag{10-2}$$

In Eq. (10-2), x is the horizontal coordinate of the water surface measured from a selected wave crest, L is the wavelength, T is

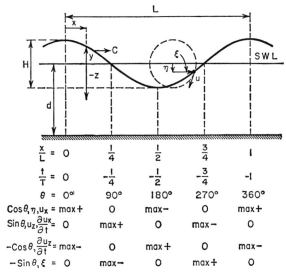

$\frac{x}{L} = 0$	$\frac{1}{4}$	$\frac{1}{2}$	$\frac{3}{4}$	1
$\frac{t}{T} = 0$	$-\frac{1}{4}$	$-\frac{1}{2}$	$-\frac{3}{4}$	-1
$\theta = 0^\circ$	$90°$	$180°$	$270°$	$360°$
$\cos\theta, \eta, u_x = \text{max}+$	0	$\text{max}-$	0	$\text{max}+$
$\sin\theta, u_z, \frac{\partial u_x}{\partial t} = 0$	$\text{max}+$	0	$\text{max}-$	0
$-\cos\theta, \frac{\partial u_z}{\partial t} = \text{max}-$	0	$\text{max}+$	0	$\text{max}-$
$-\sin\theta, \xi = 0$	$\text{max}-$	0	$\text{max}+$	0

Fig. 10-1. Definition sketch, oscillatory waves.

the wave period, and t is time measured from the instant that a wave crest is located at $x = 0$. All the terms defined above are also illustrated in Fig. 10-1. Laboratory measurements confirm that the waveform is approximately that of a sine curve for deep water and for small wave heights, whereas for shallow water and relatively large wave heights, the peaks become somewhat sharper and higher and the trough somewhat flatter and higher than would be indicated by a sine curve. In nature, waves are rarely found which do not consist of several wave trains of differing periods and lengths. Because the vertical coordinates of oscillatory waves are additive, natural waves usually appear as a series of large waves followed by smaller ones, often with much smaller waves superimposed on the entire complex system. Furthermore, the longer-period waves move much faster and thus overtake the shorter-period waves, with the result that the wave pattern is constantly changing. This effect is discussed in greater detail in connection with wave reflection (p. 10-27).

The effect of both the depth and the wave height on the form of waves, as well as any other wave characteristics, is dependent on the wavelength. For example, water having depths such that $d/L < 0.5$ is designated as shallow water because it is only in this range that depth affects the wave characteristics. Similarly, the effect of wave height is usually related to H/L, which is called the wave steepness, rather than to the depth alone.

Wave Celerity. The velocity of the waveform in relation to the body of fluid through which the waves are being propagated is called the *celerity* C. The celerity is related to wavelength and wave period by definition as shown by the equation

$$C = \frac{L}{T} \tag{10-3}$$

The Airy expression for celerity is

$$C = \sqrt{\frac{gL}{2\pi} \tanh \frac{2\pi d}{L}} \tag{10-4}$$

In deep water, $d/L \gtrless 0.5$, the value of $\tanh 2\pi d/L$ approaches 1.0 (Fig. 10-2), and the previous equation is reduced to

$$C_0 = \sqrt{\frac{gL_0}{2\pi}} \tag{10-5}$$

the subscript 0 being introduced to indicate deep-water conditions. The variation of C with d/L in accordance with Eq. (10-4) is illustrated in Fig. 10-3 for three values of deep-water wavelength L_0. The value of C_0 obtained from Eq. (10-5) for $L_0 = 100$, is also illustrated in Fig. 10-3. Computations for C by means of Eq. (10-4) are facilitated by the use of Fig. 10-2

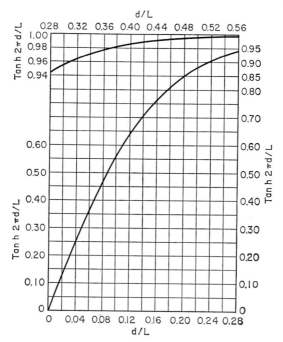

FIG. 10-2. Tanh $2\pi d/L$ versus d/L.

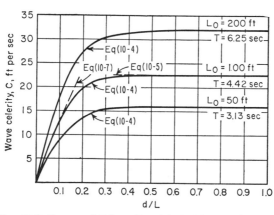

FIG. 10-3. C versus d/L from Eqs. (10-4), (10-5), and (10-7).

or by published tables.[10,11] The relation $C_0 = L_0/T$, from Eq. (10-3), may be introduced into Eq. (10-5) to obtain the following useful relationship:

$$L_0 = \frac{gT^2}{2\pi} = 5.12T^2 \qquad (10\text{-}6)$$

The values of T shown in Fig. 10-3 were computed from Eq. (10-6). Because the wave period remains nearly constant as waves enter shallow water, the subscript for deep water is not used with T. Because the wave period does not vary with depth, the deep-water wavelength may be computed by means of Eq. (10-6) from values of T observed near shore. However, it should be noted that the waves reaching shore may be complex combinations of two or more wave trains, thus making it difficult to detect the principal wave period.

When waves reach *very shallow water*, $d/L \gtreqless 0.1$, the value of tanh $2\pi d/L$ approaches the magnitude of $2\pi d/L$ (Fig. 10-2), and Eq. (10-4) may be reduced to the following approximate relationship:

$$C = \sqrt{gd} \qquad (10\text{-}7)$$

A segment of a curve obtained from Eq. (10-7) for $L_0 = 100$ ft is shown in Fig. 10-3 to illustrate the convergence of Eqs. (10-7) and (10-4) for small values of d/L.

Celerities measured by Morison[12] in a laboratory flume for $d/L \gtreqless 0.49$ agreed quite well with Eq. (10-5), although there was considerable scatter among individual values. Computations involved in obtaining values in Fig. 10-3 require the use of Eq. (10-10) and Fig. 10-4, which are presented on the following pages.

Wavelength. Because the wave characteristics depend upon the value of d/L, it is necessary to derive the equations which permit the evaluation of L for any depth. The determination of L requires that either the deep-water wavelength L_0 or the wave period T be measured or arbitrarily selected. Knowing either L_0 or T, the other can be obtained by means of Eq. (10-6). Then, by replacing C in Eq. (10-4) with L/T from Eq. (10-3), the following expression is derived:

$$\frac{L}{T^2} = \frac{g}{2\pi} \tanh \frac{2\pi d}{L} \qquad (10\text{-}8)$$

Then, because wave period does not vary with depth, T^2 may be replaced with its value in terms of deep-water wavelength as given by Eq. (10-6) to obtain Eq. (10-9):

$$\frac{L}{L_0} = \tanh \frac{2\pi d}{L} \tag{10-9}$$

and rearrangement yields

$$\frac{d}{L_0} = \frac{d}{L} \tanh \frac{2\pi d}{L} \tag{10-10}$$

Equation (10-10) is the functional relationship between d/L and d/L_0. The solution of Eq. (10-10) is facilitated by the use of

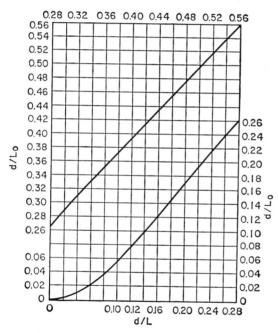

FIG. 10-4. d/L versus d/L_0 from Eq. (10-10).

Fig. 10-2, or values may be read directly from Fig. 10-4 or from published tables.[9,10] It may be noted that, as d/L increases in magnitude, it becomes more nearly equal to d/L_0, and when d/L becomes 0.5, it differs from d/L_0 by only about 0.4 per cent.

As an example of the use of Eq. (10-10), it will be shown how points on the curve in Fig. 10-3 for $L_0 = 100$ ft were obtained. After selecting $L_0 = 100$ ft, the period was found to be 4.42 sec by means of Eq. (10-6). Then, for selected values of depth, d/L_0 is computed and d/L is determined from Eq. (10-10) or Fig. 10-4. The corresponding values of C are determined from Eq. (10-4), thus giving points on the curve.

Orbital Motion. The equations for the orbital displacements, velocities, and accelerations are needed for problems dealing with wave energy and wave forces. The Airy equations for horizontal displacement ξ and vertical displacement η are given by the following equations:

$$\xi = -\frac{H}{2} \frac{\cosh 2\pi(d + z)/L}{\sinh 2\pi d/L} \sin \theta \qquad (10\text{-}11)$$

$$\eta = \frac{H}{2} \frac{\sinh 2\pi(d + z)/L}{\sinh 2\pi d/L} \cos \theta \qquad (10\text{-}12)$$

In these equations z is the distance from the water surface, upward being positive, to the point where the displacement is computed. The phase angle θ varies with x or t or both as defined by Eq. (10-2). It should be noted that z is measured from the same horizontal plane as y in Eq. (10-1); however, y is used in place of z for those points which fall on the water surface. The displacements of a point originally on the SWL ($z = 0$) are illustrated for the case of a circular orbit in Fig. 10-1.

The equations for orbital velocity and acceleration may be determined from Eqs. (10-11) and (10-12) by successive differentiations with respect to t. The equations for the horizontal and vertical components of the orbital velocity are

$$\frac{\partial \xi}{\partial t} = u_x = \frac{\pi H}{T} \frac{\cosh 2\pi(d + z)/L}{\sinh 2\pi d/L} \cos \theta \qquad (10\text{-}13)$$

and

$$\frac{\partial \eta}{\partial t} = u_z = \frac{\pi H}{T} \frac{\sinh 2\pi(d + z)/L}{\sinh 2\pi d/L} \sin \theta \qquad (10\text{-}14)$$

The corresponding expressions for orbital acceleration are

$$\frac{\partial u_x}{\partial t} = \frac{2\pi^2 H}{T^2} \frac{\cosh 2\pi(d + z)/L}{\sinh 2\pi d/L} \sin \theta \qquad (10\text{-}15)$$

and

$$\frac{\partial u_z}{\partial t} = -\frac{2\pi^2 H}{T^2} \frac{\sinh 2\pi(d + z)/L}{\sinh 2\pi d/L} \cos \theta \qquad (10\text{-}16)$$

The manner in which the quantities defined by Eqs. (10-11) to (10-16) vary with θ, x, or t is illustrated in the tabulation at the bottom of Fig. 10-1.   The manner in which the horizontal components of the orbital parameters vary with z can be illustrated by arranging all three in the following dimensionless form, assuming that the phase angle in each case is such that maximum positive values occur.

$$-\frac{\xi}{H/2} = \frac{u_x}{\pi H/T} = \frac{\partial u_x/\partial t}{2\pi^2 H/T^2} = \frac{\cosh 2\pi(d+z)/L}{\sinh 2\pi d/L} \quad (10\text{-}17a)$$

It may be seen that, for given values of H and T, the horizontal displacement, velocity, and acceleration vary with z and d/L

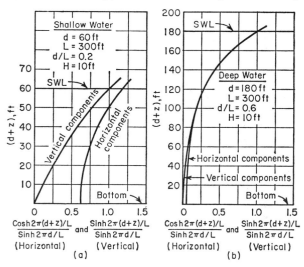

FIG. 10-5. Variation of oscillatory-wave parameters with depth.

in accordance with the right-hand term of Eq. (10-17a).   The variation of this term with z for shallow water ($d/L = 0.2$) and deep water ($d/L = 0.6$) is shown in Fig. 10-5a and b, respectively.   A corresponding dimensionless arrangement of the vertical components of the orbital parameters results in the equation

$$\frac{\eta}{H/2} = \frac{u_z}{\pi H/T} = \frac{\partial u_z/\partial t}{\pi^2 H/T^2} = \frac{\sinh 2\pi(d+z)/L}{\sinh 2\pi d/L} \quad (10\text{-}17b)$$

The variations of the vertical components with z for two values of d/L, in accordance with the right-hand term of Eq. (10-17b), are shown in Fig. 10-5. Computations of the orbital components are facilitated by the use of Fig. 10-6 or of published tables.[10,11] Figure 10-5a shows, for shallow water, that the orbits are elliptical in shape, that the horizontal components have relatively large magnitudes near the bottom, and that the vertical components all become zero at the bottom. Thus, at the bottom, the motion of the water is simply a horizontal oscillation. Figure 10-5b shows, for deep water, that the orbits

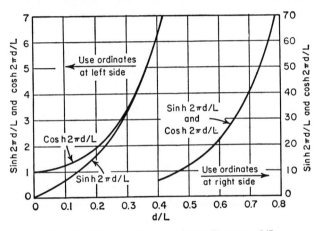

Fig. 10-6. Sinh $2\pi d/L$ and cosh $2\pi d/L$ versus d/L.

are circular near the water surface and become very small and elliptical near the bottom.

Energy. The potential energy per square foot of still-water surface for waves of small amplitude is

$$E_p = \int_0^L \frac{1}{L}\, wy\, dx\, \frac{y}{2} = \frac{w}{2L}\int_0^L y^2\, dx \qquad (10\text{-}18)$$

Substitution of y from Eq. (10-1) and integration yields the following value of potential energy per square foot of horizontal area:

$$E_p = \frac{wH^2}{16} \qquad (10\text{-}19)$$

Similarly, the kinetic energy is

$$E_k = \int_0^d \int_0^L \frac{\rho(u_x{}^2 + u_z{}^2)}{2L}\, dy\, dx \qquad (10\text{-}20)$$

Substituting u_x and u_z from Eqs. (10-13) and (10-14), respectively, and integrating results in the following expression for kinetic energy per square foot of horizontal area,

$$E_k = \frac{wH^2}{16} \qquad (10\text{-}21)$$

Thus the total energy is

$$E = \frac{wH^2}{8} \qquad (10\text{-}22)$$

Group Velocity and Energy Transmission. If a group of waves is generated, as by a limited number of strokes of a wave generator in a laboratory or by the motion of a boat, the velocity of the center of the group of waves is less than the celerity of the individual waves. This may be explained by the fact that the energy of oscillatory waves is nearly equally divided between kinetic and potential [Eqs. (10-19) and (10-21)] and that the kinetic energy is retained at any location while the potential energy is transferred forward at the same speed as the celerity of the individual waves. Then, if a newly generated group of, say, five waves is considered, half of the energy of each wave will move forward one wavelength during one wave period. This will create a new (sixth) wave at the front of the group and leave the rear wave of the original group, each with half as much energy as the original waves, while the four waves between will retain their original energy content. If, now, it is assumed that the front and rear waves will divide their half-energies equally between kinetic and potential, the next wave period will result in seven waves, the front and rear waves having one-fourth of the original energy, the second waves at front and rear having three-fourths of their original energy, and the three waves in the middle still having their original energy content. The center of the group will now have progressed forward one full wavelength, while individual waves will have moved two wavelengths. Thus, for the assumptions made, which are approximately correct for waves of small amplitude in deep water, the group velocity is one-half the wave celerity.*

* A more complete explanation of the physical nature of this phenomenon is given by Russell and MacMillan,[13] pp. 46–49.

An analytical approach to this problem based on the assumption that two trains of waves of slightly different wavelength are traveling in the same direction leads to the following expression for the group velocity:*

$$U_G = C - L \frac{dC}{dL} \tag{10-23}$$

Inserting the expression for C given by Eq. (10-4) in Eq. (10-23),

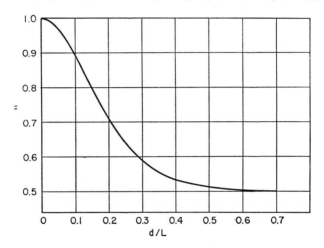

FIG. 10-7. n versus d/L.

the group velocity becomes

$$U_G = C \left(\frac{1}{2} + \frac{2\pi d/L}{\sinh 4\pi d/L} \right) \tag{10-24}$$

or

$$U_G = nC \tag{10-25}$$

where

$$n = \frac{1}{2} + \frac{2\pi d/L}{\sinh 4\pi d/L} \tag{10-26}$$

For deep water n becomes approximately $\frac{1}{2}$, which agrees with the previous discussion, while for very small values of d/L, n approaches unity as shown in Fig. 10-7. Values of n may be read from Fig. 10-7 or from published tables.[10,11]

* This derivation is presented by Ramsey, Ref. 14, who credits Stokes, Hamilton, and Rayleigh with original work on this topic.

As was indicated in the above discussion, group velocity is related to the rate of transmission of energy. If the instantaneous rate of doing work is taken as

$$W_i = \int_0^d p\,dz u_x \qquad (10\text{-}27)$$

where W_i is in foot-pounds per second per foot of wave crest and p is the pressure, then the approximate expression for the average rate of transmission of energy is[14]

$$W = \int_0^L \frac{W_i\,dx}{L} = \frac{wH^2C}{8}\left(\frac{1}{2} + \frac{2\pi d/L}{\sinh 4\pi d/L}\right) \quad (10\text{-}28)$$

Substitution of n from Eq. (10-26) yields

$$W = \frac{wH^2C}{8}\,n \qquad (10\text{-}29)$$

The group velocity as defined in Eq. (10-25) may now be introduced to obtain the following expression for the transmission of energy:

$$W = \frac{wH^2}{8}\,U_G \qquad (10\text{-}30)$$

Because $wH^2/8$ is the total energy [Eq. (10-22)], it may be seen that the energy is transmitted at the group velocity or that the potential portion of the energy is transmitted at twice the group velocity.

Refraction. Investigation of Eqs. (10-3), (10-4), and (10-10) will show that, as waves enter shallow water ($d/L < 0.50$), the wavelength and wave celerity decrease. When the waves approach the shore in such a manner that the angle between the wave crests and the bottom contours, α, is greater than zero, the depth will vary from point to point along each wave crest. Therefore the portion of the wave which encounters shallow water first will lag behind that portion of the crest which is in deep water. The wave crests then become curved in plan, and the angle between the waves and bottom contours becomes smaller as the waves approach the shoreline. This is illustrated in Fig. 10-8, in which the bottom contours are assumed to be parallel straight lines and the value of α in deep water, α_0, is taken as 63.5°. Such a refraction diagram is constructed by projecting orthogonals forward one or more wavelengths at a time at selected locations along the wave crests. In Fig. 10-8 the orthogonals were projected three wavelengths at a time; therefore only every third wave crest appears on the diagram. In order to project an orthogonal one step (three wavelengths) toward shore, the average depth over the projected distance is first estimated from the graph; then the wavelength is computed from Eq. (10-10), and the orthogonal is

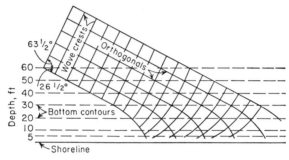

FIG. 10-8. Refraction diagram.

carried forward the required distance perpendicular to the previous crest. When this has been done for all the orthogonals, the new crest is sketched in by connecting the ends of the projections. The average depth in each projection must then be checked to ensure that the first estimate was correct. Further

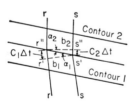

FIG. 10-9. Refraction at a bottom contour.

adjustments may then be made to provide for the change in direction of the orthogonals. A detailed description of a convenient graphical procedure for constructing refraction diagrams in this manner is provided in a publication of the Hydrographic Office of the U.S. Navy.[15]

The essential characteristics of the refraction diagram can also be determined analytically for simple topography. The analysis is similar to that used in optics. Referring to Fig. 10-9, two parallel orthogonals r and s are shown crossing contours 1 and 2, for which the depths, celerities, and wavelengths are indicated by the corresponding subscripts. It is assumed that the change in depth occurs abruptly at the mid-point between contours and that the velocity will change from C_1 to

C_2 and the value of α will change from α_1 to α_2 at that location. A wave crest in the position shown as b_1 will then continue to travel along the orthogonal r at the velocity C_1 over the distance $C_1 \Delta t$ until the mid-contour is reached. During the same time interval, the orthogonal s will progress a smaller distance $C_2 \Delta t$. At the end of the time Δt, the wave crest will extend from point r'' to s'' in such a manner that it will be perpendicular to the orthogonal s and so that s'' is the distance $C_2 \Delta t$ from s'. Thus the direction of wave motion across contour 2 is established by $s's''$, and the new distance between contours becomes b_2. The following equation, expressing α_2 in terms of α_1, may be derived from the construction shown in Fig. 10-9:

$$\sin \alpha_2 = \frac{C_2}{C_1} \sin \alpha_1 \qquad (10\text{-}31)$$

This equation may also be written in terms of wavelength by making use of Eq. (10-3) as follows:

$$\sin \alpha_2 = \frac{L_2}{L_1} \sin \alpha_1 \qquad (10\text{-}32)$$

These equations may be generalized by letting the subscript 1 refer to the original conditions in deep water and removing the subscript 2 entirely, so that they give the orientation of the waves at any depth d where the celerity is C and the wavelength is L. Equations (10-31) and (10-32) may then be rewritten as follows:

$$\sin \alpha = \frac{C}{C_0} \sin \alpha_0 = \frac{L}{L_0} \sin \alpha_0 \qquad (10\text{-}33)$$

Again referring to Fig. 10-9, the ratio of the distances between orthogonals may be expressed as follows:

$$\frac{b_1}{b_2} = \frac{\cos \alpha_1}{\cos \alpha_2} \qquad (10\text{-}34)$$

Here again the equation may be expressed in the following more general form:

$$\frac{b_0}{b} = \frac{\cos \alpha_0}{\cos \alpha} \qquad (10\text{-}35)$$

where b and α refer to conditions at any depth d and the subscript 0 refers to deep-water conditions. The square root of b_0/b is designated as K and is called the refraction coefficient;

then

$$K = \sqrt{\frac{b_0}{b}} = \sqrt{\frac{\cos \alpha_0}{\cos \alpha}} \qquad (10\text{-}36)$$

The refraction coefficient is used in computing wave heights in shallow water.

The application of Eqs. (10-31) to (10-35) is illustrated by the example given in Fig. 10-8. At the 20-ft contour the value of L computed from Eq. (10-10) is 106 ft for $L_0 = 128$ ft. Then the value of α_{20} from Eq. (10-33) is 48°. This agrees very well with values of α_{20} read from Fig. 10-8. The value of K computed from Eq. (10-36) for a depth of 20 ft is 0.82, while K computed from values of b and b_0 scaled from Fig. 10-8 has a value of approximately 0.83. After a number of computations of this type, an entire system of orthogonals and wave crests could be drawn. A number of techniques for constructing refraction diagrams based on similar analytical procedures have been devised.[16-18]

Variation of Wave Height with Depth.   One of the principal applications of a refraction diagram is in the determination of the height and orientation of the waves at various locations in shallow water for the purpose of designing structures and studying shore processes. The assumption is made in this derivation that no energy will cross the orthogonals and that no energy is lost. Dissipation of energy causes a reduction in wave height over that computed from the refraction diagram. This effect is considered in the following section. The rate at which energy progresses in the direction of wave motion was given by Eq. (10-29), which is repeated here.

$$W = \frac{wH^2C}{8} n \qquad (10\text{-}29)$$

The total energy transmission in foot-pounds per second between two orthogonals separated by the distance b (Fig. 10-8) is

$$bW = \frac{wbH^2C}{8} n \qquad (10\text{-}37)$$

For deep water this expression reduces approximately to

$$b_0 W_0 = \frac{wb_0 H_0^2 C_0}{16} \qquad (10\text{-}38)$$

If it is assumed that no energy is lost either by dissipation or by flowing across the orthogonals, then

$$bW = b_0 W_0 \qquad (10\text{-}39)$$

and

$$\frac{wbH^2C}{8} n = \frac{wb_0 H_0^2 C_0}{16} \qquad (10\text{-}40)$$

which reduces to

$$\frac{H}{H_0} = \sqrt{\frac{b_0}{b}} \sqrt{\frac{C_0/C}{2n}} \qquad (10\text{-}41)$$

The introduction of K from Eq. (10-36) leads to the following expression:

$$\frac{H}{H_0} = K \sqrt{\frac{C_0/C}{2n}} \qquad (10\text{-}42)$$

The term K, which shows the effect of refraction, can be computed from refraction diagrams or from Eq. (10-36) as previously described. When the direction of wave motion is perpendicular to straight parallel bottom contours ($\alpha = 0$), K is unity and Eq. (10-42) may be written as follows:

$$\frac{H}{H_0'} = \sqrt{\frac{C_0/C}{2n}} \qquad (10\text{-}43)$$

where H_0' is the deep-water wave height when K is unity or the hypothetical deep-water wave height corresponding to the value of H at any location, neglecting refraction. The value of H_0' is required to determine the breaker height and the depth at which waves break. Equation (10-42) can now be written in the following form:

$$\frac{H}{H_0} = K \frac{H}{H_0'} \qquad (10\text{-}44)$$

from which it can be seen that K is H_0'/H_0.

The value of H/H_0' may be computed from Eq. (10-43) by inserting the value of C_0 from Eq. (10-5), C from Eq. (10-4), and n from Eq. (10-26). Because, for a particular deep-water wave, these quantities depend only upon the depth, the refraction diagram is not needed to determine H/H_0'.

A graph showing the variation of H/H_0' with d/L_0 is shown in Fig. 10-10. Tables showing the variation of H/H_0' with d/L_0 and d/L are also available.[10,11] For the case of waves traveling directly toward a straight shoreline ($K = 1$), this graph also represents H/H_0. It may be seen that, neglecting refraction, the wave height tends to decrease until near the breaking point, when it increases again. Also shown in Fig. 10-10 is a graph of H/H_0 for the waves of Fig. 10-8, which are approaching from $\alpha_0 = 62.5°$. Computations involved are summarized in Table 10-1. Selected values of d are shown in column 1, and corresponding magnitudes of d/L_0 are given in column 2 ($L_0 = 128$ ft). Values of H/H_0' obtained from Fig. 10-10 are shown in column 3. Values of b scaled from Fig. 10-8 and corresponding values of K are shown in columns 4 and 5,

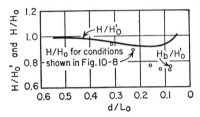

FIG. 10-10. H/H_0 and H/H_0' versus d/L_0.

respectively. The wave heights shown in column 6 were then determined from Eq. (10-44).

Breaking Waves. The previous section dealt with the change in wave height as the wave progressed into shallow water. For the case of no refraction or for converging orthogonals, the wave steepness H/L gradually increases as the waves approach the shore, until eventually the waves become unstable and break. When orthogonals are diverging, the effect of the divergence may cause the steepness to decrease as the waves first enter shallow water, but this trend is eventually reversed and then the steepness begins to increase rapidly until the breaking point is reached. Several investigators[2] have concluded that the theoretical limiting case of stability occurs when H/L becomes 0.143. Waves in shallow water usually break before this limiting condition is reached. Laboratory and field observations on the height of waves at breaking, H_b, and the still-water depth at the breaking point, d_b, serve as the basis for predicting these parameters under field conditions. The most extensive set of observations, gathered by the Hydrographic Office of the U.S. Navy,[15] are represented by the curves of d_b/H_0' versus H_0'/L_0 and H_b/H_0' versus H_0'/L_0, designated as

H.O. in Fig. 10-11a and b, respectively. The data which established these curves have a maximum scatter of about 25 per cent above and below these curves. It should be noted that the deep-water wave height used in these correlations, H_0', is a hypothetical value computed from Eq. (10-44).

The slope of the beach has an important effect on H_b and d_b.

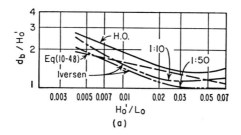

(a)

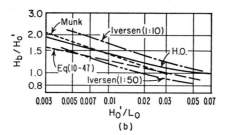

(b)

Fig. 10-11. Depth at breaking.

This is illustrated by curves, based on laboratory tests, presented by Iversen.[19] His curves for the extreme slopes, in the range of slopes tested, are reproduced in Fig. 10-11.

Figure 10-11 also includes a curve derived by Munk[20] on the basis of the theory of solitary waves. Included in this theory is the concept that the ratio of the depth at breaking to the breaker height, d_b/H_b, is 1.28. This value agrees quite well with the average of all observations. The range is from slightly less than 1.0 to about 1.5. The effect of steepness of the beach slope may be estimated from Iversen's data,[19] which showed an average value of d_b/H_b of about 1.0 for 1:10 slopes, whereas for a slope of 1:50 the average value was near 1.2.

The Airy wave equations also can be used to make an approximate analytical approach to the determination of these relationships. If Eq. (10-44) is written for the breaker location, it becomes

$$\frac{H_b}{H'_0} = \sqrt{\frac{C_0/C_b}{2n}} \tag{10-45}$$

At the breaker zone, shallow-water conditions exist and therefore n [Eq. (10-26)] may be taken at unity, and from Eq. (10-7) the value of C_b becomes·

$$C_b = \sqrt{gd_b} \tag{10-46}$$

If it is assumed that $d_b = 1.28H_b$, then the insertion of the value of C_0 from Eq. (10-5) permits the transformation of Eq. (10-45) into the following expression:

$$\left(\frac{H_b}{H'_0}\right)^5 = \frac{0.031}{H'_0/L_0} \tag{10-47}$$

This equation is plotted in Fig. 10-11b. If now H_b in Eq. (10-47) is replaced by $d_b/1.28$, the following expression for the depth at breaking is obtained:

$$\left(\frac{d_b}{H'_0}\right)^5 = \frac{0.106}{H'_0/L_0} \tag{10-48}$$

This equation is plotted in Fig. 10-11a. Here again there is fair agreement with the H.O. curve, particularly for the large values of H'_0/L_0.

These curves are used to determine the depth of breaking and the breaker height for any deep-water wave conditions in a manner which will be illustrated for the example given in Figs. 10-8 and 10-10. The wave heights are first determined for selected depths in the manner previously described and demonstrated in Table 10-1. Values of H'_0 are then obtained by dividing H by H/H'_0. These values are shown in column 7. Values of d/H'_0 and H'_0/L_0 are then computed for the smaller depths (columns 8 and 9). The depth of breaking is determined by finding the point where values in columns 8 and 9 fall on the breaker index curves of Fig. 10-11a. If the values shown in columns 8 and 9 are plotted on Fig. 10-11, it would be seen that they cross the H.O. curve for a depth slightly larger than 10 ft. Therefore, for practical purposes, the breaker zone is located at a depth of 10 ft. The corresponding breaker height,

H_b, is then determined from Fig. 10-11b. Using the H.O. curve, at H_0'/L_0 the value of H_b/H_0' is approximately 1.0, thus establishing H_b as 7.6 ft. The breaker location and height are also shown in Fig. 10-10. The lower points in Fig. 10-10 are a dimensionless representation of the variation of H with d for the example given in Fig. 10-8, with the exception that, at the point of breaking, the wave height departs from the curve and becomes H_b. It may be noted that, although the upper curve in Fig. 10-10 is completely general and applies to all conditions,

Table 10-1

(1)	(2)	(3)	(4)	(5)	(6)	(7)	(8)	(9)
d, ft	$\dfrac{d}{L_0}$	$\dfrac{H}{H_0'}$	b, ft	K	H, ft	H_0', ft	$\dfrac{d}{H_0'}$	$\dfrac{H_0'}{L_0}$
80	.63	1.0	384	1.0	10.0	10.0		
60	.47	1.0	384	1.0	10.0	10.0		
50	.39	.97	384	1.0	9.7	10.0		
40	.31	.95	390	.99	9.4	9.9		
30	.23	.93	423	.95	8.9	9.6	3.1	.075
20	.16	.91	545	.84	7.7	8.5	2.4	.067
15	.12	.92	602	.80	7.4	8.1	1.9	.063
10	.078	.96	665	.76	7.3	7.6	1.3	.059

it may also be considered as representing the variation of wave height with depth for a wave traveling perpendicular to a straight shoreline ($\alpha_0 = 0$).

Energy Dissipation. Oscillatory waves lose energy because of internal friction, wind resistance at the water surface, bottom friction, and percolation through permeable bottoms. Internal friction and wind resistance are effective in deep water, whereas the latter two factors become the important ones in shallow water.

If it is assumed that a group of waves has been generated in deep water as the result of a wind blowing over a fetch F, then, as these waves move into a region of relatively calm water, the accompanying energy loss results in a reduction in effective wave height.* Sverdrup and Munk[21] showed that the ratio of the effective wave height at the end of the generating fetch, H_F, to the effective wave height at any distance D beyond the

---

* Many of the terms used in this discussion are defined under Characteristics of Wind-generated Waves, page 10-31.

generating area, H_D, can be related to the dimensionless parameter $D/gT_F{}^2$, in which T_F is the wave period at the end of the generating fetch. Their curve was, of necessity, based on the limited number of observations then available. Another correlation, based on a larger number of data, was prepared by Bretschneider.[22,23] He plotted the data using the fetch distance F as a parameter rather than the period T_F. Inclusion of the wave period or the fetch as a variable is an indirect method of including the effect of initial wave steepness, H/L. Steep waves undergo a greater reduction in height than flatter waves in a given decay distance. The following table contains typical values for H_D/H_F from Bretschneider's revised curves[22,23] for an H_F of 10 ft. For larger waves the ratios are slightly larger, while for smaller waves they are somewhat smaller, than those shown in the table.

D, nautical miles	F, nautical miles		
	100	400	800
100	0.54	0.72	0.79
500	0.30	0.45	0.53
1,000	0.20	0.33	0.42
2,000	0.13	0.24	0.32

Under shallow-water conditions the principal energy losses result from bottom friction and percolation through permeable bottoms. Putnam and Johnson[24] have treated the loss due to bottom friction by assuming that the shear stress on the bottom is related to the bottom velocity, as obtained from Eq. (10-13), in accordance with the following expression:

$$\tau = k\rho u_x{}^2 \qquad (10\text{-}49)$$

where k is friction factor, ρ is the density, and u_x is the horizontal velocity as obtained from Eq. (10-13). The instantaneous rate of energy dissipation per unit of area is then

$$D_{f,\text{inst}} = \tau u_x = k\rho u_x{}^3 \qquad (10\text{-}50)$$

The average rate of energy dissipation due to bottom friction may then be obtained by integrating over one-half wave period and dividing by $T/2$, with the following result:

$$D_f = -k \frac{4\pi^2\rho}{3T^3} \frac{H^3}{(\sinh 2\pi d/L)^3} \qquad (10\text{-}51)$$

The friction factor k must be evaluated by means of laboratory or field observations. Bagnold[25] conducted tests by oscillating plates roughened to simulate sand ripples. He concluded that the value of k depended on the ratio of $\xi_{z=d}$, the half amplitude of water oscillation at the bottom as given by Eq. (10-11), to the ripple pitch p. His tests indicated that when $\xi_{z=d}/p < 1.0$, the value of k is 0.008, and when this ratio is greater than unity, k may be determined from the following equation:

$$k = \frac{0.072}{(\xi_{z=d}/p)^{0.75}} \qquad (10\text{-}52)$$

Values of k obtained from Eq. (10-52), together with Eqs. (10-10) and (10-11) for a pitch of 0.5 ft, are shown in Fig. 10-12. Values of k read from the curves shown in Fig. 10-12 may be modified for pitches differing from 0.5 ft. For example, values of k for pitch of 5 in. can be determined by multiplying values obtained from the curve by $(0.416/0.5)^{0.75}$. Bagnold used two pitches,

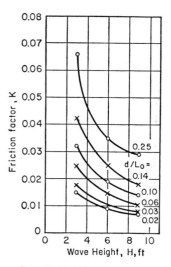

FIG. 10-12. Friction factors.

10 and 20 cm, and only one ratio of pitch height to pitch, 1:67. It is probable that the varying conditions found in nature would produce values of k which differ from those found by Bagnold.

Ripple pitch is probably affected by the wave and sand characteristics. Putnam and Johnson[24] have indicated that a typical value along the Pacific shore of the United States is 5 in. Measurements by the junior author in the Great Lakes give values varying from 5 to 8 in. Lab tests for the purpose of determining the energy loss due to bottom friction were conducted by the Beach Erosion Board.[26] Their findings were that the energy losses reach a maximum rate during the formation of ripples, but after they become stabilized for a steady-wave condition, the losses became nearly as small as for smooth-bottom conditions. The maximum losses agreed well with values computed by means of Eq. (10-51), using Bagnold's values of k.

Measurements of k have been made by the Beach Erosion Board[27] at a location in the Gulf of Mexico for wave heights of about 1 ft and values of d/L_0 of approximately 0.25. The writers expressed the opinion that the bottom material at this location was so fine the percolation would be negligible, although they indicated that the bottom tended to be somewhat fluid, which might introduce some additional loss. Values of k varied from 0.03 to 0.09. Bagnold's tests, as shown by Fig. 10-12, indicate values of k of 0.08 for this range of d/L_0 and H, if the ripple pitch is somewhere near 0.5 ft. The selection of a value of k should be guided by the use that is to be made of the results of the computations. Generally, wave heights are computed for the design of shore or offshore structures. For that purpose it would be unsafe to assume too great an energy loss, and consequently the value of k should be quite small. As indicated by Fig. 10-12, the value of k may be less than 0.01 for large waves and small values of d/L_0.

The computation of the wave height at any location, including the effect of energy loss due to bottom friction, can be carried out by successive approximations in the following manner. Knowing the deep-water wave characteristics, a refraction diagram is extended shoreward in the manner previously described (p. 10-13). Then the wave height, neglecting losses, is computed at selected locations by means of Eq. (10-42). For the example given in Fig. 10-8, these values of H are shown in column 6 of Table 10-1 and repeated in column 6 of Table 10-2. If it is assumed that the only loss of energy is that due to bottom friction and that no energy crosses the orthogonals, then the rate of energy transmission at any location, $b_x W_f$, is equal to the rate in deep water, $b_0 W_0$, less the loss in the distance x traveled by the waves after leaving deep water. This relationship is expressed by the equation

$$b_x W_f = b_0 W_0 - \Sigma\Delta(bW_f) \tag{10-53}$$

The distance x is measured midway between two orthogonals, the origin being taken at or near the location where $d/L = 0.50$

Table 10-2

(1) d, ft	(2) Δx, ft	(3) d_{av}, ft	(4) b, ft	(5) b_{av}, ft	(6) H, ft	(7) $\dfrac{d_{av}}{L_0}$	(8) $\left(\sinh \frac{2\pi d_{av}}{L_0}\right)^3$	(9) H_{av}, ft	(10) $\Delta(\delta W_f)$, ft-lb per sec	(11) $\Sigma\Delta(\delta W_f)$, ft-lb per sec	(12) $\sqrt{\dfrac{b_0 W_0 - \Sigma\Delta(\delta W_f)}{b_0 W_0}}$	(13) H_f, ft
60			384		10.0							
	1,536	50		387		.391	215.0	9.7	7,800	7,800	1.00	9.4
40			390		9.4							
	730	35		406		.273	26.2	9.2	28,200	36,000	1.00	8.9
30			423		8.9							
	580	25		484		.195	6.65	8.3	74,200	111,200	.99	7.6
20			545		7.7							
	250	17.5		578		.137	2.24	7.5	84,000	195,200	.97	7.2
								7.4	80,500	191,700	.98	7.2
15			602		7.4							
	200	12.5		634		.098	0.97	7.1	141,000	332,700	.95	7.0
10			665		7.3							

(p. 10-4).   In the example of Fig. 10-8 and Table 10-2, $x = 0$ at $d/L = 0.47$.   Introducing the expression for W_f from Eq. (10-29) and the value of W_0 from Eq. (10-38), Eq. (10-53) becomes

$$\frac{b_x w H_f^2 C_x n_x}{8} = \frac{b_0 w H_0^2 C_0}{16} - \sum \Delta(bW_f) \qquad (10\text{-}54)$$

Values of b can be read from the refraction diagram, and C_x, C_0, and n_x can be computed from Eqs. (10-4), (10-5), and (10-26), respectively, after obtaining values of d and L from the refraction diagram.   Thus the wave height after modification due to friction H_f could be computed from Eq. (10-54) once the energy loss bW_f has been evaluated.   However, the computation of H_f is simplified if Eq. (10-54) is divided by Eq. (10-39), introducing the value of W from Eq. (10-29) and the value of W_0 from Eq. (10-38) and canceling to obtain the following expression:

$$\frac{H_f^2}{H^2} = \frac{b_0 w H_0^2 C_0/16 - \Sigma\Delta(bW_f)}{b_0 w H_0^2 C_0/16} \qquad (10\text{-}55)$$

In this expression H is the wave height at any location computed by neglecting losses, shown in column 6 of Tables 10-1 and 10-2.

The value of $\Sigma\Delta(bW_f)$ can be obtained as follows:

$$\sum \Delta(bW_f) = \int_0^x D_f b \, dx \qquad (10\text{-}56)$$

The integration of Eq. (10-56) can be readily approximated by dividing the distance x into successive reaches and summing increments of loss as follows:

$$\Sigma\Delta(bW_f) = \Sigma_0^x D_{fav} b \, \Delta x \qquad (10\text{-}57)$$

The value of D_f from Eq. (10-51) is then introduced:

$$\sum \Delta(bW_f) = \sum_0^x - \left(\frac{4\pi^2 k\rho}{3T^3}\right) \left(\frac{H_{av}}{\sinh 2\pi d_{av}/L_0}\right)^3 b_{av} \Delta x \quad (10\text{-}57a)$$

The first term in parentheses on the right side of Eq. (10-57a) can be assumed to remain constant for all locations in a particular situation, although the value of k actually varies with d/L_0 and H as shown in Fig. 10-12.   For the example shown in Fig. 10-8, assuming $k = 0.015$ and fresh water, this term becomes

$$\frac{4\pi^2 k\rho}{3T^3} = \frac{4\pi^2 \times 0.015 \times 1.95}{3 \times 125} = 0.00308$$

The value of k was taken as 0.015 to give a conservative estimate of the losses. It may be seen from the values of d/L_0 and H_f in Table 10-2 that, according to Bagnold's tests (Fig. 10-12), k varies from slightly less than 0.015 to more than 0.03. Then, starting at $x = 0$, the values of d_{av} and b_{av} are determined from the refraction diagram by averaging of corresponding values at the ends of each reach, Δx, as illustrated in columns 1 to 5 of Table 10-2. For the determination of H_{av}, the correct wave height will be known at the deep-water end of each reach, but a trial value of H must be assumed at the shoreward end of the reach. As a first trial, the value of H computed by neglecting losses could be used. Sometimes several trials will be required until the computed H_f agrees with the wave height used to obtain H_{av}. The steps used in the computation are illustrated in columns 7 to 13 of Table 10-2. In this example the energy loss caused a reduction of wave height of 5 per cent at a depth of 10 ft. In cases where the bottom slope is flatter, the reduction may be much larger.

An expression for the loss of energy per unit area per second due to bottom percolation has been developed by Putnam.[28]

$$D_p = \left(\frac{-\pi P w^2}{\mu}\right) \frac{H^2}{L \cosh^2 2\pi d/L} \qquad (10\text{-}58)$$

In this equation μ is the absolute viscosity in slugs per foot-second (pp. 1–2 and 1–8), and P is the permeability in Darcys. Computations can be carried out in the manner previously described for bottom friction except that the loss term in Eqs. (10-53) to (10-57) would include the percolation loss as well as the friction term. Again, the term in parentheses on the right side of formula (10-58) would remain constant for any situation, whereas the second term in parentheses would be evaluated for successive reaches. Tests[26] have shown that the energy losses due to percolation are from one-fourth to one-tenth as large as would be indicated by the application of Eq. (10-58) and that, unless the sand is very permeable, the percolation losses are negligible. However, for sands of sizes larger than 2 mm, the losses may be substantial.

Reflection, Resonance, and Damping. Oscillatory waves are reflected from a vertical wall in such a manner that the angle of incidence is equal to the angle of reflection. The reflections take place with very little loss in energy, with the result that, in an enclosed area such as a harbor or a large slip, the wave pattern becomes very complicated and, because of resonance or focusing, wave heights at certain points may be much larger than the waves entering the harbor.   When two or more oscillatory waves are superimposed, the water motion is approximately the resultant of the various components of motion.   Thus, when two crests coincide, the resultant height will be approximately the sum of the two heights.   Similarly, the coincidence of a trough of one wave with the crest of another would cancel out all or part of the vertical motion at that point, but the horizontal amplitudes and velocities would reinforce each other. When waves are reflected from a wall at an angle less than 90°, the reflected waves cross the approaching waves and produce a pattern consisting of isolated peaks caused by the intersection of two crests surrounded by irregular troughs.   When a wave

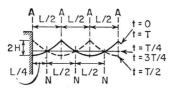

FIG. 10-13. Wave reflection.

strikes a vertical wall at a 90° angle and reflects straight back, a standing-wave pattern is formed, as illustrated schematically in Fig. 10-13.   In this figure it is assumed that waves of length L and height H approach from the right and are reflected from the vertical wall at the left.   After the first incident wave reflects from the wall and travels one-half wavelength to the right, it encounters the following incident crest. Because of the addition of the two vertical components of motion, a wave of height $2H$ is produced at this location.   Furthermore, the horizontal motions are equal and opposite, and thus the horizontal velocity is reduced to zero.   This situation is then repeated every half wavelength as the reflected waves travel seaward.   These regions of maximum vertical displacements may be called antinodes and are designated as A in Fig. 10-13.

Similarly, at a point $L/4$ from the wall, the first reflected wave encounters an oncoming trough and the vertical components of displacement are canceled, but the horizontal components of velocity are both toward the right and thus combine to produce a horizontal velocity twice as great as that for a single wave.   Such locations of zero vertical displacement and maximum horizontal displacement may be called nodes and are designated as points N in Fig. 10-13.

The variations in wave configuration are cyclic, passing

through one complete cycle during each wave period T. As illustrated in Fig. 10-13, if the solid line indicates the water surface at zero time, then, at time $t = T/4$, the water surface is a horizontal plane, at $t = T/2$, the dotted lines indicate the water surface, at $t = 3T/4$, the plane surface is repeated, and at $t = T$, conditions are the same as at $t = 0$.

The wave motion illustrated in Fig. 10-13 demonstrates the possibility of establishing resonant conditions in a harbor. For example, a vertical wall placed at one of the points A in Fig. 10-13 would not interfere with the wave motion, and waves of high amplitude could be established and maintained if wave energy in phase with the oscillations were being supplied. In general, any harbor area bounded by two parallel vertical walls would be subject to resonance if the distance between walls were

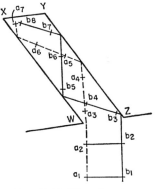

$$l = \frac{nL}{2} = \frac{nCT}{2} \quad (10\text{-}59)$$

where n is any integer.[29] The wave period is established by the waves entering the harbor, but C is a function of the depth within the

FIG. 10-14. Wave focusing.

harbor as shown by Eqs. (10-4) and (10-7). Any distance l between vertical walls, other than those which satisfy Eq. (10-59), would produce some damping, and the maximum damping action would occur for

$$l = \frac{mL}{4} \quad (10\text{-}60)$$

where m is any odd integer. This is because walls separated by a distance in accordance with Eq. (10-60) (located at points N in Fig. 10-13) would stop all particle motion in these locations.

In addition to the possibility of resonance, illustrated by the simplified example above, waves may be reflected in such a manner as to focus wave energy at particular locations. This is illustrated by the example shown in Fig. 10-14. Here waves having crests a_1b_1 approach the slip $WXYZ$. Two selected orthogonals (lines perpendicular to wave crests), designated as a_1a_2 and b_1b_2, are projected into the slip by assuming that the angle of reflection is equal to the angle of incidence.[13] The orthogonal b_1b_2 progresses into the far corner of the slip X by means of three reflections. The orthogonal a_1a_2 is deflected slightly to simulate diffraction at W and reaches the vicinity of X after only two reflections. Successive wave crests along these orthogonals are shown as a_1, a_2, etc., and b_1, b_2, etc. The crests a_7 and b_8 reach the vicinity of X at about the same time, thus illustrating one manner in which the energy from two separate portions of a wave crest may be concentrated at one location. The wave height at that location would be approximately the sum of the two original wave heights.

The most complete reflection of waves is produced by smooth vertical walls. Sloping walls, particularly walls made of rubble, will absorb some wave energy. One of the best wave absorbers is a relatively flat beach. Occasionally conditions occur in which it is possible to disperse the wave energy by reflection in many directions, as by a zigzag wall. Groin systems also act as wave absorbers when the incident angle is small. The best method of absorbing wave energy for a particular harbor can be determined with assurance only by means of a model study.[30]

Diffraction and Harbor Models. The change in wave direction as waves pass the end of a breakwater or between the tips of two breakwaters is called diffraction. Analysis of the problem, based on similarity to diffraction of light, has been carried out, and several laboratory investigations have been conducted, as reported by Dunham[31] and Johnson.[32,33] An extensive series of tests on refraction caused by a breakwater gap has been carried out by Priest.[34] Johnson and Dunham presented theoretical results in the form of diagrams which can be used to predict wave heights behind a breakwater, whereas Priest developed a set of equations, by the use of dimensional analysis, which give wave heights for a considerable range of conditions. Both the analytical and experimental results referred to above would give an indication of what reduction in wave height could be expected inside the breakwater line; however, the wave characteristics are usually influenced to such a great extent by reflections, refraction, and energy losses that actual wave conditions often differ considerably from predicted ones. Furthermore, the nature of the diffraction itself is undoubtedly influenced by the texture and shape of the ends of breakwaters.

This factor is not considered as a variable in either the analytical or laboratory results available. Because of these factors and complications from reflections, it is usually necessary to conduct model studies in order to predict the wave behavior within a harbor.

The use of hydraulic models for designing new harbors or for correcting problems in existing harbors[30] has been well established as a dependable procedure. Indeed, it is unusual for a new harbor to be designed or for a major change to be planned in an existing one without the aid of model studies.

The motion of oscillatory waves is almost completely controlled by gravitation forces. Consequently, harbor models are designed, and the results are converted to prototype values on the basis of the Froude model law (p. 3–17). Repeated tests have shown that refraction, diffraction, and reflections are accurately portrayed by undistorted models provided the model scale is such that surface tension and friction effects are minor. The effect of surface tension can be eliminated by keeping model wavelengths greater than 0.3 ft.[2] It may be impossible to minimize the effects of friction, but the reduction in wave height due to friction can be taken into account by methods previously described (p. 10–21). In most harbor model studies the exact magnitudes of prototype wave heights are not needed, the model serving merely to determine the most effective arrangements from among a number of possible choices, and thus the friction effect can be neglected.

Characteristics of Wind-generated Waves. As wind moves across a body of water, the shear stress between wind and water sets the upper layers of water into motion. As a result of the large-scale turbulence in the air, slight pressure and velocity differences exist which create small disturbances in the water surface. As soon as waves are formed, the wind produces a positive pressure on the windward sides of the waves and a reduced pressure on the leeward sides. The resultant pressure force combined with the drag force transmits energy to the water and causes the waves to grow. Because of the unsteady nature of the wind, both with respect to location and time, a spectrum of wave heights, wave periods, and wavelengths is developed. Usually a dominant pattern is developed upon which is superimposed waves of different heights and lengths. Because the wave celerity varies with wavelength [Eqs. (10-4) and (10-5)], the various wave patterns pass in and out of phase with the dominant pattern, with the result that the composite pattern is often quite irregular, consisting of alternating groups of high and low waves.

The variation in wave height within a continuous series of waves is illustrated by the following tabulation of ratios. The numerical values were selected by the author as representative of published results of wave train analyses.[35-37] The symbol H_1 is the mean of all wave heights in a series, $H_{1/3}$ is the average of the highest one-third of the waves in the series, $H_{1/10}$ is the average of the highest one-tenth of the waves, and $H_{1/100}$ is the average of the highest 1 per cent of the waves. The maximum wave height is a little larger

$$\frac{H_{1/3}}{H_1} = 1.6$$

$$\frac{H_{1/10}}{H_{1/3}} = 1.3$$

$$\frac{H_{1/100}}{H_{1/3}} = 1.7$$

than $H_{1/100}$, and the following ratio may be used to estimate its value: $H_{max}/H_{1/3} = 1.8$. $H_{1/3}$ is called the *significant wave height*. This value has been adopted as a design parameter for many purposes, and it is the wave height used in the following relations between wave height, fetch, and wind.

Correlations of wind characteristics with wave characteristics were made by Sverdrup and Munk[38,39] and revised by Bretschneider[40,41] as additional data became available. The wave characteristics used in the correlations were significant wave height and significant wave period. Knowing the wave period, the wavelength can be computed from Eq. (10-6) for deep water and from Eq. (10-8) for shallow water. The wind characteristics which must enter the correlations are velocity U, duration t, and fetch F. The fetch is the distance over which the wind is in contact with the water. On lakes this is usually the distance from shore to shore, whereas on the oceans the fetch must be scaled from synoptic charts. Wind velocities and durations may be obtained from measurements near the shorelines of lakes or from synoptic charts of pressure gradients for the oceans.[38] The wind velocity used in the correlations was taken about 26 ft above the ground or water surface. When records are obtained at other elevations, they must be reduced to this elevation by assuming that a typical velocity gradient existed.[42] Dimensional analysis suggests the arrangement of variables shown in Eq. (10-61) for relating wave characteristics to fetch and wind speed. The corresponding param-

$$\frac{gH}{U^2} \quad \text{and} \quad \frac{gT}{U} = f\left(\frac{gF}{U^2}\right) \tag{10-61}$$

eters, when wind duration is included rather than fetch, are

$$\frac{gH}{U^2} \quad \text{and} \quad \frac{gT}{U} = f\left(\frac{gt}{U}\right) \tag{10-62}$$

The data were plotted according to these functional relationships, and average curves drawn through rather widely scattered points.[38–41] Based on the most recently revised curves, the chart presented in Fig. 10-15 was prepared by Bretschneider.[41] This convenient chart includes all the variables needed to predict wave characteristics from wind. The proper use of the chart requires the following consideration of wave growth. At a particular location, assuming a certain fetch and a constant wind speed, the wave height and period continue to grow with wind duration until (at the *minimum duration*) steady (maximum) conditions are attained. During this growing period the wave characteristics at this location are a function of wind duration and velocity. However, when steady conditions are reached, the wave characteristics are established by the fetch, together with wind velocity. At locations farther downwind (larger fetch), the steady conditions are reached later (larger minimum duration) and the ultimate wave height and period have correspondingly larger values. For example, suppose that, for a fetch of 100 miles and average wind velocity of 30 miles per hr, the wind duration was 12 hr. The chart would be entered at 30 miles per hr, and proceeding from left to right, it will be noted that, for a fetch of 100 miles, the minimum duration is approximately 9.5 hr. Therefore equilibrium conditions were reached at the end of 9.5 hr and the wave height and period can be read at the intersection of the $F = 100$- and $U = 30$-miles-per-hr lines, the values being approximately 8.8 ft and 7.8 sec, respectively. If, however, the duration of the wind were only 6 hr, the duration would control and the wave height and period would be determined at the intersection of $U = 30$ miles per hr and $t = 6$ hr, the resulting values for H and T being 7.1 ft and 6.7 sec, respectively.

When water is shallow, $d/L < 0.50$, the wave height and

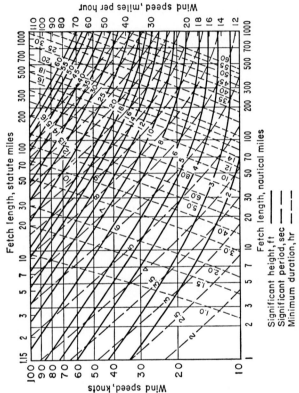

Fig. 10-15. Deep-water wave-forecasting curves as a function of wind speed, fetch length, and wind duration.

period produced by a given wind are smaller than for deep water because of the energy dissipation due to bottom friction and percolation (p. 10-21). Curves showing the probable wave height and wave period have been prepared[41,43,44] for the shallow-water conditions with unlimited wind duration. The curves are based in part on observations and in part on computations assuming the friction factor k (p. 10-22) to be 0.01 and neglecting percolation losses. Two charts derived from these curves by Bretschneider[41] are shown in Figs. 10-16 and 10-17. These apply to a constant depth. The significant wave height and wave period can be read directly from Fig. 10-16 for an unlimited fetch. When the fetch is short, values can be read from the corresponding gF/U_2 curve of Fig. 10-17, as illustrated in the following example. Suppose the fetch is 15 miles, the depth is 30 ft, and the wind velocity is 30 miles per hr. Then

$$\frac{gF}{U^2} = \frac{32.17 \times 15 \times 5,280}{30^2 \times (5,280/3,600)^2} = 1,310$$

and

$$\frac{gd}{U^2} = \frac{32.17 \times 30}{30^2 \times (5,280/3,600)^2} = 0.50$$

Then, from Fig. 10-17, interpolating between the curve for $gF/U^2 = 1,000$ and 2,000,

$$\frac{gH}{U^2} = 0.076$$

and

$$H = \frac{0.076 \times 30^2}{32.17} \times \left(\frac{5,280}{3,600}\right)^2 = 4.6$$

The wave period for this example can be estimated from Fig. 10-16 by entering at $U = 30$ miles per hr and noting that, for $H = 4.6$, $T = 5.9$ sec.

If fetch extends from deep water into relatively shallow water, the resulting wave height will be between that estimated for shallow water of a constant depth, from Figs. 10-16 and 10-17, and that determined for deep water from Fig. 10-15. The Corps of Engineers has presented curves for estimating wave heights under these conditions for three bottom slopes.[44] It is recognized that for narrow bodies of water the effective fetch to be used in estimating wave height may be less than the actual fetch. Field data are not available, but an analytical approach has been developed[45] which indicates that substantial effects

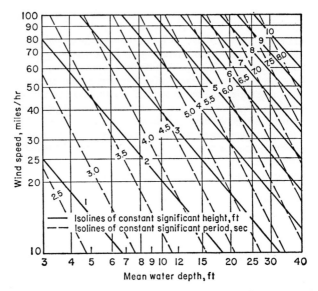

Fig. 10-16. Wave-forecasting relationships for shallow water of constant depth.

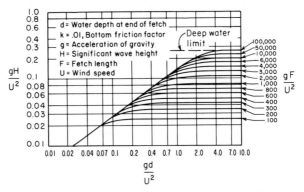

Fig. 10-17. Generation of wind waves over a bottom of constant depth for unlimited wind duration represented as dimensionless parameters.

can be expected when the fetch width becomes less than half the fetch.

Wave Run-up and Overtopping. The selection of the crest elevations of sea walls, breakwaters, revetments, and other shore structures requires information regarding the height to which waves will run up the face of the structure or an estimate of the discharge over the wall when overtopping occurs. This section presents a summary of the results of laboratory tests on these phenomena.

Run-up R is defined as the vertical distance above the still-water level that a wave will run up the slope. It should be noted that, during an onshore wind, the still-water level may rise considerably because of wind setup or wind tide (see Wind Tides, below). The run-up is a function of the wave height H, the wave period T, the depth of water at the toe of the structure d_t, the slope of the face of the structure, tan α, the roughness and permeability of the structure, and the local wind. It has been shown[46,47] that a satisfactory arrangement of variables for smooth slopes is that shown in Fig. 10-18, where R/H_0' is plotted against $H/_0' T^2$ for various values of cot α. The effect

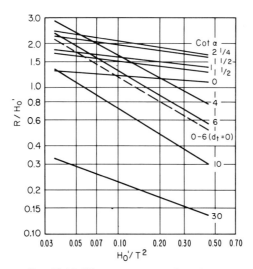

Fig. 10-18. Wave run-up, smooth surfaces.

of variations in d_t is also included in these curves, as will be explained later. R/H_0' is called the relative run-up, H_0' being the wave height in deep water if there were no refraction as defined more fully on page 10-17. H_0'/T^2 is a convenient method of expressing wave steepness, which is usually written as H/L. The close relationship between T^2 and L is shown by formula (10-6). The lines shown in Fig. 10-18 are the author's summary of values presented in the references given previously for the practical range of H_0'/T^2. The solid lines are for values of d_t such that $d_t > H_0'$. For this condition the wave breaks on the structure, and as can be seen from Fig. 10-18, there is considerable variation with α. For the case of zero depth at the face to the structure ($d_t = 0$), the slope of structure has little effect on run-up for slopes of 1:6 or steeper, and the dashed line in Fig. 10-18 can be used for all values of $\cot \alpha \gtreqless 6$. For slopes of 1:10 and 1:30, the run-up is affected very little by d_t and the solid-line curves in Fig. 10-18 may be used for all values of d_t. When $\cot \alpha \gtreqless 6$, and for values of d_t between H_0' and zero, values of run-up can be estimated by interpolating between the dashed line and the appropriate solid line.

The effects of roughness and permeability have been determined[48] by measuring run-up with material of a certain size fastened to an impermeable surface and then by using the same size of material to form the entire wall. Based on the

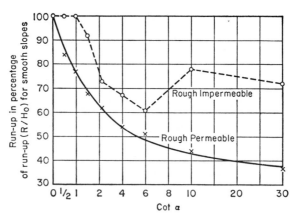

FIG. 10-19. Wave run-up, rough surfaces.

values for 10-mm stone, the author has prepared curves showing run-up on rough-impermeable and rough-permeable revetments in terms of the comparable run-up on smooth-impermeable surfaces.[47,48] These curves, shown in Fig. 10-19, are the averages for the range of H'_0/T^2 from 0.04 to 0.40. Model data have also been derived for run-up on slopes protected with various types of precast armor units.[49]

Several series of laboratory tests on *overtopping*[46,50,51] provide data from which the discharge over a sea wall can be estimated. Some of the data have been summarized by the author in Fig. 10-20a. In this figure Q is the discharge in cubic feet per second

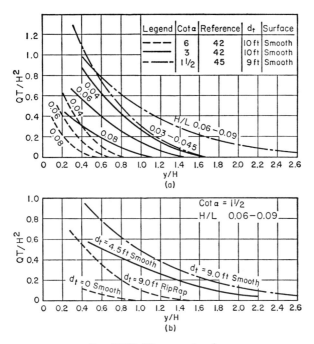

FIG. 10-20. Wave overtopping.

per foot length of wall, H is the wave height at the toe of the wall, T is the wave period, L is the wavelength at the toe of the wall, $\tan \alpha$ is the slope of the face of the wall, and y is the height of the wall above the wind-tide level. It may be seen that the group of variables QT/H^2 varies with the height of the structure relative to the wave height y/H, the wave steepness H/L, and cot α. The relative spacing of three sets of curves (each for a particular value of α) shows that overtopping increases as the slope increases (cot α decreases) up to

$$\cot \alpha = 1\tfrac{1}{2}$$

However, for a vertical wall (not shown in the figure) the values of discharge drop back to magnitudes similar to the ones for cot $\alpha = 3$. The effect of the depth at the toe of the wall, d_t, is illustrated in Fig. 10-20b, in which curves for cot $\alpha = 1\tfrac{1}{2}$ and for H/L in the range 0.06 to 0.09 for smooth slopes are shown for three values of d_t. It may be seen that overtopping increases with d_t. The effect of roughness is also demonstrated in Fig. 10-20b by comparing the location of the line, which gives results for a slope covered with riprap, to that of the smooth-surface curve for the same value of d_t.

Laboratory tests made with wind-generated waves[51] indicate that overtopping is increased by the action of the wind at the structure for winds greater than 30 miles per hr. This increase may be as much as 50 per cent. It should be noted, however, that most of the values given in the accompanying graphs are for structures having a smooth face. The one curve in Fig. 10-20b for a riprap-covered wall indicates that a roughened surface tends to reduce the overtopping and may compensate for the wind effect.

Wave Forces. The tremendous destructive forces of waves have long been the topic of writers of fact and fiction. Among the many writers, one who gathered an extensive amount of information and made many observations of his own is D. D. Gaillard.[52] Anyone interested in this topic would find his work, first published in 1904, both interesting and enlightening.

The topic of wave forces can be divided into two subdivisions, forces on shore structures and forces on submerged offshore structures. The first deals with the forces needed to design breakwaters, retaining walls, jetties, groins, and revetments, located in such a manner that long segments of the waves are reflected or absorbed. The second category deals with forces on free-standing structures located far enough from shore so that waves pass by with no distortion except that caused by the structure itself.

Forces on shore structures located in deep water are caused by the increase in depth resulting from a reflected wave, whereas structures located in shallow water must be designed to withstand the impact of breaking waves and the erosive force resulting from the uprush and return of the waves. It has already been shown that when nonbreaking waves are reflected from a vertical wall, the wave height is approximately doubled (p. 10-27). A review of methods for determining forces on a vertical wall resulting from nonbreaking waves has been presented by Hudson.[53] He suggested that one of the more dependable methods for determining this force is that of Sainflou.[54] Minikin[55] also presents the Sainflou method, together with a simplified procedure of his own which is much easier to use. Both procedures indicate that the pressure varies from zero at a distance h above the water surface to a maximum at the still-water level as shown in Fig. 10-21. The Sainflou theory indicates that the pressure at the bottom, p_1, is slightly less than that at the still-water level, p_2, whereas the Minikin method assumes a uniform pressure from the still-water level to the bottom. The diagrams shown in Fig. 10-21 show only the pressures which are produced by the wave reflection, and the hydrostatic pressure resulting from water at a depth d (shown by line SS in Fig. 10-21) must be added to obtain the total force on the wall. In most cases this force can be neglected because it is balanced by an equal and opposite pressure on the back of the wall. The equations for the various parameters are as follows:

Sainflou	*Eq.*	*Minikin*	*Eq.*
$h = H + h_0$	(10-63a)	$h = 1.66H$	(10-63b)
$h_0 = \dfrac{\pi H^2}{L} \coth \dfrac{2\pi d}{L}$	(10-64)		
$p_1 = \dfrac{wH}{\cosh(2\pi d/L)}$	(10-65a)	$p_1 = wH$	(10-65b)
$p_2 = \dfrac{h}{h+d}(wd + p_1)$	(10-66a)	$p_2 = wH$	(10-66b)

The graphs shown in Fig. 10-21 were drawn to represent the following numerical example:

$$H = 10 \text{ ft} \qquad L = 500 \text{ ft} \qquad d = 25 \text{ ft}$$

The solution for p_1 and p_2 by means of the Sainflou equations is facilitated by the use of Figs. 10-2 and 10-6.   The numerical values for this problem are as follows:

	Sainflou	*Minikin*
h	12.1 ft	16.6 ft
p_1	595 lb per sq ft	624 lb per sq ft
p_2	720 lb per sq ft	624 lb per sq ft
Total force	20,800 lb	20,800 lb
Moment at bottom	338,500 ft-lb	353,000 ft-lb

It will be noted here that the computations are much simpler using Minikin equations and that for this example the results are quite similar.   Hudson[53] has reported model test results which show that there is a systematic deviation of the measured overturning moment M_M from the moment computed by the Sainflou method M_S, depending on variations in d/L.   Hudson's curve is reproduced in Fig. 10-22.   It will be seen that, for the value of d/L in the numerical example (0.05), the measured moment would be nearly twice the computed value.   Until further investigations are made, a safe design procedure would be to multiply the computed values by the ratio from Fig. 10-22.

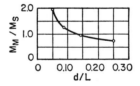

Fɪɢ. 10-21. Wave forces on sea walls, deep water.

Fɪɢ.   10-22.   Wave-force correction factors.

Forces due to *breaking waves* are caused by the impact of the onrushing water.   Laboratory measurements show that there is a great variation in the pressure intensity and that some local areas of very high pressure occur for short intervals. The intensity of pressure is also affected by the amount of entrapped air.[56]   Some observations of damage from breaking waves have provided information regarding pressures over relatively large areas.[57]   These pressures were computed by estimating the force required to move large blocks of stone, taking into consideration the coefficient of friction and the uplift. The maximum pressures were computed by assuming that the horizontal variation in pressure was such that the average pressure was from 0.50 to 0.67 times the maximum.   The two cases reported indicated maximum pressures of approximately 3,000 and 1,800 lb per sq ft for wave heights of 13.5 and 12.0 ft, respectively.   The same writers presented the following semi-empirical relationship:

$$p_{max} = 133.6H \qquad \text{lb per sq ft} \qquad (10\text{-}67)$$

This equation agrees very well with measurements made by Gaillard[52] in the Atlantic Ocean and Lake Superior, as well as the two values reported above.

Minikin[55] derived the following semiempirical equation for forces due to breaking waves:

$$p_{mi} = 2\pi wg \frac{d}{L}\left(\frac{D+d}{2D}\right) H \qquad \text{lb per sq ft} \qquad (10\text{-}68)$$

where p_{mi} is the maximum pressure occurring at the still-water level with a vertical distribution such that the pressure becomes zero a distance $H/2$ above and below the water surface, and the average pressure over the vertical distance H is $p_{mi}/3$.   The other new term introduced in Eq. (10-68) is D, which is defined in Fig. 10-23, Minikin having developed his equation for a

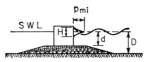

FIG. 10-23. Wave forces on sea walls, breaking waves.

composite breakwater such as the one shown.   The equation is sometimes applied to simple breakwaters (without the rubble base) by assuming that D is the depth one wavelength seaward of the wall.[44]   Equation (10-68) gives pressure somewhat higher than Eq. (10-67).   For comparison of the two, it is necessary to divide p_{mi} [Eq. (10-68)] by 3 in order to obtain the average maximum pressure in a vertical plane; then, for fresh water, and assuming $d = \frac{2}{3}D$, Eq. (10-68) becomes

$$\frac{p_{mi}}{3} = p_{max} = 3,500 \frac{d}{L} H \qquad (10\text{-}69)$$

When $d/L = 0.038$, this equation reduces to Eq. (10-67).

When breaking waves approach a breakwater from a direction such that the angle between the wave crests and the wall, β, is different from zero, the pressure is reduced from the values given by Eq. (10-67) or (10-68). As illustrated in Fig. 10-24, if the average force per square foot of wall resulting from direct wave impact would be p_{av}, then the component perpendicular to

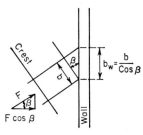

the wall is $p_{av} \cos \beta$. This component is reflected from a wall area equal to $1/\cos \beta$ sq ft and the average pressure on the wall $p_{w,av}$ may be obtained as follows:

$$p_{w,av} = p_{av} \cos^2 \beta \quad (10\text{-}70)$$

FIG. 10-24. Wave forces on sea walls.

Rubble-mound breakwaters fail because of the displacement of individual stones. Extensive model tests conducted at the U.S. Waterways Experiment Station[58] have provided information for the design of such structures. The following equation for the weight of stone required for stability was derived by Hudson.[58]

$$W_r = \frac{w_r H^3}{K_\Delta (S_r - 1)^3 \cot \alpha} \quad (10\text{-}71)$$

where W_r is the weight of a stone in pounds, w_r is the specific weight of the stone, H is the wave height in feet, K_Δ is a coefficient, depending on the shape of the stone, S_r is the specific gravity of the stone relative to the water in which it is being used, and α is the angle between the breakwater face and the horizontal. Tests were conducted for rock and formed concrete units. Values of K_Δ vary from 4 for random placed angular rock to more than 10 for formed units. The tests showed that two layers of armor, or cover stones, provided the optimum amount of protection for the volume of material used. The seaward ends of the breakwater are more vulnerable to wave attack than the body of the breakwater, and the values of K_Δ for nonbreaking waves should be reduced by about 25 per cent from those shown above. For breaking waves values of K_Δ should be about 12 per cent less than for nonbreaking waves.

Some of the formed sections tested in the laboratory were found to be exceedingly stable under wave attack, as indicated

by values of K_Δ much larger than those for quarrystones.[44,49,58]
The question of which type of construction to use in any
particular case would depend on relative costs of quarrystone
and formed units.

Wave Forces on Piling and Submerged Structures. The forces
produced on submerged structures by oscillatory waves are of
two types, the drag force, resulting from the orbital velocity,
and the inertial force, resulting from the orbital acceleration.
The drag force can be expressed as follows:

$$F_d = C_d A \frac{\rho u^2}{2} \tag{10-72}$$

where C_d is the drag coefficient, ρ is the density, A is the cross-
sectional area of the structure in a plane normal to the force,
and u is the component of the orbital velocity in the direction
of the force as given by Eqs. (10-13) and (10-14). The flow
pattern referred to is that which would occur if flow were not
disturbed by the presence of the submerged body. Because of
the nature of the velocity variation [Eq. (10-13)], the horizontal
drag force varies from a maximum downwave value under the
crest $(x/L = 0)$ to a maximum upwave value under a trough
$(x/L = 0.50)$ as illustrated in Fig. 10-1. For steady flow the
drag coefficient has been evaluated for many different shapes
and has been found to be a function of the form and of the
Reynolds number. However, for the periodic unsteady flow
associated with oscillatory wave motion, this quantity may
differ considerably from steady-flow values. An additional
complication arises for the case of large structures because of
the variation of the velocity within the dimensions of the body.

The inertial force is expressed by the equation

$$F_i = C_m \rho V \frac{\partial u}{\partial t} \tag{10-73}$$

where C_m is the coefficient of inertial resistance, V is the displaced volume, and $\partial u/\partial t$ is the component of acceleration in
the direction of the force. This type of force occurs for two
reasons. The acceleration of the fluid is caused by a pressure
gradient so that the pressure on one side of the structure is
different from that on the other side. The resulting force can
be shown to be equal to the product of the acceleration and mass
of the displaced volume. Furthermore, because of the presence
of the structure, the accelerations in the flow around the body

are increased, thus requiring an additional pressure difference. This force divided by the acceleration is called the virtual mass and is conveniently expressed by its ratio to the mass of the fluid displaced. Thus C_m is the sum of a term, approximately unity, for the pressure-gradient force and the coefficient of virtual mass. The variation of the horizontal acceleration [Eq. (10-15)] is such that the horizontal inertial force varies from a maximum downwave value at $x/L = \frac{1}{4}$ to a maximum upwave value at $x/L = \frac{3}{4}$, as illustrated in Fig. 10-1. Values of C_m must be determined experimentally.

The total force is the sum of the two given by Eqs. (10-72) and (10-73).

$$F = C_d A \frac{\rho u^2}{2} + C_m \rho V \frac{\partial u}{\partial t} \qquad (10\text{-}74)$$

Because the two forces are 90° out of phase, the maximum combined downwave force may occur at any value of x from $x/L = 0$ to $x/L = \frac{1}{4}$, depending upon the relative magnitudes of the two components. For any particular value of wave height and wave period and for a particular value of z, F is a function only of the phase angle, and Eq. (10-74) can be expressed as follows:

$$F = C_d' \cos^2 \theta + C_m' \sin \theta \qquad (10\text{-}75)$$

where

$$C_d' = C_d A \frac{p\pi^2 H^2}{2T^2} \left[\frac{\cosh 2\pi(d + z)/L}{\sinh 2\pi d/L} \right]^2 \qquad (10\text{-}76)$$

and

$$C_m' = C_m \rho V \frac{2\pi^2 H}{T^2} \frac{\cosh 2\pi(d + z)/L}{\sinh 2\pi d/L} \qquad (10\text{-}77)$$

The phase angle corresponding to the maximum force is obtained by setting $dF/d\theta = 0$, with the result shown by the equation

$$\sin \theta_{\max} = \frac{C_m'}{2C_d'} \qquad (10\text{-}78)$$

A similar derivation for the phase angle of maximum moment on piles has been presented by Morison.[60]

The equations presented above may be applied to structures having dimensions which are small in the direction of wave motion by taking the velocity and acceleration in Eq. (10-74) at the center of the structure. For large structures it is necessary to take into consideration the variation in velocity and acceleration over the dimension of the body. The methods for finding wave forces on large submerged structures are treated later in this section.

The computation of wave forces on submerged structures from the equations presented above requires information regarding values of C_d and C_m. Values must be determined from unsteady-flow conditions because, as previously explained, steady-flow values do not apply. Model tests on circular cylinders[61] indicate that a value of 2.0 for C_m will give conservative values of the inertial force. However, the same study showed values of C_d varying from 1.2 to 4.4. These tests were made by measuring moments on the model piles; thus the values of C_m and C_d include the integrated effects of distance below the water surface. The same study indicated that when three piles are placed in a row perpendicular to the direction of wave motion, the moment on the center pile will be greater than that on a single pile by amounts varying from about 7 per cent for a pile gap of $1\frac{1}{2}$ pile diameters to approximately 100 per cent for a gap of only $\frac{1}{2}$ diameter. For three piles in a row parallel to the direction of wave travel, the moment on the center pile is about 25 per cent less than that on a single pile.

Tests were also conducted on piles formed of H sections. In this case the volume term V in Eqs. (10-73) and (10-74) is taken as the volume of a cylinder having a diameter equal to the width of a projection of the section on a vertical plane perpendicular to the direction of wave motion. It was found that, when the sides of the H were either perpendicular or parallel to the direction of wave motion, the moments were about twice as large as for a circular pile of the same diameter as the height and width of the H section. When the H section was oriented so that the sides of the H were at a 45° angle with the direction of wave motion, the moment was a maximum and was about 2.75 times greater than for a circular pile of the same size. Measured values of maximum force on horizontal flat plates[63] with the face of the plate perpendicular to the wave motion could be duplicated both as to phase angle [Eq. (10-78)] and magnitude of the force [Eq. (10-74)] by using $C_d = 3.5$ and $C_m = 1.75$, when the volume term in Eq. (10-74) was taken as the volume of the circumscribing cylinder. Tests on vertical plates 1 in. wide[61] indicated that the force was approximately 1.3 times the force on a 1-in. pile.

The computation of wave forces on piles is illustrated by the following numerical examples. Assume that the depth is 100 ft, the wave height is 10 ft, and the wave period is 10 sec. Suppose that it is desired to determine the force distribution and the moment at the bottom for a circular column 3 ft in diameter. Assume that $C_d = 2.0$ and $C_m = 2.0$. From Eq. (10-6), $L_0 = 512$ ft. Then

$$\frac{d}{L_0} = 0.195$$

from Fig. 10-4, $d/L = 0.221$ and $L = 453$ ft; and from Fig. 10-6, $\sinh 2\pi d/L = 1.88$. The values of $\cosh 2\pi(d + z)/L$ given in Table 10-3 were obtained from Fig. 10-6.

Table 10-3

(1)	(2)	(3)	(4)	(5)	(6)	(7)	(8)	(9)
z	$\dfrac{d + z}{L}$	$\cosh \dfrac{2\pi(d + z)}{L}$	$\dfrac{\cosh 2\pi(d + z)/L}{\sinh 2\pi d/L}$	u_x	$\dfrac{\partial u_x}{\partial t}$	F_d	F_i	F
$+\;\;4.25$	.230	2.25	1.20	3.2	1.26	60	35	95
0	.221	2.13	1.13	3.0	1.19	52	33	85
$-\;20$	.177	1.69	.90	2.4	.95	34	26	60
$-\;40$	.133	1.38	.74	2.0	.78	23	21	44
$-\;60$	.088	1.18	.63	1.7	.66	17	18	35
$-\;80$	.044	1.04	.55	1.5	.58	13	16	29
-100	.000	1.00	.53	1.4	.56	11	15	26

The phase angle for which maximum force occurs will be determined on the basis of conditions 20 ft below the water surface ($z = -20$); then, from Eq. (10-76), $C'_d = 46.5$, and from Eq. (10-77), $C'_m = 48.75$, and from Eq. (10-78), $\theta_{\max} = 32°$. By using Eq. (10-1), it is found that the total depth at $\theta = 32°$ is 104.25 ft. Then values of $\overset{\bullet}{u}_x$ and $\partial u_x/\partial t$ may be computed from Eqs. (10-13) and (10-15), respectively. Values F_d, F_i, and F were then computed for 1-ft sections at the selected values of z by means of Eqs. (10-72) to (10-74) as shown in columns 7 to 9 of Table 10-3. The moment at any point can then be computed by breaking the load into increments of length as illustrated in columns 1 to 5 of Table 10-4 for moments at the bottom.

Table 10-4

Diameter of column = 3 ft					Diameter of column = 6 ft		
(1)	(2)	(3)	(4)	(5)	(6)	(7)	(8)
z, ft	F, lb per ft	F_{av}, lb per ft	Moment arm, ft	M, 1000's of ft-lb	F, lb per ft	F_{av}, lb per ft	M, 1,000's of ft-lb
+ 4.25	95						
		90	102	39			
0	85				260		
		72.5	90	130		230	410
− 20	60				200		
		52	70	73		180	250
− 40	44				160		
		39.5	50	40		150	150
− 60	35				140		
		32	30	19		130	78
− 80	29				120		
		27.5	10	15		110	22
−100	26				100		
Total				316			910

If the diameter of the column had been 6 ft instead of 3 ft, Eq. (10-78) would have indicated that θ_{max} is 90°. For this phase angle the force is entirely inertial and the depth would be 100 ft. The corresponding values of forces and moments are shown in columns 6 to 8, Table 10-4.

Submerged pipelines make up a special class of structures which are frequently exposed to wave forces. An extensive research program was carried out at the University of Michigan to determine inertial and drag coefficients for model circular pipes.[62] The tests were made on pipes of four diameters in a range such that for a scale ratio of 1:75, pipes varying in diameter from 8 to 23 ft would be represented. The wave height and wavelength were also varied, and the forces were measured with the pipes at four locations above the bottom, the lowest of which was with the pipe as near the bottom as possible without touching. Other tests were made with the pipe in trenches of various shapes. Forces were predominantly inertial, but for the smaller diameters and wave heights the effect of the drag force was becoming noticeable. A dimensionless criterion was developed which indicated when the drag force should be considered. This criterion is D^2/HL, in which D is the diameter of the pipe. When $D^2/HL = 0.02$, the drag force starts to influence the maximum force.

The values of C_m derived from the tests covered a wide range of experimental conditions, but it was found that a high degree of correlation occurred when C_m was related to z/L. When the pipe is above the bottom $(0.25 < -z/d < 0.75)$, Eq. (10-79) fits the data very closely.

$$C_m = 1.73 + 5.37 \frac{-z}{L} \qquad (10\text{-}79)$$

When the pipe is at the bottom,

$$C_m = 3.07 + 4.13 \frac{-z}{L} \qquad (10\text{-}80)$$

For a half-buried pipe,

$$C_m = 1.01 + 2.85 \frac{-z}{L} \qquad (10\text{-}81)$$

And when the pipe is below the bottom in a trench,

$$C_m = 1.0 + 1.4 \frac{-z}{L} \qquad (10\text{-}82)$$

Some additional refinements can be obtained by referring to the original article. Values of C_d were obtained from measured forces[62] at wave crests and troughs $(x/L = 0$ and $0.50)$ where the forces can be expected to be entirely due to drag. The values of C_d show clear trends when plotted against the Reynolds number (R). However, values of R only extended to 10,000, and prototype values of R would be much larger. The test results showed C_d dropping to 2 as R increased to 10,000 for pipes at or above the bottom.

As an example of the application of this information to a practical problem, the force per unit length will be computed for a 16-ft pipe located on the bottom in a depth of 40 ft. Waves having a height of 12 ft and a period of 8 sec pass over the pipe in a direction such that the crests are parallel to the pipe. From Eq. (10-6),

$$L_0 = 5.12T^2 = 328 \text{ ft}$$

and

$$\frac{d}{L_0} = 0.122$$

From Fig. 10-4 $\quad \frac{d}{L} = 0.160$

and then

$$L = 250 \text{ ft}$$

The value of D^2/HL is then found to be 0.09, which shows that the inertial force predominates and the maximum force can be computed from Eq. (10-73) for a phase angle of 90 or 270°. The value of z for the center of the pipe is -32 ft. The corresponding value of z/L is -0.128, and C_m may be computed from Eq. (10-80).

$$C_m = 3.07 + 4.13 \frac{-z}{L} = 3.60$$

Then

$$F_i = C_m V \frac{\partial u}{\partial t} \tag{10-83}$$
$$= 3.60 \times 201 \times 3.20 = 4,490 \text{ lb/ft}$$

Structures which have large horizontal dimensions in the direction of wave motion, for example of the order of magnitude of a quarter of a wavelength, have negligible friction forces compared with the inertial forces, and the maximum forces occur at $x/L = \frac{1}{4}$ and $\frac{3}{4}$.[62,63] When computing the inertial force from Eq. (10-73) for such large structures, it is necessary to obtain an average value of acceleration, $(\partial u/\partial t)_{av}$. A convenient way to approach this problem is to express the inertial force in terms of the difference in pressure on the two sides of the submerged body. Consider a mass of fluid of rectangular cross section, as shown in Fig. (10-25a), centered at $x/L = \frac{1}{4}$ (or $\frac{3}{4}$) with an area A perpendicular to the direction of wave motion. Then

$$F_i = V \left(\frac{\partial u}{\partial t}\right)_{av} = (p_1 - p_2)A \tag{10-84}$$

where p_1 and p_2 are the pressure intensities on the up- and down-wave sides of the fluid mass, respectively. If the fluid mass is then replaced by a solid body, Eq. (10-84) must have the coefficient of inertial resistance added, and the expression for the inertial force becomes

$$F_i = C_m V \left(\frac{\partial u}{\partial t}\right)_{av} = C_m(p_1 - p_2) \tag{10-85}$$

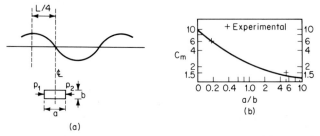

Fɪɢ. 10-25. Coefficient of inertial resistance, submerged bodies of rectangular cross-section.

The value of $p_1 - p_2$ determined from the equation of motion in the vertical direction[63] for the special case of structures centered at the location of maximum acceleration, $x/L = \frac{1}{4}$, is given by the equation.

$$p_1 - p_2 = wH \left(K - 2 \sinh^2 \frac{\pi H \cos 2\pi x_1/L}{2L} \right) \cos \frac{2\pi x_1}{L} \quad (10\text{-}86)$$

in which x_1 is the horizontal coordinate of the upwave side of the structure, i.e., the location where the pressure is p_1, and K is defined as follows:

$$K = \frac{\cosh 2\pi(d + z)/L}{\cosh 2\pi d/L} \quad (10\text{-}87)$$

An interesting application of Eq. (10-86) is to the case of the pressure difference between a crest and a trough; then, x_1/L being zero, Eq. (10-86) can be written

$$p_c - p_t = wH \left(K - 2 \sinh^2 \frac{\pi H}{2L} \right) \quad (10\text{-}88)$$

Solution of this equation for H would give the value for wave height corresponding to pressure differences recorded by a pressure gage at the bottom of the sea. Measurements made by Folsom[64] indicate that values of H computed from this equation from measured values of $p_c - p_t$ will be somewhat smaller than the actual wave heights.

Measurements of vertical and horizontal forces on large rectangular-shaped structures[63] provided values of C_m which agree reasonably well with values estimated from theory for flow without separation by Riabauchinski.[65] A curve based on his derivation is shown in Fig. 10-25b along with two experimental values.[63]   The values of C_m vary with H/L, or for a given L they vary with H as well as with the location of the structure with respect to the water surface, z.   This is illustrated in Fig. 10-26a in which C_m is plotted with respect to H/L for three

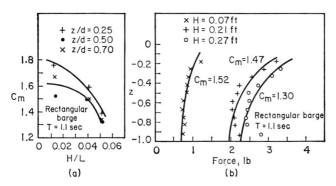

FIG. 10-26. Wave forces on submerged structures.

values of z/d.   The model from which the values were determined was a rectangular parallelepiped 2 to 6 in. long, 10 in. wide, and $1\frac{7}{8}$ high.   The large surfaces were parallel to the water surface, and the long side was perpendicular to direction of wave motion.[63]   The variation of C_m with H for a constant L is shown in Fig. 10-26b, in which force is plotted against z for three different wave heights.   The curves were computed by means of Eq. (10-85), using the value of C_m (indicated on the graph), which gave the best fit in each case.   It may be noted, however, that variations of C_m are relatively small.

The computation of forces on a large structure is illustrated by the following example.   A rectangular barge, 200 ft long, 50 ft wide, and 15 ft high, is centered 40 ft below the water surface in a depth of 100 ft.   The orientation of the barge would be as shown in Fig. 25a if a were 50 ft and b were 15 ft. The wave height is 10 ft, and the period is 10 sec, as in the problem illustrating the computation of forces on piling.   The horizontal force may be computed from Eqs. (10-85) and (10-86).   The value of C_m is estimated as 1.5 from Fig. 10-25b, knowing that a/b is $\frac{50}{15} = 3.3$. A is

$$200 \times 15 = 3{,}000 \text{ sq ft}$$

K in Eq. (10-86) is evaluated with the aid of Fig. 10-6 as $1.38/2.13 = 0.65$.

$$x_1 = \frac{L}{4} - \frac{50}{2} = \frac{453}{4} - 25 = 88 \text{ ft}$$

Then

$$\cos \frac{2\pi x_1}{L} = \cos 70_d = 0.342$$

Finally,

$$\sinh^2 \frac{\pi H \cos 2\pi x_1/L}{2L} = \sinh^2 2\pi \times 0.0019 = 0.01$$

and

$$p_1 - p_2 = 62.4 \times 10 \times (0.65 - 0.02) \times 0.342 = 135 \text{ lb per sq ft}$$

Then

$$F = 1.5 \times 135 \times 3,000 = 600,000 \text{ lb}$$

The vertical force may be computed from Eq. (10-73). In this case, $a/b = 0.3$, and from Fig. 10-25, $C_m = 4.1$. From Eq. (10-16), noting that the maximum vertical acceleration occurs at $\theta = 0$,

$$\frac{\partial u_z}{\partial t} = \frac{-2\pi^2 H}{T_2} \frac{\sinh 2\pi(d + z)/L}{\sin 2\pi d/L}$$
$$= \frac{-2\pi^2 \times 10}{100} \frac{0.94}{1.88} = 0.99 \text{ ft per sec per sec}$$

and

$$F_2 = -4.1 \times 1.94 \times 150,000 \times 0.99 = -1,200,000 \text{ lb}$$

Wind Tides. The action of wind on a body of water not only produces waves, but also induces a drag which moves surface water in the direction of the wind. Thus the water becomes deeper on the leeward end of a body of water and shallower on the windward end. The increase in depth at the leeward end is also referred to as wind setup. The difference in pressure at the two ends of a lake induces a return flow along the bottom. Wind tides must be taken into consideration in planning the crest elevations of dams and levees. The still-water level referred to in the section Wave Run-up and Overtopping, above, should be taken as the wind-tide level associated with that particular wind. The low tide on the windward end of the lake must be taken into consideration in selecting the elevations of water intakes and the bottoms of navigation channels. Wind tides as large as 7 ft above or below the mean lake level have been recorded on Lake Erie.[66]

A number of analytical laboratory and field investigations[67-72] have been made to determine the factors affecting wind tides. The analytical development used in each case leads to the differential equation

$$\frac{\partial z}{\partial x} = \frac{C\tau_s}{\rho g z} \qquad (10\text{-}89)$$

where z is the depth at any location, x is distance along the fetch, τ_s is the shear stress on the water surface due to the wind, and C is a coefficient which is related to the ratio of the shear stress on the bottom to that on the surface. The shear stress on the water surface may be expressed as follows:

$$\tau_s = C_D \rho_a U^2 \qquad (10\text{-}90)$$

where C_D is a drag coefficient, ρ_a is the density of the air, and U is a characteristic velocity of the air near the water surface. Then Eq. (10-89) can be written

$$\frac{\partial z}{\partial x} = \frac{C C_d \rho_p U^2}{\rho_w g z} \qquad (10\text{-}91)$$

For cases where the depth does not vary greatly, z may be replaced by the still-water depth. Whether or not z is replaced by d, integration of Eq. (10-91) along the entire fetch F shows that the total difference in water-surface elevation may be expressed by the following functional relationship, neglecting variations in the density of the air and water:

$$S = f\left(\frac{FU^2}{d}\right) \qquad (10\text{-}92)$$

Although the amount of increase in depth at the leeward end of the body of water, h, may not be half of S, because of the curved nature of the water surface, yet it may be assumed that h is also a function of F, U^2, and d. Sibul[71] has developed the following empirical relationships, having the general form of Eq. (10-92), which represents quite well his laboratory data and also data from larger bodies of water, including Lake Okeechobee and observations in the Baltic Sea.

$$\frac{h}{d} = 2.44 \times 10^{-5} \left(\frac{F}{d}\right)^{1.66} \left(\frac{U^2}{Fg}\right)^a \qquad (10\text{-}93)$$

and

$$a = 2.02 \left(\frac{F}{d}\right)^{-0.0768} \tag{10-94}$$

The equations may be used to estimate wind setup when no records are available. The decline in water-surface elevation at the windward end of a lake is usually slightly less than the positive tide h at the leeward end.

The following is an example of the use of Eqs. (10-93) and (10-94). Suppose the fetch is 10 miles, the wind velocity is 40 ft per sec, and the average depth is 20 ft. Then

$$\frac{U^2}{Fg} = \frac{40^2}{10 \times 5,200 \times 32.2} = 0.00094$$

and

$$\frac{F}{d} = \frac{10 \times 5,200}{20} = 2,640$$

Then

$$a = 2.02 \times 2,640^{-0.0768} = 1.1$$

and

$$\frac{h}{d} = \frac{2.44}{10^5} \times 2.640^{1.66} \times 0.00094^{1.1} = 0.0051$$

from which it is found that $h = 0.10$ ft.

More exact results can be obtained for a particular body of water with wind records,[66] thus eliminating depth and fetch as variables. Wind velocities may be corrected to a selected elevation above the water surface,[22] although this is probably not necessary. Indeed, the equations do not seem to be sensitive to small variations in the height of the wind measurements, because the values used to derive Eq. (10-93) were obtained in part from laboratory observations in a closed tunnel and in part from field observations for which no mention is made of the elevation at which values of U were measured.

The effect of bottom roughness on setup has been studied by means of laboratory tests.[72] This research indicated that, for lake bottoms covered by dense weed growth, the setup may be as much as twice the value computed for a smooth bottom when the water depth is equal to, or just a little greater than, the thickness of the roughness. For water depths varying from one to four times the height of the roughness, reasonable results can be obtained by taking the depth of the water as the depth above the roughness. For depths greater than four times the roughness, the roughness has little effect. When the depth becomes less than the roughness, the tides are reduced. For example, for a depth of half the height of the roughness, it was found that the tide was only 0.08 that for a smooth bottom.

If the wind crosses the long dimension of a lake at an angle θ, the wind setup may be estimated by applying cos θ to h. When the shape of the lake is such as to concentrate the water in a small area on the leeward end, it has been recommended that a form factor be applied.[67]

Shore-erosion Control. The shore processes resulting from waves and littoral currents cause a more or less continuous movement of shore materials called littoral drift. At some locations the deposition of littoral drift replaces the displaced material with new material, thus producing a stable shoreline. At other locations, either accretion or depletion may predominate, thus creating shorelines which are moving in seaward or landward directions. At some locations this process may change from time to time, depending on such factors as water levels and the direction of major storms. Erosion conditions may also be created artificially by the construction of jetties extending into deep water or the dredging of an inlet, either of which intercepts the littoral drift and causes erosion on the downdrift side. Littoral drift occurs at a maximum rate when the turbulence resulting from wave action loosens the heavier material and places lighter material in suspension so that it can be transported by the currents. Littoral currents may be caused by large-scale circulation of the water. However, such currents are usually small compared with those induced by wind during a major storm. Strong local currents are generated when refraction creates large waves at points of land and much smaller waves at adjacent bays. As a result, onshore currents occur at points and offshore currents, called rip currents, occur in the bays. Only a brief outline of protective measures will be presented here. Much more detailed discussions are available.[44,73]

The major portion of the movement of littoral materials occurs during unusually large storms. Not only is the erosive power of large waves and currents much greater than that of smaller waves and currents, but larger winds produce greater wind tides which bring the erosive action closer to the bluffs shoreward of the beach. As a result, the bulk of the erosion during a period of several years may occur during only a few days. The erosion process is illustrated graphically in Fig. 10-27 in which the size of the boxes shows the relative im-

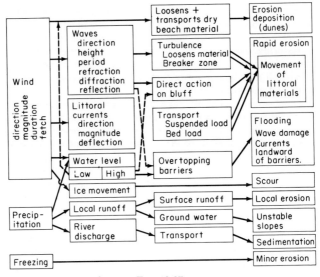

Fig. 10-27.

portance of the various factors in a qualitative way. The left column gives the energy sources, and successive columns depict the physical manifestations of the energy, the nature of the process, and the nature of the resulting erosion, respectively. The prevention of erosion in vulnerable locations requires extensive and expensive measures which must not only be carefully designed to accomplish their purpose but which must be planned to prevent increasing erosion at neighboring shore areas. Whenever possible it is best to avoid interfering with the natural processes by zoning to prevent building near the shore or by moving existing structures which are in danger. When one of these alternatives is not possible, protection may be provided by various methods which are described briefly here. More detailed discussions[44,73] are available.

The best protection against erosion is a wide beach, which causes the waves to break and dissipate their energy before attacking the rear-shore land. Consequently, the most basic and best method of preventing excessive shore damage is by means of artificial nourishment of a beach. However, because depletion of the sand is quite likely to occur in an area where erosion is in progress, the nourishment must usually be repeated at intervals. Beach material may be dredged from deep water or hauled from other sources. It should never be derived from near-shore areas. Where lack of beach is caused by the presence of an inlet, a permanent dredge installation may be made to nourish the downdrift area.

An effective method of retaining a beach is by the use of groins. Groins are walls extending from the banks behind the beach into the water. In many locations the construction of groins causes a beach to be established because of the natural littoral drift. Groins should not be so long as to interrupt permanently the movement of shore material. The most effective length and spacing of groins depend upon the severity of wave action and the nature of the shore material. For severe conditions on the Great Lakes a spacing and length of such dimensions that 70-ft squares are formed in the water have been found effective.[73] For milder conditions the spacing may be increased. The groins should extend at least a foot above the still-water level and should extend well back into the bank behind the beach. It is very important to eliminate permeability from the groins. Permeable groins are rarely effective.

Shores may also be protected by means of revetments or sea walls. Revetments are paved sections having the same slope as the bank. Care must be used to anchor the toe of the revetment and to prevent leaching through revetments constructed of rubble. Sea walls should be avoided wherever possible because the presence of a vertical smooth surface helps to maintain the wave energy and thus increases the intensity of both the turbulence and the littoral currents. As a consequence, erosion is accelerated at the wall, and the design of such walls must take into account the possibility of increased erosion in order to prevent failure from the force due to the fill on the shore side. Finally, it should be noted that an effective but expensive method of preventing erosion is by the construction of an offshore breakwater. Usually, the prevention of erosion alone would not justify such an expensive procedure.

Translatory Waves

A sudden increase or decrease in the discharge in an open channel creates a translatory wave. As the name indicates, the water is displaced during the passage of the wave. This is in contrast to oscillatory waves, in which the fluid oscillates in a nearby fixed orbit (p. 10-2). The wave shown in Fig. 10-28*a* might have been produced by the sudden opening of a gate or the failure of a dam at an upstream location. The

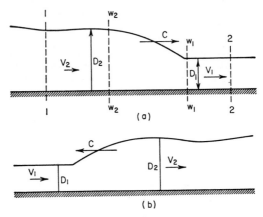

Fig. 10-28. Translatory waves.

wave of Fig. 10-28*b* would result from the sudden closing of a gate at a downstream location. The tidal bore is an example of a wave of translation which is produced on certain rivers by rising tides. A form of translatory wave which has a single crest rising above the still-water level is called a solitary wave. Waves of this type may be produced on the Great Lakes by the passage of a low-pressure area. The waves discussed so far are all positive waves in that the depth is increased. At the opposite sides of the gates which may have produced the positive waves shown in Fig. 10-28*a* and *b*, a sudden decrease in depth, called a negative wave, would be projected along the channel.

The conditions upon which the following equations are based are, in all cases, transient ones. After the passage of the initial wave there may be a series of irregular waves, including in many cases reflected waves; the flow will eventually reach a steady condition for which the depth and velocity will be controlled by friction alone.

Positive Waves. The depths and velocities on either side of a translatory wave as well as the velocity of the wave itself, C, must be such as to satisfy continuity and momentum relationships. If the conditions before the passage of the wave, D_1 and V_2, are known, there would be three unknown quantities, D_2, V_2, and C. These can be determined by applying the continuity and momentum equations, together with one known condition resulting from the cause of the wave. Most commonly, this latter condition is the new discharge. In the derivations of the equations, velocities from left to right are considered to be positive. Thus, in Fig. 10-28a, all quantities will be positive, whereas in Fig. 10-28b the value of C will be negative. The derivation will be carried out for the conditions shown in Fig. 10-28a for a unit width of a wide rectangular channel. However, the corresponding equations for Fig. 10-28b, as well as for a channel of any cross section, are presented in Table 10-5.

The discharge entering the moving wave through w_1-w_1 is

$$q_{w1} = D_1(C - V_1) \qquad (10\text{-}95a)$$

and that leaving the wave through w_2-w_2 is

$$q_{w2} = D_2(C - V_2) \qquad (10\text{-}96a)$$

If the form of the wave between w_1 and w_2 remains constant, q_{w1} is equal to q_{w2}. Equating these expressions for q_w and rearranging terms results in the following forms of the continuity equations:

$$V_2 = \frac{D_1}{D_2}(V_1 - C) + C \qquad (10\text{-}97a)$$

$$V_1 = \frac{D_2}{D_1}(V_2 - C) + C \qquad (19\text{-}98a)$$

It may be noted from Table 10-5 that Eqs. (10-97a) and (10-97b) are identical for both directions of wave travel. Continuity may also be expressed by considering the inflow, outflow, and change in volume of a fixed reach of the channel such as 1-2 in Fig. 10-28a. Then

$$D_2V_2 = D_1V_1 + C(D_2 - D_1) \qquad (10\text{-}99)$$

Rearrangement of this equation also yields Eqs. (10-97a) and (10-98a).

The momentum equation must be satisfied for the fluid passing through the wave. Neglecting shear stresses resulting from

Table 10-5

Wave travels in direction of flow (Fig. 10-28a)				Wave travels opposite to direction of flow (Fig. 10-28b)	
Wide rectangular channels	Eq.	General case	Eq.	Wide rectangular channels	Eq.
$q_{w1} = D_1(C - V_1)$ $q_{w2} = D_2(C - V_2)$	(10-95a) (10-96a)	$Q_{w1} = a_1(C - V_1)$ $Q_{w2} = a_2(C - V_2)$	(10-95a) (10-96aa)	$q_{w1} = D_1(-C + V_1)$ $q_{w2} = D_2(-C + V_2)$	(10-95b) (10-96b)
$V_2 = \dfrac{D_1}{D_2}(V_1 - C) + C$	(10-97a)	$V_2 = \dfrac{a_1}{a_2}(V_1 - C) + C$	(10-97aa)	$V_2 = \dfrac{D_1}{D_2}(V_1 - C) + C$	(10-97b)
$V_1 = \dfrac{D_2}{D_1}(V_2 - C) + C$	(10-98a)	$V_1 = \dfrac{a_2}{a_1}(V_2 - C) + C$	(10-98aa)	$V_1 = \dfrac{D_2}{D_1}(V_2 - C) + C$	(10-98b)
$C = \sqrt{\dfrac{gD_2}{2D_1}(D_2 + D_1)} + V_1$	(10-101a)	$C = \sqrt{\dfrac{g(a_2\bar{y}_2 - a_1\bar{y}_1)}{a_1(1 - a_1/a_2)}} + V_1$	(10-101aa)	$C = -\sqrt{\dfrac{gD_2}{2D_1}(D_2 + D_1)} + V_1$	(10-101b)
$C_s = \sqrt{\dfrac{gD_2}{2D_1}(D_2 + D_1)}$	(10-102a)			$C_s = -\sqrt{\dfrac{gD_2}{2D_1}(D_2 + D_1)}$	(10-102b)
$C_s = \sqrt{\dfrac{gD_1}{2}}\sqrt{\dfrac{D_2}{D_1}\left(\dfrac{D_2}{D_1}+1\right)}$	(10-103a)			$C_s = -\sqrt{\dfrac{gD_1}{2}}\sqrt{\dfrac{D_2}{D_1}\left(\dfrac{D_2}{D_1}+1\right)}$	(10-103b)
$C = C_s + V_1$	(10-104a)			$C = -C_s + V_1$	(10-104b)
$C = \sqrt{gD} + V_1$	(10-105a)	$C = \sqrt{gD_m} + V_1$	(10-105aa)	$C = -\sqrt{gD} + V_1$	(10-105b)

the resistance of the bottom, the walls, and the atmosphere and the gravitational component of force and assuming that the velocity is uniform in each cross section, the following is the expression equating force to rate of change of momentum:

$$\frac{wD_2{}^2}{2} - \frac{wD_1{}^2}{2} = \frac{q_w w}{g}(V_2 - V_1) \qquad (10\text{-}100)$$

Replacing q_w with its value from Eq. (10-95a), dividing by w, and rearranging the terms lead to the following expression for wave velocity:

$$C = \sqrt{\frac{gD_2}{2D_1}(D_2 + D_1)} + V_1 \qquad (10\text{-}101a)$$

The general form of this equation which applies to channels of any cross-sectional form [Eq. (10-101aa)] is given in Table 10-5. For the case of the wave moving upstream, it may be seen from Eq. (10-101b) of the table that the difference is in the sign of the first term on the right side of the equation. When V_1 is zero, Eq. (10-101a) becomes

$$C_s = \sqrt{\frac{gD_2}{2D_1}(D_2 + D_1)} \qquad (10\text{-}102a)$$

where C_s is the velocity of a translatory wave in still water. The expression for C_s may be written in the following form:

$$C_s = \sqrt{\frac{gD_1}{2}}\sqrt{\frac{D_2}{D_1}\left(\frac{D_2}{D_1} + 1\right)} \qquad (10\text{-}103a)$$

which lends itself to graphical presentation as shown in Fig. 10-29. Equation (10-101a) can then be written as follows:

$$C = C_s + V_1 \qquad (10\text{-}104a)$$

When the wave is very small so that $D_2 \to D_1 \to D$, Eq. (10-101a) reduces to Eq. (10-105a) of Table 10-5:

$$C = \sqrt{gD} + V_1 \qquad (10\text{-}105a)$$

In the corresponding equation for the general case [Eq. (10-105aa) of Table 10-5] the mean depth D_m is introduced, which is the area divided by the top width, a/T.

Equation (10-105a) above may be used to show why translatory waves which involve an increase in depth have abrupt faces similar to a hydraulic jump. If the total wave is considered as

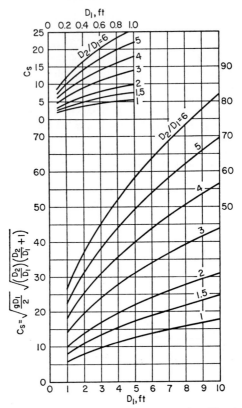

FIG. 10-29. Celerity of translatory waves in still water.

a series of small waves or steps, then, according to Eq. (10-105a), the highest wave has the largest velocity, thus tending to over-take the small waves at lower depths. The fact that a transla-tory wave is similar to a hydraulic jump may be shown by setting C equal to zero in Eq. (10-101b) of Table 10-5; then

$$V_1 = \sqrt{\frac{gD_2}{2D_1}\,(D_1 + D_2)}$$

indicating that the wave is moving upstream at the same speed that the water is carrying it downstream. Rearrangement of the above equation shows that this equation is identical with the one for a jump in rectangular channels which was derived in Sec. 8 [Eq. (8-111)].

Lansford[74] has reported a series of tests conducted in a rectangular channel 5 ft wide and 140 ft long in which sudden closure of a gate was made. His test results over a considerable range of discharges and depths indicated that Eq. (10-101b) gives reliable results. One of Lansford's test conditions will be used as a numerical example.

Example. In a rectangular channel 5 ft wide the depth D_1 is 2.5 ft and the discharge Q is 5 cu ft per sec. A gate is suddenly closed, reducing the discharge to zero ($Q_2 = 0$ and $V_2 = 0$). Determine the velocity C at which the wave will travel upstream and the depth D_2 just after closure of the gate.

$$q_1 = \frac{Q_1}{b} = \frac{5}{5} = 1.0 \text{ cu ft per sec per ft}$$

$$V_1 = \frac{q_1}{D_1} = \frac{1}{2.5} = 0.4 \text{ ft per sec}$$

Then Eqs. (10 97b) and (10-104b) of Table 10-5 become

$$0 = \frac{2.5}{D_2}(0.40 - C) + C \qquad (10\text{-}97b)$$

and

$$C = -C_s + 0.40 \qquad (10\text{-}104b)$$

These equations may be solved by trial in several ways. The method used here is to assume a value of D_2, compute C from (10-103b) and (10-104b) (see Table 10-5), and then insert these values in Eq. (10-97b), repeating until the right side of Eq. (10-97b) is zero.

Assume $D_2 = 2.60$. Then $D_2/D_1 = 1.04$, and the approximate value for C_s can be read from Fig. 10-29 as 9.2 ft per sec. Substitution in Eq. (10-104b) yields $C = -8.8$ ft per sec. Substitution of C and D_2 in Eq. (10-97b) gives

$$(2.5/2.6)(0.40 + 8.8) - 8.8 = 0.05 > 0$$

In order to determine a more exact solution, it is necessary to use Eq. (10-103b) rather than the graphs of Fig. 10-29. A trial value of $D_2 = 2.62$ yields $C = -8.9$ from Eq. (10-104b), and when these values are substituted into Eq. (10-97b), they satisfy the equation very closely. Lansford did not publish the values of D_2, but the measured value of C for this test was -8.95, which differs only a small amount from the computed value.

Tests published by the U.S. Army Corps of Engineers[75] provide data which may be used to check the translatory-wave equations for the condition of a sudden increase in discharge in the direction of flow. The tests were conducted in a long flume 4 ft wide. A dam was so constructed that a uniform discharge passed beneath the dam, and provision was made for suddenly removing all or portions of the dam. The increased discharge Q_2 was measured, and the depth and arrival time of the waves were determined at various locations up to 180 ft below the dam. Some of the results are summarized in Table 10-6. Of principal interest are the measured and computed depths. The measured depths given in the table are the depths at the crests averaged for three locations below the dam, $x = 25$ ft, $x = 80$ ft, and $x = 150$ ft. The measured wave velocities are obtained by dividing the distance below the dam, x, by the arrival time. Values are given for the three locations because they differed. The first five lines are for conditions of minimum resistance, whereas the last two lines are for the case of an artificially roughened channel. It will be noted that the computed depths D_2 agreed quite well with the measured values. Most of the computed wave velocities are in close agreement with the velocity measured at $x = 80$ ft or $x = 150$ ft for the smooth channel, whereas for the rough channel the agreement is with the velocities computed at $x = 25$ ft. This is to be expected because the channel resistance causes a gradual reduction in velocity, and this factor is not included in the equations. The following example illustrates the computations for the values in the top row of data presented in Table 10-6.

Example

$Q_1 = 1.00$ cu ft per sec

$$q_1 = \frac{Q_1}{b} = \frac{1}{4} = 0.25 \text{ cu ft per sec per ft}$$

$D_1 = 0.10$ ft

$$V_1 = \frac{q}{D_1} = \frac{0.25}{0.10} = 2.5 \text{ ft per sec}$$

$Q_2 = 6.6$ cu ft per sec

$$q_2 = \frac{Q_2}{b} = \frac{6.6}{4} = 1.65 \text{ cu ft per sec per ft}$$

Table 10-6

Test No.	D_1, ft	V_1, ft per sec	q_2, cu ft per sec per ft	D_2 Measured	D_2 Computed	C $x = 25$	C $x = 80$	C $x = 150$	C Computed
1.1 (10)	.10	2.50	1.65	.30	.30	7.8	6.7	6.8	6.9
1.1 (20)	.20	3.84	1.98	.34	.36	8.5	8.0	7.5	7.9
2.1 (10)	.10	2.50	1.25	.25	.26	7.1	6.3	6.3	6.3
2.1 (20)	.20	3.84	1.63	.31	.32	8.3	7.5	7.2	7.5
3.1 (10)	.10	2.50	.88	.20	.21	7.0	6.2	6.0	5.7
1.2 (32)	.32	0.78	1.40	.54	.53	5.4	5.0	4.6	5.5
1.2 (50)	.56	1.37	1.68	.66	.70	6.3	6.2	6.0	6.4

Assume $D_2 = 0.30$ ft; then

$$\frac{D_2}{D_1} = \frac{0.30}{0.10} = 3.0$$

and from Fig. 10-29,

$$C_s = 4.4$$

Then, from Eq. (10-104a),

$$C = C_s + V_1 = 4.4 + 2.5 = 6.9$$

The continuity equation (10-97a) is then used as a check:

$$V_2 = \frac{q_2}{D_2} = \frac{D_1}{D_2}(V_1 - C) + C$$
$$\frac{1.65}{0.30} = \frac{0.10}{0.30}(2.5 - 6.9) + 6.9$$
$$5.5 \neq 5.4$$

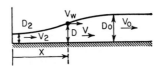

Fig. 10-30. Negative wave.

This was considered to be sufficiently near to an equality, and the computed values of D_2 and C were taken as 0.30 ft and 6.9 ft per sec, respectively. It should be noted that the suddenly increased discharge continued for only a few seconds in this case. However, even if the new discharge were maintained indefinitely, the computed value of D_2 represents only a transient condition and the depth will eventually be stabilized in accordance with the fractional resistance of the channel.

Negative Waves. A decrease in depth is produced on the downstream side of a gate, which is suddenly closed, or on the upstream side of a gate, which is suddenly opened. If the resulting wave is considered as a series of small waves, Eq. (10-105a) or (10-105b) may be applied to the individual small waves by replacing V_1 with the local velocity at the depth D as indicated in Fig. 10-30. The top wave will have the highest velocity, $C_{max} = \sqrt{gD_0} + V_0$, with the result that a rapid flattening of the wave will occur. Indeed, there is little or no appearance of a wave, but rather a gradual recession of the water surface.

The shape of a negative wave may be determined by a method suggested by Streeter.[76] If the momentum equation is written for a very small wave, the relation corresponding to Eq. (10-100) is

$$wy \, dy = \frac{w}{g} (C - V)y \, dV \qquad (10\text{-}106)$$

Inserting the value of C from Eq. (10-105a) and integrating yields

$$V = V_0 - 2\sqrt{gD_0} + 2\sqrt{gD} \qquad (10\text{-}107)$$

Combining Eqs. (10-107) and (10-105a) yields

$$C = V_0 + 3\sqrt{gD} - 2\sqrt{gD_0} \qquad (10\text{-}108)$$

Then, because $x = Ct$, the equation for the surface becomes

$$x = (V_0 + 3\sqrt{gD} - 2\sqrt{gD_0})t \qquad (10\text{-}109)$$

The depth D_2 at the gate depends on the discharge Q_2 after the gate has been partially closed. For total closure, Q_2 and V_2 are zero. For partial closure, Q_2 must be known and the equation $Q_2 = D_2 V_2 b$ may be combined with Eq. (10-109) to determine D_2.

Solitary Waves. A particular type of translatory wave which has a single crest tapering off to the original water surface in both directions as shown in Fig. 10-31 is called a solitary wave. Such a wave may be generated on the oceans by a seismic disturbance or on the Great Lakes by the passing of a localized low-pressure area. The latter type is sometimes called seiche. A laboratory investigation by Daily and Stephan[77] showed that Eq. (10-110) very closely agrees with observations. It will be noted that this equation is the same as Eq. (10-105a), previously developed.

$$C = \sqrt{gD_1} \left(1 + \frac{a}{D_1}\right)^{1/2} = \sqrt{gD_2} \qquad (10\text{-}110)$$

The water particles within a solitary wave move in the direction of wave motion with a velocity which gradually reaches a maximum u under the crest and then returns to zero as the wave passes by. An approximate value for u may be derived by applying the continuity equation to the wave as follows: In Fig. 10-31 a velocity to the left, equal to C, is applied to the entire system. Then

$$CD_1 = (C - u)D_2$$

and

$$u = C \left(1 - \frac{D_1}{D_2} \right) \tag{10-111}$$

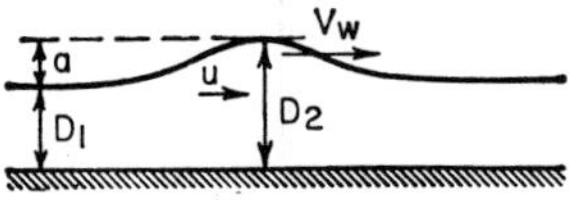

FIG. 10-31. Solitary wave.

Although it is assumed in the development of the theory that u is uniform from crest to bottom, tests have shown that there is some variation and that the velocity near the surface is somewhat larger than u.

Bibliography

1. F. Gerstner: Theorie der Wellen, *Gilberst's Ann. Phys.*, vol. 32, pp. 412–445, 1809.
2. M. P. O'Brien and M. A. Mason: A Summary of the Theory of Oscillatory Waves, *U.S. Army Corps Engrs.*, *Beach Erosion Board, Tech. Rept.* 2, 1942.
3. R. L. Wiegel and J. W. Johnson: Elements of Wave Theory, *Proc. First Conf. on Coastal Eng.*, chap. 1, Engineering Foundation, Council on Wave Research, Berkeley, Calif., 1951.
4. M. A. Mason and W. C. Hall: A Study of Progressive Oscillatory Waves in Water, *U.S. Army Corps Engrs.*, *Beach Erosion Board, Tech. Rept.* 1, 1941.
5. G. B. Airy: "On Tides and Waves," Encyclopaedia Metropolitana, vol. 5, p. 289, 1845.
6. G. G. Stokes: Cambridge Philosophical Society, vol. 3, p. 441, 1847.
7. T. Levi-Cevita: *Math. Ann.*, vol. 93, p. 264, 1925.
8. D. J. Struik: *Math. Ann.*, vol. 95, p. 595, 1926.
9. Lors Skjelbreia: Gravity Waves: Stokes' Third Order Approximations, Engineering Foundation, Council on Wave Research, Berkeley, Calif., 1958.

10. *U.S. Army Corps. Engrs., Beach Erosion Board Bull., spec. issue* 2, 1953.

11. R. L. Wiegel: Gravity Waves, Tables of Functions, Engineering Foundation, Council on Wave Research, Berkeley, Calif., 1954.

12. R. J. Morison: The Effect of Wave Steepness on Wave Velocity, *Trans. Am. Geophys. Union*, vol 32, p. 201, 1951.

13. R. C. H. Russell and D. H. MacMillan: "Waves and Tides," Hutchinson & Co. (Publishers), Ltd., London, 1952.

14. A. S. Ramsey: "A Treatise on Hydromechanics," pt. II, Hydrodynamics, G. Bell & Sons, Ltd., London, 1957.

15. Breakers and Surf: Principles in Forecasting, *U.S. Navy H.O. Publ.* 234, November, 1944.

16. J. W. Johnson, M. P. O'Brien, and J. D. Isaacs: Graphical Construction of Wave Refraction Diagrams, *H.O. Publ.* 605, 1948.

17. T. Saville, Jr., and K. Kaplan: A New Method for the Graphical Construction of Wave Refraction Diagrams, *U.S. Army Corps Engrs., Beach Erosion Board Bull.*, vol. 6, no. 3, p. 23, 1952.

18. R. S. Arthur, W. H. Munk, and J. D. Isaacs: The Direct Construction of Wave Rays, *Trans. Am. Geophys. Union*, December, 1952.

19. H. W. Iversen: Laboratory Study of Breakers, Gravity Waves, *Natl. Bur. Standards (U.S.) Circ.* 521, 1952.

20. W. H. Munk: The Solitary Wave Theory and Its Application to Wave Problems, *Ann. N.Y. Acad. Sci.*, vol. 51, p. 376, 1949.

21. H. U. Sverdrup and W. H. Munk: Wind, Sea, and Swell: Theory of Relations for Forecasting, *H.O. Publ.* 601, 1947.

22. C. L. Bretschneider: The Generation and Decay of Wind Waves in Deep Water, *Trans. Am. Geophys. Union*, June, 1952, p. 381.

23. ————: Revisions in Wave Forecasting: Deep and Shallow Water, *Proc. Sixth Conf. on Coastal Eng.*, Engineering Foundation, Council on Wave Research, 1958.

24. J. A. Putnam and J. W. Johnson: The Dissipation of Wave Energy by Bottom Friction, *Trans. Am. Geophys. Union*, vol. 30, p. 67, February, 1949.

25. R. A. Bagnold: Sand Movement by Waves: Some Small Scale Experiments with Sand of Very Low Density, *J. Inst. Civ. Eng.*, vol. 27, pp. 444–469, 1947.

26. R. P. Savage: Laboratory Study of Wave Energy Losses by Bottom Friction and Percolation, *U.S. Army Corps Engrs., Beach Erosion Board, Tech. Mem.* 31, 1953.

27. C. L. Bretschneider and H. N. Abramson: Field Investigation of Wave Energy Loss in Shallow Water Ocean Waves, *U.S. Beach Erosion Board, Tech. Mem.* 46, 1954.

28. J. A. Putnam: Loss of Wave Energy Due to Percolation in a Permeable Sea Bottom, *Trans. Am. Geophys. Union*, June, 1949, pp. 349–356.

29. G. H. Keulegan: "Engineering Hydraulics," chap. 11, Wave Motion, pp. 721–723, John Wiley & Sons, Inc., New York, 1950.

30. Ernest F. Brater: Methods of Correcting Wave Problems in Harbors, *J. Waterways Harbors Div.*, *ASCE*, December, 1959, p. 39.

31. James W. Dunham: Refraction and Diffraction Diagrams, *Proc. First Conf. on Coastal Eng.*, Engineering Foundation, Council on Wave Research, 1950.

32. J. W. Johnson: Generalized Diffraction Diagrams, *Proc. Second Conf. on Coastal Eng.*, Engineering Foundation, Council on Wave Research, 1952.

33. ———: Engineering Aspects of Diffraction and Refraction, *Trans. ASCE*, vol. 118, p. 617, 1953.

34. Melville S. Priest: "Wave Heights within a Harbor Due to Swell Entering through a Breakwater Gap," doctoral dissertation, University of Michigan Library, 1954.

35. R. R. Putz: Statistical Distribution for Ocean Waves, *Trans. Am. Geophys. Union*, vol. 33, no. 5, October, 1952, pp. 685–692.

36. R. L. Wiegel and J. Kukk: Wave measurements along the California Coast, *Trans. Am. Geophys. Union*, vol. 38, no. 5, October, 1957, pp. 667–674.

37. R. L. Wiegel: "Oceanographical Engineering," Prentice-Hall, Inc., Englewood Cliffs, N.J., 1964.

38. H. U. Sverdrup and W. H. Munk: Wind Waves and Swell: Principles in Forecasting, *H. O. Misc. Publ.* 11,275.

39. ——— and ———: Wind, Sea, and Swell: Theory of Relations for Forecasting, *H. O. Publ.* 601, 1947.

40. C. L. Bretschneider: Revised Wave Forecasting Relationships, *Proc. Second Conf. on Coastal Eng.*, Engineering Foundation, Council on Wave Research, 1952.

41. ———: Revisions in Wave Forecasting, Deep and Shallow Water, *Proc. Sixth Conf. on Coastal Eng.*, 1958.

42. C. O. Wisler and E. F. Brater: "Hydrology," John Wiley & Sons, Inc., New York, pp. 204–209. 1959.

43. C. L. Bretschneider: Generation of Wind Waves Over a Shallow Bottom, *U.S. Army Corps Engrs.*, *Beach Erosion Board*, *Tech. Mem.* 51, 1954.

44. "Shore Protection Manual," *U.S. Army Corps Engrs.*, Coastal Engineering Research Center, 1973.

45. T. Saville, Jr.: The Effect of Fetch Width on Wave Generation, *U.S. Beach Erosion Board Tech. Memo. no.* 70, 1954.

46. Wave Run-up and Overtopping, Levee Sections, Lake Okeechobee, Fla., *U.S. Army Corps Engrs. Waterways Expt. Sta. Tech. Rept.* 2-449, 1957.

47. Thorndike Saville, Jr.: Wave Run-up on Shore Structures, *Trans. ASCE*, vol. 123, pp. 139–150, 1958.

48. Rudolph P. Savage: Laboratory Data on Wave Run-up on Roughened and Permeable Slopes, *U.S. Army Corps Engrs.*, *Beach Erosion Board*, *Tech. Mem.* 109, 1959.

49. R. A. Jackson: Design of Cover Layers for Rubble-Mound Breakwaters, *U.S. Army Corps Engs. Waterways Expt. Sta. Res. Rept.* 2-11, 1968.

50. Thorndike Saville, Jr.: Laboratory Data on Wave Run-up and Overtopping on Shore Structures, *U.S. Beach Erosion Board, Tech. Mem.* 64, 1955.
51. Osvold Sibul: Model Study of Overtopping of Wind-generated Waves on Levees with Slopes of 1 : 3 and 1 : 6, *U.S. Beach Erosion Board, Tech. Mem.* 80, 1956.
52. D. D. Gaillard: Wave Action in Relation to Engineering Structures, The Engineering School, Fort Belvoir, Va., 1935.
53. R. Y. Hudson: Wave Forces on Breakwaters, *Trans. ASCE*, vol. 118, p. 653, 1953.
54. George Sainflou: Essai sur les diques maritimes verticales, *Ann. Ponts et Chaussèes*, Paris, 1928.
55. R. R. Minikin: "Winds, Waves and Maritime Structures," pp. 40–48, Charles Griffin & Company, Ltd., London, 1950.
56. Culbertson W. Ross: Laboratory Study of Shock Pressures of Breaking Waves, *U.S. Army Corps Engrs., Beach Erosion Board, Tech. Mem.* 59, 1955.
57. Luther A. Mueller, Herman A. Knutson, and A. Arthur Koch: Some Dynamic Aspects in the Design of Marine Structures on the Great Lakes, *Proc. Fourth Conf. on Coastal Eng.*, Engineering Foundation, Council on Wave Research, 1954.
58. R. Y. Hudson: Laboratory Investigation of Rubble-mound Breakwaters, *Trans. ASCE*, vol. 126, p. 492, 1961.
59. P. Danel: Tetrapods, *Proc. Fourth Conf. on Coastal Eng.*, Engineering Foundation, Council on Wave Research, 1953.
60. J. R. Morison: Design of Piling, *Proc. First Conf. on Coastal Eng.*, 1951.
61. ———, J. W. Johnson, and M. P. O'Brien: Experimental Study of Forces on Piles, *Proc. Fourth Conf. on Coastal Eng.*, Engineering Foundation, Council on Wave Research, 1954.
62. E. F. Brater and R. Wallace: Wave Forces on Submerged Pipe Lines, *Proc. 13th Coastal Engineering Conference*, ASCE, vol. III, pp. 1703–1722, 1972.
63. ———, John S. McNown, and L. D. Stair: Wave Forces on Submerged Structures, *Trans. ASCE*, vol. 126, pt. I, pp. 661–696, 191.
64. R. G. Folsom: Measurement of Ocean Waves, *Trans. Am. Geophys. Union*, October, 1949, pp. 691–699.
65. D. Riabauchinski: "Sur la restance des fluides," International Congress of Mathematics, Strasbourg, France, 1920, pp. 568–585.
66. E. F. Brater and H. W. Baynton: "Extreme Lake Levels of Lake Erie near Monroe, Michigan," 1956 (unpublished report).
67. Thorndike Saville, Jr.: Wind Set-up and Waves in Shallow Water, *U.S. Army Corps Engrs., Beach Erosion Board, Tech. Mem.* 27, 1952.
68. B. Hellstrom: Wind Effect on Lakes and Rivers, *Proc. Roy. Swedish Inst. Eng. Res.*, no. 158, Stockholm, 1941.
69. H. L. Langhaar: Wind Tides on Inland Waters, *Proc. First Midwestern Conf. on Fluid Mech.*, no. 4, Ann Arbor, Mich., 1951.

70. Garbis H. Keulegan: Wind Tides in Small Closed Channels, *Natl. Bur. Std., J. Res., Paper* 2207, vol. 46, no. 5, May, 1951.

71. O. Sibul: Laboratory Study of Wind Tides in Shallow Water, *U.S. Army Corps Engrs., Beach Erosion Board, Tech. Mem.* 61, 1955.

72. E. G. Tickner: Effect of Bottom Roughness on Wind Tide in Shallow Water, *U.S. Army Corps Engrs., Beach Erosion Board, Tech. Mem.* 95, 1957.

73. E. F. Brater: Low Cost Shore Protection Used on the Great Lakes, *Proc. Fourth Conf. on Coastal Eng.*, Engineering Foundation, Council on Wave Research, 1953.

74. W. M. Lansford: Discussion of J. H. Wilkinson, Translatory Waves in Natural Channels, *Trans. ASCE*, vol. 110, p. 1227, 1945.

75. Flood Resulting from Suddenly Breached Dams, *Rept.* 1, Conditions of Minimum Resistance, *Rept.* 2, Conditions of High Resistance, *U.S. Army Engrs. Waterways Expt. Sta. Misc. Paper* 2-374, 1962.

76. V. L. Streeter: "Fluid Mechanics," 3d ed., p. 511, McGraw-Hill Book Company, Inc., New York, 1962.

77. J. W. Daily and S. C. Stephan: Characteristics of the Solitary Wave, *Trans. ASCE*, vol. 118, p. 575, 1953.

SECTION 11

SPATIALLY VARIABLE AND UNSTEADY FLOW

This section deals with selected aspects of unsteady flow. Because the same basic equations are required for problems in spatially variable flow, this topic is also treated in this section. The first portion of the section is devoted to open-channel flow, and the second portion, to water-hammer problems.

Unsteady Open-channel Flow

When the discharge entering a channel is gradually changing with respect to time, or if water is being added or taken out throughout the length of the channel (spatially variable flow), it is necessary to deal with the basic equations of motion in

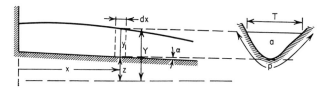

Fig. 11-1. Definition sketch, open-channel flow.

determining the water-surface profile. The equations will be derived for a general case of unsteady spatially variable flow, and thereafter the equations will be simplified to apply to steady spatially variable flow, and finally for flow in wide rectangular channels.

The derivation is carried out for a section of channel having a length dx and an area a as shown in Fig. 11-1. The depth y is taken perpendicular to the bottom, although for small slopes this distance is virtually identical with the vertical distance from the bottom to the water surface. The derivation is based on the momentum relationship embodied in Newton's second law, which states that

$$F = \frac{dM}{dt} \tag{11-1}$$

In this equation F is the sum of all external forces resolved in the direction of flow x, the positive sign indicating forces toward the right, as indicated by the equation

$$F = F_p + F_g + F_{fb} + F_{fa} \tag{11-2}$$

F_p is the pressure force, which, for parallel-walled channels, may be expressed as follows:

$$F_p = -\rho g a \frac{\partial y}{\partial x} dx \tag{11-3}$$

The minus sign is introduced so that a negative value of $\partial y/\partial x$ will produce a positive force.

If the walls are not parallel, this force must include the component of pressure forces acting on the water in the direction of flow. For very steep slopes the hydrostatic force may be approximated by multiplying this term by $\cos \alpha$.

F_g is the component of the weight which acts in the x direction. Its value is

$$F_g = \rho g a \, dx \sin \alpha \tag{11-4}$$

For small slopes

$$\sin \alpha = \tan \alpha = s_0 \tag{11-5}$$

and

$$F_g = \rho g a \, dx \, s_0 \tag{11-6}$$

F_{fb} is the shear force on the walls as expressed by the equation

$$F_{fb} = -\tau p \, dx \tag{11-7}$$

where τ is the average shear stress in pounds per square foot, and p is the wetted perimeter. The shear stress may be evaluated from uniform flow conditions as follows. For uniform steady flow the only forces acting in the direction of flow on a section of the water are the component of the gravitational force and the shear force. Therefore, from Eqs. (11-6) and (11-7),

$$F_{fb} = -\tau p \, dx = -\rho g a \, dx \, s \tag{11-8}$$

In this case, because flow is uniform, the slope of the energy gradient, s, may be used instead of the bottom slope s_0. It is assumed that the energy-gradient slope, as computed for uniform flow, will also give the correct shear force for nonuniform unsteady and spatially variable flow. The value of s is then obtained from the Manning equation [Eq. (7-50)] or from an equation of the form of Eq. (7-31). The roughness coefficients for spatially variable flow are usually larger, especially for small values of the Reynolds number, than for flow in which no such disturbance occurs.[1,2]

F_{fa} is the shear force due to the friction of the air on the water surface. This term will not be included here because it is usually very small compared with the other forces. However, for some special cases, as, for example, for wind tides (Sec. 10), it may be one of the most important terms.

The momentum term dM/dt can be expressed as follows:

$$\frac{dM}{dt} = -\rho QV + \rho \left(Q + \frac{\partial Q}{\partial x}\, dx \right) (V + dV) \qquad (11\text{-}9)$$

where

$$dV = \frac{\partial V}{\partial t}\, dt + \frac{\partial V}{\partial x}\, dx \qquad (11\text{-}10/11)$$

Then, canceling terms and eliminating higher-order differentials,

$$\frac{dM}{dt} = +\rho Q \frac{\partial V}{\partial t}\, dt + \rho Q \frac{\partial V}{\partial x}\, dx + \rho \frac{\partial Q}{\partial x}\, dx\; V \qquad (11\text{-}12)$$

Then, substituting values from Eqs. (11-3), (11-6), (11-8), and (11-12) into Eq. (11-1),

$$-\rho g a \frac{\partial y}{\partial x}\, dx + \rho g a\, dx\, s_0 - \rho g a\, dx\, s$$
$$= \rho a V \frac{\partial V}{\partial t}\, dt + \rho a V \frac{\partial V}{\partial x}\, dx + \rho \frac{\partial Q}{\partial x}\, dx\; V \qquad (11\text{-}13)$$

Dividing Eq. (11-13) by $\rho g a\, dx$ and letting inflow per foot of length $\partial Q/\partial x$ be designated by q,

$$-\frac{\partial y}{\partial x} + s_0 - s = \frac{1}{g} \frac{\partial V}{\partial t} + \frac{V}{g} \frac{\partial V}{\partial x} + \frac{qV}{ga} \qquad (11\text{-}14)$$

This is the dynamic equation for unsteady spatially variable flow.

[1] D. C. Woo and E. F. Brater, Spatially Varied Flow from Controlled Rainfall, *Proc. ASCE, J. Hydraulics Div.*, November, 1962, p. 31.

[2] Garbis H. Keuligan, Determination of Critical Depth in Spatially Variable Flow, *Proc. Second Midwestern Conf. on Fluid Mech.*, The Ohio State University, College of Engineering, Columbus, Ohio, 1952, p. 67.

For steady spatially variable flow, Eq. (11-14) becomes

$$-\frac{\partial y}{\partial x} + s_0 - s = \frac{V}{g}\frac{\partial V}{\partial x} + \frac{qV}{ga} \qquad (11\text{-}15)$$

and when flow is steady and not spatially variable, the expression is

$$-\frac{\partial y}{\partial x} + s_0 - s = \frac{V}{g}\frac{\partial V}{\partial x} \qquad (11\text{-}16)$$

Another useful form of Eq. (11-15) is obtained by noting in Fig. 11-1 that the following approximate arrangement exists:

$$Y = z + y \qquad (11\text{-}17)$$

Then

$$\frac{dY}{dx} = \frac{dz}{dx} + \frac{dy}{dx} = -s_0 + \frac{dy}{dx} \qquad (11\text{-}18)$$

and Eq. (11-15) becomes

$$-\frac{dY}{dx} - s = \frac{V}{g}\frac{\partial V}{\partial x} + \frac{qV}{ga} \qquad (11\text{-}19)$$

The continuity equation is derived as follows:

$$aV - \frac{\partial a}{\partial t}\,dx + q\,dx = \left(V + \frac{\partial V}{\partial x}\,dx\right)\left(a + \frac{\partial a}{\partial x}\,dx\right) \qquad (11\text{-}20)$$

Cancellation of terms, eliminating a higher-order differential, and division by dx yields

$$-\frac{\partial a}{\partial t} + q = V\frac{\partial a}{\partial x} + a\frac{\partial V}{\partial x} \qquad (11\text{-}21)$$

Noting that $\partial a = T\,\partial y$, the equation can be written

$$-\frac{\partial y}{\partial t}T + q = VT\frac{\partial y}{\partial x} + a\frac{\partial V}{\partial x} \qquad (11\text{-}22)$$

For steady spatially variable flow, the continuity equation becomes

$$q = VT\frac{\partial y}{\partial x} + a\frac{\partial V}{\partial x} \qquad (11\text{-}23)$$

For rectangular channels, $T = 1$ and $a = y$. Therefore

$$q = V\frac{\partial y}{\partial x} + y\frac{\partial V}{\partial x} \qquad (11\text{-}24)$$

When flow is steady and not spatially variable, the general

continuity equation becomes

$$VT \frac{\partial y}{\partial x} + a \frac{\partial V}{\partial x} = 0 \qquad (11\text{-}25)$$

which, for rectangular channels, reduces to the following form:

$$V \frac{\partial y}{\partial x} + y \frac{\partial V}{\partial x} = 0 \qquad (11\text{-}26)$$

It may be noted that substitution of Eq. (11-25) into Eq. (11-16) yields the general equation for steady, gradually varied flow in open channels [Eq. (8-131)], and a similar combination of Eq. (11-26) with Eq. (11-16) gives Eq. (8-130), which is the corresponding equation for rectangular channels.

Steady Spatially Variable Flow

One of the applications of these equations most often encountered is to the case of steady spatially variable flow. Examples of this type of flow are flow in roof and street gutters, overland flow produced by rainfall, flow in side-channel spillways, and flow in channels with side-channel outlets or inlets.[1-4] An additional continuity equation can be stated for this type of flow:

$$Q = Q_0 + qx \qquad (11\text{-}27)$$

where Q_0 is the discharge in the channel at $x = 0$. When $Q_0 = 0$,

$$q = \frac{Q}{x} = \frac{aV}{x} \qquad (11\text{-}28)$$

The solution of spatially variable flow problems may be accomplished by changing the form of Eq. (11-15) so that the differentials become finite differences, as shown in the following equation, in which the subscripts 1 and 2 apply to the upstream and downstream ends, respectively, of the reaches of length x.

$$a_{\text{av}}(y_1 - y_2) + a_{\text{av}} \Delta x(s_0 - s_{\text{av}})$$
$$= \frac{a_1 V_1 (V_2 - V_1)}{g} + \frac{q V_2 \Delta x}{g} \qquad (11\text{-}29)$$

[1] Julian Hinds, Side Channel Spillways, *Trans. ASCE*, vol. 89, p. 881, 1926.

[2] K. Hilding Beij, Flow in Roof Gutters, *U.S. Bur. Std. Res. Paper* RPG44, 1934.

[3] G. H. Keuligan, Spatially Variable Discharge over a Sloping Plane, *Trans. Am. Geophys. Union*, pt. VI, 1944, p. 956.

[4] Woo and Brater, *op. cit.*

In Eq. (11-29), $a_{av} = (a_1 + a_2)/2$ and s_{av} is computed by using this average cross-sectional area in the reach. The solution for a water-surface profile by means of Eq. (11-29) requires only that the depth be known at some point in the channel. For channels with a *mild slope* ($s_0 < s_c$) ending in a free fall, critical depth occurs near the outlet (Sec. 8), and computations can be started from this point. This is often the case with roof or street gutters and with overland flow. An illustration of the computation of a water profile for a horizontal channel ending in a downspout is given in the following example. The channel selected is one tested by Beij,[1] and the computed and measured profiles are plotted in Fig. 11-2.

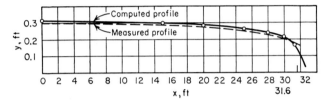

Fig. 11-2. Spatially variable flow profile, after Beij.

Example 11-1. A smooth rectangular channel 0.5 ft wide and 31.6 ft long is supplied by a discharge q, of 0.00608 cu ft per sec per ft of length. The channel is horizontal and ends in a downspout which simulates conditions at a free fall. Based on the observed data, it was assumed that critical depth would occur 0.316 ft from the end of the channel. This is only approximately $2D_c$ upstream from the fall, which is a considerably shorter distance than those reported for steady, not spatially variable flow on p. 8-18. Then the discharge at y_c is

$$31.284 \times 0.00608 = 0.190 \text{ cu ft per sec}$$

and critical depth can be computed from Eq. (8-31) as follows:

$$y_c = \sqrt[3]{\frac{(2 \times 0.190)^2}{32.2}} = 0.165 \text{ ft}$$

Computations are then carried out for selected reaches (Δx) proceeding from y_c to the upstream end. The procedure is to assume a depth y_1 at the upstream end of the reach and solve

[1] *Op. cit.*

for the terms in Eq. (11-29), repeating until this equation is satisfied. (Note that s_0 is zero for this example.) The final set of values for the first reach are shown in the accompanying table. The value of n was assumed to be 0.012. Values of s_{av} are computed by means of Eq. (7-49) and Table 7-12.

Final Computation for First Reach in Fig. 11-2

	(1)	(2)	(3)	(4)	(5)	(6)	(7)	(8)	(9)
x, ft	Δx, ft	y, ft	Q, cu ft per sec	V, ft per sec	y_{av}, ft	$\dfrac{y_{av}}{b}$	$\left(\dfrac{1}{K'}\right)^2$	Q_{av}, cu ft per sec	$\left(\dfrac{Q_{av}n}{b^{\frac{8}{3}}}\right)^2$
31.284		0.165	0.190	2.30					
	1.284				0.189	0.378	24.6	0.186	0.000205
30		0.213	0.182	1.71					

	(10)	(11)	(12)	(13)	(14)	(15)
x, ft	$-a_{av}s_{av}\,\Delta x$, cu ft	$a_{av}(y_1 - y_2)$, cu ft	$\dfrac{a_1 V_1(V_2 - V_1)}{g}$ cu ft	$qV_2\dfrac{\Delta x}{g}$ cu ft	(10) + (11)	(12) + (13)
31.284						
	−0.00061	0.0045	0.0033	0.00056	0.0039	0.0039
30						

For channels with a steep slope ($s_0 > s_c$), critical depth no longer occurs at the outlet and the solution for the water-surface profile requires the establishment of the magnitude and location of a controlling depth in order to provide a starting point for the computations. If, for example, water were entering the channel at a known depth and discharge at the upper end of the spatially variable flow region, this would establish a control, and computations could be started from this point and carried downstream in steps in the same manner that they were carried upstream for channels with a mild slope.

When the discharge is zero at the upper end of the channel, the control must be established by estimating the location of critical depth. A method suggested by Hinds[1] is based on the

[1] *Op. cit.*

assumption that, if an imaginary channel were designed in such a manner that the depth would be critical depth everywhere in the channel, then the location of critical depth in the real channel would be at the point where the bottom slope of the imaginary channel is the same as that in the real channel. This situation is shown schematically in Fig. 11-3. For this assumption to be true, it would require that the integral of all the forces and momentum changes upstream from this point (where y_c is assumed to occur) would be the same for the imaginary and real channels. The solution for the water surface and bottom profiles is made by first computing y_c at all locations, and then, starting some selected short distance away from the upstream

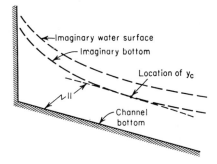

Fig. 11-3. Location of critical depth, Hinds method.

end, the water surface is computed in steps as previously described. It is convenient to use Eq. (11-19) for this computation, rearranged for finite reaches as follows:

$$a_{\mathrm{av}}(Y_1 - Y_2 - s_{\mathrm{av}} \Delta x) = \frac{a_1 V_1}{g}(V_2 - V_1) + \frac{qV_2}{g} \Delta x \quad (11\text{-}30)$$

Another method of locating critical depth in steep channels with spatially variable flow has been suggested by Keuligan.[1] Inserting the value of $\partial V/\partial x$ from the continuity equation [Eq. (11-23)] into Eq. (11-15) and solving for $\partial y/\partial x$ yields

$$\frac{\partial y}{\partial x} = \frac{s_0 - s - 2qV/ga}{1 - Q^2 T/ga^3} \quad (11\text{-}31)$$

[1] Garbis H. Keuligan, Determination of Critical Depth in Spatially Variable Flow, *Proc. Second Midwestern Conf. on Fluid Mech.*, The Ohio State University, College of Engineering, Columbus, Ohio, 1952, p. 67.

When flow is at critical depth, the term Q^2T/ga^3 is unity (p. 8-7) and the denominator becomes zero, thus indicating that $\partial y/\partial x$ is infinity. If, however, it is realized that no discontinuity exists when $y = y_c$, it can be concluded that the numerator must also be zero. Then

$$s_0 - s_c - \frac{2qV_c}{ga_c} = 0 \tag{11-32}$$

Using the continuity relationship

$$q = \frac{Q}{x} = \frac{a_cV_c}{x_c} \tag{11-28}$$

and the critical-depth relationships for the general case derived in Sec. 8,

$$y_{mc} = \frac{a_c}{T_c} \tag{11-33}$$

$$V_c^2 = gy_{mc} \tag{11-34}$$

Eq. (11-32) can be arranged into the following form:

$$x_c = \frac{8q^2}{gT_c^2(s_0 - s_c)^3} \tag{11-35}$$

In the above equations the subscript c denotes conditions at critical depth and the subscript m denotes mean depth at a particular cross section. If the Manning equation is used to solve for s_c and if it is assumed that the hydraulic radius is equal to y_m, then the value of s_c is given by Eq. (8-83).

$$s_c = \frac{n^2g}{2.21y_{mc}^{1/3}} \tag{11-36}$$

Because both T_c and y_{mc} vary with x, the solution for x_c, which gives the position of critical depth, must be made by successive approximations. For the special case of flow in wide rectangular channels, T becomes unity, and using Eq. (7-30),

$$s_c = \frac{f}{y_c}\frac{V_c^2}{2g} \tag{11-37}$$

Since $V_c^2/gy_c = 1$,

$$s_c = \frac{f}{2} \tag{11-38}$$

Then

$$x_c = \frac{8q^2}{g(s_0 - f/2)^3} \tag{11-39}$$

The weakness involved in using Eq. (11-35) or (11-39) to locate y_c is the uncertainty in estimating the exact value of the roughness coefficients.

In the discussion up to this point it has been assumed that q represents inflow in cubic feet per second per foot of channel. There are many cases where a uniform rate of outflow occurs. Examples are infiltration during overland flow and flow in conduits with side outlets. If all the momentum of the discharge leaving the channel is reduced to zero before the water leaves the channel, the term involving q would simply have its sign changed. This would probably apply to the case of infiltration during overland flow. However, for side outlets, the water leaving the channel usually retains part of its original momentum in the direction of flow after having left the channel. This situation might be handled by retaining some fractional part of the term involving q with a minus sign.

Unsteady Flow with a Free Surface

The equations developed in this section form the basis for computation of the mode of travel of a gentle wave, such as a flood wave, down a channel. Such computations, called flood routing, have usually been carried out by less elegant methods because these equations are not readily adaptable to nonprismatic channels and because the computations, even for rectangular channels, were very tedious. However, the recognition that the so-called *method of characteristics* could be used to solve the equations and the adaptability of this method to solution by means of digital computers have made it possible to use these equations for flood routing. The origination of the use of characteristic lines is credited to Massau.[1] The use of this method for flood routing in channels has been discussed by Putnam,[2] Gilcrest,[3] Lin,[4] and Stoker.[5] The method is based on the fact that Eqs. (11-14) and (11-22), with the spatially variable flow term eliminated, can be arranged into the form of

[1] J. Massau, Mémoire sur l'intégration graphique des équations aux derivés particelles, *Ann. Assoc. Ingenieurs Sortis des Écoles Spéciales de Gand*, vol. 23, p. 95, 1900.

[2] H. J. Putnam, Unsteady Flow in Open Channels, *Trans. Am. Geophys. Union*, vol. 29, p. 227, 1948.

[3] B. R. Gilcrest, Flood Routing, chap. 10, in Hunter Rouse (ed.), "Engineering Hydraulics," John Wiley & Sons, Inc., New York, 1950, p. 635.

[4] Pin-Nam Lin, Numerical Analysis of Unsteady Flow in Open Channels, *Trans. Am. Geophys. Union*, vol. 33, p. 226, April, 1952.

[5] J. J. Stoker, Numerical Solution of Flood Prediction and River Regulation Problems, *Inst. Math. and Mech. Rept.* 1, p. 200, New York University, New York, 1953.

the following expressions for total derivatives:

$$\frac{dy}{dt} = \frac{\partial y}{\partial x}\frac{dx}{dt} + \frac{\partial y}{\partial t} \tag{11-40}$$

$$\frac{dV}{dt} = \frac{\partial V}{\partial x}\frac{dx}{dt} + \frac{\partial V}{\partial t} \tag{11-41}$$

to derive the following equivalent set of equations:

$$\frac{dx}{dt} = V + C \tag{11-42a}$$

$$d(V + 2C) = g(s_0 - s)\, dt \tag{11-42b}$$

and

$$\frac{dx}{dt} = V - C \tag{11-43a}$$

$$d(V - 2C) = g(s_0 - s)\, dt \tag{11-43b}$$

where C is the celerity of a very small wave ($C = \sqrt{gy}$) as shown by Eq. (10-105a). Consider a coordinates system having the coordinates x, the distance from some initial point in a channel, and t, the time elapsed after the introduction of a

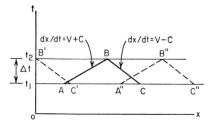

FIG. 11-4. Method of characteristics.

change in depth at $x = 0$, as, for example, the initial step in introducing a flood wave at the upper end of the channel. Then a series of lines on this coordinate system would have slopes given by Eqs. (11-42a) and (11-43a). For subcritical flow, which is the most usual situation, Eq. (11-42a) would give a positive slope, as, for example, that of AB in Fig. 11-4, and Eq. (11-43a) would give a negative slope such as that of BC in Fig. 11-4. Inherent in the derivation of Eqs. (11-42) and (11-43) is the implication that Eq. (11-42b) must be satisfied along a line having a slope given by Eq. (11-42a) and that similar relations exist for Eqs. (11-43). If y and V at some time t_1 (Fig. 11-4) are known at all points in a channel, then the slope of lines AB and CB can be computed for points A and C from Eqs. (11-42a) and (11-43a). Although the slopes are not constant from A to B and from C to B, as a first trial, they may be considered constant, and since Eqs. (11-42b) and (11-43b) must both hold at B, their simultaneous solution at that point will yield first-trial values of V_B, y_B, and C_B. The solution of Eqs. (11-42b) and (11-43b) is carried out for finite differences in t and x. Thus

$$dt \doteqdot t_2 - t_1 = \Delta t \tag{11-44}$$

and the slope of AB should be the average of the slopes at A and B. Thus

$$\frac{dx}{dt}_{\text{av}} = \tfrac{1}{2}(V_A + C_A + V_B - C_B) \tag{11-45}$$

For finite differences Eq. (11-42b) can be written

$$\Delta(V + 2C) = g(s_0 - s_{\text{av}})\,\Delta t \tag{11-46}$$

or

$$(V_B + 2C_B) - (V_A + 2C_A) = g(s_0 - s_{\text{av}})\,\Delta t \tag{11-47}$$

where

$$s_{\text{av}} = \frac{s_A + s_B}{2} \tag{11-48}$$

The corresponding rearrangement of Eq. (11-43b) yields

$$(V_B - 2C_B) - (V_C - 2C_C) = g(s_0 - s_{\text{av}})\,\Delta t \tag{11-49}$$

where

$$s_{\text{av}} = \frac{s_B + s_C}{2} \tag{11-50}$$

The value of s_{av} may be obtained from the Manning equation in one of the following forms developed in Sec. 7.

$$s = \frac{n^2 V^2}{2.208 r^{4/3}} = \left(\frac{1}{K'}\right)^2 \left(\frac{Qn}{b^{8/3}}\right)^2 \tag{11-51}$$

Note that the unknowns in Eqs. (11-47) and (11-49) are V_B, C_B, and s_B. However, s_B is related to V_B and C_B ($C_B = \sqrt{gy_B}$) by means of Eq. (11-51). Thus there are three equations, and three unknowns and solutions can be made by successive approximations.

The solution is carried forward to time t_2 in the same manner at other selected values of x, so that y and V are known at points at B, B_1, B_2, etc. The solution for the channel entrance

($x = 0$) at time t_2, which is designated as B' in Fig. 11-4, requires only the single characteristic $C'B'$ because V is the only unknown, y having been established by the nature of the flood wave which was introduced into the channel.

Lin[1] and Chow[2] give examples of graphical procedures which aid in the solution. Even with the graphical aids the solutions are tedious, and it is only by the utilization of the high-speed digital computers that this procedure becomes practical.

Water Hammer

Assume a pipe with a valve at its outlet discharging from a reservoir. If the valve is suddenly closed, a dynamic pressure, in addition to the normal static pressure, is created within the pipe. This dynamic pressure is commonly called *water hammer*. It is caused by the sudden transformation of kinetic energy to pressure energy. If P is the pressure due to water hammer and M is the mass of water in the pipe whose velocity is reduced the amount dV in the time interval dt, then

$$P = M \frac{dV}{dt} \tag{11-52}$$

If $dt = 0$, the pressure becomes infinite. Instantaneous change in velocity is not, however, possible. In the following nomenclature, all units are expressed in feet and seconds except as noted:

b = thickness of pipe walls
d = inside diameter of pipe
a = cross-sectional area of pipe, sq ft
e = modulus of elasticity of pipe walls, lb per sq ft
e' = modulus of elasticity of water, lb per sq ft
E = modulus of elasticity of pipe walls, lb per sq in.
E' = modulus of elasticity of water, lb per sq in.
g = acceleration of gravity
ΔH = head due to water hammer (in excess of static head)
H = total head producing discharge through valve
H_0 = original head in pipe
L = length of pipeline
T = time of closing valve
V_0 = mean velocity of water in pipe before closure of valve
v_w = velocity of pressure wave along pipe

[1] *Op. cit.*
[2] Ven Te Chow, "Open Channel Hydraulics," McGraw-Hill Book Company, Inc., New York, 1959, p. 587.

Let l_1, l_2, l_3, . . . , l_n represent successive infinitesimally short sections of pipe beginning at the outlet. The instant the valve is closed, the water in section l_1 is brought to rest, its kinetic energy is transformed into pressure energy, the water is somewhat compressed, and the pipe wall with which it is in contact expands slightly. Because of the enlarged cross-sectional area of l_1 and the compressed condition of the water within it, a greater mass of water is contained within this section than before the closure. A small volume of water has flowed into l_1 after the valve was closed. An instant later, a similar procedure takes place in l_2 and then in l_3, causing a wave of increased pressure to travel up the pipe. The instant this wave reaches the reservoir, the entire pipe is expanded and the water within it is compressed. There is now no moving mass of water to maintain this high pressure, and the pipe begins to contract and the water to expand, with a consequent return to normal static pressure. This process starts at the reservoir and travels as a wave to the lower end. During this second period some of the water stored within the pipe flows back into the reservoir, but on account of the inertia of this moving mass, an amount flows back greater than the excess amount stored at the end of the first period, so that the instant this second wave reaches the valve, the pressure at that point drops, not only to the normal static pressure, but also below it. A third period now follows during which a wave of pressure less than normal static pressure passes up the pipe to the reservoir. When it reaches the reservoir the entire pipe is under less than static pressure, but since all the water is again at rest, the pressure in l_n immediately returns to the normal static pressure due to the head of water in the reservoir. This starts a fourth period marked by a wave of normal static pressure moving down the pipe. When the valve is reached, the pressure there is normal, and for an instant the conditions throughout the pipe are similar to what they were when the valve was first closed. The velocity of the water (and the resultant water hammer) is now, however, somewhat less than it was at the time of closure because of friction and the imperfect elasticity of the pipe and the water.

Instantly another cycle begins similar to the one above described, and then another, and so on, each set of waves successively diminishing, until the waves finally die out.

Equation (11-52) shows that, for instantaneous closure of

valve, the pressure created would be infinite if the water were incompressible and the pipe inelastic. It is impossible to close a valve instantaneously, but if the valve is completely closed before the first pressure wave has time to return to the valve as a wave of low pressure, or in other words, if T is less than $2L/v_w$, the pressure will continue to increase up to the time of complete closure, and the resulting pressure is just the same as if the valve had been instantaneously closed. If T is greater than $2L/v_w$, the earlier pressure waves return as waves of low pressure and tend to reduce the rise of pressure resulting from the final stages of valve closure.

Hence, if T is equal to or less than $2L/v_w$, h will be the same as for instantaneous closure, but if T is greater than $2L/v_w$, h will be diminished as T increases.

The kinetic energy contained in the moving columns of water within the pipe is

$$\mathrm{KE} = \frac{MV_0{}^2}{2} = waL\,\frac{V_0{}^2}{2g} \tag{11-53}$$

This energy is used in the work of compressing the water and stretching the pipe walls. If the increase in pressure head is ΔH ft, the compression of the water column absorbs $(w\,\Delta H)^2aL/2e'$ ft-lb of energy because the average pressure force of the water is $w\,\Delta Ha/2$ and the distance through which this force moves is $w\,\Delta HL/e'$.

In a similar manner the work done in stretching the pipe walls is $(w\,\Delta H)^2LaD/2eb$. Then, relating the energy of the water to the work done in stopping it,

$$waL\,\frac{V_0{}^2}{2g} = \frac{(w\,\Delta H)^2aL}{2e'} + \frac{(w\,\Delta H)^2LaD}{2eb} \tag{11-54}$$

or

$$H = \frac{V_0}{g}\,\sqrt{\frac{1}{w/g(1/e' + D/eb)}} \tag{11-55}$$

As this pressure wave moves along the pipe with a velocity v_w, the force may be equated to the rate of change in momentum as follows:

$$w\,\Delta Ha = \frac{w}{g}\,v_w aV_0 \tag{11-56}$$

or

$$\Delta H = \frac{v_w}{g}\,V_0 \tag{11-57}$$

and

$$v_w = \sqrt{\dfrac{1}{w/g(1/e' + D/eb)}} \tag{11-58}$$

This derivation is approximate in that the stress in the longitudinal direction is neglected. When this is included Eq. (11-57) becomes[1]

$$v_w = \sqrt{\dfrac{1}{w/g(1/e' + Dc/eb)}} \tag{11-59}$$

where c is related to Poisson's ratio and the manner in which the pipe is held in place. Values of c are somewhat less than unity;[2] however, it is on the safe side to use Eq. (11-57), in which c is assumed to be unity. The analysis presented here is credited to Professor N. Jankovsky of Moscow.[3] The analysis may also be carried out by writing the basic dynamic and continuity equations in a manner similar to the derivation presented for open channels in the first part of this section.[4,5]

Pressure When $T \gtreqless 2L/v_w$. For this case ΔH may be computed directly from Eq. (11-55) or from Eq. (11-57) after v_w is determined from Eq. (11-58).

If, for example, v_w is 4,680 ft per sec and V_0 is 11.75 ft per sec, closure of a valve in a time $T \gtreqless 2L/v_w$ will create an additional pressure head of the gate of

$$\Delta H = \dfrac{v_w V_0}{g} = 1,770 \text{ ft}$$

Pressure When $T \gtreqless 2L/v_w$. For slow gate closure the computations may be carried out in steps by a method suggested by Gibson[6] or by means of a graphical solution. Both methods will be described and illustrated by means of a numerical example. In the step solution Eq. (11-57) is written as follows:

$$\Delta H = \dfrac{v_w}{g} \Delta V \tag{11-60}$$

[1] John Parmakian, "Water Hammer Analysis," Prentice-Hall, Inc., Englewood Cliffs, N.J., 1955.

[2] *Ibid.*

[3] O. Simin, Water Hammer, with Special Reference to Researches of Professor N. Jankovsky, *Proc. Am. Water Works Assoc.*, vol. 24, 1904.

[4] *Ibid.*

[5] George R. Rich, "Hydraulic Transients," McGraw-Hill Book Company, Inc., New York, 1951.

[6] N. R. Gibson, Pressures in Penstocks Caused by the Gradual Closing of Turbine Gates, *Trans. ASCE*, vol. 83, 1919.

where ΔH is the increase in pressure head resulting from one step in the valve closure, which reduces the velocity in the pipe by the amount ΔV. It is convenient to write Eq. (11-60) in terms of the initial condition as follows:

$$\frac{\Delta H}{H_0} = \frac{v_w V_0}{g H_0} \frac{\Delta V}{V_0} \tag{11-61}$$

Relations between head and pipe velocity for various gate openings must next be developed. It is assumed that this relationship can be expressed as follows:

$$Q = aV = C_d A_g \sqrt{2gH} \tag{11-62}$$

where a is the area of the pipe, V is the average velocity in the pipe, $C_d A_g$ is the product of the coefficients of discharge and the area of the gate, and H is the head at the gate. Then, for full gate opening,

$$Q = aV_0 = (C_d A_g)_0 \sqrt{2gH_0} \tag{11-63}$$

and, in general,

$$\frac{V}{V_0} = \frac{C_d A_g}{(C_d A_g)_0} \sqrt{\frac{H}{H_0}} \tag{11-64}$$

or, for simplicity,

$$\frac{V}{V_0} = \tau \sqrt{\frac{H}{H_0}} \tag{11-65}$$

where τ is $C_d A_g / (C_d A_g)_0$. Values of τ vary from 1.0 for a fully open gate to zero when the gate is closed. Solutions of slow closure problems consist of the step-by-step simultaneous solution of Eqs. (11-61) and (11-65), as will be illustrated by the following example.

Example 11-2. Determine the rise in pressure in a penstock leading to a power plant if the turbine gates are closed in 2.1 sec. $H_0 = 165$ ft, $L = 820$ ft, $V_0 = 11.75$ ft per sec, and $v_w = 4,680$ ft per sec. The solution of the problem will be carried forward in six time increments of $2.1/6 = 0.35$ sec, arbitrarily chosen equal to the travel time of the pressure wave from the gate to reservoir and back to the gate

$$\frac{2L}{v_w} = 0.35 \text{ sec}$$

A sketch of the penstock is shown in Fig. 11-5. The gate is closed in such a manner that six uniform decrements of area occur during each of the six time intervals. Then τ has the values shown in column 2 of the accompanying table. In

Time interval	(1) t, sec	(2) τ	(3) $\dfrac{\Delta V}{V_0}$	(4) $\dfrac{\Delta H}{H_0}$	(5) $\dfrac{V}{V_0}$	(6) V, ft per sec	(7) $\dfrac{H}{H_0}$	(8) H, ft
0	0	1.00	0	0	1	11.75	1	165
1	0.35	0.833	0.033	0.34	0.967	11.35	1.34	221
2	0.70	0.667	0.067	0.69	0.867	10.18	1.69	279
3	1.05	0.500	0.095	0.98	0.705	8.28	1.98	327
4	1.40	0.333	0.117	1.19	0.493	5.79	2.19	362
5	1.75	0.167	0.123	1.29	0.253	2.97	2.29	378
6	2.10	0	0.130	1.32	0	0	2.32	382

solving the problem it helps to visualize that the head at the gate is increasing linearly during the time of uniform closure. Then, at $t = 0.167$ sec, the front of the pressure wave has just reached the reservoir and the pressure in the pipe is as shown by

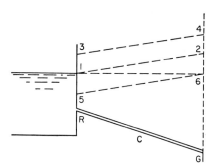

Fig. 11-5. Definition sketch, water hammer.

line 1-2 in Fig. 11-5. At $t = 0.35$ sec, the pressure is the sum of the positive pressures indicated by the line 3-4 and the negative pressures indicated by the line 5-6. Thus, at $t = 0.35$ sec, the pressure wave has just returned to the gate G but has zero value at that point. Therefore, at time $t = 0.35$ sec, there is only an increase in pressure at G computed as follows, noting first that $V_1 = V_0 - \Delta V_1$, $H_1 = H_0 + \Delta H_1$, and $\tau = 0.833$, the subscripts indicating values at the end of the first time interval. Equation (11-65) becomes

$$\frac{V_1}{V_0} = 1 - \frac{\Delta V_1}{V_0} = \tau \sqrt{\frac{H_1}{H_0}} = 0.833 \sqrt{1 + \frac{\Delta H_1}{H_0}} \quad (11\text{-}65a)$$

Also, Eq. (11-61) becomes

$$\frac{\Delta H_1}{H_0} = \frac{v_w V_0}{g H_0} \frac{\Delta V_1}{V_0} = \frac{4{,}680 \times 11.75}{32.2 \times 165} \frac{\Delta V_1}{V_0} = 10.36 \frac{\Delta V_1}{V_0}$$
$$(11\text{-}61a)$$

These two equations are then solved by successive approximations. As a first trial assume $\Delta V_1/V_0 = 0.10$. Then, from Eq. (11-61a),

$$\frac{\Delta H_1}{H_0} = 10.36 \times 0.10 = 1.04$$

and Eq. (11-65a) becomes

$$1 - \frac{\Delta V_1}{V_0} = 0.833 \sqrt{1 + \frac{\Delta H_1}{H_0}}$$
$$1 - 0.10 = 0.833 \sqrt{1 + 1.04}$$
$$0.90 \neq 1.19$$

Because this is not an equality, further trials must be carried out. The final solution for this time interval gave values of

$$\Delta V_1/V_0 = 0.033$$

and $\Delta H/H_0 = 0.34$. Then $V_1/V_0 = 0.967$ and

$$V_1 = 0.967 \times 11.75 = 11.35 \text{ ft per sec}$$

Similarly, $H_1/H_0 = 1.34$ and $H_1 = 1.34 \times 165 = 221$ ft. These values are recorded in the table.

During the second time interval the solution of Eq. (11-61a) is carried out as before, except for the subscripts, because this equation deals only with the pressure increment resulting from another reduction in velocity.

$$\frac{\Delta H_2}{H_0} = 10.36 \frac{\Delta V_2}{V_0} \qquad (11\text{-}61a)$$

However, Eq. (11-65a) must be revised because there is superimposed upon the positive pressure wave the negative wave returning from the reservoir. At $T = 0.70$ sec this negative wave will cause a reduction in velocity equal to the increment from the first interval denoted here as ΔV_1 ($\Delta V_1/V_0 = 0.033$) and a reduction in pressure ΔH_0 ($\Delta H_1/H_0 = 0.34$). These values must be included in the discharge relationship at the gate as given by Eq. (11-65a) as follows:

$$\frac{V_2}{V_0} = \frac{V_1}{V_0} - \frac{\Delta V_1}{V_0} - \frac{\Delta V_2}{V_0} = \tau \sqrt{\frac{H_2}{H_0}}$$
$$= \tau \sqrt{\frac{H_1}{H_0} - \frac{\Delta H_1}{H_0} + \frac{\Delta H_2}{H_0}} \quad (11\text{-}65a)$$

Inserting numerical values,

$$0.967 - 0.033 - \frac{\Delta V_2}{V_0} = 0.667 \sqrt{1.34 - 0.34 + \frac{\Delta H_2}{H_0}}$$

or

$$0.934 - \frac{\Delta V_2}{V_0} = 0.667 \sqrt{1 + \frac{\Delta H_2}{H_0}} \quad (11\text{-}65a)$$

Solution yields $\Delta V_2/V_0 = 0.067$ and $\Delta H_2/H_0 = 0.693$. Then $V_2/V_0 = 0.867$ and $H_2/H_0 = 1.693$. Corresponding values of V_2 and H_2 are shown in the table. Computations were continued in this manner, and the results are tabulated.

Much less tedious than the step computations described above is a *graphical method*[1] of solving slow-closure problems. The equations upon which this method is based are obtained by solving the differential equations for dynamic equilibrium and continuity.[2] For any two points in a pipeline such as R and G in Fig. 11-5, the following equations can be written:

$$h_{Gt_1} - h_{Rt_2} = \frac{v_w V_0}{g H_0} (v_{Gt_1} - v_{Rt_2}) \quad (11\text{-}66)$$

$$h_{Rt_2} - h_{Gt_3} = -\frac{v_w V_0}{g H_0} (v_{Rt_2} - v_{Gt_3}) \quad (11\text{-}67)$$

In these equations $h = H/H_0$ and $v = V/V_0$ and t_1, t_2, and t_3 are successive times separated by uniform time intervals. Furthermore, h_{Gt_1}, v_{Gt_1} and h_{Rt_2}, v_{Rt_2} are coordinates of points on a graph such as that shown in Fig. 11-6, and Eq. (11-66) represents a straight line having a slope $v_w V_0/g H_0$ connecting these

[1] Parmakian, *op. cit.*

[2] R. W. Angus, Simple Graphical Solution for Pressure Rise in Pipes and Pump Discharge Lines, *J. Eng. Inst. Canada*, February, 1935, p. 72.

two points. The points are designated in Fig. 11-6 by the subscripts only. A similar line is represented by Eq. (11-67), except that it has a negative slope. These two equations are derived from the dynamic relationship resulting from the water hammer and thus correspond to Eq. (11-61). The discharge relationship at the gate is taken care of in the graphical solution by plotting the parabolas represented by Eqs. (11-64) and (11-65) for various values of τ as shown in Fig. 11-6. The use of these equations in making a graphical solution will be illustrated by applying them to the same problem solved in the previous example by the step method.

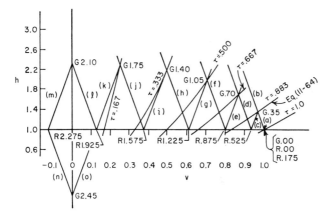

Fig. 11-6. Graphical solution, Example 11-3.

Example 11-3. The graphical solution is conveniently made by writing the equations for time intervals equal to half the round-trip travel time of the wave, or $L/v_w = 0.175$ sec. Then the first four required forms of Eqs. (11-66) and (11-67) are:

$$h_{G.0} - h_{R.175} = 10.36(v_{G.0} - v_{R.175}) \qquad (a)$$
$$h_{R.175} - h_{G.35} = -10.36(v_{R.175} - v_{G.35}) \qquad (b)$$
$$h_{G.35} - h_{R.525} = 10.36(v_{G.35} - v_{R.525}) \qquad (c)$$
$$h_{R.525} - h_{G.667} = -10.36(v_{R.525} - v_{G.667}) \qquad (d)$$

Once the pattern of the equations is envisioned, they can be represented diagrammatically[1] as shown in Fig. 11-7, in which

[1] This scheme is patterned after one shown by Parmakian, *op. cit.*

the four equations shown above are represented by lines a to d. It need only be remembered that equations showing a time sequence from G to R have a positive slope, and those proceeding in the opposite direction have a negative slope.

At zero time $V = V_0$ and $H = H_0$; therefore $h_{G.0}$ and $v_{G.0}$ both have the value 1.0 and the point $G.0$ is plotted at that location in Fig. 11-6. Furthermore, at the reservoir, the original conditions exist at time $t = 0$ and $t = 0.175$ sec, so that points $R.0$ and $R.175$ are also plotted at $v = 1$, $h = 1$. Because

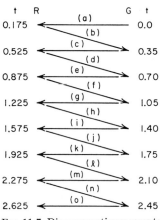

both ends of the line a, as represented by Eq. (a), occur at the same point, Eq. (a) is also represented by the same point as shown in the figure. The gate-discharge relationship also is satisfied by this point because, with $\tau = 1.0$, Eq. (11-65) passes through $h = 1$, $v = 1$. However, at time $t = 0.35$ sec, the conditions at the gate are represented by Eq. (b) as well as by Eq. (11-65), with τ equal to 0.833. This value of τ may be read from the table shown in Example 11-2. Equation (11-65),

FIG. 11-7. Diagrammatic representation of equations, Example 11-3.

with $\tau = 0.833$, and Eq. (b) are plotted, and their intersection locates point $G.35$. Values of $h = H_{.35}/H_0$ and $v = V_{.35}/V_0$ may be read from this point and compared with the tabulated values computed by the step method in Example 11-2.

Equation (c) is plotted through $G.35$ with a positive slope, and the location of $R.525$ is found at $h = 1.0$ because the head at the reservoir must remain constant at the original value H_0. Point $G.70$ is then located by extending Eq. (d) with a negative slope from point $R.525$ to its intersection with Eq. (11-65) with $\tau = 0.667$. The solution is then continued in the same manner until the valve is completely closed, after which, because friction has been neglected, the pressure continues to fluctuate from a maximum positive to a maximum negative value as shown by the loop at the left end of the figure. It may be noted that the graphical solution gives results identical with the step solution shown in the previous example.

The graphical solution is much faster than the step solution, which usually involves a considerable number of trials for each step. An additional advantage of the graphical solution is that it can be readily set up to find the pressure at other locations in the pipe. This is illustrated by means of the following example.

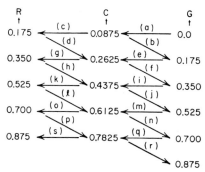

FIG. 11-8. Diagrammatic representation of equations, Example 11-4.

Example 11-4. For the same penstock used in Examples 11-2 and 11-3, find the variations in the pressure at mid-length (point c in Fig. 11-5) as well as at the gate during valve closure. In this problem Eqs. (11-66) and (11-67) are written between G and C and also between C and R. The first few equations are given below, and the simpler scheme of representing the equations described in the previous example is shown in Fig. 11-8. For this example the equations are written for time intervals of $L/2v_w = 0.0875$ sec.

$$h_{G.0} - h_{C.0875} = 10.36(v_{G.0} - v_{C.0875}) \qquad (a)$$

$$h_{C.0875} - h_{G.175} = -10.36(v_{C.0875} - v_{G.175}) \qquad (b)$$

$$h_{C.0875} - h_{R.175} = 10.36(v_{C.0875} - v_{R.175}) \qquad (c)$$

$$h_{R.175} - h_{C.2625} = -10.36(v_{R.175} - v_{C.2625}) \qquad (d)$$

$$h_{G.175} - h_{C.2625} = 10.36(v_{G.175} - v_{C.2625}) \qquad (e)$$

$$h_{C.2625} - h_{G.35} = -10.36(v_{C.2625} - v_{G.35}) \qquad (f)$$

Several steps in the graphical solution are shown in Fig. 11-9. The reasoning is the same as that of Example 11-3, except that points at the center of the pipe are located by the intersection of two of the straight lines. For example, $C.4375$ is at the intersection of lines h and i. The location of line h is established by its starting point at $R.35$ and its negative slope, and the location of i is determined by its starting point at $G.35$ and its positive slope. It may be noted that points such as $G.35$, $G.70$, $R.525$, and $R.70$ have the same coordinates as determined in Example 11-3 and shown in Fig. 11-6.

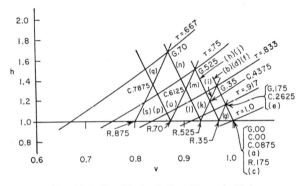

FIG. 11-9. Graphical solution, Example 11-4.

Although the graphical solution is much quicker and easier than the analytical solution previously described, it also becomes cumbersome when very complicated conditions are encountered. Under such conditions water-hammer problems can probably be solved most expeditiously by means of the digital computer.[1,2] A convenient method of applying the computer to water-hammer problems is the method of characteristics.[2,3] The procedure is carried forward in steps in a manner similar to that described in the first portion of this section, in which the method characteristics were applied to flow with a free surface.

[1] F. D. Ezekiel and H. M. Paynter, "Computer Representations of Engineering Systems Involving Fluid Transients," *Trans. ASME*, vol. 79, p. 1840, 1957.

[2] V. L. Streeter and Chintu Lai, Water-hammer Analysis Including Fluid Friction, *Proc. ASCE, J. Hydraulics Div.*, May, 1962, p. 79.

[3] C. A. M. Gray, Analysis of Water Hammer by Characteristics, *Trans. ASCE*, vol. 119, p. 1176, 1954.

SECTION 12

MEASUREMENT OF FLOWING WATER

In general, all methods of measuring flowing water may be classed in one of two divisions, which, together with a list of the more important methods coming under each classification, are as follows:

1. Velocity-area methods, velocity measured by:
   a. Current meter
   b. Pitot tube
   c. Color method
   d. Salt-velocity method
2. Direct-discharge methods
   a. Gravimetric
   b. Volumetric
   c. Weirs
   d. Orifices
   e. Gibson method
   f. Venturi meter
   g. Pipe orifice
   h. Flow nozzle
   i. California-pipe method
   j. Venturi flume
   k. Critical-depth meter
   l. Contracted opening
   m. Chemical gaging
   n. Electromagnetic flow meter

In general, the current meter, the weir, the venturi flume, the contracted section, and the critical-depth meter are used for the measurement of the flow in open channels. The color method, the salt-velocity method, the Gibson method, the venturi meter, the orifice in pipe, the flow nozzle, and the

California-pipe method are used for measuring the flow in pipes. Pitot tubes and chemical gaging are used for both open and closed conduits. Orifices are used only for measuring comparatively small quantities of water.

Velocity-area methods require the determination by actual measurement of the mean velocity of the water. The discharge is the product of the area and mean velocity. The traveling-screen, color, and salt-velocity methods determine the mean velocity from a single observation. The current meter and pitot tube give velocities at one point for each observation, and floats give the mean velocity in the path traveled. The current meter is generally preferred for measuring velocities in open channels where extreme accuracy is not required, and it is used almost exclusively for gaging rivers.

Direct-discharge methods do not involve velocity measurements. In some of the methods the determination of velocity is a step in the proceedings, but no actual measurement of velocity is made. Gravimetric and volumetric methods of measuring water, which require the determination of the weight and volume, respectively, of water flowing in a given time, are adapted primarily to experimental work in laboratories and can be used only for measuring comparatively small flows. These methods are simple and require no explanation. The use of orifices and weirs is explained in the chapters under these headings. All the other methods listed above are described in the following pages.

The Current Meter

The actuating element of a current meter is a wheel, comprising a series of vanes or cups, which is impelled by the current. The rate at which the wheel revolves varies with the velocity of the water. There are several arrangements for determining the speed of the wheel. Usually this is accomplished by means of a mechanism which, at each revolution or at a given number of revolutions, makes and breaks an electric circuit in which is included a telephone receiver or other suitable electrical indicating or recording device. The acoustic meter has an attachment which strikes a drum at a given number of revolutions, the sound being conveyed to the observer through the tube by which the meter is held. Other meters are arranged with mechanical recording devices. Current meters are suspended from a cable or attached to a rod.

For gaging large streams the former arrangement is preferable. Meters attached to rods are convenient for gaging small streams.

There are two general types of current meters—the differential, or cup, type, consisting of a vertical axis carrying a series of cups which revolve by the excess pressure on the concave side over that on the convex side; and the direct, or propeller, type, having vanes set on a horizontal axis which revolve by the direct action of the current. The cup meter always registers the full velocity regardless of the direction of the current or the direction in which the meter is pointed. Moving the meter vertically, either up or down, causes the wheel to move in a positive direction. There is therefore a tendency

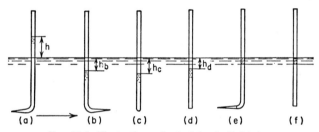

Fig. 12-1. Illustrations of principle of pitot tube.

for the cup meter always to indicate a velocity too high. The propeller type of meter does not have this objectionable feature, at least not to the same degree as the cup meter. It is probable, however, that any of the standard makes of current meters, if used properly, under the conditions to which they are best suited, will prove satisfactory in ordinary stream-gaging work.[1]

The pitot tube, in its simplest form, is a pipe with open ends and a right-angled bend near one end. When held with the opening in the shorter portion directed against the current, as indicated in Fig. 12-1a, the velocity at the opening being v, water will rise in the tube a distance $v^2/2g$ above the surface of the stream. It has been proved experimentally that this relation holds rigidly regardless of the dimensions of the tube or the size of opening. In this simple form the pitot tube has

[1] For a more complete discussion of the use of current meters, see C. O. Wisler and E. F. Brater, "Hydrology," 2d ed, John Wiley & Sons, Inc., New York, 1959.

little practical value, since the distance above the surface of the stream which the water in the tube will rise cannot be accurately measured.

In Fig. 12-1b and c are tubes exactly like tube a, except that tube b is pointed downstream and tube c is pointed across the current. A suction is created in both, the amount of suction being measured by the respective distances h_b and h_c, by which the water surface in each tube is drawn below the surface of the stream. Approximate values of h_b and h_c, from experiments by Darcy, are

$$h_b = 0.43 \frac{v^2}{2g} \qquad \text{and} \qquad h_c = 0.68 \frac{v^2}{2g}$$

Similarly, for tube d, a straight tube open at both ends, there is a depression h_d. Tube e is the same as tube a, except that the lower end is closed and there is a small hole in each side wall. If this tube is pointed either upstream or downstream so that the walls of the tube are parallel to the direction of flow, the water surface in the tube will remain at about the same elevation as the surface of the stream. In other words, a tube of this type records very closely the true static pressure. Tube f is a straight pipe closed at its lower end with a small hole on each side. If this tube is held so that the surfaces containing the holes are parallel to the current, it records approximately the static pressure, but probably not so closely as tube e.

A device designed by Darcy to measure velocities in open channels is shown in Fig. 12-2. A kinetic leg and a static leg, Fig. 12-1a and b, respectively, have glass tubes attached to their upper ends and are connected to an air suction pump through a common chamber containing a valve. There are two valves on one stem just below the glass tubes. To obtain a velocity measurement, the kinetic leg (either leg for this particular design) is held to point against the current. Then, by operating the pump, air is rarefied sufficiently to draw both water columns into the glass tubes. The valves are then closed, and the instrument is lifted from the water and read. Any one of the forms of static leg c, d, e, or f, of Fig. 12-1, as well as other designs not shown, could be substituted for leg b.

If $h_1 - h_2$ (Fig. 12-2) is the difference in height of water columns in feet and c is a coefficient, constant for each instrument, the velocity is

$$v = c \sqrt{2g(h_1 - h_2)} \tag{12-1}$$

Approximate values of c for some of the forms of static leg shown in Fig. 12-1 are

$$\text{For } b: c = 0.84$$
$$\text{For } c: c = 0.77$$
$$\text{For } e \text{ and } f: c = 1$$

For accurate work each instrument should be rated by moving it through still water, and c obtained for several velocities.

The pitot tube shown in Fig. 12-3 is a form for pipes contained in the Report of the Special Research Committee[1] on Fluid

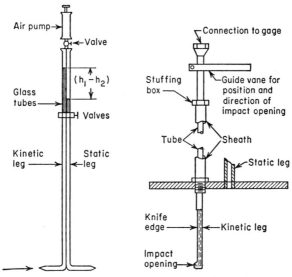

FIG. 12-2. Darcy tube.

FIG. 12-3. Single-opening pitot tube for pipes.

Meters of the ASME. With this arrangement, the static head is taken in the wall of the pipe entirely separate from the kinetic leg. There should be not less than two pairs of diametrically opposed holes to transmit the static head. These openings should not exceed $\frac{1}{4}$ in. in diameter, and their edges should be sharp. The tubes leading from them should be normal to

[1] Clemens Herschel, "Fluid Meters: Their Theory and Application," Report of Special Research Committee on Fluid Meters, ASME, 1924.

the internal surface of the conduit wall. The difference in pressure in the two legs may be measured with a U tube.

The Color Method.   This method is used for determining the discharge in pipes or other closed conduits.   It is not necessary that the conduit be of uniform or regular cross section.   A small quantity of a concentrated solution of some powerful coloring matter is injected into the conduit, and the time it requires to travel to some point of observation is determined. The length of reach, that is, the distance between the point where the coloring matter is introduced and the point where it is observed, is measured.

Scobey[1] found that the coloring matter is contained in a prism having a length equal to about 10 per cent of the distance traveled.   He used three chemicals for coloring—fluorescein, congo red, and potassium permanganate.   One teaspoonful of fluorescein dissolved in a pint of water gives sufficient coloring matter for four injections in a pipe carrying 60 sec-ft of water. Congo red and potassium permanganate each require about ten times this amount of chemical to produce the same intensity in color.

The coloring matter can be introduced at the intake, or it can be injected by a force pump or gun through an opening in the wall of the conduit.   The point of observation must be where the water can be seen, as at the outlet or when a valve can be opened.   The length of reach in feet should not be less than two hundred times the velocity.   Time observations should be made at the instant the coloring matter is introduced and at the first and last appearances of the coloring matter at the point of observation.   The average of these time intervals is considered the time of travel.   In a pipe or conduit of uniform cross-sectional area the length of reach divided by the time of travel equals the mean velocity, and the discharge is the product of this mean velocity and the cross-sectional area of the conduit.   If the cross section of the conduit is not uniform, the volume of the reach must be determined.   This volume divided by the time of travel equals the discharge.

The Salt-velocity Method.   This is a modification of the color method and was used by Slichter,[2] in 1901, to measure the

[1] Fred C. Scobey, The Flow of Water in Concrete Pipe, *U.S. Dept. Agr. Bull.* 852, 1920.

[2] C. S. Slichter, Motion of Underground Waters, *U.S. Geol. Survey Water Supply and Irrigation Paper* 67, 1902.

rate of flow of ground water. Its application to the measurement of flow in pipes was described by the author[1] in 1918. Later the method was used by Allen and Taylor[2] to measure the discharge of penstocks in making turbine tests.

A concentrated salt brine is introduced at the intake or through openings in the conduit wall. The salt increases the electrical conductivity of the water. Electrodes, connected to an ammeter or electrical recording meter, are installed at one or more points of observation below the place where salt is introduced. An increase in electric current is indicated when the prism of water containing the salt passes the electrodes.

If an ammeter is used, with but one point of observation, time observations are made at the instant the salt is introduced and also at the beginning and end of increased deflection of the ammeter needle. The average of these time intervals is considered the time of travel. If there are two or more points of observation, particularly if one of the points is near the place where salt is introduced, it is not usual to record the time of introducing the salt. The time of travel between two points of observation is the average of the times between the beginnings and the ends of increased deflection. Readings at one point of observation, in addition to the two readings necessary for a discharge measurement, provide an independent check on the result.

If a recording meter is used, the time when the salt is considered to pass a point of observation is given by the center of gravity of the area included between the line of normal current extended and the line showing excess current. The method of computing discharge is identical with that described for the color method. The volume of the conduit for the reach being considered must be determined. The discharge equals this volume in cubic feet divided by the time of travel in seconds.

The Gibson Method. This can be used only for measuring the discharge in a pipe or other closed conduit which has a valve, or some other means of gradually shutting off the water, at least 25 and preferably 50 ft or more below the intake. The conduit need not be of uniform cross-sectional area. The method is particularly adapted to measuring the discharge in

[1] H. W. King, "Handbook of Hydraulics," 1st ed., p. 247, McGraw-Hill Book Company, Inc., New York, 1918.

[2] C. M. Allen and E. A. Taylor, The Salt-velocity Method of Water Measurement, *Trans. ASME*, vol. 86, 1923.

penstocks in which the flow of water is controlled by turbine gates.

A mercury U tube attached to the penstock above the gates indicates the hydrostatic pressure. In making a measurement the gates are closed gradually, and a continuous photographic record showing equal time intervals and the height of the mercury in the U tube is made by the Gibson apparatus.[1] This is a time-pressure diagram which shows the total impulse necessary to bring the column of water to rest and from which the discharge can be computed.

Figure 12-4 is reproduced from one of Gibson's time-pressure diagrams. The vertical lines 1, 2, 3, etc., are equal time

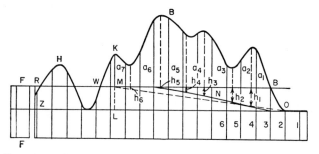

Fig. 12-4. Gibson time-pressure diagram. h_1, h_2, h_3, etc., are measured on line separating areas a_1, a_2, a_3, etc., between lines FB and MNO.

intervals, preferably 1 sec. The curved line $OBBKH$ is the locus of elevations of the surface of mercury in the U tube. The detached rectangle FF is a short record of pressure after the gates are closed and oscillations have ceased. The horizontal line OZ shows the pressure before the gates began to close, and the line FB is the hydrostatic pressure at zero velocity. The vertical distance between these lines is therefore the sum of the velocity head and friction head when the gates are open. At O the gates began to close, and at K they

[1] N. R. Gibson, The Gibson Method and Apparatus for Measuring the Flow of Water in Closed Conduits, *Trans. ASME*, vol. 86, pp. 343–376, 1923. Method and apparatus patented in United States, Oct. 13 and Nov. 22, 1921. A brief description of the method is given here. For fuller details, the theory involved, minor corrections to be made, and a description of the Gibson apparatus, the reader is referred to Gibson's paper.

are completely closed. The position of K is determined by drawing the ordinate MK, the point M being approximately one-fourth of a complete wavelength, $\frac{1}{4}RW$, to the right of W.

The line ONM eliminates the area produced by the recovery of friction and velocity heads, the area above this line being a measure of the rate of discharge in the conduit at the moment the gates began to close. Trial and error are used to locate the position of the line ONM. As a first assumption, the straight line OM may be taken, but usually it will be found easy to estimate by inspection the approximate position so that only one correction will be necessary.

A number of vertical lines are drawn from the pressure line BBK to intersect the line OM, and the areas a_1, a_2, a_3, etc., enclosed by these lines are measured by planimeter or by scaling in square inches. The sum of these areas will be called A_1. The distance LM, the sum of the friction and velocity heads, is measured in inches and called Y. Let

$$P_1 = \frac{a_1}{A_1}, P_2 = \frac{a_1 + a_2}{A_1}, P_3 = \frac{a_1 + a_2 + a_3}{A_1}, \ldots$$

and let

$$h_1 = Y(1 - P_1)^2, h_2 = Y(1 - P_2)^2, \ldots$$

Having determined the values of h_1, h_2, h_3, etc., from these equations, a point is located on the line separating the areas a_1 and a_2, or this line produced by measuring down vertically from FB a distance equal to h_1. A distance equal to h_2 is measured down vertically from FB on the line separating the areas a_2 and a_3. Similarly, a distance equal to each of the values h_3, h_4, etc., is measured down from FB on the respective lines separating the areas a_3, a_4, etc. The points so plotted are then joined, forming a line from O to M. If this line fails to coincide with the assumed line, a second trial is made using the new line in place of the one first assumed. This process is repeated until a base line ONM is found such that, when h_1, h_2, etc., are computed as before but using the new areas a_1, a_2, a_3, etc., above the line ONM, the line joining the ends of h_1, h_2, etc., will coincide with ONM.

Referring to Fig. 12-4, let

A = area, sq in. of surface $OBBKMNO$

r = vertical height, in., corresponding to 1 ft of pressure change in conduit

S = horizontal length, in., corresponding to 1 sec of time

Then, if $K = g/r$, g being the acceleration due to gravity, and L = length of pipe in feet,

$$v = \frac{KA}{SL} \qquad (12\text{-}2)$$

This is a convenient form of the final equation for a pipe of uniform cross-sectional area. The mean velocity v is multiplied by the area to obtain the discharge.

When the conduit is not of uniform cross-sectional area throughout its length but is made up of a series of different sections of lengths l_1, l_2, l_3, etc., having average cross-sectional areas a_1, a_2, a_3, etc., respectively, the discharge is given by the formula

$$Q = \frac{KA}{SF} \qquad (12\text{-}3)$$

where $F = \Sigma(l/a)$, that is, the sum of the quotients obtained by dividing the length of each section by its average cross-sectional areas.

The above method can be modified by substituting for the simple U tube with a single piezometer connection a differential U tube with connections to the conduit at two points at least 25 ft apart. The procedure in preparing and using the diagrams in the two cases is substantially the same.

Venturi Meters.   The principle of the venturi meter was first stated in 1797 by J. B. Venturi, an Italian, and was first applied by Herschel[1] to the measurement of flow in pipes in 1887. Figure 12-5 shows a venturi meter which is reproduced from a drawing contained in the Report of the Special Committee[2] on Fluid Meters of the ASME. It consists of a constricted portion which may be inserted between two flanges in a pipeline for the purpose of accelerating the water and lowering its static pressure. The proportions of the venturi meters now used are much the same as those originally adopted by Herschel and shown in Fig. 12-5. The basic principles involved in the use of the venturi meter are discussed on page 3-9 and methods of computing the discharge at which cavitation will begin in a venturi are shown on page 3-10.

[1] *Trans. ASCE*, vol. 17, p. 228, 1887.
[2] Clemens Herschel, "Fluid Meters: Their Theory and Application," Report of Special Research Committee on Fluid Meters, ASME, 1924. The figure and most of the information contained in the above description are taken from this report.

Starting at the upstream flange, there is, first, a short cylindrical portion which continues the pipeline but is machined inside or cast smooth so that its diameter may be accurately determined. In this portion a side hole is drilled through the wall, or several holes lead into a piezometer ring, so that a connection may be made for measuring the static pressure of

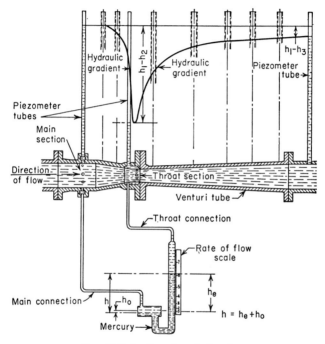

Fig. 12-5. Section of venturi meter.

the fluid before it enters the constriction. Following this preliminary straight part, the entrance cone of about 21°, total angle, leads to the short cylindrical throat which is accurately machined and is provided with a side hole or holes for taking off the static pressure in the throat. The transition from the entrance cone into the straight throat is rounded off to an easy tangential curve to avoid the resistance caused by a sharp corner and to preclude the possibility that the fluid might break away from the wall at high speeds and so not fill the throat completely. The diameter of the throat is usually between one-half and one-fourth of the entrance or pipeline diameter, and there is usually a joint, a handhole, or even a manhole in large sizes, at the throat which facilitates inspection of the condition of the throat and side holes and permits of accurate measurement of the throat diameter. The end of the throat leads, by another easy curve, into the exit cone or diffuser, which has a total angle of about 5 to 7°. This terminates in the downstream flange for connecting the venturi to the following pipeline. A pressure connection is sometimes provided at the downstream flange for the purpose of determining the overall loss of head caused by the resistance of the venturi as a whole.

Very small venturis—say, for pipelines less than 2 in. in diameter—are commonly made of brass or bronze and smoothly finished all over the inside to reduce the resistance. Larger venturis are usually of cast iron, the throat and sometimes the straight entrance portion being lined with brass or bronze and machined to a smooth finish. Very large venturis, up to 20 ft in diameter, have been made of smooth-surface concrete, only the throat being of machined bronze. Wood staves and steel plate have also been used for the cones of large venturis.

Venturi tubes, especially in large sizes, are usually set horizontally or nearly so, although this position is not at all essential to the operation of the meter. If reliable measurements are required, it is essential that the venturi should not follow immediately after a valve, elbow, or other irregularity in the pipeline, which would tend to cause great turbulence or set up permanent crosscurrents or whirls, but should be preceded by a length of 5 or more diameters of straight pipe in which the flow may steady down after any such cause of disturbance. There is probably never any appreciable advantage in accuracy to be gained by using more than 20 diameters of straight pipe ahead of the venturi. When it is impossible to provide a sufficient line of pipe, the flow should be steadied by straightening vanes. A sheet-metal cross, 1 or 2 diameters long, inserted in the pipe just ahead of the venturi, will serve this purpose.

The function of the long diverging cone is to retard or decelerate the fluid smoothly and restore the pressure as nearly as possible to the value it had at the entrance. This restoration is imperfect because there is always some resistance to flow through the venturi and some loss of head is unavoidable. The overall loss is 10 to 20 per cent of the venturi head, or differential from entrance to throat. In other words, between 80 and 90 per cent of the fall of pressure at the throat is restored in the diverging cone. The percentage loss decreases as the speed of flow increases or as the meter is made larger.

Let h_1 and h_2 represent the height above the axis of the meter to which the water rises in the piezometer tubes at the entrance and throat of the meter, respectively, and let V_1, d_1, and a_1 and V_2, d_2, and a_2 be the corresponding velocities, diameters, and areas. Then, from Bernoulli's theorem, neglecting friction,

$$\frac{V_2{}^2 - V_1{}^2}{2g} = h_1 - h_2 \tag{12-4}$$

and since

$$Q = a_1 V_1 = a_2 V_2$$

the formula for discharge through a venturi meter, including the empirical coefficient c, becomes

$$Q = \frac{c a_1 a_2}{\sqrt{a_1{}^2 - a_2{}^2}} \sqrt{2g(h_1 - h_2)} \tag{12-5}$$

or, expressed in terms of diameter,

$$Q = \frac{c \pi d_1{}^2 d_2{}^2}{4 \sqrt{d_1{}^4 - d_2{}^4}} \sqrt{2g(h_1 - h_2)} \tag{12-6}$$

which reduces to

$$Q = c K d_2{}^2 \sqrt{h_1 - h_2} \tag{12-7}$$

where

$$K = \frac{4}{\pi} \sqrt{\frac{2g}{1 - (d_2/d_1)^4}} \tag{12-8}$$

Values of K corresponding to different values of d_2/d_1 and values of c are given in the following tables. Coefficients of discharge c were obtained from experiments by Ledoux[1] on 19 different venturi meters, in which the throat diameter varied from 0.4 to 18 in. Discharges were measured volumetrically, and heads were measured with hook gages. It is believed that these experiments provide the most reliable data available for com-

[1] J. W. Ledoux, Venturi Tube Characteristics, *Trans. ASCE*, vol. 91, 1927.

puting venturi coefficients. The table values represent the approximate mean of the experimental values. Individual measurements vary by 1 per cent or more from the tabulated values. The experiments include throat velocities of 1 to 30 ft per sec, approximately. Values in the table for the higher

Coefficients of Discharge c for Venturi Meters

Diameter of throat, in.	Throat velocity, ft per sec								
	3	4	5	10	15	20	30	40	50
1	.935	.945	.949	.958	.963	.966	.969	.970	.972
2	.939	.948	.953	.965	.970	.973	.974	.975	.977
4	.943	.952	.957	.970	.975	.977	.978	.979	.980
8	.948	.957	.062	.974	.978	.980	.981	.982	.983
12	.955	.962	.967	.978	.981	.982	.983	.984	.985
18	.963	.969	.973	.981	.983	.984	.985	.986	.986
48	.970	.977	.980	.984	.985	.986	.987	.988	.988

velocities as well as for the throat diameter of 48 in. were obtained by extending curves plotted from the experiments. The Ledoux experiments indicated values of the coefficient to be about 2 per cent smaller for throat velocities of 5 ft per sec and about 1 per cent smaller for the higher velocities than the values given by the Report of the Special Committee on Fluid Meters of the ASME.

The coefficients of discharge c are for temperatures of 60°F. The following are corrective factors for other temperatures:

Temperature	40	60	80	100	120	150	200
f	1.4	1.0	0.8	0.6	0.5	0.4	0.3

To determine c for a temperature other than 60°, multiply the actual throat velocity by f and take the coefficient corresponding to the equivalent throat velocity from the table.

Measurements by Ledoux on a 4- by $1\frac{17}{32}$-in. venturi meter, with heavy deposits in cone but clean throat, gave a coefficient about 2.5 per cent less before cleaning than the coefficient obtained for the same meter after cleaning. Snow[1] found that

[1] B. F. Snow, Venturi Tube Characteristics, discussion, *Trans. ASCE*, vol. 91, p. 581, 1927.

a venturi meter in a sewage main, after having been in service 20 years, had its throat diameter reduced from 15 to $12\frac{1}{4}$ in. by the deposition of carbonate of lime which came from trade wastes.

Values of K in Formula for Venturi Meters

$\dfrac{d_2}{d_1}$	K	$\dfrac{d_2}{d_1}$	K	$\dfrac{d_2}{d_1}$	K	$\dfrac{d_2}{d_1}$	K	$\dfrac{d_2}{d_1}$	K
.20	6.31	.33	6.34	.46	6.45	.59	6.72	.72	7.37
.21	6.31	.34	6.34	.47	6.46	.60	6.75	.73	7.45
.22	6.31	.35	6.35	.48	6.47	.61	6.79	.74	7.53
.23	6.31	.36	6.35	.49	6.49	.62	6.82	.75	7.62
.24	6.31	.37	6.36	.50	6.51	.63	6.86	.76	7.72
.25	6.31	.38	6.37	.51	6.52	.64	6.91	.77	7.82
.26	6.31	.39	6.37	.52	6.54	.65	6.95	.78	7.94
.27	6.32	.40	6.38	.53	6.56	.66	7.00	.79	8.06
.28	6.32	.41	6.39	.54	6.59	.67	7.05	.80	8.20
.29	6.32	.42	6.40	.55	6.61	.68	7.11	.81	8.35
.30	6.33	.43	6.41	.56	6.64	.69	7.17	.82	8.51
.31	6.33	.44	6.42	.57	6.66	.70	7.23	.83	8.69
.32	6.33	.45	6.43	.58	6.69	.71	7.30	.84	8.89

Pipe Orifices. The equation for discharge through a circular sharp-edged orifice was derived in Sec. 4, page 4-14. This equation may be restated in the following form:

$$Q = Ka \sqrt{2g \left(\frac{p_1}{w} - \frac{p_2}{w} \right)} \qquad (12\text{-}9)$$

where K is defined as follows:

$$K = \frac{C}{\sqrt{1 - C^2(a/a_1)^2}} \qquad (12\text{-}10)$$

In Eqs. (12-9) and (12-10), Q is the discharge in second-feet; a and a_1 are the areas of the orifice and the pipe, respectively, in square feet; p_1 and p_2 are the pressures at the upstream and downstream sides of the orifice, respectively, in pounds per square foot; and w is the unit weight of the liquid in pounds per cubic foot. It will be noted from the derivation on page 4-3 that C takes care of the energy loss and the contraction of the jet. It follows from Eq. (12-10) that the coefficient K includes these factors as well as the velocity of approach.

Values of K for square-edged pipe orifices have been presented by the ASME[1] for three different types of pressure taps. These are flange taps, vena contracta taps, and radius taps. Flange taps are located with the center of the high-pressure tap 1 in. from the upstream face of the orifice plate and the center of the low-pressure tap 1 in. from the downstream side of the plate.   For vena contracta taps, the high-pressure tap is located 1 pipe diameter, d_1, upstream from the face of the orifice plate, and the low-pressure tap is located at the vena contracta.   The mean distance from the orifice plate to the vena contracta, in terms of pipe diameters, for various values of the ratio of orifice diameter to the pipe diameter, d/d_1, is

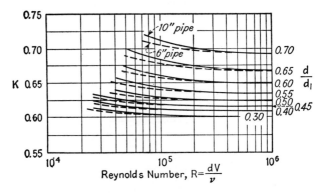

Fig. 12-6. Pipe-orifice coefficients for flange taps.

given in Sec. 4, page 4-17.   Radius taps are located 1 pipe diameter upstream and 12 pipe diameter downstream from the orifice plate.

Values of K are presented in terms of the Reynolds number

$$R = \frac{dV}{\nu} \tag{12-11}$$

where d is the orifice diameter in feet, V is the velocity at the orifice in feet per second, and ν is the kinematic viscosity of the fluid in square feet per second.   Values of ν for water may be obtained from Table 1-2.   Values of K to be used with

[1] ASME, "Flow Measurement by Means of Standardized Nozzles and Orifice Plates," Power Test Codes, Supplement on Instruments and Apparatus, pt. 5, chap. 4, 1949.   This supplement was prepared and published by ASME under the auspices of the Power Test Codes Committee.

flange taps for 6- and 10-in. pipe are shown in Fig. 12-6. These were taken from the ASME Power Test Codes previously referred to.[1] The curves for 6-in. pipe are quite similar to those for 3- and 4-in. pipe, while those for 10-in. pipe are similar to those for 8- and 14-in. pipe. Values of K for 2-in. pipe are somewhat lower than those for 6-in. pipe for $R < 10^5$ and slightly higher for $R > 2 \times 10^5$. If an installation of a pipe orifice is to be made without a calibration, it is recommended

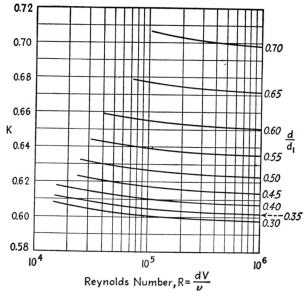

FIG. 12-7. Pipe-orifice coefficients for vena contracta taps.

that reference be made to the original data for the particular pipe size, as well as to detailed installation requirements.[1]

Curves giving values of K for vena contracta taps are shown in Fig. 12-7. These curves were presented for 6-in. pipe.[1] They are, however, nearly identical with those for other pipe diameters.

Values of K for a pipe orifice in any particular location may be expected to differ somewhat from values given in Figs. 12-6

[1] *Ibid.*

and 12-7 unless installation recommendations are carefully followed. Detailed instructions are available.[1] Some of the more important restrictions have to do with the location of pipe fittings in the vicinity of the orifice. For example, elbows or open valves must be located 5 pipe diameters upstream from the orifice for small values of d/d_1 and as many as 25 diameters upstream from the orifice for large values of d/d_1. No elbow should be placed nearer than 5 diameters from the downstream side of the orifice. Partially open valves should not be located upstream from the orifice. Where these restrictions cannot be followed, flow straighteners must be used or the orifice must be calibrated in place. Studies regarding the effect of pipe fittings

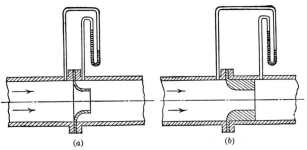

Fig. 12-8. Flow nozzles. (a) Spun type; (b) thick-plate type.

on orifice flow are being conducted, and preliminary information is available.[2]

The ISA (International Federation of National Standardizing Associations) standard orifice is also a square-edged circular-pipe orifice. The pressure taps, however, are located immediately adjacent to the orifice plate. Coefficients for this type of taps have been published by the Verein Deutscher Ingenieure, translated into English by the ASME, and recently published by the National Advisory Committee for Aeronautics.[3]

Standardized Nozzles. This method of measuring the flow in pipes is the same as the pipe-orifice method, except that the orifice has rounded corners and prolonged sides (Fig. 12-8)

[1] *Ibid.*

[2] "Investigation of Orifice Meter Installation Requirements," Interim Research Report, American Gas Association and ASME, March, 1951.

[3] "Standards for Discharge Measurement with Standardized Nozzles and Orifices," German Industrial Standard 1952, 4th ed., *NACA Tech. Mem.* 952.

which lead the water smoothly to the orifice so that it issues without contraction in a straight cylindrical jet of the same diameter as the orifice. In effect, the flow nozzle is a venturi meter with the long diffuser omitted. Discharge coefficients have been published for two standard types of nozzles. The ISA nozzle was developed in Germany. Discharge coefficients have been published in the United States by the ASME[1] and the NACA.[2] The ASME long-radius nozzle,[1] as the name implies, is longer and constricts the flow more gently than the ISA nozzle. The installation requirements described for pipe orifices, page 12-18, also apply to standardized nozzles.

California-pipe Method. This is a method, developed by Van Leer,[3] for determining the rate of flow from the open end of a partially filled horizontal pipe discharging freely into the

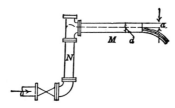

FIG. 12-9. Illustrating California-pipe method of measuring discharge.

air. It is particularly adapted to the measurement of comparatively small flows in pipes. It can also be used to measure flows in small open channels if the water can be diverted into a pipe which it does not completely fill and which discharges without any submergence of the outlet.

The discharge pipe should be level and at least 6 diameters long. If the pipe is flowing nearly full, there should be an air vent a few diameters back from the outlet to provide for the free circulation of air in the unfilled portion of the discharge pipe. Water should enter the discharge pipe without excessive velocity of approach. The equipment required is simple, and it can be easily installed and used.

One arrangement for measuring the flow in a pipeline is shown in Fig. 12-9. The nipple N connects at its lower end to

[1] ASME, 1949, *op. cit.*

[2] NACA, *op. cit.*

[3] B. R. Van Leer, The California-pipe Method of Water Measurement, *Eng. News-Rec.*, Aug. 3, 1922, Aug. 21, 1924.

the supply pipe, and at the upper end it is connected by a tee to the discharge pipe M. The open end of the tee permits a free circulation of air.

Let d equal the internal diameter of the pipe in feet and a equal the distance in feet, measured in the plane of the end of the pipe, from the top of the inside surface of the pipe to the water surface. This distance can be measured approximately with a rule or more accurately with calipers. The discharge in second-feet is given by the formula

$$Q = 8.69 \left(1 - \frac{a}{d}\right)^{1.88} d^{2.48} \qquad (12\text{-}12)$$

This formula is based on experimental data for pipes 3 to 10 in. in diameter, and it applies accurately within these limits.

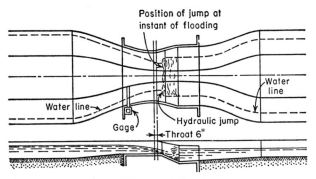

FIG. 12-10. Control meter.

There appears no reason to doubt, however, that it can be used with considerable assurance for larger pipes.

Venturi Flumes. This is a method of adapting the venturi principle to the measurement of flow in open channels. A venturi[1] flume consists of a constricted portion, or throat, with a gradually contracting portion leading to the throat and a gradually expanding portion leading from it. It is illustrated

[1] V. M. Cone, The Venturi Flume, *J. Agr. Research*, vol. 9, no. 4, 1917. R. L. Parshall and Carl Rohwer, The Venturi Flume, *Colo. Agr. Exp. Sta. Bull.* 265, 1921. P. S. Wilson and C. A. Wright, A Study of the Venturi Flume, *Eng. News-Rec.*, vol. 85, Sept. 2, 1920. R. L. Parshall, The Improved Venturi Flume, *Trans. ASCE*, vol. 89, 1926.

in Fig. 12-10, with the exception that in the true venturi flume the floor is laid substantially to the canal grade, and stilling wells for measuring head are provided at both the entrance and throat. The difference in level in the two wells represents the change from potential head to velocity head plus friction and is a measure of the discharge. Figure 12-10 represents a flume having a trapezoidal section, but the section may be rectangular, triangular, or of any other regular form.

The venturi flume is particularly adapted to the measurement of irrigation water. It has advantages over the weir in that it does not back up materially the water in the channel and its accuracy is not apt to be interfered with by the deposition of silt or floating matter.

The derivation of the formula for discharge is identical with that for venturi meters (p. 3-9). If a_1 and a_2 are the respective cross-sectional areas of stream and h the difference in water levels at the entrance and throat, the formula for discharge through the flume, including the empirical coefficient c, is

$$Q = cMa_2 \sqrt{h} \qquad (12\text{-}13)$$

where

$$M = \sqrt{\frac{2g}{1 - (a_2/a_1)^2}} \qquad (12\text{-}14)$$

Values of M for Venturi Flume and Contracted-section Formulas

$\frac{a_2}{a_1}$	M	$\frac{a_2}{a_1}$	M	$\frac{a_2}{a_1}$	M	$\frac{a_2}{a_1}$	M	$\frac{a_2}{a_1}$	M	$\frac{a_2}{a_1}$	M
.00	8.02	.10	8.06	.20	8.19	.30	8.41	.40	8.75	.50	9.26
.01	8.02	.11	8.07	.21	8.20	.31	8.44	.41	8.79	.51	9.32
.02	8.02	.12	8.08	.22	8.22	.32	8.47	.42	8.84	.52	9.39
.03	8.02	.13	8.09	.23	8.24	.33	8.50	.43	8.88	.53	9.46
.04	8.03	.14	8.10	.24	8.26	.34	8.53	.44	8.93	.54	9.53
.05	8.03	.15	8.11	.25	8.28	.35	8.56	.45	8.98	.55	9.60
.06	8.03	.16	8.12	.26	8.31	.36	8.60	.46	9.03	.56	9.68
.07	8.04	.17	8.14	.27	8.33	.37	8.63	.47	9.09	.57	9.76
.08	8.05	.18	8.15	.28	8.35	.38	8.67	.48	9.14	.58	9.84
.09	8.05	.19	8.17	.29	8.38	.39	8.71	.49	9.20	.59	9.93

Values of M corresponding to different values of a_2/a_1 are given in the above table. The value of c will ordinarily lie between 0.95 and 1.00.   It can be kept at 0.98 or higher if care is taken to have smooth surfaces and to round off all corners so as to lead the water to the throat of the flume without contractions or unnecessary turbulence.

Critical-depth Meters.   This is a modified venturi flume. The main feature is a constriction in the channel, so proportioned as to produce flow at critical depth.   The principles, formulas, and tables which apply are described in Sec. 8.   The adaptation of this device to the measurement of irrigation water was first described by Hinds.[1]   Figure 12-10 shows a structure of trapezoidal form which was installed at the hydraulic laboratory of the U.S. Bureau of Reclamation at Boise, Idaho.   The constriction is provided by drawing in the sides and raising the floor above the bed of the channel.   A slight drop, to prevent interference from backwater, is provided just below the throat. Other types of control meters are illustrated by Fig. 8-9.

It is essential that flow at critical depth should occur without interference from backwater.   A standing wave (hydraulic jump) usually forms in the lower channel.   This will not affect the proper functioning of the device so long as the wave forms so far downstream that the control is not flooded.   Figure 12-10 illustrates a test run which was made to determine the conditions under which flooding of the control will occur.   By means of checks the water surface in the lower channel was slowly raised while conditions at the control were studied.   It was found that there was no submergence (that is, the depth at the control was not greater than critical depth) until the standing wave reached approximately the location of the control.   The figure shows the characteristic appearance of the wave just before submergence.   After submergence the wave usually changes to a series of ripples which may be practically as rough as the last stage of the wave but which have a distinctly different appearance.   After the control is flooded, the device becomes in principle a venturi flume.

A large number of tests on different structures by the U.S. Bureau of Reclamation give an average coefficient of discharge of practically unity; that is to say, the theoretical formulas [formulas (8-35), (8-69), and (8-74)] apply without any empirical modification.   These formulas include no correction for fric-

[1] Julian Hinds, Venturi Flume Data Throws Light upon "Control Weir," *Eng. News-Rec.*, vol. 85, Dec. 23, 1920; also discussion, The Improved Venturi Flume, *Trans. ASCE*, vol. 89, 1926.

tion or the effects of nonuniform velocities in the channel of approach. Since these corrections are of opposite sign, they tend to offset each other, and this may, to some extent, explain the close agreement between theoretical and measured results.

Until more experiments are available it is probable that the best that can be done is to use the theoretical formulas for determining discharges by the control meter. Even under these circumstances it appears to compare favorably in accuracy with the sharp-crested weir. It is at a disadvantage in that it may be flooded when the lower channel is obstructed. Otherwise it has all the advantages of the venturi flume and the additional advantage of requiring but a single head measurement.

Contracted Opening. This method of measuring discharge in open channels is particularly adapted to the measurement of floods. It can be used where a constriction in the channel produces a foot or more drop in the water surface. The method is described in European literature. It was used to measure flood flows by the Miami Conservancy District. The details of these measurements were described by Houk.[1] The principle is that of the venturi flume (p. 12-20), but any constriction, such as might be caused by a bridge or similar obstruction, is utilized.

The formula for discharge through a contracted opening, the same as for a venturi flume (p. 12-21), is

$$Q = CMa_2 \sqrt{h} \qquad (12\text{-}13)$$

where

$$M = \sqrt{\frac{2g}{1 - (a_2/a_1)^2}} \qquad (12\text{-}14)$$

In these expressions, h is the drop in water surface and a_1 and a_2 are, respectively, the effective cross-sectional area of the stream just above the beginning of the pronounced drop in water surface and the area at the smallest cross section of the opening. Values of M corresponding to different values of a_2/a_1 are given in the preceding table. Following the analysis used for orifices (p. 4-3),

$$C = C_c C_v$$

[1] I. E. Houk, Calculations of Flow in Open Channels, *Tech. Reports.* pt. IV, The Miami Conservancy District, Dayton, Ohio, 1918.

where C_c is the coefficient of contraction and C_v is the coefficient of velocity. The latter corrects for all losses due to friction and turbulence.

A correction for contraction is required wherever there is a sharp-edged entrance such as the corner of a bridge pier or abutment. It is probable that for a vertical right-angled corner the Francis correction for end contractions (that is, reducing the length of the opening by 0.1 the depth of water for each contraction) will apply approximately. The contraction will be less for piers having rounded or pointed heads. Wherever practicable, the estimated contraction should be checked by field measurements.

For openings of fairly regular form which permit the water to approach the section of minimum area without undue turbulence, C_v will probably have a value of 0.90 or more. For extremely rough or irregular openings, C_v may be 0.50 or even less. The mean value of C_v from 23 measurements by the Miami Conservancy District was 0.86, 20 of the values being above 0.80. The minimum value was 0.45, and the maximum 0.97.

Cross sections should be obtained just above the pronounced drop in water surface and at the smallest part of the opening. Elevations of water surface at these sections are also necessary. Their difference is the drop in water surface. Where the drop in water surface cannot be obtained by direct measurement, as occurs when it is desired to determine the maximum flood discharge after the crest has passed, high-water marks may be utilized.

Chemical gaging consists in determining discharges by introducing a chemical at a known rate into flowing water and determining the quantity of the chemical in the stream at a section far enough downstream to ensure a thorough mixture of the chemical with the water. Common salt (NaCl) is the chemical usually employed. For convenience the salt is dissolved in water before being introduced into the stream.

Let Q represent the discharge of the stream in second-feet. If w lb per sec of salt is introduced and after thorough mixture a sample taken from the stream shows that 1 lb of water contains n lb of salt in addition to the salt which the water already contained, then

$$\frac{w}{62.4Q} = \frac{n}{1} \qquad \text{or} \qquad Q = \frac{w}{62.4n} \qquad (12\text{-}15)$$

The determination of n requires precise laboratory techniques. The successful use of this method depends on thorough mixing which requires a high degree of turbulence. Therefore the method does not lend itself to the measurement of slugish, slow-moving water. Detailed discussions of this method of measuring discharge have been presented by Groat[1] and Nagler.[2]

Electromagnetic Flowmeters. When a fluid which is an electric conductor moves across a magnetic field at 90° as shown in Fig. 12-11, an electromotive force is induced in the fluid at right angles to both the flux of the magnetic field and the velocity of the fluid. The induced voltage is proportional to the average velocity of the fluid, V. In Fig. 12-11, S and N are magnetic poles, M is a voltmeter, and the electrodes are designated as E. If the pipe is a conductor, it is not necessary for the electrodes to penetrate the pipe walls.

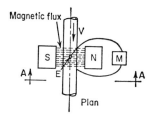

Plan

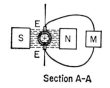

Section A-A

Fɪɢ. 12-11

This method is particularly useful where corrosive materials are being gaged or where it is undesirable to penetrate the conduit, as in the case of the flow of blood in blood vessels.   The original development of this flow-measuring procedure has been ascribed to Faraday by Shirer, Shackelford, and Jochim.[3] Their article also provides a detailed description of the procedure and a historical account of the development of the method. Applications to the gaging of mercury have been made[4] which show a good relation between analytical consideration and test results.

[1] R. F. Groat, Chemi-hydrometry and Precise Turbine Testing, *Trans. ASCE*, vol. 80, 1916.

[2] F. A. Nagler, Verification of Bazin Weir Formula by Hydrochemical Gaging, *Trans. ASCE*, vol. 83, 1919.

[3] Hampton W. Shirer, Richard B. Shackelford, and Kenneth E. Jochim, A Magnetic Flowmeter for Recording Cardiac Output, *Proc. IRE*, vol. 47, p. 1901, 1959.

[4] H. G. Elrod, Jr., and R. R. Fouse, An Investigation of Electromagnetic Flow Meters, *Trans. ASME*, vol. 24, p. 589, 1952.

SECTION 13

APPLICATIONS OF NUMERICAL METHODS AND DIGITAL COMPUTERS TO HYDRAULIC ENGINEERING

E. B. Wylie and E. F. Brater

Almost all engineering fields have benefited from the introduction of digital computers to aid in making numerical calculations. Some types of problems which require many repetitive operations can be solved economically and completely only since the introduction of the digital computer. Examples are optimization problems and many types of transient problems. Most engineering offices either have a computer of some type within the organization or have relatively easy access to a machine through time-sharing systems that are commercially available. The objectives of this section are to provide a basic introduction to computer programming and the requisite numerical methods, and to formulate a number of common hydraulic engineering problems in a form suitable for computation on a digital computer. Examples, with computer programs, are presented to help illustrate programming techniques as well as some of the capabilities of digital computers. In preparing this section it was assumed that some readers may have no previous training in the use of the digital computer.

Computers, Input-Output, and Coding Languages

There are at least as many computers on the market as there are manufacturers, and each contains its own special characteristics. From an engineering computational point of view, the digital computer can be viewed as a device that can perform arithmetic calculations, make comparisons, make certain logical decisions, perform iterative and repetitive operations, and store data, results, and instructions. The differentiating characteristics among various computers lie largely in the available storage capacity and the speed with which the various operations are performed. The size of a computer is generally described by the number of words of available storage. A word represents a unit of storage which may contain a numerical value or an instruction in binary notation. Each unit of information is assigned a specific location in the storage device. Once a quantity is stored in a particular location, it remains unchanged and available for future use until an instruction is issued to replace the original quantity with a new quantity. Typically a small computer may have 16,000 (16 K) or 32,000 (32 K) words of memory. Operational speeds vary with the machine and the operation, but simple addition, including memory core access, is measured in microseconds.

The procedures for communicating to the computer the algorithm and data for the solution of a problem and retrieving the solution are vital but sometimes confusing steps. Most commonly the input is from punched cards, but it may be introduced from a tape or by means of a remote teletype. Certain set procedures or data collections can also be stored in the computer and called upon when needed. Output is most frequently printed out, but it may be placed on punched cards. It would be of little value to the reader to discuss input-output in much more detail here because each computer facility has its own system and the user must refer to the instructions provided with each facility.

A number of "automatic" or procedure-oriented languages are available including Fortran, Algol, PL1, Basic, etc. Generally engineering computations are formulated in one of these languages. All machines operate from a set of machine-code instructions; therefore, a compiler program must be available on each particular machine to translate the procedure-oriented code to machine code. It is not necessary that a technical programmer be familiar with the machine language, although most professional programmers are entirely competent in this area. A number of subject-oriented computer languages have been developed. Examples include Strudal, Cogo, and Sepol, developed under ICES,[1] and Hydro.[2] The latter, Hydro, is directed to the field of water resources engineering and has the capability of handling a few hydraulic problems. These programs are very useful for some of the common problems to which they have been adapted, requiring only that the data be properly organized. However, if the engineering problem is slightly different from the ordinary, the program may not cover the situation, and the user is forced to revert to a procedure-oriented method or to a hand calculation. Therefore, even through this chapter deals with computer applications to hydraulic engineering problems, it is desirable to provide an introduction to a more generally applicable procedure-oriented language. Inasmuch as most computing facilities have Fortran[3,4] capabilities, Fortran IV is used as the programming language in this chapter. A number of programs are developed as programming examples. Some of these could be used directly on, or easily adapted to, the reader's computer facility.

Fortran

Excellent references[5,6] are available that describe in detail the elements of Fortran programming. A brief introduction is presented here for those engineers who have had no previous training.

Fortran consists of a series of statements, some of which are English, others are constants and variables, combined with simple algebraic symbols. The rules of the language must be followed precisely, however, as all statements must be grammatically correct and completely unambiguous. In order to write statements, it is first necessary to gain familiarity with the elements of which statements are composed, namely, constants, variables, operations, expressions, and functions.

Simple statements in a Fortran program are executed in sequence. Computer cards have a total of 72 columns available

[1] D. Ross, "ICES System Design," MIT Press, Cambridge, Mass., 1966.

[2] G. Bugliarello et al., HYDRO, a Computer Language for Water Resources Engineering, *ASCE, Civil Engineering*, November, 1966, pp. 69–71.

[3] E. I. Organik, "A FORTRAN IV Primer," Addison-Wesley Publishing Company, Inc., Reading, Mass., 1966.

[4] FORTRAN IV Language, OS 44PS DOS, File No. S360, IBM Corp., New York, 10020.

[5] E. I. Organik, *op. cit.*

[6] IBM Corp., *op. cit.*

for characters, and statements must be written in columns 7 to 72. Columns 1 to 5 are reserved for statement labels, and column 6 is used to show a continuation from the previous card. The following basic symbols are available on the keyboard of the card punch console:

> Alphabetic: Capital letters, A,B,C, . . . , X,Y,Z
> Numeric: digits 0,1,2, . . . , 9
> Special: $+$ $-$ $*$ $/$ $($ $)$ $.$ $,$ $;$ $\$$ $\&$ $=$ $'$

Two kinds of constants are commonly used: integers which are whole numbers without a decimal, and real numbers which are decimal numbers. Variables are referred to by name and can take on many values during execution of a program. Variable names are selected by the programmer. They can be made up of one to six alphanumeric characters of which the first must be alphabetic, for example, PRESS, PIPE1, or PIPE21. Variables that begin with I, J, K, L, M, or N are of integer mode, and all others are real variables unless the mode is changed with a declaration statement.

If it is desirable to denote a series of numbers as one variable, the variable can be subscripted by placing the subscript in parentheses, for example, Q(J) or PIPE(5). A DIMENSION statement is necessary to reserve space for each subscripted variable. Example: DIMENSION X(10), A(20). This means that 10 values of X can be stored as the variables X(1), X(2), . . . , X(10), and 20 values of A can be stored as the variables A(1), A(2), . . . , A(20).

Five arithmetic operations are available and are symbolized by $+$ $-$ $*$ $/$ $**$, for addition, subtraction, multiplication, division, and raising a number to a power, respectively. If more than one operation appears in a statement, an order of precedence exists: (1) exponentiation, $**$, (2) multiplication and division, $*$ $/$, (3) addition and subtraction, $+$ $-$. In the case of equal precedence, as multiplication and division, the order is from left to right. Closed parentheses are very helpful to indicate desired groupings of operations with variables. The expression within the innermost parentheses is always evaluated first. Examples:

$$(A + B)**2. \text{ means } (A + B)^2$$
$$2. + X/Y*2. \text{ means } 2. + \left(\frac{X}{Y}\right) (2.)$$

2. $+ X/Y**2$ means $2. + \dfrac{X}{Y^2}$

$(2 + X/Y)**2 - 3.$ means $\left(2 + \dfrac{X}{Y}\right)^2 - 3.$

Most of the common mathematical functions are directly available for use in statements. These include, among others, the trigonometric functions SIN and COS; square root, SQRT; absolute value, ABS; arc tangent, ATAN; and natural logarithm, ALOG.

The assignment or substitution statement is the most used statement, $\nu = \xi$. It means evaluate the expression on the right of the equals sign and substitute the result in the variable location ν. Examples: A = X + Y; N = N − 1; RATIO = 3./13.

If an order of execution other than sequential is desired in a program, a transfer of control statement can be used. One possibility is a GO TO statement, GO TO n, where n is a statement label. Another possibility is an arithmetic IF statement, for example, IF (ξ) n_1, n_2, n_3, where n_1, n_2, and n_3 are statement labels. The meaning is as follows: if the expression ξ is negative, the next statement executed is the one labeled n_1; if ξ is zero, the next statement executed is the one labeled n_2; if ξ is positive, the next statement executed is the one labeled n_3. Example:

```
        I = 0
    10 IF (I-10) 20,20,30
    20 I = I + 1
        Q(I) = 3.4*I**2.5
        GO TO 10
    30 CONTINUE
```

This series of statements will add 1 to the integer variable I until I = 11 and compute values of Q_1 for all values of I from 1 to 11 inclusive.

Logical IF statements can be used to transfer control or to cause a statement to be executed only under special conditions. Logical expressions are written with the relational operators .LT., .LE., .GT., .GE., .EQ., .NE., meaning less than, less than or equal, greater than, greater than or equal, equal, and not equal, respectively. The form of the logical IF is IF (e) S, where e is a logical expression and S is another statement. If e is true, S is executed; if e is false, S is not executed, and the next statement is executed.   Example:

$$I = 0$$
$$10 \ IF \ (I.GT.10) \ GO \ TO \ 20$$
$$I = I + 1$$
$$Q(I) = 3.4*I**2.5$$
$$GO \ TO \ 10$$
$$20 \ CONTINUE$$

This series of statements will perform the same operation as in the previous example.

The DO statement is one of the most powerful features in a program as it provides the capability to execute a portion of the program repeatedly.   It has the form DO n $i = m_1, m_2, m_3$, where n is a statement number, i is an integer variable, and m_1, m_2, and m_3 are integer constants or variables.   The meaning conveyed is that the statements following the DO statement up to and including the statement labeled n are executed repeatedly, first with $i = m_1$, then with $i = m_1 + m_3$, and so on until i exceeds m_2; then the statement following the one labeled n is executed.   If m_3 is left off the DO statement, it is assumed to be unity.   Example:

$$DO \ 10 \ I = 1,11$$
$$10 \ Q(I) = 3.4*I**2.5$$
$$CONTINUE$$

This series of statements accomplishes the same objective as each of the previous two examples.

Computational Concepts

The various steps involved in producing a usable program to solve a particular problem include (1) a decision as to the scope of the problem, (2) the mathematical description, (3) programming, which may include a flowchart and the actual coding, (4) program checkout, and (5) production and interpretation. The problem identification is no different than if a computer were not available as a tool.   It is necessary to establish the problem scope completely prior to attempting to obtain a programmed solution or an algorithm.   The mathematical description may involve simple algebra, or it may involve sophisticated numerical simultaneous algebraic equations.   A flow diagram is often quite useful in establishing the computational procedure to solve a problem.   It is a graphical representation of the logic of the program.   It may be a basic diagram that shows only the major steps in a problem, but ideally it is a diagram that displays all the operations and decisions, including their order of execution. Successful production runs are only possible after a complete checkout of any newly developed program.

There are three identifiable computational methods that may be used in solving a technical problem. Examples 13-1 to 13-4 illustrate the use of these methods to solve hydraulic problems by means of digital computers. Most programs used in hydraulic engineering will contain more than one of the computational concepts. Examples 13-5 to 13-9 provide additional programs for solving problems. It is believed by the authors that following through these flowcharts and program listings will enable the reader to gain familiarity with programming. Increased capability can best be attained by doing more real problems.

Direct Method. If an explicit equation is available to yield the desired answer, the computer can be used in place of the slide rule, desk calculator, or direct hand calculation. A simple program to illustrate this direct approach follows.

Example 13-1. Given an open channel of trapezoidal section, with known roughness and bottom slope, evaluate the discharge corresponding to a given normal depth, D, by use of Manning's Equation [Eq. (7-34a) and (b)],

$$Q = \frac{1.486}{n} ar^{2/3}s^{1/2} \tag{13-1}$$

The flow diagram which shows the various steps in the program is shown in Fig. 13-1. A listing of the Fortran program is shown in Fig. 13-2. Each line except the last is a listing of one card of the deck of cards submitted to the computer. The first line is a comment statement which identifies the program. Comment statements are identified by the letter C and may be used anywhere in a program. The second, third, and eleventh statements constitute the input information for the program. The NAMELIST name is DATA, and it instructs the computer to find values of n, s, and D on the DATA card (line 11). The ampersand symbols (&) used at the beginning of the line and preceding the word END at the end of the line are necessary to convey the data to the computer. The notation in line 11 is self-evident with the exception of Manning's roughness n, denoted by the symbol RN, and bottom slope s_0, which is given the symbol SO. The first statements in lines 3 to 7 correspond exactly with the instruction boxes in Fig. 13-1. Line 3 instructs the computer to store these variables, obtained from input device 5, in memory. Lines 4 to 6 are the steps in the algorithm needed to solve the problem. Lines 7 to 9 are the output statements. Line 7 instructs the computer to print the answer by means of output device 6 according to the format prescribed in lines 8 and 9. This is done in the last line. The statement, END, signifies the end of the program.

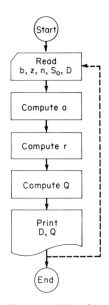

A slight alteration in this program would enable the user to compute values of discharge corresponding to different values of depth, slope, roughness, channel width, or side slope. The necessary changes include the addition of a statement to cause a return to the READ statement, as shown by the dashed line in Fig. 13-1, and the addition of more data cards listing the new variables for which discharge is desired. This can also be accomplished by using the iteration procedure described below.

Fig. 13-1. Flow diagram for computation of discharge in an open channel by direct method.

Iteration Method. A number of statements in a program that can be used repetitively are very effective in the solution of technical problems. The following problem illustrates this technique.

Example 13-2. Develop a table of discharge versus depth for the conditions given in Example 13-1. Figure 13-3 displays

```
1      C DETERMINATION OF DISCHARGE IN MANNING EQUATION
2             NAMELIST/DATA/B,Z,RN,S0,D
3             READ(5,DATA)
4             A=(B+Z*D)*D
5             R=A/(B+2.*D*SQRT(Z*Z+1.))
6             Q=1.486*A*R**.6667*SQRT(S0)/RN
7             WRITE(6,1) D,Q
8           1 FORMAT(' DISCHARGE CORRESPONDING TO A DEPTH OF',F5.2,' FEET'
9           2' IS',F8.2,' CFS')
10            END
11     &DATA B=10.,Z=1.5,RN=0.015,S0=.0002,D=5 &END

       DISCHARGE CORRESPONDING TO A DEPTH OF 5.00 FEET IS   261.87 CFS
```

Fig. 13-2. Program for computation of discharge in an open channel by direct method.

the flow diagram, and Fig. 13-4 shows the Fortran program, input data, and the tabulated computer output. The repetition in this program is controlled by the unconditional transfer statement of line 11, GO TO 20, which forces the computer to return to line 5. Line 5 instructs the computer to increase the previous value of D by DD, which is given in line 15 as 0.5 ft, and then the computations are continued. A DO loop such as is used in Example 13-3 could have been used to accomplish the same objective. The logical IF statement (IF(D.GT.D2) GO TO 10), which appears as line 6, is used to stop the iteration. Its meaning is, when the current value of D is greater than D2 (predetermined as 10 in line 15), return to statement 10 (line 3); otherwise continue with the computations. When the computer returns to line 3 and finds no additional data, it terminates the program. The output instruction in line 10 causes successive values of depth and the corresponding discharges to be printed out as they are computed. If subscripted variables had been used, all the computed values could have been stored in memory and printed at the end of the program. Another example of the iteration method is presented in the next subsection.

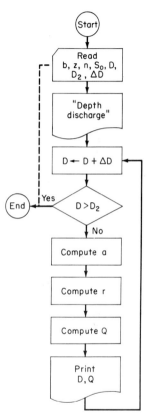

Fig. 13-3. Flow diagram for making a series of solutions for discharge in an open channel by the iterative method.

Solution ₜby Successive Approximation—Logical Decisions. The iteration technique can be used to facilitate a trial-and-error solution of many complex equations. Programmed logical decisions are also helpful in arriving at the desired result.

```
 1      C DEPTH VERSUS DISCHARGE FROM MANNING EQUATION
 2            NAMELIST/DATA/B,Z,RN,S0,D ,D2,DD
 3         10 READ(5,DATA)
 4            WRITE(6,1)
 5         20 D=D +DD
 6            IF(D.GT.D2) GO TO 10
 7            A=(B+Z*D)*D
 8            R=A/(B+2.*D*SQRT(Z*Z+1.))
 9            Q=1.486*A*R**.6667*SQRT(S0)/RN
10            WRITE(6,2) D,Q
11            GO TO 20
12          1 FORMAT('0      DEPTH DISCHARGE')
13          2 FORMAT(1H ,2F10.2)
14            END
15        &DATA B=10.,Z=1.5,RN=0.015,S0=.0002,D=1.,DD=0.5,D2=10. &END
```

DEPTH	DISCHARGE
1.50	28.95
2.00	47.96
2.50	71.47
3.00	99.62
3.50	132.55
4.00	170.44
4.50	213.48
5.00	261.87
5.50	315.79
6.00	375.44
6.50	441.01
7.00	512.71
7.50	590.70
8.00	675.20
8.50	766.38
9.00	864.43
9.50	969.54
10.00	1081.88

Fig. 13-4. Program for making a series of solutions for discharge in an open channel by the iterative method.

As an illustration, if it were desired to find normal depth associated with a particular flow in a trapezoidal channel, a direct solution of Manning's equation is not possible, and the direct method is not applicable. Successive values of depth could be substituted as in Example 13-2 until the computed flow matches the actual flow, but this may involve many trials. Ideally, a systematic procedure should be established so that normal depth can be determined within a specified degree of accuracy and in a minimum number of trials. In any successive approximation scheme a trial value is assumed, substituted, then improved upon until the final answer is obtained. An important consideration is that a method should be used that seeks an improved value which ensures rapid convergence to the final result. The bisection and Newton's methods are used in the following examples.

Example 13.3. Determine normal depth using the bisection method for a flow of 400 cfs for the channel used in Example 13-1, in which $z = 1.5$, $n = 0.015$, $b = 10$ ft, and $S_0 = 0.0002$.

The Manning formula is written in the following form, and the value of D is sought so that the function is zero.

$$F(D) = 1 - \frac{Qnp^{2/3}}{1.486a^{5/3}s^{1/2}} = 0 \qquad (13\text{-}2)$$

The bisection or half-interval method, which is described in the Appendix to this section, is used to solve for normal depth.

Figure 13-5 displays the flow diagram and Fig. 13-6 shows the program (lines 6 to 15), input (lines 4, 5, and 19), output instructions (lines 16 and 17), and solution (line 20). An estimated value of normal depth is required as input data and is given as DN = 10 in the data list shown in line 19. The lower and upper limits of normal depth (y_L and y_U in the Appendix) are designated as YMIN and YMAX, respectively, in the program, and their initial values are set in lines 6 and 7. The solution by the bisection method begins with line 8 which initiates a DO loop. This is an iteration statement which requires that all succeeding instructions through statement 40 (line 15) be executed repeatedly as the counter I varies from 1 to 15 in increments of unity. Equation (13-2) is shown in lines 9 and 10 with $F(D)$ designated as FUNCTN and with values of (p) and (a) written in forms similar to Eqs. (7-6) and (7-4), respectively. Line 11 is an arithmetic IF statement. It instructs the computer to go to statement 20, 50, or 30 if FUNCTN is less than, equal to, or greater than zero, respectively. This problem can also be solved without successive approximations by the use of Tables 7-11 and 7-19.

Example 13-4. Determine critical depth using Newton's method for the conditions given in Example 13-3 in which $Q = 400$ cfs, $z = 1.5$, $n = 0.015$, $b = 10$ ft, and $S_o = 0.0002$. The critical depth relationship (see Critical Depth—General Case in Sec. 8) is written in the following form.

$$f(D) = 1 - \frac{Q^2 T}{ga^3} = 0 \qquad (13\text{-}3)$$

Newton's method is used in the program to solve Equation (13-3); it is described in the Appendix to this section. Alternatively, the bisection method could be used with equal success.

In Newton's method the derivative of $f(D)$, Eq. (13-3), is needed.

$$\frac{df(D)}{dD} = -\frac{Q^2}{ga^3}\left(2z - \frac{3T^2}{a}\right) \qquad (13\text{-}4)$$

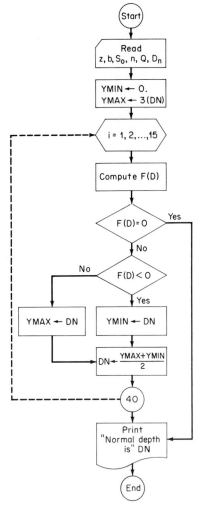

FIG. 13-5. Flow diagram for computing normal depth in a trapezoidal channel by the bisection method.

```
1     C DETERMINATION OF NORMAL DEPTH, DN, IN TRAPEZOIDAL CHANNEL
2     C SOLUTION OF MANNING EQUATION BY USE OF BISECTION METHOD
3     C ESTIMATED VALUE OF DN IS GIVEN AS INPUT DATA.
4           NAMELIST/DATA/Z,B,S0,RN,Q,DN
5        10 READ(5,DATA)
6           YMIN=0.
7           YMAX=3.*DN
8           DO 40 I=1,15
9           FUNCTN=1.-Q*RN*(B+2.*DN*SQRT(Z*Z+1))**.6667/(1.486*((B+Z*DN)
10       2*DN)**1.6667*SQRT(S0))
11          IF(FUNCTN) 20,50,30
12       20 YMIN=DN
13          GO TO 40
14       30 YMAX=DN
15       40 DN=(YMIN+YMAX)*.5
16       50 WRITE(6,1) DN
17        1 FORMAT('0 NORMAL DEPTH IS',F8.2)
18          END
19    &DATA Z=1.5,B=10.,RN=0.015,S0=.0002,Q=400.,DN=10. &END

      NORMAL DEPTH IS    6.19
```

FIG. 13-6. Program for computing normal depth in a trapezoidal channel by the bisection method.

According to Newton's method, the correction to the current depth, D_k, at the kth iteration is

$$\Delta D = \frac{-f(D)}{df(D)/dD} \tag{13-5}$$

and the newly corrected depth is

$$D_{k+1} = D_k + \Delta D \tag{13-6}$$

The flow diagram for this problem is shown in Fig. 13-7, and the Fortran listing, data, and computed output are shown in Fig. 13-8. Single-line functions are used for AREA and top width, TOP. These functions are defined with a dummy argument at the beginning of the program (lines 4 and 5); then when the area or top width is required during computation, for a particular depth, DC, it can be obtained by writing AREA(DC) or TOP(DC). The Newton iteration procedure begins at line 8 with the statement DO 20 I = 1,18, and ends at the statement labeled 20. Equation (13-4) is defined by the variable DFDD, and the correction, ΔD, computed with Eq. (13-5) is defined as DD. The iteration procedure continues until the correction ΔD is less than a prescribed quantity, ϵ (EPS in line 13), or in the case of no convergence it will iterate a total of 18 times (line 8) and indicate an "unsuccessful solution" in the printout (lines 15 and 17). Line 12 guards against the possibility of a large negative value of DD creating a negative value of D. The input data shown in line 21 include the

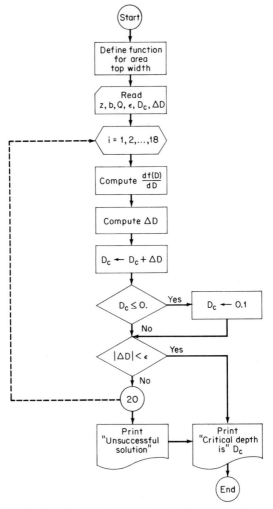

Fig. 13-7. Flow diagram for computing critical depth in a trape-zoidal channel by Newton's method.

```
1    C DETERMINATION OF CRITICAL DEPTH, DC, IN A TRAPEZOIDAL CHANNEL
2    C SOLUTION OF CRITICAL DEPTH EQUATION BY USE OF NEWTON'S METHOD
3    C ESTIMATED VALUE OF DC IS GIVEN AS INPUT DATA
4          AREA(YY)=(B+YY*Z)*YY
5          TOP(YY)=B+2.*Z*YY
6          NAMELIST/DATA/Z,B,Q,EPS,DC,DD
7       10 READ(5,DATA)
8          DO 20 I=1,18
9          DFDD=*Q*Q*(2.*Z-3.*TOP(DC)**2/AREA(DC))/(32.2*AREA(DC)**3)
10         DD=(1.-Q*Q*TOP(DC)/(32.2*AREA(DC)**3))/DFDD
11         DC=DC+DD
12         IF(DC.LE.0.) DC=0.1
13         IF(ABS(DD).LT.EPS) GO TO 30
14      20 CONTINUE
15         WRITE(6,1)
16      30 WRITE(6,2) DC
17       1 FORMAT('0 UNSUCCESSFUL SOLUTION, INITIAL VALUE OF DC IS NOT
18       2   GOOD')
19       2 FORMAT('0 CRITICAL DEPTH IS',F8.2)
20         GO TO 10
21         END
22    &DATA Z=1.5,B=10.,Q=400.,EPS=.001,DC=10. &END

      CRITICAL DEPTH IS    3.12
```

FIG. 13-8. Program for computing critical depth in a trapezoidal channel by Newton's method.

quantity ϵ and an initial estimate of the critical depth, $DC = 10$. The computed result is shown on the last line. This problem can also be solved without the need for successive approximations by the use of Table 8-5.

Steady Nonuniform Flow in Prismatic Open Channels by Numerical Integration

The computation of gradually varied water surface profiles is readily adaptable to digital computer solution. Several different approaches could be applied, any of which might be fully satisfactory in most situations. One of the most direct approaches is to program the hand calculation proposed in Section 8, namely the solution of Eq. (8-135b). Another approach is to start with the basic differential equation, Eq. (8-131),

$$\frac{dD}{dx} = \frac{s_0 - s}{1 - Q^2 T/ga^3} \tag{13-7}$$

and use a standard numerical integration procedure. If the above equation is inverted it can be expressed

$$x = \int_{D_0}^{D_1} f(D) \, dD \tag{13-8}$$

since the right side is a function of depth only. At $x = 0$, the depth is D_0, and at any distance x the depth is D_1. Evaluation of this integral can be accomplished by use of one of the equal-interval rules such as the trapezoidal rule or Simpson's rule. These methods are described in the Appendix to this section. Simpson's rule is applied in the following example.

Example 13-5.   Determine the water surface profile, the energy grade line, and sufficient information so that the location of the hydraulic jump can be determined for the open-channel problem solved in Example 8-1.

A flow diagram, which outlines the major computational steps, is shown in Fig. 13-9.   The actual program, input data, and computed output are shown in Fig. 13-10.   Statement functions are used for the evaluation of top width, area, wetted perimeter, energy, and force plus momentum, each as a function of depth.   The latter is evaluated by use of the force equation, Eq. (8-98b), and is used to locate the hydraulic jump. Newton's method is used to compute both critical and normal depths.   A subroutine is used to compute the water surface profile information, that is, to evaluate the integral in Eq. (13-8) by use of Simpson's rule.   The first statement after the comment lines, COMMON, which also appears in the subroutine PROFIL, is necessary so that variables in the main program are available in the subroutine.   The input data line describes the channel characteristics, gives the depth at the gate, $D_0 = 8.$, gives a tolerance value for the computation of critical and normal depths, EPS = .005, and sets the number of intervals of depth, between the level at the gate and critical depth, to which distance is to be computed, N = 12.

The computed output shows the length measured from the gate to a particular depth, energy, and force plus momentum. The last line shows the energy and force plus momentum corresponding to normal depth.   The hydraulic jump could be located by use of the computer, but with the force plus momentum information available as a function of depth, shown as computed output, it is an easy matter to graphically locate the position where the force plus momentum is equal upstream and downstream of the jump.   This is shown along with the profile and energy gradient in Fig. 13-11.

If it were necessary to evaluate the depth at a particular location in the previous example, as at XL feet from the gate, the profile would be evaluated beyond this position to a depth of D at location SL; then a linear interpolation can be used to determine the depth at the position XL.   By reference to Fig. 13-12,

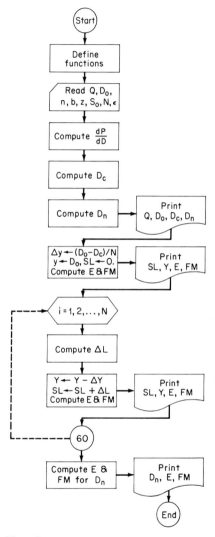

FIG. 13-9. Flow diagram for computing the water-surface profile in an open channel by numerical integration.

```
C COMPUTATION OF WATER SURFACE PROFILE AND ENERGY GRADE LINE IN STEEP
C TRAPEZOIDAL CHANNEL, AND FORCE + MOMENTUM VALUES TO LOCATE THE
C HYDRAULIC JUMP.
      COMMON Q,B,Z,RN,S0,DPDD
      TOP(YY)=B+2.*Z*YY
      AREA(YY)=(B+Z*YY)*YY
      PER(YY)=B+YY*DPDD
      ENERGY(YY)=YY+Q*Q/(64.4*AREA(YY)**2)
      FPM(YY)=62.4*(YY*YY*(B/2.+Z*YY/3.)+Q*Q/(32.2*AREA(YY)))
      NAMELIST/DATA/Q,D0,RN,B,Z,S0,N,EPS
   10 READ(5,DATA)
      DPDD=2.*SQRT(Z*Z+1.)
C CRITICAL DEPTH EVALUATION
      DC=D0
      DO 20 I=1,18
      DFDD=Q*Q*(2.*Z-3.*TOP(DC)**2/AREA(DC))/(32.2*AREA(DC)**3)
      DD=(1.-Q*Q*TOP(DC)/(32.2*AREA(DC)**3))/DFDD
      DC=DC+DD
      IF (DC.LE.0.) DC=0.1
      IF(ABS(DD).LT.EPS) GO TO 30
   20 CONTINUE
C NORMAL DEPTH EVALUATION
   30 DN=D0
      CON=1.486*SQRT(S0)/RN
      DO 40 I=1,18
      DFDD=CON*(AREA(DN)/PER(DN))**0.6667*(1.6667*TOP(DN)-AREA(DN)/PER(D
     2N)*0.6667*DPDD)
      DD=(-CON*AREA(DN)**1.6667/PER(DN)**0.6667+Q)/DFDD
      DN=DN+DD
      IF(ABS(DD).LT.EPS) GO TO 50
   40 CONTINUE
   50 WRITE(6,1) Q,D0,DC,DN
C WATER SURFACE PROFILE, ENERGY AND FORCE + MOMENTUM EVALUATION
      DY=(D0-DC)/N
      Y=D0
      SL=0.
      E=ENERGY(Y)
      FM=FPM(Y)
      WRITE(6,2)
      WRITE(6,3) SL,Y,E,FM
      DO 60 I=1,N
      CALL PROFIL(Y,DY,DL)
      Y=Y-DY
      SL=SL+DL
      E=ENERGY(Y)
      FM=FPM(Y)
   60 WRITE(6,3) SL,Y,E,FM
      E=ENERGY(DN)
      FM=FPM(DN)
      WRITE(6,4) DN,E,FM
    1 FORMAT('0 Q=',F8.2,' D0=',F8.3,' DC=',F8.3,' DN=',F8.3)
    2 FORMAT('0    LENGTH      DEPTH      ENERGY  FORCE + MOMENTUM')
    3 FORMAT(1H ,F12.1,2F12.2,F12.0)
    4 FORMAT(1H ,12X,2F12.2,F12.0)
      END
C WATER SURFACE PROFILE USING SIMPSONS RULE
      SUBROUTINE PROFIL(D,DD,DX)
      COMMON Q,B,Z,RN,S0,DPDD
      AREA(YY)=(B+Z*YY)*YY
      DIST(YY)=(1.-Q*Q*(B+2.*Z*YY)/(32.2*AREA(YY)**3))/(S0-(Q*RN/1.486)
     2**2*(B+YY*DPDD)**1.333/AREA(YY)**3.333)
      Y2=D-DD/2.
      Y3=D-DD
      DX=(DIST(D)+4.*DIST(Y2)+DIST(Y3))*DD/6.
      RETURN
      END
&DATA Q=200.,D0=8.,RN=0.011,B=8.,Z=1.,S0=0.03,N=12,EPS=.005 &END
```

See opposite page for legend.

```
Q=  200.00 DO=   8.000 DC=   2.416 DM=    1.044
      LENGTH      DEPTH      ENERGY  FORCE + MOMENTUM
         0.0       8.00        8.04      27230.
        15.3       7.53        7.58      23730.
        30.5       7.07        7.12      20550.
        45.6       6.60        6.67      17681.
        60.6       6.14        6.22      15111.
        75.5       5.67        5.78      12832.
        90.1       5.21        5.34      10835.
       104.4       4.74        4.91       9116.
       118.1       4.28        4.50       7671.
       131.1       3.81        4.12       6501.
       142.6       3.35        3.78       5617.
       151.6       2.88        3.51       5042.
       155.6       2.42        3.40       4831.
                   1.04        9.02       3508.
```

FIG. 13-10. Program for computing the water-surface profile in an open channel by numerical integration.

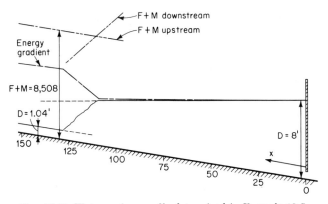

FIG. 13-11. Water-surface profile determined in Example 13-5.

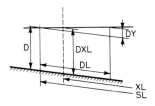

FIG. 13-12. Definition sketch for computation of an intermediate depth in Example 13-5.

the depth, DXL, is given by

$$DXL = D + (SL - XL) \frac{DY}{DL} \qquad (13\text{-}9)$$

For example, the depth at 110.8 ft from the gate is $DXL = 4.28 + (118.1 - 110.8)(4.74 - 4.28)/(118.1 - 104.4) = 4.53$ ft. Numerical values are from Fig. 13-10.

Flow in Pipes

Problems associated with the flow of liquids in pipelines can be separated into three types: determination of the head loss, the discharge, or the pipe size. The Darcy-Weisbach equation, Eq. (6-19), is normally used to relate the loss to the discharge in a straight section of a particular pipe.

$$h_f = \frac{fl}{d} \frac{V^2}{2g} \qquad (13\text{-}10)$$

When flow is turbulent, the friction factor, f, from the Moody diagram is dependent upon the relative roughness of the pipe, ϵ, and the Reynolds number, R (see Turbulent Flow in Pipes in Sec. 6). When the digital computer is used, it is convenient to express the information from the Moody diagram as an explicit relationship between relative roughness, Reynolds number, and friction factor. Wood[1] recommends the use of the following expressions:

$$f = a + bR^{-c} \qquad (13\text{-}11)$$

where

$$a = 0.094 \left(\frac{\epsilon}{D}\right)^{0.225} + 0.53 \left(\frac{\epsilon}{D}\right)$$

$$b = 88.0 \left(\frac{\epsilon}{D}\right)^{0.44}$$

$$c = 1.62 \left(\frac{\epsilon}{D}\right)^{0.134} \qquad (13\text{-}12)$$

If these expressions are used, a program to compute the head loss of a particular liquid flowing in a given pipe in which discharge, length, diameter, roughness, and fluid viscosity are given becomes an application of the direct method of Example 13-1. The procedure is to compute the Reynolds number,

---

[1] Don J. Wood, An explicit friction factor relationship, *Civil Engineering*, *ASCE*, December, 1966, pp. 60–61.

the relative roughness, and the friction factor; then the head loss can be found directly from the Darcy-Weisbach equation. This procedure is illustrated in Example 6-1 using the Moody diagram and Table 6-2.

The second type of pipe problem in which the discharge is to be computed involves an iterative solution. In this case, since the discharge is unknown, the friction factor cannot be explicitly evaluated. An initial value is assumed for f, the discharge is computed, f is corrected, and the process is repeated until the new value of f is within an acceptable tolerance of the previous value. A typical computer solution to such a problem is presented in Example 13-6.

Example 13-6. Determine the flow of water in a 6-in.-diameter commercial steel pipe 4,000 ft long if the head loss is 30.5 ft, $\nu = 0.00001$ ft^2/sec, $d = 0.505$ ft, and $\epsilon = 0.00015$ ft.

The flow diagram for this calculation is shown in Fig. 13-13, and the actual program listing appears in Fig. 13-14. Equation (13-10) is solved for v and the terms which are constant are called CON as shown in Eq. (13-10a).

$$V = \sqrt{\frac{dh_f 2g}{fl}} = \sqrt{\frac{CON}{f}} \qquad (13\text{-}10a)$$

Note that the program execution continues until the change in f is less than the tolerance value that is given in the input data, TOLER = 0.001. If this never happens, a comment is printed to indicate that the solution did not converge to a satisfactory solution. This is a possibility if unrealistic data have been submitted. The computed result shows the discharge to be 0.731 cfs. Inasmuch as the friction factor equations are valid only for turbulent flow, this program should not be used for a condition of laminar flow in the pipeline.

The third type of pipe flow problem is the determination of a suitable pipe size to transport a certain flow to a specific destination within a limited pressure drop. In addition to the diameter the variables velocity, relative roughness, and fraction factor are also unknown. A typical problem is solved in the following example.

Example 13-7. Determine the size of cast-iron pipe necessary to handle a flow of 5 cfs of water with a head loss of not more than 30 ft. The length of pipeline is 2,100 ft, and $\nu = 0.00001$ ft^2/sec.

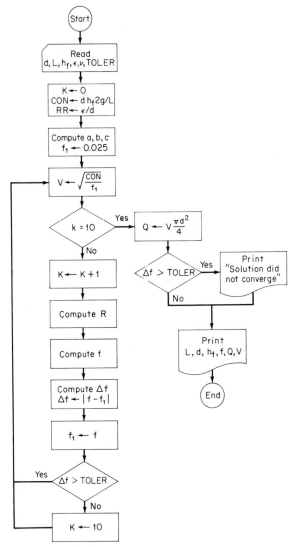

Fig. 13-13. Flow diagram for computing discharge in a pipe.

```
1      C DETERMINATION OF DISCHARGE IN CFS IN PIPE OF GIVEN DIAMETER (D),
2      C ROUGHNESS(ROUGH), LENGTH (L), HEAD LOSS (HF) IN FEET, AND FLUID
3      C VISCOSITY (NU IN FT*FT/SEC).
4            REAL L,NU
5            NAMELIST/DATA/D,L,HF,ROUGH,NU,TOLER
6         10 READ(5,DATA)
7            K=0
8            CON=D*HF*64.4/L
9            RR=ROUGH/D
10           A=0.094*RR**.225+0.53*RR
11           B=88.*RR**0.44
12           C=1.62*RR**0.134
13           F1=.025
14         20 V=SQRT(CON/F1)
15           IF(K.EQ.10) GO TO 30
16           K=K+1
17           REY=V*D/NU
18           F=A+B/REY**C
19           DF=ABS(F-F1)
20           F1=F
21           IF(DF.GT.TOLER) GO TO 20
22           K=10
23           GO TO 20
24         30 Q=V*.7854*D*D
25           IF(DF.GT.TOLER) WRITE(6,1)
26           WRITE(6,2) L,D,HF,F,Q,V
27           GO TO 10
28          1 FORMAT('0   SOLUTION DID NOT CONVERGE')
29          2 FORMAT('   LENGTH   DIAMETER   HEAD LOSS   FRICTION FACTOR'
30           2'DISCHARGE   VELOCITY'/F8.1,2F11.3,F16.4,2F11.3)
31           END
32      &DATA D=.505,L=4000.,HF=30.5,ROUGH=.00015,NU=.00001,TOLER=.001 &END
```

LENGTH	DIAMETER	HEAD LOSS	FRICTION FACTOR	DISCHARGE	VELOCITY
4000.0	0.505	30.500	0.0186	0.731	3.652

FIG. 13-14. Program listing for computing discharge in a pipe.

The program flow diagram and Fortran coding are shown in Figs. 13-15 and 13-16. The computational procedure is to assume a friction factor, compute a trial diameter by use of the Darcy-Weisbach equation, then determine relative roughness, Reynolds number, and a new f value. The procedure is repeated until the newly calculated f does not change within a specified tolerance. The computed pipe size is then used to select the nominal pipe from a list of commercially available sizes. The head loss corresponding to the given flow through the actual pipe is also computed. The output, which is also shown in Fig. 13-16, shows that a 12-in-diameter pipe will handle the 5 cfs flow with a head loss of 27.08 ft.

Experimental Measurements—Least Squares Analysis

The calibration of many fluid metering devices such as weirs, venturi meters, and orifice meters requires gathering data involving at least two variables. The digital computer is a valuable tool for analyzing such data. The calibration of a weir along with statistical tests of the derived equation will be used as an example. In the case of a weir these data are flow

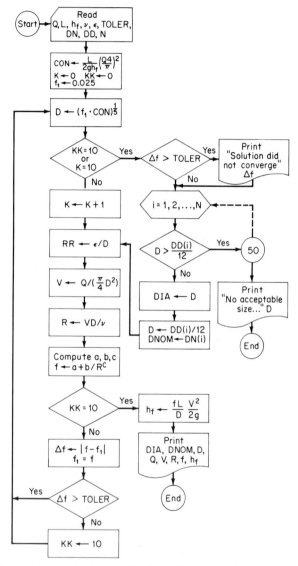

Fɪɢ. 13-15. Flow diagram for determining pipe diameter for a given discharge.

```
1    C DETERMINE THE PIPE SIZE REQUIRED TO TRANSPORT A FLOW Q(CFS) OVER A
2    C DISTANCE L(FT) WITH A MAXIMUM HEAD LOSS OF HF(FT, OF FLUID).
3    C PIPE ROUGHNESS (ROUGH IN FT) AND FLUID VISCOSITY (NU IN FT*FT/SEC)
4    C ARE GIVEN. TOTAL OF N POSSIBLE PIPE SIZES ARE AVAILABLE FROM WHICH
5    C THE PIPE SELECTION CAN BE MADE.  THE NOMINAL AND ACTUAL PIPE SIZES
6    C (INCHES) ARE STORED IN ARRAYS DN(I) AND DD(I) RESPECTIVELY, IN
7    C ORDER OF INCREASING SIZE.
8          REAL L, NU
9          DIMENSION DN(50),DD(50)
10         NAMELIST/DATA/Q,L,HF,NU,ROUGH,TOLER,DN,DD,N
11      10 READ(5,DATA)
12         CON=L*Q*Q/(.7854*.7854*64.4*HF)
13         K=0
14         KK=0
15         F1=0.025
16      20 D=(F1*CON)**0.2
17         IF(KK.EQ.10.OR.K.EQ.10) GO TO 40
18         K=K+1
19      30 RR=ROUGH/D
20         V=Q/(.7854*D*D)
21         REY=V*D/NU
22         A=0.094*RR**0.225+0.53*RR
23         B=88.*RR**0.44
24         C=1.62*RR**0.134
25         F=A+B/REY**C
26         IF(KK.EQ.10) GO TO 60
27         DF=ABS(F-F1)
28         F1=F
29         IF(DF.GT.TOLER) GO TO 20
30         KK=10
31         GO TO 20
32      40 IF(DF.GT.TOLER) WRITE(6,4) DF
33         DO 50 I=1,N
34         IF(D.GT.DD(I)/12.) GO TO 50
35         DIA=D
36         D=DD(I)/12.
37         DNOM=DN(I)
38         GO TO 30
39      50 CONTINUE
40         WRITE(6,1) D
41         GO TO 10
42      60 HF=F*L*V*V/(D*64.4)
43         WRITE(6,2)
44         WRITE(6,3) DIA,DNOM,D,Q,V,REY,F,HF
45         GO TO 10
46       1 FORMAT('0   NO ACCEPTABLE PIPE SIZE IN DATA LIST, COMPUTED '
47         2'DIAMETER=',F7.2)
48       2 FORMAT('               DIAMETERS'//'  CALC,FT  NOM,IN  ACTUAL,FT '
49         2'DISCH  VELOC  REYNOLDS      F      LOSS')
50       3 FORMAT(1H ,5F8.3,F11.0,F9.4,F7.2)
51       4 FORMAT('0   SOLUTION DID NOT CONVERGE, POOR INPUT DATA  DF=',
52         2F10.5)
53         END
54      &DATA Q=5.,L=2100.,HF=30.,NU=.00001,ROUGH=.00085,TOLER=.0001,
55      DD=3.,4.,6.,8.,10.,12.,14.,16.,18.,20.,24.,30.,36., N=13,
56      DN=3.,4.,6.,8.,10.,12.,14.,16.,18.,20.,24.,30.,36.  &END
```

	DIAMETERS						
CALC,FT	NOM,IN	ACTUAL,FT	DISCH	VELOC	REYNOLDS	F	LOSS
0.980	12.000	1.000	5.000	6.366	636618.	0.0205	27.08

FIG. 13-16. Program for determining pipe diameter for a given discharge.

rates (Q) at various levels of fluid above the weir notch (H). The calibration of the device is completed by correlating the data in some manner so that an explicit relationship is available between the variables.

Flow over a notched weir (see V-notch Weirs in Sec. 5) is expressed by an equation in the following form:

$$Q = CH^m \qquad (13\text{-}13)$$

where C and m are the unknown weir coefficients to be determined by calibration. Taking the logarithm of Eq. (13-13) yields Eq. (13-14):

$$\ln Q = m \ln H + \ln C \qquad (13\text{-}14)$$

which has the form of the straight-line equation:

$$y = mx + b \qquad (13\text{-}15)$$

The values of m and b are desired so that the line best matches the data points. The process of arriving at these values is known as the *method of least squares* and the straight line is known as the *regression line of y on x*, where y and x correspond to values of $\ln H$ and $\ln Q$, respectively. A line fitted to the data (x_i, y_i), $i = 1, 2, \ldots, n$, by the method of least squares is the one that minimizes the sum of squares of the deviations of the measured values (y_i) from corresponding points on the line (y). The sum of the squares of the deviations is a function of the unknowns m and b and is given by

$$\sum_{i=1}^{n} (y_i - y)^2 = \sum_{i=1}^{n} (y_i - mx_i - b)^2 \qquad (13\text{-}16)$$

By taking the separate partial derivatives of this equation with respect to each unknown and setting them equal to zero, two equations are obtained.

$$\Sigma y_i - m\Sigma x_i - nb = 0$$
$$\Sigma x_i y_i - m\Sigma x_i^2 - b\Sigma x_i = 0 \qquad (13\text{-}17)$$

It is understood that the summations are for i varying from 1 to n. By designating the mean values of the variables as $\bar{x}$, $\bar{y}$, defined by $n\bar{y} = \Sigma y_i$ and $n\bar{x} = \Sigma x_i$, the solutions for the unknowns can be written

$$m = \frac{\Sigma x_i y_i - n\bar{x}\bar{y}}{\Sigma x_i^2 - n\bar{x}^2} \qquad (13\text{-}18)$$

$$b = \bar{y} - m\bar{x} \qquad (13\text{-}19)$$

These values of m and b define the best fit straight line on the log-log graph of Q vs. H. The value of m is the exponent of H in the weir equation, Eq. (13-13), and $C = e^b$.

The scatter of the data points in the y direction is measured by the *sample standard deviation of the regression* given by

$$s = \sqrt{\frac{\Sigma(Y_i - y)^2}{n - 2}} \qquad (13\text{-}20)$$

This quantity is a measure of the failure of the line to fit the data.

The sample linear correlation coefficient is defined by

$$r = \frac{\Sigma xy - n\bar{x}\bar{y}}{\sqrt{(\Sigma x^2 - n\bar{x}^2)(\Sigma y^2 - n\bar{y}^2)}} \qquad (13\text{-}21)$$

and always lies between -1 and $+1$. If all points lie on the regression line, then $r = \pm 1$. If $r = 0$, no linear relation exists between the two variables x and y. The sign of r merely agrees with the sign of the slope of the regression.

Example 13-8. Experimental data are available from a calibration of a 90° V-notch weir. Determine the coefficients for

```
C LEAST SQUARES ANALYSIS OF CALIBRATION DATA FOR EVALUATION OF
C WEIR COEFFICIENTS, SAMPLE STANDARD DEVIATION AND SAMPLE CORRELATION
C COEFFICIENT.
      DIMENSION Q(30),H(30),ELH(30),ELQ(30)
      NAMELIST/DATA/N,Q,H/OUT/C,EM,S,R
   10 READ(5,DATA)
      X=0.
      Y=0.
      XX=0.
      YY=0.
      XY=0.
      D2=0.
      DO 20 I=1,N
      ELH(I)=ALOG(H(I))
      ELQ(I)=ALOG(Q(I))
      X=X+ELH(I)
      Y=Y+ELQ(I)
      XX=XX+ELH(I)**2
      YY=YY+ELQ(I)**2
   20 XY=XY+ELH(I)*ELQ(I)
      XBAR=X/N
      YBAR=Y/N
      EM=(XY-N*XBAR*YBAR)/(XX-N*XBAR*XBAR)
      B=YBAR-EM*XBAR
      C=EXP(B)
C CORRELATION COEFFICIENT
      R=(XY-N*XBAR*YBAR)/SORT((XX-N*XBAR*XBAR)*(YY-N*YBAR*YBAR))
      DO 30 I=1,N
   30 D2=D2+(ELQ(I)-EM*ELH(I)-B)**2
C SAMPLE STANDARD DEVIATION
      S=SQRT(D2/(N-2.))
      WRITE(6,OUT)
      GO TO 10
      END
&DATA Q=.0362,.0534,.0897,.1272,.1973,.2568,.3155,.3775,.4265,.4790,.5305,
H=.179,.210,.260,.300,.357,.398,.431,.463,.486,.510,.530, N=11 &END

&OUT
C= 0.2532825E 01,EM= 0.2475050E 01,S= 0.7132269E-02,R= 0.9999587E 00,&END
```

Fig. 13-17. Fortran listing for weir calibration and statistical analysis of repression.

the weir equation by use of the least squares analysis, and find the sample standard deviation of the regression and the sample linear correlation coefficient.

Figure 13-17 shows the Fortran listing of this program, a set of input data, and the results of the calculation.   The computed output is also shown, and for these data the weir equation is $Q = 2.533\ H^{2.475}$.

Distribution Networks

In Sec. 6 two methods were presented for the computation of the distribution of flow in complex piping networks.   The Hardy Cross[1] approach is widely used and is programmable for digital computer solution.   It is described and demonstrated with a numerical example in Sec. 6 (see Hardy Cross Solution). However, certain complications are encountered when the distribution network contains more than one reservoir, pump, or controlled pressure zone within the system.   The nodal method[2] has the flexibility to handle these situations and is also easily programmed.   Although convergence is sometimes quite slow, its adaptability to relatively small computers for the solution of large networks makes the method very practical.   The method requires that pressure heads be initially assumed at each junction in the system.   If these are estimated with reasonably good engineering judgment, the solution is rapid and very satisfactory.   The method is more fully described and demonstrated with an example in Sec. 6 (see Nodal Method). The following example illustrates the development of a computer program to solve the pipe network problems used as examples in Sec. 6.

Example 13-9*a* and 13-9*b*.   Determine the flow distribution in the network presented in Example 6-5 (Example 13-9*a*) and Example 6-4 (Example 13-9*b*) by use of the nodal method.   A schematic diagram of the system is shown in Fig. 13-18.   Note that in Example 13-9*a* (Example 6-5) a pump, with characteristics shown in Fig. 6-9, is located at node 1, and the flow at the reservoir (junction 2) is determined from the analysis, whereas in Example 13-9*b* (Example 6-4) a flow of 5 cfs is forced into the system at node 1 by a pressure head which is

[1] Hardy Cross, Analysis of Flow in Networks of Conduits or Conductors, *University of Illinois Bull. 286*, November, 1946.

[2] V. L. Streeter, Water Hammer Analysis of Distribution Systems, *J. of the Hydraulic Div. ASCE*, vol. 93, no. HY5, September, 1967.

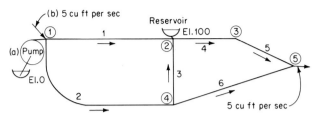

Fig. 13-18. Pipe network.

determined as part of the solution, and there is no flow into or out of the reservoir.

The program listing and input data are shown in Fig. 13-19. The input data are shown near the end of Fig. 13-19. Following the first data sign (&DATA), all data are shown which apply to Example 13-9a. Following the second data sign are given the data which apply only to Example 13-9b. One of the primary difficulties associated with a computer solution of a complex network is the adequate description of the physical and geometric properties of the system. In this program the network is described by an indexing system of numbers stored in array IX which is the first array listed under &DATA. Each junction or node has such a series of numbers associated with it.

The first number in the array is simply the number assigned to the node or junction as shown in Fig. 13-18. The second number, called JTYPE, gives the type of junction. JTYPE = 1 describes a junction with two or more pipes, JTYPE = 2 indicates a junction with a pump, JTYPE = 3 is used for a junction with a reservoir, and a node with outflow is designated by JTYPE = 4. The next three numbers in the array describe one of the pipes at that junction. The third number is the number assigned to one of the pipes at the junction as shown in Fig. 13-18. The fourth number gives the number of the opposite junction for this pipe. The fifth number gives the direction of flow in the pipe: the number 1 indicates flow is into the node and 2 that flow is away from the node. The sixth, seventh, and eighth numbers describe another pipe at the node in the same way as the previous three numbers, and this series of three numbers can be repeated as often as necessary until all pipes at the node are described. Eight numbers are required to describe a JTYPE = 1 node with two pipes, and 11 numbers

```
C NODAL METHOD TO COMPUTE FLOWS AND PRESSURE HEADS IN A DISTRIBUTION
C NETWORK.  HAZEN-WILLIAMS EQUATION IS USED TO EVALUATE LOSSES IN EACH
C PIPE, H=Rk*Q**EN, OR Q=RR*H**RN.
C EACH NODE IS DESCRIBED AS A CERTAIN JUNCTION TYPE, JTYPE=1 NODE WITH
C ONE OR MORE PIPES, JTYPE=2 NODE WITH PUMP, JTYPE=3 NODE AT RESERVOIR,
C JTYPE=4 NODE WITH OUTFLOW.
C PUMP CURVE IS DESCRIBED BY TABULAR DATA IN QP.
C INFLOWS TO THE SYSTEM ARE CONSIDERED POSITIVE.
      REAL L
      DIMENSION IX(46),DH(20),QV(20),HH(20),D(20),L(20),QQ(20),RR(20),
     2RK(20),QP(20),N(6)
      NAMELIST/DATA/IX,N,HH,D,L,QV,JU,JP,QP,DDH,H0,HWC,EN,TOLER,ITER, IP
     2RINT
   10 READ(5,DATA)
      WRITE(6,1)
      DO 50 NPIPE=1,JP
      QQ(NPIPE)=0.
      RN=1./EN
      RK(NPIPE)=L(NPIPE)/(1.318*HWC*(D(NPIPE)/4.)**0.63*.7854*D(NPIPE)**
     22)**1.85
   50 RR(NPIPE)=1./RK(NPIPE)**RN
      RN1=RN-1.
      DO 120 II=1,ITER
      NBEG=1
      TL=0.
      DO 105 M=1,3
      IF(M.GT.1) NBEG=NBEG+(N(M-1)*NP)
      NP=2+3*M
      NEND=NBEG+N(M)*NP-1
      DO 105 NJ=NBEG,NEND,NP
      IF(NBEG.GE.NEND) GO TO 105
      A=0.
      C=0.
      I=IX(NJ)
      JTYPE=IX(NJ+1)
      DO 90 IP=1,M
      J=IX(NJ+3*IP)
      NPIPE=IX(NJ+3*IP-1)
      IF(JTYPE.EQ.3) GO TO 70
      GO TO 80
   70 C=1.
      A=0.
      GO TO 92
   80 DELH=HH(J)-HH(I)
      IF(DELH) 86,86,85
   85 A=A+RR(NPIPE)*DELH**RN
      C=C+RR(NPIPE)*DELH**RN1*RN
      GO TO 90
   86 IF(DELH.EQ.0.) DELH=-.00001
      A=A-RR(NPIPE)*(-DELH)**RN
      C=C+RR(NPIPE)*(-DELH)**RN1*RN
   90 CONTINUE
   92 GO TO (95,96,95,97),JTYPE
   95 DH(I)=A/C
      GO TO 100
   96 JI=(HH(I)-H0)/DDH+1
      IF(JI.LE.1) JI=2
      IF(JI.GE.20) JI=19
      HP1=(JI-1)*DDH+H0
      C3=(QP(JI+1)+QP(JI-1)-2.*QP(JI))/(2.*DDH*DDH)
      C2=(QP(JI)-QP(JI-1))/DDH-C3*(DDH+2.*HP1)
      C1=QP(JI)-HP1*(C2+C3*HP1)
      DH(I)=(A+C1+HH(I)*(C2+C3*HH(I)))/(C-C2-2.*C3*HH(I))
      GO TO 100
   97 DH(I)=(A+QV(I))/C
  100 TL=TL+ABS(DH(I))
  105 CONTINUE
      DO 110 I=1,JU
  110 HH(I)=HH(I)+DH(I)
      IF(TL.LT.TOLER) GO TO 130
  120 IF(II/IPRINT*IPRINT.EQ.II) WRITE(6,2) II,TL,(HH(I),I=1,JU)
  130 NBEG=1
      DO 140 M=1,3
      IF(M.GT.1) NBEG=NBEG+(N(M-1)*NP)
      NP=2+3*M
      NEND=NBEG+N(M)*NP-1
      DO 140 NJ=NBEG,NEND,NP
      IF(NBEG.GE.NEND) GO TO 140
      I=IX(NJ)
      DO 140 IP=1,M
      J=IX(NJ+3*IP)
      NPIPE=IX(NJ+3*IP-1)
      IF(QQ(NPIPE).EQ.0.) GO TO 132
      GO TO 140
```

See opposite page for legend.

```
132 S=1.
    IF(IX(NJ+3*IP+1).EQ.2) S=-1.
    DELH=HH(J)-HH(I)
    IF(DELH) 136,136,135
135 QQ(NPIPE)=S*RR(NPIPE)*DELH**RN
    GO TO 140
136 QQ(NPIPE)=-S*RR(NPIPE)*(-DELH)**RN
140 CONTINUE
    IF(IX(2).EQ.2) QV(1)=C1+C2*HH(1)+C3*HH(1)**2
    QV(2)=QQ(4)-QQ(1)-QQ(3)
    WRITE(6,3)
    WRITE(6,4) (J,L(J),D(J),RK(J),EN,RR(J),QQ(J),J=1,JP)
    WRITE(6,5)
    WRITE(6,6) (I,HH(I),QV(I),I=1,JU)
    GO TO 10
  1 FORMAT('0 ITERATION TOLERANCE          HH(1...5)')
  2 FORMAT(1H ,I9,F8.2,5F8.1)
  3 FORMAT('0     PIPE LENGTH DIAMETER     RK      EN      RR  DISCHARG
   2E')
  4 FORMAT(1H ,I9,F8.0,5F8.3)
  5 FORMAT('0      NODE   HEAD   OUTFLOW')
  6 FORMAT(1H ,I9,2F8.2)
    END
&DATA IX=1,2,1,2,2,2,4,2, 3,1,4,2,1,5,5,2, 5,4,6,4,1,5,3,1, 2,3,1,1,1,3,4,1,4,
3,2, 4,1,2,1,1,3,2,2,6,5,2, N=0,3,2, HH=110.,100.,90.,105.,85.,
D=1.,1.,1.,1.,.833,.667, L=2000.,3000.,1000.,1000.,1000.,2000.,
QV=4*0.,-5., JU=5, JP=6, QP=13.4,13.2,12.9,12.65,12.3,11.75,11.25,10.6,9.8,
8.8,7.6,5.8,3.7,7*0., DDH=5, H0=60., HWC=100., EN=1.85, TOLER=0.01,
ITER=25, IPRINT=1 &END
&DATA HH=110.,100.,95.,105.,85.,IX(2)=4,QV=5.,3*0.,-5.,TOLER=.05 &END
```

FIG. 13-19. Fortran listing for determining discharge and pressures in a pipe network.

would be required if there were three pipes at the node. All two-pipe junctions are listed first, followed by three-pipe junctions, etc.

For example, the first data designation, IX = 1,2,1,2,2,2,4,2 . . . , describes node 1 (Fig. 13-18) as a type-2 junction having pipe 1 with opposite junction 2 flowing away from the node, and pipe 2 with opposite junction 4 flowing away from the node. Junction 3 is described with the next series of eight numbers.

A second array in this same data listing, called N, lists the number of one-, two-, three-, etc., pipe junctions in the system. In this case there are no single-pipe nodes, 3 two-pipe nodes, and 2 three-pipe nodes, so N = 0,3,2. The lengths and diameters of each pipe are designated in this data list as L and D, respectively. Also given in this data list are the number of junctions (JU), the number of pipes (JD), the Hazen-Williams roughness coefficient (HWC), and the exponent on the velocity in the Hazen-Williams equation (EN). The estimated heads at each junction are given by HH, and the fixed flow demands or inputs are shown for each node by QV. Inflows are considered positive. Execution of the program is stopped by exceeding the number of iterations given by ITER, or by finding the sum of the junction head corrections on any iteration to be less than

ITERATION TOLERANCE   HH(1...5)
```
        1   30.47   118.2   100.0   95.7   99.8    73.7
        2    8.81   115.5   100.0   92.7  101.3    72.2
        3    3.33   115.7   100.0   91.9  100.8    70.3
        4    1.37   115.6   100.0   91.3  100.8    69.5
        5    0.68   115.6   100.0   91.1  100.7    69.1
        6    0.32   115.6   100.0   91.0  100.7    68.9
        7    0.16   115.6   100.0   91.0  100.7    68.8
        8    0.07   115.6   100.0   90.9  100.7    68.8
        9    0.04   115.6   100.0   90.9  100.7    68.8
       10    0.02   115.6   100.0   90.9  100.7    68.8
```

PIPE LENGTH DIAMETER   RK   EN   RR DISCHARGE
```
    1   2000.   1.000    1.884   1.850   0.710    3.137
    2   3000.   1.000    2.825   1.850   0.570    2.456
    3   1000.   1.000    0.942   1.850   1.033    0.864
    4   1000.   1.000    0.942   1.850   1.033    3.407
    5   1000.   0.833    2.291   1.850   0.639    3.407
    6   2000.   0.667   13.511   1.850   0.245    1.592
```

NODE   HEAD   OUTFLOW
```
    1  115.62    5.59
    2  100.00   -0.59
    3   90.90    0.0
    4  100.72    0.0
    5   68.77   -5.00
```

(a)

ITERATION TOLERANCE   HH(1...5)
```
        1   20.14   114.2   100.0   95.6   99.8    74.9
        2    8.63   112.3   100.0   92.9  101.0    72.1
        3    4.01   112.9   100.0   91.9  100.4    70.4
        4    1.84   112.6   100.0   91.4  100.5    69.4
        5    0.76   112.6   100.0   91.1  100.4    69.1
        6    0.37   112.6   100.0   91.0  100.4    68.8
        7    0.16   112.6   100.0   90.9  100.4    68.8
        8    0.08   112.6   100.0   90.9  100.4    68.7
```

PIPE LENGTH DIAMETER   RK   EN   RR DISCHARGE
```
    1   2000.   1.000    1.884   1.850   0.710    2.794
    2   3000.   1.000    2.825   1.850   0.570    2.206
    3   1000.   1.000    0.942   1.850   1.033    0.621
    4   1000.   1.000    0.942   1.850   1.033    3.411
    5   1000.   0.833    2.291   1.850   0.639    3.413
    6   2000.   0.667   13.511   1.850   0.245    1.586
```

NODE   HEAD   OUTFLOW
```
    1  112.60    5.00
    2  100.00   -0.00
    3   90.88    0.0
    4  100.39    0.0
    5   68.68   -5.00
```

(b)

Fig. 13-20. Output for program shown in Fig. 13-19.

a tolerance called TOLER. The pump characteristic curve is given as tabular data with the discharge (QP) given in cubic feet per second for every 5 ft of change in head (DDH) starting with an initial head (HO) of 60 ft.

The second set of input data makes the necessary changes to handle Example 13-9b (Example 6-4); notably the junction type at node 1 is changed to type 4 corresponding to a node with inflow, and the inflow at node 1 is QV = 5.

The programmed solution follows the procedure outlined in Sec. 6 with the exception that the pump characteristics curve is described by a parabola rather than a straight line. The parabola is passed through points adjacent to the operating point, and the equation is

$$Q = C_1 + C_2 \Delta H_i + C_3 \Delta H_i^2$$

Since the suction reservoir is at zero elevation, the linearized form of the equation in terms of the head at the junction is

$$Q \cong C_1 + C_2(H_i + DH) + C_3(H_i^2 + 2H_iDH)$$

This equation combined with continuity at the junction yields

$$\Sigma A - DH \, \Sigma C + C_1 + C_2H_i + C_3H_i^2 + DH(C_2 + 2C_3H_i) = 0$$

and

$$DH = \frac{\Sigma A + C_1 + C_2H_i + C_3H_i^2}{\Sigma C - C_2 - 2C_3H_i}$$

The results for both examples are tabulated in Fig. 13-20. The first table in Fig. 13-20 shows the variation in pressure level with each iteration. The second table shows the flow in each pipe. The last table displays the head at each node and the flow into the node as positive values and flow out of the node as negative values.

APPENDIX: NUMERICAL METHODS

Simple numerical techniques that are useful in many computer-programmed solutions of practical problems are presented. These include methods of solution of algebraic equations in a single variable, numerical integration, and numerical approximation by linear and quadratic interpolation.

Solution of Algebraic Equations by Bisection Method

Any algebraic expression in one variable can be written $F(y) = 0$. The problem is to find the value of y that will make the function equal or approximately equal to zero. The bisection method provides a systematic substitution procedure to locate the value of y. A graphical representation of the evaluation of normal depth in a trapezoidal channel will illustrate the method.

The following equation is to be solved for y [see Eq. (13-2)].

$$F(y) = 1 - \frac{Qnp^{2/3}}{1.486a^{5/3}s^{1/2}} = 0 \qquad (13\text{-}22)$$

Figure 13-21 shows the shape of the graph of Eq. (13-22). An upper and lower limit are selected for normal depth designated y_U and y_L. When these values are substituted into Eq. (13-22),

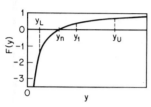

FIG. 13-21. Bisection method.

they produce values of $F(y)$ having opposite signs. The interval $y_U - y_L$ is bisected, and the value

$$y_1 = (y_U + y_L)/2$$

is substituted into the function $F(y)$. If the sign of $F(y_1)$ is the same as the sign of $F(y_U)$, it is known that normal depth does not lie between y_U and y_1, so this portion of the y scale can be eliminated. A new value of y, namely, $y_2 = (y_1 + y_L)/2$, is substituted, and the interval may be halved again based on the sign of $F(y_2)$.

Inasmuch as the interval that is known to contain normal depth is halved in each substitution, the bisection method is also known as the *half-interval method*. If the original interval between the upper and lower limiting depths is $\Delta y = y_U - y_L$, the interval after n substitutions is $\delta = \Delta y/2^n$. The number of iterations to reduce the interval to δ is given by

$$n = \frac{\ln \Delta y/\delta}{\ln 2} \qquad (13\text{-}23)$$

For example, if Δy is 30 ft and it is desired to find normal depth to the nearest 0.001 ft, 15 iterations would be required.

The bisection method is a very direct and reliable method of solution of algebraic equations. If the function $F(y)$ crosses the zero axis more than once in the vicinity of the desired answer, caution must be used in selecting the original limiting value of y. Example 13-3 illustrates the use of the bisection method.

Solutions of Algebraic Equations by Newton's Method

This method of solution of an algebraic equation in one variable, or of a set of simultaneous nonlinear algebraic equations, has the highly desirable characteristic of rapid convergence properties if good initial assumptions are available for the

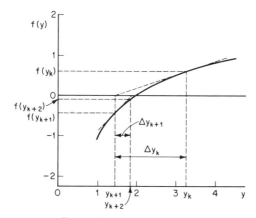

Fig. 13-22. Newton's method.

variables. In the solution of a single equation, say $f(y) = 0$, a correction to the value of y after k iterations is found by

$$\Delta y = \frac{-f(y)}{[df(y)]/dy} \qquad (13\text{-}24)$$

where the right side of the equation is evaluated using y_k. The derivation of Eq. (13-24) can be made by noting in Fig. 13-22 that

$$\frac{f(y)}{-\Delta y} = \frac{df(y)}{dy}$$

In this figure $df(y)/dy$ is positive. When $df(y)/dy$ is negative, Δy is positive, and the expression for Δy is the same. The new value of y is $y_{k+1} = y_k + \Delta y_k$. Iteration is carried on until the value of Δy is less than some selected value ϵ.

As an example, find critical depth in a trapezoidal channel having a fixed discharge [see Eq. (13-3)].

$$f(y) = 1 - \frac{Q^2 T}{g a^3} = 0 \qquad (13\text{-}25)$$

Figure 13-22 graphs this equation and shows schematically several steps in the evaluation of the correction, Δy. The derivative of Eq. (13-25) is

$$\frac{df(y)}{dy} = -\frac{Q^2}{ga^3}\left(2z - \frac{3T^2}{a}\right) \qquad (13\text{-}26)$$

in which the substitutions $da = T\,dy$ and $dT = 2z\,dy$ have been made. Equations (13-25) and (13-26) are substituted into Eq. 13-24 to evaluate Δy.

When a good initial estimate for the unknown variable is made, convergence to the actual value is generally rapid. Unfortunately, if a poor estimate is made, the method may fail to converge. For example, if a large depth were estimated as the initial value of critical depth, an examination of Fig. 13-22 shows that the first iteration would produce a negative depth, an answer that is not acceptable. Newton's method is used in Example 13-4 to evaluate critical depth in a channel.

Numerical Integration

The evaluation of the integral

$$L = \int_{D_0}^{D} F(y)\,dy \qquad (13\text{-}27)$$

where $F(y)$ is a complicated function such that analytical inte-

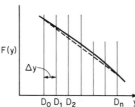

FIG. 13-23. Trapezoidal rule and Simpson's rule.

gration is difficult if not impossible is a common engineering problem. The integral is shown graphically as the area under the curve in Fig. 13-23. Two methods of approximate evaluation of the integral follow.

Trapezoidal Rule. One of the simplest approximations to the area under the curve is to evaluate the area of the trapezoid by multiplying the base times the average height.

$$L = \int_{D_0}^{D_1} F(y) \cong (D_n - D_0)\frac{F(D_0) + F(D_n)}{2} \qquad (13\text{-}28)$$

The error can be seen to be the area between the curved line and the dashed straight line in Fig. 13-23. The error can be reduced by increasing the number of sections between D_0 and D_n.

Simpson's Rule. A better approximation may be made by use of Simpson's rule. The interval between D_0 and D_n is divided into equal subintervals of width ΔY, Fig. 13-23. The value of L between D_0 and D_2 is given by

$$L = \int_{D_0}^{D_2} F(y)\ dy \cong \frac{\Delta y}{3}\ [F(D_0) + 4F(D_1) + F(D_2)] \quad (13\text{-}29)$$

and the value of L between D_0 and D_n is

$$L = \int_{D_0}^{D_n} F(y)\ dy \cong \frac{\Delta y}{3}\ [F(D_0) + 4F(D_1) + 2F(D_2) \\ + 4F(D_3) + \cdots + F(D_n)] \quad (13\text{-}30)$$

where the number of equal intervals is even. Example 13-5 illustrates the use of Simpson's rule to integrate the differential equation that describes the gradually varied water surface profile.

Interpolation Methods

Experimental or tabular data are often needed in computer programs. For example, the volume of a reservoir may be tabulated as a function of depth at equal intervals of depth (ΔD), Fig. 13-24. If the volume is needed at an intermediate

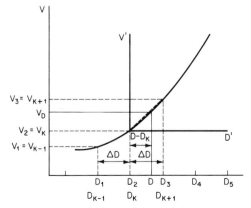

FIG. 13-24. Interpolation methods.

value, it can be approximated by an interpolation procedure. A linear interpolation and second-order interpolation method are presented.

Linear Interpolation. If, for example, the volume (VOL) corresponding to a depth D is to be computed, a straight line is passed through points D_2, V_2 and D_3, V_3 or in more general terms through the points D_K, V_K and D_{K+1}, V_{K+1} as shown in Fig. 13-24, and the point D, V_D is assumed to fall on this line. Then from similar triangles

$$\frac{V_D - V_K}{D - D_K} = \frac{V_{K+1} - V_K}{\Delta D} \tag{13-31}$$

and

$$V_D = \frac{D - D_K}{\Delta D} (V_{K+1} - V_K) + V_K \tag{13-32}$$

It is convenient to replace the ration $(D - D_K)/\Delta D$ by θ. Then

$$\frac{D - D_K}{\Delta D} = \theta \tag{13-33}$$

and

$$V_D = \theta(V_{K+1} - V_K) + V_K$$

or

$$V_D = V_{K+1}\theta + V_K(1 - \theta) \tag{13-34}$$

Three Fortran statements for computing VOL are shown below. It is assumed that values of V are known at regular intervals of $D(\Delta D)$ beginning at D_1 as shown graphically in Fig. 13-24. The variable θ is represented by TH and ΔD by DD.

```
1.    K = (D − D1)/DD + 1
2.    TH = (D − D1 − (K − 1) * DD)/DD
3.    V(D) = V(K+1) * TH + V(K) * (1. − TH)
```

Statement 1 is obvious if it is understood that K is an integer. Statement 2 is Eq. (13-33) with D_K replaced by D1 + (K − 1) * DD. Statement 3 is Eq. (13-34).

Parabolic Interpolation. A better interpolation along the curve represented by tabulated data can be obtained by fitting a second-order equation to three adjacent tabulated points. Again it is assumed that the tabulated data are for uniform increments along the D axis designated as ΔD.

The coordinate axes (D', V') are passed through point D_K, V_K as shown in Fig. 13-24. Then the second-order equation has the form

$$V' = aD'^2 + bD' \tag{13-35}$$

The V' coordinate for $D' = \Delta D$ is $(V_{K+1} - V_K)$ and for $D' = -\Delta D$ is $(V_{K-1} - V_K)$. Substitution of these values into Eq. (13-35) yields the following two equations:

$$V_{K+1} - V_K = a\,\Delta D^2 + b\,\Delta D$$
$$V_{K-1} - V_K = a\,\Delta D^2 - b\,\Delta D$$

which may be solved to obtain the expression for a and b shown in Eqs. (13-36) and (13-37), respectively.

$$a = \frac{V_{K+1} + V_{K-1} - 2V_K}{2\,\Delta D^2} \tag{13-36}$$

and

$$b = \frac{V_{K+1} - V_{K-1}}{2\,\Delta D} \tag{13-37}$$

If these values are substituted into Eq. (13-35) noting that $D' = D - D_K$ and $V' = V_D - V_K$ and again introducing θ in place of $(D - D_K)/\Delta D$, the following expression for V_D is obtained:

$$V_D = V_K + \frac{\theta^2}{2}\,(V_{K+1} + V_{K-1} - 2V_K) + \frac{\theta}{2}\,(V_{K+1} - V_{K-1}) \tag{13-38}$$

The following four Fortran statements could be used to interpolate for V_D by this method:

```
1.    K = (D − D1)/DD + 1
2.    IF (K.EQ.1)K = 2
3.    TH = (D − D1 − (K−1) * DD)/DD
4.    V(D) = V(K) + .5 * TH ** 2 (V(K+1) + V(K−1)
      − 2. * V(K)) + .5 * TH (V(K+1) − V(K−1))
```

Statements 1 and 3 are the same as for linear interpolation and Statement 4 is Eq. (13-38). Statement 2 takes care of the case where D is in the first interval and avoids a zero subscript.

SECTION 14

TABLES

Following each section is a group of tables pertaining more particularly to the subject matter contained in that section. Tables useful in general hydraulic computations are included in the following pages. By familiarizing himself with the location and purpose of the tables contained in this volume, the engineer will be able to simplify the processes involved in hydraulic calculations.

Many problems may be worked with sufficient accuracy with a slide rule. A log-log slide rule will be found particularly convenient in evaluating hydraulic formulas. Where greater accuracy is required, logarithms should be used. Table 14-1 contains five-place logarithms of numbers up to 10,000, and Table 14-2 gives the corresponding cologarithms of numbers. The latter table will be found especially useful in problems involving mixed operations of multiplication and division and in raising to any powers numbers less than unity. The principle of logarithms and typical problems involving their use are given below.

Tables 14-3 to 14-5 give the natural trigonometric functions to five decimal places for intervals of 10 min.

Use of Logarithms

The common, or Briggs, logarithms are the only ones used in ordinary calculations. In this system the logarithm of a number is the power to which 10 must be raised to equal the number. Thus the logarithms of 1, 10, 100, 1,000, 10,000, etc., are, respectively, 0, 1, 2, 3, 4, etc., and the logarithms of 0.1, 0.01, 0.001, . . . , and 0 are, respectively, −1, −2, −3, . . . , and − ∞. All numbers greater than unity have positive logarithms, and those less than unity have negative logarithms.

The logarithms of all numbers which are not integral powers of 10 are fractional and consist of an integer called the *characteristic* and a decimal fraction termed the *mantissa*. The logarithms of numbers greater than unity have characteristics one less than the number of places to the left of the decimal point, and for a given sequence of figures the mantissas are equal. The following examples will illustrate:

$$\text{Logarithm of } 4.45 = 0.64836$$
$$\text{Logarithm of } 44.5 = 1.64836$$
$$\text{Logarithm of } 445 = 2.64836$$
$$\text{Logarithm of } 4{,}450 = 3.64836$$

Negative logarithms, that is, the logarithms of numbers less than unity, are generally expressed with negative characteristics and positive mantissas. This gives a common mantissa for a given sequence of figures regardless of whether the number is greater or less than unity. A minus sign over the characteristic indicates that the characteristic is negative and the mantissa positive. Usually, 10 is added to such logarithms to make the whole logarithm positive, it being understood that the logarithm is 10 less than indicated. The following examples illustrate different methods of expressing the logarithms of numbers less than unity:

$$\text{Logarithm of } 4.45 = +0.64836 = 0.64836 = 0.64836$$
$$\text{Logarithm of } 0.445 = -0.35164 = \bar{1}.64836 = 9.64836 - 10$$
$$\text{Logarithm of } 0.0445 = -1.35164 = \bar{2}.64836 = 8.64836 - 10$$
$$\text{Logarithm of } 0.00445 = -2.35164 = \bar{3}.64836 = 7.64836 - 10$$
$$\text{Logarithm of } 0.000445 = -3.35164 = \bar{4}.64836 = 6.64836 - 10$$

If the logarithm of a number if subtracted from zero, the difference is called the *cologarithm* of the number. The cologarithm of a number is thus the logarithm of its reciprocal, and the cologarithm of a number less than unity is positive. The following are logarithms and corresponding cologarithms of various numbers, the mantissas in all cases being positive, and the characteristics positive or negative as required.

Number	Logarithm	Cologarithm
4,450	3.64836	$\bar{4}$.35164
445	2.64836	$\bar{3}$.35164
44.5	1.64836	$\bar{2}$.35164
4.45	0.64836	$\bar{1}$.35164
0.445	$\bar{1}$.64836	0.35164
0.0445	$\bar{2}$.64836	1.35164
0.00445	$\bar{3}$.64836	2.35164
0.000445	$\bar{4}$.64836	3.35164

Logarithmic tables contain only manitssas, since characteristics can be determined from the position of the decimal point.

Below are indicated solutions of a few fundamental problems involving the use of logarithms The words logarithm and cologarithm are abbreviated to log and colog, respectively.

$$\log abc = \log a + \log b + \log c$$
$$\log \frac{ab}{c} = \log a + \log b - \log c = \log a + \log b + \operatorname{colog} c$$
$$\log b^x = x \log b = -x \operatorname{colog} b$$
$$\log \frac{1}{b^x} = -x \log b = x \operatorname{colog} b$$
$$\log ab^x = \log a + x \log b = \log a - x \operatorname{colog} b$$
$$\log \frac{a}{b^x} = \log a - x \log b = \log a + x \operatorname{colog} b$$

Since it is confusing to multiply logarithms having a negative characteristic and positive mantissa, it is simpler to use cologarithms when a number less than unity is to be raised to any power. The following numerical examples indicate the simplest method of procedure:

Problem. Given $y = 3.127 \times 0.04156^{0.217}$; to determine y.

$$\begin{aligned}
\log y &= \log 3.127 - 0.217 \operatorname{colog} 0.04156 \\
&= 0.49513 - 0.217 \times 1.38132 \\
&= 0.19538 \\
y &= 1.568
\end{aligned}$$

Problem. Given $y = \dfrac{0.07658}{0.1917^{0.251}}$; to determine y.

$$\begin{aligned}
\log y &= \log 0.07658 + 0.251 \operatorname{colog} 0.1917 \\
&= \bar{2}.88412 + 0.251 \times 0.71738 \\
&= \bar{1}.06418 \\
y &= 0.1159
\end{aligned}$$

Table 14-1. Logarithms of Numbers

N.	L. 0	1	2	3	4	5	6	7	8	9
100	00 000	043	087	130	173	217	260	303	346	389
101	432	475	518	561	604	647	689	732	775	817
102	860	903	945	988	*030	*072	*115	*157	*199	*242
103	01 284	326	368	410	452	494	536	578	620	662
104	703	745	787	828	870	912	953	995	*036	*078
105	02 119	160	202	243	284	325	366	407	449	490
106	531	572	612	653	694	735	776	816	857	898
107	938	979	*019	*060	*100	*141	*181	*222	*262	*302
108	03 342	383	423	463	503	543	583	623	663	703
109	743	782	822	862	902	941	981	*021	*060	*100
110	04 139	179	218	258	297	336	376	415	454	493
111	532	571	610	650	689	727	766	805	844	883
112	922	961	999	*038	*077	*115	*154	*192	*231	*269
113	05 308	346	385	423	461	500	538	576	614	652
114	690	729	767	805	843	881	918	956	994	*032
115	06 070	108	145	183	221	258	296	333	371	408
116	446	483	521	558	595	633	670	707	744	781
117	819	856	893	930	967	*004	*041	*078	*115	*151
118	07 188	225	262	298	335	372	408	445	482	518
119	555	591	628	664	700	737	773	809	846	882
120	918	954	990	*027	*063	*099	*135	*171	*207	*243
121	08 279	314	350	386	422	458	493	529	565	600
122	636	672	707	743	778	814	849	884	920	955
123	991	*026	*061	*096	*132	*167	*202	*237	*272	*307
124	09 342	377	412	447	482	517	552	587	621	656
125	691	726	760	795	830	864	899	934	968	*003
126	10 037	072	106	140	175	209	243	278	312	346
127	380	415	449	483	517	551	585	619	653	687
128	721	755	789	823	857	890	924	958	992	*025
129	11 059	093	126	160	193	227	261	294	327	361
130	394	428	461	494	528	561	594	628	661	694
131	727	760	793	826	860	893	926	959	992	*024
132	12 057	090	123	156	189	222	254	287	320	352
133	385	418	450	483	516	548	581	613	646	678
134	710	743	775	808	840	872	905	937	969	*001
135	13 033	066	098	130	162	194	226	258	290	322
136	354	386	418	450	481	513	545	577	609	640
137	672	704	735	767	799	830	862	893	925	956
138	988	*019	*051	*082	*114	*145	*176	*208	*239	*270
139	14 301	333	364	395	426	457	489	520	551	582
140	613	644	675	706	737	768	799	829	860	891
141	922	953	983	*014	*045	*076	*106	*137	*168	*198
142	15 229	259	290	320	351	381	412	442	473	503
143	534	564	594	625	655	685	715	746	776	806
144	836	866	897	927	957	987	*017	*047	*077	*107
145	16 137	167	197	227	256	286	316	346	376	406
146	435	465	495	524	554	584	613	643	673	702
147	732	761	791	820	850	879	909	938	967	997
148	17 026	056	085	114	143	173	202	231	260	289
149	319	348	377	406	435	464	493	522	551	580
150	609	638	667	696	725	754	782	811	840	869
N.	L. 0	1	2	3	4	5	6	7	8	9

P. P.

	44	43	42
1	4.4	4.3	4.2
2	8.8	8.6	8.4
3	13.2	12.9	12.6
4	17.6	17.2	16.8
5	22.0	21.5	21.0
6	26.4	25.8	25.2
7	30.8	30.1	29.4
8	35.2	34.4	33.6
9	39.6	38.7	37.8

	41	40	39
1	4.1	4.0	3.9
2	8.2	8.0	7.8
3	12.3	12.0	11.7
4	16.4	16.0	15.6
5	20.5	20.0	19.5
6	24.6	24.0	23.4
7	28.7	28.0	27.3
8	32.8	32.0	31.2
9	36.9	36.0	35.1

	38	37	36
1	3.8	3.7	3.6
2	7.6	7.4	7.2
3	11.4	11.1	10.8
4	15.2	14.8	14.4
5	19.0	18.5	18.0
6	22.8	22.2	21.6
7	26.6	25.9	25.2
8	30.4	29.6	28.8
9	34.2	33.3	32.4

	35	34	33
1	3.5	3.4	3.3
2	7.0	6.8	6.6
3	10.5	10.2	9.9
4	14.0	13.6	13.2
5	17.5	17.0	16.5
6	21.0	20.4	19.8
7	24.5	23.8	23.1
8	28.0	27.2	26.4
9	31.5	30.6	29.7

	32	31	30
1	3.2	3.1	3.0
2	6.4	6.2	6.0
3	9.6	9.3	9.0
4	12.8	12.4	12.0
5	16.0	15.5	15.0
6	19.2	18.6	18.0
7	22.4	21.7	21.0
8	25.6	24.8	24.0
9	28.8	27.9	27.0

Table 14-1. Logarithms of Numbers (*Continued*)

N.	L. 0	1	2	3	4	5	6	7	8	9
150	17 609	638	667	696	725	754	782	811	840	869
151	898	926	955	984	*013	*041	*070	*099	*127	*156
152	18 184	213	241	270	298	327	355	384	412	441
153	469	498	526	554	583	611	639	667	696	724
154	752	780	808	837	865	893	921	949	977	*005
155	19 033	061	089	117	145	173	201	229	257	285
156	312	340	368	396	424	451	479	507	535	562
157	590	618	645	673	700	728	756	783	811	838
158	866	893	921	948	976	*003	*030	*058	*085	*112
159	20 140	167	194	222	249	276	303	330	358	385
160	412	439	466	493	520	548	575	602	629	656
161	683	710	737	763	790	817	844	871	898	925
162	952	978	*005	*032	*059	*085	*112	*139	*165	*192
163	21 219	245	272	299	325	352	378	405	431	458
164	484	511	537	564	590	617	643	669	696	722
165	748	775	801	827	854	880	906	932	958	985
166	22 011	037	063	089	115	141	167	194	220	246
167	272	298	324	350	376	401	427	453	479	505
168	531	557	583	608	634	660	686	712	737	763
169	789	814	840	866	891	917	943	968	994	*019
170	23 045	070	096	121	147	172	198	223	249	274
171	300	325	350	376	401	426	452	477	502	528
172	553	578	603	629	654	679	704	729	754	779
173	805	830	855	880	905	930	955	980	*005	*030
174	24 055	080	105	130	155	180	204	229	254	279
175	304	329	353	378	403	428	452	477	502	527
176	551	576	601	625	650	674	699	724	748	773
177	797	822	846	871	895	920	944	969	993	*018
178	25 042	066	091	115	139	164	188	212	237	261
179	285	310	334	358	382	406	431	455	479	503
180	527	551	575	600	624	648	672	696	720	744
181	768	792	816	840	864	888	912	935	959	983
182	26 007	031	055	079	102	126	150	174	198	221
183	245	269	293	316	340	364	387	411	435	458
184	482	505	529	553	576	600	623	647	670	694
185	717	741	764	788	811	834	858	881	905	928
186	951	975	998	*021	*045	*068	*091	*114	*138	*161
187	27 184	207	231	254	277	300	323	346	370	393
188	416	439	462	485	508	531	554	577	600	623
189	646	669	692	715	738	761	784	807	830	852
190	875	898	921	944	967	989	*012	*035	*058	*081
191	28 103	126	149	171	194	217	240	262	285	307
192	330	353	375	398	421	443	466	488	511	533
193	556	578	601	623	646	668	691	713	735	758
194	780	803	825	847	870	892	914	937	959	981
195	29 003	026	048	070	092	115	137	159	181	203
196	226	248	270	292	314	336	358	380	403	425
197	447	469	491	513	535	557	579	601	623	645
198	667	688	710	732	754	776	798	820	842	863
199	885	907	929	951	973	994	*016	*038	*060	*081
200	30 103	125	146	168	190	211	233	255	276	298

P. P.

	29	28		27	26		25		24	23		22	21
1	2.9	2.8	1	2.7	2.6	1	2.5	1	2.4	2.3	1	2.2	2.1
2	5.8	5.6	2	5.4	5.2	2	5.0	2	4.8	4.6	2	4.4	4.2
3	8.7	8.4	3	8.1	7.8	3	7.5	3	7.2	6.9	3	6.6	6.3
4	11.6	11.2	4	10.8	10.4	4	10.0	4	9.6	9.2	4	8.8	8.4
5	14.5	14.0	5	13.5	13.0	5	12.5	5	12.0	11.5	5	11.0	10.5
6	17.4	16.8	6	16.2	15.6	6	15.0	6	14.4	13.8	6	13.2	12.6
7	20.3	19.6	7	18.9	18.2	7	17.5	7	16.8	16.1	7	15.4	14.7
8	23.2	22.4	8	21.6	20.8	8	20.0	8	19.2	18.4	8	17.6	16.8
9	26.1	25.2	9	24.3	23.4	9	22.5	9	21.6	20.7	9	19.8	18.9

Table 14-1. Logarithms of Numbers (*Continued*)

N.	L.0	1	2	3	4	5	6	7	8	9
200	30 103	125	146	168	190	211	233	255	276	298
201	320	341	363	384	406	428	449	471	492	514
202	535	557	578	600	621	643	664	685	707	728
203	750	771	792	814	835	856	878	899	920	942
204	963	984	*006	*027	*048	*069	*091	*112	*133	*154
205	31 175	197	218	239	260	281	302	323	345	366
206	387	408	429	450	471	492	513	534	555	576
207	597	618	639	660	681	702	723	744	765	785
208	806	827	848	869	890	911	931	952	973	994
209	32 015	035	056	077	098	118	139	160	180	201
210	222	243	263	284	305	325	346	366	387	408
211	428	449	469	490	510	531	552	572	593	613
212	634	654	675	695	715	736	756	777	797	818
213	838	858	879	899	919	940	960	980	*001	*021
214	33 041	062	082	102	122	143	163	183	203	224
215	244	264	284	304	325	345	365	385	405	425
216	445	465	486	506	526	546	566	586	606	626
217	646	666	686	706	726	746	766	786	806	826
218	846	866	885	905	925	945	965	985	*005	*025
219	34 044	064	084	104	124	143	163	183	203	223
220	242	262	282	301	321	341	361	380	400	420
221	439	459	479	498	518	537	557	577	596	616
222	635	655	674	694	713	733	753	772	792	811
223	830	850	869	889	908	928	947	967	986	*005
224	35 025	044	064	083	102	122	141	160	180	199
225	218	238	257	276	295	315	334	353	372	392
226	411	430	449	468	488	507	526	545	564	583
227	603	622	641	660	679	698	717	736	755	774
228	793	813	832	851	870	889	908	927	946	965
229	984	*003	*021	*040	*059	*078	*097	*116	*135	*154
230	36 173	192	211	229	248	267	286	305	324	342
231	361	380	399	418	436	455	474	493	511	530
232	549	568	586	605	624	642	661	680	698	717
233	736	754	773	791	810	829	847	866	884	903
234	922	940	959	977	996	*014	*033	*051	*070	*088
235	37 107	125	144	162	181	199	218	236	254	273
236	291	310	328	346	365	383	401	420	438	457
237	475	493	511	530	548	566	585	603	621	639
238	658	676	694	712	731	749	767	785	803	822
239	840	858	876	894	912	931	949	967	985	*003
240	38 021	039	057	075	093	112	130	148	166	184
241	202	220	238	256	274	292	310	328	346	364
242	382	399	417	435	453	471	489	507	525	543
243	561	578	596	614	632	650	668	686	703	721
244	739	757	775	792	810	828	846	863	881	899
245	917	934	952	970	987	*005	*023	*041	*058	*076
246	39 094	111	129	146	164	182	199	217	235	252
247	270	287	305	322	340	358	375	393	410	428
248	445	463	480	498	515	533	550	568	585	602
249	620	637	655	672	690	707	724	742	759	777
250	794	811	829	846	863	881	898	915	933	950
N.	L.0	1	2	3	4	5	6	7	8	9

P. P.

	22	21
1	2.2	2.1
2	4.4	4.2
3	6.6	6.3
4	8.8	8.4
5	11.0	10.5
6	13.2	12.6
7	15.4	14.7
8	17.6	16.8
9	19.8	18.9

	20
1	2.0
2	4.0
3	6.0
4	8.0
5	10.0
6	12.0
7	14.0
8	16.0
9	18.0

	19
1	1.9
2	3.8
3	5.7
4	7.6
5	9.5
6	11.4
7	13.3
8	15.2
9	17.1

	18
1	1.8
2	3.6
3	5.4
4	7.2
5	9.0
6	10.8
7	12.6
8	14.4
9	16.2

	17
1	1.7
2	3.4
3	5.1
4	6.8
5	8.5
6	10.2
7	11.9
8	13.6
9	15.3

Table 14-1. Logarithms of Numbers (*Continued*)

N.	L.0	1	2	3	4	5	6	7	8	9
250	39 794	811	829	846	863	881	898	915	933	950
251	967	985	*002	*019	*037	*054	*071	*088	*106	*123
252	40 140	157	175	192	209	226	243	261	278	295
253	312	329	346	364	381	398	415	432	449	466
254	483	500	518	535	552	569	586	603	620	637
255	654	671	688	705	722	739	756	773	790	807
256	824	841	858	875	892	909	926	943	960	976
257	993	*010	*027	*044	*061	*078	*095	*111	*128	*145
258	41 162	179	196	212	229	246	263	280	296	313
259	330	347	363	380	397	414	430	447	464	481
260	497	514	531	547	564	581	597	614	631	647
261	664	681	697	714	731	747	764	780	797	814
262	830	847	863	880	896	913	929	946	963	979
263	996	*012	*029	*045	*062	*078	*095	*111	*127	*144
264	42 160	177	193	210	226	243	259	275	292	308
265	325	341	357	374	390	406	423	439	455	472
266	488	504	521	537	553	570	586	602	619	635
267	651	667	684	700	716	732	749	765	781	797
268	813	830	846	862	878	894	911	927	943	959
269	975	991	*008	*024	*040	*056	*072	*088	*104	*120
270	43 136	152	169	185	201	217	233	249	265	281
271	297	313	329	345	361	377	393	409	425	441
272	457	473	489	505	521	537	553	569	584	600
273	616	632	648	664	680	696	712	727	743	759
274	775	791	807	823	838	854	870	886	902	917
275	933	949	965	981	996	*012	*028	*044	*059	*075
276	44 091	107	122	138	154	170	185	201	217	232
277	248	264	279	295	311	326	342	358	373	389
278	404	420	436	451	467	483	498	514	529	545
279	560	576	592	607	623	638	654	669	685	700
280	716	731	747	762	778	793	809	824	840	855
281	871	886	902	917	932	948	963	979	994	*010
282	45 025	040	056	071	086	102	117	133	148	163
283	179	194	209	225	240	255	271	286	301	317
284	332	347	362	378	393	408	423	439	454	469
285	484	500	515	530	545	561	576	591	606	621
286	637	652	667	682	697	712	728	743	758	773
287	788	803	818	834	849	864	879	894	909	924
288	939	954	969	984	*000	*015	*030	*045	*060	*075
289	46 090	105	120	135	150	165	180	195	210	225
290	240	255	270	285	300	315	330	345	359	374
291	389	404	419	434	449	464	479	494	509	523
292	538	553	568	583	598	613	627	642	657	672
293	687	702	716	731	746	761	776	790	805	820
294	835	850	864	879	894	909	923	938	953	967
295	982	997	*012	*026	*041	*056	*070	*085	*100	*114
296	47 129	144	159	173	188	202	217	232	246	261
297	276	290	305	319	334	349	363	378	392	407
298	422	436	451	465	480	494	509	524	538	553
299	567	582	596	611	625	640	654	669	683	698
300	712	727	741	756	770	784	799	813	828	842
N.	L.0	1	2	3	4	5	6	7	8	9

P.P.

18
1	1.8
2	3.6
3	5.4
4	7.2
5	9.0
6	10.8
7	12.6
8	14.4
9	16.2

17
1	1.7
2	3.4
3	5.1
4	6.8
5	8.5
6	10.2
7	11.9
8	13.6
9	15.3

16
1	1.6
2	3.2
3	4.8
4	6.4
5	8.0
6	9.6
7	11.2
8	12.8
9	14.4

15
1	1.5
2	3.0
3	4.5
4	6.0
5	7.5
6	9.0
7	10.5
8	12.0
9	13.5

14
1	1.4
2	2.8
3	4.2
4	5.6
5	7.0
6	8.4
7	9.8
8	11.2
9	12.6

Table 14-1. Logarithms of Numbers (*Continued*)

N.	L. 0	1	2	3	4	5	6	7	8	9
300	47 712	727	741	756	770	784	799	813	828	842
301	857	871	885	900	914	929	943	958	972	986
302	48 001	015	029	044	058	073	087	101	116	130
303	144	159	173	187	202	216	230	244	259	273
304	287	302	316	330	344	359	373	387	401	416
305	430	444	458	473	487	501	515	530	544	558
306	572	586	601	615	629	643	657	671	686	700
307	714	728	742	756	770	785	799	813	827	841
308	855	869	883	897	911	926	940	954	968	982
309	996	*010	*024	*038	*052	*066	*080	*094	*108	*122
310	49 136	150	164	178	192	206	220	234	248	262
311	276	290	304	318	332	346	360	374	388	402
312	415	429	443	457	471	485	499	513	527	541
313	554	568	582	596	610	624	638	651	665	679
314	693	707	721	734	748	762	776	790	803	817
315	831	845	859	872	886	900	914	927	941	955
316	969	982	996	*010	*024	*037	*051	*065	*079	*092
317	50 106	120	133	147	161	174	188	202	215	229
318	243	256	270	284	297	311	325	338	352	365
319	379	393	406	420	433	447	461	474	488	501
320	515	529	542	556	569	583	596	610	623	637
321	651	664	678	691	705	718	732	745	759	772
322	786	799	813	826	840	853	866	880	893	907
323	920	934	947	961	974	987	*001	*014	*028	*041
324	51 055	068	081	095	108	121	135	148	162	175
325	188	202	215	228	242	255	268	282	295	308
326	322	335	348	362	375	388	402	415	428	441
327	455	468	481	495	508	521	534	548	561	574
328	587	601	614	627	640	654	667	680	693	706
329	720	733	746	759	772	786	799	812	825	838
330	851	865	878	891	904	917	930	943	957	970
331	983	996	*009	*022	*035	*048	*061	*075	*088	*101
332	52 114	127	140	153	166	179	192	205	218	231
333	244	257	270	284	297	310	323	336	349	362
334	375	388	401	414	427	440	453	466	479	492
335	504	517	530	543	556	569	582	595	608	621
336	634	647	660	673	686	699	711	724	737	750
337	763	776	789	802	815	827	840	853	866	879
338	892	905	917	930	943	956	969	982	994	*007
339	53 020	033	046	058	071	084	097	110	122	135
340	148	161	173	186	199	212	224	237	250	263
341	275	288	301	314	326	339	352	364	377	390
342	403	415	428	441	453	466	479	491	504	517
343	529	542	555	567	580	593	605	618	631	643
344	656	668	681	694	706	719	732	744	757	769
345	782	794	807	820	832	845	857	870	882	895
346	908	920	933	945	958	970	983	995	*008	*020
347	54 033	045	058	070	083	095	108	120	133	145
348	158	170	183	195	208	220	233	245	258	270
349	283	295	307	320	332	345	357	370	382	394
350	407	419	432	444	456	469	481	494	506	518
N.	L. 0	1	2	3	4	5	6	7	8	9

P. P.

15
1	1.5
2	3.0
3	4.5
4	6.0
5	7.5
6	9.0
7	10.5
8	12.0
9	13.5

14
1	1.4
2	2.8
3	4.2
4	5.6
5	7.0
6	8.4
7	9.8
8	11.2
9	12.6

13
1	1.3
2	2.6
3	3.9
4	5.2
5	6.5
6	7.8
7	9.1
8	10.4
9	11.7

12
1	1.2
2	2.4
3	3.6
4	4.8
5	6.0
6	7.2
7	8.4
8	9.6
9	10.8

Table 14-1. Logarithms of Numbers (*Continued*)

N.	L. 0	1	2	3	4	5	6	7	8	9	P. P.	
350	54 407	419	432	444	456	469	481	494	506	518		
351	531	543	555	568	580	593	605	617	630	642		
352	654	667	679	691	704	716	728	741	753	765		
353	777	790	802	814	827	839	851	864	876	888		
354	900	913	925	937	949	962	974	986	998	*011		**13**
355	55 023	035	047	060	072	084	096	108	121	133		
356	145	157	169	182	194	206	218	230	242	255	1	1.3
357	267	279	291	303	315	328	340	352	364	376	2	2.6
358	388	400	413	425	437	449	461	473	485	497	3	3.9
359	509	522	534	546	558	570	582	594	606	618	4	5.2
											5	6.5
360	630	642	654	666	678	691	703	715	727	739	6	7.8
											7	9.1
361	751	763	775	787	799	811	823	835	847	859	8	10.4
362	871	883	895	907	919	931	943	955	967	979	9	11.7
363	991	*003	*015	*027	*038	*050	*062	*074	*086	*098		
364	56 110	122	134	146	158	170	182	194	205	217		
365	229	241	253	265	277	289	301	312	324	336		**12**
366	348	360	372	384	396	407	419	431	443	455		
367	467	478	490	502	514	526	538	549	561	573	1	1.2
368	585	597	608	620	632	644	656	667	679	691	2	2.4
369	703	714	726	738	750	761	773	785	797	808	3	3.6
											4	4.8
370	820	832	844	855	867	879	891	902	914	926	5	6.0
											6	7.2
371	937	949	961	972	984	996	*008	*019	*031	*043	7	8.4
372	57 054	066	078	089	101	113	124	136	148	159	8	9.6
373	171	183	194	206	217	229	241	252	264	276	9	10.8
374	287	299	310	322	334	345	357	368	380	392		
375	403	415	426	438	449	461	473	484	496	507		
376	519	530	542	553	565	576	588	600	611	623		**11**
377	634	646	657	669	680	692	703	715	726	738		
378	749	761	772	784	795	807	818	830	841	852	1	1.1
379	864	875	887	898	910	921	933	944	955	967	2	2.2
											3	3.3
380	978	990	*001	*013	*024	*035	*047	*058	*070	*081	4	4.4
											5	5.5
381	58 092	104	115	127	138	149	161	172	184	195	6	6.6
382	206	218	229	240	252	263	274	286	297	309	7	7.7
383	320	331	343	354	365	377	388	399	410	422	8	8.8
384	433	444	456	467	478	490	501	512	524	535	9	9.9
385	546	557	569	580	591	602	614	625	636	647		
386	659	670	681	692	704	715	726	737	749	760		
387	771	782	794	805	816	827	838	850	861	872		**10**
388	883	894	906	917	928	939	950	961	973	984		
389	995	*006	*017	*028	*040	*051	*062	*073	*084	*095	1	1.0
											2	2.0
390	59 106	118	129	140	151	162	173	184	195	207	3	3.0
											4	4.0
391	218	229	240	251	262	273	284	295	306	318	5	5.0
392	329	340	351	362	373	384	395	406	417	428	6	6.0
393	439	450	461	472	483	494	506	517	528	539	7	7.0
394	550	561	572	583	594	605	616	627	638	649	8	8.0
395	660	671	682	693	704	715	726	737	748	759	9	9.0
396	770	780	791	802	813	824	835	846	857	868		
397	879	890	901	912	923	934	945	956	966	977		
398	988	999	*010	*021	*032	*043	*054	*065	*076	*086		
399	60 097	108	119	130	141	152	163	173	184	195		
400	206	217	228	239	249	260	271	282	293	304		
N.	**L. 0**	**1**	**2**	**3**	**4**	**5**	**6**	**7**	**8**	**9**	**P. P.**	

Table 14-1. Logarithms of Numbers (*Continued*)

N.	L. 0	1	2	3	4	5	6	7	8	9
400	60 206	217	228	239	249	260	271	282	293	304
401	314	325	336	347	358	369	379	390	401	412
402	423	433	444	455	466	477	487	498	509	520
403	531	541	552	563	574	584	595	606	617	627
404	638	649	660	670	681	692	703	713	724	735
405	746	756	767	778	788	799	810	821	831	842
406	853	863	874	885	895	906	917	927	938	949
407	959	970	981	991	*002	*013	*023	*034	*045	*055
408	61 066	077	087	098	109	119	130	140	151	162
409	172	183	194	204	215	225	236	247	257	268
410	278	289	300	310	321	331	342	352	363	374
411	384	395	405	416	426	437	448	458	469	479
412	490	500	511	521	532	542	553	563	574	584
413	595	606	616	627	637	648	658	669	679	690
414	700	711	721	731	742	752	763	773	784	794
415	805	815	826	836	847	857	868	878	888	899
416	909	920	930	941	951	962	972	982	993	*003
417	62 014	024	034	045	055	066	076	086	097	107
418	118	128	138	149	159	170	180	190	201	211
419	221	232	242	252	263	273	284	294	304	315
420	325	335	346	356	366	377	387	397	408	418
421	428	439	449	459	469	480	490	500	511	521
422	531	542	552	562	572	583	593	603	613	624
423	634	644	655	665	675	685	696	706	716	726
424	737	747	757	767	778	788	798	808	818	829
425	839	849	859	870	880	890	900	910	921	931
426	941	951	961	972	982	992	*002	*012	*022	*033
427	63 043	053	063	073	083	094	104	114	124	134
428	144	155	165	175	185	195	205	215	225	236
429	246	256	266	276	286	296	306	317	327	337
430	347	357	367	377	387	397	407	417	428	438
431	448	458	468	478	488	498	508	518	528	538
432	548	558	568	579	589	599	609	619	629	639
433	649	659	669	679	689	699	709	719	729	739
434	749	759	769	779	789	799	809	819	829	839
435	849	859	869	879	889	899	909	919	929	939
436	949	959	969	979	988	998	*008	*018	*028	*038
437	64 048	058	068	078	088	098	108	118	128	137
438	147	157	167	177	187	197	207	217	227	237
439	246	256	266	276	286	296	306	316	326	335
440	345	355	365	375	385	395	404	414	424	434
441	444	454	464	473	483	493	503	513	523	532
442	542	552	562	572	582	591	601	611	621	631
443	640	650	660	670	680	689	699	709	719	729
444	738	748	758	768	777	787	797	807	816	826
445	836	846	856	865	875	885	895	904	914	924
446	933	943	953	963	972	982	992	*002	*011	*021
447	65 031	040	050	060	070	079	089	099	108	118
448	128	137	147	157	167	176	186	196	205	215
449	225	234	244	254	263	273	283	292	302	312
450	321	331	341	350	360	369	379	389	398	408
N.	L. 0	1	2	3	4	5	6	7	8	9

P. P.

	11
1	1.1
2	2.2
3	3.3
4	4.4
5	5.5
6	6.6
7	7.7
8	8.8
9	9.9

	10
1	1.0
2	2.0
3	3.0
4	4.0
5	5.0
6	6.0
7	7.0
8	8.0
9	9.0

	9
1	0.9
2	1.8
3	2.7
4	3.6
5	4.5
6	5.4
7	6.3
8	7.2
9	8.1

Table 14-1. Logarithms of Numbers (*Continued*)

N.	L. 0	1	2	3	4	5	6	7	8	9	P. P.
450	65 321	331	341	350	360	369	379	389	398	408	
451	418	427	437	447	456	466	475	485	495	504	
452	514	523	533	543	552	562	571	581	591	600	
453	610	619	629	639	648	658	667	677	686	696	
454	706	715	725	734	744	753	763	772	782	792	
455	801	811	820	830	839	849	858	868	877	887	
456	896	906	916	925	935	944	954	963	973	982	
457	992	*001	*011	*020	*030	*039	*049	*058	*068	*077	
458	66 087	096	106	115	124	134	143	153	162	172	
459	181	191	200	210	219	229	238	247	257	266	
460	276	285	295	304	314	323	332	342	351	361	
461	370	380	389	398	408	417	427	436	445	455	
462	464	474	483	492	502	511	521	530	539	549	
463	558	567	577	586	596	605	614	624	633	642	
464	652	661	671	680	689	699	708	717	727	736	
465	745	755	764	773	783	792	801	811	820	829	
466	839	848	857	867	876	885	894	904	913	922	
467	932	941	950	960	969	978	987	997	*006	*015	
468	67 025	034	043	052	062	071	080	089	099	108	
469	117	127	136	145	154	164	173	182	191	201	
470	210	219	228	237	247	256	265	274	284	293	
471	302	311	321	330	339	348	357	367	376	385	
472	394	403	413	422	431	440	449	459	468	477	
473	486	495	504	514	523	532	541	550	560	569	
474	578	587	596	605	614	624	633	642	651	660	
475	669	679	688	697	706	715	724	733	742	752	
476	761	770	779	788	797	806	815	825	834	843	
477	852	861	870	879	888	897	906	916	925	934	
478	943	952	961	970	979	988	997	*006	*015	*024	
479	68 034	043	052	061	070	079	088	097	106	115	
480	124	133	142	151	160	169	178	187	196	205	
481	215	224	233	242	251	260	269	278	287	296	
482	305	314	323	332	341	350	359	368	377	386	
483	395	404	413	422	431	440	449	458	467	476	
484	485	494	502	511	520	529	538	547	556	565	
485	574	583	592	601	610	619	628	637	646	655	
486	664	673	681	690	699	708	717	726	735	744	
487	753	762	771	780	789	797	806	815	824	833	
488	842	851	860	869	878	886	895	904	913	922	
489	931	940	949	958	966	975	984	993	*002	*011	
490	69 020	028	037	046	055	064	073	082	090	099	
491	108	117	126	135	144	152	161	170	179	188	
492	197	205	214	223	232	241	249	258	267	276	
493	285	294	302	311	320	329	338	346	355	364	
494	373	381	390	399	408	417	425	434	443	452	
495	461	469	478	487	496	504	513	522	531	539	
496	548	557	566	574	583	592	601	609	618	627	
497	636	644	653	662	671	679	688	697	705	714	
498	723	732	740	749	758	767	775	784	793	801	
499	810	819	827	836	845	854	862	871	880	888	
500	897	906	914	923	932	940	949	958	966	975	
N.	L. 0	1	2	3	4	5	6	7	8	9	P. P.

P. P.

10

1	1.0
2	2.0
3	3.0
4	4.0
5	5.0
6	6.0
7	7.0
8	8.0
9	9.0

9

1	0.9
2	1.8
3	2.7
4	3.6
5	4.5
6	5.4
7	6.3
8	7.2
9	8.1

8

1	0.8
2	1.6
3	2.4
4	3.2
5	4.0
6	4.8
7	5.6
8	6.4
9	7.2

Table 14-1. Logarithms of Numbers (*Continued*)

N.	L.0	1	2	3	4	5	6	7	8	9
500	69 897	906	914	923	932	940	949	958	966	975
501	984	992	*001	*010	*018	*027	*036	*044	*053	*062
502	70 070	079	088	096	105	114	122	131	140	148
503	157	165	174	183	191	200	209	217	226	234
504	243	252	260	269	278	286	295	303	312	321
505	329	338	346	355	364	372	381	389	398	406
506	415	424	432	441	449	458	467	475	484	492
507	501	509	518	526	535	544	552	561	569	578
508	586	595	603	612	621	629	638	646	655	663
509	672	680	689	697	706	714	723	731	740	749
510	757	766	774	783	791	800	808	817	825	834
511	842	851	859	868	876	885	893	902	910	919
512	927	935	944	952	961	969	978	986	995	*003
513	71 012	020	029	037	046	054	063	071	079	088
514	096	105	113	122	130	139	147	155	164	172
515	181	189	198	206	214	223	231	240	248	257
516	265	273	282	290	299	307	315	324	332	341
517	349	357	366	374	383	391	399	408	416	425
518	433	441	450	458	466	475	483	492	500	508
519	517	525	533	542	550	559	567	575	584	592
520	600	609	617	625	634	642	650	659	667	675
521	684	692	700	709	717	725	734	742	750	759
522	767	775	784	792	800	809	817	825	834	842
523	850	858	867	875	883	892	900	908	917	925
524	933	941	950	958	966	975	983	991	999	*008
525	72 016	024	032	041	049	057	066	074	082	090
526	099	107	115	123	132	140	148	156	165	173
527	181	189	198	206	214	222	230	239	247	255
528	263	272	280	288	296	304	313	321	329	337
529	346	354	362	370	378	387	395	403	411	419
530	428	436	444	452	460	469	477	485	493	501
531	509	518	526	534	542	550	558	567	575	583
532	591	599	607	616	624	632	640	648	656	665
533	673	681	689	697	705	713	722	730	738	746
534	754	762	770	779	787	795	803	811	819	827
535	835	843	852	860	868	876	884	892	900	908
536	916	925	933	941	949	957	965	973	981	989
537	997	*006	*014	*022	*030	*038	*046	*054	*062	*070
538	73 078	086	094	102	111	119	127	135	143	151
539	159	167	175	183	191	199	207	215	223	231
540	239	247	255	263	272	280	288	296	304	312
541	320	328	336	344	352	360	368	376	384	392
542	400	408	416	424	432	440	448	456	464	472
543	480	488	496	504	512	520	528	536	544	552
544	560	568	576	584	592	600	608	616	624	632
545	640	648	656	664	672	679	687	695	703	711
546	719	727	735	743	751	759	767	775	783	791
547	799	807	815	823	830	838	846	854	862	870
548	878	886	894	902	910	918	926	933	941	949
549	957	965	973	981	989	997	*005	*013	*020	*028
550	74 036	044	052	060	068	076	084	092	099	107

P. P.

9

1	0.9
2	1.8
3	2.7
4	3.6
5	4.5
6	5.4
7	6.3
8	7.2
9	8.1

8

1	0.8
2	1.6
3	2.4
4	3.2
5	4.0
6	4.8
7	5.6
8	6.4
9	7.2

7

1	0.7
2	1.4
3	2.1
4	2.8
5	3.5
6	4.2
7	4.9
8	5 6
9	6.3

N.	L.0	1	2	3	4	5	6	7	8	9	P. P.

Table 14-1. Logarithms of Numbers (*Continued*)

N.	L. 0	1	2	3	4	5	6	7	8	9	P. P.
550	74 036	044	052	060	068	076	084	092	099	107	
551	115	123	131	139	147	155	162	170	178	186	
552	194	202	210	218	225	233	241	249	257	265	
553	273	280	288	296	304	312	320	327	335	343	
554	351	359	367	374	382	390	398	406	414	421	
555	429	437	445	453	461	468	476	484	492*	500	
556	507	515	523	531	539	547	554	562	570	578	
557	586	593	601	609	617	624	632	640	648	656	
558	663	671	679	687	695	702	710	718	726	733	
559	741	749	757	764	772	780	788	796	803	811	
560	819	827	834	842	850	858	865	873	881	889	**8**
561	896	904	912	920	927	935	943	950	958	966	1 0.8
562	974	981	989	997	*005	*012	*020	*028	*035	*043	2 1.6
563	75 051	059	066	074	082	089	097	105	113	120	3 2.4
564	128	136	143	151	159	166	174	182	189	197	4 3.2
565	205	213	220	228	236	243	251	259	266	274	5 4.0
566	282	289	297	305	312	320	328	335	343	351	6 4.8
567	358	366	374	381	389	397	404	412	420	427	7 5.6
568	435	442	450	458	465	473	481	488	496	504	8 6.4
569	511	519	526	534	542	549	557	565	572	580	9 7.2
570	587	595	603	610	618	626	633	641	648	656	
571	664	671	679	686	694	702	709	717	724	732	
572	740	747	755	762	770	778	785	793	800	808	
573	815	823	831	838	846	853	861	868	876	884	
574	891	899	906	914	921	929	937	944	952	959	
575	967	974	982	989	997	*005	*012	*020	*027	*035	
576	76 042	050	057	065	072	080	087	095	103	110	
577	118	125	133	140	148	155	163	170	178	185	
578	193	200	208	215	223	230	238	245	253	260	
579	268	275	283	290	298	305	313	320	328	335	
580	343	350	358	365	373	380	388	395	403	410	**7**
581	418	425	433	440	448	455	462	470	477	485	1 0.7
582	492	500	507	515	522	530	537	545	552	559	2 1.4
583	567	574	582	589	597	604	612	619	626	634	3 2.1
584	641	649	656	664	671	678	686	693	701	708	4 2.8
585	716	723	730	738	745	753	760	768	775	782	5 3.5
586	790	797	805	812	819	827	834	842	849	856	6 4.2
587	864	871	879	886	893	901	908	916	923	930	7 4.9
588	938	945	953	960	967	975	982	989	997	*004	8 5.6
589	77 012	019	026	034	041	048	056	063	070	078	9 6.3
590	085	093	100	107	115	122	129	137	144	151	
591	159	166	173	181	188	195	203	210	217	225	
592	232	240	247	254	262	269	276	283	291	298	
593	305	313	320	327	335	342	349	357	364	371	
594	379	386	393	401	408	415	422	430	437	444	
595	452	459	466	474	481	488	495	503	510	517	
596	525	532	539	546	554	561	568	576	583	590	
597	597	605	612	619	627	634	641	648	656	663	
598	670	677	685	692	699	706	714	721	728	735	
599	743	750	757	764	772	779	786	793	801	808	
600	815	822	830	837	844	851	859	866	873	880	
N.	**L. 0**	**1**	**2**	**3**	**4**	**5**	**6**	**7**	**8**	**9**	**P. P.**

Table 14-1. Logarithms of Numbers (*Continued*)

N.	L. 0	1	2	3	4	5	6	7	8	9	P. P.
600	77 815	822	830	837	844	851	859	866	873	880	
601	887	895	902	909	916	924	931	938	945	952	
602	960	967	974	981	988	996	*003	*010	*017	*025	
603	78 032	039	046	053	061	068	075	082	089	097	
604	104	111	118	125	132	140	147	154	161	168	
605	176	183	190	197	204	211	219	226	233	240	
606	247	254	262	269	276	283	290	297	305	312	
607	319	326	333	340	347	355	362	369	376	383	
608	390	398	405	412	419	426	433	440	447	455	
609	462	469	476	483	490	497	504	512	519	526	
610	533	540	547	554	561	569	576	583	590	597	
611	604	611	618	625	633	640	647	654	661	668	
612	675	682	689	696	704	711	718	725	732	739	
613	746	753	760	767	774	781	789	796	803	810	
614	817	824	831	838	845	852	859	866	873	880	
615	888	895	902	909	916	923	930	937	944	951	
616	958	965	972	979	986	993	*000	*007	*014	*021	
617	79 029	036	043	050	057	064	071	078	085	092	
618	099	106	113	120	127	134	141	148	155	162	
619	169	176	183	190	197	204	211	218	225	232	
620	239	246	253	260	267	274	281	288	295	302	
621	309	316	323	330	337	344	351	358	365	372	
622	379	386	393	400	407	414	421	428	435	442	
623	449	456	463	470	477	484	491	498	505	511	
624	518	525	532	539	546	553	560	567	574	581	
625	588	595	602	609	616	623	630	637	644	650	
626	657	664	671	678	685	692	699	706	713	720	
627	727	734	741	748	754	761	768	775	782	789	
628	796	803	810	817	824	831	837	844	851	858	
629	865	872	879	886	893	900	906	913	920	927	
630	934	941	948	955	962	969	975	982	989	996	
631	80 003	010	017	024	030	037	044	051	058	065	
632	072	079	085	092	099	106	113	120	127	134	
633	140	147	154	161	168	175	182	188	195	202	
634	209	216	223	229	236	243	250	257	264	271	
635	277	284	291	298	305	312	318	325	332	339	
636	346	353	359	366	373	380	387	393	400	407	
637	414	421	428	434	441	448	455	462	468	475	
638	482	489	496	502	509	516	523	530	536	543	
639	550	557	564	570	577	584	591	598	604	611	
640	618	625	632	638	645	652	659	665	672	679	
641	686	693	699	706	713	720	726	733	740	747	
642	754	760	767	774	781	787	794	801	808	814	
643	821	828	835	841	848	855	862	868	875	882	
644	889	895	902	909	916	922	929	936	943	949	
645	956	963	969	976	983	990	996	*003	*010	*017	
646	81 023	030	037	·043	050	057	064	070	077	084	
647	090	097	104	111	117	124	131	137	144	151	
648	158	164	171	178	184	191	198	204	211	218	
649	224	231	238	245	251	258	265	271	278	285	
650	291	298	305	311	318	325	331	338	345	351	
N.	**L. 0**	**1**	**2**	**3**	**4**	**5**	**6**	**7**	**8**	**9**	**P. P.**

P. P.

8
1	0.8
2	1.6
3	2.4
4	3.2
5	4.0
6	4.8
7	5.6
8	6.4
9	7.2

7
1	0.7
2	1.4
3	2.1
4	2.8
5	3.5
6	4.2
7	4.9
8	5.6
9	6.3

6
1	0.6
2	1.2
3	1.8
4	2.4
5	3.0
6	3.6
7	4.2
8	4.8
9	5.4

Table 14-1. Logarithms of Numbers (*Continued*)

N.	L. 0	1	2	3	4	5	6	7	8	9	P. P.
650	81 291	298	305	311	318	325	331	338	345	351	
651	358	365	371	378	385	391	398	405	411	418	
652	425	431	438	445	451	458	465	471	478	485	
653	491	498	505	511	518	525	531	538	544	551	
654	558	564	571	578	584	591	598	604	611	617	
655	624	631	637	644	651	657	664	671	677	684	
656	690	697	704	710	717	723	730	737	743	750	
657	757	763	770	776	783	790	796	803	809	816	
658	823	829	836	842	849	856	862	869	875	882	
659	889	895	902	908	915	921	928	935	941	948	
660	954	961	968	974	981	987	994	*000	*007	*014	**7**
661	82 020	027	033	040	046	053	060	066	073	079	
662	086	092	099	105	112	119	125	132	138	145	1 0.7
663	151	158	164	171	178	184	191	197	204	210	2 1.4
664	217	223	230	236	243	249	256	263	269	276	3 2.1
665	282	289	295	302	308	315	321	328	334	341	4 2.8
666	347	354	360	367	373	380	387	393	400	406	5 3.5
667	413	419	426	432	439	445	452	458	465	471	6 4.2
668	478	484	491	497	504	510	517	523	530	536	7 4.9
669	543	549	556	562	569	575	582	588	595	601	8 5.6
670	607	614	620	627	633	640	646	653	659	666	9 6.3
671	672	679	685	692	698	705	711	718	724	730	
672	737	743	750	756	763	769	776	782	789	795	
673	802	808	814	821	827	834	840	847	853	860	
674	866	872	879	885	892	898	905	911	918	924	
675	930	937	943	950	956	963	969	975	982	988	
676	995	*001	*008	*014	*020	*027	*033	*040	*046	*052	
677	83 059	065	072	078	085	091	097	104	110	117	
678	123	129	136	142	149	155	161	168	174	181	
679	187	193	200	206	213	219	225	232	238	245	
680	251	257	264	270	276	283	289	296	302	308	**6**
681	315	321	327	334	340	347	353	359	366	372	1 0.6
682	378	385	391	398	404	410	417	423	429	436	2 1.2
683	442	448	455	461	467	474	480	487	493	499	3 1.8
684	506	512	518	525	531	537	544	550	556	563	4 2.4
685	569	575	582	588	594	601	607	613	620	626	5 3.0
686	632	639	645	651	658	664	670	677	683	689	6 3.6
687	696	702	708	715	721	727	734	740	746	753	7 4.2
688	759	765	771	778	784	790	797	803	809	816	8 4.8
689	822	828	835	841	847	853	860	866	872	879	9 5.4
690	885	891	897	904	910	916	923	929	935	942	
691	948	954	960	967	973	979	985	992	998	*004	
692	84 011	017	023	029	036	042	048	055	061	067	
693	073	080	086	092	098	105	111	117	123	130	
694	136	142	148	155	161	167	173	180	186	192	
695	198	205	211	217	223	230	236	242	248	255	
696	261	267	273	280	286	292	298	305	311	317	
697	323	330	336	342	348	354	361	367	373	379	
698	386	392	398	404	410	417	423	429	435	442	
699	448	454	460	466	473	479	485	491	497	504	
700	510	516	522	528	535	541	547	553	559	566	
N.	L. 0	1	2	3	4	5	6	7	8	9	P. P.

Table 14-1. Logarithms of Numbers (*Continued*)

N.	L. 0	1	2	3	4	5	6	7	8	9
700	84 510	516	522	528	535	541	547	553	559	566
701	572	578	584	590	597	603	609	615	621	628
702	634	640	646	652	658	665	671	677	683	689
703	696	702	708	714	720	726	733	739	745	751
704	757	763	770	776	782	788	794	800	807	813
705	819	825	831	837	844	850	856	862	868	874
706	880	887	893	899	905	911	917	924	930	936
707	942	948	954	960	967	973	979	985	991	997
708	85 003	009	016	022	028	034	040	046	052	058
709	065	071	077	083	089	095	101	107	114	120
710	126	132	138	144	150	156	163	169	175	181
711	187	193	199	205	211	217	224	230	236	242
712	248	254	260	266	272	278	285	291	297	303
713	309	315	321	327	333	339	·345	352	358	364
714	370	376	382	388	394	400	406	412	418	425
715	431	437	443	449	455	461	467	473	479	485
716	491	497	503	509	516	522	528	531	540	546
717	552	558	564	570	576	582	588	594	600	606
718	612	618	625	631	637	643	649	655	661	667
719	673	679	685	691	697	703	709	715	721	727
720	733	739	745	751	757	763	769	775	781	788
721	794	800	806	812	818	824	830	836	842	848
722	854	860	866	872	878	884	890	896	902	908
723	914	920	926	932	938	944	950	956	962	968
724	974	980	986	992	998	*004	*010	*016	*022	*028
725	86 034	040	046	052	058	064	070	076	082	088
726	094	100	106	112	118	124	130	136	141	147
727	153	159	165	171	177	183	189	195	201	207
728	213	219	225	231	237	243	249	255	261	267
729	273	279	285	291	297	303	308	314	320	326
730	332	338	344	350	356	362	368	374	380	386
731	392	398	404	410	415	421	427	433	439	445
732	451	457	463	469	475	481	487	493	499	504
733	510	516	522	528	534	540	546	552	558	564
734	570	576	581	587	593	599	605	611	617	623
735	629	635	641	646	652	658	664	670	676	682
736	688	694	700	705	711	717	723	729	735	741
737	747	753	759	764	770	776	782	788	794	800
738	806	812	817	823	829	835	841	847	853	859
739	864	870	876	882	888	894	900	906	911	917
740	923	929	935	941	947	953	958	964	970	976
741	982	988	994	999	*005	*011	*017	*023	*029	*035
742	87 040	046	052	058	064	070	075	081	087	093
743	099	105	111	116	122	128	134	140	146	151
744	157	163	169	175	181	186	192	198	204	210
745	216	221	227	233	239	245	251	256	262	268
746	274	280	286	291	297	303	309	315	320	326
747	332	338	344	349	355	361	367	373	379	384
748	390	396	402	408	413	419	425	431	437	442
749	448	454	460	466	471	477	483	489	495	500
750	506	512	518	523	529	535	541	547	552	558

P. P.

7
1 0.7
2 1.4
3 2.1
4 2.8
5 3.5
6 4.2
7 4.9
8 5.6
9 6.3

6
1 0.6
2 1.2
3 1.8
4 2.4
5 3.0
6 3.6
7 4.2
8 4.8
9 5.4

5
1 0.5
2 1.0
3 1.5
4 2.0
5 2.5
6 3.0
7 3.5
8 4.0
9 4.5

Table 14-1. Logarithms of Numbers (*Continued*)

N.	L. 0	1	2	3	4	5	6	7	8	9
750	87 506	512	518	523	529	535	541	547	552	558
751	564	570	576	581	587	593	599	604	610	616
752	622	628	633	639	645	651	656	662	668	674
753	679	685	691	697	703	708	714	720	726	731
754	737	743	749	754	760	766	772	777	783	789
755	795	800	806	812	818	823	829	835	841	846
756	852	858	864	869	875	881	887	892	898	904
757	910	915	921	927	933	938	944	950	955	961
758	967	973	978	984	990	996	*001	*007	*013	*018
759	88 024	030	036	041	047	053	058	064	070	076
760	081	087	093	098	104	110	116	121	127	133
761	138	144	150	156	161	167	173	178	184	190
762	195	201	207	213	218	224	230	235	241	247
763	252	258	264	270	275	281	287	292	298	304
764	309	315	321	326	332	338	343	349	355	360
765	366	372	377	383	389	395	400	406	412	417
766	423	429	434	440	446	451	457	463	468	474
767	480	485	491	497	502	508	513	519	525	530
768	536	542	547	553	559	564	570	576	581	587
769	593	598	604	610	615	621	627	632	638	643
770	649	655	660	666	672	677	683	689	694	700
771	705	711	717	722	728	734	739	745	750	756
772	762	767	773	779	784	790	795	801	807	812
773	818	824	829	835	840	846	852	857	863	868
774	874	880	885	891	897	902	908	913	919	925
775	930	936	941	947	953	958	964	969	975	981
776	986	992	997	*003	*009	*014	*020	*025	*031	*037
777	89 042	048	053	059	064	070	076	081	087	092
778	098	104	109	115	120	126	131	137	143	148
779	154	159	165	170	176	182	187	193	198	204
780	209	215	221	226	232	237	243	248	254	260
781	265	271	276	282	287	293	298	304	310	315
782	321	326	332	337	343	348	354	360	365	371
783	376	382	387	393	398	404	409	415	421	426
784	432	437	443	448	454	459	465	470	476	481
785	487	492	498	504	509	515	520	526	531	537
786	542	548	553	559	564	570	575	581	586	592
787	597	603	609	614	620	625	631	636	642	647
788	653	658	664	669	675	680	686	691	697	702
789	708	713	719	724	730	735	741	746	752	757
790	763	768	774	779	785	790	796	801	807	812
791	818	823	829	834	840	845	851	856	862	867
792	873	878	883	889	894	900	905	911	916	922
793	927	933	938	944	949	955	960	966	971	977
794	982	988	993	998	*004	*009	*015	*020	*025	*031
795	90 037	042	048	053	059	064	069	075	080	086
796	091	097	102	108	113	119	124	129	135	140
797	146	151	157	162	168	173	179	184	189	195
798	200	206	211	217	222	227	233	238	244	249
799	255	260	266	271	276	282	287	293	298	304
800	309	314	320	325	331	336	342	347	352	358

P. P.

6

1	0.6
2	1.2
3	1.8
4	2.4
5	3.0
6	3.6
7	4.2
8	4.8
9	5.4

5

1	0.5
2	1.0
3	1.5
4	2.0
5	2.5
6	3.0
7	3.5
8	4.0
9	4.5

Table 14-1. Logarithms of Numbers (*Continued*)

N.	L. 0	1	2	3	4	5	6	7	8	9	P. P.	
800	90 309	314	320	325	331	336	342	347	352	358		
801	363	369	374	380	385	390	396	401	407	412		
802	417	423	428	434	439	445	450	455	461	466		
803	472	477	482	488	493	499	504	509	515	520		
804	526	531	536	542	547	553	558	563	569	574		
805	580	585	590	596	601	607	612	617	623	628		
806	634	639	644	650	655	660	666	671	677	682		
807	687	693	698	703	709	714	720	725	730	736		
808	741	747	752	757	763	768	773	779	784	789		
809	795	800	806	811	816	822	827	832	838	843		
810	849	854	859	865	870	875	881	886	891	897		**6**
811	902	907	913	918	924	929	934	940	945	950	1	0.6
812	956	961	966	972	977	982	988	993	998	*004	2	1.2
813	91 009	014	020	025	030	036	041	046	052	057	3	1.8
814	062	068	073	078	084	089	094	100	105	110	4	2.4
815	116	121	126	132	137	142	148	153	158	164	5	3.0
816	169	174	180	185	190	196	201	206	212	217	6	3.6
817	222	228	233	238	243	249	254	259	265	270	7	4.2
818	275	281	286	291	297	302	307	312	318	323	8	4.8
819	328	334	339	344	350	355	360	365	371	376	9	5.4
820	381	387	392	397	403	408	413	418	424	429		
821	434	440	445	450	455	461	466	471	477	482		
822	487	492	498	503	508	514	519	524	529	535		
823	540	545	551	556	561	566	572	577	582	587		
824	593	598	603	609	614	619	624	630	635	640		
825	645	651	656	661	666	672	677	682	687	693		
826	698	703	709	714	719	724	730	735	740	745		
827	751	756	761	766	772	777	782	787	793	798		
828	803	808	814	819	824	829	834	840	845	850		
829	855	861	866	871	876	882	887	892	897	903		
830	908	913	918	924	929	934	939	944	950	955		**5**
831	960	965	971	976	981	986	991	997	*002	*007	1	0.5
832	92 012	018	023	028	033	038	044	049	054	059	2	1.0
833	065	070	075	080	085	091	096	101	106	111	3	1.5
834	117	122	127	132	137	143	148	153	158	163	4	2.0
835	169	174	179	184	189	195	200	205	210	215	5	2.5
836	221	226	231	236	241	247	252	257	262	267	6	3.0
837	273	278	283	288	293	298	304	309	314	319	7	3.5
838	324	330	335	340	345	350	355	361	366	371	8	4.0
839	376	381	387	392	397	402	407	412	418	423	9	4.5
840	428	433	438	443	449	454	459	464	469	474		
841	480	485	490	495	500	505	511	516	521	526		
842	531	536	542	547	552	557	562	567	572	578		
843	583	588	593	598	603	609	614	619	624	629		
844	634	639	645	650	655	660	665	670	675	681		
845	686	691	696	701	706	711	716	722	727	732		
846	737	742	747	752	758	763	768	773	778	783		
847	788	793	799	804	809	814	819	824	829	834		
848	840	845	850	855	860	865	870	875	881	886		
849	891	896	901	906	911	916	921	927	932	937		
850	942	947	952	957	962	967	973	978	983	988		
N.	**L. 0**	**1**	**2**	**3**	**4**	**5**	**6**	**7**	**8**	**9**	**P. P.**	

Table 14-1. Logarithms of Numbers (*Continued*)

N.	L. 0	1	2	3	4	5	6	7	8	9
850	92 942	947	952	957	962	967	973	978	983	988
851	993	998	*003	*008	*013	*018	*024	*029	*034	*039
852	93 044	049	054	059	064	069	075	080	085	090
853	095	100	105	110	115	120	125	131	136	141
854	146	151	156	161	166	171	176	181	186	192
855	197	202	207	212	217	222	227	232	237	242
856	247	252	258	263	268	273	278	283	288	293
857	298	303	308	313	318	323	328	334	339	344
858	349	354	359	364	369	374	379	384	389	394
859	399	404	409	414	420	425	430	435	440	445
860	450	455	460	465	470	475	480	485	490	495
861	500	505	510	515	520	526	531	536	541	546
862	551	556	561	566	571	576	581	586	591	596
863	601	606	611	616	621	626	631	636	641	646
864	651	656	661	666	671	676	682	687	692	697
865	702	707	712	717	722	727	732	737	742	747
866	752	757	762	767	772	777	782	787	792	797
867	802	807	812	817	822	827	832	837	842	847
868	852	857	862	867	872	877	882	887	892	897
869	902	907	912	917	922	927	932	937	942	947
870	952	957	962	967	972	977	982	987	992	997
871	94 002	007	012	017	022	027	032	037	042	047
872	052	057	062	067	072	077	082	086	091	096
873	101	106	111	116	121	126	131	136	141	146
874	151	156	161	166	171	176	181	186	191	196
875	201	206	211	216	221	226	231	236	240	245
876	250	255	260	265	270	275	280	285	290	295
877	300	305	310	315	320	325	330	335	340	345
878	349	354	359	364	369	374	379	384	389	394
879	399	404	409	414	419	424	429	433	438	443
880	448	453	458	463	468	473	478	483	488	493
881	498	503	507	512	517	522	527	532	537	542
882	547	552	557	562	567	571	576	581	586	591
883	596	601	606	611	616	621	626	630	635	640
884	645	650	655	660	665	670	675	680	685	689
885	694	699	704	709	714	719	724	729	734	738
886	743	748	753	758	763	768	773	778	783	787
887	792	797	802	807	812	817	822	827	832	836
888	841	846	851	856	861	866	871	876	880	885
889	890	895	900	905	910	915	919	924	929	934
890	939	944	949	954	959	963	968	973	978	983
891	988	993	998	*002	*007	*012	*017	*022	*027	*032
892	95 036	041	046	051	056	061	066	071	075	080
893	085	090	095	100	105	109	114	119	124	129
894	134	139	143	148	153	158	163	168	173	177
895	182	187	192	197	202	207	211	216	221	226
896	231	236	240	245	250	255	260	265	270	274
897	, 279	284	289	294	299	303	308	313	318	323
898	328	332	337	342	347	352	357	361	366	371
899	376	381	386	390	395	400	405	410	415	419
900	424	429	434	439	444	448	453	458	463	468

P. P.

6
1	0.6
2	1.2
3	1.8
4	2.4
5	3.0
6	3.6
7	4.2
8	4.8
9	5.4

5
1	0.5
2	1.0
3	1.5
4	2.0
5	2.5
6	3.0
7	3.5
8	4.0
9	4.5

4
1	0.4
2	0.8
3	1.2
4	1.6
5	2.0
6	2.4
7	2.8
8	3.2
9	3.6

Table 14-1. Logarithms of Numbers (*Continued*)

N.	L.0	1	2	3	4	5	6	7	8	9	P.P.
900	95 424	429	434	439	444	448	453	458	463	468	
901	472	477	482	487	492	497	501	506	511	516	
902	521	525	530	535	540	545	550	554	559	564	
903	569	574	578	583	588	593	598	602	607	612	
904	617	622	626	631	636	641	646	650	655	660	
905	665	670	674	679	684	689	694	698	703	708	
906	713	718	722	727	732	737	742	746	751	756	
907	761	766	770	775	780	785	789	794	799	804	
908	809	813	818	823	828	832	837	842	847	852	
909	856	861	866	871	875	880	885	890	895	899	
910	904	909	914	918	923	928	933	938	942	947	
911	952	957	961	966	971	976	980	985	990	995	**5**
912	999	*004	*009	*014	*019	*023	*028	*033	*038	*042	1 0.5
913	96 047	052	057	061	066	071	076	080	085	090	2 1.0
914	095	099	104	109	114	118	123	128	133	137	3 1.5
915	142	147	152	156	161	166	171	175	180	185	4 2.0
916	190	194	199	204	209	213	218	223	227	232	5 2.5
917	237	242	246	251	256	261	265	270	275	280	6 3.0
918	284	289	294	298	303	308	313	317	322	327	7 3.5
919	332	336	341	346	350	355	360	365	369	374	8 4.0
920	379	384	388	393	398	402	407	412	417	421	9 4.5
921	426	431	435	440	445	450	454	459	464	468	
922	473	478	483	487	492	497	501	506	511	515	
923	520	525	530	534	539	544	548	553	558	562	
924	567	572	577	581	586	591	595	600	605	609	
925	614	619	624	628	633	638	642	647	652	656	
926	661	666	670	675	680	685	689	694	699	703	
927	708	713	717	722	727	731	736	741	745	750	
928	755	759	764	769	774	778	783	788	792	797	
929	802	806	811	816	820	825	830	834	839	844	
930	848	853	858	862	867	872	876	881	886	890	
931	895	900	904	909	914	918	923	928	932	937	**4**
932	942	946	951	956	960	965	970	974	979	984	1 0.4
933	988	993	997	*002	*007	*011	*016	*021	*025	*030	2 0.8
934	97 035	039	044	049	053	058	063	067	072	077	3 1.2
935	081	086	090	095	100	104	109	114	118	123	4 1.6
936	128	132	137	142	146	151	155	160	165	169	5 2.0
937	174	179	183	188	192	197	202	206	211	216	6 2.4
938	220	225	230	234	239	243	248	253	257	262	7 2.8
939	267	271	276	280	285	290	294	299	304	308	8 3.2
940	313	317	322	327	331	336	340	345	350	354	9 3.6
941	359	364	368	373	377	382	387	391	396	400	
942	405	410	414	419	424	428	433	437	442	447	
943	451	456	460	465	470	474	479	483	488	493	
944	497	502	506	511	516	520	525	529	534	539	
945	543	548	552	557	562	566	571	575	580	585	
946	589	594	598	603	607	612	617	621	626	630	
947	635	640	644	649	653	658	663	667	672	676	
948	681	685	690	695	699	704	708	713	717	722	
949	727	731	736	740	745	749	754	759	763	768	
950	772	777	782	786	791	795	800	804	809	813	
N.	L.0	1	2	3	4	5	6	7	8	9	P.P.

Table 14-1. Logarithms of Numbers (*Concluded*)

N.	L. 0	1	2	3	4	5	6	7	8	9	P. P.
950	97 772	777	782	786	791	795	800	804	809	813	
951	818	823	827	832	836	841	845	850	855	859	
952	864	868	873	877	882	886	891	896	900	905	
953	909	914	918	923	928	932	937	941	946	950	
954	955	959	964	968	973	978	982	987	991	996	
955	98 000	005	009	014	019	023	028	032	037	041	
956	046	050	055	059	064	068	073	078	082	087	
957	091	096	100	105	109	114	118	123	127	132	
958	137	141	146	150	155	159	164	168	173	177	
959	182	186	191	195	200	204	209	214	218	223	
960	227	232	236	241	245	250	254	259	263	268	**5**
961	272	277	281	286	290	295	299	304	308	313	1 0.5
962	318	322	327	331	336	340	345	349	354	358	2 1.0
963	363	367	372	376	381	385	390	394	399	403	3 1.5
964	408	412	417	421	426	430	435	439	444	448	4 2.0
965	453	457	462	466	471	475	480	484	489	493	5 2.5
966	498	502	507	511	516	520	525	529	534	538	6 3.0
967	543	547	552	556	561	565	570	574	579	583	7 3.5
968	588	592	597	601	605	610	614	619	623	628	8 4.0
969	632	637	641	646	650	655	659	664	668	673	9 4.5
970	677	682	686	691	695	700	704	709	713	717	
971	722	726	731	735	740	744	749	753	758	762	
972	767	771	776	780	784	789	793	798	802	807	
973	811	816	820	825	829	834	838	843	847	851	
974	856	860	865	869	874	878	883	887	892	896	
975	900	905	909	914	918	923	927	932	936	941	
976	945	949	954	958	963	967	972	976	981	985	
977	989	994	998	*003	*007	*012	*016	*021	*025	*029	
978	99 034	038	043	047	052	056	061	065	069	074	
979	078	083	087	092	096	100	105	109	114	118	
980	123	127	131	136	140	145	149	154	158	162	**4**
981	167	171	176	180	185	189	193	198	202	207	1 0.4
982	211	216	220	224	229	233	238	242	247	251	2 0.8
983	255	260	264	269	273	277	282	286	291	295	3 1.2
984	300	304	308	313	317	322	326	330	335	339	4 1.6
985	344	348	352	357	361	366	370	374	379	383	5 2.0
986	388	392	396	401	405	410	414	419	423	427	6 2.4
987	432	436	441	445	449	454	458	463	467	471	7 2.8
988	476	480	484	489	493	498	502	506	511	515	8 3.2
989	520	524	528	533	537	542	546	550	555	559	9 3.6
990	564	568	572	577	581	585	590	594	599	603	
991	607	612	616	621	625	629	634	638	642	647	
992	651	656	660	664	669	673	677	682	686	691	
993	695	699	704	708	712	717	721	726	730	734	
994	739	743	747	752	756	760	765	769	774	778	
995	782	787	791	795	800	804	808	813	817	822	
996	826	830	835	839	843	848	852	856	861	865	
997	870	874	878	883	887	891	896	900	904	909	
998	913	917	922	926	930	935	939	944	948	952	
999	957	961	965	970	974	978	983	987	991	996	
1000	00 000	004	009	013	017	022	026	030	035	039	
N.	L. 0	1	2	3	4	5	6	7	8	9	P. P.

Table 14-2. Cologarithms of Numbers

No.	0	1	2	3	4	5	6	7	8	9
100	.00 000	*957	*913	*870	*827	*783	*740	*697	*654	*611
1	.99 568	525	482	439	396	353	311	268	225	183
2	140	097	055	012	*970	*928	*885	*843	*801	*758
3	.98 716	674	632	590	548	506	464	422	380	338
4	297	255	213	172	130	088	047	005	*964	*922
5	.97 881	840	798	757	716	675	634	593	551	510
6	469	428	388	347	306	265	224	184	143	102
7	062	021	*981	*940	*900	*859	*819	*778	*738	*698
8	.96 658	617	577	537	497	457	417	377	337	297
9	257	218	178	138	098	059	019	*979	*940	*900
110	.95 861	821	782	742	703	664	624	585	546	507
1	468	429	390	350	311	273	234	195	156	117
2	078	039	001	*962	*923	*885	*846	*808	*769	*731
3	.94 692	654	615	577	539	500	462	424	386	348
4	310	271	233	195	157	119	082	044	006	*968
5	.93 930	892	855	817	779	742	704	667	629	592
6	554	517	479	442	405	367	330	293	256	219
7	181	144	107	070	033	*996	*959	*922	*885	*849
8	.92 812	775	738	702	665	628	592	555	518	482
9	445	409	372	336	300	263	227	191	154	118
120	082	046	010	*973	*937	*901	*865	*829	*793	*757
1	.91 721	686	650	614	578	542	507	471	435	400
2	364	328	293	257	222	186	151	116	080	045
3	009	*974	*939	*904	*868	*833	*798	*763	*728	*693
4	.90 658	623	588	553	518	483	448	413	379	344
5	309	274	240	205	170	136	101	066	032	*997
6	.89 963	928	894	860	825	791	757	722	688	654
7	620	585	551	517	483	449	415	381	347	313
8	279	245	211	177	143	110	076	042	008	*975
9	.88 941	907	874	840	807	773	739	706	673	639
130	606	572	539	506	472	439	406	372	339	306
1	273	240	207	174	140	107	074	041	008	*976
2	.87 943	910	877	844	811	778	746	713	680	648
3	615	582	550	517	484	452	419	387	354	322
4	290	257	225	192	160	128	095	063	031	*999
5	.86 967	934	902	870	838	806	774	742	710	678
6	646	614	582	550	519	487	455	423	391	360
7	328	296	265	233	201	170	138	107	075	044
8	012	*981	*949	*918	*886	*855	*824	*792	*761	*730
9	.85 699	667	636	605	574	543	511	480	449	418
140	387	356	325	294	263	232	201	171	140	109
1	078	047	017	*986	*955	*924	*894	*863	*832	*802
2	.84 771	741	710	680	649	619	588	558	527	497
3	466	436	406	375	345	315	285	254	224	194
4	164	134	103	073	043	013	*983	*953	*923	*893
5	.83 863	833	803	773	744	714	684	654	624	594
6	565	535	505	476	446	416	387	357	327	298
7	268	239	209	180	150	121	091	062	033	003
8	.82 974	944	915	886	857	827	798	769	740	711
9	681	652	623	594	565	536	507	478	449	420
150	391	362	333	304	275	246	218	189	160	131

P.P. (Proportional Parts)

Nos. 100–109:

	44	43	42
1	4	4	4
2	9	9	8
3	13	13	13
4	18	17	17
5	22	22	21
6	26	26	25
7	31	30	29
8	35	34	34
9	40	39	38

Nos. 110–119:

	41	40	39
1	4	4	4
2	8	8	8
3	12	12	12
4	16	16	16
5	21	20	20
6	25	24	23
7	29	28	27
8	33	32	31
9	37	36	35

Nos. 120–129:

	38	37	36
1	4	4	4
2	8	7	7
3	11	11	11
4	15	15	14
5	19	19	18
6	23	22	22
7	27	26	25
8	30	30	29
9	34	33	32

Nos. 130–139:

	35	34	33
1	4	3	3
2	7	7	7
3	11	10	10
4	14	14	13
5	18	17	17
6	21	20	20
7	25	24	23
8	28	27	26
9	32	31	30

Nos. 140–149:

	32	31	30
1	3	3	3
2	6	6	6
3	10	9	9
4	13	12	12
5	16	16	15
6	19	19	18
7	22	22	21
8	26	25	24
9	29	28	27

Table 14-2. Cologarithms of Numbers (*Continued*)

No.	0	1	2	3	4	5	6	7	8	9	P.P.
150	.82 391	362	333	304	275	246	218	189	160	131	**29 28**
1	102	074	045	016	*987	*959	*930	*901	*873	*844	1 3 3
2	.81 816	787	759	730	702	673	645	616	588	559	2 6 6
3	531	502	474	446	417	389	361	333	304	276	3 9 8
4	248	220	192	163	135	107	079	051	023	*995	4 12 11
5	.80 967	939	911	883	855	827	799	771	743	715	5 15 14
6	688	660	632	604	576	549	521	493	465	438	6 17 17
7	410	382	355	327	300	272	244	217	189	162	7 20 20
8	134	107	079	052	024	*997	*970	*942	*915	*888	8 23 22
9	.79 860	833	806	778	751	724	697	670	642	615	9 26 25
160	588	561	534	507	480	452	425	398	371	344	**27 26**
1	317	290	263	237	210	183	156	129	102	075	1 3 3
2	048	022	*995	*968	*941	*915	*888	*861	*835	*808	2 5 5
3	.78 781	755	728	701	675	648	622	595	569	542	3 8 8
4	516	489	463	436	410	383	357	331	304	278	4 11 10
5	252	225	199	173	146	120	094	068	042	015	5 14 13
6	.77 989	963	937	911	885	859	833	806	780	754	6 16 16
7	728	702	676	650	624	599	573	547	521	495	7 19 18
8	469	443	417	392	366	340	314	288	263	237	8 22 21
9	211	186	160	134	109	083	057	032	006	*981	9 24 23
170	.76 955	930	904	879	853	828	802	777	751	726	**25**
1	700	675	650	624	599	574	548	523	498	472	1 3
2	447	422	397	371	346	321	296	271	246	221	2 5
3	195	170	145	120	095	070	045	020	*995	*970	3 8
4	.75 945	920	895	870	845	820	796	771	746	721	4 10
5	696	671	647	622	597	572	548	523	498	473	5 13
6	449	424	399	375	350	326	301	276	252	227	6 15
7	203	178	154	129	105	080	056	031	007	*982	7 18
8	.74 958	934	909	885	861	836	812	788	763	739	8 20
9	715	690	666	642	618	594	569	545	521	497	9 23
180	473	449	425	400	376	352	328	304	280	256	**24 23**
1	232	208	184	160	136	112	088	065	041	017	1 2 2
2	.73 993	969	945	921	898	874	850	826	802	779	2 5 5
3	755	731	707	684	660	636	613	589	565	542	3 7 7
4	518	495	471	447	424	400	377	353	330	306	4 10 9
5	283	259	236	212	189	166	142	119	095	072	5 12 12
6	049	025	002	*979	*955	*932	*909	*886	*862	*839	6 14 14
7	.72 816	793	769	746	723	700	677	654	630	607	7 17 16
8	584	561	538	515	492	469	446	423	400	377	8 19 18
9	354	331	308	285	262	239	216	193	170	148	9 22 21
190	125	102	079	056	033	011	*988	*965	*942	*919	**22 21**
1	.71 897	874	851	829	806	783	760	738	715	693	1 2 2
2	670	647	625	602	579	557	534	512	489	467	2 4 4
3	444	422	399	377	354	332	309	287	265	242	3 7 6
4	220	197	175	153	130	108	086	063	041	019	4 9 8
5	.70 997	974	952	930	908	885	863	841	819	797	5 11 11
6	774	752	730	708	686	664	642	620	597	575	6 13 13
7	553	531	509	487	465	443	421	399	377	355	7 15 15
8	333	312	290	268	246	224	202	180	158	137	8 18 17
9	115	093	071	049	027	006	*984	*962	*940	*919	9 20 19
200	.69 897	875	854	832	810	789	767	745	724	702	

Table 14-2. Cologarithms of Numbers (*Continued*)

No.	0	1	2	3	4	5	6	7	8	9
200	.69 897	875	854	832	810	789	767	745	724	702
1	680	659	637	616	594	572	551	529	508	486
2	465	443	422	400	379	357	336	315	293	272
3	250	229	208	186	165	144	122	101	080	058
4	037	016	*994	*973	*952	*931	*909	*888	*867	*846
5	.68 825	803	782	761	740	719	698	677	655	634
6	613	592	571	550	529	508	487	466	445	424
7	403	382	361	340	319	298	277	256	235	215
8	194	173	152	131	110	089	069	048	027	006
9	.67 985	965	944	923	902	882	861	840	819	799
210	778	757	737	716	695	675	654	634	613	592
1	572	551	531	510	490	469	448	428	407	387
2	366	346	325	305	285	264	244	223	203	182
3	162	142	121	101	081	060	040	020	*999	*979
4	.66 959	938	918	898	878	857	837	817	797	776
5	756	736	716	696	675	655	635	615	595	575
6	555	535	514	494	474	454	434	414	394	374
7	354	334	314	294	274	254	234	214	194	174
8	154	134	115	095	075	055	035	015	*995	*975
9	.65 956	936	916	896	876	857	837	817	797	777
220	758	738	718	699	679	659	639	620	600	580
1	561	541	521	502	482	463	443	423	404	384
2	365	345	326	306	287	267	247	228	208	189
3	170	150	131	111	092	072	053	033	014	*995
4	.64 975	956	936	917	898	878	859	840	820	801
5	782	762	743	724	705	685	666	647	628	608
6	589	570	551	532	512	493	474	455	436	417
7	397	378	359	340	321	302	283	264	245	226
8	207	187	168	149	130	111	092	073	054	035
9	016	*997	*979	*960	*941	*922	*903	*884	*865	*846
230	.63 827	808	789	771	752	733	714	695	676	658
1	639	620	601	582	564	545	526	507	489	470
2	451	432	414	395	376	358	339	320	302	283
3	264	246	227	209	190	171	153	134	116	097
4	078	060	041	023	004	*986	*967	*949	*930	*912
5	.62 893	875	856	838	819	801	782	764	746	727
6	709	690	672	654	635	617	599	580	562	543
7	525	507	489	470	452	434	415	397	379	361
8	342	324	306	288	269	251	233	215	197	178
9	160	142	124	106	088	069	051	033	015	*997
240	.61 979	961	943	925	907	888	870	852	834	816
1	798	780	762	744	726	708	690	672	654	636
2	618	601	583	565	547	529	511	493	475	457
3	439	422	404	386	368	350	332	314	297	279
4	261	243	225	208	190	172	154	137	119	101
5	083	066	048	030	013	*995	*977	*959	*942	*924
6	.60 906	889	871	854	836	818	801	783	765	748
7	730	713	695	678	660	642	625	607	590	572
8	555	537	520	502	485	467	450	432	415	398
9	380	363	345	328	310	293	276	258	241	223
250	206	189	171	154	137	119	102	085	067	050

P.P.

	22	21
1	2	2
2	4	4
3	7	6
4	9	8
5	11	11
6	13	13
7	15	15
8	18	17
9	20	19

	20
1	2
2	4
3	6
4	8
5	10
6	12
7	14
8	16
9	18

	19
1	2
2	4
3	6
4	8
5	10
6	11
7	13
8	15
9	17

	18
1	2
2	4
3	5
4	7
5	9
6	11
7	13
8	14
9	16

	17
1	2
2	3
3	5
4	7
5	9
6	10
7	12
8	14
9	15

Table 14-2. Cologarithms of Numbers (*Continued*)

No.	0	1	2	3	4	5	6	7	8	9	P.P.	
250	.60 206	189	171	154	137	119	102	085	067	050		**18**
1	033	015	*998	*981	*963	*946	*929	*912	*894	*877	1	2
2	.59 860	843	825	808	791	774	757	739	722	705	2	4
3	688	671	654	636	619	602	585	568	551	534	3	5
4	517	500	482	465	448	431	414	397	380	363	4	7
5	346	329	312	295	278	261	244	227	210	193	5	9
6	176	159	142	125	108	091	074	057	040	024	6	11
7	007	*990	*973	*956	*939	*922	*905	*889	*872	*855	7	13
8	.58 838	821	804	788	771	754	737	720	704	687	8	14
9	670	653	637	620	603	586	570	553	536	519	9	16
260	503	486	469	453	436	419	403	386	369	353		**17**
1	336	319	303	286	269	253	236	220	203	186	1	2
2	170	153	137	120	104	087	071	054	037	021	2	3
3	004	*988	*971	*955	*938	*922	*905	*889	*873	*856	3	5
4	.57 840	823	807	790	774	757	741	725	708	692	4	7
5	675	659	643	626	610	594	577	561	545	528	5	9
6	512	496	479	463	447	430	414	398	381	365	6	10
7	349	333	316	300	284	268	251	235	219	203	7	12
8	187	170	154	138	122	106	089	073	057	041	8	14
9	025	009	*992	*976	*960	*944	*928	*912	*896	*880	9	15
270	.56 864	848	831	815	799	783	767	751	735	719		**16**
1	703	687	671	655	639	623	607	591	575	559	2	2
2	543	527	511	495	479	463	447	431	416	400	2	3
3	384	368	352	336	320	304	288	273	257	241	3	5
4	225	209	193	177	162	146	130	114	098	083	4	6
5	067	051	035	019	004	988	*972	*956	*941	*925	5	8
6	.55 909	893	878	862	846	830	815	799	783	768	6	10
7	752	736	721	705	689	674	658	642	627	611	7	11
8	596	580	564	549	533	517	502	486	471	455	8	13
9	440	424	408	393	377	362	346	331	315	300	9	14
280	284	269	253	238	222	207	191	176	160	145		**15**
1	129	114	098	083	068	052	037	021	006	*990	1	2
2	.54 975	960	944	929	914	898	883	867	852	837	2	3
3	821	806	791	775	760	745	729	714	699	683	3	5
4	668	653	638	622	607	592	577	561	546	531	4	6
5	516	500	485	470	455	439	424	409	394	379	5	8
6	363	348	333	318	303	288	272	257	242	227	6	9
7	212	197	182	166	151	136	121	106	091	076	7	11
8	061	046	031	016	000	*985	*970	*955	*940	*925	8	12
9	.53 910	895	880	865	850	835	820	805	790	775	9	14
290	760	745	730	715	700	685	670	655	641	626		**14**
1	611	596	581	566	551	536	521	506	491	477	1	1
2	462	447	432	417	402	387	373	358	343	328	2	3
3	313	298	284	269	254	239	224	210	195	180	3	4
4	165	150	136	121	106	091	077	062	047	033	4	6
5	018	003	*988	*974	*959	*944	*930	*915	*900	*886	5	7
6	.52 871	856	841	827	812	798	783	768	754	739	6	8
7	724	710	695	681	666	651	637	622	608	593	7	10
8	578	564	549	535	520	506	491	476	462	447	8	11
9	433	418	404	389	375	360	346	331	317	302	9	13
300	288	273	259	244	230	216	201	187	172	158		

Table 14-2. Cologarithms of Numbers (*Continued*)

No.	0	1	2	3	4	5	6	7	8	9	P.P.
300	.52 288	273	259	244	230	216	201	187	172	158	**15**
1	143	129	115	100	086	071	057	042	028	014	1 2
2	.51 999	985	971	956	942	927	913	899	884	870	2 3
3	856	841	827	813	798	784	770	756	741	727	3 5
4	713	698	684	670	656	641	627	613	599	584	4 6
5	570	556	542	527	513	499	485	470	456	442	5 8
6	428	414	399	385	371	357	343	329	314	300	6 9
7	286	272	258	244	230	215	201	187	173	159	7 11
8	145	131	117	103	089	074	060	046	032	018	8 12
9	004	*990	*976	*962	*948	*934	*920	*906	*892	*878	9 14
310	.50 864	850	836	822	808	794	780	766	752	738	**14**
1	724	710	696	682	668	654	640	626	612	598	1 1
2	585	571	557	543	529	515	501	487	473	459	2 3
3	446	432	418	404	390	376	362	349	335	321	3 4
4	307	293	279	266	252	238	224	210	197	183	4 6
5	169	155	141	128	114	100	086	073	059	045	5 7
6	031	018	004	*990	*976	*963	*949	*935	*921	*908	6 8
7	.49 894	880	867	853	839	826	812	798	785	771	7 10
8	757	744	730	716	703	689	675	662	648	635	8 11
9	621	607	594	580	567	553	539	526	512	499	9 13
320	485	471	458	444	431	417	404	390	377	363	**13**
1	349	336	322	309	295	282	268	255	241	228	1 1
2	214	201	187	174	160	147	134	120	107	093	2 3
3	080	066	053	039	026	013	*999	*986	*972	*959	3 4
4	.48 945	932	919	905	892	879	865	852	838	825	4 5
5	812	798	785	772	758	745	732	718	705	692	5 7
6	678	665	652	638	625	612	598	585	572	559	6 8
7	545	532	519	505	492	479	466	452	439	426	7 9
8	413	399	386	373	360	346	333	320	307	294	8 10
9	280	267	254	241	228	214	201	188	175	162	9 12
330	149	135	122	109	096	083	070	057	043	030	**12**
1	017	004	*991	*978	*965	*952	*939	*925	*912	*899	1 1
2	.47 886	873	860	847	834	821	808	795	782	769	2 2
3	756	743	730	716	703	690	677	664	651	638	3 4
4	625	612	599	586	573	560	547	534	521	508	4 5
5	496	483	470	457	444	431	418	405	392	379	5 6
6	366	353	340	327	314	301	289	276	263	250	6 7
7	237	224	211	198	185	173	160	147	134	121	7 8
8	108	095	083	070	057	044	031	018	006	*993	8 10
9	.46 980	967	954	942	929	916	903	890	878	865	9 11
340	852	839	827	814	801	788	776	763	750	737	
1	725	712	699	686	674	661	648	636	623	610	
2	597	585	572	559	547	534	521	509	496	483	
3	471	458	445	433	420	407	395	382	369	357	
4	344	332	319	306	294	231	268	256	243	231	
5	218	206	193	180	168	155	143	130	118	105	
6	092	080	067	055	042	030	017	005	*992	*980	
7	.45 967	955	942	930	917	905	892	880	867	855	
8	842	830	817	805	792	780	767	755	742	730	
9	717	705	693	680	668	655	643	630	618	606	
350	593	581	568	556	544	531	519	506	494	482	

Table 14-2. Cologarithms of Numbers (*Continued*)

No.	0	1	2	3	4	5	6	7	8	9	P.P.	
350	.45 593	581	568	556	544	531	519	506	494	482		**13**
1	469	457	445	432	420	407	395	383	370	358	1	1
2	346	333	321	309	296	284	272	259	247	235	2	3
3	223	210	198	186	173	161	149	136	124	112	3	4
4	100	087	075	063	051	038	026	014	002	*989	4	5
5	.44 977	965	953	940	928	916	904	892	879	867	5	7
6	855	843	831	818	806	794	782	770	758	745	6	8
7	733	721	709	697	685	672	660	648	636	624	7	9
8	612	600	587	575	563	551	539	527	515	503	8	10
9	491	478	466	454	442	430	418	406	394	382	9	12
360	370	358	346	334	322	309	297	285	273	261		**12**
1	249	237	225	213	201	189	177	165	153	141	1	1
2	129	117	105	093	081	069	057	045	033	021	2	2
3	009	*997	*985	*973	*962	*950	*938	*926	*914	*902	3	4
4	.43 890	878	866	854	842	830	818	806	795	783	4	5
5	771	759	747	735	723	711	699	688	676	664	5	6
6	652	640	628	616	604	593	581	569	557	545	6	7
7	533	522	510	498	486	474	462	451	439	427	7	8
8	415	403	392	380	368	356	344	333	321	309	8	10
9	297	286	274	262	250	239	227	215	203	192	9	11
370	180	168	156	145	133	121	109	098	086	*074		**11**
1	063	051	039	028	016	004	*992	*981	*969	957	1	1
2	.42 946	934	922	911	899	887	876	864	852	841	2	2
3	829	817	806	794	783	771	759	748	736	724	3	3
4	713	701	690	678	666	655	643	632	620	608	4	4
5	597	585	574	562	551	539	527	516	504	493	5	6
6	481	470	458	447	435	424	412	400	389	377	6	7
7	366	354	343	331	320	308	297	285	274	262	7	8
8	251	239	228	216	205	193	182	170	159	148	8	9
9	136	125	113	102	090	079	067	056	045	033	9	10
380	022	010	*999	*987	*976	*965	*953	*942	*930	*919		**10**
1	.41 908	896	885	873	862	851	839	828	816	805	1	1
2	794	782	771	760	748	737	726	714	703	691	2	2
3	680	669	657	646	635	623	612	601	590	578	3	3
4	567	556	544	533	522	510	499	488	476	465	4	4
5	454	443	431	420	409	398	386	375	364	353	5	5
6	341	330	319	308	296	285	274	263	251	240	6	6
7	229	218	206	195	184	173	162	150	139	128	7	7
8	117	106	094	083	072	061	050	039	027	016	8	8
9	005	*994	*983	*972	*960	*949	*938	*927	*916	*905	9	9
390	.40 894	882	871	860	849	838	827	816	805	793		
1	782	771	760	749	738	727	716	705	694	682		
2	671	660	649	638	627	616	605	594	583	572		
3	561	550	539	528	517	506	494	483	472	461		
4	450	439	428	417	406	395	384	373	362	351		
5	340	329	318	307	296	285	274	263	252	241		
6	230	220	209	198	187	176	165	154	143	132		
7	121	110	099	088	077	066	055	044	034	*023		
8	012	001	*990	*979	*968	*957	*946	*935	*924	914		
9	.39 903	892	881	870	859	848	837	827	816	805		
400	794	783	772	761	751	740	729	718	707	696		

Table 14-2. Cologarithms of Numbers (*Continued*)

No.	0	1	2	3	4	5	6	7	8	9	P.P.	
400	.39 794	783	772	761	751	740	729	718	707	696		
1	686	675	664	653	642	631	621	610	599	588		
2	577	567	556	545	534	523	513	502	491	480		
3	469	459	448	437	426	416	405	394	383	373		
4	362	351	340	330	319	308	297	287	276	265		
5	254	244	233	222	212	201	190	179	169	158		**11**
6	147	137	126	115	105	094	083	073	062	051	1	1
7	041	030	019	009	*998	*987	*977	*966	*955	*945	2	2
8	.38 934	923	913	902	891	881	870	860	849	838	3	3
9	828	817	806	796	785	775	764	753	743	732	4	4
410	722	711	700	690	679	669	658	648	637	626	5	6
1	616	605	595	584	574	563	552	542	531	521	6	7
2	510	500	489	479	468	458	447	437	426	416	7	8
3	405	394	384	373	363	352	342	331	321	310	8	9
4	300	289	279	269	258	248	237	227	216	206	9	10
5	195	185	174	164	153	143	132	122	112	101		
6	091	080	070	059	049	038	028	018	007	*997		
7	.37 986	976	966	955	945	934	924	914	903	893		
8	882	872	862	851	841	830	820	810	799	789		
9	779	768	758	748	737	727	716	706	696	685		
420	675	665	654	644	634	623	613	603	592	582		**10**
1	572	561	551	541	531	520	510	500	489	479	1	1
2	469	458	448	438	428	417	407	397	387	376	2	2
3	366	356	345	335	325	315	304	294	284	274	3	3
4	263	253	243	233	222	212	202	192	182	171	4	4
5	161	151	141	130	120	110	100	090	079	069	5	5
6	059	049	039	028	018	008	*998	*988	*978	*967	6	6
7	.36 957	947	937	927	917	906	896	886	876	866	7	7
8	856	845	835	825	815	805	795	785	775	764	8	8
9	754	744	734	724	714	704	694	683	673	663	9	9
430	653	643	633	623	613	603	593	583	572	562		
1	552	542	532	522	512	502	492	482	472	462		
2	452	442	432	421	411	401	391	381	371	361		
3	351	341	331	321	311	301	291	281	271	261		
4	251	241	231	221	211	201	191	181	171	161		
5	151	141	131	121	111	101	091	081	071	061		**9**
6	051	041	031	021	012	002	*992	*982	*972	*962	1	1
7	.35 952	942	932	922	912	902	892	882	872	863	2	2
8	853	843	833	823	813	803	793	783	773	763	3	3
9	754	744	734	724	714	704	694	684	674	665	4	4
440	655	645	635	625	615	605	596	586	576	566	5	5
1	556	546	536	527	517	507	497	487	477	468	6	5
2	458	448	438	428	418	409	399	389	379	369	7	6
3	360	350	340	330	320	311	301	291	281	271	8	7
4	262	252	242	232	223	213	203	193	184	174	9	8
5	164	154	144	135	125	115	105	096	086	076		
6	067	057	047	037	028	018	008	*998	*989	*979		
7	.34 969	960	950	940	930	921	911	901	892	882		
8	872	863	853	843	833	824	814	804	795	785		
9	775	766	756	746	737	727	717	708	698	688		
450	679	669	659	650	640	631	621	611	602	592		

Table 14-2. Cologarithms of Numbers (*Continued*)

No.	0	1	2	3	4	5	6	7	8	9	P.P.	
450	.34 679	669	659	650	640	631	621	611	602	592		
1	582	573	563	553	544	534	525	515	505	496		
2	486	477	467	457	448	438	429	419	409	400		
3	390	381	371	361	352	342	333	323	314	304		
4	294	285	275	266	256	247	237	228	218	208		
5	199	189	180	170	161	151	142	132	123	113		10
6	104	094	084	075	065	056	046	037	027	018	1	1
7	008	*999	*989	*980	*970	*961	*951	*942	*932	*923	2	2
8	.33 913	904	894	885	876	866	857	847	838	828	3	3
9	819	809	800	790	781	771	762	753	743	734	4	4
460	724	715	705	696	686	677	668	658	649	639	5	5
1	630	620	611	602	592	583	573	564	555	545	6	6
2	536	526	517	508	498	489	479	470	461	451	7	7
3	442	433	423	414	404	395	386	376	367	358	8	8
4	348	339	329	320	311	301	292	283	273	264	9	9
5	255	245	236	227	217	208	199	189	180	171		
6	161	152	143	133	124	115	106	096	087	078		
7	068	059	050	040	031	022	013	003	*994	*985		
8	.32 975	966	957	948	938	929	920	911	901	892		
9	883	873	864	855	846	836	827	818	809	799		
470	790	781	772	763	753	744	735	726	716	707		9
1	698	689	679	670	661	652	643	633	624	615	1	1
2	606	597	587	578	569	560	551	541	532	523	2	2
3	514	505	496	486	477	468	459	450	440	431	3	3
4	422	413	404	395	386	376	367	358	349	340	4	4
5	331	321	312	303	294	285	276	267	258	248	5	5
6	239	230	221	212	203	194	185	175	166	157	6	6
7	148	139	130	121	112	103	094	084	075	066	7	7
8	057	048	039	030	021	012	003	*994	*985	*976	8	8
9	.31 966	957	948	939	930	921	912	903	894	885		
480	876	867	858	849	840	831	822	813	804	795		
1	785	776	767	758	749	740	731	722	713	704		
2	695	686	677	668	659	650	641	632	623	614		
3	605	596	587	578	569	560	551	542	533	524		
4	515	506	498	489	480	471	462	453	444	435		
5	426	417	408	399	390	381	372	363	354	345		8
6	336	327	319	310	301	292	283	274	265	256	1	1
7	247	238	229	220	211	203	194	185	176	167	2	2
8	158	149	140	131	122	114	105	096	087	078	3	3
9	069	060	051	042	034	025	016	007	*998	*989	4	4
490	.30 980	972	963	954	945	936	927	918	910	901	5	4
1	892	883	874	865	856	848	839	830	821	812	6	5
2	803	795	786	777	768	759	751	742	733	724	7	6
3	715	706	698	689	680	671	662	654	645	636	8	6
4	627	619	610	601	592	583	575	566	557	548	9	7
5	539	531	522	513	504	496	487	478	469	461		
6	452	443	434	426	417	408	399	391	382	373		
7	364	356	347	338	329	321	312	303	295	286		
8	277	268	260	251	242	233	225	216	207	199		
9	190	181	173	164	155	146	138	129	120	112		
500	103	094	086	077	068	060	051	042	034	025		

Table 14-2. Cologarithms of Numbers (Continued)

No.	0	1	2	3	4	5	6	7	8	9	P.P.	
500	.30 103	094	086	077	068	060	051	042	034	025		
1	016	008	*999	*990	*982	*973	*964	*956	*947	*938		
2	.29 930	921	912	904	895	886	878	869	860	852		
3	843	835	826	817	809	800	791	783	774	766		
4	757	748	740	731	722	714	705	697	688	679		
5	671	662	654	645	636	628	619	611	602	594		9
6	585	576	568	559	551	542	533	525	516	508	1	1
7	499	491	482	474	465	456	448	439	431	422	2	2
8	414	405	397	388	379	371	362	354	345	337	3	3
9	328	320	311	303	294	286	277	269	260	251	4	4
510	243	234	226	217	209	200	192	183	175	166	5	5
1	158	149	141	132	124	115	107	098	090	081	6	5
2	073	065	056	048	039	031	022	014	005	*997	7	6
3	.28 988	980	971	963	954	946	937	929	921	912	8	7
4	904	895	887	878	870	861	853	845	836	828	9	8
5	819	811	802	794	786	777	769	760	752	743		
6	735	727	718	710	701	693	685	676	668	659		
7	651	643	634	626	617	609	601	592	584	575		
8	567	559	550	542	534	525	517	508	500	492		
9	483	475	467	458	450	441	433	425	416	408		
520	400	391	383	375	366	358	350	341	333	325		8
1	316	308	300	291	283	275	266	258	250	241	1	1
2	233	225	216	208	200	191	183	175	166	158	2	2
3	150	142	133	125	117	108	100	092	083	075	3	2
4	067	059	050	042	034	025	017	009	001	*992	4	3
5	.27 984	976	968	959	951	943	934	926	918	910	5	4
6	901	893	885	877	868	860	852	844	835	827	6	5
7	819	811	802	794	786	778	770	761	753	745	7	6
8	737	728	720	712	704	696	687	679	671	663	8	6
9	654	646	638	630	622	613	605	597	589	581	9	7
530	572	564	556	548	540	531	523	515	507	499		
1	491	482	474	466	458	450	442	433	425	417		
2	409	401	393	384	376	368	360	352	344	335		
3	327	319	311	303	295	287	278	270	262	254		
4	246	238	230	221	213	205	197	189	181	173		
5	165	157	148	140	132	124	116	108	100	092		7
6	084	075	067	059	051	043	035	027	019	011	1	1
7	003	*994	*986	*978	*970	*962	*954	*946	*938	*930	2	1
8	.26 922	914	906	898	889	881	873	865	857	849	3	2
9	841	833	825	817	809	801	793	785	777	769	4	3
540	761	753	745	737	728	720	712	704	696	688	5	4
1	680	672	664	656	648	640	632	624	616	608	6	4
2	600	592	584	576	568	560	552	544	536	528	7	5
3	520	512	504	496	488	480	472	464	456	448	8	6
4	440	432	424	416	408	400	392	384	376	368	9	6
5	360	352	344	336	328	321	313	305	297	289		
6	281	273	265	257	249	241	233	225	217	209		
7	201	193	185	177	170	162	154	146	138	130		
8	122	114	106	098	090	082	074	067	059	051		
9	043	035	027	019	011	003	*995	*987	*980	*972		
550	.25 964	956	948	940	932	924	916	908	901	893		

Table 14-2. Cologarithms of Numbers (*Continued*)

No.	0	1	2	3	4	5	6	7	8	9	P.P.
550	.25 964	956	948	940	932	924	916	908	901	893	
1	885	877	869	861	853	845	838	830	822	814	
2	806	798	790	782	775	767	759	751	743	735	
3	727	720	712	704	696	688	680	673	665	657	
4	649	641	633	626	618	610	602	594	586	579	
5	571	563	555	547	539	532	524	516	508	500	
6	493	485	477	469	461	453	446	438	430	422	
7	414	407	399	391	383	376	368	360	352	344	
8	337	329	321	313	305	298	290	282	274	267	
9	259	251	243	236	228	220	212	204	197	189	**8**
560	181	173	166	158	150	142	135	127	119	111	1 1
1	104	096	088	080	073	065	057	050	042	034	2 2
2	026	019	011	003	*995	*988	*980	*972	*965	*957	3 2
3	.24 949	941	934	926	918	911	903	895	887	880	4 3
4	872	864	857	849	841	834	826	818	811	803	5 4
5	795	787	780	772	764	757	749	741	734	726	6 5
6	718	711	703	695	688	680	672	665	657	649	7 6
7	642	634	626	619	611	603	596	588	580	573	8 6
8	565	558	550	542	535	527	519	512	504	496	9 7
9	489	481	474	466	458	451	443	435	428	420	
570	413	405	397	390	382	374	367	359	352	344	
1	336	329	321	314	306	298	291	283	276	268	
2	260	253	245	238	230	222	215	207	200	192	
3	185	177	169	162	154	147	139	132	124	116	
4	109	101	094	086	079	071	063	056	048	041	
5	033	026	018	011	003	*995	*988	*980	*973	*965	
6	.23 958	950	943	935	928	920	913	905	897	890	
7	882	875	867	860	852	845	837	830	822	815	
8	807	800	792	785	777	770	762	755	747	740	
9	732	725	717	710	702	695	687	680	672	665	**7**
580	657	650	642	635	627	620	612	605	597	590	1 1
1	582	575	567	560	552	545	538	530	523	515	2 1
2	508	500	493	485	478	470	463	455	448	441	3 2
3	433	426	418	411	403	396	388	381	374	366	4 3
4	359	351	344	336	329	322	314	307	299	292	5 4
5	284	277	270	262	255	247	240	232	225	218	6 4
6	210	203	195	188	181	173	166	158	151	144	7 5
7	136	129	121	114	107	099	092	084	077	070	8 6
8	062	055	047	040	033	025	018	011	003	*996	9 6
9	.22 988	981	974	966	959	952	944	937	930	922	
590	915	907	900	893	885	878	871	863	856	849	
1	841	834	827	819	812	805	797	790	783	775	
2	768	760	753	746	738	731	724	717	709	702	
3	695	687	680	673	665	658	651	643	636	629	
4	621	614	607	599	592	585	578	570	563	556	
5	548	541	534	526	519	512	505	497	490	483	
6	475	468	461	454	446	439	432	424	417	410	
7	403	395	388	381	373	366	359	352	344	337	
8	330	323	315	308	301	294	286	279	272	265	
9	257	250	243	236	228	221	214	207	199	192	
600	185	178	170	163	156	149	141	134	127	120	

Table 14-2. Cologarithms of Numbers (*Continued*)

No.	0	1	2	3	4	5	6	7	8	9	P.P.
600	.22 185	178	170	163	156	149	141	134	127	120	
1	113	105	098	091	084	076	069	062	055	048	
2	040	033	026	019	012	004	*997	*990	*983	*975	
3	.21 968	961	954	947	939	932	925	918	911	903	
4	896	889	882	875	868	860	853	846	839	832	
5	824	817	810	803	796	789	781	774	767	760	**8**
6	753	746	738	731	724	717	710	703	695	688	1 1
7	681	674	667	660	653	645	638	631	624	617	2 2
8	610	602	595	588	581	574	567	560	553	545	3 2
9	538	531	524	517	510	503	496	488	481	474	4 3
610	467	460	453	446	439	431	424	417	410	403	5 4
1	396	389	382	375	367	360	353	346	339	332	6 5
2	325	318	311	304	296	289	282	275	268	261	7 6
3	254	247	240	233	226	219	211	204	197	190	8 6
4	183	176	169	162	155	148	141	134	127	120	9 7
5	112	105	098	091	084	077	070	063	056	049	
6	042	035	028	021	014	007	000	*993	*986	*979	
7	.20 971	964	957	950	943	936	929	922	915	908	
8	901	894	887	880	873	866	859	852	845	838	
9	831	824	817	810	803	796	789	782	775	768	
620	761	754	747	740	733	726	719	712	705	698	**7**
1	691	684	677	670	663	656	649	642	635	628	1 1
2	621	614	607	600	593	586	579	572	565	558	2 1
3	551	544	537	530	523	516	509	502	495	489	3 2
4	482	475	468	461	454	447	440	433	426	419	4 3
5	412	405	398	391	384	377	370	363	356	350	5 4
6	343	336	329	322	315	308	301	294	287	280	6 5
7	273	266	259	252	246	239	232	225	218	211	7 5
8	204	197	190	183	176	169	163	156	149	142	8 6
9	135	128	121	114	107	100	094	087	080	073	9 6
630	066	059	052	045	038	031	025	018	011	004	
1	.19 997	990	983	976	970	963	956	949	942	935	
2	928	921	915	908	901	894	887	880	873	866	
3	860	853	846	839	832	825	818	812	805	798	
4	791	784	777	771	764	757	750	743	736	729	
5	723	716	709	702	695	688	682	675	668	661	**6**
6	654	647	641	634	627	620	613	607	600	593	1 1
7	586	579	572	566	559	552	545	538	532	525	2 1
8	518	511	504	498	491	484	477	470	464	457	3 2
9	450	443	436	430	423	416	409	402	396	389	4 2
640	382	375	368	362	355	348	341	335	328	321	5 3
1	314	307	301	294	287	280	274	267	260	253	6 4
2	246	240	233	226	219	213	206	199	192	186	7 4
3	179	172	165	159	152	145	138	132	125	118	8 5
4	111	105	098	091	084	078	071	064	057	051	9 5
5	044	037	031	024	017	010	004	*997	*990	*983	
6	.18 977	970	963	957	950	943	936	930	923	916	
7	910	903	896	889	883	876	869	863	856	849	
8	842	836	829	822	816	809	802	796	789	782	
9	776	769	762	755	749	742	735	729	722	715	
650	709	702	695	689	682	675	669	662	655	649	

Table 14-2. Cologarithms of Numbers (*Continued*)

No.	0	1	2	3	4	5	6	7	8	9
650	.18 709	702	695	689	682	675	669	662	655	649
1	642	635	629	622	615	609	602	595	589	582
2	575	569	562	555	549	542	535	529	522	515
3	509	502	495	489	482	475	469	462	456	449
4	442	436	429	422	416	409	402	396	389	383
5	376	369	363	356	349	343	336	329	323	316
6	310	303	296	290	283	277	270	263	257	250
7	243	237	230	224	217	210	204	197	191	184
8	177	171	134	158	151	144	138	131	125	118
9	111	105	098	092	085	079	072	065	059	052
660	046	039	032	026	019	013	006	000	*993	*986
1	.17 980	973	967	960	954	947	940	934	927	921
2	914	908	901	895	888	881	875	868	862	855
3	849	842	836	829	822	816	809	803	796	790
4	783	777	770	764	757	751	744	737	731	724
5	718	711	705	698	692	685	679	672	666	659
6	653	646	640	633	627	620	613	607	600	594
7	587	581	574	568	561	555	548	542	535	529
8	522	516	509	503	496	490	483	477	470	464
9	457	451	444	438	431	425	418	412	405	399
670	393	386	380	373	367	360	354	347	341	334
1	328	321	315	308	302	295	289	282	276	270
2	263	257	250	244	237	231	224	218	211	205
3	198	192	186	179	173	166	160	153	147	140
4	134	128	121	115	108	102	095	089	082	076
5	070	063	057	050	044	037	031	025	018	012
6	005	*999	*992	*986	*980	*973	*967	*960	*954	*948
7	.16 941	935	928	922	915	909	903	896	890	883
8	877	871	864	858	851	845	839	832	826	819
9	813	807	800	794	787	781	775	768	762	755
680	749	743	736	730	724	717	711	704	698	692
1	685	679	673	666	660	653	647	641	634	628
2	622	615	609	602	596	590	583	577	571	564
3	558	552	545	539	533	526	520	513	507	501
4	494	488	482	475	469	463	456	450	444	437
5	431	425	418	412	406	399	393	387	380	374
6	368	361	355	349	342	336	330	323	317	311
7	304	298	292	285	279	273	266	260	254	247
8	241	235	229	222	216	210	203	197	191	184
9	178	172	165	159	153	147	140	134	128	121
690	115	109	103	096	090	084	077	071	065	058
1	052	046	040	033	027	021	015	008	002	*996
2	.15 989	983	977	971	964	958	952	945	939	933
3	927	920	914	908	902	895	889	883	877	870
4	864	858	852	845	839	833	827	820	814	808
5	802	795	789	783	777	770	764	758	752	745
6	739	733	727	720	714	708	702	695	689	683
7	677	670	664	658	652	646	639	633	627	621
8	614	608	602	596	590	583	577	571	565	558
9	552	546	540	534	527	521	515	509	503	496
700	490	484	478	472	465	459	453	447	441	434

P.P.

7	
1	1
2	1
3	2
4	3
5	4
6	4
7	5
8	6
9	6

6	
1	1
2	1
3	2
4	2
5	3
6	4
7	4
8	5
9	5

Table 14-2. Cologarithms of Numbers (*Continued*)

No.	0	1	2	3	4	5	6	7	8	9
700	.15 490	484	478	472	465	459	453	447	441	434
1	428	422	416	410	403	397	391	385	379	372
2	366	360	354	348	342	335	329	323	317	311
3	304	298	292	286	280	274	267	261	255	249
4	243	237	230	224	218	212	206	200	193	187
5	181	175	169	163	156	150	144	138	132	126
6	120	113	107	101	095	089	083	076	070	064
7	058	052	046	040	033	027	021	015	009	003
8	.14 997	991	984	978	972	966	960	954	948	942
9	935	929	923	917	911	905	899	893	886	880
710	874	868	862	856	850	844	837	831	825	819
1	813	807	801	795	789	783	776	770	764	758
2	752	746	740	734	728	722	715	709	703	697
3	691	685	679	673	667	661	655	648	642	636
4	630	624	618	612	606	600	594	588	582	575
5	560	563	557	551	545	539	533	527	521	515
6	509	503	497	491	484	478	472	466	460	454
7	448	442	436	430	424	418	412	406	400	394
8	388	382	375	369	363	357	351	345	339	333
9	327	321	315	309	303	297	291	285	279	273
720	267	261	255	249	243	237	231	225	219	212
1	206	200	194	188	182	176	170	164	158	152
2	146	140	134	128	122	116	110	104	098	092
3	086	080	074	068	062	056	050	044	038	032
4	026	020	014	008	002	*996	*990	*984	*978	*972
5	.13 966	960	954	948	942	936	930	924	918	912
6	906	900	894	888	882	876	870	864	859	853
7	847	841	835	829	823	817	811	805	799	793
8	787	781	775	769	763	757	751	745	739	733
9	727	721	715	709	703	697	692	686	680	674
730	668	662	656	650	644	638	632	626	620	614
1	608	602	596	590	585	579	573	567	561	555
2	549	543	537	531	525	519	513	507	501	496
3	490	484	478	472	466	460	454	448	442	436
4	430	424	419	413	407	401	395	389	383	377
5	371	365	359	354	348	342	336	330	324	318
6	312	306	300	295	289	283	277	271	265	259
7	253	247	241	236	230	224	218	212	206	200
8	194	188	183	177	171	165	159	153	147	141
9	136	130	124	118	112	106	100	094	089	083
740	077	071	065	059	053	047	042	036	030	024
1	018	012	006	001	*995	*989	*983	*977	*971	*965
2	.12 960	954	948	942	936	930	925	919	913	907
3	901	895	889	884	878	872	866	860	854	849
4	843	837	831	825	819	814	808	802	796	790
5	784	779	773	767	761	755	749	744	738	732
6	726	720	714	709	703	697	691	685	680	674
7	668	662	656	651	645	639	633	627	621	616
8	610	604	598	592	587	581	575	569	563	558
9	552	546	540	534	529	523	517	511	505	500
750	494	488	482	477	471	465	459	453	448	442

P.P.

7	
1	1
2	1
3	2
4	3
5	4
6	4
7	5
8	6
9	6

6	
1	1
2	1
3	2
4	2
5	3
6	4
7	4
8	5
9	5

5	
1	1
2	1
3	2
4	2
5	3
6	3
7	4
8	4
9	5

Table 14-2. Cologarithms of Numbers (*Continued*)

No.	0	1	2	3	4	5	6	7	8	9	P.P.
750	.12 494	488	482	477	471	465	459	453	448	442	
1	436	430	424	419	413	407	401	396	390	384	
2	378	372	367	361	355	349	344	338	332	326	
3	321	315	309	303	297	292	286	280	274	269	
4	263	257	251	246	240	234	228	223	217	211	
5	205	200	194	188	182	177	171	165	159	154	
6	148	142	136	131	125	119	113	108	102	096	
7	090	085	079	073	067	062	056	050	045	039	
8	033	027	022	016	010	004	*999	*993	*987	*982	
9	.11 976	970	964	959	953	947	942	936	930	924	
760	919	913	907	902	896	890	884	879	873	867	**6**
1	862	856	850	844	839	833	827	822	816	810	1 1
2	805	799	793	787	782	776	770	765	759	753	2 1
3	748	742	736	730	725	719	713	708	702	696	3 2
4	691	685	679	674	668	662	657	651	645	640	4 2
5	634	628	623	617	611	605	600	594	588	583	5 3
6	577	571	566	560	554	549	543	537	532	526	6 4
7	520	515	509	503	498	492	487	481	475	470	7 4
8	464	458	453	447	441	436	430	424	419	413	8 5
9	407	402	396	390	385	379	373	368	362	357	9 5
770	351	345	340	334	328	323	317	311	306	300	
1	295	289	283	278	272	266	261	255	250	244	
2	238	233	227	221	216	210	205	199	193	188	
3	182	176	171	165	160	154	148	143	137	132	
4	126	120	115	109	103	098	092	087	081	075	
5	070	064	059	053	047	042	036	031	025	019	
6	014	008	003	*997	*991	*986	*980	*975	*969	*963	
7	.10 958	952	947	941	936	930	924	919	913	908	
8	902	896	891	885	880	874	869	863	857	852	
9	846	841	835	830	824	818	813	807	802	796	
780	791	785	779	774	768	763	757	752	746	740	**5**
1	735	729	724	718	713	707	702	696	690	685	1 1
2	679	674	668	663	657	652	646	640	635	629	2 1
3	624	618	613	607	602	596	591	585	579	574	3 2
4	568	563	557	552	546	541	535	530	524	519	4 2
5	513	508	502	496	491	485	480	474	469	463	5 3
6	458	452	447	441	436	430	425	419	414	408	6 3
7	403	397	391	386	380	375	369	364	358	353	7 4
8	347	342	336	331	325	320	314	309	303	298	8 4
9	292	287	281	276	270	265	259	254	248	243	9 5
790	237	232	226	221	215	210	204	199	193	188	
1	182	177	171	166	160	155	149	144	138	133	
2	127	122	117	111	106	100	095	089	084	078	
3	073	067	062	056	051	045	040	034	029	023	
4	018	012	007	002	*996	*991	*985	*980	*974	*969	
5	.09 963	958	952	947	941	936	931	925	920	914	
6	909	903	898	892	887	881	876	871	865	860	
7	854	849	843	838	832	827	821	816	811	805	
8	800	794	789	783	778	773	767	762	756	751	
9	745	740	734	729	724	718	713	707	702	696	
800	691	686	680	675	669	664	658	653	648	642	

Table 14-2. Cologarithms of Numbers (*Continued*)

No.	0	1	2	3	4	5	6	7	8	9
800	.09 601	686	680	675	669	664	658	653	648	642
1	637	631	626	620	615	610	604	599	593	588
2	583	577	572	566	561	555	550	545	539	534
3	528	523	518	512	507	501	496	491	485	480
4	474	469	464	458	453	447	442	437	431	426
5	420	415	410	404	399	393	388	383	377	372
6	366	361	356	350	345	340	334	329	323	318
7	313	307	302	297	291	286	280	275	270	264
8	259	253	248	243	237	232	227	221	216	211
9	205	200	194	189	184	178	173	168	162	157
810	151	146	141	135	130	125	119	114	109	103
1	098	093	087	082	076	071	066	060	055	050
2	044	039	034	028	023	018	012	007	002	*996
3	.08 991	986	980	975	970	964	959	954	948	943
4	938	932	927	922	916	911	906	900	895	890
5	884	879	874	868	863	858	852	847	842	.836
6	831	826	820	815	810	804	799	794	788	783
7	778	772	767	762	757	751	746	741	735	730
8	725	719	714	709	703	698	693	688	682	677
9	672	666	661	656	650	645	640	635	629	624
820	619	613	608	603	597	592	587	582	576	571
1	566	560	555	550	545	539	534	529	523	518
2	513	508	502	497	492	486	481	476	471	465
3	460	455	449	444	439	434	428	423	418	413
4	407	402	397	391	386	381	376	370	365	360
5	355	349	344	339	334	328	323	318	313	307
6	302	297	291	286	281	276	270	265	260	255
7	249	244	239	234	228	223	218	213	207	202
8	197	192	186	181	176	171	166	160	155	150
9	145	139	134	129	124	118	113	108	103	097
830	092	087	082	076	071	066	061	056	050	045
1	040	035	029	024	019	014	009	003	*998	*993
2	.07 988	982	977	972	967	962	956	951	946	941
3	935	930	925	920	915	909	904	899	894	889
4	883	878	873	868	863	857	852	847	842	837
5	831	826	821	816	811	805	800	795	790	785
6	779	774	769	764	759	753	748	743	738	733
7	727	722	717	712	707	702	696	691	686	681
8	676	670	665	660	655	650	645	639	634	629
9	624	619	613	608	603	·598	593	588	582	577
840	572	567	562	557	551	546	541	536	531	526
1	520	515	510	505	500	495	489	484	479	474
2	469	464	458	453	448	443	438	433	428	422
3	417	412	407	402	397	391	386	381	376	371
4	366	361	355	350	345	340	335	330	325	319
5	314	309	304	299	294	289	284	278	273	268
6	263	258	253	248	242	237	232	227	222	217
7	212	207	201	196	191	186	181	176	171	166
8	160	155	150	145	140	135	130	125	119	114
9	109	104	099	094	089	084	079	073	068	063
850	058	053	048	043	038	033	027	022	017	012

P.P.

6
1	1
2	1
3	2
4	2
5	3
6	4
7	4
8	5
9	5

5
1	1
2	1
3	2
4	2
5	3
6	3
7	4
8	4
9	5

Table 14-2. Cologarithms of Numbers (*Continued*)

No.	0	1	2	3	4	5	6	7	8	9	P.P.	
850	.07 058	053	048	043	038	033	027	022	017	012		
1	007	002	*997	*992	*987	*982	*976	*971	*966	*961		
2	.06 956	951	946	941	936	931	925	920	915	910		
3	905	900	895	890	885	880	875	869	864	859		
4	854	849	844	839	834	829	824	819	814	808		
5	803	798	793	788	783	778	773	768	763	758	**6**	
6	753	748	742	737	732	727	722	717	712	707	1	1
7	702	697	692	687	682	677	672	666	661	656	2	1
8	651	646	641	636	631	626	621	616	611	606	3	2
9	601	596	591	586	580	575	570	565	560	555	4	2
860	550	545	540	535	530	525	520	515	510	505	5	3
1	500	495	490	485	480	474	469	464	459	454	6	4
2	449	444	439	434	429	424	419	414	409	404	7	4
3	399	394	389	384	379	374	369	364	359	354	8	5
4	349	344	339	334	329	324	318	313	308	303	9	5
5	298	293	288	283	278	273	268	263	258	253		
6	248	243	238	233	228	223	218	213	208	203		
7	198	193	188	183	178	173	168	163	158	153		
8	148	143	138	133	128	123	118	113	108	103		
9	098	093	088	083	078	073	068	063	058	053		
870	048	043	038	033	028	023	018	013	008	003	**5**	
1	.05 998	993	988	983	978	973	968	963	958	953	1	1
2	948	943	938	933	928	923	918	914	909	904	2	1
3	899	894	889	884	879	874	869	864	859	954	3	2
4	849	844	839	834	829	824	819	814	809	804	4	2
5	799	794	789	784	779	774	769	764	760	755	5	3
6	750	745	740	735	730	725	720	715	710	705	6	3
7	700	695	690	685	680	675	670	665	660	655	7	4
8	651	646	641	636	631	626	621	616	611	606	8	4
9	601	596	591	586	581	576	571	567	562	557	9	5
880	552	547	542	537	532	527	522	517	512	507		
1	502	497	493	488	483	478	473	468	463	458		
2	453	448	443	438	433	429	424	419	414	409		
3	404	399	394	389	384	379	374	370	365	360		
4	355	350	345	340	335	330	325	320	315	311		
5	306	301	296	291	286	281	276	271	266	262	**4**	
6	257	252	247	242	237	232	227	222	217	213	1	0
7	208	203	198	193	188	183	178	173	168	164	2	1
8	159	154	149	144	139	134	129	124	120	115	3	1
9	110	105	100	095	090	085	081	076	071	066	4	2
890	061	056	051	046	041	037	032	027	022	017	5	2
1	012	007	002	*998	*993	*988	*983	*978	*973	*968	6	2
2	.04 964	959	954	949	944	939	934	929	925	920	7	3
3	915	910	905	900	895	891	886	881	876	871	8	3
4	866	861	857	852	847	842	837	832	827	823	9	4
5	818	813	808	803	798	793	789	784	779	774		
6	769	764	760	755	750	745	740	735	730	726		
7	721	716	711	706	701	697	692	687	682	677		
8	672	668	663	658	653	648	643	639	634	629		
9	624	619	614	610	605	600	595	590	585	581		
900	576	571	566	561	556	552	547	542	537	532		

Table 14-2 Cologarithms of Numbers (*Continued*)

No.	0	1	2	3	4	5	6	7	8	9	P.P.	
900	.04 576	571	566	561	556	552	547	542	537	532		
1	528	523	518	513	508	503	499	494	489	484		
2	479	475	470	465	460	455	450	446	441	436		
3	431	426	422	417	412	407	402	398	393	388		
4	383	378	374	369	364	359	354	350	345	340		
5	335	330	326	321	316	311	306	302	297	292		
6	287	282	278	273	268	263	258	254	249	244		
7	239	234	230	225	220	215	211	206	201	196		
8	191	187	182	177	172	168	163	158	153	148		
9	144	139	134	129	125	120	115	110	105	101		
910	096	091	086	082	077	072	067	062	058	053	**5**	
1	048	043	039	034	029	024	020	015	010	005	1	1
2	001	*996	*991	*986	*981	*977	*972	*967	*962	*958	2	1
3	.03 953	948	943	939	934	929	924	920	915	910	3	2
4	905	901	896	891	886	882	877	872	867	863	4	2
5	858	853	848	844	839	834	829	825	820	815	5	3
6	810	806	801	796	791	787	782	777	773	768	6	3
7	763	758	754	749	744	739	735	730	725	720	7	4
8	716	711	706	702	697	692	687	683	678	673	8	4
9	668	664	659	654	650	645	640	635	631	626	9	5
920	621	616	612	607	602	598	593	588	583	579		
1	574	569	565	560	555	550	546	541	536	532		
2	527	522	517	513	508	503	499	494	489	485		
3	480	475	470	466	461	456	452	447	442	438		
4	433	428	423	419	414	409	405	400	395	391		
5	386	381	376	372	367	362	358	353	348	344		
6	339	334	330	325	320	315	311	306	301	297		
7	292	287	283	278	273	269	264	259	255	250		
8	245	241	236	231	226	222	217	212	208	203		
9	198	194	189	184	180	175	170	166	161	156		
930	152	147	142	138	133	128	124	119	114	110	**4**	
1	105	100	096	091	086	082	077	072	068	063	1	0
2	058	054	049	044	040	035	030	026	021	016	2	1
3	012	007	003	*998	*993	*989	*984	*979	*975	*970	3	1
4	.02 965	961	956	951	947	942	937	933	928	923	4	2
5	919	914	910	905	900	896	891	886	882	877	5	2
6	872	868	863	858	854	849	845	840	835	831	6	2
7	826	821	817	812	808	803	798	794	789	784	7	3
8	780	775	770	766	761	757	752	747	743	738	8	3
9	733	729	724	720	715	710	706	701	696	692	9	4
940	687	683	678	673	669	664	660	655	650	646		
1	641	636	632	627	623	618	613	609	604	600		
2	595	590	586	581	576	572	567	563	558	553		
3	549	544	540	535	530	526	521	517	512	507		
4	503	498	494	489	484	480	475	471	466	461		
5	457	452	448	443	438	434	429	425	420	415		
6	411	406	402	397	393	388	383	379	374	370		
7	365	360	356	351	347	342	337	333	328	324		
8	319	315	310	305	301	296	292	287	283	278		
9	273	269	264	260	255	251	246	241	237	232		
950	228	223	218	214	209	205	200	196	191	187		

Table 14-2 Cologarithms of Numbers (*Concluded*)

No.	0	1	2	3	4	5	6	7	8	9	P.P.	
950	.02 228	223	218	214	209	205	200	196	191	187		
1	182	177	173	168	164	159	155	150	145	141		
2	136	132	127	123	118	114	109	104	100	095		
3	091	086	082	077	072	068	063	059	054	050		
4	045	041	036	032	027	022	018	013	009	004		
5	000	*995	*991	*986	*981	*977	*972	*968	*963	*959		
6	.01 954	950	945	941	936	932	927	922	918	913		
7	909	904	900	895	891	886	882	877	873	868		
8	863	859	854	850	845	841	836	832	827	823		
9	818	814	809	805	800	796	791	786	782	777		
960	773	768	764	759	755	750	746	741	737	732	**5**	
1	728	723	719	714	710	705	701	696	692	687	1	1
2	682	678	673	669	664	660	655	651	646	642	2	1
3	637	633	628	624	619	615	610	606	601	597	3	2
4	592	588	583	579	574	570	565	561	556	552	4	2
5	547	543	538	534	529	525	520	516	511	507	5	3
6	502	498	493	489	484	480	475	471	466	462	6	3
7	457	453	448	444	439	435	430	426	421	417	7	4
8	412	408	403	399	395	390	386	381	377	372	8	4
9	368	363	359	354	350	345	341	336	332	327	9	5
970	323	318	314	309	305	300	296	291	287	283		
1	278	274	269	265	260	256	251	247	242	238		
2	233	229	224	220	216	211	207	202	198	193		
3	189	184	180	175	171	166	162	157	153	149		
4	144	140	135	131	126	122	117	113	108	104		
5	100	095	091	086	082	077	073	068	064	059		
6	055	051	046	042	037	033	028	024	019	015		
7	011	006	002	*997	*993	*988	*984	*979	*975	*971		
8	.00 966	962	957	953	948	944	939	935	931	926		
9	922	917	913	908	904	900	895	891	886	882		
980	877	873	869	864	860	855	851	846	842	838	**4**	
1	833	829	824	820	815	811	807	802	798	793	1	0
2	789	784	780	776	771	767	762	758	753	749	2	1
3	745	740	736	731	727	723	718	714	709	705	3	1
4	700	696	692	687	683	678	674	670	665	661	4	2
5	656	652	648	643	639	634	630	626	621	617	5	2
6	612	608	604	599	595	590	586	581	577	573	6	2
7	568	564	559	555	551	546	542	537	533	529	7	3
8	524	520	516	511	507	502	498	494	489	485	8	3
9	480	476	472	467	463	458	454	450	445	441	9	4
990	436	432	428	423	419	415	410	406	401	397		
1	393	388	384	379	375	371	366	362	358	353		
2	349	344	340	336	331	327	323	318	314	309		
3	305	301	296	292	288	283	279	274	270	266		
4	261	257	253	248	244	240	235	231	226	222		
5	218	213	209	205	200	196	192	187	183	178		
6	174	170	165	161	157	152	148	144	139	135		
7	130	126	122	117	113	109	104	100	096	091		
8	087	083	078	074	070	065	061	056	052	048		
9	043	039	035	030	026	022	017	013	009	004		
1000	000											

Table 14-3. Natural Sines and Cosines

Degrees	\multicolumn{7}{c}{SINES}	Cosines
	0'	10'	20'	30'	40'	50'	60'	
0	0.00000	0.00291	0.00582	0.00873	0.01164	0.01454	0.01745	89
1	0.01745	0.02036	0.02327	0.02618	0.02908	0.03199	0.03490	88
2	0.03490	0.03781	0.04071	0.04362	0.04653	0.04943	0.05234	87
3	0.05234	0.05524	0.05814	0.06105	0.06395	0.06685	0.06976	86
4	0.06976	0.07266	0.07556	0.07846	0.08136	0.08426	0.08716	85
5	0.08716	0.09005	0.09295	0.09585	0.09874	0.10164	0.10453	84
6	0.10453	0.10742	0.11031	0.11320	0.11609	0.11898	0.12187	83
7	0.12187	0.12476	0.12764	0.13053	0.13341	0.13629	0.13917	82
8	0.13917	0.14205	0.14493	0.14781	0.15069	0.15356	0.15643	81
9	0.15643	0.15931	0.16218	0.16505	0.16792	0.17078	0.17365	80
10	0.17365	0.17651	0.17937	0.18224	0.18509	0.18795	0.19081	79
11	0.19081	0.19366	0.19652	0.19937	0.20222	0.20507	0.20791	78
12	0.20791	0.21076	0.21360	0.21644	0.21928	0.22212	0.22495	77
13	0.22495	0.22778	0.23062	0.23345	0.23627	0.23910	0.24192	76
14	0.24192	0.24474	0.24756	0.25038	0.25320	0.25601	0.25882	75
15	0.25882	0.26163	0.26443	0.26724	0.27004	0.27284	0.27564	74
16	0.27564	0.27843	0.28123	0.28402	0.28680	0.28959	0.29237	73
17	0.29237	0.29515	0.29793	0.30071	0.30348	0.30625	0.30902	72
18	0.30902	0.31178	0.31454	0.31730	0.32006	0.32282	0.32557	71
19	0.32557	0.32832	0.33106	0.33381	0.33655	0.33929	0.34202	70
20	0.34202	0.34475	0.34748	0.35021	0.35293	0.35565	0.35837	69
21	0.35837	0.36108	0.36379	0.36650	0.36921	0.37191	0.37461	68
22	0.37461	0.37730	0.37999	0.38268	0.38537	0.38805	0.39073	67
23	0.39073	0.39341	0.39608	0.39875	0.40142	0.40408	0.40674	66
24	0.40674	0.40939	0.41204	0.41469	0.41734	0.41998	0.42262	65
25	0.42262	0.42525	0.42788	0.43051	0.43313	0.43575	0.43837	64
26	0.43837	0.44098	0.44359	0.44620	0.44880	0.45140	0.45399	63
27	0.45399	0.45658	0.45917	0.46175	0.46433	0.46690	0.46947	62
28	0.46947	0.47204	0.47460	0.47716	0.47971	0.48226	0.48481	61
29	0.48481	0.48735	0.48989	0.49242	0.49495	0.49748	0.50000	60
30	0.50000	0.50252	0.50503	0.50754	0.51004	0.51254	0.51504	59
31	0.51504	0.51753	0.52002	0.52250	0.52498	0.52745	0.52992	58
32	0.52992	0.53238	0.53484	0.53730	0.53975	0.54220	0.54464	57
33	0.54464	0.54708	0.54951	0.55194	0.55436	0.55678	0.55919	56
34	0.55919	0.56160	0.56401	0.56641	0.56880	0.57119	0.57358	55
35	0.57358	0.57596	0.57833	0.58070	0.58307	0.58543	0.58779	54
36	0.58779	0.59014	0.59248	0.59482	0.59716	0.59949	0.60182	53
37	0.60182	0.60414	0.60645	0.60876	0.61107	0.61337	0.61566	52
38	0.61566	0.61795	0.62024	0.62251	0.62479	0.62706	0.62932	51
39	0.62932	0.63158	0.63383	0.63608	0.63832	0.64056	0.64279	50
40	0.64279	0.64501	0.64723	0.64945	0.65166	0.65386	0.65606	49
41	0.65606	0.65825	0.66044	0.66262	0.66480	0.66697	0.66913	48
42	0.66913	0.67129	0.67344	0.67559	0.67773	0.67987	0.68200	47
43	0.68200	0.68412	0.68624	0.68835	0.69046	0.69256	0.69466	46
44	0.69466	0.69675	0.69883	0.70091	0.70298	0.70505	0.70711	45
Sines	60'	50'	40'	30'	20'	10'	0'	Degrees
	\multicolumn{7}{c}{COSINES}	

Table 14-3. Natural Sines and Cosines (*Concluded*)

| Degrees | COSINES | | | | | | | Sines |
	0′	10′	20′	30′	40′	50′	60′	
0	1.00000	1.00000	0.99998	0.99996	0.99993	0.99989	0.99985	89
1	0.99985	0.99979	0.99973	0.99966	0.99958	0.99949	0.99939	88
2	0.99939	0.99929	0.99917	0.99905	0.99892	0.99878	0.99863	87
3	0.99863	0.99847	0.99831	0.99813	0.99795	0.99776	0.99756	86
4	0.99756	0.99736	0.99714	0.99692	0.99668	0.99644	0.99619	85
5	0.99619	0.99594	0.99567	0.99540	0.99511	0.99482	0.99452	84
6	0.99452	0.99421	0.99390	0.99357	0.99324	0.99290	0.99255	83
7	0.99255	0.99219	0.99182	0.99144	0.99106	0.99067	0.99027	82
8	0.99027	0.98986	0.98944	0.98902	0.98858	0.98814	0.98769	81
9	0.98769	0.98723	0.98676	0.98629	0.98580	0.98531	0.98481	80
10	0.98481	0.98430	0.98378	0.98325	0.98272	0.98218	0.98163	79
11	0.98163	0.98107	0.98050	0.97992	0.97934	0.97875	0.97815	78
12	0.97815	0.97754	0.97692	0.97630	0.97566	0.97502	0.97437	77
13	0.97437	0.97371	0.97304	0.97237	0.97169	0.97100	0.97030	76
14	0.97030	0.96959	0.96887	0.96815	0.96742	0.96667	0.96593	75
15	0.96593	0.96517	0.96440	0.96363	0.96285	0.96206	0.96126	74
16	0.96126	0.96046	0.95964	0.95882	0.95799	0.95715	0.95630	73
17	0.95630	0.95545	0.95459	0.95372	0.95284	0.95195	0.95106	72
18	0.95106	0.95015	0.94924	0.94832	0.94740	0.94646	0.94552	71
19	0.94552	0.94457	0.94361	0.94264	0.94167	0.94068	0.93969	70
20	0.93969	0.93869	0.93769	0.93667	0.93565	0.93462	0.93358	69
21	0.93358	0.93253	0.93148	0.93042	0.92935	0.92827	0.92718	68
22	0.92718	0.92609	0.92499	0.92388	0.92276	0.92164	0.92050	67
23	0.92050	0.91936	0.91822	0.91706	0.91590	0.91472	0.91355	66
24	0.91355	0.91236	0.91116	0.90996	0.90875	0.90753	0.90631	65
25	0.90631	0.90507	0.90383	0.90259	0.90133	0.90007	0.89879	64
26	0.89879	0.89752	0.89623	0.89493	0.89363	0.89232	0.89101	63
27	0.89101	0.88968	0.88835	0.88701	0.88566	0.88431	0.88295	62
28	0.88295	0.88158	0.88020	0.87882	0.87743	0.87603	0.87462	61
29	0.87462	0.87321	0.87178	0.87036	0.86892	0.86748	0.86603	60
30	0.86603	0.86457	0.86310	0.86163	0.86015	0.85866	0.85717	59
31	0.85717	0.85567	0.85416	0.85264	0.85112	0.84959	0.84805	58
32	0.84805	0.84650	0.84495	0.84339	0.84182	0.84025	0.83867	57
33	0.83867	0.83708	0.83549	0.83389	0.83228	0.83066	0.82904	56
34	0.82904	0.82741	0.82577	0.82413	0.82248	0.82082	0.81915	55
35	0.81915	0.81748	0.81580	0.81412	0.81242	0.81072	0.80902	54
36	0.80902	0.80730	0.80558	0.80386	0.80212	0.80038	0.79864	53
37	0.79864	0.79688	0.79512	0.79335	0.79158	0.78980	0.78801	52
38	0.78801	0.78622	0.78442	0.78261	0.78079	0.77897	0.77715	51
39	0.77715	0.77531	0.77347	0.77162	0.76977	0.76791	0.76604	50
40	0.76604	0.76417	0.76229	0.76041	0.75851	0.75661	0.75471	49
41	0.75471	0.75280	0.75088	0.74896	0.74703	0.74509	0.74314	48
42	0.74314	0.74120	0.73924	0.73728	0.73531	0.73333	0.73135	47
43	0.73135	0.72937	0.72737	0.72537	0.72337	0.72136	0.71934	46
44	0.71934	0.71732	0.71529	0.71325	0.71121	0.70916	0.70711	45
Cosines	60′	50′	40′	30′	20′	10′	0′	Degrees
	SINES							

Table 14-4. Natural Tangents and Cotangents

Degrees	TANGENTS							Co-tangents
	0′	10′	20′	30′	40′	50′	60′	
0	0.00000	0.00291	0.00582	0.00873	0.01164	0.01455	0.01746	89
1	0.01746	0.02036	0.02328	0.02619	0.02910	0.03201	0.33492	88
2	0.03492	0.03783	0.04075	0.04366	0.04658	0.04949	0.05241	87
3	0.05241	0.05533	0.05824	0.06116	0.06408	0.06700	0.06993	86
4	0.06993	0.07285	0.07578	0.07870	0.08163	0.08456	0.08749	85
5	0.08749	0.09042	0.09335	0.09629	0.09923	0.10216	0.10510	84
6	0.10510	0.10805	0.11099	0.11394	0.11688	0.11983	0.12278	83
7	0.12278	0.12574	0.12869	0.13165	0.13461	0.13758	0.14054	82
8	0.14054	0.14351	0.14648	0.14945	0.15243	0.15540	0.15838	81
9	0.15838	0.16137	0.16435	0.16734	0.17033	0.17333	0.17633	80
10	0.17633	0.17933	0.18233	0.18534	0.18835	0.19136	0.19438	79
11	0.19438	0.19740	0.20042	0.20345	0.20648	0.20952	0.21256	78
12	0.21256	0.21560	0.21864	0.22169	0.22475	0.22781	0.23087	77
13	0.23087	0.23393	0.23700	0.24008	0.24316	0.24624	0.24933	76
14	0.24933	0.25242	0.25552	0.25862	0.26172	0.26483	0.26795	75
15	0.26795	0.27107	0.27419	0.27732	0.28046	0.28360	0.28675	74
16	0.28675	0.28990	0.29305	0.29621	0.29938	0.30255	0.30573	73
17	0.30573	0.30891	0.31210	0.31530	0.31850	0.32171	0.32492	72
18	0.32492	0.32814	0.33136	0.33460	0.33783	0.34108	0.34433	71
19	0.34433	0.34758	0.35085	0.35412	0.35740	0.36068	0.36397	70
20	0.36397	0.36727	0.37057	0.37388	0.37720	0.38053	0.38386	69
21	0.38386	0.38721	0.39055	0.39391	0.39727	0.40065	0.40403	68
22	0.40403	0.40741	0.41081	0.41421	0.41763	0.42105	0.42447	67
23	0.42447	0.42791	0.43136	0.43481	0.43828	0.44175	0.44523	66
24	0.44523	0.44872	0.45222	0.45573	0.45924	0.46277	0.46631	65
25	0.46631	0.46985	0.47341	0.47698	0.48055	0.48414	0.48773	64
26	0.48773	0.49134	0.49495	0.49858	0.50222	0.50587	0.50953	63
27	0.50953	0.51320	0.51688	0.52057	0.52427	0.52798	0.53171	62
28	0.53171	0.53545	0.53920	0.54296	0.54674	0.55051	0.55431	61
29	0.55431	0.55812	0.56194	0.56577	0.56962	0.57348	0.57735	60
30	0.57735	0.58124	0.58513	0.58905	0.59297	0.59691	0.60086	59
31	0.60086	0.60483	0.60881	0.61280	0.61681	0.62083	0.62487	58
32	0.62487	0.62892	0.63299	0.63707	0.64117	0.64528	0.64941	57
33	0.64941	0.65355	0.65771	0.66189	0.66608	0.67028	0.67451	56
34	0.67451	0.67875	0.68301	0.68728	0.69157	0.69588	0.70021	55
35	0.70021	0.70455	0.70891	0.71329	0.71769	0.72211	0.72654	54
36	0.72654	0.73100	0.73547	0.73996	0.74447	0.74900	0.75355	53
37	0.75355	0.75812	0.76272	0.76733	0.77196	0.77661	0.78129	52
38	0.78129	0.78598	0.79070	0.79544	0.80020	0.80498	0.80978	51
39	0.80978	0.81461	0.81946	0.82434	0.82923	0.83415	0.83910	50
40	0.83910	0.84407	0.84906	0.85408	0.85912	0.86419	0.86929	49
41	0.86929	0.87441	0.87955	0.88473	0.88992	0.89515	0.90040	48
42	0.90040	0.90569	0.91099	0.91633	0.92170	0.92709	0.93252	47
43	0.93252	0.93797	0.94345	0.94896	0.95451	0.96008	0.96569	46
44	0.96569	0.97133	0.97700	0.98270	0.98843	0.99420	1.00000	45
Tangents	60′	50′	40′	30′	20′	10′	0′	Degrees
	COTANGENTS							

Table 14-4. Natural Tangents and Cotangents (*Concluded*)

| Degrees | COTANGENTS | | | | | | | Tangents |
	0'	10'	20'	30'	40'	50'	60'	
0	∞	343.77371	171.88540	114.58865	85.93979	68.75009	57.28996	89
1	57.28996	49.10388	42.96408	38.18846	34.36777	31.24158	28.63625	88
2	28.63625	26.43160	24.54176	22.90377	21.47040	20.20555	19.08114	87
3	19.08114	18.07498	17.16934	16.34986	15.60478	14.92442	14.30067	86
4	14.30067	13.72674	13.19688	12.70621	12.25051	11.82617	11.43005	85
5	11.43005	11.05943	10.71191	10.38540	10.07803	9.78817	9.51436	84
6	9.51436	9.25530	9.00983	8.77689	8.55555	8.34496	8.14435	83
7	8.14435	7.95302	7.77035	7.59575	7.42871	7.26873	7.11537	82
8	7.11537	6.96823	6.82694	6.69116	6.56055	6.43484	6.31375	81
9	6.31375	6.19703	6.08444	5.97576	5.87080	5.76937	5.67128	80
10	5.67128	5.57638	5.48451	5.39552	5.30928	5.22566	5.14455	79
11	5.14455	5.06584	4.98940	4.91516	4.84300	4.77286	4.70463	78
12	4.70463	4.63825	4.57363	4.51071	4.44942	4.38969	4.33148	77
13	4.33148	4.27471	4.21933	4.16530	4.11256	4.06107	4.01078	76
14	4.01078	3.96165	3.91364	3.86671	3.82083	3.77595	3.73205	75
15	3.73205	3.68909	3.64705	3.60588	3.56557	3.52609	3.48741	74
16	3.48741	3.44951	3.41236	3.37594	3.34023	3.30521	3.27085	73
17	3.27085	3.23714	3.20406	3.17159	3.13972	3.10842	3.07768	72
18	3.07768	3.04749	3.01783	2.98869	2.96004	2.93189	2.90421	71
19	2.90421	2.87700	2.85023	2.82391	2.79802	2.77254	2.74748	70
20	2.74748	2.72281	2.69853	2.67462	2.65109	2.62791	2.60509	69
21	2.60509	2.58261	2.56046	2.53865	2.51715	2.49597	2.47509	68
22	2.47509	2.45451	2.43422	2.41421	2.39449	2.37504	2.35585	67
23	2.35585	2.33693	2.31826	2.29984	2.28167	2.26374	2.24604	66
24	2.24604	2.22857	2.21132	2.19430	2.17749	2.16090	2.14451	65
25	2.14451	2.12832	2.11233	2.09654	2.08094	2.06553	2.05030	64
26	2.05030	2.03526	2.02039	2.00569	1.99116	1.97680	1.96261	63
27	1.96261	1.94858	1.93470	1.92098	1.90741	1.89400	1.88073	62
28	1.88073	1.86760	1.85462	1.84177	1.82907	1.81649	1.80405	61
29	1.80405	1.79174	1.77955	1.76749	1.75556	1.74375	1.73205	60
30	1.73205	1.72047	1.70901	1.69766	1.68643	1.67530	1.66428	59
31	1.66428	1.65337	1.64256	1.63185	1.62125	1.61074	1.60033	58
32	1.60033	1.59002	1.57981	1.56969	1.55966	1.54972	1.53987	57
33	1.53987	1.53010	1.52043	1.51084	1.50133	1.49190	1.48256	56
34	1.48256	1.47330	1.46411	1.45501	1.44598	1.43703	1.42815	55
35	1.42815	1.41934	1.41061	1.40195	1.39336	1.38484	1.37638	54
36	1.37638	1.36800	1.35968	1.35142	1.34323	1.33511	1.32704	53
37	1.32704	1.31904	1.31110	1.30323	1.29541	1.28764	1.27994	52
38	1.27994	1.27230	1.26471	1.25717	1.24969	1.24227	1.23490	51
39	1.23490	1.22758	1.22031	1.21310	1.20593	1.19882	1.19175	50
40	1.19175	1.18474	1.17777	1.17085	1.16398	1.15715	1.15037	49
41	1.15037	1.14363	1.13694	1.13029	1.12369	1.11713	1.11061	48
42	1.11061	1.10414	1.09770	1.09131	1.08496	1.07864	1.07237	47
43	1.07237	1.06613	1.05994	1.05378	1.04766	1.04158	1.03553	46
44	1.03553	1.02952	1.02355	1.01761	1.01170	1.00583	1.00000	45
Co-tangents	60'	50'	40'	30'	20'	10'	0'	Degrees

TANGENTS

Table 14-5. Natural Secants and Cosecants

Degrees	\multicolumn{7}{SECANTS}							Cosecants
	0′	10′	20′	30′	40′	50′	60′	
0	1.00000	1.00000	1.00002	1.00004	1.00007	1.00011	1.00015	89
1	1.00015	1.00021	1.00027	1.00034	1.00042	1.00051	1.00061	88
2	1.00061	1.00072	1.00083	1.00095	1.00108	1.00122	1.00137	87
3	1.00137	1.00153	1.00169	1.00187	1.00205	1.00224	1.00244	86
4	1.00244	1.00265	1.00287	1.00309	1.00333	1.00357	1.00382	85
5	1.00382	1.00408	1.00435	1.00463	1.00491	1.00521	1.00551	84
6	1.00551	1.00582	1.00614	1.00647	1.00681	1.00715	1.00751	83
7	1.00751	1.00787	1.00825	1.00863	1.00902	1.00942	1.00983	82
8	1.00983	1.01024	1.01067	1.01111	1.01155	1.01200	1.01247	81
9	1.01247	1.01294	1.01342	1.01391	1.01440	1.01491	1.01543	80
10	1.01543	1.01595	1.01649	1.01703	1.01758	1.01815	1.01872	79
11	1.01872	1.01930	1.01989	1.02049	1.02110	1.02171	1.02234	78
12	1.02234	1.02298	1.02362	1.02428	1.02494	1.02562	1.02630	77
13	1.02630	1.02700	1.02770	1.02842	1.02914	1.02987	1.03061	76
14	1.03061	1.03137	1.03213	1.03290	1.03368	1.03447	1.03528	75
15	1.03528	1.03609	1.03691	1.03774	1.03858	1.03944	1.04030	74
16	1.04030	1.04117	1.04206	1.04295	1.04385	1.04477	1.04569	73
17	1.04569	1.04663	1.04757	1.04853	1.04950	1.05047	1.05146	72
18	1.05146	1.05246	1.05347	1.05449	1.05552	1.05657	1.05762	71
19	1.05762	1.05869	1.05976	1.06085	1.06195	1.06306	1.06418	70
20	1.06418	1.06531	1.06645	1.06761	1.06878	1.06995	1.07115	69
21	1.07115	1.07235	1.07356	1.07479	1.07602	1.07727	1.07853	68
22	1.07853	1.07981	1.08109	1.08239	1.08370	1.08503	1.08636	67
23	1.08636	1.08771	1.08907	1.09044	1.09183	1.09323	1.09464	66
24	1.09464	1.09606	1.09750	1.09895	1.10041	1.10189	1.10338	65
25	1.10338	1.10488	1.10640	1.10793	1.10947	1.11103	1.11260	64
26	1.11260	1.11419	1.11579	1.11740	1.11903	1.12067	1.12233	63
27	1.12233	1.12400	1.12568	1.12738	1.12910	1.13083	1.13257	62
28	1.13257	1.13433	1.13610	1.13789	1.13970	1.14152	1.14335	61
29	1.14335	1.14521	1.14707	1.14896	1.15085	1.15277	1.15470	60
30	1.15470	1.15665	1.15861	1.16059	1.16259	1.16460	1.16663	59
31	1.16663	1.16868	1.17075	1.17283	1.17493	1.17704	1.17918	58
32	1.17918	1.18133	1.18350	1.18569	1.18790	1.19012	1.19236	57
33	1.19236	1.19463	1.19691	1.19920	1.20152	1.20386	1.20622	56
34	1.20622	1.20859	1.21099	1.21341	1.21584	1.21830	1.22077	55
35	1.22077	1.22327	1.22579	1.22833	1.23089	1.23347	1.23607	54
36	1.23607	1.23869	1.24134	1.24400	1.24669	1.24940	1.25214	53
37	1.25214	1.25489	1.25767	1.26047	1.26330	1.26615	1.26902	52
38	1.26902	1.27191	1.27483	1.27778	1.28075	1.28374	1.28676	51
39	1.28676	1.28980	1.29287	1.29597	1.29909	1.30223	1.30541	50
40	1.30541	1.30861	1.31183	1.31509	1.31837	1.32168	1.32501	49
41	1.32501	1.32838	1.33177	1.33519	1.33864	1.34212	1.34563	48
42	1.34563	1.34917	1.35274	1.35634	1.35997	1.36363	1.36733	47
43	1.36733	1.37105	1.37481	1.37860	1.38242	1.38628	1.39016	46
44	1.39016	1.39409	1.39804	1.40203	1.40606	1.41012	1.41421	45
Secants	60′	50′	40′	30′	20′	10′	0′	Degrees
	\multicolumn{7}{COSECANTS}							

Table 14-5. Natural Secants and Cosecants (*Concluded*)

Degrees	COSECANTS							Secants
	0'	10'	20'	30'	40'	50'	60'	
0	∞	343.77516	171.88831	114.59301	85.94561	68.75736	57.29869	89
1	57.29869	49.11406	42.97571	38.20155	34.38232	31.25758	28.65371	88
2	28.65371	26.45051	24.56212	22.92559	21.49368	20.23028	19.10732	87
3	19.10732	18.10262	17.19843	16.38041	15.63679	14.95788	14.33559	86
4	14.33559	13.76312	13.23472	12.74550	12.29125	11.86837	11.47371	85
5	11.47371	11.10455	10.75849	10.43343	10.12752	9.83912	9.56677	84,
6	9.56677	9.30917	9.06515	8.83367	8.61379	8.40466	8.20551	83
7	8.20551	8.01565	7.83443	7.66130	7.49571	7.33719	7.18530	82
8	7.18530	7.03962	6.89979	6.76547	6.63633	6.51208	6.39245	81
9	6.39245	6.27719	6.16607	6.05886	5.95536	5.85539	5.75877	80
10	5.75877	5.66533	5.57493	5.48740	5.40263	5.32049	5.24084	79
11	5.24084	5.16359	5.08863	5.01585	4.94517	4.87649	4.80973	78
12	4.80973	4.74482	4.68167	4.62023	4.56041	4.50216	4.44541	77
13	4.44541	4.39012	4.33622	4.28366	4.23239	4.18238	4.13357	76
14	4.13357	4.08591	4.03938	3.99393	3.94952	3.90613	3.86370	75
15	3.86370	3.82223	3.78166	3.74198	3.70315	3.66515	3.62796	74
16	3.62796	3.59154	3.55587	3.52094	3.48671	3.45317	3.42030	73
17	3.42030	3.38808	3.35649	3.32551	3.29512	3.26531	3.23607	72
18	3.23607	3.20737	3.17920	3.15155	3.12440	3.09774	3.07155	71
19	3.07155	3.04584	3.02057	2.99574	2.97135	2.94737	2.92380	70
20	2.92380	2.90063	2.87785	2.85545	2.83342	2.81175	2.79043	69
21	2.79043	2.76945	2.74881	2.72850	2.70851	2.68884	2.66947	68
22	2.66947	2.65040	2.63162	2.61313	2.59491	2.57698	2.55930	67
23	2.55930	2.54190	2.52474	2.50784	2.49119	2.47477	2.45859	66
24	2.45859	2.44264	2.42692	2.41142	2.39614	2.38107	2.36620	65
25	2.36620	2.35154	2.33708	2.32282	2.30875	2.29487	2.28117	64
26	2.28117	2.26766	2.25432	2.24116	2.22817	2.21535	2.20269	63
27	2.20269	2.19019	2.17786	2.16568	2.15366	2.14178	2.13005	62
28	2.13005	2.11847	2.10704	2.09574	2.08458	2.07356	2.06267	61
29	2.06267	2.05191	2.04128	2.03077	2.02039	2.01014	2.00000	60
30	2.00000	1.98998	1.98008	1.97029	1.96062	1.95106	1.94160	59
31	1.94160	1.93226	1.92302	1.91388	1.90485	1.89591	1.88708	58
32	1.88708	1.87834	1.86970	1.86116	1.85271	1.84435	1.83608	57
33	1.83608	1.82790	1.81981	1.81180	1.80388	1.79604	1.78829	56
34	1.78829	1.78062	1.77303	1.76552	1.75808	1.75073	1.74345	55
35	1.74345	1.73624	1.72911	1.72205	1.71506	1.70815	1.70130	54
36	1.70130	1.69452	1.68782	1.68117	1.67460	1.66809	1.66164	53
37	1.66164	1.65526	1.64894	1.64268	1.63648	1.63035	1.62427	52
38	1.62427	1.61825	1.61229	1.60639	1.60054	1.59475	1.58902	51
39	1.58902	1.58333	1.57771	1.57213	1.56661	1.56114	1.55572	50
40	1.55572	1.55036	1.54504	1.53977	1.53455	1.52938	1.52425	49
41	1.52425	1.51918	1.51415	1.50916	1.50422	1.49933	1.49448	48
42	1.49448	1.48967	1.48491	1.48019	1.47551	1.47087	1.46628	47
43	1.46628	1.46173	1.45721	1.45274	1.44831	1.44391	1.43956	46
44	1.43956	1.43524	1.43096	1.42672	1.42251	1.41835	1.41421	45
Cosecants	60'	50'	40'	30'	20'	10'	0'	Degrees
	SECANTS							

INDEX